ShaderX⁵

Advanced Rendering Techniques

ShaderX⁵
Advanced Rendering Techniques

Edited by Wolfgang Engel

CHARLES RIVER MEDIA

Boston, Massachusetts

Cover Design: Tyler Creative
Cover Image: Rockstar Games

CHARLES RIVER MEDIA
25 THOMSON PLACE
BOSTON, MA 02210
617-757-7900
617-757-7969 (FAX)
crm.info@thomson.com
www.charlesriver.com

This book is printed on acid-free paper.

Wolfgang Engel. *ShaderX^5: Advanced Rendering Techniques.*
ISBN: 1-58450-499-4

All brand names and product names mentioned in this book are trademarks or service marks of their respective companies. Any omission or misuse (of any kind) of service marks or trademarks should not be regarded as intent to infringe on the property of others. The publisher recognizes and respects all marks used by companies, manufacturers, and developers as a means to distinguish their products.

Library of Congress Cataloging-in-Publication Data
Engel, Wolfgang F.
  ShaderX^5 : advanced rendering techniques / Wolfgang Engel. -- 1st ed.
    p. cm.
  Includes index.
  ISBN 1-58450-499-4 (hc : alk. paper, CD-ROM)
  1. Computer graphics. 2. Three-dimensional display systems. I. Title.

  T385.E38559 2006
  006.6'93--dc22
2006034609

Printed in the United States of America
07 7 6 5 4 3 2 First Edition

CHARLES RIVER MEDIA titles are available for site license or bulk purchase by institutions, user groups, corporations, etc. For additional information, please contact the Special Sales Department at 781-740-0400.

Requests for replacement of a defective CD-ROM must be accompanied by the original disc, your mailing address, telephone number, date of purchase, and purchase price. Please state the nature of the problem, and send the information to CHARLES RIVER MEDIA, 25 Thomson Place, Boston, Massachusetts 02210. CRM's sole obligation to the purchaser is to replace the disc, based on defective materials or faulty workmanship, but not on the operation or functionality of the product.

This book is dedicated to Ida Hurley,
who passed away during the editing of this book.

This book is dedicated to Ida Hurley,
who passed away during the editing of this book.

Contents

About the Editors

Wessam Bahnassi

Wessam's professional career started about eight years ago when he started the development of the real-time 3D engine DirectSkeleton and its pipeline tools for In|Framez. He led the development team for several games and real-time demos based on the same engine in addition to his many contributions and publications in graphics and programming in general. Wessam has been a Microsoft® Most Valuable Professional (MVP) for DirectX® technologies for the past four years. Currently, he works at Electronic Arts Montreal, doing console and PC graphics and game programming for some of EA's great titles.

Kristof Beets

Kristof is the third-party relations manager for PowerVR in the Business Development Group at Imagination Technologies. Through the PowerVR Insider program he manages technical support and comarketing activities for the Mobile Graphics Ecosystem. He has a background in electrical engineering and received a master's degree in artificial intelligence. Prior to joining the Business Development Group he worked on SDKs and tools for both PC and mobile products as a member of the PowerVR Developer Relations Team. Previous work has been published in *ShaderX²*, *ARM IQ Magazine*, and online by 3Dfx Interactive and Beyond3D.

Carsten Dachsbacher

Carsten Dachsbacher is a postdoctoral fellow at REVES/INRIA in Sophia-Antipolis, France. His research focuses on interactive and hardware-assisted computer graphics; in particular, he is working on interactive global illumination techniques, procedural models and point-based rendering. He has worked as a freelancer for various (game) companies programming mainly real-time 3D graphics and published some of his work at conferences and in books and magazines.

Wolfgang Engel

Wolfgang is a senior graphics programmer in the core technology group at Rockstar San Diego. He is the editor of the *ShaderX* book series and the author of *Programming Vertex and Pixel Shaders*. Wolfgang is a frequent speaker at conferences worldwide and publishes articles on several Web sites. Since July 2006 he has been a Microsoft MVP in DirectX.

Tom Forsyth

Tom Forsyth works at RAD Game Tools on Granny3D and Pixomatic. He is one of the best-known industry professionals in the graphics programming area and has spoken frequently at GDC and other events, most recently focusing on shadow mapping techniques.

Kenneth Hurley

Kenneth has worked for notable game and technology companies such as Electronic Arts® and Intel® and most recently was a senior engineer at NVIDIA® Corporation. While there, he participated in the XBox hardware and numerous video games including *Tiger Woods Golf*. Kenneth has been a consultant for several Silicon Valley companies and worked with the United States government on the latest military equipment, including the highly acclaimed Land Warrior. Kenneth's passion and experience for the gaming industry is what brings him to the helm of Signature Devices. With over 20 years of experience, this is Kenneth's second start-up as an independent developer, giving him perspective and a strong understanding of the demands of running an up-and-coming development company. He has contributed to best-selling computer books on 3D graphics, and he is a requested speaker at conventions and workshops around the country. Kenneth received his bachelor of science degree in computer science from the University of Maryland.

Sebastien St-Laurent

Sebastien St-Laurent holds a degree in computer engineering from Sherbrooke University in Quebec (Canada), where he graduated at top of his class in 1999. Since then, he has worked on many video game titles including *Space Invaders*, *Dave Mira Freestyle BMX*, *Dave Mira Freestyle BMX2*, *Aggressive Inline*, and *BMX XXX*. Sebastien is currently employed with the Microsoft Corporation, where he is a graphics developer for the Microsoft Game Studios. Sebastien St-Laurent is also a published author who has written *Shaders for Game Programmers and Artists* and *The COMPLETE Effect and HLSL Guide*.

Natalya Tatarchuk

Natalya is a senior software engineer in the ATI Research, Inc. 3D Application Research Group, where she is investigating innovative graphics techniques in the real-time domain for current and future platforms as a contributor in the demo group. In the past she has been the lead for the tools group at the 3D Application Research Group, working on a pioneering real-time shader development environment RenderMonkeyTM IDE. Natalya has been in the graphics industry for many years, previously working on award-winning haptic 3D modeling software, scientific visualization libraries, and various other projects. She has published articles in the *ShaderX* books, *Game Programming Gems*, *Game Developer* magazine, and Gamasutra.com, among others. She has presented novel techniques at conferences throughout the world, including Siggraph sketches and presentations, GDC, GDC-Europe, Microsoft Meltdown, and Russian GDCs. Natalya graduated with B.A.s in computers science and mathematics from Boston University and is currently pursuing an S.M. in computer science with concentration in graphics at Harvard University.

Matthias Wloka

Matthias Wloka is a software engineer in the technical developer relations group at NVIDIA. His primary responsibility is to collaborate with game developers to enhance the image quality and graphics performance of their games; he is also a regular contributor at game developer conferences, such as GDC. Matthias's passion for computer gaming started at age 15 when he discovered that that his school's Commodore PET 2001 computers also played black jack. He started writing his own games soon thereafter and continues to use the latest graphics hardware to explore the limits of interactive real-time rendering. Before joining NVIDIA, Matthias was a game developer at GameFX/THQ, Inc. He received his M.Sc in computer science from Brown University in 1990 and his B.Sc from Christian Albrechts University in Kiel, Germany, in 1987.

About the Contributors

Brief biographies are included here for those contributors who submitted them.

Barnabás Aszódi

Barnabás Aszódi is a Ph.D. student in computer graphics at the Budapest University of Technology and Economics. He works on multimedia systems and GPU algorithms aiming at photo-realistic real-time rendering.

Homam Bahnassi

Homam holds a B.C. in engineering management. Working in the computer graphics industry for nearly a decade, he developed pipelines for gaming production at several leading companies, in addition to supervision, special effects development, and technical direction of several computer graphics productions. He has many publications and researches in the fields of media management, technical directing, and special effects development for both real-time and offline rendering systems. He enjoys the merging of his engineering skills into the computer graphics industry that he always liked.

Wessam Bahnassi

Wessam's professional career started about eight years ago when he started the development of the real-time 3D engine DirectSkeleton and its pipeline tools for In|Framez. He led the development team for several games and real-time demos based on the same engine in addition to his many contributions and publications in graphics and programming in general. Wessam has been a Microsoft Most Valuable Professional (MVP) for DirectX technologies for the past four years. Currently, he works at Electronics Arts Montreal, doing console and PC graphics and game programming for some of EA's great titles.

Kristof Beets

Kristof is the third-party relations manager for PowerVR in the Business Development Group at Imagination Technologies. Through the PowerVR Insider program he manages technical support and comarketing activities for the Mobile Graphics Ecosystem. He has a background in electrical engineering and received a master's degree in artificial intelligence. Prior to joining the Business Development Group he worked on SDKs and tools for both PC and mobile products as a member of the PowerVR Developer Relations Team. Previous work has been published in *ShaderX²*, *ARM IQ Magazine*, and online by 3Dfx Interactive and Beyond3D.

Ali Botorabi

Ali is a researcher in a German automotive company. He works in a department with a focus on software/methods and tools. He has a strong preference for development of entertaining multimedia applications and leads the open source project Yag2002 at SourceForge.

João Luiz Dihl Comba

João Luiz Dihl Comba received a B.S. degree in computer science from the Federal University of Rio Grande do Sul, Brazil, an M.S. degree in computer science from the Federal University of Rio de Janeiro, Brazil, and a Ph.D. degree in computer science from Stanford University. He is an associate professor of computer science at the Federal University of Rio Grande do Sul, Brazil. His main research interests are in graphics, visualization, spatial data structures, and applied computational geometry. His current projects include the development of algorithms for large-scale scientific visualization, data structures for point-based modeling and rendering, and general-purpose computing using graphics hardware. He is a member of the ACM Siggraph.

Carsten Dachsbacher

Carsten Dachsbacher is a postdoctoral fellow at REVES/INRIA in Sophia-Antipolis, France. His research focuses on interactive and hardware-assisted computer graphics; in particular, he is working on interactive global illumination techniques, procedural models, and point-based rendering. He has worked as a freelancer for various (game) companies programming mainly real-time 3D graphics and published some of his work at conferences and in books and magazines.

Carlos Augusto Dietrich

Carlos Augusto Dietrich received a B.S. degree in computer science from the Federal University of Santa Maria, Brazil, and an M.S. degree in computer science from the Federal University of Rio Grande do Sul, Brazil. His research interests include graphics, visualization, and the use of GPUs as general purpose processors. He is currently a second-year Ph.D. student working in the Computer Graphics Group at the Federal University of Rio Grande do Sul, Brazil.

Alexander Ehrath

Alex started programming on a TI-99/4a 25 years ago. Always fascinated by technology, he taught himself machine language at age 14 on a Commodore 64 and got his start in the game industry professionally 8 years later. He then picked up 3D programming as video game consoles became more powerful. Alex is currently senior programmer at a top game development firm in the San Diego area.

Wolfgang Engel

Wolfgang is a senior graphics programmer in the core technology group at Rockstar San Diego. He is the editor of the *ShaderX* book series and the author of *Programming Vertex and Pixel Shaders*. Wolfgang is a frequent speaker at conferences worldwide and publishes articles on several Web sites. Since July 2006 he has been a Microsoft MVP in DirectX.

Dustin Franklin

Dustin is the lead graphics programmer for middleware provider Mystic Game Development, where he specializes in developing renderers and animation software. He also does undergraduate work at Johns Hopkins University, in Baltimore, Maryland. Dustin has previously written for the *ShaderX* series of books, as well as published content on his personal site, *www.circlesoft.org*. For his participation in online forums such as GameDev.net, he was awarded Microsoft MVP status in the area of DirectX.

David Gillham

David Gillham graduated in 2002 from Middlesex University with a first-class honors degree in computer science, which focused on graphics and games programming. He is a member of Climax Brighton's Core Technology Group and has recently worked on the debug rendering libraries, water, and depth of field HLSL shader effects for MotoGP06 XBox 360.

Dan Ginsburg

Dan is a software engineer on the handheld team in the 3D Application Research Group at ATI, where he works on demos and tools for ATI's handheld graphics chips. Prior to joining the 3DARG, Dan worked on ATI's OpenGL driver team for over four years. Before joining ATI, Dan worked for n-Space, Inc., an Orlando-based game development company.

Pheng-Ann Heng

Pheng-Ann Heng is a professor in the Department of Computer Science and Engineering in the Chinese University of Hong Kong (CUHK). In 1999 he set up the CUHK Virtual Reality, Visualization, and Imaging Research Centre and has served as the center's director since then. He works on medical imaging, medical visualization, image-based rendering, virtual reality applications in medicine, and interactive graphics. His recent work includes GPU-accelerated volume rendering, real-time visualization of Chinese Visible Human (CVH), and photorealistic virtual anatomy. His research group has also constructed the world's first virtual acupuncture human based on an ultra-high resolution CVH data set. He received the IEEE Transactions on Multimedia Prize Paper Award 2005 and Asia Pacific ICT Award 2005.

Benjamín Hernández

Benjamín Hernández received a B.S. degree in computer systems engineering from the Instituto Politécnico Nacional in 2001 and an M.S. degree in computer science from the Instituto Tecnológico y de Estudios Superiores de Monterrey (ITESM-CEM) in 2004. He is currently a Ph.D. student and research assistant at ITESM-CEM. His research interests are in virtual human modeling, animation, and rendering; GPGPU applications; and virtual environments.

Aick in der Au

Aick is a computer science student at the Ilmenau University of Technology, Germany. He works at Phenomic Game Development, where he is responsible for getting the render core to work with multiple threads. While fighting with spin locks, sync points, job chains, and other threading issues, he enjoys having the fastest SMP machine in the office. Other interests include procedural generated graphics and demoscene-related things.

István Lazányi

István Lazányi has been a Ph.D. student at the Budapest University of Technology and Economics since 2003. His research interests include material models, global illumination algorithms, and GPU programming for realistic rendering.

Max Dennis Luesebrink

Currently a student of cognitive science focusing on AI, he formerly worked as a graphics programmer at Codecult on the Codecreatures 3D-Engine and several technology demos (Transrapid Simulation for SIEMENS AG, launch demo for the GF4TI release of NVIDIA). Also, he has taken part in the development of the engine used for *Gothic*, *Gothic II*, and the add-on *Night of the Raven*.

Erik Millán

Erik Millán is a Ph.D. student of computer science at the Instituto Tecnológico y de Estudios Superiores de Monterrey, Campus Estado de México. He is completing his thesis on specification and simulation of crowd behavior. He received his master's degree at the same institution, working on plant modeling based on particle systems. His research interests include crowd simulation, GPGPU, procedural modeling, level of detail techniques, and computer vision.

Jason L. Mitchell

Jason is a Software Engineer at Valve, where he works on real-time 3D graphics techniques on a variety of projects. Prior to joining Valve, Jason was the lead of the 3D Application Research Group at ATI Research for eight years. Jason received a B.S. in Computer Engineering from Case Western Reserve University in 1994 and an M.S. in Electrical Engineering from the University of Cincinnati in 1996. He has also studied at the University of New South Wales in Sydney, Australia and worked in Tsukuba, Japan through the National Science Foundation Summer Institute in Japan. Other publications and conference materials can be found on Jason's website: *http://www.pixelmaven.com/jason/*

Luciana Porcher Nedel

Luciana Porcher Nedel received a Ph.D. in computer science from the Swiss Federal Institute of Technology, Lausanne, Switzerland, under the supervision of Prof. Daniel Thalmann in 1998. She received an M.S. degree in computer science from the Federal University of Rio Grande do Sul, Brazil, and a B.S. degree in computer science from the Pontifical Catholic University, Brazil. In 2005, during a sabbatical year, she spent two months at the Université Paul Sabatier, Toulouse, France, and two months at the Université Catholique de Louvain, Louvain-la-Neuve, Belgium, doing research on interaction. She is an assistant professor at the Federal University of Rio Grande do Sul, Brazil. Since 1991 she has been involved in computer animation research, and since 1996 she has been doing research in virtual reality. Her current projects include deformation methods, virtual human simulation, interactive animation, and 3D interaction using virtual reality devices.

Frank Nielsen

Frank Nielsen defended his Ph.D. thesis on adaptive computational geometry prepared at INRIA Sophia-Antipolis (France) in 1996. In 1998 he joined Sony Computer Science Laboratories, Inc., Tokyo (Japan), as a researcher. His current research interests include geometry, vision, graphics, learning, and optimization. He recently published the book *Visual Computing: Geometry, Graphics, and Vision*, Charles River Media, 2005 (ISBN 1584504277). His papers, projects, and activities are further described at *http://www.csl.sony.co.jp/person/nielsen/*.

Chris Oat

Chris Oat is a senior software engineer in the 3D Application Research Group at ATI, where he explores novel rendering techniques for real-time 3D graphics applications. As the technical lead of ATI's demo team, Chris focuses on shader development for current and future graphics platforms. He has published several articles in the *ShaderX* and *Game Programming Gems* series and has presented at game developer conferences around the world. Chris received a B.A. in computer science from Boston University.

Manuel M. Oliveira

Manuel M. Oliveira received his Ph.D. in computer science from the University of North Carolina at Chapel Hill (2000). He is currently a professor at the Instituto de Informática, Universidade Federal do Rio Grande do Sul (UFRGS), in Brazil. Before joining the faculty at UFRGS, he worked for two years as an assistant professor of computer science at the State University of New York at Stony Brook. His interests include image-based modeling and rendering, real-time rendering, innovative uses of graphics hardware, 3D photography, surface reconstruction from point clouds, medical applications of imaging technologies, and the construction of virtual replicas of real environments. His homepage is *http://www.inf.ufrgs.br/~oliveira*.

Wai-Man Pang

Wai-Man Pang is currently a Ph.D. candidate in the Department of Computer Science and Engineering at the Chinese University of Hong Kong (CUHK). His research interests include image-based relighting, GPU techniques, and non-photo-realistic rendering. During his master's study, He proposed a vision-based capturing system to acquire relighting data from real environments (IEEE CG&A 2004 May). He loves programming, especially vision and graphics applications, and he has explored GPU programming for several years.

Kurt Pelzer

Kurt Pelzer is a software engineer with over seven years experience in team-oriented projects within the game industry. He has been involved in all stages of development from conceptual and technical design to implementation, debugging, und testing. Currently Kurt works as senior software engineer at Piranha Bytes, where he has taken part in the development of the new PC game *Gothic 3*, including the next-generation engine Genome. Kurt has also worked on the predecessors *Gothic*, and *Gothic II* and the add-on *Gothic II - The Night of the Raven*. Prior to that, he was a senior programmer at Codecult, developed Codecult's 3D-Engine Codecreatures, and built several real-time simulations and tech-demos on that technology (for example, a simulation of the Shanghai "Transrapid" track for SIEMENS AG, a tech-demo for NVIDIA's GeForce 4 Ti launch, and the well-known Codecreatures Benchmark Pro). Kurt has published in *GPU Gems*, *GPU Gems 2*, *Game Programming Gems 4*, *ShaderX²*, and *ShaderX⁴*.

Aurelio Reis

As a young child, Aurelio dreamed of fantastical new worlds and the endless possibilities for adventure within them. As a game developer, he's been able to turn his dreams into reality. Aurelio has been making games for a number of years now and is currently employed as a software engineer at Firaxis Games, specializing in graphics and engine technologies.

Guodong Rong

Guodong Rong received a B.Eng. degree and a M.Eng. degree, both in computer science, from Shandong University in 2000 and 2003, respectively. He is currently a Ph.D. candidate in the School of Computing, University of Singapore. His research interests include computer graphics, virtual reality, and visualization. He is currently working on general-purpose computation on GPUs and real-time soft shadows.

Isaac Rudomín

Isaac Rudomín received his Ph.D. in computer science from the University of Pennsylvania. He has been a professor at the Instituto Tecnológico y de Estudios Superiores de Monterrey, Campus Estado de México since 1991. He is the author of about 50 technical papers. His research interests include human modeling and crowd animation as well as the use of graphics processors.

Pedro V. Sander

Pedro attended college at Stony Brook University, in New York, USA, where he received a Bachelor of Science in Computer Science. He then attended graduate school at Harvard University, in Cambridge, USA, where he received Master of Science and Doctor of Philosophy degrees in 1999 and 2003, respectively. While attending graduate school at Harvard, he was a Microsoft Research fellow from 2000-2002. Most of his research during graduate school focused on geometry processing, more specifically on mesh parametrization. After graduating in 2003, Dr. Sander was a senior member of the 3D Application Research Group at ATI Research, where he conducted advanced real-time rendering research using the latest graphics hardware. In August 2006, he moved to Hong Kong to join the Faculty of Computer Science and Engineering at The Hong Kong University of Science and Technology. Other work of Pedro's can be found on his website: *http://www.cse.ust.hk/~psander/*

Rahul Sathe

Rahul Sathe is currently working as senior application engineer at Intel Corp. and is involved in enabling Intel's multicore platforms. He consults various game companies on optimizing their games on Intel hardware. Prior to this, he worked in various aspects of CPU architecture and design. He holds a B.E. degree in electronics engineering from Mumbai University (1997) and an M.S. in computer engineering from Clemson University (1999). He has prior publications in the computer architecture area. His current interests include graphics, mathematics, and computer architecture.

Christian Schüler

Christian Schüler is software engineer at Phenomic Game Development in Ingelheim, Germany, where he is responsible for engine development. He worked on the graphics engine of the game *Spellforce 2*. Previous projects include engine work for smaller studios and medical visualization. He joined the games industry in 2002.

László Szirmay-Kalos

László Szirmay-Kalos is a full professor and the head of the Computer Graphics Group at the Budapest University of Technology and Economics. He graduated from this university in 1987 and received a Ph.D. degree in 1990. He is the author of 150 technical papers and 5 books. His current research interests include global illumination algorithms and the application of GPUs to speed up these methods.

Tiow-Seng Tan

Tiow-Seng Tan graduated with a Ph.D. from the University of Illinois at Urbana-Champaign in 1993. By training, he specializes in computational geometry. He is currently an associate professor at the School of Computing, National University of Singapore. His recent research interest is in the area of interactive 3D graphics. His graphics research group has contributed in designing novel algorithms such as simplification, collision detection, occlusion culling, and real-time shadow generation.

Natalya Tatarchuk

Natalya Tatarchuk is a staff research engineer in the demo group of ATI's 3D Application Research Group, where she likes to push the GPU boundaries investigating innovative graphics techniques and creating striking interactive renderings. Her recent achievements include leading creation of the state-of-the-art realistic rendering of city environments in the ATI demo "ToyShop." In the past she has been the lead for the tools group at ATI Research. She has published articles in technical book series such as *ShaderX* and *Game Programming Gems* and has presented talks at SIGGRAPH and at game developers conferences worldwide. Natalya holds a B.A. in computer science and mathematics from Boston University and is currently pursuing a graduate degree in computer science with a concentration in graphics at Harvard University.

Tamás Umenhoffer

Tamás Umenhoffer has been a Ph.D. student in computer graphics at the Budapest University of Technology and Economics since 2005. His research has focused on real-time animation and rendering of atmospheric phenomena and the application of these effects in games.

Tien-Tsin Wong

Tien-Tsin Wong is an associate professor in the Department of Computer Science and Engineering at the Chinese University of Hong Kong (CUHK). He has been programming for the past 18 years, including writing publicly available codes/libraries/demos and codes for all his graphics research. He works on GPU techniques, rendering, image-based relighting, natural phenomenon modeling, computerized manga, and multimedia data compression. He is a SIGGRAPH author. He proposed a method to simulate dust accumulation (IEEE CGA 1995) and other surface imperfections (SIGGRAPH 2005). In SIGGRAPH 2006 he proposed a technique for manga colorization. He also proposed the apparent BRDF, one of the earliest techniques for relighting (precomputed lighting) in 1997. Besides academic papers, he has written game development–related articles in *Graphics Gems 5*, *Graphics Programming Methods*, *ShaderX³*, *ShaderX⁴*, and *ShaderX⁵*. Recently, he has been working on projects for general purpose usage of GPUs, such as evolutionary computing (such as genetic algorithms), and discrete wavelet transform. He received the IEEE Transaction on Multimedia Prize Paper Award 2005 and CUHK Young Researcher Award 2004.

Kim Hyoun Woo

Kim Hyoun Woo started his game development career in 1996. He is currently the manager of the program team on RF-online, an MMORPG game that has been exported to several countries including Japan, Taiwan, the Philippines, China, the United Kingdom, and others. Since 2003, he has been involved in his spare time in the open source 3D engine project Nebula Device. He wrote the Nebula2 3DSMax Toolkit that was used by several commercial and noncommercial projects.

Chris Wyman

Chris Wyman is an assistant professor in the Department of Computer Science at the University of Iowa. Before joining the faculty at Iowa, he graduated in 2004 with his Ph.D. from the University of Utah. His interests include real-time rendering, interactive global illumination, interactive rendering of specular and other complex materials, and perceptually guided simplification of lighting models. More information is available at his Web page: *http://www.cs.uiowa.edu/~cwyman/*.

Preface

The talented editors and contributors of this book spent eight months writing, selecting, editing, and finalizing the articles for this newest volume of the *ShaderX* series. We hope you find these state-of-the-art graphics-programming articles useful in your own work. As with the other *ShaderX* books, all of the topics cover ready-to-use ideas and procedures that can solve many of your daily graphics-programming challenges.

I would like to thank the section editors for the fantastic job they did. The work of Kenneth Hurley, Wessam Bahnassi, Sebastien St-Laurent, Natalya Tatarchuk, Tom Forsyth, Kristof Beets, Carsten Dachsbacher, and Matthias Wloka ensures that the quality of the series stands up to the expectations of our readers.

The great looking cover images come from Rockstar's *Table-Tennis*. I have to thank Sam Hauser and Josh Needleman for allowing us to use them. Additionally I have to thank Allan Wasserman, Steve Reed, Derek Tarvin, Eugene Foss, David Etherton, and all the other great people at Rockstar San Diego for the great time I am having there.

The team at Charles River Media/Thomson made the whole project happen: Dave Pallai, Jenifer Niles, and the production team, who took the articles and made them into a book.

Special thanks go out to our families and friends, who spent many evenings and weekends during the long book production cycle without us.

I hope you have as much fun reading this book as we had creating it.

Wolfgang Engel

P.S. Plans for an upcoming *ShaderX*[6] are already in progress. Any comments, proposals, and suggestions are highly welcome (*wolf@shaderx.com*).

GEOMETRY
MANIPULATION

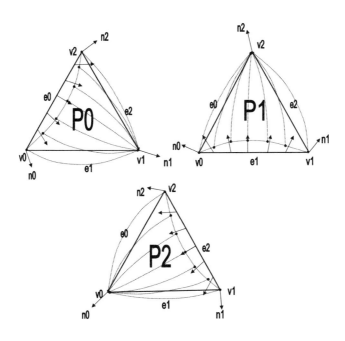

Introduction

Wolfgang Engel

The Geometry Manipulation section of the book focuses on the ability of graphic processor units (GPUs) to process and generate geometry in exciting and interesting ways.

The first article in the section is "Smoothed N-Patches," by Holger Gruen. This article introduces a way to improve N-Patches to make them visually smooth across edges. The method described does not resort to using subdivision surfaces and ideally only needs the normals of neighboring faces. The surfaces generated by the method described will in general look smoother than normal N-Patches for objects with a low polygon count.

Homam and Wessam Bahnassi introduce with their article "Micro-beveled Edges" a simple way to achieve beveling. Beveling is a technique that gets rid of sharp edges in 3D rendered objects by rounding or chamfering these sharp edges. This produces more natural scenes because hard and sharp edges rarely exist in nature, where most everything has rounded edges on many different scales.

The next article in the section, written by Jörn Loviscach, is "Dynamic Wrinkle Patterns and Hatching on Animated Meshes." This article shows how to create dynamic, seamless, self-organizing surface patterns that adapt to a varying shape of the mesh and don't even require texture coordinate data. Generating wrinkles as described in the article might be used in addition to a physically approximated dynamic cloth simulation.

Finally, the second article written by Homam and Wessam Bahnassi, "Cloth without Cloth," proposes a cheap (yet good-looking) technique to render those small bumpy cloth details that appear at the inner sides of bent cloth pieces. The technique replaces the unnatural static baked cloth bumps that are usually found in game characters.

1.1

Smoothed N-Patches

Holger Gruen, Intel Corp.

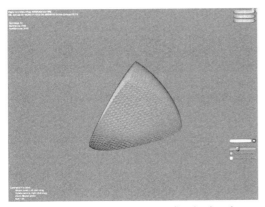

FIGURE 1.1.1A A tetrahedron refined using the original N-Patch.

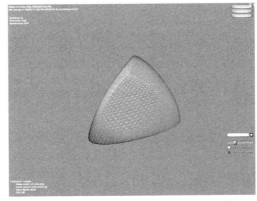

FIGURE 1.1.1B A tetrahedron refined using the new patch.

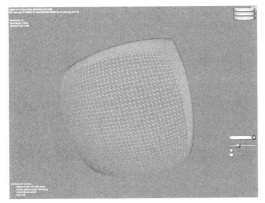

FIGURE 1.1.1C A cube refined using the original N-Patch.

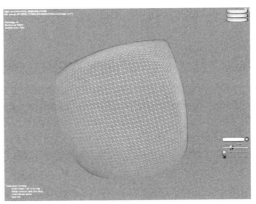

FIGURE 1.1.1D A cube refined using the new N-Patch.

Abstract

N-Patches [Vlachos01] provide a simple way to visually smoothen triangular objects. The smoothing suffers, though, because the composite surface generated by two N-Patches is visually only smooth at the vertices and along edges shared by two object triangles. If you consider directions across (e.g., not parallel to) a shared edge, the generated surface does not necessarily look smooth. This is especially obvious for objects with very low triangle counts.

This article introduces a way to improve N-Patches to make them visually smooth across edges also. The method described does not resort to using subdivision surfaces and ideally only needs the normals of neighboring faces. The surfaces generated by the method in general look smoother than normal N-Patches for objects with low polygon counts.

With the introduction of DirectX10® Geometry Shaders and techniques such as *tessellation through instancing* [Gruen05], it is possible to evaluate the described patches on-the-fly and efficiently for complete objects on the GPU and even on DirectX9 class hardware. Also, for many pass-rendering architectures, an efficient multithreaded CPU implementation that makes use of SSE and writes to dynamic vertex buffers is possible.

Introduction

The idea of having a low-polygon-count (low-poly) object representation that can be refined later on and smoothed on-the-fly is very desirable. A technology like that will result in smooth silhouettes and produce an organic look. Relatively low-poly objects can then be used to save precious video memory, something that is especially relevant for game consoles.

The downside of a low-poly mesh is obvious; it simply does not look as good as a high-polygon-count (high-poly) object. Some aspects of this low-poly look can be improved by using normal maps to emulate fine details through per-pixel lighting (see, e.g., [Cloward]). Still, the silhouettes of such an object look crude.

Several researchers have tackled the problem of how to improve silhouettes of low-poly object approximations. These solutions range from view-dependent level-of-detail (LOD) techniques for high-poly objects (see, e.g., [Hoppe97]) to approaches that only draw an improved silhouette (see, e.g., [Loviscach03], [Sander00], or [Sander01]). The downside of view-dependent LOD techniques is that they need at least as much memory as a high-poly object. Approaches to only improve the silhouette are more interesting in terms of memory footprint. Unfortunately they put a high burden on the CPU to identify silhouette edges and usually issue a large number of batches. All this does not contribute to optimal performance. Applying such approaches to a potentially large number of objects as featured by many games is problematic.

A completely different approach to generate nice silhouettes for low-poly objects is to replace triangles of the object with curved surface patches. Alternatively, one can represent the object completely by the control points necessary to define these patches. The kind of curved surfaces to be used ranges from parametric patches to subdivision surfaces.

A large body of work describes how to realize efficient refinement and tessellation of objects and patches on the CPU (see, e.g., [Lien87] or [Bolz02]). Using these techniques, high-poly representations for every LOD needed can be generated. It is also possible to use even finer tessellations for patches that border silhouette edges of the mesh. The resulting meshes then automatically feature the desired smooth silhouettes. If cached properly, the different LODs of such an object can be computed without putting too much strain on the CPU. If the rendering pipeline used does use many render passes, for example, for lighting it can be faster to use objects that are tessellated on the CPU as opposed to tessellation on the GPU. Recent CPUs feature several cores. These can be successfully utilized to speed up object tessellation (see [Gruen06]).

Using subdivision surfaces to smoothen triangular objects results in smoothed objects with a good visual quality. The thing that makes subdivision surfaces undesirable is that one needs to consider a potentially unlimited number of vertices in the neighborhood of an irregular vertex of the subdivision to evaluate the surface.

NP-Triangles (also called N-Patches [Vlachos01]) were introduced to realize object refinement without any knowledge of neighboring triangles or vertices. N-Patches and other curved surfaces are part of DirectX but are supported in GPU hardware only by a very limited installed hardware base. This limited hardware base resulted in almost zero adoption of this tessellation technology. Current graphics hardware does not support on-the-fly N-Patches any more. Fortunately DirectX offers CPU-based routines to generate refined meshes.

Since N-Patches don't consider any neighboring vertices or faces, refinements of low-poly objects don't feature the visual smoothness of objects refined with subdivision schemes. The way N-Patches are defined implies that the overall surface is not always visually smooth in directions across edges shared by two triangles of an object. The goal of this article is to find an improved patch that behaves like the N-Patch in the interior of a triangle but also produces a reasonably smoothed surface along the directions across shared edges.

The upcoming Shader Model 4.0 supports *geometry shaders* that will enable GPU programs that introduce new vertices and triangles [Tatarchuk06]. Still, game developers need to support older platforms as well; fortunately, tessellation through instancing (see [Gruen05]) enables tessellation on the GPU on DirectX9-class hardware if tessellation on the CPU is not an option.

Before a new way to generate a smoother N-Patch is described, this article first describes how the original N-Patch is constructed. The curved surface patches that will be discussed are defined on a triangular parameter domain. Therefore, barycentric coordinates and Gregory coordinates [Farin99] will be covered as well since these coordinates are commonly used for defining triangular parameter domains.

The Original N-Patch

N-Patches [Vlachos01] are triangular Bezier patches of degree three. These patches are defined by 10 control points as shown in Figure 1.1.2.

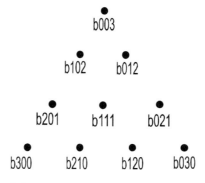

FIGURE 1.1.2   The control points of a bicubic triangular Bezier patch.

Each control point is derived from the three corners of an original triangle and the three normals at the corners. If $v0$, $v1$, and $v2$ are the vertices and $n0$, $n1$, and $n2$ are the normals of a triangle, then the control points can be computed using Equation 1.1.1.

$$b_{300} = v0$$
$$b_{030} = v1$$
$$b_{003} = v2$$
$$b_{210} = (\ 2v0 + v1 - dot(\ v1 - v0,\ n0\ )\ ^* n0\ )\ /\ 3$$
$$b_{120} = (\ 2v1 + v0 - dot(\ v0 - v1,\ n1\ )\ ^* n1\ )\ /\ 3$$
$$b_{021} = (\ 2v1 + v2 - dot(\ v2 - v1,\ n1\ )\ ^* n1\ )\ /\ 3$$
$$b_{012} = (\ 2v2 + v1 - dot(\ v1 - v2,\ n2\ )\ ^* n2\ )\ /\ 3$$
$$b_{201} = (\ 2v0 + v2 - dot(\ v2 - v0,\ n0\ )\ ^* n0\ )\ /\ 3$$
$$b_{102} = (\ 2v2 + v0 - dot(\ v0 - v2,\ n2\ )\ ^* n2\ )\ /\ 3$$
$$b_{111} = 3\ (\ b_{210} + b_{120} + b_{021} + b_{012} + b_{102} + b_{201}\ )\ /\ 12 - (\ v0 + v1 + v2\ )\ /\ 6 \qquad (1.1.1)$$

To compute points on the surface of an N-Patch Equation 1.1.2 needs to be evaluated for a triplet of barycentric coordinates $b0$, $b1$, $b2$. How barycentric coordinates are defined on a triangle will be described later.

$$P(b0,b1,b2) = v0\ b0^3 + v1\ b1^3 + v2\ b2^3 +$$
$$3b_{102}\ b0\ b2^2 + 3\ b_{012}\ b1\ b2^2 +$$
$$3b_{201}\ b0^2\ b2 + 3\ b_{021}\ b1^2\ b2 +$$
$$3b_{210}\ b0^2\ b1 + 3\ b_{120}\ b0\ b1^2 +$$
$$6b_{111}\ b0\ b1\ b2 \qquad (1.1.2)$$

If shared triangle edges agree on the normals at the shared vertices, N-Patches will produce a closed surface along shared edges.

Barycentric Coordinates and Gregory Coordinates

N-Patches are triangular Bezier patches. These patches are defined over a barycentric parameter domain. To understand how barycentric coordinates are defined, consider Figure 1.1.3.

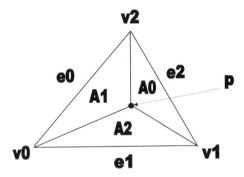

FIGURE 1.1.3 If *A* is the area of a triangle, barycentric coordinates of a point *p* are defined by the ratios of *A0/A, A1/A,* and *A2/A.*

A is the area of the full triangle defined by *v0, v1,* and *v2. A0, A1,* and *A2* are the areas of the corresponding subtriangles defined by a point *p* as shown in Figure 1.1.3. Given these triangles, the barycentric coordinates *b0, b1,* and *b2* of the point *p* are defined by the following equation:

$$b0 = \frac{A0}{A}$$
$$b1 = \frac{A1}{A}$$
$$b2 = \frac{A2}{A}$$
$$b0 + b1 + b2 = 1. \quad (1.1.3)$$

Equation 1.1.3 also implies that *b0 = 1.0* at *v0, b1 = 1.0* at *v1,* and *b2 = 1.0* at *v2.*

Gregory coordinates (see [Farin99]) are the equivalent of barycentric coordinates. Each of the three Gregory coordinates equals 1.0 on exactly one of the edges of a triangle as opposed to one vertex for the barycentric coordinates. Later on this article describes the need for three blending factors that sum up to 1.0 everywhere in a triangle but that only one of them is supposed to be one on each of the edges. Gregory coordinates are defined in terms of barycentric coordinates as described by the following equation:

$$g0 = b0 \cdot b2 \Big/ \left(b0 \cdot b1 + b0 \cdot b2 + b1 \cdot b2 \right)$$

$$g1 = b0 \cdot b1 \Big/ \left(b0 \cdot b1 + b0 \cdot b2 + b1 \cdot b2 \right)$$

$$g2 = b1 \cdot b2 \Big/ \left(b0 \cdot b1 + b0 \cdot b2 + b1 \cdot b2 \right)$$

$$g0 + g1 + g2 = 1. \hspace{3cm} (1.1.4)$$

Equation 1.1.4 implies that $g0$ = *1.0* on *e0* (see Figure 1.1.3), $g1$ = *1.0* on *e,1* and $g2$ = *1.0* on *e0*. It has to be noted that Gregory coordinates are not defined at the vertices of the triangle, since $b0 \cdot b1 + b0 \cdot b2 + b1 \cdot b2$ is 0 at the vertices. As will be shown later, this does not really limit their usability for the purpose of this article.

First Step Toward a Smoother N-Patch

The way N-Patches are defined already generates a visually smooth surface along shared triangle edges and at the triangle's vertices. In order to make it smooth across the edges, one wants to ideally change the surface in a way that guarantees the same surface normal for two patches that meet along a curve above a shared triangle edge.

The exterior (e.g., not b_{111}) control points of the N-Patch as defined by Equation 1.1.1 define three cubic Bezier border curves. The plane normal formed by the cross product of the derivatives of two of these curves at every vertex of the triangle will be the same normal as the one provided as input for Equation 1.1.1. Considering this, to achieve overall visual smoothness, it could be a viable way to make sure that the surface on the edges has a normal that is a linear blend of the normals of the two vertices forming the edge.

The border curves of the original N-Patch are defined by four Bezier control points (see Figure 1.1.4).

FIGURE 1.1.4 The start and end derivatives of a cubic Bezier curve point toward the inner control points.

The two control points $b30$ and $b03$ are the starting point and the endpoint of the curve and are interpolated by the curve. The interior control points are placed along the intended directions of the start and end derivatives $d0$ and $d1$ and are not interpolated. These derivatives are derived from the two points defining an edge and the corresponding normals *n0* and *n1*. Note that *d0* is perpendicular to *n0* and *d1* is perpendicular to *n1*. Equation 1.1.5 describes how to compute these interior control points if two vertices and two normals are given.

$$b_{21} = (2 \, b_{30} + b_{03} - dot(b_{03} - b_{30}, \, n0) * n0) / 3$$
$$b_{12} = (2 \, b_{03} + b_{30} - dot(b_{30} - b_{03}, \, n1) * n1) / 3 \qquad (1.1.5)$$

For every point *p* on a curve (e.g., the curve for edge *e1*), as defined by the original N-Patch, a new curve can be set up. For this curve, *p* is chosen as the starting point and *v2* as the end point. The interior control points are derived from Equation 1.1.5. The starting normal is chosen to be a linear blend of *n0* and *n1*. The end-normal is *n2* (see top right of Figure 1.1.5).

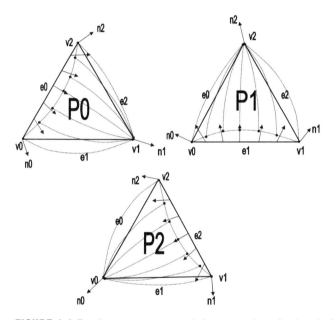

FIGURE 1.1.5 One creates one patch for every edge *e0, e1,* and *e2*.

The overall surface generated by all these curves forms a new patch definition. The derivative of each curve at its starting point will be perpendicular to the interpolated (blended) normal, and the curves of an adjacent patch (sharing *e1*) will also be perpendicular to this normal. Since the shared Bezier curves of two adjacent triangles also agree on derivatives along the curve, the surface normals of both patches will be identical along a shared edge. Also note that a patch defined like this reproduces exactly the border curves of the original N-Patch.

Using this train of thought, a similar patch can be defined for every of the three edges (see patches *P0, P1,* and *P2* in Figure 1.1.5) of the triangle. If Gregory coordinates (see Equation 1.1.4) are used to trilinearly blend these three patches, one ends up with surface patches that would agree on their normals on shared curves or edges. The following equation defines this blending operation:

$$P = g0^n \cdot P0 + g1^n \cdot P1 + g2^n \cdot P2 \tag{1.1.6}$$

The only thing left to define is how to evaluate the new patch, given a triplet of barycentric coordinates. The first thing to do for each of *P0, P1,* and *P2* is to find the appropriate starting points on the corresponding border curves. To compute these points, one needs to know where or when to evaluate the curves to get the starting points. In other words, three curve parameters (*st0, st1,* and *st2*) have to be derived from the barycentric coordinates *b0, b1,* and *b2*. As it turns out, it is easy to choose these parameters. Consult Equation 1.1.7 to understand how to choose them.

$$st0 = \frac{b1}{1 - b2}\ for \quad b2 \neq 1$$
$$st0 = 0.5\ for \quad b2 = 1$$
$$st1 = \frac{b2}{1 - b0}\ for \quad b0 \neq 1$$
$$st1 = 0.5\ for \quad b0 = 1$$
$$st2 = \frac{b0}{1 - b1}\ for \quad b1 \neq 1$$
$$st2 = 0.5\ for \quad b1 = 1. \tag{1.1.7}$$

Given *st0, st1,* and *st2,* one can evaluate the border curves to find the starting points of the current curves (e.g., *c0, c1,* and *c2*) for every patch *P0, P1,* and *P2.* After setting up the three curves, for every curve, one finally only needs to find the actual curve parameter. If these curve parameters are called *ct0, ct1,* and *ct2,* then the following equation shows how to choose them:

$$ct0 = b1$$
$$ct1 = b2$$
$$ct2 = b0 \tag{1.1.8}$$

Now everything is in place to test the patch. The initial implementation shown below (see Listing 1.1.1) is realized with an HLSL vertex shader that is intended to work within the context of tessellation through instancing (see [Gruen05]). The basic idea is to instance a vertex buffer that contains a flat barycentric tessellation of a triangle (see Figure 1.1.6) with vertex data that only contain barycentric coordinates for every triangle of a mesh that needs to be refined. As per instance data, a second vertex buffer contains the vertices, normals, and texture coordinates of one mesh triangle. Note that the shader simply uses trilinearly interpolated normals and does not try to compute real normals. This is also the way normals are computed for N-Patches. Alternatively, a quadratic Bezier patch can be used for normal approximation (see [Vlachos01]).

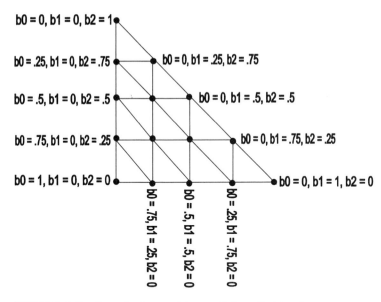

FIGURE 1.1.6 A regular barycentric tessellation of a triangle.

LISTING 1.1.1 Initial Implementation

```
// evaluate a curve defined by two vertices and two normals at b
   (see Equation 1.1.5)
float3 evaluateCurve( float3 v0,
                      float3 v1,
                      float3 n0,
                      float3 n1,
                      float  b
                    )
{
float  b_   = 1.0 - b;

// compute internal control points
   float3 b21 = ( 2 * v0 + v1 - dot( v1 - v0, n0 ) * n0 );
   float3 b12 = ( 2 * v1 + v0 - dot( v0 - v1, n1 ) * n1 );

   // evaluate curve
   return   b_ *b_* b_  * v0  +
            b * b * b   * v1  +
            b_ *b_* b   * b21 +
            b_ *b * b   * b12;
}

void VSInstancedPatch( float3 b    : POSITION,  // barycentric
                                                        coords
                       float3 v0            : TEXCOORD0,
                                             // v0 of triangle
                       float3 v1            : TEXCOORD1,
                                             // v1 of triangle
```

```
                                float3 v2          : TEXCOORD2,
                                                   // v2 of triangle
                                float3 n0          : TEXCOORD3,
                                                   // normal for v0
                                float3 n1          : TEXCOORD4,
                                                   // normal for v1
                                float3 n2          : TEXCOORD5,
                                                   // normal for v2
                                float2 t0          : TEXCOORD6,
                                                   // texcoord for v0
                                float2 t1          : TEXCOORD7,
                                                   // texcoord for v1
                                float2 t2          : TEXCOORD8,
                                                   // texcoord for v2
                                out float4 oPos    : POSITION,
                                out float2 oTex    : TEXCOORD0,
                                out float4 Diffuse : COLOR0   )
{
float3 g; // gregory coords
float3 c; // parameters for border curves/edges

   float  b0b2 = b.x * b.z, b0b1 = b.x * b.y, b1b2 = b.y * b.z;
float  sum = b0b2 + b0b1 + b1b2;

   // compute gregory coords from barycentric coords
   if( b.x > 0.999f || b.y > 0.999f || b.z > 0.999f )
   {
     if( b.x > 0.999f )
       g.x = 1.0f, g.y = g.z = 0.0f;
     else if( b.y > 0.999f )
       g.y = 1.0f, g.x = g.z = 0.0f;
     else
       g.z = 1.0f, g.x = g.y = 0.0f;
   }
   else
   {
     g.x = b0b2/sum;
     g.y = b0b1/sum;
     g.z = b1b2/sum;
   }

// compute parameters for border curves
   if( 1.0f - b.z != 0.0f )
     c.x = b.y / ( 1.0f - b.z );
   else
     c.x = 0.5f;
   if( 1.0f - b.x != 0.0f )
     c.y = b.z / ( 1.0f - b.x );
   else
     c.y = 0.5f;
   if( 1.0f - b.y != 0.0f )
     c.z = b.x / ( 1.0f - b.y );
   else
     c.z = 0.5f;
```

```
    // compute points on border curves
    float3 pos0  = evaluateCurve( v0, v1, n0, n1, c.x );
    float3 pos1  = evaluateCurve( v1, v2, n1, n2, c.y );
    float3 pos2  = evaluateCurve( v2, v0, n2, n0, c.z );

    // compute interpolated normals
    float3 norm0 = normalize( lerp( n0, n1, c.x ) );
    float3 norm1 = normalize( lerp( n1, n2, c.y ) );
    float3 norm2 = normalize( lerp( n2, n0, c2.z ) );

    // evaluate points on each of the three curves
    pos0 = evaluateCurve( pos0, v2, norm0, n2, b.z );
    pos1 = evaluateCurve( pos1, v0, norm1, n0, b.x );
    pos2 = evaluateCurve( pos2, v1, norm2, n1, b.y );

    // gregory blend points on curves
    float3 pos = g.x * pos2 + g.y * pos0 + g.z * pos1;

    // transform
    oPos = mul( float4( pos, 1 ), g_mWorldViewProjection );

    float3 Normal = mul( normalize( b.x * n0 + b.y * n1 + b.z * n2
), (float3x3)g_mWorld );
    Diffuse = saturate( dot( Normal, float3( 0.0f, 0.0f, -1.0f ) )
) * g_vDiffuse;
    Diffuse.w = 1.0;

    oTex = b.x * t0 + b.y * t1 + b.z * t2;
}
```

An initial test of the patch for a tetrahedron produces the results shown in Figures 1.1.7. It can be seen that the new patch produces a visually smoother result than the original N-Patch. Obviously more tests need to be run to check if the patch works properly for other objects as well.

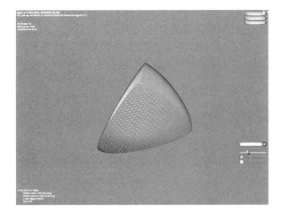

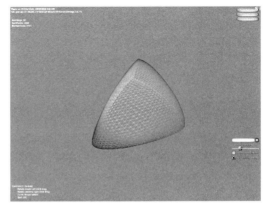

FIGURE 1.1.7A A tetrahedron refined using the original N-Patch.

FIGURE 1.1.7B A tetrahedron refined using the new intermediate patch.

Unfortunately the next test object, which is a cube (part of the media that comes with the DirectX SDK), already reveals that the new patch does not always behave nicely. Figure 1.1.8 shows a refined cube. Although it certainly is visually smooth, it produces a smooth but undesirable valley along the edges of triangles that form one of the six faces of the cube.

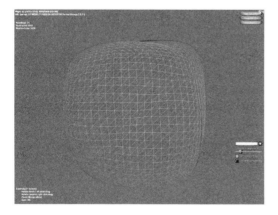
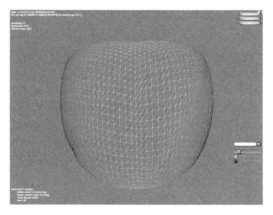

FIGURE 1.1.8A   Refined cube showing smooth edges where cube faces meet.

FIGURE 1.1.8B   Refined cube showing ridges along the coplanar triangles that form the faces of the cube.

One way to explain these ridges is shown in Figure 1.1.9 and explained in the following text.

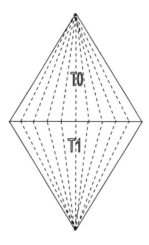

FIGURE 1.1.9   Parameter space lines take off into different directions from the shared position on a shared triangle edge.

Along the edges of coplanar triangles (e.g., triangles forming a face of a cube), patches share the same normal on the shared curve, but each of the curves (see dashed lines in Figure 1.1.9; two triangles *T0* and *T1* are shown) are not parallel when they meet. The normal of the surface is still the same, but a small local neighborhood of these nonparallel curves forms a little wedge. The visible valley is created when the curves sweep this wedge. In addition to this, the patch bulges out more than the original N-Patch does near the center of the triangle. This makes the valleys even more prominent.

Interestingly, the surface looks smooth without ridges where edges from adjacent cube faces meet. The angle between the surface normals of the triangles that meet at these edges is 90°. Therefore, the wedge sweeps a ridge that bulges out and does not hamper visual smoothness.

From observation, the original N-Patch does a good job producing visual smoothness if the normals of adjacent triangles are equal or if they are pointing in similar directions. This suggests that a method to blend the N-Patch and the new patch needs to be found. This method needs to create a patch that behaves like the N-Patch near the center of the triangle and near shared edges with triangles with almost parallel normals.

Finalizing the Smoother N-Patch

In accordance with what has just been discussed, the first thing to find is a term that is 1 at the center of the triangle and slowly goes down to 0 on the edges. Equation 1.1.2 luckily already contains a term that can be used. It is the polynomial $b_{111} b0 \cdot b1 \cdot b2$. Since its value does not go up to 1.0 at the center of the triangle, it needs to be scaled up by 3^3. The resulting blending term is one ingredient of the solution that is about to be described.

$$bl = 3^3 b_{111} b0 \cdot b1 \cdot b2 \qquad (1.1.9)$$

The second ingredient is the absolute value of the dot product of the face normals of two of the triangles that are adjacent along an edge. Since there are usually three shared edges, there are also three of these values *fn0*, *fn1*, and *fn2*. In order to really control the transition from the edge to the center, for every triangle edge one needs three blending factors to blend between the new patch and the N-Patch. Equation 1.1.10 shows how to set up these blending factors.

$$bf0 = \min\left(1, fn0 + bl\right)$$
$$bf1 = \min\left(1, fn1 + bl\right)$$
$$bf2 = \min\left(1, fn2 + bl\right) \qquad (1.1.10)$$

To use these factors, one first evaluates the original N-Patch () resulting in a point *np*. Then for every patch *P0, P1,* and *P2* (see Figure 1.1.5), blend between *np* and the position on the corresponding patch. This results in the following equation:

$$pos0 = lerp\left(P0, np, bf\,0\right)$$

$$pos1 = lerp\left(P1, np, bf\,1\right)$$

$$pos2 = lerp\left(P2, np, bf\,2\right) \qquad\qquad (1.1.11)$$

Now the only thing left is to do a Gregory blend of theses three positions. Bringing it all together, an implementation—again in a vertex shader designed to run within a tessellation through instancing context—looks like this:

LISTING 1.1.2   Implementation

```
float3 evaluateNPatch( float3 v0,
                       float3 v1,
                       float3 v2,
                       float3 n0,
                       float3 n1,
                       float3 n2,
                       float3 b
                     )
{
  float3 b102 = ( 2 * v2 + v0 - dot( v0 - v2, n2 ) * n2 );
  float3 b012 = ( 2 * v2 + v1 - dot( v1 - v2, n2 ) * n2 );
  float3 b201 = ( 2 * v0 + v2 - dot( v2 - v0, n0 ) * n0 );
  float3 b021 = ( 2 * v1 + v2 - dot( v2 - v1, n1 ) * n1 );
  float3 b210 = ( 2 * v0 + v1 - dot( v1 - v0, n0 ) * n0 );
  float3 b120 = ( 2 * v1 + v0 - dot( v0 - v1, n1 ) * n1 );

  return  b.x*b.x*b.x * v0 + b.y*b.y*b.y * v1 + b.z*b.z*b.z * v
2 + b.x*b.z*b.z * b102 +
      b.y*b.z*b.z * b012 + b.x*b.x*b.z * b201 + b.y*b.y*b.z*
      b021 +
      b.x*b.x*b.y * b210 + b.x*b.y*b.y * b120 +
      b.x*b.y*b.z * ( 0.5 * ( b210 + b120 + b021 + b012.xyz +
      b102 + b201 ) -
                          v0 - v1 - v2 );
}

void VSInstancedPatch( float3 b              : POSITION,
                                             // barycentric coords
                       float3 v0             : TEXCOORD0,
                                             // v0 of triangle
                       float3 v1             : TEXCOORD1,
                                             // v1 of triangle
                       float3 v2             : TEXCOORD2,
                                             // v2 of triangle
                       float3 n0             : TEXCOORD3,
                                             // normal for v0
                       float3 n1             : TEXCOORD4,
                                             // normal for v1
                       float3 n2             : TEXCOORD5,
                                             // normal for v2
```

```
                                 float3 v0_          : TEXCOORD6,
                                                     // vtx opposite v0
                                                     // across shared edge
                                 float3 v1_          : TEXCOORD7,
                                                     // vtx opposite v1
                                                     // across shared edge
                                 float3 v2_          : TEXCOORD8,
                                                     // vtx opposite v2
                                                     // across shared edge
                                 float2 t0           : TEXCOORD9,
                                                     // texcoord for v0
                                 float2 t1           : TEXCOORD10,
                                                     // texcoord for v1
                                 float2 t2           : TEXCOORD11,
                                                     // texcoord for v2
                                 out float4 oPos     : POSITION,
                                 out float2 oTex     : TEXCOORD0,
                                 out float4 Diffuse  : COLOR0   )
     {
     float3 g; // gregory coords
     float3 c; // parameters for border curves/edges

       float  b0b2 = b.x * b.z, b0b1 = b.x * b.y, b1b2 = b.y * b.z;
     float  sum = b0b2 + b0b1 + b1b2;

       // compute gregory coords from barycentric coords
       if( b.x > 0.999f || b.y > 0.999f || b.z > 0.999f )
       {
         if( b.x > 0.999f )
           g.x = 1.0f, g.y = g.z = 0.0f;
         else if( b.y > 0.999f )
           g.y = 1.0f, g.x = g.z = 0.0f;
         else
           g.z = 1.0f, g.x = g.y = 0.0f;
       }
       else
       {
         g.x = b0b2/sum;
         g.y = b0b1/sum;
         g.z = b1b2/sum;
       }

     // compute parameters for border curves
       if( 1.0f − b.z != 0.0f )
         c.x = b.y / ( 1.0f − b.z );
       else
         c.x = 0.5f;
       if( 1.0f − b.x != 0.0f )
         c.y = b.z / ( 1.0f − b.x );
       else
         c.y = 0.5f;
       if( 1.0f − b.y != 0.0f )
         c.z = b.x / ( 1.0f − b.y );
       else
         c.z = 0.5f;
```

```
    // compute points on border curves
    float3 pos0  = evaluateCurve( v0, v1, n0, n1, c.x );
    float3 pos1  = evaluateCurve( v1, v2, n1, n2, c.y );
    float3 pos2  = evaluateCurve( v2, v0, n2, n0, c.z );

    // compute interpolated normals
    float3 norm0 = normalize( lerp( n0, n1, c.x ) );
    float3 norm1 = normalize( lerp( n1, n2, c.y ) );
    float3 norm2 = normalize( lerp( n2, n0, c2.z ) );

    // evaluate points on each of the three curves
    pos0 = evaluateCurve( pos0, v2, norm0, n2, b.z );
    pos1 = evaluateCurve( pos1, v0, norm1, n0, b.x );
    pos2 = evaluateCurve( pos2, v1, norm2, n1, b.y );

    // face normal based blending factors
    float  fn0 = abs( dot( n, normalize( cross( v2_ - v0 ,
                                                 v1  - v0 ) ) ) );
    float  fn1 = abs( dot( n, normalize( cross( v0_ - v1,
                                                 v2  - v1 ) ) ) );
    float  fn2 = abs( dot( n, normalize( cross( v2  - v0 ,
                                                 v1_ - v0 ) ) ) );

    // evaluate N-Patch
float3 posN  = evaluateNPatch( v0, v1, v2, n0, n1, n2, b );

// blend factor to blend towards N-Patch based on vicinity of the
// center of the tri
    float bl = 3 * 3 * 3 * b.x*b.y*b.z;

// blend each patch towards the N-Patch
    pos0 = lerp( pos0, posN, min( 1, fn0 + bl ) );
    pos1 = lerp( pos1, posN, min( 1, fn1 + bl ) );
    pos2 = lerp( pos2, posN, min( 1, fn2 + bl ) );

    // gregory blend points on curves and blend with N-Patch again
    float3 pos = lerp( g.x * pos2 + g.y * pos0 + g.z * pos1, posN,
    bl );

    // transform
    oPos = mul( float4( pos, 1 ), g_mWorldViewProjection );

    float3 Normal = mul( normalize( b.x * n0 + b.y * n1 + b.z *
    n2 ), (float3x3)g_mWorld );
    Diffuse = saturate( dot( Normal, float3( 0.0f, 0.0f, -1.0f ) ) )
    * g_vDiffuse;
    Diffuse.w = 1.0;

    oTex = b.x * t0 + b.y * t1 + b.z * t2;
}
```

Note that in order to compute face normals of adjacent faces inside the shader, the per-instance data has to be augmented with the vertices of the adjacent triangles. Obviously one only needs to add the vertices that oppose shared edges.

Running this shader on the cube produces the results shown in Figure 1.1.10. It is obvious that the final patch improves the smoothness of the cube.

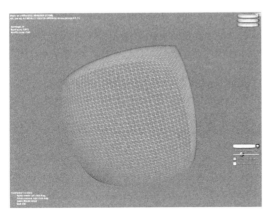

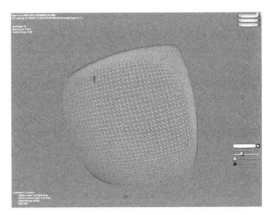

FIGURE 1.1.10A A cube refined using the original N-Patch.

FIGURE 1.1.10B A cube refined using the final new patch.

Now that it has been shown that it is possible to construct a smoother N-Patch, performance considerations and conclusions will be discussed.

Performance Considerations and Conclusions

It is clear that it is more expensive to evaluate the new patches described in this article than it is to evaluate the N-Patch. Luckily enough, the original N-Patch can be mixed with the new patches across an object since the new patches create the same shared border curves that N-Patches create. Depending on the angle between triangles, it may not be necessary to evaluate *P0, P1,* or *P2* but to stick to the original N-Patch. Using per-edge information and appropriate *if()* statements inside the vertex shader can speed up patch evaluation enormously if there is proper hardware support for these statements.

The new patches show improved smoothness when compared to the original N-Patch for low-poly objects. As indicated for N-Patches in [Gruen05] they could also be used as a basis for surface compression.

Even if one concludes that the new patches are too slow to run inside a shader, it is still possible to evaluate them on the CPU and cache the results. Hardware that features several parallel processor cores, in particular, can be utilized easily. This is possible since tessellation scales in a data-parallel way (see [Gruen06]).

Conclusions

Geometry Shaders, which are part of DirectX10, allow geometry generation on the GPU. They can therefore be used to tessellate triangles and to evaluate patches. Interestingly DirectX10 also allows Geometry Shader to access adjacency information for triangles. These features can therefore be easily used to access the additional vertices that the patches proposed here need. Once there is DirectX10-capable hardware, it would be straightforward to implement the smoother N-Patch with Geometry Shaders. Currently the reference software device does not make such an experiment a very pleasurable experience because of speed considerations.

References

[Bolz02] Bolz, Jeffrey and Peter Schröder, "Rapid Evaluation of Catmull-Clark Subdivision Surfaces," February 2002, Proceeding of the Seventh International Conference on 3D Web Technology.

[Cloward] Cloward, Ben, "Creating and Using Normal Maps." Available online at *http://www.monitorstudios.com/bcloward/tutorials_normal_maps1.html*.

[Farin96] Farin, Gerald E., *Curves and Surfaces for Computer-Aided Geometric Design*, Academic Press Inc., 1996.

[Farin99] Farin, Gerald E."*Nurbs,*" A K Peters, Ltd., 1999.

[Gruen05] Gruen, Holger, "Efficient Tessellation on the GPU through Instancing," *Journal of Game Development, 1*(3), December 2005.

[Gruen06] Gruen, Holger, "Multi-threaded Terrain Smoothing." Available online at *www.gamasutra.com*, June 2006.

[Hoppe97] Hoppe, Hugues, "View-Dependent Refinement of Progressive Meshes," ACM SIGGRAPH, 1997, pp, 189–198.

[Lien87] Sheue-Ling, Lien, Michael Shantz, and Vaughan Pratt, "Adaptive Forward Differencing for Rendering Curves and Surfaces," ACM SIGGRAPH Computer Graphics, Proceedings of the 14th Annual Conference on Computer Graphics and Interactive Techniques, *21*(4), August 1987.

[Loviscach03] Loviscach, Jörn, "Silhouette Geometry Shaders," *ShaderX³ Advanced Rendering with DirectX and OpenGL*, Charles River Media, 2003.

[Sander00] Sander, P., X. Gu, S. Gortler, H. Hoppe, and J. Snyder, "Silhouette Clipping." ACM SIGGRAPH 2000: pp. 327–334.

[Sander01] Sander, P., H. Hoppe, J. Snyder, and S. Gortler, "Discontinuity Edge Overdraw," ACM Symposium on Interactive 3D Graphics 2001: pp. 167–174.

[Vlachos01] Vlachos, Alex, Jörg Peters, Chas Boyd, and Jason L. Mitchell, "Curved PN Triangles," *Proceedings of the 2001 Symposium on Interactive 3D Graphics*, March 2001.

1.2

Micro-beveled Edges

Homam Bahnassi (In|Framez) and
Wessam Bahnassi (Electronic Arts)

Introduction

Beveling is a technique that gets rid of sharp edges in 3D rendered objects by rounding or chamfering these sharp edges. This produces more natural scenes because hard and sharp edges rarely exist in nature, where almost everything has rounded edges on many different scales. Thinking of it more, even most man-made objects have rounded edges. For example, boxes and crates, buildings, bricks, many electrical appliances (TVs, fridges, and ovens), and even robots.

Beveling is usually carried out on the geometric level. That is, it changes the topology of the 3D object by adding more faces at the edges to gradually round the angle between perpendicular faces.

However, modeling this effect can be tedious and, more importantly, expensive for rendering. The number of vertices and edges can easily multiply by at least 20 times for even a simple cube, which is a waste of performance relative to the overall outcome (see Figure 1.2.1).

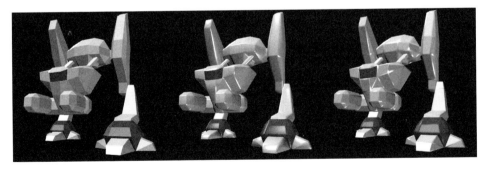

FIGURE 1.2.1   (Left) Robot model without micro-beveled edges; mesh composed of 752 triangle faces. (Middle) Robot model with geometric micro-beveling; mesh composed of 5000 faces. (Right) Robot model micro-beveled with the technique described in this article; mesh composed of 752 triangle faces, just like the original version

ON THE CD

This article discusses a simple technique to approximate rounded edges cheaply and without the huge increase in modeling data. A variation of this technique was presented before [Bahnassi05] for offline renderers (e.g., mentalRay), in which it resulted in a good performance gain, especially in heavily populated scenes. This method can work on objects lit with either per-pixel lighting or per-vertex lighting, and it allows the faking of only a small amount of beveling (hence it is called micro-beveling), which is enough to give back the natural look.

The Goal

While beveling can be done in many different ways, the technique described here tries to add rounding and slight imperfections to objects' edges, with the following considerations in mind:

- Save tedious modeling time.
- Avoid the huge increase in the number of triangles.
- Make use of existing data as much as possible.
- Allow enough control to flexibly express and tune the effect.

With these goals in mind, we will discuss techniques that "fake" beveling without actually modifying topology (i.e., similar to bump mapping).

First Approach

For objects lit with per-pixel lighting, a straightforward solution is to just "bake" the rounded normals into the tangent-space normal map where the texture goes around the edges. This would result in a normal map like that in Figure 1.2.2.

FIGURE 1.2.2   (Left) The normal map of a micro-beveled cube. (Right) The cube shaded with this normal map.

However, in reality this solution can be impractical. Normal maps consume a lot of memory even when they are compressed. Thus, objects are rarely flattened to cover a whole sheet of texture. Instead, the same normal map texture is mostly reused many times across the different faces of the object and across different objects in the scene* (Figure 1.2.3).

FIGURE 1.2.3   Textures are usually reused across different faces of the same object or reused across different objects in the same scene.

For this kind of texture mapping, however, it might be problematic or too restrictive to incorporate rounded normals into the right place on the map.

Moreover, baking normals into the normal map requires modeling the real thing and then pulling out the details onto the normal map using some high detail to low detail conversion tool, and this can be a very time-consuming and tedious task.

Finally, the technique should not be restricted to normal-mapped objects only. It is highly preferable that works for objects that use simple per-vertex lighting too.

If the First Did Not Succeed . . .

Before going deeper into finding a better solution, it might be helpful to see how normals look when beveling is applied the classic way (Figure 1.2.4).

If we borrow these normals from the high-detail model and apply them over the low-detail model, we would end up with something like Figure 1.2.5.

Because normals are simply interpolated across the face, wrong shading occurs across the whole box, which gives rounded shading over flat areas, and that is clearly wrong.

*Which is the main purpose of using tangent-space normal maps as opposed to object-space normal maps.

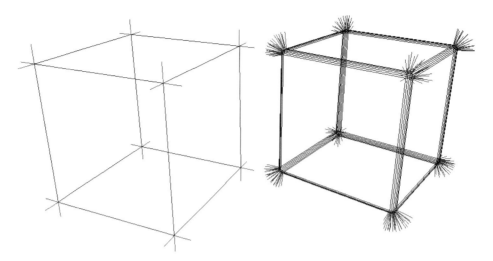

FIGURE 1.2.4   (Left) Normals of a box made of six faces only. Note that they are all perpendicular to the box's faces, which produces the general flat shading. (Right) The box with micro-beveled edges. Note how the normals smoothly wrap around the edges.

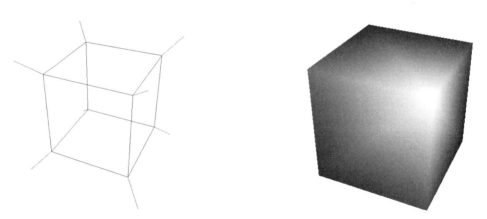

FIGURE 1.2.5   (Left) The same simple box as in Figure 1.2.4, but with smoothed normals. (Right) The shaded version of the box on the left. As expected, the result is totally incorrect shading across the faces.

However, both versions of the same object (smoothed and nonsmoothed) can be combined in a special way to give flat shading over flat surfaces and rounded shading over the edges. The combination is done with the aid of a mask that selects which normal is used for which part of the object. Such a mask would look like Figure 1.2.6 for the box object.

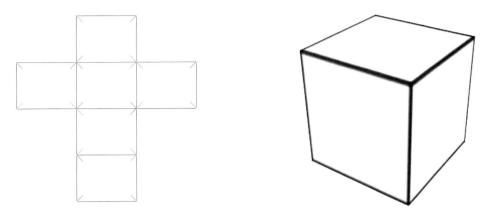

FIGURE 1.2.6   (Left) The mask texture. (Right) The 3D box with this texture applied.

Let us assume that the object has two sets of normals specified per-vertex. The first set is generated by calculating face normals and storing them at the vertices. The second set is generated by calculating the average normal for each vertex from all faces sharing that vertex.

So, given the face normal and the average normal and a mask, the calculation goes like this on a per-pixel basis (in HLSL terminology):

```
FinalNormal = Lerp(FaceNormal, AverageNormal, MaskIntensity);
// ...normalize and use FinalNormal through
// the following lighting calculations
```

In these lines, as the mask gets brighter at a position, the average normal will contribute more to the final lighting normal. Thus, a mask like the one in Figure 1.2.6 would produce smooth lighting across the edges and flat lighting over the interior of the polygons. The final result would look similar to Figure 1.2.7.

FIGURE 1.2.7   The box shaded with this technique.

The creation of the mask texture is very simple and allows for flexible hand-tuning as shown in Figure 1.2.8. The texture can be generated by *stamping* the UV coordinates of the texture that the object is using. Stamping is an operation commonly used by 3D artists when they need to make changes to the texture as they adjust the object's UV coordinates. By doing so, they ensure proper mapping while modifying the image. The UV coordinates are stamped over the texture, and the result is saved into a new image.

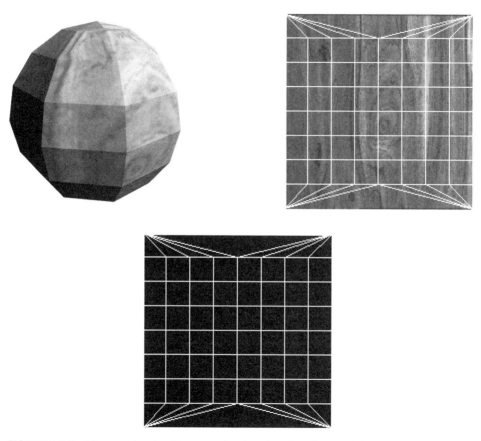

FIGURE 1.2.8   The steps involved in generating the micro-beveling mask for a textured 3D sphere. The sphere on the left is mapped onto the texture in the middle, and the stamp of the primitives making this sphere is extracted to a separate image for further hand-tuning.

In our case, only the wireframe is needed in the mask image, so the stamp should be generated against a black background. Then, this image can be modified freely in any image-editing tool. For example, blurring the lines will result in more roundedness and fewer sharp transitions over the edges; increasing the lines' thickness results in rounding covering more area on the sides of the edges, and finally, the lines can be touched to give varying thickness and blurring that results in imperfect edges that are useful to give the impression of abused objects.

The Ins and Outs

Before we come to a conclusion, it is worth noting some important points about this technique.

The technique requires two sets of normals and the mask texture only. The first set is the original normals set and can be specified in different ways, such as from a normal map or from simple per-vertex normals. The second normals set is for the averaged normals, and it should be stored per-vertex.

Keep in mind that during calculation, both normals should exist in the same space (either object or tangent space) before they can be blended meaningfully.

For objects using per-vertex lighting, this technique can still be applicable. However, instead of sending the two normals to the pixel shader, the vertex shader calculates lighting for both normals individually and sends the resulting two colors to the pixel shader for blending in accordance with the mask texture.

The mask texture carries a grayscale value used for the blending. Thus, the mask should be stored in a single-channel texture or even combined in an unused channel of a texture that is already applied to the object. Also, it does not have to be stored at full resolution. It might be preferable to use a low-resolution texture to store the mask. This, combined with linear filtering, can help give additional blurring to the edges for free while lowering texture memory consumption and ultimately increasing performance.

The mask texture should be generated with caution. If the stamping tool stamps triangulated primitives over the texture, rounding can appear at the wrong places across flat faces. If the stamping is done by a hand-written tool, edges shared between triangles that form a single plane should be ignored.

Finally, since this technique does not modify the real 3D geometry, a box will keep being a box. That is, the silhouette is still sharp, but the shading is smooth. However, we still believe that this approximation is good enough to remove the unnatural look of real-time nonorganic objects.

Conclusion

This article has proposed a cheap method to fake micro-beveling in real-time. The concept builds on a special mask that selects between rounded and flat normals on a per-pixel basis. The mask is a simple stamp of the textured primitives, blurred and tweaked freely to control the amount and shape of micro-beveling.

The technique integrates well with normal mapping, as well as objects rendered with per-vertex lighting.

References

[Bahnassi05] Bahnassi, Homam, "Faking Micro-bevel with MentalRay," In|Framez Papers. Available online at *http://www.inframez.com/papers/xsi_microbevel.htm*

1.3

Dynamic Wrinkle Patterns and Hatching on Animated Meshes

Jörn Loviscach

(jlovisca@informatik.hs-bremen.de)

Introduction

Commonly, textures are generated from fixed bitmap images or through procedures that are not affected by animation. However, current GPUs allow one to create dynamic, seamless, self-organizing surface patterns that adapt to a varying shape of the mesh and don't require texture coordinate data. This chapter demonstrates two technically similar uses of this idea. The first use is an ultra-fast cloth simulation: the local deformation of an animated mesh can be employed to create believable fold and wrinkle patterns in real-time.

These patterns may be rendered very efficiently with bump and parallax mapping on coarse, polygonal objects [Loviscach06] (see Figure 1.3.1). As a second use, the principal directions of the mesh's local curvature can be used to form stripe patterns that resemble hatching as applied by an artist [Loviscach06a] (see Figure 1.3.2). In contrast to earlier solutions such as in [Praun01], the hatching conforms to the animated shape and does not require a texture parameterization.

For both the wrinkling and the hatching patterns, a smooth overall layout of the patterns is vital. Thus, a major feature of the method is a relaxation process to shift local patterns so that they form a globally consistent field. Typically, such a global perspective of the mesh is alien to GPU-based algorithms.

The full process requires four rendering passes with vertex and pixel shaders. This number sounds high; however, the first three passes produce one pixel for every vertex of the mesh, so that they run at high speed for typical game-like objects. Some input data and all intermediate results are stored in floating-point pseudo-textures. The first rendering pass evaluates matrix-palette skinning. The second pass computes the local wavelength and direction of the pattern. The third pass comprises a gradual relaxation to align the local patterns globally. The fourth pass generates the image on screen.

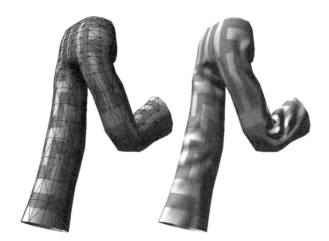

FIGURE 1.3.1   From the mesh's bare animation (left), dynamic
fold and wrinkle patterns can be created and rendered with bump
and parallax mapping (right).

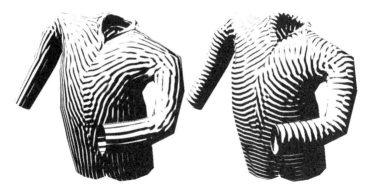

FIGURE 1.3.2   Stripe patterns aligned to the principal curvature directions
resemble hatching in hand-drawn illustrations.

ON THE CD

The prototype as contained in this article's folder on the accompanying CD-ROM
has been built in C# 2.0 and HLSL Shader Model 3.0 on top of .NET 2.0 and Managed DirectX 1.0 from the DirectX 9.0c SDK (April 2006). For easy reproducibility,
the input files are prerecorded animations from .x files, even though the method can
handle an interactive control.

Since the 3D mesh is animated, one has to distinguish between its original shape
(the rest pose) and its deformed shape after skinning. Vector quantities referring to
the rest pose are denoted by boldface characters such as $\mathbf{x}$; vector quantities referring
to the deformed shape are denoted by boldface characters with a prime such as $\mathbf{x}'$.

Seam Welding and Skinning

Typical meshes do not contain seamless *uv* texture coordinates but are equipped with a texture atlas. The patches of the atlas are glued together by duplicated vertices, which occupy a single 3D position but differ in their *uv* values. To produce a seamless wave pattern, a preprocessing step welds such multiple copies of a single vertex into one. Nonetheless, the mesh's *uv* coordinates may still be used, for instance, to control color textures (see Figure 1.3.1). To this end, yet another copy of the original vertices is produced: in this buffer, each original vertex is augmented by the number of its representative in the unified list.

The first of the four rendering passes evaluates matrix-palette skinning for every vertex of the mesh in a standard fashion. Its vertex shader computes weighted sums of the vectors resulting from the action of the bones onto every vertex's original position and normal vector. However, the result is not used directly for rendering. Rather, the graphics card is set to point rendering mode; every vertex is treated on its own, and the pixel shader stores the resulting position and normal vector in two separate floating-point buffers, making use of Multiple Render Target functionality. The *uv* position in these buffers is determined from the vertex's index number, which has been added to the vertex attributes during the preprocessing step.

Local Patterns from Curvature

The second rendering pass is slightly different, depending on whether one wants to produce a hatching pattern or cloth-like wrinkles. Let's start with the former application, since it involves fewer steps. In this case, the job of the second rendering pass is to produce a direction vector $\mathbf{k'}$ per vertex. Again, the list of unique vertices is traversed in point-rendering mode. The resulting $\mathbf{k'}$ is written to a floating-point RGBA texture, with every texel representing one vertex.

The vector $\mathbf{k'}_0$ describes the local shape of the pattern: a plane sinusoidal wave,

$$\cos\left(\tfrac{2\pi}{W}\,\mathbf{k'}_0 \cdot \left(\mathbf{x'} - \mathbf{x'}_0\right) + \varphi_0\right),\qquad\qquad(1.3.1)$$

as used in physics to describe, among other things, phenomena of light or sound (see Figure 1.3.3). The primed quantities are being used, since this computation is done after the deformation. The pattern's width is equal to $W\,/\left|\mathbf{k'}_0\right|$. The value φ_0 acts as a phase offset, given at the point $\mathbf{x'}_0$.

The objective is now to compute a vector $\mathbf{k'}$ for every vertex in such a way that

- $\mathbf{k'}$ is perpendicular to the normal, so that the pattern is applied along the surface,
- $\mathbf{k'}$ points in the direction of the strongest or the least magnitude of local curvature (up to the user's choice), so that the stripe pattern is, for instance, aligned with the long axis of a cylinder.

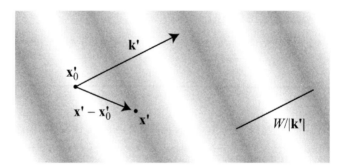

FIGURE 1.3.3   The vector $\mathbf{k}'_0$ is perpendicular to the plane wave's peaks and valleys.

The local curvature can't be determined from one vertex alone; it's a property of the neighborhood. Since the positions and the normals of all vertices are readily available from the pseudo-textures created in the first rendering pass, to access these data it suffices to have the ID numbers of the neighbor vertices available.

These ID numbers may not be stored as part of the vertex's attributes, since their number is virtually unbounded. Imagine, for instance, the number of triangles adjacent to the poles of a sphere tessellated as usual. On initialization, the neighborhood data are stored as pseudo-colors in a texture. Owing to the current size limitations for textures, the data do not fit into a 1D texture, but require a 2D texture.

The ID numbers are stored texel by texel in standard writing order: first, the ID numbers of the neighbors of the first vertex and then those of the second vertex and so on (see Figure 1.3.4). If there is not enough space on the current line, its remaining texels are left unused, and the data continue on the next line. This speeds up the address computation on retrieval. Every vertex in the vertex buffer is equipped with the start address of its neighbors in this texture and with their count.

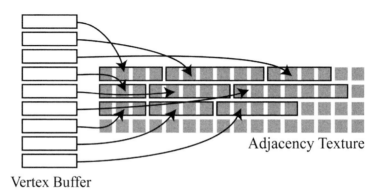

FIGURE 1.3.4   The neighborhood data are prepared in a 2D pseudo-texture.

Given the position and normal vectors of a vertex and its neighbors, one can estimate the local bending of the surface. The curvature is proportional to the speed with which the normal vectors tilt away from the central vertex's normal as one moves away from its position (see Figure 1.3.5). This speed and thus the curvature vary with direction; we aim to find the direction with the highest speed, which is one of the two principal directions of curvature. The other principal direction will be perpendicular to this. It is up to the user to decide which one of these two directions is to be returned as the vector $\mathbf{k}'$.

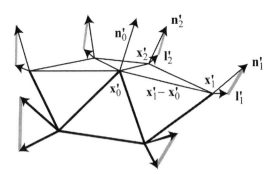

FIGURE 1.3.5 The curvature can be determined from the speed with which the lateral components of the normal vectors grow.

One could immediately find out for which adjacent vertex the speed is highest. However, this would lead to artificial discontinuities on the mesh and in the temporal development of an animation, since the adjacent vertices represent only a sparse sample of the neighborhood. Thus, one needs to find a smooth interpolation of this sparse sample. Since we're interested in how quickly the normal tilts as we move away from the central vertex in a tangential direction, it is natural to look for a matrix $\mathbf{M}$ that approximately maps every tangent vector $\mathbf{t}'_i = \mathbf{x}'_i - \mathbf{x}'_0 - ((\mathbf{x}'_i - \mathbf{x}'_0) \cdot \mathbf{n}'_0)\mathbf{n}'_0$ to the lateral component $\mathbf{l}'_i = \mathbf{n}'_i - (\mathbf{n}'_i \cdot \mathbf{n}'_0)\mathbf{n}'_0$ of the corresponding normal (see Figure 1.3.5).

Linear Regression and Maximum Curvature

We're seeking a matrix $\mathbf{M}$ that maps every $\mathbf{t}'_i$ approximately to the corresponding $\mathbf{l}'_i$ and incurs the least overall error, that is,

$$\sum_i \left| \mathbf{l}'_i - \mathbf{M}\mathbf{t}'_i \right|^2 \overset{!}{=} \min.$$

This is an example of data fitting—in this case multidimensional linear regression. All derivatives of the left-hand side with respect to any entry of **M** have to vanish. After some lengthy computations one finds [Alpaydin04]

$$\mathbf{M} = \sum_i \mathbf{l'}_i \otimes \mathbf{t'}_i \left(\sum_j \mathbf{t'}_j \otimes \mathbf{t'}_j \right)^{-1},$$

where the exponent –1 denotes the inverse matrix and $\mathbf{a} \otimes \mathbf{b}$ is the tensor product matrix of two vectors **a** and **b**:

$$\mathbf{a} \otimes \mathbf{b} = \begin{bmatrix} a_x b_x & a_x b_y & a_x b_z \\ a_y b_x & a_y b_y & a_y b_z \\ a_z b_x & a_z b_y & a_z b_z \end{bmatrix}.$$

M describes how the local curvature at the vertex 0 depends on the direction. The objective was to find a direction vector **k'** with the quickest or slowest variation of the normal, that is $|\mathbf{Mk'}| = \max$ for $|\mathbf{k'}| = 1$. Geometrically speaking, one applies **M** to every position vector on the unit sphere. The shape resulting from that is an ellipsoid, as for all linear transformations. We're looking for a vector mapped to the major principal axis of the ellipsoid.

It is equivalent but easier to look for the max of the square of $|\mathbf{Mk'}|$:

$$|\mathbf{Mk'}|^2 = (\mathbf{Mk'}) \cdot (\mathbf{Mk'}) = \mathbf{k'} \cdot (\mathbf{M}^T \mathbf{Mk'})$$

where $\mathbf{M}^T$ denotes the transposed matrix. If **k'** fulfills $|\mathbf{k'}| = 1$ and maximizes the former expression, **k'** has to be parallel to $\mathbf{M}^T\mathbf{Mk'}$. Otherwise, one could change **k'** to point a little more in the direction of $\mathbf{M}^T\mathbf{Mk'}$ and achieve a strictly larger value.

k' being parallel to $\mathbf{M}^T\mathbf{Mk'}$ only means that **k'** is an eigenvector of $\mathbf{M}^T\mathbf{M}$; that is $\mathbf{M}^T\mathbf{Mk'} = \lambda\mathbf{k'}$ with some number λ. We're looking for the largest such eigenvalue λ. The direction of **k'** is only determined up to sign, an ambiguity of which later stages have to take care.

These computations don't need to be executed in 3D space, since the input and output vectors stem only from a 2D space: the tangent plane at vertex 0. One can employ the normal and one neighbor $\mathbf{x'}_1$ to create a coordinate frame in the tangent plane, spanned by the two vectors

$$\mathbf{t'} = \text{normalize}(\mathbf{x'}_1 - \mathbf{x'}_0 - ((\mathbf{x'}_1 - \mathbf{x'}_0) \cdot \mathbf{n'}_0)\mathbf{n'}_0),$$

$$\mathbf{b'} = \mathbf{n'}_0 \times \mathbf{t'}.$$

The position and normal data are converted to this frame by forming dot products with **t'** and **b'**.

In principle, the GPU can execute 3D and 2D computations at the same speed, barring a slight chance of folding two 2D instructions into one 4D instruction. The main reason to do this computation in 2D is that this makes it much easier to determine the largest eigenvalue and a corresponding eigenvector. Actually, in 2D there can only be two eigenvalues at the most: one larger and one smaller.

Let the matrix $\mathbf{M}$ be given as

$$\begin{pmatrix} a & b \\ c & d \end{pmatrix}.$$

Then the larger eigenvalue λ of $\mathbf{M}^T\mathbf{M}$ can be found through

$$\lambda = 0.5(a^2 + b^2 + c^2 + d^2) + \sqrt{0.25(a^2 + b^2 + c^2 + d^2) + (ab + cd)^2 - (a^2 + c^2)(b^2 + d^2)}, \quad (1.3.2)$$

and the smaller eigenvalue has a minus in front of the square root. This looks overly complex on first sight. However, all terms can be computed relatively quickly using 2D dot products such as

$$ab + cd = \begin{bmatrix} a \\ c \end{bmatrix} \cdot \begin{bmatrix} b \\ d \end{bmatrix}$$

An eigenvector corresponding to the eigenvalue λ is given as

$$\begin{bmatrix} ab + cd \\ \lambda - (a^2 + c^2) \end{bmatrix}$$

where two of the subexpressions for λ can be reused.

The sought direction vector $\mathbf{k'}$ has to have unit length, so one can use the above eigenvector divided by its length. However, there is a numerical issue when this length is near zero. A closer inspection of the matrix $\mathbf{M}^T\mathbf{M}$ reveals that it is approximately equal to

$$\begin{bmatrix} \lambda & 0 \\ 0 & b^2 + d^2 \end{bmatrix}$$

in this case, so that one can set the direction vector to $\begin{bmatrix} 1 \\ 0 \end{bmatrix}$.

For perfectly spherical or planar parts of a mesh, the two eigenvalues will be equal and there will be no preferred directions. Thus, curvature-based hatching has to break down in such a case and the described method produces seemingly random directions that depend on the structure of the mesh.

Local Patterns from Deformation

The second rendering pass may determine the mesh's curvature, which is the basis for hatching, but may also extract the compression of the mesh for cloth folds. The major difference lies in the determination of the direction vector per vertex. Instead of looking at how quickly the surrounding normal vectors bend away, one has to find the local direction of maximum compression applied by the animation. Folds and wrinkles should form perpendicular to this direction.

Again, there is a matrix $\mathbf{M}$ that pictures the local situation. But now, $\mathbf{M}$ does not describe the curvature, but the deformation. It connects rest-pose space coordinates $\mathbf{x}$ to post-deformation coordinates $\mathbf{x'}$. In particular, $\mathbf{M}$ generalizes the mapping that converts $\mathbf{t}_i = \mathbf{x}_i - \mathbf{x}_0 - ((\mathbf{x}_i - \mathbf{x}_0) \cdot \mathbf{n}_0)\mathbf{n}_0$ to $\mathbf{t'}_i = \mathbf{x'}_i - \mathbf{x'}_0 - ((\mathbf{x'}_i - \mathbf{x'}_0) \cdot \mathbf{n'}_0)\mathbf{n'}_0$ (see Figure 1.3.6).

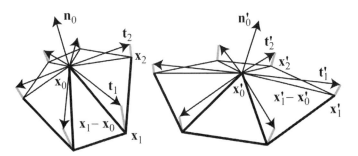

FIGURE 1.3.6   To create fold and wrinkle patterns, the matrix $\mathbf{M}$ approximates the local effect of the deformation.

$\mathbf{M}$ can again be found through regression in 2D. The input to this computation consists of the positions of all vertices before and after deformation plus the normal of vertex 0 before and after deformation. The post-deformation position and normal vectors are already available from pseudo-textures written in the first rendering pass. The rest-space position and normal of vertex 0 is part of its attributes in the vertex buffer. In addition to that, the rest-space positions of all vertices are available from a pseudo-texture, which is created during the initialization.

To determine the direction of maximum compression, one has to use the smaller eigenvector of $\mathbf{M}$. Since this matrix describes the square of the deformation, the length expansion/compression factor will be $\sqrt{\lambda}$. In contrast to the hatching method, one can't only store the direction vector per vertex, but also has to store the amplitude of wrinkles to be created. Through a coarse triangular approximation, one finds that the amplitude should equal $\frac{4}{W}\sqrt{\max(1-\lambda,0)}$ (see Figure 1.3.7). Note that taking the maximum is necessary to also handle the case of expansion, in which the amplitude is set to zero. To model the tension wrinkles generated by expansion, one may introduce an ad-hoc formula that also covers the case $\lambda > 1$. Preliminary experiments revealed, however, that this leads to abundant wrinkles.

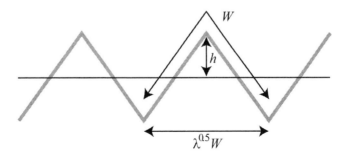

FIGURE 1.3.7   For accordion-type wrinkles, the relation between compression and amplitude can be derived from Pythagoras's law.

If there is an exactly uniform deformation, there are no preferred directions, and the method will produce seemingly random directions, not unlike the behavior of real cloth. This is analogous to the case of planar or spherical meshes for the hatching method. However, if there is no deformation at all, the wrinkle patterns behave well, since their amplitude is zero.

The direction vector with unit length determined from the eigenanalysis is a vector referring to the rest pose. The resulting plane waves according to

$$\cos\left(\tfrac{2\pi}{W}\mathbf{k}_0 \cdot (\mathbf{x} - \mathbf{x}_0) + \varphi_0\right) \tag{1.3.3}$$

thus "live" in rest-pose space. This is helpful, because in this way the width W of the pattern is constant on the original mesh. However, all following computations are executed on the deformed mesh. Thus, one has to find a post-deformation tangent vector $\mathbf{k}'_0$ so that Equation 1.3.1 produces the same pattern in post-deformation space $\mathbf{x}'$ as Equation 1.3.3 does in rest-pose space $\mathbf{x}$.

Since $\mathbf{M}$ describes the local deformation, the tangential part of $\mathbf{x}' - \mathbf{x}'_0$ is approximately equal to $\mathbf{M}$ applied to the tangential part of $\mathbf{x} - \mathbf{x}_0$. Both $\mathbf{k}'$ and $\mathbf{k}'_0$ are tangent vectors, so that one can discard nontangent components in the dot products. This yields

$$\mathbf{k}_0 \cdot (\mathbf{x} - \mathbf{x}_0) \approx \mathbf{k}_0 \cdot \mathbf{M}^{-1}(\mathbf{x}' - \mathbf{x}'_0) = ((\mathbf{M}^T)^{-1}\mathbf{k}_0) \cdot (\mathbf{x}' - \mathbf{x}'_0)$$

This leads to the conclusion that $\mathbf{k}'_0$ is transformed by the inverse transpose of $\mathbf{M}$:

$$\mathbf{k}'_0 = (\mathbf{M}^T)^{-1}\mathbf{k}_0$$

a transformation well known to shader developers from the treatment of normal vectors with the `WorldInverseTranspose` matrix. In general, $\mathbf{k}'_0$ will no longer be normalized, which is precisely what is needed to produce wrinkle patterns that are compressed in the same way the mesh is.

ON THE CD

The demo software included on the CD-ROM provides additional real-time functionality to paint wrinkles onto the mesh's rest position. This is realized through a distortion of **M** [Loviscach06].

Relaxation

At this point, the patterns are defined in the neighborhood of every vertex. There, they form plane waves with known wavelength, direction up to sign and (in the case of wrinkling) amplitude. However, the phase φ_0 in the waves' equation (Equation 1.3.1) is still unknown. It is optimized in the third rendering pass to diminish the mismatch between the waves defined at adjacent vertices (see Figure 1.3.8).

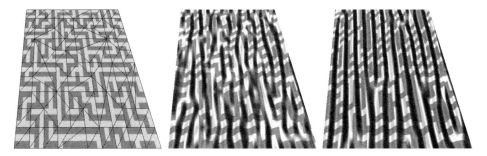

FIGURE 1.3.8   An appropriate phase shift of the local plane waves determined in the former steps (middle) can be used to create a globally consistent field (right).

Real-time applications in general and GPUs in particular do not lend themselves to global optimization processes. Thus, a gradual, local process is employed: the third rendering pass computes the local mismatch around every vertex and introduces a corresponding small correction to the wave's phase at that vertex. During the course of, say, 10 or 20 frames of the animation the wave field will relax toward an optimal shape. If the amount of correction is too large, oscillations may occur; if it's too small, the process takes too long, resulting in flowing, silk-like motion. The optimum shape found through the iterative process may not be the best solution imaginable but may contain some bifurcations that can't be fixed by small corrections. However, this seemingly imperfect behavior lets the solution look even more plausible (see Figure 1.3.8).

Similar to the first two rendering passes, the third pass processes every vertex of the mesh (again the copy with welded seams) to create one pixel in a one-channel floating-point pseudo-texture. This texture represents the phase values. Since the third pass has to take the current phase into account to compute the mismatch, it must also be able to read the phase, not only to write it. However, current GPUs can't write to and read from the same texture in a single pass. Thus, there have to be two copies of that texture: one for reading and one for writing. Their roles alternate every frame.

To compute the mismatch between a vertex and its neighbors, one can try to come up with an analytical formula or to sample the errors in a deterministic or a stochastic manner. A sparse deterministic sampling strategy turns out to work effectively and efficiently: The samples are taken on the centers of the edges connecting a vertex to its neighbors (see Figure 1.3.9).

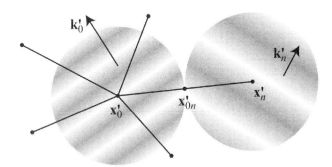

FIGURE 1.3.9 The phase mismatch is determined at the centers of the edges connecting a vertex to its neighbors.

Let's look at the contribution of the error sample at the center, $\mathbf{x'}_{0n} = 0.5(\mathbf{x'}_0 + \mathbf{x'}_n)$, of the edge between vertex 0 and its neighbor n. It should measure the local mismatch between $\cos(\frac{2\pi}{W}\mathbf{k'}_n \cdot (\mathbf{x'} - \mathbf{x'}_n) + \varphi_n)$ and $\cos(\frac{2\pi}{W}\mathbf{k'}_0 \cdot (\mathbf{x'} - \mathbf{x'}_0) + \varphi_0)$ for all $\mathbf{x'}$ in the vicinity of $\mathbf{x'}_{0n}$.

A naïve solution would be to directly compare the phases $\psi_n = \frac{2\pi}{W}\mathbf{k'}_n \cdot (\mathbf{x'} - \mathbf{x'}_n) + \varphi_n$ and $\psi_0 = \frac{2\pi}{W}\mathbf{k'}_0 \cdot (\mathbf{x'} - \mathbf{x'}_0) + \varphi_0$. However, such an approach would be overly strict, since the cosine is both an even and a periodic function. Changing a phase to its negative or adding an integer multiple of 2π to it would not change the appearance of the waves. Note that this also hides the indeterminacy of the sign of all vectors $\mathbf{k'}$. A change in such a sign can be perfectly hidden by changing the sign of the corresponding phase φ as well. The relaxation process will automatically take care of finding the right sign for the phase.

To accommodate for the cosine being even, one has to take the directions $\mathbf{k'}_n$ and $\mathbf{k'}_0$ into account. If these two directions form an obtuse angle, one of them needs to be flipped. Thus, a meaningful quantity is $\Delta\psi = \text{sgn}(\mathbf{k'}_n \cdot \mathbf{k'}_0)\psi_n - \psi_0$. The periodicity of the cosine still needs to be taken into account. If $\Delta\psi$ is an integer multiple of 2π, that's as good as if it was zero. Thus, a measure of mismatch can be defined through

$$E_n = \left| \frac{1}{2\pi}\Delta\psi - \text{floor}(\frac{1}{2\pi}\Delta\psi + 0.5) \right|^2$$

The contributions E_n of all edges around a given vertex 0 are average to form the complete error of the phase at that vertex.

The shader of the third rendering pass determines this per-vertex error and tries to diminish it using a gradient descent. It changes ψ_0 slightly in such a way that the error tends to decrease. One looks at the derivative of the error with respect to ψ_0 and changes ψ_0 by a small negative number times this derivative. If the derivative is positive, the error tends to increase with growing ψ_0; thus, it has to be reduced, and vice versa. Actually, the error itself doesn't have to be computed; one only needs its derivative, which is the average of

$$-\tfrac{1}{\pi}(\tfrac{1}{2\pi}\Delta\psi - \text{floor}(\tfrac{1}{2\pi}\Delta\psi + 0.5))$$

over all adjacent vertices.

The hatching patterns extend over the entire mesh, but the wrinkle pattern will appear only in specific places—namely, where the animation contacts the mesh. The phase adjustments within one of the wrinkled parts should not affect the others. That is, the relaxation must not spread across flat parts. The easiest way to achieve this is to clamp the error to zero for flat parts. To get a soft cutoff instead, one can weigh the errors E_n by $\max(\min(4H - 0.2, 1), 0)$, where H is wrinkle amplitude scaled to range between 0 and 1.

Wave Interpolation and Rendering

The fourth and final rendering pass computes the waves around every vertex, blends them, and generates illumination and texturing to produce the pixels displayed to the user.

Given the $\mathbf{k'}$ direction vector, the phase φ, and—in the case of wrinkles—the wave's amplitude per vertex, one has to interpolate these data to find the wave's actual height at every pixel. A naive approach would be to compute the height at every vertex and interpolate the result linearly across every triangle. Then there would no be oscillations on the triangles, so that the wavelength would have to be much larger than a triangle's diameter.

The implemented solution computes the waves corresponding to all three vertices of a triangle for all of its pixels. These are blended using linearly varying weights that are 1 at one vertex are 0 at the others. This requires having $\mathbf{k'}$, φ, and the amplitude of all three vertices available at every pixel. Thus, the fourth rendering pass draws triangle after triangle with no index buffer. No vertices are shared between triangles; the attributes of every vertex contain the ID numbers of all three vertices of the corresponding triangle. In addition, the texture coordinates of all three vertices in that triangle are stored per vertex. As a side effect, this allows reproduction of the texture seams, even though duplicated seam vertices have been welded in the preprocessing step.

The vertex shader of the fourth rendering pass uses the ID numbers to retrieve the deformed positions and normal vectors, as well as the $\mathbf{k'}$, φ, and amplitude data. The phases of the waves corresponding to a triangle's vertices A, B, C are $\frac{2\pi}{W}\mathbf{k'}_A \cdot (\mathbf{x'} - \mathbf{x'}_A) + \varphi_A$ and so on. They depend linearly on the position $\mathbf{x'}$ and can be computed at the vertices to be automatically interpolated between vertex shader and pixel shader. The pixel shader then computes the cosine, applies the amplitude, and blends the three waves linearly. The same happens for the sine part, which turns out to be needed in later steps.

In the case of wrinkling, the cosine data are employed as a height field over the surface, and the sine data are used to determine the gradient of that height:

$$-\frac{2\pi}{W}\mathbf{k'}_A \sin(\frac{2\pi}{W}\mathbf{k'}_A \cdot (\mathbf{x'} - \mathbf{x'}_A) + \varphi_A)$$

and similarly for B and C. To save a huge computational burden, the height field is not used to deform the surfaces. Rather, the deformation is simulated on the flat triangular faces through texture deformation according to the parallax mapping approach and by illumination analogous to bump mapping.

Furthermore, the included demo software allows one to change the wrinkle's profile. The profile need not be sinusoidal, as long as it possesses even symmetry, to cater for the indeterminacy of the signs of the $\mathbf{k'}$. Both the profile and its derivative are read from a texture, which is not only more general than sine and cosine but also reduces the number of complex arithmetic functions being called.

Parallax Mapping

Parallax mapping [Kankekot01] assumes that the height field varies slowly and that the viewing angle is not overly oblique. Assume that the surface is offset by an amount h in the normal direction $\mathbf{k'}$ and the user is placed far away in the direction given by the unit vector $\mathbf{v}$. Then the viewing ray intersects the surface with an offset of $\Delta\mathbf{x'} = (\frac{\mathbf{v}}{\mathbf{v}\cdot\mathbf{n'}} - \mathbf{n'})h$ (see Figure 1.3.10).

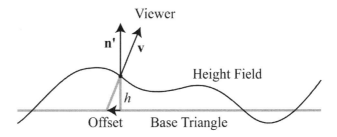

FIGURE 1.3.10   Parallax mapping computes the offset introduced by a vertical shift of the surface.

The basic idea of parallax mapping is to use this offset vector $\Delta\mathbf{x'}$ to determine which point of the texture should appear below the viewing ray. However, in the application to 3D characters this requires some elaborate computations, since one is dealing with highly irregular *uv* parameterizations.

Within every triangle ABC, the *uv* coordinates vary linearly. That is, if we shift a point $\mathbf{x}'$ by some vector $\beta(\mathbf{x}'_B - \mathbf{x}'_A) + \gamma(\mathbf{x}'_C - \mathbf{x}'_A)$, the coordinate *u* will change by $\beta(u_B - u_A) + \gamma(u_C - u_A)$ and similarly for *v*. Thus, if one finds β and γ to write $\Delta\mathbf{x}'$ as $\beta(\mathbf{x}'_B - \mathbf{x}'_A) + \gamma(\mathbf{x}'_C - \mathbf{x}'_A)$, one can immediately read off the necessary change in *u* and *v*. The quantity β can be computed by

$$\beta = \frac{\mathbf{n}' \times (\mathbf{x}'_C - \mathbf{x}'_A)}{\mathbf{n}' \cdot ((\mathbf{x}'_C - \mathbf{x}'_A) \times (\mathbf{x}'_B - \mathbf{x}'_A))} \cdot \Delta\mathbf{x}'$$

γ can be found by switching the roles of B and C. These formulas can easily be verified by plugging in the decomposition of $\Delta\mathbf{x}'$ and applying the properties of the vector product. Because of the linear dependence on $\Delta\mathbf{x}'$, much of this can be precomputed in the vertex shader.

Some limits of this approach become obvious for large folds. First, the formula for $\Delta\mathbf{x}'$ returns exploding values for oblique angles. This can be fixed by an ad hoc cutoff such as $\Delta\mathbf{x}' = \frac{(\mathbf{v} - (\mathbf{v} \cdot \mathbf{n}')\mathbf{n}')(\mathbf{v} \cdot \mathbf{n}')}{(\mathbf{v} \cdot \mathbf{n}')^2 + 0.1|\mathbf{v}|^2} h$, which doesn't require a normalized $\mathbf{v}$. Second, if $\Delta\mathbf{x}'$ points outside of the triangle, possibly even across a texture seam, the limits of the approach become visible.

Bump Mapping

Whereas parallax mapping is employed to distort the texture, bump mapping changes the normal vectors to conform to the orientation of a mesh that is actually deformed. Standard GPU-based algorithms employ a normal map that directly stores the changed normals. This is very efficient for static deformations. Wrinkling, however, demands a real-time update of the normals and can't be handled with a fixed normal texture. Thus, the method employed starts from the height field, like Blinn's original version of bump mapping [Blinn78].

Bump mapping typically relies on computing a height field's derivatives with respect to *uv* texture coordinates. However, via Equation 1.3.1 we are instead given a dependency on the position $\mathbf{x}'$ so that the computations can be simplified: The original normal vector $\mathbf{n}'$ is simply changed by the negative gradient of the height field (see Figure 1.3.11). The resulting (unnormalized) normal is flipped according to the face register of the pixel shader to always point to the viewer and thus create a two-sided surface.

Another option that seems to be viable on first sight is to compute the gradient of the height field with respect to a screen through HLSL's ddx and ddy instructions. However, this requires a transformation back from screen space into the x' frame and leads to several artifacts. First, the GPU treats 2 × 2 pixels in parallel to compute ddx and ddy, which results in a blocky look. Second, the undistorted positions of every rendered triangle lie in a plane, which produces a constant normal and thus a faceted look.

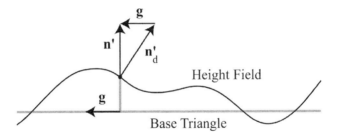

FIGURE 1.3.11 The deformed normal $\mathbf{n}'_d$ of the height field can be determined from its gradient $\mathbf{g}$ and the undeformed normal $\mathbf{n}'$.

Hatching and Prefiltering

The hatching effect has to produce either black or white pixels, barring the antialiasing to be covered later. However, if one generates a stripe pattern for every vertex of a triangle and then blends the three patterns, the result contains lots of intermediary shades of gray. Thus, it is imperative to first obtain a single phase value per pixel, from which the stripe pattern is computed.

Directly computing such an average phase from the phases of the three partial waves is difficult, because the phase values do not reflect the waves's periodicity. However, one can interpret every phase φ as a point $(\cos\varphi, \sin\varphi)$ on the unit circle. One could separately blend the sine waves and the cosine waves belonging to the three vertices and then apply the arc tangent atan2 to both results to recover an average phase φ_M (see Figure 1.3.12). However, the signs of the $\mathbf{k}'$ are not uniquely fixed, so we can only meaningfully blend even functions, not the sine. A loophole is to blend the square of the sine, which is even, and to form the square root after blending. The angle determined by the arc tangent will then oscillate between 0 and π instead of starting at $-\pi$, increasing to π and starting from $-\pi$ again.

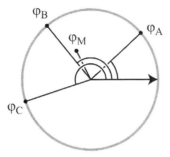

FIGURE 1.3.12 Phases can be blended naturally by interpreting them as points on the unit circle.

The resulting phase is fed into an even function representing a stripe pattern with a black/white ratio corresponding to the diffuse illumination. This hard-edged pattern, if applied as such, would lead to strong aliasing. Thanks to the simplicity of the stripe pattern, it is possible to apply analytical prefiltering, that is, to use formulas to determine spatial averages of the pattern's colors.

The first step in prefiltering is to determine the amount of filtering to be applied. Every pixel of the screen should approximately contain the average color of the points mapped to its tiny square. For the stripe pattern, this translates into a number or a fraction of periods of the pattern to be averaged over. Let L be the number of periods of the pattern appearing behind a certain pixel of the screen (see Figure 1.3.13). Then the following has to hold true because of the intercept theorem:

$$\frac{2\tan(\text{fov}/2)}{\text{Screen Height in Pixels}} = \frac{\left|\mathbf{k}' - (\mathbf{k}' \cdot \mathbf{p})\mathbf{p}\right|}{-\mathbf{v} \cdot \mathbf{p}} \frac{LW}{\left|\mathbf{k}'\right|^2}$$

where $\mathbf{v}$ is the vector from the current point to the camera and the unit vector $\mathbf{p}$ points along the camera's central direction. From this, L can be determined. It may be changed by a constant factor to control the crispness of the image.

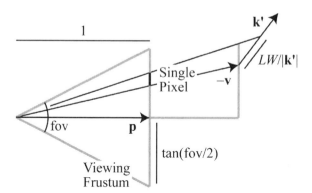

FIGURE 1.3.13　The area mapped to a pixel depends both on the distance and the field of view (fov) angle.

Now we are given the fractional or integer number L of periods to average over. The demo implementation employs the simplest of all prefilters, a box filter—not a triangular or even Gaussian filter (see Figure 1.3.14). The box filter is easy to evaluate and offers a clear visual improvement, even though heavily oscillating patterns still produce some moiré effects. To compute the effect of the box filter, one can easily count how many complete periods are contained and then add the contributions of the sliced periods left and right. Note that complete periods will only be contained if the pattern appears very small on the screen and is merely reduced to a shade of gray.

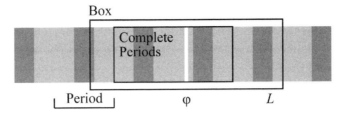

FIGURE 1.3.14   The box filter computes the average color inside a "box" around the current phase value.

Conclusion and Outlook

The presented solution offers illustration-style shading and believable cloth effects with a minor computational load. The main reason for the efficiency is that the mesh does not have to be decomposed into tiny triangles. Rather, one can employ 3D objects in resolutions that are typical for games.

This efficiency comes at a price, however. The most noticeable artifacts happen with large folds and result from using parallax mapping instead of real deformation. One option would be to geometrically deform a finely tessellated mesh. Another option would be to employ GPU-based ray-casting approaches such as relief mapping [Policarpo06].

The presented methods will strongly benefit from new features to appear on GPUs. Microsoft® DirectX 10 will allow one to stream data directly from the vertex shader into memory. Currently, one is forced to rasterize the vertex shader's output (if only into one pixel per vertex), writing vertices as pseudo-pixels.

Geometry shaders, another novel feature of Microsoft DirectX 10, will facilitate and speed up several of the computations: In the second and third rendering pass of the method, they can be used to retrieve data from adjacent vertices. In the fourth rendering pass, they can treat all three vertices of one triangle at the same time; thus, one can easily interpolate each vertex's phase across the triangle. Up to now this requires equipping every vertex with the data of the other two vertices of a triangle; this means having to recompute the vertex for every triangle in which it appears.

References

[Alpaydin04] Alpaydin, Ethem, *Introduction to Machine Learning*, MIT Press, 2004.

[Blinn78] Blinn, J. F., "Simulation of Wrinkled Surfaces," *Proceedings of SIGGRAPH '78* (1978): pp. 286–292.

[Kankekot01] Kankekot, T., T. Takahei, M. Inami, N. Kawakami, Y. Yanagida, T. Maeda, and S. Tachi, "Detailed Shape Representation with Parallax Mapping," *Proceedings of ICAT 2001: International Conference on Artificial Reality and Telepresence* (2001): pp. 205–208.

[Loviscach06] Loviscach, Jörn, "Wrinkling Coarse Meshes on the GPU," *Computer Graphics Forum*, *25*(3) (Eurographics 2006).

[Loviscach06a] Loviscach, Jörn, "Visualization of Bone Weights," SIGGRAPH 2006 Poster.

[Policarpo06] Policarpo, Fabio, and Manuel M. Oliveira, "Rendering Surface Details in Games with Relief Mapping Using a Minimally Invasive Approach." *ShaderX⁴: Advanced Rendering Techniques*, edited by Wolfgang Engel, Charles River Media Inc., 2006: pp. 109–119.

[Praun01] Praun, E., H. Hoppe, M. Webb, and A. Finkelstein, "Real-time Hatching," Proceedings of SIGGRAPH '01, pp. 581–587.

1.4

Cloth without Cloth

Homam Bahnassi (In|Framez) and *Wessam Bahnassi* (Electronic Arts)

Introduction

Almost all games have characters in them, and almost all game characters wear something. The complexity of the characters' clothing style ranges from sticky rubber cloth, to wide dresses with scarves floating around the hero's body. While the first example does not involve clothes that are affected by wind or gravity, it still does not look fully correct because in-game cloth simulators will not go down to the level of calculating the deep bumps caused at the joints and waist of the animated character.

While wide rags are usually affected by dynamics calculations and behave somewhat naturally with respect to gravity, they still miss detailed smooth bumps that appear across the whole sheet (Figure 1.4.1).

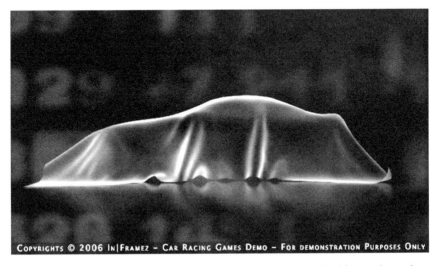

FIGURE 1.4.1 Although wide rags usually look nice when simulated in run-time, a lot of detail can be added cheaply by the method described in this article, as is the case with the car cover shown above. (© Car Games Technical Preview reprinted with permission from In|Framez / *www.inframez.com*.)

This article proposes a cheap (yet good-looking) technique to render those small bumpy cloth details that appear at the inner side of bent cloth pieces. The technique replaces the unnatural static baked cloth bumps that are usually found on game characters.

The Technique 101

Before describing the technique, it is a good idea to identify the parts in a character that make the most use out of this technique. Figure 1.4.2 shows that joints are the number one candidates for such an improvement. For a human character, joints can be elbows, knees, the waist, and so on.

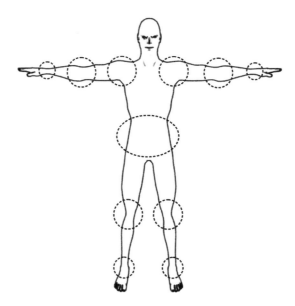

FIGURE 1.4.2   The joints of a human character are the number one candidates for use of this technique (e.g., waist and elbows).

   As the figure suggests, most characters require some sort of dynamic cloth bumping around five main places in their bodies: two of them around the elbows, two around the knees and last one around the waist. Of course, this depends a lot on the character dressing, but these are the areas that benefit the most.

   One of the goals here is to provide artists with the ability to control the shape and details of these small bumps. For that, the technique depends on the concept of masking, which is simple and well-known. Masking can be implemented in many different ways, which depend on the technique used to shade the character. Since normal mapping is very common nowadays, the implementation here will concentrate on this case.

The basic method requires that the character's model has two normal maps (Figure 1.4.3). One is the usual base version, and the other is a copy that is filled with cloth bumps and wrinkles. Finally, a special texture is used to mask the place where the wrinkled normal map should be used instead of the nonwrinkled version.

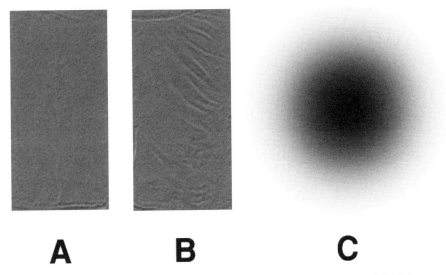

A   **B**   **C**

FIGURE 1.4.3   (Left) The usual (nonwrinkled) normal map for a character. (Middle) The wrinkled version of the same normal map. (Right) The masking texture.

As a start, the case of a simple joint as the elbow will be studied. First, the textures shown in Figure 1.4.3 need to be mapped appropriately, which is a simple task. The two normal maps share exactly the same set of UV coordinates, and the third texture is mapped in whatever method works so that it covers the joint's inner area (Figure 1.4.4).

Now, given that the textures are correctly mapped, all that is required at runtime is to decide whether the wrinkles should appear or not, which is a simple computation. As can be seen, the amount of cloth that wrinkles is constrained to the amount the character bends his arm. So, when the arm is fully straight, no wrinkles should appear. When the arm is fully bent, the wrinkles should appear at maximum. This determination is done by taking the dot product between the two vectors representing the bones that are connected at that joint (Figure 1.4.5):

$$BlendValue = \overrightarrow{Bone1Dir} \bullet \overrightarrow{Bone2Dir}$$

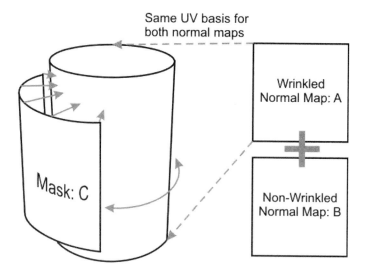

FIGURE 1.4.4   The mapping of the normal maps along with the mask.

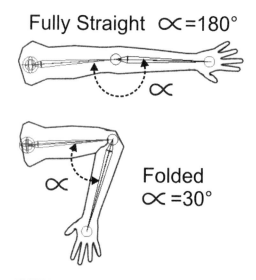

FIGURE 1.4.5   The angle ∝ formed at the elbow joint can range from 180° to around 30° (based on how muscular our hero is).

For an angle spanning the range [0°, 180°], this value will span a matching range of [+1,−1], but before it can be used in further calculations, it needs to be remapped to [0, 1] where 0 means no wrinkles and 1 means fully wrinkled clothes. It is preferred to map [180°, ~30°] into [0, 1] instead of mapping [180°, 0°] into [0, 1], because even when the human arm is fully bent, the bones do not make a 0° angle. Rather, it is some higher value (the value 30° is used here only as a suggestion).

An example of a basic remapping would go like this:

$$FinalBlendValue = \min\left(\frac{1 - BlendValue}{1 - \cos(pi - MinAngle)}, 1\right)$$

where `MinAngle` is the minimum angle that can be formed by the joint, which is assumed to be 30° in our case.

So when `FinalBlendValue` reaches 1, the wrinkled normal map is used, and as it approaches 0, the wrinkled normal map slowly fades away and gets replaced by the original normal map.

For the pixel shader implementation, this can look like (in HLSL)

```
float3 vec3OrgNormal = tex2D(sampOrgNormalMap, vec2NrmUV).xyz;
float3 vec3WrnkNormal = tex2D(sampWrnkNormalMap,vec2NrmUV).xyz;
float3 vec3Mask = tex2D(sampMask,vec2MaskUV).xyz;
vec3Mask *= fFinalBlendValue;
float3 vec3Normal = lerp(vec3OrgNormal, vec3WrnkNormal,vec3Mask);
// Use vec3Normal in your favorite lighting equation as usual
// after normalizing it of course...
```

The Technique 201

So far, the technique described works fine only for simple joints such as the elbow and the knee. However, it is about time to move to something more interesting. The elbow and knee joints are simple because they are 2D joints in nature. They only work in the space of a plane, but for a joint such as the waist, the story is different. The waist acts more as a ball joint, which allows the upper part of the body to bend in any direction (Figure 1.4.6).

That being the case, a fixed UV mapping for the mask texture can no longer be assumed. The mask now has to follow the area of pressure to correctly show the wrinkles at the right area, so the calculations have to be modified a little bit.

Nothing will change for the textures themselves. The technique still needs the two normal maps and the mask texture. The mapping is also the same for the normal maps, but for the mask, it is now different. Because the area of pressure can dynamically change in position as the waist bends in different directions, these UV coordinates need to correctly position the mask over the right area. The intensity of the mask is still calculated the same way, but some more calculations need to be added for correct positioning.

For the sake of simplicity, the calculations here are based on the assumption that the bones are skinned by a cylinder, which is a good enough representation of most characters' waists (Figure 1.4.7). Also, the 3D coordinate system assumes that X+ goes to the right, Y+ goes up, and Z+ goes out of the screen (right-handed coordinate system).

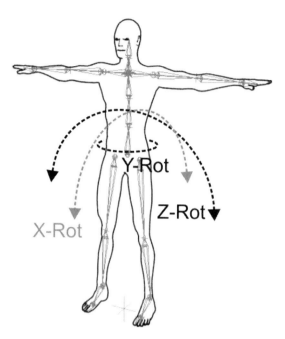

FIGURE 1.4.6   The waist can rotate freely around all axes (with limitations). This allows the upper body to lean in any direction. This generates wrinkles in cloth at the area where the pressure is currently occurring.

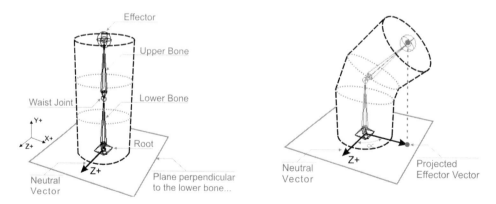

FIGURE 1.4.7   For simplicity, the body is assumed to be a cylinder, with the waist joint being at the middle of its height. The different components used in the calculations are marked here for reference.

In Figure 1.4.7 the neutral vector is a normalized vector starting from the waist's joint and pointing toward the center of the mask texture as it is mapped on the cylinder's body. For the illustration, the neutral vector points along the Z+ axis.

The goal is to know the direction in which the waist is bending and use that information to push the mask texture's UV so the mask covers the area of pressure formed at the bending direction.

For this task, the upper bone is first projected onto a plane perpendicular to the lower bone. Next, the angle between the projected upper bone and the neutral vector is taken. Finally, this angle is used rotate the UVs around until the mask matches the pressure area (Figure 1.4.8).

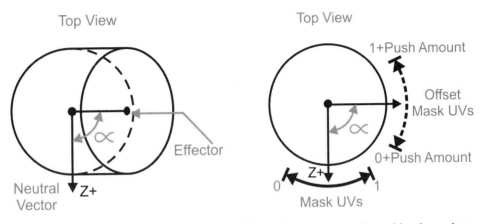

FIGURE 1.4.8 A top view that shows how the UV coordinates are altered to position the mask at the area of pressure.

Mathematically speaking, the first part can be done by:

1. Transforming the effector's global position into the lower bone's space.
2. Projecting the point onto the plane perpendicular to the lower bone.
3. Normalizing the projected point position to form a direction.

Step 1 requires transforming the effector's position by the inverse of the global transform matrix for the lower bone:

$$LocalEffectorPos = GlobalEffectorPos \times LowerBoneMatrix^{-1}$$

After transformation, step 2 simply boils down to setting the Y component of the transformed point to 0 and then normalizing the vector:

$$UpperBoneDir = Normalize(LocalEffectorPos.x, 0, LocalEffectorPos.z)$$

where UpperBoneDir is the projected upper bone direction.

The next step is to find the angle between the neutral vector and the projected upper bone vector. This is done by calculating the dot product between both vectors and ensuring that it spans the full range of [0°, 360°]:

$$Dot = UpperBoneDir \bullet NeutralVector$$

$$PushAmount = \left(\frac{Dot - (-1)}{1 - (-1)} \right) \times 0.5$$

$$FinalPushAmount = \begin{cases} PushAmount + 0.5, & if \ UpperBoneDir.x < 0 \\ PushAmount, & otherwise \end{cases}$$

`FinalPushAmount` is now in the range [0,1], which matches an angular range of [0°, 360°].

The last step is to use this push amount to rotate the UVs around until the mask matches the pressure area. This is done prior to passing the UVs to the pixel shader for sampling, so it ends up as a single additional operation in the vertex shader:

```
vsOutput.vec2UVMask.x = vsInput.vec2UVMask.x + g_FinalPushAmount;
vsOutput.vec2UVMask.y = vsInput.vec2UVMask.y;
```

The value `FinalPushAmount` might need to be scaled prior to using it directly to offset the UVs.

The pixel shader is still the same and has not changed since the previous section.

Note that the mask is not required to be big. A mask texture of 64×64 would work just fine in most cases. Of course, clamping is essential when sampling from this texture.

Additional Thoughts

The pixel shader described at the beginning of the chapter was used to blend normal maps, but this can be changed to blend other kinds of textures also. For example, assume a character that does not use per-pixel lighting; it just uses baked lighting for the details and leaves general lighting to be done per-vertex. For this, the same technique can be used to blend between two diffuse maps. Again, the first is the usual nonwrinkled texture, and the second is the one with wrinkles and bumps all over it.

Although the technique was applied to a humanoid character, there should not be any problems with applying the same technique for other kinds of creatures or objects in general. For example, tentacles, tails, and all other monster limbs can use the same method to add detail when and where needed.

With some care, the technique can be used to model not only pressure areas in cloth, but also tension areas (Figure 1.4.9). As an example, for an elbow, a special mask texture can be fully wrapped around the joint so that from one side it shows pressure and from the other side it shows tension.

Finally, this technique has one requirement to work perfectly. The object must have some kind of uniform texture mapping over its vertices so that pushing UV coordinates can be properly done by the simple addition operation.

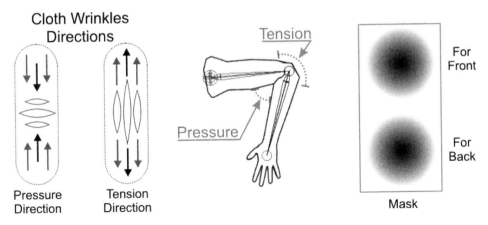

FIGURE 1.4.9 The wrinkled texture can express pressure as well as tension in cloth. The mask has to be carefully constructed and mapped so that it always covers both sides of the joint.

Conclusion

This article described a simple and practical way of adding bump detail to skinned joints. The simple case of 2D joints was first explained, followed by the case of ball joints. The calculations result in two values: a blend value, and a UV push value. The blend value is used to transition between a wrinkled texture and a nonwrinkled texture based on the joint's angle. The UV push amount is used to position the bumps at the correct place for ball joints. A special mask uses this UV set to control the appearance of the bumps from the wrinkled texture.

Finally, the article suggested additional uses for the technique and mentioned a certain requirement about the importance of uniform texture mapping for proper results.

Acknowledgments

Special thanks go to Sergei Savchenko from EA and Abdo Haji-Ali from In|Framez for reviewing this article.

RENDERING TECHNIQUES

Introduction

Kenneth Hurley

The "Rendering Techniques" section of this book has become one of my favorite sections of the *ShaderX* series. I've always enjoyed writing vertex and pixel shaders, so I decided I wanted to edit this section. The articles selected for this section are very diverse and very informative. The seven articles are entitled, "A Simple Area Light Model for GPUs," "Animating Vegetation Using GPU Programs," "Alpha-to-Coverage in Depth," "Preprocessing of Complex, Static Scenes for Fast Real-time Graphics," "Overcoming Deferred Shading Drawbacks," "Normal Mapping without Precomputed Tangents," "Practical Parallax Occlusion Mapping with Approximate Soft Shadows for Detailed Surface Rendering," and "ZT-Buffer Algorithm."

The article "A Simple Area Light Model for GPUs" uses extensions to the Blinn and Phong lighting equation to render area lights without resorting to ray-tracing or radiosity techniques. As can be seen from the figures, this technique can work well for disc-shaped and rectangular area lights.

Kevin Myers from NVIDIA was kind enough to present his article on "Alpha-to-coverage in Depth." His article delves into how alpha-to-coverage is screen door transparency applied at the subpixel level through multisampling. This type of rendering is useful for natural-looking vegetation, realistic fur, as well as complex particle systems for smoke and clouds.

Natalya Tatarchuk from ATI contributes a nice article on parallax mapping with soft shadows. The article presents a per-pixel ray-tracing algorithm with dynamic lighting of surfaces in real-time on the GPU. The article is much more than just a rehash of parallax mapping techniques and describes an adaptive level-of-detail system that uses the information supplied by the graphics hardware during rendering to automatically manage shader complexity without artifacts. The artist isn't left out either, as the article discusses integrating these techniques into game pipelines.

Two articles that deal with deferred shading are presented. The first article, entitled "Preprocessing of Complex, Static Scenes for Fast Real-time Graphics," deals with things other articles have not. Spherical harmonics, local point lights with shadows, and other topics are discussed in detail in the article. The techniques presented are suitable for games such as adventures with fixed camera position, top-down scroller with orthogonal projection, and 3D games with portals that render farsighted scenes and will allow rendering these with a high level of detail.

The second article on deferred shading presents techniques for optimal performance and discusses an entire system for a deferred shading pipeline. The solutions overcome or reduce most of the deferred shading drawbacks and give tips on how to implement a scalable system that can run on most graphic cards. The system uses less memory and optimizes the whole process, not only in the shaders, but also inside the application by implementing high-level managers that run on the CPU.

"Normal Mapping without Precomputed Tangents" presents methods to generate tangent frames inside the pixel shader by using derivative instructions. The tangent frame is computed per pixel so there is no need to store precomputed tangent frames. This can really save vertex buffer stream size and help alleviate bottlenecks across the bus. These methods also help solve many of the problems seen with tangent space by placing no constraints on the way texture coordinates are assigned to vertices. This allows UV-mirroring or procedural texture coordinates with normal mapping.

The techniques in the article "Animating Vegetation Using GPU Programs" are extremely useful in games and have been implemented in an open source 3D application known as Virtual Reality Chat. VRC island is an especially beautiful rendered scene. The article shows step-by-step development of a vertex and fragment shader for animating vegetation. The author was kind enough to provide reference code, which uses GLSL, but it can be easily ported to other GPU programming languages.

Finally, the last article in the section, "ZT-Buffer Algorithm," presents a novel algorithm for real-time order-independent rendering of arbitrary transparent objects. It describes a general transparency algorithm with a detailed hardware-based implementation and outline pipelines for most common rendering methods.

It has been my pleasure to edit this section on rendering techniques. Wolfgang and I worked together many times on the *ShaderX* series, and it has always been enjoyable. As a final note, I want to dedicate this section to my mother, Ida Hurley, who passed away during the editing of this book. Her love for her children showed no bounds, but she ended up finally losing the battle with her diabetes. I'll miss her dearly.

2.1

A Simple Area Light Model for GPUs

Aick in der Au

Introduction

Using area lights in computer-generated images has been mainly limited to the domain of ray tracing or radiosity rendering techniques. This article introduces an extension to the standard Blinn and Phong lighting equations to cope with disc-shaped and rectangular area lights.

The basic notion behind this is that on a limited area light plane there exists an infinite number of omni-directional point light sources. Since we have no chance to integrate over that plane, numerical approximations, if they are found, would still be too slow and complex to run on a shader. Another approach must be implemented. We limit ourselves to selecting one point light per fragment, which has the greatest influence. If the point light position on the area light plane is found, we proceed with standard diffuse/specular lighting term calculation.

Finding Point Light Source Positions

What follows are some equations that can be easily processed in a pixel shader. To find the light position LP for every fragment, we do a three-step approximation:

1. Set LP near the surface of geometry.
2. Project LP onto area light planes.
3. Clamp LP to area light boundaries.

Each area light has several parameters:

- AP is the center position of the area light source.
- $\mathbf{D_z}$ is the normalized light plane vector of the light source.
- $\mathbf{D_x}$ and $\mathbf{D_y}$ span the light plane ($\mathbf{D_x}$, $\mathbf{D_y}$, and $\mathbf{D_z}$ are orthogonal to each other).
- Use *radius* if it is a disc-shaped light.
- Use *length*, *width* if it is rectangular-shaped light.
- *Inset* a light control parameter (explained later on).

Other light-specific parameters such as colors, attenuation factors, spotlight cut-off angles, and so on are left open to a concrete shader implementation and therefore are not discussed here.

Step One: Set LP Near the Surface of Geometry

Since we are in fragment level, "near the surface" means setting LP above or below the current fragment position (Equation 2.1.1). This gives us maximum contribution in diffuse range, since $\mathbf{N}$ dot $\mathbf{L}$ are equal then.

$$LP = P + inset \cdot \mathrm{N}. \tag{2.1.1}$$

where P is the fragment position in eye space, *inset* influences the behavior if our area light surface cuts geometry. If the inset is less than zero, polygons cutting the area light plane would not be illuminated. Small positive values would generate sharp transitions, and large positive values would generate smooth transitions. Setting *inset* to zero is not defined. Figure 2.1.1 demonstrates this.

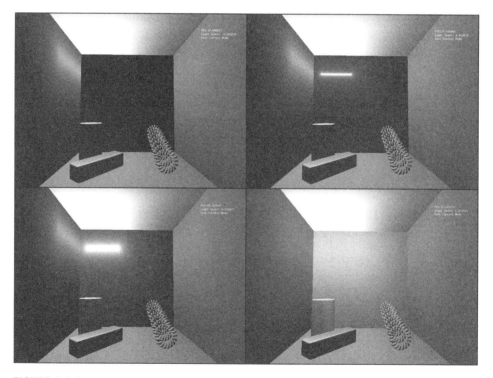

FIGURE 2.1.1 Influence of *inset*. The Cornell box rear wall cuts the area light. *inset* < 0; *inset* = 0.01; *inset* = 0.05; *inset* = 1.0.

Step Two: Project *LP* onto Area Light Plane

Applying step one alone would result in full intensity for each fragment—not an optimal solution for a light model. In the next step we project the light position onto the area light plane (Equation 2.1.2):

$$LP = LP - \mathbf{D}_z \times (\mathbf{D}_z \cdot LP - \mathbf{D}_z \cdot AP). \qquad (2.1.2)$$

Using vector $\mathbf{D}_z$ as a straight line for the projection does not always gives the optimum position with the most influence, but the results are numerically stable in contrast to using $\mathbf{N}$ (see Figure 2.1.2).

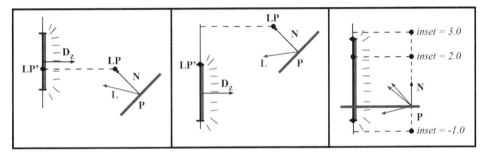

FIGURE 2.1.2   Calculation of *LP* (*LP'* marks the final position) and *L*. The gray line is acting as geometry. (Left) *LP* is projected onto the light plane. (Center) *LP* is clamped to lights boundary. (Right) Demonstration of how *inset* influences *L*.

Step Three: Clamp *LP* to Area Light Boundaries

For disc-shaped area lights,

$$LP = \begin{cases} LP & \text{if } |LP\text{-}AP| < radius \\ AP + (LP - AP)/|LP\text{-}AP| & \text{else} \end{cases}. \qquad (2.1.3)$$

LP for rectangular area lights is

$$l = clamp((LP - AP) \cdot \mathbf{D}_x, -length/2, length/2)$$
$$w = clamp((LP - AP) \cdot \mathbf{D}_y, -width/2, width/2)$$
$$LP = AP + \mathbf{D}_x \times l + \mathbf{D}_y \times w. \qquad (2.1.4)$$

Equation 2.1.4 also includes the light plane projection, so we can skip step two for rectangular light sources.

Proceed with the Classic Blinn or Phong Lighting Equation

Now that the new light position *LP* has been found, we can calculate the corresponding light vector (Equation 2.1.5) and proceed with standard diffuse and specular lighting terms. For example, [Shishkovtsov05] uses an excellent model with lookup tables for N dot L and N dot H.

$$L = LP - P\big/\big|LP - P\big|. \tag{2.1.5}$$

Further Experiments

Other light shapes are possible to achieve by changing the clamp function (step three). Extending the model to an elliptic-shaped light is one possibility. Another interesting effect can be achieved by adding a height field to the light plane (see Figure 2.1.3). Though it has nothing to do with real world lighting situations, your special-FX department surely will find an application for that.

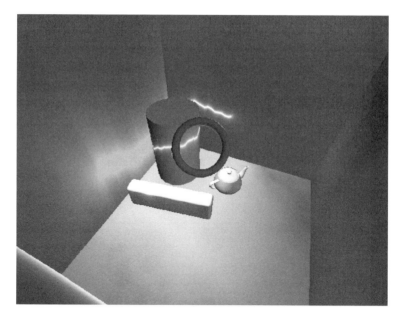

FIGURE 2.1.3 A rectangular area light with a Perlin noise height field on the resulting light positions—not very realistic, but it looks interesting.

Conclusion

Now you are able to light your scenes with area lights; Listing 2.1.1 summarizes the computation. The demo on the CD-ROM includes the full shader source. Special

ON THE CD

thanks to to Michael Saenger for providing the RenderMole DemoSystem for this demo. Implementing a hyper-realistic shadow algorithm with smooth penumbra edges is left as an exercise for the reader. Luckily, Tomas Akenine-Möller and Ulf Assarsson published a shadow volume algorithm in [Akenine-Möller02] that can handle arbitrary convex light sources.

LISTING 2.1.1 Area Light Source

```
vec3 LP = P + inset * N;

if (rectangular)
{
    // clamp light position to rectangle
    vec3 DIR = LP - AP;
    float dirdotx = dot( DIR, DX );
    float dirdoty = dot( DIR, DY );
    LP = AP + DX * clamp( dirdotx, -width/2, width/2 ) +
        DY * clamp( dirdoty, -length/2, length/2 );
}
else
{
    // project onto light plane
    LP = LP — DZ * (dot( DZ, LP ) - dot( DZ, AP) );

    // clamp light position to disc
    vec3 DIR = LP-AP;
    float le = length( DIR );
    DIR = normalize( DIR );
    LP = AP + DIR * min( radius, le );
}

// new light vector
L = LP-P;
```

References

[Akenine-Möller02] Akenine-Möller, Tomas and Ulf Assarsson, "Approximate Soft Shadows on Arbitrary Surfaces using Penumbra Wedges," *13th Eurographics Workshop on Rendering,* June 2002: pp. 297–305.

[Shishkovtsov05] Shishkovtsov, Oles, "Deferred Shading in S.T.A.L.K.E.R." *GPU Gems 2: Programming Techniques for High-Performance Graphics and General-Purpose Computation,* edited by Randima Fernando and Matt Pharr, Addison-Wesley, 2005.

2.2

Alpha-to-Coverage in Depth

Kevin Myers, NVIDIA Corporation

Realistic simulation of the real world depends on realistic rendering of highly detailed organic objects. Natural-looking vegetation, lifelike fur, as well as complex particle systems for smoke and clouds are among those objects. Physically based descriptions of such objects relying on geometric data are onerous for both artists and efficient hardware implementations. Modern GPUs are excellent at pixel shading, but not exceptionally adept at handling a large number of small triangles. Owing to these limitations, many solutions that stress fragment-level shading have been developed over the years.

A simple solution that is well understood is alpha testing (Figure 2.2.1). With alpha testing a fourth 1-bit color channel, alpha, is used to parameterize the image. With more than 1 bit of alpha we can define a ratio of source color to destination color (Figure 2.2.2). The common algorithm for so-called alpha blending is dest color = source color * source alpha + current dest color * (1 − source alpha). As you can see, this calculation is not commutable; order does matter. This burdens us with maintaining strict back to front rendering, which also forces us to sort all blended objects. Blending also reduces pixels throughput, typically by half, because of the overhead of reading back the current pixel's color.

FIGURE 2.2.1 Alpha testing results.

FIGURE 2.2.2 Alpha Blending results.

A simpler idea that does not rely on in-order rendering is screen door transparency. This technique gets its name from the observation that a screen covering a window will darken the view through the window as the eye interpolates the color of the screen with the color behind the screen. Screen door transparency relies on the human eye's ability to fill in the gaps between discrete samples. The more solid the screen is, the less background color gets through. If the screen varies in transparency, we can achieve different levels of blending. This is the basis for modern alpha-to-coverage.

Alpha-to-coverage is screen door transparency applied at the subpixel level through multisampling. API support exists in both OpenGL and DirectX 10. As a reminder, multisampling rasterizes more than one sample (typically four) per pixel, while shading once for all subsamples. This produces smooth polygon edges without the overhead of additional shading. When using alpha-to-coverage, multisampling is handled as usual, but the alpha value is used to decrease coverage when alpha is less than 1. The result can be seen in Figure 2.2.3. Notice the softly dithered edges compared to the hard edge in the case of simple alpha testing. Figure 2.2.4 shows a close-up view of one of the blades. One can clearly see the hard edge that occurs if alpha is interpreted as 0 or 1. In Figure 2.2.5 alpha is used to determine coverage. The black holes represent where alpha was determined to be below a particular threshold, therefore preventing a sample from being generated. Remember, this is being done at the antialiased resolution. Blending occurs during the multisample resolve, where the image is down-sampled to the display's resolution. Figure 2.2.6 shows a blown up picture of the final leaf.

FIGURE 2.2.3   Alpha to coverage result.

FIGURE 2.2.4   Close up view of one blade.

Alpha-to-coverage is then limited in quality by the number of subsamples. With only four subsamples per pixel, it would seem we could only have five discrete levels of coverage (zero to four samples covered). Fortunately we can do better. Figure 2.2.7

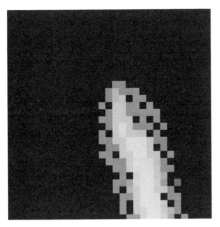

FIGURE 2.2.5 Alpha is used to determine coverage.

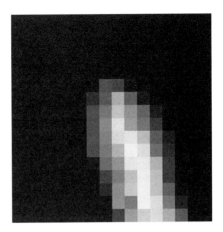

FIGURE 2.2.6 Alpha to coverage result of one blade.

was produced by linearly increasing alpha from right to left with 4x MSAA and alpha-to-coverage on. As we can see, there are clearly more than five levels of coverage. In order to get more levels of coverage than existing subsamples, an implementation must dither coverage levels at the pixel level and not the subsample level. Alpha-to-coverage as dictated by the OpenGL specification simply says coverage must be 0 when alpha == 0 and 1 when alpha == 1. Between 0 and 1 the specification indicates that coverage must increase, but it does not specify how it must increase. Various implementations then have freedom in how this is implemented as long as these three rules are followed.

FIGURE 2.2.7 Result of linearly increasing alpha from right to left with 4x MSAA.

What can be gleaned from the spec is that alpha-to-coverage differs from normal screen-door transparency in its inability to handle multiple layers of transparency effectively. Because the spec only states that coverage should increase with increasing alpha, two triangles with the same alpha value will occupy the same samples. In Figure 2.2.8 two triangles with the same alpha are rasterized to the same pixel, represented by the four subsamples inside the square. We first render the pink triangle and then the blue triangle. Since both have an alpha value of 0.5, only two samples will be written, but they are the same two each time. This is why we only see blue and the background color in our subsamples. This is a serious limitation if we are trying to use alpha-to-coverage to simulate general blending. Particle simulations that depend heavily on alpha blending will not benefit from alpha-to-coverage because only the most recently written layer's color will survive.

FIGURE 2.2.8   Two triangles with the same alpha.

This doesn't mean alpha-to-coverage is useless (or we wouldn't have this article). Alpha-to-coverage is especially useful when alpha is used to define geometric primitives, as often occurs with foliage. In this case, alpha is equal to 1 wherever the primitive is defined, and 0 elsewhere. Only at the edges is alpha < 1 and alpha > 0. It is here that we get interesting coverage. As is shown in Figure 2.2.3, as alpha tapers off to 0, more and more of the background will fill the samples not occupied by the blades of grass. When the multisample resolve occurs, the leaf edge will be blended with the background to create a soft transition without aliasing. The limitations cited before are not of great concern in this case because the region where alpha-to-coverage is occurring is very small (only at the edges), thus reducing the chance for multiple layers to intersect.

This works great for vegetation, but what about smoke or other particle systems? In Figure 2.2.9 we see the result of alpha-blending several quads to create a smoke cloud. Figure 2.2.10 shows what happens when alpha-to-coverage is used instead of blending. Notice the mid-section of the cloud. A couple of quads are completely missing because the final quads killed off the quads in the back. One way to work around the limitation is to use commutative blending in addition to alpha-to-coverage. Instead of doing typical src alpha/inv src alpha blending, we do simple additive blending where destination color = current dest color + source for color. Using multiple render targets which work with AA in DirectX 10, we maintain a pixel count per pixel by incrementing a single-channel texture. This allows us to, in the final pass, renormalize color to avoid saturating color. The result is Figure 2.2.11, which more closely mimics the alpha-blended reference image. This renormalization process was done to an FP16 render target. To mitigate the dithering artifacts, in Figure 2.2.12 we applied a filter that takes the current pixel and the four neighbors, blending them together if they contain smoke.

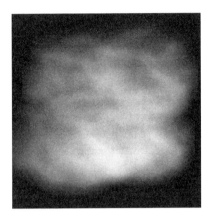

FIGURE 2.2.9 Alpha blending to create a smoke cloud.

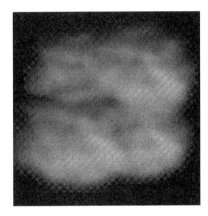

FIGURE 2.2.10 Alpha to coverage to create a smoke cloud.

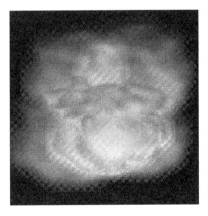

FIGURE 2.2.11 Alpha to coverage and commutative blending.

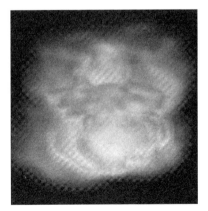

FIGURE 2.2.12 Alpha to coverage, commutative blending and filtering the result.

Another common artifact with alpha-to-coverage is shimmering with very far away or very small primitives. This will vary from implementation to implementation but is the result of dithering being used to achieve a greater variance in coverage. Since small triangles are inherently under-sampled (they represent a small portion of the screen), alpha values tend to jump rather quickly at the edges of such primitives. This in turn causes rapid variations in coverage as the alpha value assumes vastly different coverage values. One way to mitigate this problem is to supersample small, distant primitives. One can also adjust the mip-chain such that the smaller mip levels are more blurred. The important thing to remember is that alpha directly relates to coverage and coverage directly relates to the blended pixel.

References

Mulder, J. D., F. C. A. Groen, and J. J. van Wijk, *Pixel Masks for Screen-Door Transparency*, IEEE Computer Society Press, 1998.

OpenGL 2.0 Spec. Available online at *http://www.opengl.org/documentation/specs/version2.0/glspec20.pdf#search=%22OpenGL%202.0%20Spec%20%22*.

Alpha-to-coverage whitepaper–NVIDIA. Available at *http://download.developer.nvidia.com/developer/SDK/Individual_Samples/DEMOS/Direct3D9/src/AntiAliasingWithTransparency/docs/AntiAliasingWithTransparency.pdf*.

2.3

Practical Parallax Occlusion Mapping with Approximate Soft Shadows for Detailed Surface Rendering

Natalya Tatarchuk, ATI Research

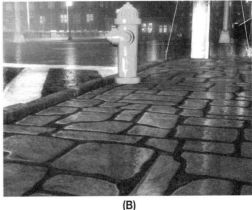

(A)   (B)

FIGURE 2.3.1   Realistic city scene rendered using parallax occlusion mapping applied to the cobblestone sidewalk in (**A**) and using the normal mapping technique in (**B**).

Overview

This chapter presents a per-pixel ray-tracing algorithm with dynamic lighting of surfaces in real-time on the GPU. First, we will describe a method for increased precision of the critical ray–height field intersection and adaptive height field sampling. We achieve higher-quality results than the existing inverse displacement-mapping algorithms. Second, soft shadows are computed by estimating light visibility for the displaced surfaces. Third, we describe an adaptive LOD system that uses the information supplied by the graphics hardware during rendering to automatically manage shader complexity. This

LOD scheme maintains smooth transitions between the full displacement computation and a simplified representation at a lower LOD without visual artifacts. Finally, algorithm limitations will be discussed along with the practical considerations for integration into game pipelines. Specific attention will be given to the art asset authoring, providing guidelines, tips, and concerns. The algorithm performs well for animated objects and supports dynamic rendering of height fields for a variety of interesting displacement effects. The presented method is scalable for a range of consumer-grade GPU products. It exhibits a low memory footprint and can be easily integrated into existing art pipelines for games and effects rendering.

Introduction

The advances in the programmability of consumer GPUs in recent years have revolutionized the visual complexity of interactive worlds found in games and similar real-time applications. However, the balance between the concept and realism dictates that in order to make the objects in these virtual worlds appear photo-realistic, the visual intricacy demands a significant amount of detail. Simply painting a few broken bricks will not serve the purpose of displaying a dilapidated brick wall in a forlorn city any longer. With the raised visual fidelity of the latest games, players want to be immersed in these worlds—they want to *experience* the details of their environments. That demands that each object maintains its three-dimensional appearance accurately regardless of the viewing distance or angle.

This brings us to an age-old problem of computer graphics: how do we render detailed objects with complex surface detail without paying the price in performance? We must balance the desire to render intricate surfaces with the cost of the millions of triangles associated with high-polygonal surfaces typically necessary to represent that geometry. Although the geometric throughput of graphics hardware has increased immensely in recent years, there still exist many obstacles in throwing huge amounts of geometry onto the GPU. There is an associated memory footprint for storing large meshes (typically measured in many megabytes of vertex and connectivity data) and the performance cost for vertex transformations and animations of those meshes.

If we want the players to think they're near a brick wall, it should look and behave like one. The bricks should have deep grooves and an assortment of bumps and scratches. There should be shadows between individual bricks. As the player moves around the object, it needs to maintain its depth and volume. We want to render these complex surfaces, such as this mythical brick wall, accurately—which means we must do the following:

- Preserve depth at all angles.
- Support dynamic lighting.
- Ensure that self-occlusions on the surface result in correct self-shadowing on the surface without aliasing.

Throughout history, artists have specialized in creating the illusion of detail and depth without actually building a concrete model of reality on the canvas. Similarly, in computer graphics we frequently want to create a compelling impression of a realistic scene without the full cost of complex geometry. Texture mapping is essential for that purpose; it allows generation of detail-rich scenes without the full geometric content representation. Bump mapping was introduced in the early days of computer graphics in [Blinn78] to avoid rendering high-polygonal-count models.

Bump mapping is a technique for making surfaces appear detailed and uneven by perturbing the surface normal using a texture. This approach creates a visual illusion of surface detail that would otherwise consume most of a project's polygon budget (such as fissures and cracks in terrain and rocks, textured bark on trees, clothes, wrinkles, etc.). Since the early days, there have been many extensions to the basic bump-mapping technique including emboss bump mapping, environment map bump mapping, and the highly popular dot product bump mapping (normal mapping). See [Akenine-Möller02] for a more detailed description of these techniques. In Figure 2.3.1b, we can see the per-pixel bump-mapping technique (also called *normal mapping*) applied to the cobblestone sidewalk.

Despite its low computational cost and ease of use, bump mapping fails to account for important visual cues such as shading because of interpenetrations and self-occlusion. It also does not display perspective-correct depth at all angles. Since the bump-mapping technique doesn't take into consideration the geometric depth of the surface, it does not exhibit parallax. This technique displays various visual artifacts, and thus several approaches have been introduced to simulate parallax on bump-mapped geometry. However, many of the existing parallax generation techniques cannot account for self-occluding geometry or add shadowing effects. Indeed, shadows provide a very important visual cue for surface detail.

The main contribution of this chapter is an advanced technique for simulating the illusion of depth on uneven surfaces without increasing the geometric complexity of rendered objects. This is accomplished by computing a perspective-correct representation while maintaining accurate parallax by using an inverse displacement-mapping technique. We also describe a method for computing self-shadowing effects for self-occluding objects. The resulting approach allows us to simulate pseudo-geometry displacement in the pixel shader instead of modeling geometric details in the polygonal mesh. This allows us to render surface detail providing a convincing visual impression of depth from varying viewpoints, utilizing the programmable pixel pipelines of commercial graphics hardware. The results of applying parallax occlusion mapping can be seen in Figure 2.3.1a, where the method is used to render the cobblestone sidewalk.

We perform per-pixel ray tracing for inverse displacement mapping with an easy-to-implement, efficient algorithm. Our method allows interactive rendering of displaced surfaces with dynamic lighting, soft shadows, self-occlusions, and motion parallax. Previous methods displayed strong aliasing at grazing angles, thus limiting potential applications' view angles, making these approaches impractical in realistic game scenarios. We present a significant improvement in the rendering quality necessary for production-level results. This work was originally presented in [Tatarchuk06].

Our method's contributions include:

- A high-precision computation algorithm for critical height field–ray intersection and an adaptive height field-sampling scheme, well designed for a range of consumer GPUs. This method significantly reduces visual artifacts at oblique angles.
- Estimation of light visibility for displaced surfaces allowing real-time computation of soft shadows owing to self-occlusion.
- Adaptive LOD control system with smooth transitions for controlling shader complexity using per-pixel LOD information.

The contributions presented in this chapter are important for easy integration of inverse displacement mapping into interactive applications such as games. They improve visual quality while taking full advantage of programmable GPU pixel and texture pipelines' efficiency. Our technique can be applied to animated objects and fits well within established art pipelines of games and effects rendering. The algorithm allows scalability for a range of existing GPU products.

Why Reinvent the Wheel? Common Artifacts and Related Work

Although standard bump mapping offers a relatively inexpensive way to add surface detail, there are several downsides to this technique. Common bump-mapping approaches lack the ability to represent view-dependent unevenness of detailed surfaces and therefore fail to represent motion parallax—the apparent displacement of the object owing to viewpoint change. In recent years, new approaches for simulating displacement on surfaces have been introduced. An approach to parallax mapping for representing surface detail using normal maps is described in [Kaneko01] and [Welsh04], and [Wang03] introduced a technique for view-dependent displacement mapping that improved on displaying surface detail as well as silhouette detail.

Displacement mapping, introduced by [Cook84], addressed the issues above by modifying the underlying surface geometry. Ray-tracing-based approaches dominated in the offline domain ([Pharr96], [Heidrich98]). These methods adapt poorly to current programmable GPUs and are not applicable to the interactive domain because of high computational costs. Additionally, displacement mapping requires fairly high tessellated models to achieve satisfactory results, negating the polygon-saving effect of bump mapping.

Other approaches included software-based image-warping techniques for rendering perspective-correct geometry [Oliveira00] and precomputed visibility information [Wang03], [Wang04] [Donnelly05]. Wang describes a per-pixel technique for self-shadowing view-dependent rendering capable of handling occlusions and correct display of silhouette detail [Wang03]. The precomputed surface description is stored in multiple texture maps (the data is precomputed from a supplied height map). The view-dependent displacement-mapping textures approach displays a convincing parallax effect by storing the texel relationship from several viewing directions. However, the cost of storing multiple additional texture maps for surface description is prohibitive for most real-time applications. Our proposed method requires a low memory footprint and can be used for dynamically rendered height fields.

Recent inverse displacement-mapping approaches take advantage of the parallel nature of GPU pixel pipelines to render displacement directly on the GPU [Doggett00], [Kautz01], [Hirche04], [Brawley04], [Policarpo05]. One of the significant disadvantages of these approaches is the lack of correct object silhouettes since these techniques do not modify the actual geometry. Accurate silhouettes can be generated by using view-dependent displacement data as in [Wang03] and [Wang04] or by encoding the surface curvature information with quadric surfaces as in [Oliveira05].

Another limitation of bump-mapping techniques is the inability to properly model self-shadowing of the bump-mapped surface, adding an unrealistic effect to the final look. The horizon-mapping technique [Max88] [Sloan00] allows shadowing of bump-mapped surfaces using precomputed visibility maps. With this approach, the height of the shadowing horizon at each point on the bump map for eight cardinal directions is encoded in a series of textures that are used to determine the amount of self-shadowing for a given light position during rendering. A variety of other techniques were introduced for this purpose. Again, the reader may refer to an excellent survey in [Akenine-Möller02].

A precomputed three-dimensional distance map for a rendered object can be used for surface extrusion along a given view direction ([Donnelly05]). This technique stores a *slab* of distances to the height field in a volumetric texture. It then uses this distance field texture to perform ray *walks* along the view ray to arrive at the displaced point on the extruded surface. The highly prohibitive cost of a three-dimensional texture and dependent texture fetches' latency make this algorithm less attractive and in many cases simply not applicable in most real-time applications. Additionally, as this approach does not compute an accurate intersection of the rays with the height field, it suffers from aliasing artifacts at a large range of viewing angles. Since the algorithm requires precomputed distance fields for each given height field, it is not suitable for dynamic height-field rendering approaches.

Mapping relief data in tangent space for per-pixel displacement mapping in real-time was proposed in [Brawley04], [Policarpo05], and [McGuire05] and further extended in [Oliveira05] to support silhouette generation. The latter work was further extended to support rendering with non-height field data in [Policarpo06]. These methods take advantage of the programmable pixel pipeline efficiency by performing height field–ray intersection in the pixel shader to compute the displacement information. These approaches generate dynamic lighting with self-occlusion, shadows, and motion parallax. Using the visibility horizon to compute hard shadows as in [Policarpo05], [McGuire05], and [Oliveira05] can result in shadow aliasing artifacts. All of the preceding approaches exhibit strong aliasing and excessive flattening at steep viewing angles. No explicit LOD schemes were provided with these approaches, relying on the texture-filtering capabilities of the GPUs.

Adaptive LOD control systems are beneficial to any computationally intensive algorithm, and there have been many contributors in the field of rendering. An LOD system for bump-mapped surfaces using prefiltered maps was presented in [Fournier92]. RenderMan® displacement maps were automatically converted to bump maps and BRDF representations in [Becker93]. An automatic shader simplification system presented in [Olano03] uses controllable parameters to manage system complexity. The resulting LOD shader appearance is adjustable based on distance, size, importance, and hardware limits.

Parallax Occlusion Mapping

This section will provide a brief overview of concepts of the parallax occlusion-mapping method. We encode the displacement information for the surface in a height map as shown in Figure 2.3.2b. The inherent planarity of the tangent space allows us to compute displacement for arbitrary polygonal surfaces. Height field–ray intersections are performed in tangent space. The lighting can be computed in any space using a variety of illumination models. Efficient GPU implementation allows us to compute per-pixel shading, self-occlusion effects, and soft shadows, dynamically scaling the computations.

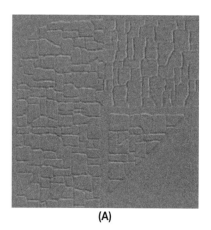
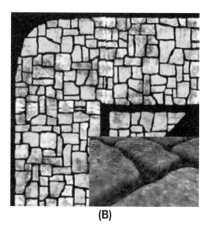

(A)   (B)

FIGURE 2.3.2   (**A**) Tangent space normal map used to render the cobblestone sidewalk in Figure 2.3.1a. (**B**) Corresponding height field encoding the displacement information in the range [0;1] for that sidewalk object and a close-up view of the rendered sidewalk.

The effect of motion parallax for a surface can be computed by applying a height map and offsetting each pixel in the height map using the geometric normal and the view vector. As we move the geometry away from its original position using that ray, the parallax is obtained by the fact that the highest points on the height map would move the farthest along that ray, and the lower extremes would not appear to be moving at all. To obtain satisfactory results for true perspective simulation, one would need to displace every pixel in the height map using the view ray and the geometric normal. We trace a ray through the height field to find the closest visible point on the surface.

The input mesh provides the reference plane for displacing the surface downward. The height field is normalized for correct ray–height field intersection computation, 0 representing the reference polygon surface values and 1 representing the extrusion valleys.

The parallax occlusion-mapping algorithm execution can be summarized as follows:

1. Compute the tangent-space viewing direction $\hat{V}_{ts}$ and the light direction $\hat{L}_{ts}$ per-vertex, interpolate, and normalize in the pixel shader
2. Compute the parallax offset vector P (either per-vertex or per-pixel) to determine the maximum visual offset in texture-space for the current level (as described in [Brawley04]).

In the pixel shader:

1. Ray cast the view ray $\hat{V}_{ts}$ along P to compute the height profile–ray intersection point. Sample the height field profile along P to determine the correct displaced point on the extruded surface. This yields the texture coordinate offset necessary to arrive at the desired point on the extruded surface as shown in Figure 2.3.3. Add this parallax offset amount to the original sample coordinates to yield the shifted texture coordinates t_{off}:

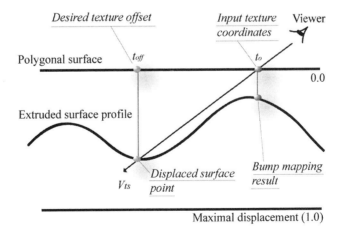

FIGURE 2.3.3 Displacement based on sampled height field and current view direction.

2. Estimate the light visibility coefficient v by casting the light direction ray $\hat{L}_{ts}$ and sampling the height profile for occlusions.

3. Shade the pixel using v, $\hat{L}_{ts}$, and the pixel's attributes (such as the albedo, color map, normal, etc.) sampled at the texture coordinate offset t_{off}.

Figure 2.3.6 later in the chapter illustrates the process above for a given pixel on a polygonal face. We will now discuss each of the above steps in greater detail.

Height Field–Ray Intersection

Techniques such as those described in [Policarpo05] and [Oliveira05] determine the intersection point by a combination of linear and binary search routines. These approaches sample the height field as a piecewise constant function. The linear search allows arriving at a point below the extruded surface intersection with the view ray. The following binary search helps in finding an approximate height-field intersection utilizing bilinear texture filtering to interpolate the intersection point.

The intersection of the surface is approximated with texture filtering, thus only using 8 bits of precision for the intersection computation. This results in visible stair-stepping artifacts at steep viewing angles (as seen in Figure 2.3.4a). Depth biasing toward the horizon hides these artifacts but introduces excessive feature flattening at oblique angles (Figure 2.3.4b).

FIGURE 2.3.4A   Relief mapping rendered with both linear and binary search but without depth bias applied. Notice the visual artifacts resulting from sampling aliasing at grazing angles.

FIGURE 2.3.4B   Relief mapping rendered with both linear and binary search and with depth bias applied. Notice the flattening of surface features toward the horizon.

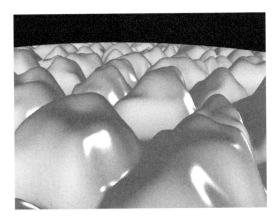

FIGURE 2.3.4C Parallax occlusion mapping rendered with the high-precision height field intersection computation. Notice the lack of aliasing artifacts and feature flattening toward the horizon.

The binary search from [Policarpo05] requires dependent texture fetches for computation. These incur a latency cost that is not offset by any ALU ok computations in the relief mapping ray–height field intersection routine. Increasing the sampling rate during the binary search increases the latency of each fetch by increasing the dependency depth for each successive fetch.

Using a linear search from [Policarpo05] without an associated binary search exacerbates the stair-stepping artifacts even with a high sampling rate (as in Figure 2.3.5a).

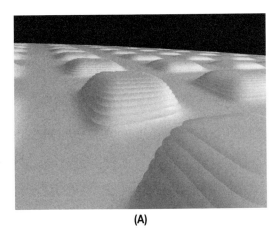

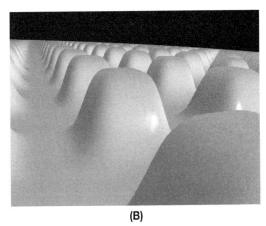

(A) (B)

FIGURE 2.3.5 Comparison of height field intersection precision using the linear search only (same assets). **(A)** Relief mapping. **(B)** Parallax occlusion mapping.

The advantage of a linear search for an intersection root finding lies in an effective use of texturing hardware with low latency, as it does not require dependent texture fetches. Simply using a linear search requires higher precision for the root finding.

We sample the height field using a linear search and approximating the height profile as a piecewise linear curve (as illustrated in Figure 2.3.6). This allows us to combine the 8-bit precision owing to bilinear texture filtering with the full 32-bit precision for root finding during the line intersection. Figure 2.3.4c displays the improved visual results with the lack of aliasing with using our approach.

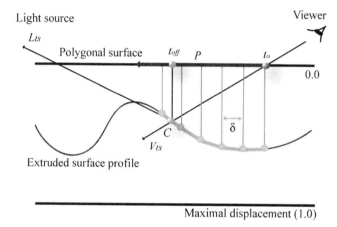

FIGURE 2.3.6   We start at the input texture coordinates t_o and sample the height field profile for each linear segment of the green piecewise linear curve along parallax offset vector **P**. The height field profile–view ray intersection yields parallax-shifted texture coordinate offset t_{off}. δ is the interval step size. Then we perform the visibility tracing. We start at texture offset t_{off} and trace along the light direction vector $\mathbf{L_{ts}}$ to determine any occluding features in the height field profile.

Since we do not encode feature information into additional look-up tables, the accuracy of our technique corresponds to the sampling interval δ (as well as for [Policarpo05]). Both algorithms suffer from some amount of aliasing artifacts if too few samples are used for a relatively high-frequency height field, though the amount differs between the techniques.

Automatically determining δ by using the texture resolution is currently impractical. At grazing angles, the parallax amount is quite large, and thus we must march along a long parallax offset vector to arrive at the displaced point. In that case, the step size is frequently much larger than a texel and thus unrelated to the texture resolution. To solve this, we provide both directable and automatic controls.

The artists can control the sampling size bounds with artist-editable parameters. This is convenient in real game scenarios, as it allows control per texture map. If dynamic flow control (DFC) is available, we can automatically adjust the sampling rate during ray tracing. We express the sampling rate as a linear function of the angle between the geometric normal and the view direction ray:

$$n = n_{\min} + \hat{N} \cdot \hat{V}_{ts}(n_{\max} - n_{\min}), \qquad (2.3.1)$$

where $n_{\min}$ and $n_{\max}$ are the artist-controlled sampling rate bounds, and $\hat{N}$ is the interpolated geometric unit normal vector at the current pixel. This ensures that we increase the sampling rate along the steep viewing angles. We increase the efficiency of the linear search by using the early out functionality of DFC to stop sampling the height field when a point below the surface is found.

Soft Shadows

The height map can cast shadows on itself. This is accomplished by substituting the light vector for the view vector when computing the intersection of the height profile to determine the correct displaced texel position during the reverse height-mapping step. Once we arrive at the point on the displaced surface (the point C in Figure 2.3.6), we can compute its visibility from the any light source. For that, we cast a ray toward the light source in question and perform horizon visibility queries of the height field profile along the light direction ray $\hat{L}_{ts}$.

If there are intersections of the height field profile with $\hat{L}_{ts}$, then there are occluding features, and the point in question will be in shadow. This process allows us to generate shadows owing to the object features' self-occlusions and object interpenetration.

If we repeated the process for the height field profile–view direction ray tracing for the visibility query by stopping sampling at the first intersection, we would arrive at the horizon-shadowing value that describes whether the displaced pixel is in shadow. Using this value during the lighting computation (as in [Policarpo05]) generates hard shadows that can display aliasing artifacts in some scenes (Figure 2.3.7a).

We can use the height-field profile samples h_i along the light direction ray to determine the occlusion coefficient. We sample the height value h_0 at the shifted texture coordinate t_{off}. Starting at this offset ensures that the shadows do not appear floating on top of the surface. The sample h_0 is our reference (surface) height. We then sample n other samples along the light ray, subtracting h_0 from each of the successive samples h_i. This allows us to compute the blocker-to-receiver ratio as in Figure 2.3.9. The closer the blocker is to the surface, the smaller the resulting penumbra. We compute the penumbra coefficient (the visibility coefficient v) by scaling the contribution of each sample by the distance of this sample from h_0, and using the maximum value sampled. Additionally we can weight each visibility sample to simulate the blur kernel for shadow filtering.

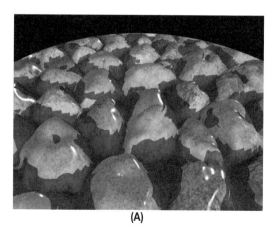

(A)   (B)

FIGURE 2.3.7   (**A**) Hard shadows generated with the relief-mapping horizon-visibility threshold computation. (**B**) Soft shadows generated with the parallax occlusion-mapping penumbra approximation technique. With our approach, we sample n samples $h_1 - h_n$ along the light direction ray (Figure 2.3.8). We assume that we are lighting the surface with an area light source and, similar to [Chan03] and [Wyman02], we heuristically approximate the size of penumbra for the occluded pixel. Figure 2.3.9 demonstrates the penumbra-size computation given an area light source, a blocker, and a receiver surface.

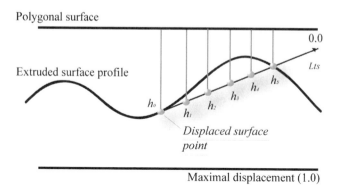

FIGURE 2.3.8   Sampling the height field profile along the light ray direction L_{ts} to obtain height samples $h_1 - h_8$ ($n = 8$).

We apply the visibility coefficient v during the lighting computation for generation of smooth soft shadows. This allows us to obtain well-behaved soft shadows without any edge aliasing or filtering artifacts. Figures 2.3.7b and 2.3.10 show examples of smooth shadows using our technique. One limitation of our technique is the lack of hard surface contact shadow for extremely high-frequency height maps.

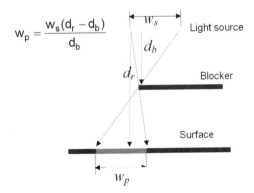

$$w_p = \frac{w_s(d_r - d_b)}{d_b}$$

FIGURE 2.3.9   Penumbra size approximation for area light sources, where w_s is the light source width, w_p is the penumbra width, d_r is the receiver depth, and d_b is the blocker depth from the light source.

FIGURE 2.3.10   Smooth soft shadows and perspective-correct depth details generated with the parallax occlusion-rendering algorithm.

Remember that estimating light visibility increases shader complexity. We perform the visibility query only for areas where the dot product between the geometric normal and the light vector is nonnegative by utilizing dynamic branching (see the actual pixel shader in Listing 2.3.2 in the Appendix). This allows us to compute soft shadows only for areas that are facing the light source.

Adaptive LOD Control System

We compute the current mip level explicitly in the pixel shader and use this information to transition between different levels of detail from the full effect to bump mapping. Simply using mip mapping for LOD management is ineffective since it does not reduce shader complexity during rendering. Using the full shader for the height field profile intersection with the view ray and the light ray, the visibility and lighting is expensive. Although at lower mip levels the fill is reduced, without our LOD system, the full shader will be executed for each pixel regardless of its proximity to the viewer. Instead, with our algorithm, only a simple bump-mapping shader is executed for mip levels higher than the specified threshold value.

This in-shader LOD system provides a significant rendering optimization and smooth transitions between the full parallax occlusion mapping and a simplified representation without visual artifacts such as ghosting or popping. Since all calculations are performed per pixel, the method robustly handles extreme close-ups of the object surface, thus providing an additional LOD management.

We compute the mip level directly in the pixel shader (as described in [Shreiner05]) on SM 3.0 hardware (see the actual pixel shader in Listing 2.3.2 in the Appendix). The lowest LOD is rendered using bump mapping. As we determine that the currently rendered LOD is close enough to the threshold, we interpolate the parallax occlusion-mapped lit result with the bump-mapped lit result using the fractional part of the current mip level as the interpolation parameter. There is almost no associated visual quality degradation as we move into a lower LOD, and the transition appears quite smooth (Figure 2.3.11).

(A)   (B)

FIGURE 2.3.11   A complex scene with parallax occlusion mapping on the sidewalk and the brick wall. The strength of the blue tint in (**B**) denotes the decreasing LOD (deepest blue being bump mapping and no blue displays full computation). Note the lack of visual artifacts and smooth transition owing to the LOD transition discernable in (**A**). The transition region is very small.

We expose the threshold-level parameter to the artists to provide directability for game-level editing. In our examples we used a threshold value of 4. Thus, even at steep grazing angles the close-up views of surfaces will maintain perspective correct depth.

Results

We have implemented the techniques described in this paper using DirectX 9.0c shader programs on a variety of graphics cards. An example of an educational version of this shader is shown in Listings 2.3.1 (for the vertex shader implementation using DirectX 9.0c Shader Model 3.0) and Listing 2.3.2 (for the pixel shader implementation using DirectX 9.0c Shader Model 3.0). We use different texture sizes based on the desired feature resolution. For Figures 2.3.1, 2.3.2, 2.3.11, 2.3.12, and 2.3.13 we apply

FIGURE 2.3.12A A 1100-polygon game soldier character with parallax occlusion mapping.

FIGURE 2.3.12B A 1.5 million–polygon soldier character with diffuse lighting.

FIGURE 2.3.13 Displaced text rendering with the sign rendered using parallax occlusion mapping technique .

1024×1024 RGBα textures with noncontiguous texture coordinates. For Figures 2.3.4 and 2.3.7 we apply repeated 256×256 RGBα textures, and for Figures 2.3.5 and 2.3.10 we use repeated 128×128 RGBα textures.

We applied parallax occlusion mapping to the 1100-polygon soldier character shown in Figure 2.3.12a. We compared this result to a 1.5 million polygon version of the soldier model used to generate normal maps for the low resolution version (Figure 2.3.12b). (Note that the two images in Figure 2.3.12 are from slightly different viewpoints though extracted from a demo sequence with similar viewpoint paths.) We apply a 2048×2048 RGBα texture map to the low-resolution object. We render the low resolution soldier using DirectX on ATI Radeon X1600 XL at 255 fps. The sampling rate bounds were set to the range of [8, 50]. The memory requirement for this model was 79 K for the vertex buffer, 6 K for the index buffer, and 13 MB of texture memory (using 3DC texture compression).

The high-resolution soldier model is rendered on the same hardware at a rate of 32 fps. The memory requirement for this model was 31 MB for the vertex buffer and 14 MB for the index buffer. Because of memory considerations, the vertex transform cost for rendering, animation, and authoring issues, characters matching the high-resolution soldier are impractical in current game scenarios. However, using our technique on an extremely low-resolution model provided significant frame rate increase, with 32 MB of memory being saved, at a comparable quality of rendering.

This demonstrates the usefulness of the presented technique for texture-space displacement mapping via parallax occlusion mapping. In order to render the same objects interactively with equal levels of detail, the meshes would need an extremely detailed triangle subdivision, which is impractical even with the currently available GPUs.

Our method can be used with a dynamically rendered height field and still produce perspective-correct depth results. In that case, the dynamically updated displacement values can be used to derive the normal vectors at rendering time by convolving the height map with a Sobel operator in the horizontal and vertical direction (as described in detail in [Tatarchuk06a]). The rest of the algorithm does not require any modification.

We used this technique extensively in the interactive demo called *ToyShop* [Toyshop05] for a variety of surfaces and effects. As seen in Figures 2.3.1 and 2.3.12, we've rendered the cobblestone sidewalk using this technique (using a sampling range from 8 to 40 samples per pixel). In Figure 2.3.14 we have applied it to the brick wall (with the same sampling range), and in Figure 2.3.13 we see parallax occlusion mapping used to render the extruded wood-block letters of the *ToyShop* store sign. We were able to integrate a variety of lighting models with this technique, ranging from a single diffusely lit material in Figure 2.3.14 to shadows and specular illumination in Figure 2.3.13, and shadow-mapping integrated and dynamic view-dependent reflections in Figure 2.3.1a.

FIGURE 2.3.14 A portion of a realistic city environment with the cobblestone sidewalk and the brick wall rendered with parallax occlusion mapping (left) and bump mapping (right). We are able to use shadow mapping on the surfaces and dynamically rendered reflections from objects in the scene.

Considerations for Practical Use of Parallax Occlusion Mapping and Game Integration

Algorithm Limitations and Relevant Considerations

Although parallax occlusion mapping is a very powerful and flexible technique for computing and lighting extruded surfaces in real-time, it does have its limitations. Parallax occlusion mapping is a sampling-based algorithm at its core, and as such, it can exhibit aliasing. The frequencies of the height field will determine the required sampling rate for the ray-tracing procedures—otherwise aliasing artifacts will be visible (as seen in Figures 2.3.4a and 2.3.5a). One must increase the sampling rate significantly if the height field contains very sharp features (as visible in the text and sharp conic features in Figure 2.3.15). However, as we can note from Figures 2.3.15a and 2.3.15b, the visual quality of the results rendered with parallax occlusion mapping is high enough to render such traditionally difficult objects as extruded text or sharp peaks at highly interactive rates (fps > 15 fps on ATI Radeon X1600 XL rendering at 1600x1200 resolution). To render the same objects interactively with equal levels of detail, the meshes would need an extremely detailed triangle subdivision (with triangles being nearly pixel sized), which is impractical even with the currently available GPUs.

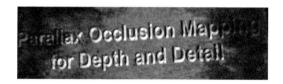
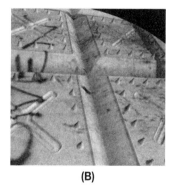

(A)   (B)

FIGURE 2.3.15   Rendering extruded text objects in (**A**) and sharp conic features in (**B**) with parallax occlusion mapping.

The sampling limitation is particularly evident in the DirectX 9.0c Shader Model 2.0 implementation of the parallax occlusion-mapping algorithm if the height field used has high spatial frequency content. This shader model suffers from a small instruction count limit, and thus we are unable to compute more than eight samples during ray tracing in a single pass. However, several passes can be used to compute the results of ray tracing by using offscreen buffer rendering to increase the resulting precision of computations using SM 2.0 shaders. As in the analog-to-digital sound conversion process, sampling during the ray tracing at slightly more than twice the frequency of the height map features will make up for not modeling the surfaces with implicit functions and performing the exact intersection of the ray with the implicit representation of the extruded surface.

Another limitation of our technique is the lack of detailed silhouettes, betraying the low-resolution geometry rendered with our method. This is an important feature for enhancing the realism of the effect, and we are investigating ideas for generating correct silhouettes. However, in many scenarios, the artists can work around this issue by placing specific *border* geometry to hide the artifacts. One can see this at work in the *ToyShop* demo, as the artists placed the curb stones at the edge of the sidewalk object with parallax occlusion-mapped cobblestones or with a special row of bricks at the corner of the brick building shown in Figure 2.3.16.

The parallax occlusion-mapping algorithm will not automatically produce surfaces with correct depth buffer values (since it simply operates in screen space on individual pixels). This means that in some situations this will result in apparent object interpenetration or incorrect object collision. The algorithm can be extended to output accurate depth quite easily. Since we know the reference surface's geometric depth, we can compute the displacement amount by sampling the height field at the t_{off} location and

FIGURE 2.3.16 Additional brick geometry placed at the corners of parallax occlusion-mapped brick objects to hide inaccurate silhouettes in an interactive environment of the *ToyShop* demo. (© ATI Research Inc. Reprinted with permission.)

adding or subtracting this displacement amount to the reference depth value (as described in [Policarpo05]) by outputting it as the depth value from the pixel shader.

Art Content Authoring Suggestions for Parallax Occlusion Mapping

Adding art asset support for parallax occlusion mapping requires a minimal increase in memory footprint (for an additional 8-bit height map) if the application already supports normal mapping and contains appropriate assets. There are many reliable methods for generating height maps useful for this technique:

- Normal maps can be generated from a combination of a low- and high-resolution models with the NormalMapper software [NormalMapper03]. The tool has an option to simultaneously output the corresponding displacement values in a height map.
- A height map may be painted in thee-dimensional painting software such as ZBrush™.
- It also can be created in a two-dimensional painting software such as Adobe® Photoshop™.

The parallax occlusion-mapping technique is an efficient and compelling technique for simulating surface details. However, as with other bump-mapping techniques, its quality depends strongly on the quality of its art content. Empirically, we found that lower-frequency height map textures result in higher-performance (owing to fewer samples required for ray tracing) and better-quality results (since fewer height field features are missed). For example, when creating height maps for rendering bricks or cobblestones, one may widen the grout region and apply a soft blur to smooth the transition and thus lower the height-map frequency content. As discussed in the previous section, when using high-frequency height maps (such as those in Figure 2.3.15a or 2.3.15b), we must increase the range of sampling for ray tracing.

An important consideration for authoring art assets for use with this algorithm lies in the realization that the algorithm always extrudes surfaces "pushing down"—unlike the traditional displacement mapping. This affects the placement of the original low-resolution geometry. The surfaces must be placed slightly higher than where the anticipated extruded surface should be located. Additionally this means that the peaks in the extruded surface will correspond to the brightest values in the height map (white), and the valleys will correspond to the darkest (black).

Conclusions

We have presented a pixel-driven displacement-mapping technique for rendering detailed surfaces under varying light conditions and generating soft shadows resulting from self-occlusion. We have described an efficient algorithm for computing intersections of the height field profile of rays with high precision. Our method includes estimation of light visibility for generation of soft shadows. An automatic LOD control system manages shader complexity efficiently at runtime, generating smooth LOD transitions without visual artifacts. Our technique takes advantage of the programmable GPU pipeline, resulting in highly interactive frame rates coupled with a low memory footprint.

Parallax occlusion mapping can be used effectively to generate an illusion of very detailed geometry exhibiting correct motion parallax as well as producing very convincing self-shadowing effects. We provide a high level of directability to the artists and significantly improve visual quality over the previous approaches. We hope to see more games implementing compelling scenes using this technique.

Acknowledgments

We thank Dan Roeger, Daniel Szecket, Abe Wiley, and Eli Turner for their help with the artwork and Zoë Brawley from Relic Entertainment for her ideas in the original implementation of the 2004 technique.

Sample Code

ON THE CD

On the CD-ROM accompanying this book, we have provided the following samples demonstrating the power of parallax occlusion mapping:

- RenderMonkey version 1.62 samples:
  1. Parallax Occlusion Mapping—RM 1.62; contains sample with and without LOD calculations
  2. POM Rotating Light—RM 1.62.zip
- ParallaxOcclusionMapping—DX9; a DirectX 9.0c sample using SM 3.0 shaders

We also recommend taking a look at ATI's *ToyShop* demo (also provided on the CD-ROM in the folder path: 05 Environment Effects/5.4 Rendering Multiple Layers of Rain with a Post-Processing Composite Effect/ati-demo-toyshop-v1.2.exe) since that demo is the best showcase for the parallax occlusion mapping technology.

References

[Akenine-Möller02] Akenine-Möller, T. and E. Heines. *Real-time Rendering*, 2nd ed. A.K. Peters, July 2002.

[Becker93] Becker, B. G. and N. L. Max. "Smooth Transitions between Bump Rendering Algorithms." *ACM Transactions on Graphics* (Siggraph 1993 Proceedings). ACM Press, 1993: pp. 183–190.

[Blinn78] Blinn, J. F. "Simulation of Wrinkled Surfaces." *Proceedings of the 5th Annual Conference on Computer Graphics and Interactive Techniques*. ACM Press, 1978: pp. 286–292.

[Brawley04] Brawley, Z. and N. Tatarchuk. "Parallax Occlusion Mapping: Self-Shadowing, Perspective-Correct Bump Mapping Using Reverse Height Map Tracing." *ShaderX³: Advanced Rendering with DirectX and OpenGL*, edited by W. Engel, Charles River Media, 2004: pp. 135–154.

[Chan03] Chan, E., and F. Durand, "Rendering Fake Soft Shadows With Smoothies" *Eurographics Symposium on Rendering Proceedings*. ACM Press, 2003: pp. 208–218.

[Cook84] Cook, R. L. "Shade Trees." *Proceedings of the 11th Annual Conference on Computer Graphics and Interactive Techniques*. ACM Press, 1984: pp. 223–231.

[Doggett00] Doggett, M. and J. Hirche. "Adaptive View Dependent Tessellation of Displacement Maps." *HWWS '00: Proceedings of the ACM SIGGRAPH/EUROGRAPHICS Workshop on Graphics Hardware*. ACM Press, 2000: pp. 59–66.

[Donnelly05] Donnelly, W. "Per-Pixel Displacement Mapping with Distance Functions." *GPU Gems 2*, edited by M. Pharr. Addison-Wesley, 2005: pp. 123–136.

[Fournier92] Fournier, A. "Filtering Normal Maps and Creating Multiple Surfaces." Technical report, University of British Columbia, 1992.

[Heidrich98] Heidrich, W. and H.-P. Seidel. "Ray-tracing Procedural Displacement Shaders." *Graphics Interface*, 1998: pp. 8–16.

[Hirche04] Hirche, J., A. Ehlert, S. Guthe, and M. Doggett. "Hardware Accelerated Per-Pixel Displacement Mapping." *Graphics Interface*, 2004: pp. 153–158.

[Kaneko01] Kaneko, T., T. Takahei, M. Inami, N. Kawakami, Y. Yanagida, T. Maeda, and S. Tachi. "Detailed Shape Representation with Parallax Mapping." *Proceedings of ICAT 2001*, 2001: pp. 205–208.

[Kautz01] Kautz, J. and H.-P. Seidel. "Hardware Accelerated Displacement Mapping for Image Based Rendering. *Proceedings of Graphics Interface 2001*, edited by B. Watson and J.W. Buchanan. 2001: pp. 61–70.

[Max88] Max, N. "Horizon Mapping: Shadows for Bump-Mapped Surfaces." *Visual Computer 4*(2) (1988): pp. 109–117.

[McGuire05] Mcguire, M. and M. Mcguire. "Steep Parallax Mapping." I3D 2005 Poster.

[NormalMapper03] Normalmapper Tool, 2003. ATI Research, Inc. Available online at *http://www2.ati.com/developer/NormalMapper-3_2_2.zip*.

[Olano03] Olano, M., B. Kuehne, and M. Simmons. "Automatic Shader Level of Detail." *Siggraph/Eurographics Workshop on Graphics Hardware Proceedings*, ACM Press, 2003: pp. 7–14.

[Oliveira00] Oliveira, M. M., G. Bishop, and D. Mcallister. "Relief texture mapping." *Siggraph 2000, Computer Graphics Proceedings*, edited by K. Akeley. ACM Press/ACM SIGGRAPH/Addison Wesley Longman, 2000: pp. 359–368.

[Oliveira05] Oliveira, M. M. and F. Policarpo. "An Efficient Representation for Surface Details." UFRGS Technical Report RP-351, 2005.

[Pharr96] Pharr, M. and P. Hanrahan. "Geometry Caching for Ray-Tracing Displacement Maps." *Eurographics Rendering Worshop 1996*, edited by X. Pueyo and P. Schröder. Springer Wien, New York 1996: pp. 31–40.

[Policarpo05] Policarpo, F., M. M. Oliveira, and J. Comba. "Real-time Relief Mapping on Arbitrary Polygonal Surfaces." *ACM SIGGRAPH Symposium on Interactive 3D Graphics Proceedings*. ACM Press, 2005: pp. 359–368.

[Policarpo06] Policarpo, F. and M. M. Oliveira. "Relief Mapping of Non-Height-Field Surface Details." *ACM SIGGRAPH Symposium on Interactive 3D Graphics and Games Proceedings*. ACM Press, 2006: pp. 55–52.

[Shreiner05] Shreiner, D., M. Woo, J. Neider, and T. Davis. *OpenGL® Programming Guide: The Official Guide to Learning OpenGL®*, version 2. Addison-Wesley, 2005.

[Sloan00] Sloan, P.-P. J. and M. F. Cohen. "Interactive Horizon Mapping." *11th Eurographics Workshop on Rendering Proceedings*. ACM Press, 2000: pp. 281–286.

[Tatarchuk06] Tatarchuk, N. "Dynamic Parallax Occlusion Mapping with Approximate Soft Shadows." *Proceedings of ACM SIGGRAPH Symposium on Interactive 3D Graphics and Games*. 2006: pp. 63-69.

[Tatarchuk06a] Tatarchuk, N. "Practical Parallax Occlusion Mapping for Highly Detailed Surface Rendering." *Proceedings of Game Developer Conference*. 2006.

[Toyshop05] Toyshop Demo, 2005. ATI Research, Inc. Available online at *http://www.ati.com/developer/demos/rx1800.html*.

[Wang03] Wang, L., X. Wang, X. Tong, S. Lin, S. Hu, B. Guo, and H.-Y. Shum. "View-Dependent Displacement Mapping." *ACM Trans. Graph. 22*(3) (2003): pp. 334–339.

[Wang04] Wang, X., X. Tong, S. Lin, S. Hu, B. Guo, and H.-Y. Shum. "Generalized Displacement Maps." *Eurographics Symposium on Rendering 2004, EUROGRAPHICS*, edited by Keller and Jensen. EUROGRAPHICS, 2004, pp. 227–233.

[Welsh04] Welsh, T. "Parallax Mapping." *ShaderX³: Advanced Rendering with DirectX and OpenGL*, edited by W. Engel. A.K. Peters, 2004.

[Wyman02] Wyman, C. and C. Hansen. "Penumbra Maps: Approximate Soft Shadows in Real-time." *Eurographics Workshop on Rendering 2003, EUROGRAPHICS*, edited by Keller and Jensen. EUROGRAPHICS, 2002: pp. 202–207.

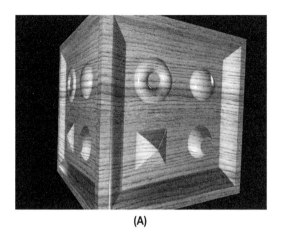 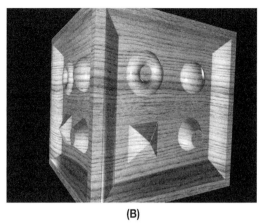

(A)   (B)

FIGURE 2.3.17   Simple cube model rendered with detailed surface from the same viewpoint. In (**A**) relief mapping is used to create surface complexity. In (**B**) parallax occlusion mapping is used to render perspective-correct extruded surfaces. Notice the differences on the left face of the cube as the surface is viewed at a steep angle.

Appendix: DirectX Shader Code Implementation of Parallax Occlusion Mapping

LISTING 2.3.1   Parallax Occlusion Mapping Algorithm Implementation (Vertex Shader, DirectX 9.0c Shader Model 3.0)

```
float4x4 matViewInverse;
float4x4 matWorldViewProjection;
float4x4 matView;

float    fBaseTextureRepeat;
float    fHeightMapRange;
float4   vLightPosition;

struct VS_INPUT
{
   float4 positionWS  : POSITION;
   float2 texCoord    : TEXCOORD0;
   float3 vNormalWS   : NORMAL;
   float3 vBinormalWS : BINORMAL;
   float3 vTangentWS  : TANGENT;
};

struct VS_OUTPUT
{
   float4 position : POSITION;
   float2 texCoord : TEXCOORD0;
```

```
    // Light vector in tangent space, not normalized
    float3 vLightTS : TEXCOORD1;

    // View vector in tangent space, not normalized
    float3 vViewTS : TEXCOORD2;

    // Parallax offset vector in tangent space
    float2 vParallaxOffsetTS : TEXCOORD3;

    // Normal vector in world space
    float3 vNormalWS : TEXCOORD4;

    // View vector in world space
    float3 vViewWS : TEXCOORD5;
};

VS_OUTPUT vs_main( VS_INPUT i )
{
    VS_OUTPUT Out = (VS_OUTPUT) O;

    // Transform and output input position
    Out.position = mul( matWorldViewProjection, i.positionWS );

    // Propagate texture coordinate through:
    Out.texCoord = i.texCoord;

    // Uncomment this to repeat the texture
    // Out.texCoord *= fBaseTextureRepeat;

    // Propagate the world vertex normal through:
    Out.vNormalWS = i.vNormalWS;

    // Compute and output the world view vector:
    float3 vViewWS = mul( matViewInverse,
                    float4(0,0,0,1)) - i.positionWS;

    Out.vViewWS = vViewWS;

    // Compute denormalized light vector in world space:
    float3 vLightWS = vLightPosition - i.positionWS;

    // Normalize the light and view vectors and transform
    // it to the tangent space:
    float3x3 mWorldToTangent =
        float3x3( i.vTangentWS, i.vBinormalWS, i.vNormalWS );

    // Propagate the view and the light vectors (in tangent space):
    Out.vLightTS = mul( mWorldToTangent, vLightWS );
    Out.vViewTS  = mul( mWorldToTangent, vViewWS  );

    // Compute the ray direction for intersecting the height field
    // profile with current view ray. See the above paper for
    // derivation
    // of this computation.
```

```
                    // Compute initial parallax displacement direction:
                    float2 vParallaxDirection = normalize(  Out.vViewTS.xy );

                    // The length of this vector determines the furthest amount
                    // of displacement:
                    float fLength = length( Out.vViewTS );
                    float fParallaxLength = sqrt( fLength * fLength - Out.vViewTS.z
                            * Out.vViewTS.z ) / Out.vViewTS.z;

                    // Compute the actual reverse parallax displacement vector:
                    Out.vParallaxOffsetTS = vParallaxDirection * fParallaxLength;

                    // Need to scale the amount of displacement to account for
                    // different height ranges in height maps. This is controlled by
                    // an artist-editable parameter:
                    Out.vParallaxOffsetTS *= fHeightMapRange;

                    return Out;

                }   // End of VS_OUTPUT vs_main(..)
```

LISTING 2.3.2 Parallax Occlusion Mapping Algorithm Implementation (Pixel Shader, DirectX 9.0c Shader Model 3.0)

```
                    // NOTE: Since for this particular example want to make convenient
                    // ways
                    // to turn features rendering on and off (for example, for turning
                    // on /
                    // off visualization of current level of details, shadows, etc.),
                    // the
                    // shader presented uses more flow control instructions than it
                    // would
                    // in a game engine.

                    // Uniform shader parameters declarations
                    bool bVisualizeLOD;
                    bool bVisualizeMipLevel;
                    bool bDisplayShadows;

                    // This parameter contains the dimensions of the height map /
                    // normal map
                    // pair and is used for determination of current mip level value:
                    float2 vTextureDims;

                    int    nLODThreshold;
                    float fShadowSoftening;
                    float fSpecularExponent;
                    float fDiffuseBrightness;
                    float fHeightMapRange;

                    float4 cAmbientColor;
                    float4 cDiffuseColor;
                    float4 cSpecularColor;
```

```
       int nMinSamples;
       int nMaxSamples;

       sampler tBaseMap;
       sampler tNormalMap;

       // Note: centroid sampling should be specified if multisampling is
       // enabled
       struct PS_INPUT
       {
          float2 texCoord : TEXCOORD0;

          // Light vector in tangent space, denormalized
          float3 vLightTS : TEXCOORD1_centroid;

          // View vector in tangent space, denormalized
          float3 vViewTS : TEXCOORD2_centroid;

          // Parallax offset vector in tangent space
          float2 vParallaxOffsetTS : TEXCOORD3_centroid;

          // Normal vector in world space
          float3 vNormalWS : TEXCOORD4_centroid;

          // View vector in world space
          float3 vViewWS : TEXCOORD5_centroid;
       };



//...................................................................
   // Function:    ComputeIllumination
   //
   // Description: Computes phong illumination for the given pixel
      using
   //              its attribute textures and a light vector.

//...................................................................
   float4 ComputeIllumination( float2 texCoord, float3 vLightTS,
                               float3 vViewTS, float  fOcclusion-
                               Shadow )
   {
      // Sample the normal from the normal map for the given texture
      // sample:
      float3 vNormalTS = normalize( tex2D( tNormalMap, texCoord ) *
      2 - 1 );

      // Sample base map:
      float4 cBaseColor = tex2D( tBaseMap, texCoord );

      // Compute diffuse color component:
      float4 cDiffuse = saturate( dot( vNormalTS, vLightTS )) *
                                  cDiffuseColor;

      // Compute specular component:
```

```
                  float3 vReflectionTS = normalize( 2 * dot( vViewTS,
                  vNormalTS ) *
                                                  vNormalTS - vViewTS );

                  float fRdotL = dot( vReflectionTS, vLightTS );

                  float4 cSpecular = saturate( pow( fRdotL, fSpecularExponent )) *
                                  cSpecularColor;

                  float4 cFinalColor = (( cAmbientColor + cDiffuse ) * cBaseColor +
                                  cSpecular ) * fOcclusionShadow;

                  return cFinalColor;
              }



    //..................................................................
        // Function:    ps_main
        //
        // Description: Computes pixel illumination result due to applying
        //              parallax occlusion mapping to simulation of view-
        //              dependent surface displacement for a given height
        //              map

    //..................................................................
    float4 ps_main( PS_INPUT i ) : COLOR0
        {
          //  Normalize the interpolated vectors:
          float3 vViewTS   = normalize( i.vViewTS  );
          float3 vViewWS   = normalize( i.vViewWS  );
          float3 vLightTS  = normalize( i.vLightTS );
          float3 vNormalWS = normalize( i.vNormalWS );

          float4 cResultColor = float4( 0, 0, 0, 1 );

          // Adaptive in-shader level-of-detail system implementation.
          // Compute the current mip level explicitly in the pixel shader
          // and use this information to transition between different
          // levels of detail from the full effect to simple bump mapping.

          // Compute the current gradients:
          float2 fTexCoordsPerSize = i.texCoord * vTextureDims;

          // Compute all 4 derivatives in x and y in a single instruction
          //  to optimize:
          float2 dxSize, dySize;
          float2 dx, dy;

          float4( dxSize, dx ) = ddx( float4( fTexCoordsPerSize,
          i.texCoord ) );
          float4( dySize, dy ) = ddy( float4( fTexCoordsPerSize,
          i.texCoord ) );

          float  fMipLevel;
          float  fMipLevelInt;    // mip level integer portion
```

```
float  fMipLevelFrac;   // mip level fractional amount for
                        // blending in between levels

float  fMinTexCoordDelta;
float2 dTexCoords;

// Find min of change in u and v across quad: compute du and dv
// magnitude across quad
dTexCoords = dxSize * dxSize + dySize * dySize;

// Standard mipmapping uses max here
fMinTexCoordDelta = max( dTexCoords.x, dTexCoords.y );

// Compute the current mip level  (* 0.5 is effectively
// computing a square root before )
fMipLevel = max( 0.5 * log2( fMinTexCoordDelta ), 0 );

// Start the current sample located at the input texture
// coordinate, which would correspond to computing a bump
// mapping result:
float2 texSample = i.texCoord;

// Multiplier for visualizing the level of detail
float4 cLODColoring = float4( 1, 1, 3, 1 );

float fOcclusionShadow = 1.0;

if ( fMipLevel <= (float) nLODThreshold )
{
    //=============================================//
    // Parallax occlusion mapping offset computation //
    //=============================================//

    // Utilize dynamic flow control to change the number of
    // samples per ray depending on the viewing angle for the
    // surface. Oblique angles require smaller step sizes to
    // achieve more accurate precision for computing displacement.
    // We express the sampling rate as a linear function of the
    // angle between the geometric normal and the view
    // direction ray:
    int nNumSteps = (int) lerp( nMaxSamples, nMinSamples,
                               dot( vViewWS, vNormalWS ) );

    // Intersect the view ray with the height field profile along
    // the direction of the parallax offset ray (computed in the
    // vertex shader. Note that the code is designed specifically
    // to take advantage of the dynamic flow control constructs
    // in HLSL and is very sensitive to the specific language
    // syntax. When converting to other examples, if still want
    // to use dynamic flow control in the resulting assembly
    // shader, care must be applied.
    // In the below steps we approximate the height field profile
    // as piecewise linear curve. We find the pair of endpoints
    // between which the intersection between the height field
```

```
// profile and the view ray is found and then compute line
// segment intersection for the view ray and the line
// segment formed by the two endpoints. This intersection
// is the displacement offset from the original texture
// coordinate.

float fCurrHeight = 0.0;
float fStepSize   = 1.0 / (float) nNumSteps;
float fPrevHeight = 1.0;
float fNextHeight = 0.0;

int    nStepIndex = 0;
bool   bCondition = true;

float2 vTexOffsetPerStep = fStepSize * i.vParallaxOffsetTS;
float2 vTexCurrentOffset = i.texCoord;
float  fCurrentBound     = 1.0;
float  fParallaxAmount    = 0.0;

float2 pt1 = 0;
float2 pt2 = 0;

float2 texOffset2 = 0;

while ( nStepIndex < nNumSteps )
{
   vTexCurrentOffset -= vTexOffsetPerStep;

   // Sample height map which in this case is stored in the
   // alpha channel of the normal map:
   fCurrHeight = tex2Dgrad( tNormalMap, vTexCurrentOffset,
                            dx, dy ).a;

   fCurrentBound -= fStepSize;

   if ( fCurrHeight > fCurrentBound )
   {
      pt1 = float2( fCurrentBound, fCurrHeight );
      pt2 = float2( fCurrentBound + fStepSize, fPrevHeight );

      texOffset2 = vTexCurrentOffset - vTexOffsetPerStep;

      nStepIndex = nNumSteps + 1;
   }
   else
   {
      nStepIndex++;
      fPrevHeight = fCurrHeight;
   }
}   // End of while ( nStepIndex < nNumSteps )

float fDelta2 = pt2.x - pt2.y;
float fDelta1 = pt1.x - pt1.y;
fParallaxAmount = (pt1.x * fDelta2 - pt2.x * fDelta1 ) /
                  ( fDelta2 - fDelta1 );
```

```
float2 vParallaxOffset = i.vParallaxOffsetTS *
                    (1 - fParallaxAmount );

// The computed texture offset for the displaced point
// on the pseudo-extruded surface:
float2 texSampleBase = i.texCoord - vParallaxOffset;
texSample = texSampleBase;

// Lerp to bump mapping only if we are in between,
// transition section:
cLODColoring = float4( 1, 1, 1, 1 );

if ( fMipLevel > (float)(nLODThreshold - 1) )
{
   // Lerp based on the fractional part:
   fMipLevelFrac = modf( fMipLevel, fMipLevelInt );

   if ( bVisualizeLOD )
   {
      // For visualizing: lerping from regular POM-
      // resulted color through blue color for transition
      // layer:
      cLODColoring = float4( 1, 1, max(1, 2 * fMipLevel-
      Frac), 1 );
   }

   // Lerp the texture coordinate from parallax occlusion
   // mapped coordinate to bump mapping smoothly based on
   // the current mip level:
   texSample = lerp( texSampleBase, i.texCoord,
   fMipLevelFrac );

} // End of if ( fMipLevel > fThreshold - 1 )

if ( bDisplayShadows == true )
{
   float2 vLightRayTS = vLightTS.xy * fHeightMapRange;

   // Compute the soft blurry shadows taking into account
   // self-occlusion for features of the height field:

   float sh0 =  tex2Dgrad( tNormalMap, texSampleBase, dx, dy
   ).a;
   float shA = (tex2Dgrad( tNormalMap, texSampleBase +
   vLightRayTS
       * 0.88, dx, dy ).a - sh0 - 0.88 ) *  1 *
       fShadowSoftening;
   float sh9 = (tex2Dgrad( tNormalMap, texSampleBase +
   vLightRayTS *
       0.77, dx, dy ).a - sh0 - 0.77 ) *  2 * fShadowSoft-
       ening;
   float sh8 = (tex2Dgrad( tNormalMap, texSampleBase +
   vLightRayTS *
       0.66, dx, dy ).a - sh0 - 0.66 ) *  4 * f
       ShadowSoftening;
```

```
            float sh7 = (tex2Dgrad( tNormalMap, texSampleBase +
            vLightRayTS *
                0.55, dx, dy ).a - sh0 - 0.55 ) *  6 * fShadowSoft-
                ening;
            float sh6 = (tex2Dgrad( tNormalMap, texSampleBase +
            vLightRayTS *
                0.44, dx, dy ).a - sh0 - 0.44 ) *  8 * fShadowSoft-
                ening;
            float sh5 = (tex2Dgrad( tNormalMap, texSampleBase +
            vLightRayTS *
                0.33, dx, dy ).a - sh0 - 0.33 ) * 10 * fShadowSoft-
                ening;
            float sh4 = (tex2Dgrad( tNormalMap, texSampleBase +
            vLightRayTS *
                0.22, dx, dy ).a - sh0 - 0.22 ) * 12 * fShadowSoft-
                ening;

            // Compute the actual shadow strength:
            fOcclusionShadow = 1 - max( max( max( max( max( max( shA,
            sh9 ),
                sh8 ), sh7 ), sh6 ), sh5 ), sh4 );

            // The previous computation overbrightens the image;
               let's adjust
            // for that:
            fOcclusionShadow = fOcclusionShadow * 0.6 + 0.4;

        }   // End of if ( bAddShadows )

    }   // End of if ( fMipLevel <= (float) nLODThreshold )

    // Compute resulting color for the pixel:
    cResultColor = ComputeIllumination( texSample, vLightTS,
                                        vViewTS, fOcclusionShadow );

    if ( bVisualizeLOD )
    {
        cResultColor *= cLODColoring;
    }

    // Visualize currently computed mip level, tinting the color blue
    // if we are in the region outside of the threshold level:
    if ( bVisualizeMipLevel )
    {
        cResultColor = fMipLevel.xxxx;
    }

    // If using HDR rendering, make sure to tonemap the result color
    // prior to outputting it. But since this example isn't doing
    // that, we just output the computed result color here:
    return cResultColor;


}   // End of float4 ps_main(..)
```

2.4

Preprocessing of Complex, Static Scenes for Fast Real-time Graphics

Max Dennis Luesebrink, University of Osnabrueck

Kurt Pelzer, Piranha Bytes

The idea of the technique presented in this article is to store complex static scenes in a handful of textures and use them to reconstruct a fully lit scene with dynamic objects and postrender effect shaders. This technique will allow the scene to be rendered a lot faster, with higher subpixel accuracy than is usually possible.

This will be especially useable for games of these genres:

- Adventures with fixed camera position (camera may also rotate free with a 360 degree picture like in *Riven,* the *Myst* sequel)
- Top-down scroller with orthogonal projection
- 3D games with portals that render farsighted scenes and will allow one to render these with a high level of detail

Thus, the technique can be used on classic PC/console applications as well as mobile and handheld devices.

Overview

The basic idea is that the scene will be rendered in a preprocessing step with a fixed camera position to some specialized textures. These textures contain, for example, Z-buffer, RGB-buffer with unlit material colors, vertex normals and projected normal maps in camera space, and scene positions in world or camera space (dependent on the effects you want to implement).

In the end, this will also save memory since you don't have to store all the material textures for all objects, but just one for the overall scene. The whole scene is just a handful of textures that will be rendered using a pixel shader to complete the scene (see Figure 2.4.1). This can include lighting and diverse postrendering effects (including high-dynamic range [HDR] bloom effect, blur effect, depth of field). For the lighting of the scene you can either use the texture that contains the normals or a texture of projected

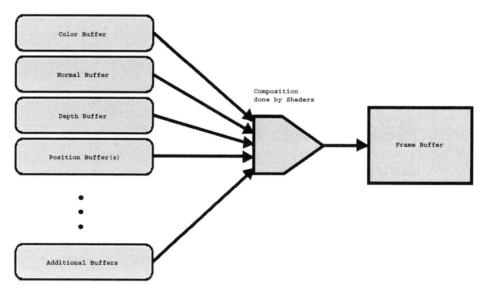

FIGURE 2.4.1   Overview.

spherical harmonic (SH) coefficients. Using textures with a higher resolution than the screen will get you full-screen anti-aliasing and subpixel accuracy of the scene for free.

Color, Normal, Depth, and Position Buffers via Textures

We need to render the scene to some specialized buffers. These buffers are textures that are used in the final composition done by shaders (see Figures 2.4.2 and 2.4.3).

Color Buffer: Scene rendered without any lights, which is just ambient lighting set to a midlevel. This is the usual scene without shadows and lighting. To be able to lighten and darken this buffer, we chose a midlevel ambient light. The format of this buffer is just the usual 32-bit X8R8G8G8 format, which can be compressed to DXT1 format.

Normal Buffer: The normal buffer is the scene rendered with all normal maps switched on without any lighting at all. Thus, you obtain the scene with the normals in camera space. This is of course easily achievable by just switching on the normal maps and rendering the scene with only the normal map shader. Since you can't render into compressed textures, you will need to render into a normal 32-bit X8R8G8B8 formatted buffer and then compress it into a compressed normal texture format such as DXT5. The normal buffer then contains all the normals of the normal mappings in camera space coordinates.

Depth Buffer: The depth buffer is obtained by rendering the distances of the pixels from the near clipping plane. Just accessing the usual 32-bit Z-buffer of the rendered scene can do this.

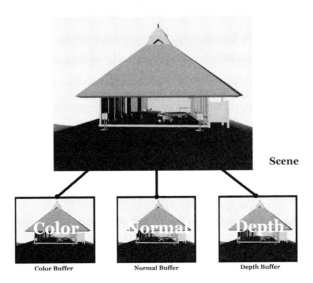

FIGURE 2.4.2 Color, normal, and depth buffers.

Position Buffer: The position buffer renders the position of every visible pixel in word or camera space. The vertex shader to create this buffer writes the vertex position to a three-component texture coordinate register, and the pixel shader receives the interpolated values and writes them per pixel. Thus, you can write the x, y, and z position to a texture. If the x, y, and z values need to be high-resolution 32-bit floats, you will have to render this position buffer into three separate textures with 32-bit format R32G0B0A0, R0G32B0A0, and R0G0B32A0.

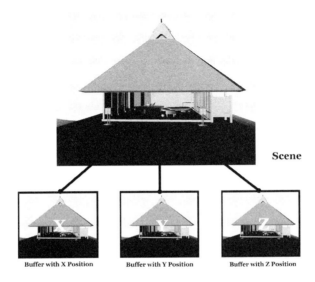

FIGURE 2.4.3 Position buffers (three separate textures).

All these buffers can also be rendered in standard 3D applications with appropriate plug-ins. This way the artist can render all the needed preprocessed textures in his known environment.

Spherical Harmonics Buffers for Directional Lights

SH lighting has the big advantage of looking very natural. It is very smooth, which usually is what you want to achieve for directional light as light cast by the sun. It also allows you to light the scene with not only a single directional component, but with a lighting transfer function that resembles the light distribution of virtually any lighting function you want to have. That is, the light that is cast onto each element of the scene is also distributed on a unit sphere.

SH coefficients are projections of the light distribution from a point on a surface into a polynomial space that resembles the unit sphere on which the light distribution is mapped. Usually you do this for all texels or vertices in the scene. In our case we only need to process the pixels that can be seen, so we can use the position buffer from the previous section, because it just shows the pixels that can be seen from our point of view and also gives us the position for casting the rays that are needed to establish the light distribution on the unit sphere.

We process the whole buffer and end up with n coefficients that are written into textures depending on the range of the coefficients (see Figure 2.4.4).

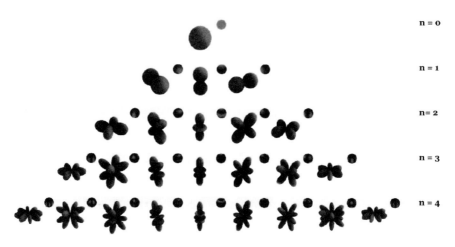

FIGURE 2.4.4   Spherical harmonics (the first five unsigned spherical functions).

Local Point Lights with Shadows

There are three types of light sources we have to handle in different ways: static, pseudo-dynamic, and dynamic.

Static Lights

Static lights are quite easily implemented with our technique. This just requires us to render the shadow buffer once and save it for later usage and proceed as usual with shadow mapping. For light attenuation you can use the position buffer.

Another technique would be to render the scene as a cube map from every visible point in the scene (every point in the position buffer you can see), adding the light contribution from only the light-emitting objects. This buffer keeps information that tells you what objects the light is reaching in the scene.

The third technique takes into account the scene-projected shadow buffer and inverts it. This roughly resembles the second technique with harder edges.

Pseudo-dynamic Lights

Pseudo-dynamic lights are lights that have constant motion, for example, a swinging light or a rotating fan in a scene. The same applies for all motion that is known in advance. For these kinds of lights you need to render a shadow buffer texture sequence or video so you can pick the appropriate prerendered buffer for the light's state at position x.

Dynamic Lights

Dynamic lights require you to still be able to use the 3D scene. If you want to have access to these lights, you will have to have a simple representation of the scene as blockers in a 3D format. For example, if you want to have a flashlight in the scene, you would just apply the usual shadow-mapping techniques, then use the simplified scene objects as blockers and map this shadow onto the scene.

Composition of the Buffers to the Full Scene Blend

Composition of the final scene is dependent on the specific application and the required textures. Let's assume that you wanted to build a scrolling 2D adventure. You would require the color buffer, depth buffer, SH buffer, and simplified version of the 3D scene you used to render the buffers. The composition of the textures would roughly follow the steps below. For all the desired dynamic lights in the scene, first render the shadow map using the depth buffer and a simplified 3D scene. Then set up the texture slots with the buffers and the dynamic rendered shadow map as shown in Figure 2.4.5.

1. The first step in the composition shader is to do the lighting on the SH buffer and the corresponding lighting transfer function of the scene (for example, sunlight or any other directional light). The results are the lighting coefficients for the scene.

2. To add up the shadows of the local dynamic lights, you would have to multiply these with the entries in the shadow map. You would then end up with the final shadow and light information for the scene. This coefficient is the usual lighting function that can be multiplied with the color buffer for lighting.

3. Further postprocessing effects might be applied in the shader or later on. (See enhancements section.)

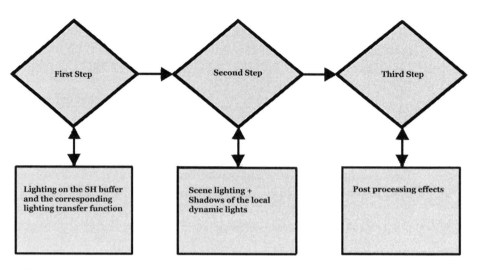

FIGURE 2.4.5   Composition of the buffers.

Applications: Scroller, Rotating Camera, and Distant Scenes in 3D Environments

Scroller

Scrollers such as classical top-down ones like Hybris or Xenon can be implemented with respect to lighting because the depth buffer of the landscape is a height map and we can apply relief mapping to them to get good-looking shadows on the landscape.

Rotating Camera

This is done by rendering all needed textures to a cube map centered around the viewer, just like a skybox. This is not unlike a 360-degree image. All of the above techniques are used for rendering the scene.

Distant Scenes

An example of an application for this would be a window. Depending on the distance to the window, two different techniques might be applied.

The first is applicable if you are not able to get close to the window and you see the same scene from whichever direction you look into the window. In this case you would just render the whole outside scene into the buffers and render a single quad behind the window so you have the impression that it resembles the outside.

The second technique is used when you can get close to the window and have to adjust the angle of the scene. In this case, you would either render the whole scene on a hemisphere or an open cube (half cube) and then place the object in front of the window such that it covers the complete hole.

Enhancements

HDR Rendering

In order to make the light look very natural, an HDR pass should be added. The HDR pass is easily achieved with techniques shown in DirectX's Demo Browser such as the HDR Lighting Demo. It will add a lot of atmosphere with little cost.

Colored SH Lighting

Since you do not have to calculate many coefficients for the scene and you only have to calculate and store information for pixels that are seen, you can store three SH buffers—one for each color channel. This produces scenes that have colored windows like those in a church or have some nice lighting in the scene, such as a colorful sky (for example the setting sun).

Depth of Field

Since you store the depth buffer, you also can implement a depth of field effect. This can only use the underlying depth of the scene if it has a far range for the Z values in the scene.

AA through Subpixel Accuracy

Since you can store the buffers in different resolutions, you can choose to use a bigger buffer (pixel-wise) then the screen resolution, achieving anti-aliasing for free.

Conclusion

By reconstructing a fully lit, complex static scene with additional dynamic objects from a handful of textures (which store all needed scene information), we achieved a technique that allows us to render scenes a lot faster, with higher subpixel accuracy. Our technique can be used successfully on classic PC/console applications as well as mobile and handheld devices.

References

A technique similar to the one introduced here, specialized for computer-animated feature films: "Lpics: A Hybrid Hardware-Accelerated Relighting Engine for Computer Cinematography," F. Pellacini, K. Vidimce, A. Lefohn, A. Mohr, M. Leone, J. Warren, Pixar Animation Studios, 2005. For paper and video see *http://www.vidimce.org/publications/lpics/*.

You can find information in detail about spherical harmonic lighting here: "Spherical Harmonic Lighting: The Gritty Details," Robin Green, Sony Computer Entertainment America, 2003. For paper see *http://www.research.scea.com/gdc2003/spherical-harmonic-lighting.pdf*.

2.5

Overcoming Deferred Shading Drawbacks

Frank Puig Placeres
(*fpuig@fpuig.cjb.net*)

Lighting in today's applications is performed by batching light sources together into small groups of three to eight lights that can be managed by current shaders. For each of these groups, the scene is rendered and the light's contribution is added into the frame buffer that, at the end, contains the influence of all lights in the world.

When targeting today's graphics, it may be justified to use a multipass solution for lighting, but that can only be justified when targeting graphics that generally consist of low- and medium-poly-count scenes with no complex materials, a very small number of light types, and where illumination comes from a few lights spread all over the scene.

However, next-generation games have heavily increased the poly count and number of lights on screen while raising the material's complexity. Performing several passes on those heavy scenes clearly overwhelms the hardware capabilities even when most of the passes can be accelerated by the use of early rejection features.

Special effects such as high dynamic range, depth of field, heat haze, and dynamic volumetric fogs, among others, are going to be the standard; this means that traditional multipass rendering systems are next to impossible because most of those effects require rerendering the scene several times.

A better solution is presented that uses deferred shading. This technique overcomes most of the above drawbacks while simplifying the rendering of multiple special effects. It also reduces the overhead of performing several passes on the scene by reducing it to only rendering a full screen quad for each pass instead of the complete scene geometry.

Deferred shading also allows the reduction of lighting, shadow, special effects, complex materials, and other computations on the pixels that are visible, which is required when materials get really heavy and lighting involves more realistic models. In addition, forward shadow mapping fits incredibly easily on a deferred shading system. Not only do shadows work well with the system, but so do other special effects since everything becomes image postprocessing work.

Nonetheless, deferred shading has several disadvantages. It needs a lot of memory to store the geometric buffer, it produces a noticeable impact on fill rate, it can't handle transparency efficiently, and it can suffer from antialiasing effects.

This article presents solutions to overcome or reduce most of the deferred shading drawbacks and gives tips on how to implement a scalable system that can run on more graphic cards. The system uses less memory and optimizes the whole process not only in the shaders but also from the application itself by implementing high-level managers that run on the CPU.

Memory Optimization

Contrary to classic forward rendering, in a deferred shading system, lighting and other special effects are not computed in the same pass in which the scene geometry is processed. Instead, there is a first pass in which the scene geometry is rendered and per-pixel attributes such as `Position` and `Normal` are saved into several textures composing an auxiliary buffer called a *geometric buffer* (G-buffer). Those textures are then used on subsequent passes to get the pixel's geometric data without processing the scene again.

As there is no need to reprocess the scene's geometry in each pass, executing multiple passes to create special effects becomes simple 2D image postprocessing. However, using the G-buffer comes with its own drawbacks. For each pixel, all the geometrical attributes that are needed for lighting, shadow, or any other effect must be saved into the buffer's texels.

Common attributes such as `Position` and `Normal` can use up to three floats each, and there's also a need to store material values such as `specular power`, `glow factor`, and `occlusion term`, among others. This can increase the memory footprint between 10 and 40 MB just to store auxiliary values for standard game resolutions.

With the increase in the memory footprint comes the need to use multiple render targets or perform multiple passes to save all the values in the G-buffer. Next, we are going to present some tips to reduce the memory footprint and the other problems.

When designing a deferred shading system, special care must be taken with respect to which values should be stored in the G-buffer. Cleverly packing those values allows the reduction of the memory footprint.

Normal Vector

The easiest and a faster way to store the normal is to save each of its components to the G-buffer. However, knowing that each normal component is a float, it would take 12 bytes per pixel to store them.

Using normals that are unit length vectors, it's possible to compute one component, given the other two, by applying the equation:

$$z = \pm\sqrt{1 - x^2 - y^2}$$

The computed component could be a positive or negative number. However, if all the lighting is performed in view space, then the front-faced polygons are always going to have negative or positive Z components, depending on the frame of reference used. Thus, it is possible to only save the *x* and *y* component in the G-buffer and recreate the complete vector using the stored data.

The math involved in unpacking the *z* component can add up to five extra lines to the shader code. Those instructions can be safely removed by using a simple look-up texture, having in each texel the value of the *z* component corresponding to its *u* and *v* values. So a texture fetch where the *u* and *v* values correspond to the *x* and *y* normal components returns the *z* without extra math instructions.

Using the texture look-up could help improve performance on some applications and make things slower on others. This depends on the texture cache and how much texture bandwidth the application uses. So when replacing the math code with the texture fetch, it is advisable to compare the performance of both paths.

Further optimizations could reduce the precision in which the normal components are stored from a whole float down to a single byte or even just four to five bits per component. A byte is commonly used for a normal component when dealing with normal maps or other precomputed textures. It creates a nice trade-off between graphics quality and memory consumption.

Position

Instead of storing all the three components of the position vector, it's possible to only save one value in the G-buffer. Saving the distance the pixel is from the camera allows recreation of the complete position vector. When rendering the first pass (geometry phase), the position of the pixel in view space is stored as a single value into the buffer by using:

```
G_Buffer.z = length(Input.PosInViewSpace);
```

When it's necessary to retrieve the position from the G-buffer, the following code is used:

```
(Vertex Shader)
out.vEyeToScreen = float3( Input.ScreenPos.x * ViewAspect,
                    Input.ScreenPos.y, invTanHalfFOV );

(Pixel Shader)
float3 PixelPos = normalize(Input.vEyeToScreen) * G_Buffer.z;
```

This code computes a ray from the eye location to the screen position of the pixel, maintaining the view aspect that defines the relation between the screen width and height and the field of view angle. The ray is normalized and then multiplied by the distance from the eye location to the pixel, generating the position of the pixel as shown in Figure 2.5.1.

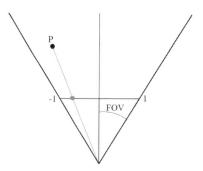

FIGURE 2.5.1   Generating the pixel position from the distance to the eye.

When storing the computed distance from the eye to the pixel position in the G-buffer, the value can be saved using several sizes, from a 32-bit float down to 24 or 16 bits. The selected size determines the final image quality, but as shown in Figure 2.5.2, these lower-precision results can be acceptable as fallback solutions because most of the time the results are indistinguishable from the high-resolution version.

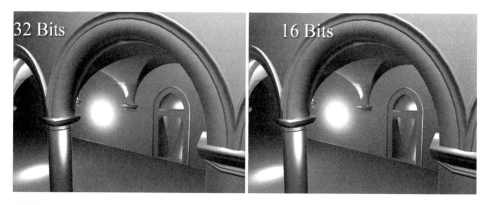

FIGURE 2.5.2   Scene rendered using different depth precisions.

Using 24 or 16 bits will not only match the depth buffer resolution and save memory space, but also gets rid of floating point textures on systems that don't support them. In later sections, we will present how it also allows better integration into the G-buffer, which will reduce the number of render targets used or the number of passes to be performed to fill the Geometry buffer.

Functions to pack and unpack a float 32 into 24 bits are presented in [Buttza05]. A similar approach can be followed for other target precisions or for changing the game view range.

Material Attributes

While it could be ideal to store all material attributes such as specular power, glow factor, occlusion term, and so on in the G-buffer, they consume too much memory. Applications that use one or two attributes could store them directly by first adjusting the number of bits assigned to them. For example, when the specular power is constrained to the values [1, 4, 10, 30], it can be saved using two bits, which gives four distinct values. The value then can be computed from the component inside the shader.

In most situations more attributes are needed; however, they don't change their value per pixel, but per surface. Where there are just a few materials in the scene, it's possible to pack all the attributes describing a material and only save an index of the material into the G-buffer. Depending on the number of materials in the scene, the index can be adjusted to use a certain number of bits that fits the maximum value.

Depending on the number of materials and the graphics hardware, the material attributes can be accessed in one of several ways. When all the attributes fit in the available unused shader constants, the shader is fed input values that can be used to do an indexed look-up.

When the number of materials and attributes exceeds the unused shader constants, the values can be packed into a texture where each row represents a different material, and the attributes can be accessed from the shader by using a texture fetch.

Designing the G-Buffer

Selecting the number of textures comprising the G-buffer, their format, and how the needed values are going to be distributed is one of the aspects that will deeply influence the resulting performance and memory footprint.

When designing the configuration of the G-buffer, special care must be taken to take advantage of the available features in the graphic hardware. Are multiple render targets supported? Can the hardware use floating point textures? What about other formats such as A16B16G16R16? How complex are the shaders that produce the lighting and special effects? Will the application rely heavily on texture access?

Several combinations appear to produce faster results, while others will reduce the memory footprint and minimize texture cache misses. It's possible to store values without packing them so they can be easily recovered in the lighting phase. However, this technique will consume a large amount of memory and will involve a higher number of passes to fill the G-buffer. It might also require multiple render targets and will rely on the target texture caches that might increase cache misses and texture fill rate.

Other configurations can use lower-resolution targets by packing the elements before storing them. The examples on the CD-ROM show several combinations to pack the Diffuse Color, Normal Vector, Position, and Material into two RGBA8 textures with different precision ranges. Those configurations heavily reduce cache misses and the memory footprint but introduce some overhead while packing and unpacking

ON THE CD

the values of the G-buffer. Some of the other configurations that are possible use precision ranges that can diminish the graphic quality of the resulting image, but generally the quality is acceptable.

Fill-Rate Reduction

Given that deferred shading systems rely on filtering image pixels, they are likely to become fill-rate limited. Most implementations, after filling the G-buffer, just loop through every light source and special effect and apply the shader to each pixel. This is done by rendering a full-screen quad over the scene using the G-buffers as a source and letting the shader combine the values for the final output. When using this technique the shader will still have to process all view-port pixels, including those that are not affected by the light or the effect.

Instead of linearly looping through the list of lights and special effects and sending each of them to the deferred shading pipeline, it's possible to implement a high-level manager. The application acts as a firewall, only sending to the pipeline the sources that influence the final image and executing the shaders only on the pixels that are influenced by the effect or light.

The high-level manager receives the list of all sources that should modulate the resulting render and all the information about them. One such piece of information is a bounding object that contains information on how strong the source effect should be applied to the rendering equation (for a light it could be the brightness, etc.).

Using that list, the manager executes two phases. The first phase is called the social phase since it performs general algorithms to reduce the number of sources that have to be sent to the pipeline. The second phase is called the individual phase and will configure the shaders to reduce the processing cost of each source.

Social Stage

During this first stage, the manager filters the lights and effects on the scene, producing a smaller list of sources to be processed. To filter the list, the following pseudo code is applied:

1. Execute visibility and occlusion algorithms to discard lights whose influence is not appreciable.
2. Project visible sources bounding objects into screen space.
3. Combine similar sources that are too close in screen space or influence almost the same screen area.
4. Discard sources with a tiny contribution because of their projected bounding object being too small or too far.
5. Check that more than a predefined number of sources do not affect each screen region. Choose the biggest, strongest, and closer sources.

In the first step, using the source-bounding object, the manager finds which lights and effects are not occluded by the scene geometry and are inside the view frustum, thus affecting the visible screen. Sources that are not visible are discarded.

Subsequent steps analyze the source influence on the screen using the projection of the source-bounding object into screen space. As shown, there is no restriction about which bounding object can be used. It is possible to combine several objects to define the source region of influence. When projecting, all bounding objects are transformed into bidimensional shapes describing the source area of influence.

Further reductions to the source list produce a nonconservative result, which implies a loss of image quality. However, properly adjusting the settings of the next steps minimizes the quality impact. In most cases it is better to have a performance improvement than trying to achieve perfect images when the results are almost indistinguishable from the lower quality image.

Once the bounding objects have been projected into screen space, sources that are too close and affecting almost the same region are combined (see Figure 2.5.3a). These sources are combined into one source and then are applied using an intensity that simulates the result of the mixed sources.

Isolated sources that are too far or have an area of influence of just a few pixels can be omitted. Remember that the visual quality difference may not be worth the expensive operation of setting all the stages in the graphics pipeline to process these few pixels. An example is shown in Figure 2.5.3b.

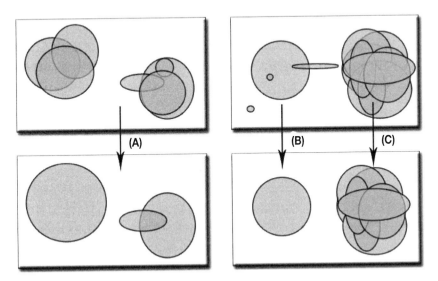

FIGURE 2.5.3   (A) Similar sources are combined. **(B)** Small sources are discarded. **(C)** There are no more than a fixed number of sources per pixel.

The previous actions are targeted to reduce the number of sources being processed according to their geometrical and visual properties. However, a last step can be added to help application performance. In this step the application can limit the number of sources affecting each pixel. For quicker computations, screen regions can be used instead of pixels. This is shown in Figure 2.5.3c.

When the average frame rate is high enough, the limiting number is raised. If the frame rate drops, the limiting number is lowered. This is a fast way to control the fill rate of the application and allows maintenance of smooth frame rates. A similar approach can be used for steps 3 and 4. Having variables track how far or small the sources should be before they are discarded or how different the sources should be, so that they are not combined, helps performance. These factors can also be tweaked according to the resulting performance.

Individual Stage

Lights and special effects in general can be classified in two main groups: global sources and local sources. Each group allows custom setup and optimization for the graphics pipeline to minimize overhead. The individual phase of the high-level manager classifies each source in the list returned by the social phase and applies the following steps according to the group each source belongs to.

Global Sources

These are meant to affect all screen pixels, implying that the effects' shaders must be executed on all pixels by processing a complete screen quad. Examples of these sources are big lights illuminating the entire world, such as the sun, smaller lights containing the camera, or special effects applied to the whole screen such as depth of field, fog, and so on.

Realizing that in a deferred shading system the shading cost is proportional to the number of affected pixels, global sources are one of the most fill-rate expensive. Fortunately, most of the time there are just a few of them.

These sources don't allow any specific optimization and heavily depend on how optimized the shaders being used are. In general, the individual stage performs the following steps for the global lights. For each global source:

1. Enable the appropriated shaders.
2. Render a quad covering the screen.

Local Sources

Unlike global sources, these only affect regions of the scene. Thus, any source whose influence is restricted to just a world sector falls under this category. Classic examples include small lights spread over the scene, effects such as volumetric fog, or heat haze, among others.

The benefit of local sources is that only the pixels that are inside the source bounding object have to be processed. Application of the shader only on those pixels can be implemented in several ways. The easiest is to render the source bounding object and discard back-faced polygons since bounding objects are generally convex volumes.

Even when using this approach, and almost all of the pixels are influenced by the shader, it can be slower. Applications that are vertex-transform bottlenecked and send the polygons that shape the bounding object to the graphics pipeline can result in a slower performance than only rendering all the screen pixels. This is especially true when using sphere bounding objects that are composed of a lot of polygons.

Another approach to shading only the pixels influenced by the bounding object involves rendering a full screen quad, just like for global sources, but enabling clipping and rejection features to discard as many noninfluenced pixels as possible should result in less of a performance impact.

The scissor test can be enabled using the rectangle that surrounds the screen projection of the source bounding object that was computed in the social stage. While the scissor test quickly rejects pixels at the fragment level, clipping planes can also be used to further restrain the pixels that get into the fragment stage from the transform level.

Using the scissor and clipping tests allows the system to quickly reject the pixels that are out of the projected bounding object area. The defined bidimensional region can still be very different from the real bounding object projection, and all pixels in that area are going to be shaded even if they are in front of or behind the bounding volume, as shown in Figure 2.5.4.

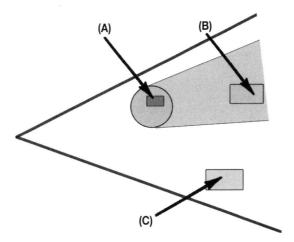

FIGURE 2.5.4 Pixels in front of and behind the bounding volume. **(A)** Inside screen projected volume. **(B)** Inside screen projected volume but not influenced. **(C)** Outside screen projected volume.

Dynamic branching can be used to discard all those pixels at the shader level. In the shaders of the lighting phase, if the pixel position is not found to be in the influence area of the bounding object, which is being passed through the shader registers, then the pixel is discarded and no lighting or effects are processed.

When dealing with spheres, the individual stage passes the sphere radius and center to the shaders, and if they find that a pixel's distance to the center is greater than the radius, the pixel is discarded. For axis-aligned bounding boxes, the process is even easier and only involves checking if the components of the position are inside the box.

The drawback is that dynamic branching is not widely supported. However, the stencil buffer can be used to emulate the dynamic branching behavior on systems that don't support it. The approach uses a cheap extra pass to create a mask on the stencil buffer, using a given condition that in this case should be if the pixel in the G-buffer is inside the influence area or not. The technique is described in [ATI05].

Using the previously described optimizations reduces the number of pixels processed and the fill rate of the deferred system. However, fill rate also relies on the processing cost of the shaded pixels.

Another nonconservative optimization that can be applied is to use a sort of level of detail to decide how many instructions each pixel uses to compute the source effect, keeping in mind that farther and smaller sources don't have to be computed with the same quality than closer sources, so it is possible to save some instructions on them.

Figure 2.5.5 shows a source rendered with three levels of detail according to how far the source is from the camera. In the first level the light is computed using the diffuse and specular components, while in the last level the specular component is not computed. However, owing to the distance at which the source is rendered, the resulting image is not distinguishable from its counterpart that renders the source with the full equation at all times.

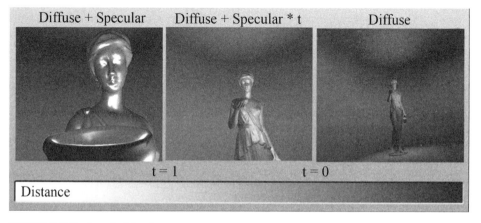

FIGURE 2.5.5   Level of detail.

When removing components from the effects equations, some artifacts and sudden popping can appear at the points where the source transitions from one level to the next. To avoid those artifacts, transition levels can be inserted that blend the previous and next level to make a smooth transition. In the presented example, the transition level multiplies the specular component by a factor that starts off being 1 to fully show the specular contribution and gradually fades to 0, fading according to the distance.

Using the presented optimizations, the individual stage of the high-level manager can be outlined as follows. For each local source:

1. Select the appropriate level of detail.
2. If dynamic branching is not supported, render a mask in the stencil buffer.
3. Enable and configure the source shaders.
4. Compute the minimum and maximum screen cord values of the projected bounding object.
5. Enable the scissor test.
6. Enable the clipping planes.
7. Render a screen quad or the bounding object.

Other Performance Optimizations

Even when the above solutions have being used to reduce the memory footprint and fill rate, they are likely to improve the general performance as well. For instance, using less memory to store the G-buffer allows a better use of the texture cache, which reduces texture transfers, thereby reducing the performance impact of packing the pixel attributes in the buffer.

This has the same effect on fill-rate reduction, which is directly bound to performance. It eliminates the fill-rate bottleneck, which is the most frequent problem in high-end graphic applications. The reduction of the fragment unit usage allows computing more complicated effects and more sources.

Together with the presented optimizations, the deferred shading system can be further optimized. As has been shown, the individual stage of the high-level manager scans all sources that need to be rendered and configures them to reduce its processing cost.

However, the sources' bounding object or a full screen quad has to be sent to the pipeline for each source. On sources that are going to be computed with the same shaders, it's possible to batch the polygons. These batched polygons can then be processed with just one draw call. They can even be collapsed into several source shapes and processed with a single shader that computes the contribution of more than one source.

When setting sources' shaders, call states can be minimized by first finding those shaders that are going to be used for each source and sorting the sources according to those shaders. Then to minimize state changes, each shader is set and all sources that use it are processed without changing the shader state.

Further nonconservative optimizations can be applied when performance is dropping. For instance, the texture that stores the pixels' colors in the G-buffer can be rendered at full size, but the other textures can be stored at lower resolutions. This way, the lighting and postprocessing phase could be computed to a render target that is half or one-quarter of the viewport dimensions and then modulated by the full-resolution color texture.

When the performance falls to unacceptable levels, lights and other effects can be computed at half or lower screen resolution while still maintaining good results if the color buffer is still rendered at full resolution. The quality loss is acceptable, given that there's a big reduction in fill rate, and therefore it is possible to add more lights and effects to modulate the scene.

While the above solutions enhance the performance of the lighting and postprocessing phase, other optimizations are applied to the geometry phase where the G-buffer is filled. For instance, when processing the scene geometry to fill the G-buffer, lights, fog, and all other unneeded effects at that stage should be disabled.

Also, it's possible to batch the scene geometry. In this instance, how the scene is batched doesn't have to match the batching used during normal rendering. This way, two different representations of the scene can be used, both presenting the same geometry but batched differently. One representation is used to render the color texture in the G-buffer. It maintains a group of polygons for each texture, and each group can be rendered with just one draw call.

The other representation is used for rendering position and normal into the G-buffer. There's no need to separate the textures and the complete geometry, so the batch can be submitted to the pipeline with just one draw call.

In practical situations the batching also has to account for occlusion and visibility, so there should be more groups to represent visibility sectors, objects, or any other visibility structure that can be used to cull out nonvisible objects and effects. However, when it's possible to keep both geometry representations in memory, the performance increases by decreasing the draw calls and other state changes, such as vertex buffer switching.

When multiple render targets are not supported, or when there are not enough to render all the textures composing the G-buffer in one pass, several passes should be done. The order in which those passes are performed can also impact performance. Before rendering the first pass, the depth buffer should be cleared, and while the rendering is performed, the buffer is filled. This first pass can suffer from overdraw, but subsequent passes use the depth values stored in the z-buffer to avoid overdraw.

The cheapest pass should be executed first to handle overdraw with the lowest penalty, and then the more intense passes should be run with the benefit of not reprocessing the same pixels. The pass that stores the normal components and the material ID should be performed before the pass that stores pixel colors from the polygon texture, vertex color, and so on.

Other possibilities are to combine forward lighting and effects with the deferred system. The per-vertex influence of some lights should be written while filling color values in the G-buffer. This technique can be used when the geometry is highly tessellated or light sources are far or don't rely on complicated lighting calculations. The difference to the per-pixel version is not very noticeable, improving the performance when the per-vertex solution can be used.

This approach can enhance performance in some situations and reduce it on others, depending on where the application bottleneck is located. The geometry properties of the surface and how many pixels compose the geometry can also influence performance, so this method should be used carefully.

Also bear in mind that most general shader optimizations can be applied to further enhance performance in a deferred shading system. Typical examples are the use of half data instead of floats when the extra precision is not needed. For materials ID and normal components, they can be stored at lower precision, and fetching the value from a lookup texture can compute the attenuation factors.

Transparency

The Alpha test is easy to integrate with a deferred shading system, but alpha blending requires several pixels to be shaded and combined. However, the G-buffer only stores information about a single pixel in each texel, so blending on a deferred shading system is not as simple as on forward rendering.

Still, some hacks can be done to allow blending on a deferred shading system. The easiest is not doing deferred rendering on polygons that need to be blended. In a first pass the application can perform the deferred path for solid polygons and then forward rendering on all the transparent polygons with alpha blending enabled.

Another approach is the rarely used technique called *screen door transparency*. It uses a stippling pattern to mask the transparent polygons so that some pixels of the background can be seen through the mask. For instance, a pattern used to represent 50% transparency will skip all the even pixels in one row and all the odd pixels in the next. When the stippling pattern is applied to a polygon, the background can be seen through the masked pixels. The holes are so small that they aren't picked up by the eye, and the eye blends the nearest pixels, giving the illusion of a transparent polygon.

Screen door transparency can be implemented directly on the deferred shading pipeline and doesn't require depth sorting. However, the screen resolution needs to be relatively high to hide the masking pattern. To make it even harder to spot the mask, the pattern can be changed and offset every frame, which also has the advantage of producing better-looking results when the transparency has a high depth complexity.

Other approaches can use depth peeling to break blended complexity into layers, which then can be rendered and blended one after the other by using a deferred shading path. This technique involves executing the complete deferred pipeline for each layer, from filling the G-buffer to source shading, which can seriously impact performance.

Anti-Aliasing

The deferred shading system can suffer from aliasing problems since the anti-aliasing pass has to be performed after the accumulation is done in the lighting and postprocessing phase.

Even when the graphics hardware can natively support multisampling in the G-buffer, lighting and other effects can create artifacts near the polygon edges. This happens because there's no multisampling support on the shading phase and because the work is performed in image space. When dealing with floating-point textures composing the G-buffer, the graphics card may not even support multisampling when writing to the G-buffer.

Several solutions can reduce the aliasing problems on a deferred shading system. The easiest approach is to use over-sampling. That technique is implemented by performing the entire rendering at higher screen resolutions and then blurring down to the desired output resolution. For instance, the rendering can be performed at 1600×1200 and then in a final pass scaled down to 800×600 using a bilinear filter.

Over-sampling has the advantage of noticeably reducing the aliasing artifacts in the scene; however, it requires more memory to store the G-buffer. This heavily increases the application fill rate, becoming prohibitively expensive in most applications.

Another solution for implementing anti-aliasing is to use an edge-smoothing filter [Fabio05]. This filter is implemented as another source effect, which is introduced as the last source in the postprocessing phase of the deferred pipeline. The filter performs two steps.

First an edge-detection scan is applied to the screen. To perform the edge detection, the filter uses the discontinuities in the positions and normal stored in the G-buffer. The results can be stored in the stencil buffer as a mask for the next step.

Later the screen is blurred using only the pixels that are edges. This is accomplished by performing a blurring only on the pixels that are masked in the stencil buffer. A by-product of the blurring is that the color will bleed into the edges of the polygons. This can result in the background bleeding into the character, producing undesired results. To eliminate the color bleeding, the blurring process should be refined. A kernel is applied to the edge pixels, but instead of blurring all the pixels that lie in the kernel, only the closest to the camera are combined.

This way the closest polygons are smoothed and no color bleeding will happen when the polygons are overlapped. ATI [ATIGDC] has a more in-depth description of the color bleeding reduction algorithm. It is oriented toward depth of field, but the process is the same.

This technique allows the reduction of the aliasing artifacts without increasing the memory footprint required to store the G-buffer. Even when the fill rate is increased, the use of the stencil buffer to quickly discard the nonedge pixels on the second step helps reduce the fill-rate impact of the blurring. This technique can be disabled if there is a severe performance drop and dynamically enabled again when the performance gets back to a tolerable level.

Another way to simulate anti-aliasing is to perform a separate pass when storing the color in the G-buffer. In this pass we don't render the colors to a floating-point texture, but to the classical RGBA8 frame-buffer with anti-aliasing enabled.

This way, only the colors receive anti-aliasing; lights and effects don't. When lighting is not anti-aliased, the results can be acceptable, but when colors are not anti-aliased, the results are not good.

It's also possible to combine the color anti-aliasing with the edge detection filter, blurring, and color bleeding reduction for the lighting and effects, which improves the quality of the resulting anti-aliasing image.

Conclusions

Deferred shading is a nice solution to deal with multiple lights influencing a scene. It keeps everything simple and separated and allows handling next-generation scenes with a high number of polygons, complex materials, and lots of special effects and lights.

However, as has been shown, deferred shading has some huge disadvantages such as memory use, high fill-rate, and the inability to handle transparency nicely, and most implementations suffer from aliasing problems.

This article has presented several techniques to reduce each of these drawbacks. Proper planning in the low-level pipeline, with respect to the shader implementation, and use of G-buffer capabilities help improve performance. The high-level mangers in the application layer and general optimizations increase the performance and scalability of the system. Using all these techniques makes it possible to overcome or manage most of the major drawbacks.

Most of the presented solutions can be controlled in real-time, which allows for adjusting the image quality according to the average frame rate. This helps maintain a constant frame rate, which in the end plays a major role in the user immersion experience.

When combining these techniques and the potential of a deferred shading system to handle next-generation scenes simply and fast, it makes a very attractive solution for highly detailed graphics on current and next-generation systems.

References

[ATI05] ATI, "Dynamic Branching Using Stencil Test." ATI Software Developer's Kit, June 2005.

[ATIGDC] ATI, "Advanced Depth of Field." Available online at *www.ati.com/developer/gdc/Scheuermann_DepthOfField.pdf.*

[Buttza05] Butterfield, Ryan. "Packing a Float into a Texture." Available online at *http://www.gamedev.net/community/forums/topic.asp?topic_id=322318&whichpage=1&#2078865.*

[Calver03] Calver, Dean. "Photo-realistic Deferred Lighting." Available online at *http://www.beyond3d.com/articles/deflight/*, July 31, 2003.

[Delphi3D] "Deferred Shading." available online at *http://www.delphi3d.net/articles/viewarticle.php?article=deferred.htm*, October 24, 2002.

[Fabio05] Policarpo, Fabio and Francisco Fonseca. "Deferred Shading Tutorial." Available online at *http://fabio.policarpo.nom.br/docs/Deferred_Shading_Tutorial_SBGAMES2005.pdf*.

[Geldreich04] Geldreich, Rich. "Gladiator Deferred Shading Demo." Available online at *http://www.gdconf.com/conference/archives/2004/geldreich_rich.ppt*, March 16, 2004.

[NVIDIA04] Hargreaves, Shawn and Mark Harris. "Deferred Shading." Available online at *http://download.nvidia.com/developer/presentations/2004/6800_Leagues/6800_Leagues_Deferred_Shading.pdf*, March 26, 2004.

[Pritchard04] Pritchard, Matt. "Deferred Lighting and Shading." Available online at *http://www.gdconf.com/conference/archives/2004/pritchard_matt.ppt*, March 7, 2004.

[Puig05] Puig, Frank. "Deferred Shading Demo." Available online at *http://fpuig.cjb.net*, February 15, 2005.

[Puig06] Puig, Frank. "Fast Per-Pixel Lighting with Many Lights." *Game Programming Gems 6*, edited by Michael Dickheiser. Charles River Media, 2006.

2.6

Normal Mapping without Precomputed Tangents

Christian Schüler, Phenomic

Introduction

Tangent-space normal mapping is a well-known technique to compute per-pixel lighting with small surface perturbations stored in a texture map, as pioneered by [Kilgard00] and [Peercy97]. In virtually every implementation today, a tangent frame needs to be precomputed from partial derivatives of texture coordinates at each vertex of a surface and stored as vertex attributes.

This article shows how the tangent frame can be generated inside the pixel shader using derivative instructions. Since the tangent frame is computed per pixel, there is no need to store precomputed tangent frames. No constraints are placed on the way texture coordinates are assigned to vertices. For instance, UV-mirroring and procedural texture coordinates are perfectly possible.

Review of Tangent Space Normal Mapping

A normal map is a texture that stores information about how to rotate a normal vector into a perturbed position. The operation is

$$\mathbf{N'} = \underline{\mathbf{R}}(\mathbf{N}),$$

where $\mathbf{N'}$ is the perturbed normal we want to produce, $\mathbf{N}$ is the interpolated surface normal we know from the vertices, and $\underline{\mathbf{R}}$ is a rotation operator somehow stored in the normal map. From the many ways possible to encode a rotation operator, a certain representation is particularly easy in tangent space.

Tangent space is a coordinate system that is locally aligned with the surface, such that the surface normal $\mathbf{N}$ is a constant unit vector (usually in the z-direction). In this space one can express a rotation matrix acting on $\mathbf{N}$ with just its bottom row, since the first two components of $\mathbf{N}$ are zero. Assuming that $\mathbf{R}$ is a rotation matrix in tangent space, it follows that [Kilgard00]

$$\mathbf{N'} = \mathbf{N}\,\mathbf{R} \rightarrow$$
$$\mathbf{N'} = (0,0,1)\,\mathbf{R} \rightarrow$$
$$\mathbf{N'} = (\mathbf{R}_{31}, \mathbf{R}_{32}, \mathbf{R}_{33}).$$

In essence, a tangent space normal map contains the bottom row of the rotation matrix **R** as a three-component vector.

The coordinate basis for the tangent space, the *tangent frame*, is usually given as a set of three vectors: the *tangent* **T**, *binormal* **B**, and surface normal **N**. The first two (the *tangents*, for short) lie in the surface plane. A code snippet to perform normal perturbation using a tangent-space normal map could look like this:

```
float3 perturb_normal( float3 T, float3 B, float3 N, float2 texcoord )
   {
        // build a tangent frame as float3x3 for convenience
        float3x3 tangent_frame = float3x3( T, B, N );

        // read the perturbed normal from the normal map
        float3 perturbed_normal = tex2D( normalmap, texcoord );

        // sign-expand (for a normal map in unsigned RGB format)
        perturbed_normal = 2 * perturbed_normal - 1;

        // and transform the perturbed normal out of tangent space
        // (into whatever space T, B and N were originally expressed in,
        // usually world).
        return normalize( mul( perturbed_normal, tangent_frame ) );
   }
```

Computation of Tangent Frames

As mentioned in the introduction, normal mapping involves precomputing tangent frames and storing them as vertex attributes. Usually **T** is taken from the partial derivative of the u texture coordinate, and **B** is taken from the partial derivative of the v texture coordinate with respect to a point $\mathbf{p}(u,v)$ in world space $x,\ y,\ z$:

$$\mathbf{T} \propto \frac{\partial u}{\partial \mathbf{p}} = \left(\frac{\partial u}{\partial x}, \frac{\partial u}{\partial y}, \frac{\partial u}{\partial z} \right), \quad \mathbf{B} \propto \frac{\partial v}{\partial \mathbf{p}} = \left(\frac{\partial v}{\partial x}, \frac{\partial v}{\partial y}, \frac{\partial v}{\partial z} \right).$$

In other words, the tangent vector points to the direction of increasing u, and the binormal points toward increasing v (see Figure 2.6.1). As long as the surface $\mathbf{p}(u,v)$ consists of a set of planar polygons with interpolated u and v, the partial derivatives are constant across each polygon and can be calculated once per face. The partial derivatives are unbounded in magnitude and in general not orthogonal. The tangent frame, on the other hand, is usually orthonormalized and averaged at each vertex from adjacent polygons.

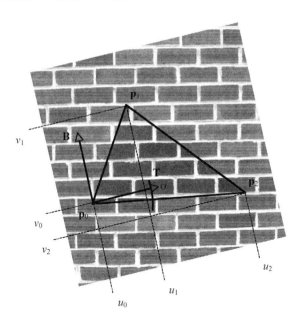

FIGURE 2.6.1   Textured triangle with texture coordinates, tangent, and binormal.

If all that is known is a triangle with vertices $\mathbf{p}_0$, $\mathbf{p}_1$, and $\mathbf{p}_2$ and texture coordinates at these vertices, u_0, u_1, u_2, and v_0, v_1, v_2, how are tangents computed? First, we introduce edge differences:

$$\begin{array}{ccc} \Delta\mathbf{p}_1 = \mathbf{p}_1 - \mathbf{p}_0 & \Delta u_1 = u_1 - u_0 & \Delta v_1 = v_1 - v_0 \\ \Delta\mathbf{p}_2 = \mathbf{p}_2 - \mathbf{p}_0 & \Delta u_2 = u_2 - u_0 & \Delta v_2 = v_2 - v_0 \end{array}.$$

In the next step we observe that $\Delta\mathbf{p}$ can be related to Δu and Δv via dot products. For example, Figure 2.6.1 has the angle α between the lower triangle edge $\Delta\mathbf{p}_2$ and the tangent vector $\mathbf{T}$. Assume for this time that the length of $\mathbf{T}$ corresponds to the magnitude of the u-gradient. Then we can write

$$\Delta u = \Delta\mathbf{p}\,|\mathbf{T}|\cos\alpha \quad \rightarrow \quad \Delta u = \Delta\mathbf{p}\cdot\mathbf{T},$$

and similarly for the binormal and Δv. It is therefore easy to formulate three conditions that we can use to solve for both tangent and binormal. Two conditions stem from the dot product relations, and the third condition constrains the vector in question to the triangle plane; the latter is expressed as a dot product with a perpendicular vector $\Delta\mathbf{p}_1 \times \Delta\mathbf{p}_2$ (the plane normal). Taken together, all conditions that must be met, are.

$$\Delta\mathbf{p}_1 \cdot \mathbf{T} = \Delta u_1 \qquad\qquad \Delta\mathbf{p}_1 \cdot \mathbf{B} = \Delta v_1$$

$$\Delta\mathbf{p}_2 \cdot \mathbf{T} = \Delta u_2 \qquad\qquad \Delta\mathbf{p}_2 \cdot \mathbf{B} = \Delta v_2$$

$$(\Delta\mathbf{p}_1 \times \Delta\mathbf{p}_2) \cdot \mathbf{T} = 0 \qquad (\Delta\mathbf{p}_1 \times \Delta\mathbf{p}_2) \cdot \mathbf{B} = 0 \quad .$$

These systems of equations can be solved in matrix form. We construct a matrix with the rows $\Delta\mathbf{p}_1$, $\Delta\mathbf{p}_2$ and $\Delta\mathbf{p}_1 \times \Delta\mathbf{p}_2$ to be multiplied with one of $\mathbf{T}$ or $\mathbf{B}$, and an inversion then yields the solution. Following $\mathbf{T}$ as an example we have

$$\begin{pmatrix} \Delta\mathbf{p}_1 \\ \Delta\mathbf{p}_2 \\ \Delta\mathbf{p}_1 \times \Delta\mathbf{p}_2 \end{pmatrix} \mathbf{T} = \begin{pmatrix} \Delta u_1 \\ \Delta u_2 \\ 0 \end{pmatrix} \quad \rightarrow \quad \mathbf{T} = \begin{pmatrix} \Delta\mathbf{p}_1 \\ \Delta\mathbf{p}_2 \\ \Delta\mathbf{p}_1 \times \Delta\mathbf{p}_2 \end{pmatrix}^{-1} \begin{pmatrix} \Delta u_1 \\ \Delta u_2 \\ 0 \end{pmatrix} .$$

A similar expression yields $\mathbf{B}$ when u is replaced with v.

Since each polygon has its own set of tangents, no vertex containing a tangent frame could be shared with another polygon. An involved procedure usually follows, which averages tangent frames from adjacent polygons while respecting hard edges between polygons and duplicating vertices at borders where regions of left- and right-handed (mirrored) texture mapping intersect. All this complexity is of course not needed if tangent frames are not stored as vertex attributes.

Moving to the Pixel Shader

The computation of the tangent frame can be done in the pixel shader. All we need are edges of triangles at which to throw our algorithm. It turns out that we can construct such triangles at every pixel by means of the ddx and ddy derivative instructions. On current hardware, if a position vector and a pair of texture coordinates are fed to the pixel shader, the ddx and ddy instructions will calculate the edge differences of triangles over a 2×2 pixel area (see Figure 2.6.2).

A straightforward implementation of the algorithm from the previous section using pixel triangles is very easy. The only advanced prerequisite we need is a function to invert a 3×3 matrix, since there is no built-in function to perform this task in a pixel shader. Later we will find ways to optimize this expensive operation to something cheaper, but for now let's consider a full matrix inversion:

```
float3x3 invert_3x3( float3x3 M )
{
    float det = dot( cross( M[0], M[1] ), M[2] );
    float3x3 T = transpose( M );
    return float3x3(
        cross( T[1], T[2] ),
        cross( T[2], T[0] ),
        cross( T[0], T[1] ) ) / det;    }
```

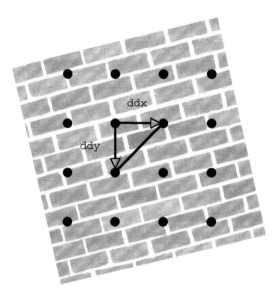

FIGURE 2.6.2   A 2 × 2 pixel triangle spanned by the ddx and ddy instructions on the pixel grid.

Using this function, we create a function that takes an interpolated surface normal **N**, a position vector **p**, and texture coordinates u and v and returns a complete tangent frame that is ready to be used in lighting calculations:

```
float3x3 compute_tangent_frame( float3 N, float3 p, float2 uv )
{
    // get edge vectors of the pixel triangle
    float3 dp1 = ddx( p );
    float3 dp2 = ddy( p );
    float2 duv1 = ddx( uv );
    float2 duv2 = ddy( uv );

    // solve the linear system
    float3x3 M = float3x3( dp1, dp2, cross( dp1, dp2 ) );
    float3x3 inverseM = invert_3x3( M );
    float3 T = mul( inverseM, float3( duv1.x, duv2.x, 0 ) );
    float3 B = mul( inverseM, float3( duv1.y, duv2.y, 0 ) );

    // construct tangent frame
    // (* see discussion regarding the square patch assumption)
    float maxLength = max( length(T), length(B) );
    return float3x3( T / maxLength, B / maxLength, N );
}
```

Note that it is possible to replace **p** with a vector other than the proper vertex position. Since only differences matter, a constant offset on **p** does not change the result. The view vector **V**, which is often used in lighting calculations, already contains the vertex position subtracted by the camera position. Since the camera position is constant, the view vector is a suitable replacement for **p** with respect to tangent frame computation, so no additional attributes are needed if texture coordinates and **V** are already fed to the pixel shader.

Figure 2.6.3a shows a shot from a normal-mapped model with per-pixel Blinn-Phong lighting, with orthonormalized per-vertex tangent frames provided per default in NVIDIA's FX Composer [NVIDIA06]. Figure 2.6.3b shows the same model using per-pixel tangent frames computed by the algorithm discussed above. By and large, both methods tend to produce very similar results. A notable difference, however, can be seen at regions of high texture anisotropy. Compare the region around the nozzle of the teapot where the texture is severely squashed (magnified respectively in the inlets). In Figure 2.6.3a, the light direction is wrong on some of the circular spots, and the stripes seem to fade out toward higher anisotropy. In Figure 2.6.3b, no such problems are apparent. The reason behind this is that we have relaxed the requirement of an orthonormal tangent frame, which is discussed in the next section.

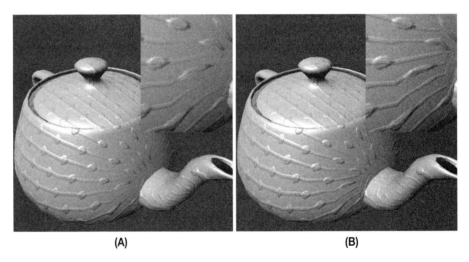

(A) (B)

FIGURE 2.6.3 Normal mapping under differently calculated tangent frames. **(A)** Tangent frame from interpolated vertex attributes. **(B)** Tangent frame calculated inside pixel shader.

The Square Patch Assumption

The authors [Peercy97] and [Kilgard00] employed the *square patch assumption*, which states that the *u*- and *v*-gradients are assumed to be equal in magnitude and orthogonal to each other. In other words, the texture image on the mapped surface should look like a square patch, neither stretched nor sheared. With this assumption, the tangent frame was constrained to be orthonormal.

It is not strictly necessary for us to keep up the square patch assumption; quite to the contrary, it may be beneficial to give it up for special applications. Consider Figure 2.6.4, which shows an array of embossed points, lit from the upper-left corner. In Figure 2.6.4a, the square patch assumption holds. In Figures 2.6.4b to 2.6.4d, the texture image was stretched and sheared by means of texture coordinate manipulation inside the pixel shader. An orthonormal tangent frame becomes obsolete, and the produced lighting is wrong (Figure 2.6.4b). A tangent frame not bound to orthogonality has no problems adjusting to the stretched texture, and the lighting is correct (Figure 2.6.4c; observe the location of the specular highlights).

The alert reader might have noticed that our pixel shader from the previous section contains a quasi normalization for **T** and **B** by their common maximal length. This is a hack, but if it was left out, he bump depth would also have been dependent on object scale—the larger the object in world space, the fainter the bumps. In terms of partial derivatives, this is a correct behavior (think of a height field being stretched), but probably not desired.

A last word on nonorthogonal tangent frames: you have probably been freely using tangent frames given in **T**, **B**, **N** form as transforms for going to and from tangent space. In the general case, the transpose does not equal the inverse, and you can use the tangent frame only to transform out of tangent space, not into it.

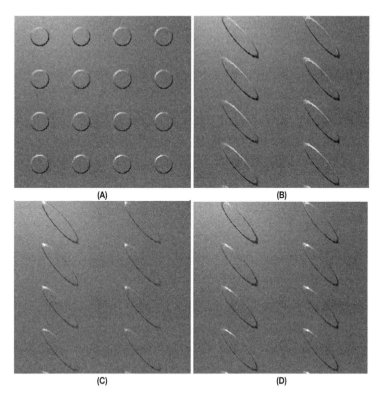

FIGURE 2.6.4   Discussion of the square patch assumption. (**A**) Square patch condition; (**B**) lighting with orthonormalized tangent frame; (**C**) lighting with general tangent frame; (**D**) lighting with normalized tangent frame.

Optimization

The function `compute_tangent_frame` as presented above accounts for an overhead of 46 pixel shader instructions when compared to the case when the tangent frame is simply read and normalized from vertex attributes.

The first step in optimization is to independently normalize the tangents **T** and **B** to unit length, while still allowing them to be nonorthogonal with each other. This produces lighting as shown in Figure 2.6.4d. The specular highlight on the stretched texture is a little off when compared to the general solution in Figure 2.6.4c, but this error is well worth the performance gain. Since the tangents are constrained to unit length at the end of the computation, we can disregard any scale factors on the way up to the result. This allows us to eliminate the determinant from the matrix inverse. The first optimized version of the `compute_tangent_frame` function thus might look like this:

```
float3x3 compute_tangent_frame_01( float3 N, float3 p, float2 uv )
{
    ...
    // no determinant since result gets normalized
    float3x3 inverseM = invert_3x3_nodet( M );
    ...

    // construct tangent frame
    return float3x3( normalize(T), normalize(B), N );
}
```

Here, the function `invert_3x3_nodet` is just a variant of the matrix inversion code that doesn't compute a determinant. With this optimization, the cost of tangent frame computation has come down to 31 instructions.

The next step of the optimization exploits the zero components found in the solution vectors and collapses a hidden double transpose. Consider these lines:

```
float3 T = mul( inverseM, float3( duv1.x, duv2.x, 0 ) );
float3 B = mul( inverseM, float3( duv1.y, duv2.y, 0 ) );
```

If these multiplications could be transposed, the zero components could eliminate an entire matrix row. To achieve this, we need the inverse transpose of **M**, instead of just the inverse, which turns out to be less expensive to compute, since we can eliminate the transpose already happening in the inverse. The modified code should then look like this:

```
float3x3 compute_tangent_frame_02( float3 N, float3 p, float2 uv )
{
    ...
    // solve linear system
```

```
// hidden double transpose revealed, only needs float2x3
float3x3 M = float3x3( dp1, dp2, cross( dp1, dp2 ) );
float2x3 inversetransposeM =
    float2x3( cross( M[1], M[2] ), cross( M[2], M[0] ) );
float3 T = mul( float2( duv1.x, duv2.x ), inversetransposeM );
float3 B = mul( float2( duv1.y, duv2.y ), inversetransposeM );
...
}
```

In this function the calculation of the inverse transpose has been inlined into the function body since it is nothing more than two cross products. Note also how the inverse transpose matrix has been reduced to a `float2x3`, since the last row doesn't contribute. This step of optimization reduces the cost of tangent frame computation to 17 pixel shader instructions and is visually equivalent to the previous step.

The last step of optimization exploits the fact that we have made an inverse transpose explicit. An inverse transpose reduces to a nonoperation (up to a scale factor, but scale doesn't matter already) if the underlying matrix is orthogonal. Let's assume that **M** is orthogonal:

```
float3x3 compute_tangent_frame_03( float3 N, float3 p, float2 uv
)
{
    ...
    // solve linear system
    // (not much solving is left going here)
    float2x3 M = float2x3( dp1, dp2 );
    float3 T = mul( float2( duv1.x, duv2.x ), M );
    float3 B = mul( float2( duv1.y, duv2.y ), M );
    ...
}
```

In this minimalist version the cross products have been eliminated and the edge differences just multiply with themselves. This version has a cost of 14 pixel shader instructions for the tangent frame computation, not much less than the version before, but how likely is it that the matrix M will be orthogonal anyway? The matrix **M** consists of the edge differences of the vertex positions of the screen triangles in world space. So **M** is reasonably orthogonal if the square patch assumption holds for the *screen projection*. In other words, as long as perspective distortion is low, the assumption holds. We have to expect artifacts, however, if there is screen-space anisotropy. Compare Figure 2.6.5a (rendered with `compute_tangent_frame_02`) to Figure 2.6.5b (rendered with `compute_tangent_frame_03`) on a perspective plane. While the close-up region of the figures agrees very well, there are notable differences in the farther away region.

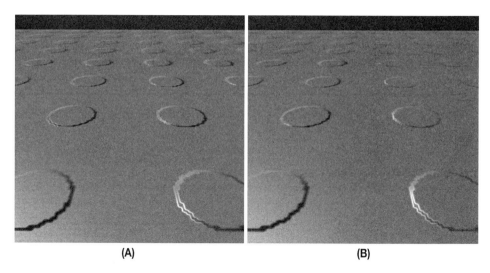

(A)   (B)

FIGURE 2.6.5   Dependency of optimized tangent frame conputation of perspective distortion.
(**A**) Normalized tangent frame. (**B**) Normalized plus assuming the inverse transpose to be a
non-operation.

Conclusion

ON THE CD

The main contribution of this article is to show a way to transfer the tangent frame
computation into the pixel shader. This eliminates the need to store precomputed
tangent frames as vertex attributes and their associated complexity. A general solution
for the pixel shader is presented that can handle arbitrary texture space configurations,
such as procedurally distorted texture coordinates. Several optimizations from the
general solution are discussed both on a theoretical and practical level. Per-pixel tangent frames can be bought for as low as 14 pixel shader instructions. The complete
source code of the Shader can be found on the CD-ROM.

References

[Kilgard00] Mark J. Kilgard. "A Practical and Robust Bump-mapping Technique for
    Today's GPUs." Game Developers Conference 2000. Available online at
    http://www.nvidia.com/object/Practical_Bumpmapping_Tech.html.
[NVIDIA06] FX Composer 1.8. NVIDIA Corporation. Available online at *http://
    developer.nvidia.com.*
[Peercy97] Mark Peercy, John Airey, and Brian Cabral. "Efficient Bump Mapping
    Hardware." *Computer Graphics* (Proc. Siggraph '97) (1997): pp. 303–306. Avail-
    able online at *http://citeseer.ist.psu.edu/peercy97efficient.html.*

2.7

Animating Vegetation Using GPU Programs

Ali Botorabi

(botorabi@users.sourceforge.net)

Introduction

One of the important aspects of outdoor scenes is the visual appearance of trees, weeds, grass, and other types of vegetation. Animated trees and weeds help create the illusion of more realistic and picturesque outdoor scenes, while static vegetation is often less visually appealing.

Various techniques already exist for animating vegetation in an interactive application. Most of them use the programmability of a modern GPU. We refer to GPU programs as a shader in this text. This article describes a technique that uses vertex animation in combination with a static lightmap. The static lightmap ensures better visual quality in contrast to dynamically lit vegetation without shadows, but it introduces a limitation on the light sources: the relevant light sources must be static too. An example where this technique can be used is in outdoor scenes where the sun is the only relevant light source and it does not move; that is, no night and day simulation is performed.

The animation technique explained here is used for the open-source 3D application Virtual Reality Chat [VRC]. Every chat member has an avatar and can explore a small island surrounded by an ocean. VRC supports Internet Relay Chat IRC and its own dedicated chat protocol. Figure 2.7.1 and Figure 2.7.2 show two screenshots of the VRC island.

The following sections introduce the step-by-step development of a vertex and fragment shader for animating vegetation. We assume that the reader has at least intermediate skills in GPU programming. The reference code described in this article uses GLSL, but it can be easily ported to other GPU programming languages.

FIGURE 2.7.1   Vegetation on the VRC island.

FIGURE 2.7.2   More vegetation on the VRC island.

What Will the Animation Look Like?

The basic idea is to use harmonic swaying of the vertices for animation. The amplitude increases from zero to maximum along the vegetation mesh's height. Taking a tree as an example, at its root the amplitude would be zero, resulting in no swaying;

the tip of tree would sway, with highest amplitude. As we use harmonic swaying for animation, it fits well into a scene having a mild wind. It is less suited to stormy scenes. However, experimenting with a few lines of the vertex shader introduced later can provide interesting results.

What Kind of Vegetation Can this Technique Be Used For?

We have seen good results for the following species ("good" is our subjective impression; try out the technique and judge yourself).

- Trees such as palms and birches
- Mushrooms
- Grass
- Weeds
- Flowers
- Scrub

Certainly, every vegetation species has its own properties and behaves differently under the influence of wind. What we have tried to do is to work out a rather simple technique providing an overall appealing look on the island, instead of being precise concerning individual species' animation characteristics.

Accompanying Material on CD-ROM

ON THE CD

The accompanying CD-ROM contains a Microsoft Windows executable for every step explained in the next sections. All scenes are stored in human-readable OpenScene-Graph (OSG) format and can be viewed using osgViewer. The viewer is also available for other platforms, for example, Linux. Visit the OSG web site [OSG] for more details.

Prerequisites

Before we begin to develop the vegetation shaders, we must take following prerequisites into account.

Coordinate System

We assume a Z-up right-hand coordinate system. However, it is easy to change the shaders for handling a Y-up coordinate system.

Mesh Data

The vertex positions of vegetation meshes should be in absolute world coordinates. This makes the vertex position and Model View matrix multiplication in the vertex shader unnecessary and saves GPU performance. Usually, visualization packages can preprocess all mesh data at initialization and try to perform some optimizations. One of the optimizations is flattening the model hierarchy for static meshes, and as result all mesh-local vertex positions are converted to absolute world coordinates. Skipping this step does not hurt, but makes the matrix multiplication in the vertex shader necessary. In the special case that the vegetation mesh is not static—think of a flower in a vase that is sitting on a movable platform—this step can be ignored, and the vertex shader has to perform the vertex position/matrix multiplication.

Lightmap and Height Bias

The lightmap information is stored in the vertex colors. Four-component colors are needed, as we have to store a *height bias* in the alpha component in addition to the RGB colors. Later, we will explain in detail why we need the height bias for every mesh. The height bias is the *z* component of lowest vertex position in a vegetation mesh—remember we use a Z-up coordinate system. The bias must be in world space. It is preferably determined during the mesh creation process, for example, in the mesh exporter of your 3D modeling package. Alternatively, one can determine the height bias during application initialization and store it in the mesh colors' alpha component. The same bias must be stored in all mesh colors belonging to the same vegetation asset such as a tree. Here, care must be taken; for instance, a tree is often built of at least two sorts of meshes: a stem and a bunch of flat polygons for leaves. Assume that we use polygon clouds for leaves. In a simple approach the height bias for the complete tree can be determined by finding the lowest vertex in the stem mesh and setting its *z* component as the height bias in the alpha component of all stems and the leaves' polygons' vertex colors.

First Attempt to Animate Vegetation

We will begin with a simple animation of vegetation without lightmaps. We take a tree with a stem, polygon clouds for leaves, and trunks as a reference mesh, as it helps to better imagine the visual impact of the animation shaders. In this section we focus on the vertex animation. The code below shows how *x* and *y* components of mesh vertices are animated using the functions sine and cosine of uniform *time*. Using sine and cosine functions results in a harmonically swaying animation. The only interesting note to mention here is the increasing movement amplitude along the height.

```
/* Vertex program 1 - First attempt */
uniform float time;
const   float magnitude = 0.006;
varying vec2  texCoords;

void main(void)
{
   // increase amplitude along height component z
   float amplitude = magnitude * gl_Vertex.z;

   // calculate sine / cosine of time
   vec4 wave = amplitude *
               vec4(
                 sin(time),
                 cos(time),
```

```
                          0, 0
                        );

        // update the vertex position
        vec4  vert = gl_Vertex + wave;
        vert.w     = 1.0;

        gl_Position = gl_ModelViewProjectionMatrix * vert;
        texCoords   = gl_MultiTexCoord0.xy;
    }
```

Parameter *magnitude* can be adjusted to fit your needs. It determines the magnitude of increasing amplitude along the mesh height. To keep things simple, we use a constant value for magnitude, but it can also be defined as a uniform constant and be passed to the shader by the application code. The uniform *time* can be current system time or the time passed since application start in milliseconds and must be passed to the shader by the application at every frame. The variable vector texCoords is used for passing the texture coordinates to the fragment shader, which will be explained later.

One note to mention is related to near/far clipping and frustum culling performed on the CPU in application code. The application considers the vertex data as static and does not know about the modifications on the GPU; that is, the near/far clipping and frustum culling in the application is not accurate. This can lead to a situation where vertices on mesh boundaries should be rendered, but they get clipped. However, as the vertex moving amplitude for animating our vegetation is relatively small, there will be no noticeable clipping problem. One possible work-around would be choosing a slightly bigger bounding geometry for culling and clipping.

The code below already performs a nice animation for a single tree. However, the shader is not well suited when it comes to several trees close to each other, as they all would sway in the same rhythm. This is because all vegetation meshes are passed through the same vertex shader and have the same *time* variable, although when the tree meshes differ, this effect often makes them look as though they are moving in an unnatural way. What we need is an individual offsetting of *time*. First attempts during the development of this technique used a constant offset for each mesh group. A mesh group is the complete mesh built for the complete tree, including the stem and leaves. The results were not satisfactory, as that allowed only offsetting the swaying phase for an entire group. We figured out that we needed an individual offsetting of *time* for every vertex, not just for every group.

In the next section we introduce a way that adds chaos to the vertex movement, resulting in a more natural vegetation animation.

Adding Chaos to Vertex Movement

A simple trick to bring the desired chaos into the vertex movement is to add a vertex-specific offset to the sine and cosine arguments, instead of just using the sine and cosine of *time*:

```
...
vec4 wave = amplitude *
            vec4(
             sin(time),
             cos(time),
             0, 0
             );
...
```

We add sine and cosine of (*time* + vertex's *x* and *y* components):

```
    ...
vec4 wave = amplitude *
            vec4(
             sin(time + gl_Vertex.x),
             cos(time + gl_Vertex.y),
             0, 0
             );
...
```

As neighboring vertices are a small distance from each other, offsetting *time* with their *x* and *y* components causes a smooth change in the swaying phase from vertex to vertex, which results in good-looking chaos added to the vertex movements.

The following code shows the new shader, which shows better-looking animation of many trees close to each other.

```
/* Vertex program 2 - Animation of vertices */
uniform float time;
const   float magnitude = 0.006;
varying vec2  texCoords;

void main(void)
{
   // increase amplitude along height component z
   float amplitude = magnitude * gl_Vertex.z;

   // calculate sine / cosine of time + offset
   vec4 wave = amplitude *
               vec4(
                sin(time + gl_Vertex.x),
                cos(time + gl_Vertex.y),
                0, 0
                );

   // update the vertex position
   vec4  vert = gl_Vertex + wave;
   vert.w     = 1.0;

   gl_Position = gl_ModelViewProjectionMatrix * vert;
   texCoords   = gl_MultiTexCoord0.xy;
}
```

Be aware that this shader assumes that all vertices are in absolute world coordinates (see Prerequisites section). If not, the shader has to perform the vertex position/Model View multiplication:

```
...
// multiply with Model View matrix if vertex position
// is not in world space!
vec4 Vertex = gl_Vertex * ModelView;

// increase amplitude along height component z
float amplitude = magnitude * Vertex.z;

// calculate sine / cosine of time + offset
vec4 wave = amplitude *
            vec4(
            sin(time + gl_Vertex.x),
            cos(time + gl_Vertex.y),
            0, 0
            );

// update the vertex position
vec4  vert = gl_Vertex + wave;
vert.w     = 1.0;
...
```

Now we have a shader, which animates the vertices with harmonic functions depending on vertices' heights and their positions in world space. It works fine as long as all vegetation meshes are positioned at zero height. For instance, if a tree is positioned at height 10, then it gets too much movement amplitude starting at its local lowest vertex. We need a way to bias the height for every mesh. The next section shows how to fix this problem in conjunction with lightmaps.

What About the Lightmap and Height Bias?

The scene can be statically lightmapped using your favorite tool. We assume that the vegetation meshes get their lightmap data via vertex colors. In the Prerequisites section we mentioned the problem of biasing the mesh group's height. We can use the alpha component *a* of vertex colors for this purpose. This means the meshes must be preprocessed offline or during application initialization for setting the proper height bias in the colors' *a* component. The simplest way would be to take the lowest vertex position in a meshes group as the bias. *Amplitude* is increased locally to individual vegetation mesh groups by first subtracting the *height bias* from the vertices' z component and then multiplying the result with the *magnitude*. The shader now looks like the following:

```
/* Vertex program 3 - Lightmap + Mesh Height Bias */
uniform float time;
const   float magnitude = 0.006;
varying vec2  texCoords;
```

```
void main(void)
{
   // increase amplitude along height component z
   // consider the height bias in color's w component
   float amplitude = magnitude * (gl_Vertex.z - gl_Color.a);

   // calculate sine / cosine of time + offset
   vec4 wave = amplitude *
                vec4(
                 sin(time + gl_Vertex.x),
                 cos(time + gl_Vertex.y),
                     0, 0
                );

   // update the vertex position
   vec4  vert = gl_Vertex + wave;
   vert.w     = 1.0;

   gl_Position = gl_ModelViewProjectionMatrix * vert;
   texCoords   = gl_MultiTexCoord0.xy;
}
```

The next section shows the final shader including the fragment shader, which also fixes transparency artifacts occurring on boundaries of opaque areas (leaves, trunks, etc.). This is caused by alpha blending and texture filtering/mip-mapping.

Final Shader

We've come to the final version of our vertex shader. Here, we show the fragment shader, which mixes the lightmaps encoded in vertex colors with the base texture building the final fragment color.

```
/* Vertex program 4 - Final version */
uniform float time;
const   float magnitude = 0.006;
varying vec2  texCoords;
varying vec4  vertColor;

void main(void)
{
   // increase amplitude along height component z
   // consider the height bias in color's w component
   float amplitude = magnitude * (gl_Vertex.z - gl_Color.a);

   // calculate sine / cosine of time + offset
   vec4 wave = amplitude *
                vec4(
                 sin(time + gl_Vertex.x),
                 cos(time + gl_Vertex.y),
                 0, 0
                );
```

```
    // update the vertex position
    vec4  vert = gl_Vertex + wave;
    vert.w     = 1.0;

    gl_Position = gl_ModelViewProjectionMatrix * vert;
    texCoords   = gl_MultiTexCoord0.xy;
    vertColor   = gl_Color;
}

/* Fragment program 4 - Mixing colors and removing transparency
   artifacts */
uniform sampler2D baseMap;
varying vec4      vertColor;
varying vec2      texCoords;

void main(void)
{
    // get texture color and mix it with lightmap
    vec4 mapColor  = texture2D(baseMap, texCoords);
    vec3 fragColor = mapColor.rgb * vertColor.rgb;

    // use step function to remove transparent silhouettes
    float trans = step(0.5, mapColor.a);

    // set final fragment color considering transparency
    gl_FragColor = vec4(fragColor.rgb, trans);
}
```

The leaves and other alpha-blended materials on meshes often get an unpleasant silhouette around the boundary of opaque parts. This is caused by texture filtering and mip-mapping on the graphics card. The fragment shader makes use of GLSL's Step function to sharpen the transition between transparent and opaque areas.

```
...
float trans      = step(0.5, mapColor.a);
...
```

The opacity data is encoded in the base texture's alpha channel. We've achieved good results using a cut-off threshold of 0.5 in the Step function.

Runtime Performance

Our reference system is an AMD 3200+ based PC with 1 GByte memory and a Nvidia 6600 GT graphics card. The VRC island (in version 1.1.0) has about 25,000 primitives and 23,000 vertices for vegetation and about 90,000 primitives and 66,000 vertices for nonvegetation meshes. On a Windows XP™ and Linux system it runs at more than 60 frames/second. Note that the actual frame rate may be much higher than 60. VRC has a software throttle for saving CPU and GPU power, preventing higher frame rates than 60; VRC is meant to be a chat application, which runs without using too much from other applications' resources.

Conclusions and Future Directions

This article showed the step-by-step development of a vertex and fragment shader for animating vegetation. The issues addressed by animating vegetation meshes such as trees, weeds, and grass were

- Animation of the meshes in a more natural way by introducing a kind of chaos in vertex movements using harmonic functions *sine* and *cosine* in combination with proper offsetting
- Vertex movement amplitude considering vertices' height in a mesh group
- Combining the height bias with lightmap data in vertex colors
- Elimination of transparent silhouettes on leaves and other alpha-blended materials by using GLSL's Step function

The introduced technique allows the animation of a high count of vegetation meshes at an acceptable frame rate, making it usable in interactive multimedia applications such as games.

Further work on this technique could deal with supporting some environmental influences such as wind and earthquake. Its integration with a precomputed radiance transfer [PRT] approach for a better dynamic lighting would also be interesting, enabling the development of a night and day simulation.

Acknowledgment

I thank Mike Weiblen from 3Dlabs [TDL] for his useful hints on GLSL programming and technical review and Mark Dollery for proofreading. Special thanks go to OpenSceneGraph [OSG] developer Robert Osfield for his excellent OSG library, which we successfully used in our project. I can't forget to mention the OSG's IRC community in channel #openscenegraph on freenode for their emotional and technical support during the whole time of development, in particular, nhv, dtidrow, neighborlee, and wallaba. Last, but not least, I thank my project team members [VRC], who always work hard on improving and extending VRC.

References

[OSG] OpenSceneGraph: 3D Renderer And Scenegraph Manager. Available online at *http://www.openscenegraph.org*.

[PRT] "Pre-computed Radiance Transfer." Available online at *http://en.wikipedia.org/wiki/Precomputed_Radiance_Transfer*.

[TDL] 3Dlabs: Specialists on Graphics Card Hardware and Software. Web site at *http://www.3dlabs.com*.

[VRC] Virtual Reality Chat: Project Yag2002 at SourceForge. Available online at *http://yag2002.sourceforge.net*.

2.8

ZT-Buffer Algorithm

David Pangerl (david@zootfly.com)

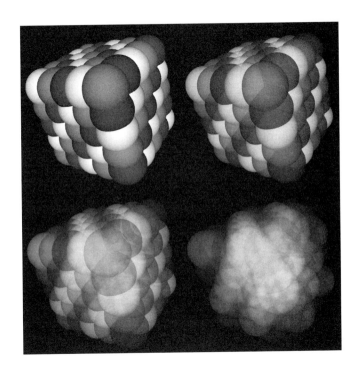

Abstract

This paper presents a novel algorithm for real-time order-independent rendering of arbitrary transparent objects. It describes a general transparency algorithm with a detail hardware–based implementation and outline pipelines for most common rendering methods. Additionally, the chapter includes notes of future work.

Requirements:

- Multirender target (current implementation)
- Float render target alpha blending (current implementation)
- Pixel shader 2.0 or higher
- Use of active render target as a source texture

Advantages:

* Order-independent rendering
* Correct transparency sorting
* Simple to implement

Disadvantages:

* Correct alpha sorting only for limited transparency layers
* One additional render of transparent objects

Introduction

To correctly render intersected and overlaid transparent triangles, it is required to do per-pixel (fragment) depth sorting to properly calculate transparency factors. ZT-buffer is an algorithm for real-time order-independent rendering of arbitrary transparent objects.

The idea of this paper is to present a ZT-buffer algorithm and enable other developers to implement it and further explore its possibilities. The ZT-buffer algorithm is easy enough to be implemented in graphics hardware.

ZT-Buffer

ZT-buffer is basically a multilayer Z-buffer with a per-layer transparency factor. ZT-buffer layers are sorted by ZT-buffer Z values. ZT-buffer T values are precalculated transparency factors. With n-layer ZT-buffer we get a fragment closest to n layers of depth and transparency. Figure 2.8.1 provides a diagrammatic view of ZT-buffer.

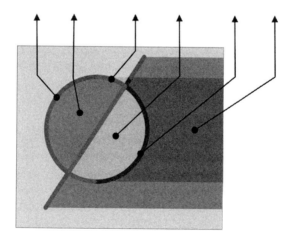

FIGURE 2.8.1   TA layered structure of the ZT-buffer. The frame below the table shows the ZT-buffer depth layers; the nearest layer, Z_0, is the dark red line; the next layer, Z_1, is the dark green line; the next layer, Z_2, is the blue line.

An *n*-layer ZT-buffer can correctly sort *n* − 1 transparency layers. The last ZT-buffer T value is used for all transparency layers after layer *n* − 1.

ZT4-Buffer

A ZT4-buffer is a four-layer ZT-buffer. With a ZT4-buffer, we get a correct three-layer transparency.

Four layers are a logical choice since render targets have four color channels (RGBA) that we can use for layers. Additionally, the tests have proven that humans cannot distinguish between many more than four layers of transparency.

Implementation

For current implementation we use two A16B16G16R16F render targets (RT) and a multirender target (MRT). One RT is used for Z values and the other for T values. Each or RT RGBA channel is used for one layer (see the Future Work section for additional implementation information). Figure 2.8.2 outlines the implementation.

FIGURE 2.8.2 ZT4-buffer RT implementation with two A16B16G16R16F RTs. The same color channel of RT_0 and RT_1 is used for one ZT-buffer layer.

ZT-Buffer Construction

This section explains how to construct the ZT-buffer with additional implementation details for ZT4-buffer construction. The ZT-buffer construction is done in three steps.

Initialize

ZT-buffer Z values are set to clip far plane values and T values to 1 (opaque object alpha value). ZT4-buffer initialization is done with a full screen quad render since DirectX can't clear RTs in MRTs to a different values or set values outside the [0..1] range.

Render Transparent Objects

Render all transparent objects into the ZT-buffer. The transparency alpha factors are written into the ZT-buffer T value. The ZT-buffer is used as a source texture and an RT.
   Render state:

1. Use normal (copy) blending (src*1 + dest*0).
2. Disable Z-buffer writing.
3. Use Z-buffer test if it is valid (optimization).
4. Activate ZT-Buffer as a render target.

Vertex shader:

1. Prepare screen space (x,y) position for pixel shader ZT-buffer sampling.
2. Prepare depth position (z) for pixel shader ZT-buffer sorting.

```
pos=inpos * CameraMatrix
outpos=pos * ProjectionMatrix
screen=(outpos + outpos.w) * 0.5
```

Pixel shader:

1. Sample ZT-buffer with pixel screen (x,y) position.
2. Use the pixel depth position (z) to sort the current pixel (z,a) value into the sampled ZT-buffer and output the sorted ZT-buffer value.
3. ZT4-buffer sorting:

```
        if( z < Z0 ) ZT=((z,a), ZT0, ZT1, ZT2 )
   else if( z < Z1 ) ZT=(ZT0, (z,a), ZT1, ZT2 )
   else if( z < Z2 ) ZT=(ZT0, ZT1, (z,a), ZT2 )
   else if( z < Z3 ) ZT=(ZT0, ZT1, ZT2, (z,a) )
```

Transparency Calculation

We calculate the transparency values (t_n) from alpha factors (a_n) stored in the ZT-buffer T value:

$$t_n = a_n \prod_{i=0}^{n-1} (1 - a_i)$$

The ZT-buffer is used as a source texture and an RT.
   ZT4-buffer transparency calculation is done with a full-screen quad render. The render is preformed only in the ZT4-buffer T value.

$$T_0 = A_0$$
$$T_1 = (1 - A_0)A_1$$
$$T_2 = (1 - A_0)(1 - A_1)A_2$$
$$T_3 = (1 - A_0)(1 - A_1))(1 - A_2)A_3$$

Rendering with ZT-Buffer

To render with ZT-buffer requires minimal vertex shader and pixel shader changes.
Render state:

1. Use additive blending (dest*1 + src *1).
2. Disable Z-buffer writing.
3. Use the Z-buffer test if it is valid (optimization).

Vertex shader:

1. Prepare screen space (x,y) position for pixel shader ZT-buffer sampling.
2. Prepare depth position (z) for pixel shader ZT-buffer layer selection.

Pixel shader:

1. Use a custom pixel shader to calculate a user pixel color (user pixel shader).
2. Sample ZT-buffer with pixel screen (x,y) position.
3. Use pixel depth position (z) to select the sampled ZT-buffer layer T value and output the pixel color multiplied with the selected layer T value.
4. ZT4-buffer T value selection:

```
t=1
        if( z >= Z3 ) t=T3
else         if( z >= Z2 ) t=T2
else         if( z >= Z1 ) t=T1
else         if( z >= Z0 ) t=T0
```

Rendering

This chapter outlines the rendering pipeline using the ZT-buffer.

Conventional rendering

This is the most common way of rendering, where a Z-buffer is created while doing the main render.

1. ZT-buffer construction. Use the method described previously. Don't use the Z-buffer test.
2. Render all opaque objects. Render all opaque objects using ZT-buffer. Write the Z-buffer.
3. Render transparent objects.
4. Render all transparent objects using ZT-buffer.

Conventional Rendering with Z-Buffer Prepass

This method is similar to the previous one. The only difference is that the Z-buffer is created prior to the main render to exploit the hardware-fast Z-buffer creation and early Z rejection for rendering.

1. Render the Z-buffer. Render all opaque objects into the Z-buffer. You should render objects sorted front to back to further utilize the early Z rejection. Disable Z-buffer write after this step.
2. ZT-buffer construction. Use the method described previously. Use the Z-buffer test.
3. Render all opaque and transparent objects. Render all objects using ZT-buffer. Use the Z-buffer test.

Future Work

We are currently analyzing the simultaneous render target read/write restriction. This is still the major problem with the algorithm since the support of this feature is undocumented and so is the hardware implementation. However, it should be possible to solve this problem with minor hardware changes.

Using a single A32B32G32R32F RT for a ZT4-buffer (decimal part for Z value and fraction part for T value) would save one texture sampler (the total bandwidth would remain the same) and remove the algorithm requirement for MRT with minimal additional pixel shader instructions used for decompression. Using an integer render target would additionally remove the float alpha blend requirement (unsupported by ATI X*** GPU series).

ZT-buffer construction might be faster if the implementation could be adapted to work with all MRTs' initial values set to 0 (one full screen pass less).

Transparency calculation should be performed only on pixels that have actually been set. This can be done with a stencil buffer by masking set pixels in a previous pass.

Much of our attention is directed to the ZT-buffer extension for the deferred rendering method, volume transparency rendering, and subsurface scattering (whitepapers on these topics to follow soon). All of these applications are the logical consequences of the multiple depth layers stored within the ZT-buffer.

Conclusion

I presented a simple and fast algorithm for correct alpha sorting for limited transparency layers. The algorithm requires only one render pass of transparent objects and it makes good use of graphics hardware. Additionally there are many useful applications for ZT-buffer information.

Gallery

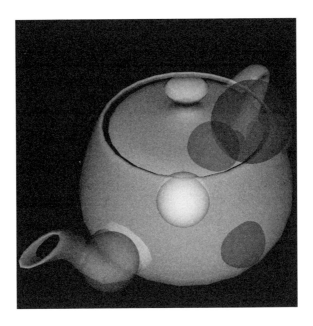

IMAGE SPACE

© 2006 MotoGP'06 for XBox 360, developed by Climax Racing and published by THQ.

Introduction

Natalya Tatarchuk

This section covers all techniques that happen in image space. Because of the increasing pixel shader power of current graphics cards, techniques that were done on the CPU or just avoided due to their expensiveness are now possible.

In the first article of the section, "Real-time Depth-of-Field Implemented with a Postprocessing-Only Technique," David Gillham covers how to implement a depth-of-field effect as a posteffect that was used in *MotoGP 3*.

Emil Persson proposes in his article, "Selective Supersampling," a hybrid solution supersampling that uses regular multisampling for edge anti-aliasing, and lets the application deal with the internal aliasing in the pixel shader. With his approach, the application will have control of where to apply supersampling, thus reducing the cost of supersampling from being directly proportional to the number of samples to a much more reasonable value.

The last article in the section, "Jump Flooding: An Efficient and Effective Communication Pattern for Use on GPUs," by Guodong Rong and Tiow-Seng Tan, introduces an efficient and effective communication pattern—the jump flooding algorithm (JFA)—and demonstrates some of its applications.

3.1

Real-time Depth-of-Field Implemented with a Postprocessing-Only Technique

David Gillham, Climax Brighton

Introduction

Depth-of-field is a visual artifact that causes parts of an image to appear blurred while preserving focus in others. It is caused by the physical properties of camera lenses and can be observed in both photography and cinematography. While possibly considered undesirable, it is now a commonly used tool in bringing a viewer's attention to specific areas of a scene, enhancing the visual experience.

Since the introduction of powerful programmable graphics hardware, it has been possible to simulate depth-of-field in games and other real-time applications. This has provided for a more photo-realistic look in rendered scenes and allows the players attention to be focused on areas of the scene to enhance the playing experience.

Several popular techniques for implementing real-time depth-of-field using programmable hardware have already been presented in considerable detail in previous *ShaderX* articles [Riguer03] [Scheuermann04]. Despite producing varying results in terms of quality, performance, and flexibility, these algorithms all follow a similar pattern. They begin by producing a blurriness factor for each rendered pixel during the scene-rendering pass, which describes the amount to blur each pixel based on parameters defined by the author. Then, in a final postprocessing pass, the per-pixel blur factor is combined with various techniques to produce the final depth-of-field scene rendered pixel. Although being different in terms of how the final pixels are produced, all of these algorithms still use the scene rendering pass to aid in computing a blur factor for each pixel, and herein lies the problem.

Typically, blur factor is computed by adding additional code to every scene vertex shader, which outputs the depth of every vertex in camera space to an interpolator. This interpolated depth value is then passed as input to every accompanying pixel shader, and with additional code is used in computing a blurriness factor. Even if we have a system that can automatically append the necessary code to all involved shaders, this approach can be inconvenient for the following reasons:

- It adds cost to all scene vertex and pixel shaders.
- It requires an extra interpolator, which adds additional overhead and could break existing shaders that are already on the interpolator limit.
- Having to add additional code to all scene shaders is something that will almost certainly require maintenance throughout the lifetime of a project as shaders evolve.

Wouldn't it be nice if we could avoid having to add code to all these shaders and avoid the above pitfalls? Well, we can.

This chapter presents a modified version of the *ShaderX²* depth-of-field article, "Depth of Field Rendering by Blurring with Separate Gaussian Filter" [Riguer03], which is confined entirely to the postprocessing stage of rendering and alleviates the need to append code to an application's scene shaders.

Pixel Depth and Blurriness Factor

Our Approach

Figure 3.1.1 shows the pipeline for the traditional approach to depth-of-field rendering as explained in the Introduction.

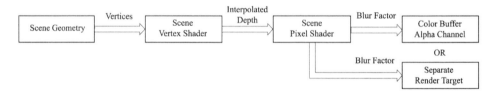

FIGURE 3.1.1   Scene rendering pass with the traditional approach to obtaining scene depth and blurriness factor for each pixel.

Note that another interpolated scene depth for each pixel is also calculated and stored into an off-screen buffer. This of course is the depth buffer. We may then ask why the above technique is still used if pixel scene depth is already calculated and stored by the system.

First, values in the depth buffer cannot be used directly in blur factor calculations, as they do not represent scene depth in relation to camera space. The values are computed by multiplying camera space coordinates by the perspective projection matrix and then dividing by w. The value placed in depth buffer is the z component of this transformed camera space position.

Second, gaining access to the z or depth buffer for sampling within a pixel shader is not a clear-cut task. It may require proficient knowledge of the target platform's graphics API, which could mean learning several APIs if an application is cross platform.

If we want to avoid the pitfalls of the traditional approach to obtaining depth and blurriness factor, we must first solve two problems: first, transforming values stored in the depth buffer back into camera space, and second, a way of making the depth buffer available as a texture that can then be sampled from within a pixel shader. Once solved, this will give us an alternative method for computing scene depth and blur factor for each pixel, which is independent of scene rendering.

The next two sections describe our solution to these problems. In the subsequent sections we outline a depth-of-field technique that is confined entirely to postprocessing by incorporating these solutions.

Resolving the Depth Buffer

In order to derive an equation that converts depth buffer values into camera space, we must first understand how these values are obtained. Below is a standard row-major perspective projection matrix, which is used to transform camera space coordinates to clip space.

$$\begin{bmatrix} x & y & z & 1 \end{bmatrix} \begin{bmatrix} Zoom_x & 0 & 0 & 0 \\ 0 & Zoom_y & 0 & 0 \\ 0 & 0 & Q & 1 \\ 0 & 0 & -Z_nQ & 0 \end{bmatrix} = \begin{bmatrix} x' & y' & z' & z \end{bmatrix}, \quad (3.1.1)$$

where

$$Q = \frac{Z_f}{Z_f - Z_n} \quad (1.3.2)$$

$$Z_f = \text{far clip}$$
$$Z_n = \text{near clip}.$$

$Zoom_x$ and $Zoom_y$ are equations that define the field of view behavior of the matrix, and a good explanation of how these are derived can be found in "*Real-time Rendering,*" second edition [Akenine02]. However, they are not important for our purposes here, so we choose not to define them.

Q is defined such that resultant z values will satisfy the inequality, $0 \le z \le w$, with $w = 1$. This is similar to a DirectX style clip matrix, but different than an OpenGL one, where $-w \le z \le w$. However, for our purposes, we will use the DirectX style matrix, as this is more commonly used in games. Of course, this is not the only way to create a perspective projection matrix, but what we have here is standard enough and sufficient to demonstrate our solution.

To clearly see how depth buffer values are obtained, let's start by writing out in full the equation that results from multiplying a 4D homogenous vector with the third column of the above matrix:

$$z' = (zQ) + (-Z_n Q). \tag{3.1.3}$$

Now factor into Equation 3.1.3 the homogenous divide by w, in the case of the above matrix $w = z$, and we have the final depth buffer equation:

$$Z_d = \frac{(zQ) + (-Z_n Q)}{z}. \tag{3.1.4}$$

All we have to do now is solve Equation 3.1.4 for z and we will have a means to back-transform depth buffer values into camera space:

$$Z_d = \frac{zQ - Z_n Q}{z}. \tag{3.1.5}$$

$$z = \frac{-Z_n Q}{Z_d - Q}. \tag{3.1.6}$$

We could precompute the $-Z_n Q$ part, and then computing z will amount to just one subtraction and a divide.

Note that Equation 3.1.6 will be different depending on how one constructs the clip space perspective projection matrix. So before blindly using the above, we need to check how the matrix is constructed and factor in any differences before solving for z again.

One other note worth mentioning: values stored in the depth buffer are usually limited to a 24-bit fixed-point format, and as a result, precision is limited. This has the unwanted side-effect of nearer depth values being much more precise than values that are farther away. The degree of this nonlinearity is controlled by the ratio between the near and far clip planes (the closer the near clip is to the camera, the less precision there will be for distant objects) [Baker06]. This loss of precision will also be carried through when using our equation to back-transform values from the depth buffer, meaning our transformed depth values to camera space will not be 100% accurate for every pixel. However, when viewing an image rendered with depth-of-field, it is practically impossible to tell exactly how blurry a pixel should appear [Scheuermann04]. Therefore, this loss of precision will not have a noticeable impact on the final rendered scene.

Accessing the Depth Buffer

To put our new equation to use, the depth buffer (or a copy of it) must be made available as a texture to a pixel shader for sampling. How this is achieved will depend strongly on the target platform and rendering API, and covering all available methods is beyond the scope of this chapter. Instead, we will look at several ways to achieve this by using the two most common rendering APIs in use today. These approaches may not be the most optimal for all applications, but they should at least provide a means to get people started.

OpenGL

For OpenGL we can use the `GL_EXT_framebuffer_object` extension [Juliano05]. The good thing about this extension is that it is supported in both OpenGL 2.0 and PSGL for PS3.

With the `framebuffer` object extension, there are two ways to create a depth buffer texture. The more accepted approach is to use the RenderBuffer API, but render buffer targets cannot be used as textures to be sampled from [Green05]. The alternative is to create an empty texture object, which can then be bound to a frame buffer object and used as the depth/stencil render target. This is done by creating a 2D texture object using the standard GL calls `glGenTextures()`, `glBindTexture()`, and `glTexImage2D()`. Be sure to only create a texture object with one mipmap, though, and use the following texture parameters:

```
GL_TEXTURE_MAX_LEVEL = 1
GL_TEXTURE_MAX_ANISOTROPY_EXT = 1
GL_TEXTURE_MAG_FILTER = GL_NEAREST
GL_TEXTURE_MIN_FILTER = GL_NEAREST_MIPMAP_NEAREST
```

The first two parameters are to avoid GL warnings when using texture objects with just one mipmap. The last two parameters are to ensure that the value sampled from the depth texture is not a weighted average of the surrounding texels, which would produce incorrect results when computing blur factor. Note that this filtering rule will need to be adhered to, whichever API one uses.

Before scene rendering, we will need to bind the depth buffer texture object to the frame buffer object being used for rendering. Because we are not using the RenderBuffer API, instead of calling `glFramebufferRenderbufferEXT()`, we can use `glFramebufferTexture2DEXT()` to bind the depth texture. We need to make sure, though, that we pass `GL_DEPTH_ATTACHMENT_EXT` as the second argument to this function [Green05].

Once scene rendering is complete, we need to first unbind the depth texture object from the frame buffer object, and then we are free to use it as a normal texture for sampling.

DirectX

Unfortunately, in DirectX9, obtaining a copy of the depth buffer is not quite as straightforward as in OpenGL2.0. This is mainly due to formats of depth buffers being proprietary, and independent hardware vendors (IHVs) do not want to encourage reliance on proprietary data. As a result, several methods are currently available, but no one approach will work best on all hardware. We will now discuss these options with the pros and cons of each.

Copying The Depth Buffer

The following steps outline a method for obtaining a copy of the depth buffer, which involves locking the system depth buffer surface and copying its contents to a texture surface.

First, when creating a system depth/stencil surface, we must use a format of either `D3DFMT_D16_LOCKABLE` or `D3DFMT_D32F_LOCKABLE`. These are the only two formats that allow a depth/stencil surface to be locked. Once the D3D device has been created, we need to gain access to the system depth/stencil surface interface by calling the `IDirect3DDevice9::GetDepthStencilSurface()` method.

Next we need to manually create a D3D texture resource with just one surface, with dimensions and format compatible with that of the device depth/stencil surface. This is done using the `IDirect3DDevice9::CreateTexture()` method. The reason for creating this texture is that only D3D texture objects can be associated with pixel shader samplers. The format should be equal in terms of both bit depth and polarity (unsigned for depth). For example, if using `D3DFMT_D16_LOCKABLE`, then `D3DFMT_L16` will be a compatible format.

The final step is to copy the data from the system depth buffer surface to the surface of our manually created depth buffer texture. This can be accomplished either manually or by using the D3DX helper function `D3DXLoadSurfaceFromSurface()`. Once completed, we will have a texture containing an up-to-date copy of the system depth buffer.

The advantage of this method is that it uses only generic features of DX9 and should work on a wide variety of hardware, but be aware that not all cards support the lockable depth buffer formats. The downside is that it may kill an application's performance, as reading from the system depth buffer surface can be extremely slow.

Depth Textures

Another technique for accessing the depth buffer, similar to the technique discussed using OpenGL2.0, is the use of depth textures. Assuming the hardware supports it, an application can create a texture with a depth buffer format and set this texture's surface as the system depth/stencil buffer. Once scene rendering is complete, this same depth texture can be used like a normal texture and sampled from within a pixel shader.

This technique should prove to be considerably faster, as copying the depth buffer is no longer required. However, creating textures with depth buffer formats is only supported on select hardware. Most NVIDIA cards should support this, but support by ATI is limited to DX9 cards only. Drivers for these cards have added special four-CC coded depth buffer formats, and only Radeon X1900, X1600, and X1300 cards support a 24-bit depth format [Riguer06]. A more detailed explanation of depth textures and their use can be found in *The Radeon X1000 Series Programming Guide* [Riguer06].

DirectX 10

Fortunately, DirectX 10 provides a means to efficiently access the depth buffer that will work across all DirectX 10–compatible hardware, putting an end to this problem. Through the use of resource views, once scene rendering is complete, the depth buffer can be viewed as a shader resource (a texture) for read access.

This can be achieved by first creating two views for a depth texture: a depth buffer view and a shader resource view. Before scene rendering begins, bind a texture using the depth buffer view, and when scene rendering is complete, bind this depth texture as an input to your shader using the shader resource view. The DirectX 10 documentation in the latest DirectX SDK explains the API for this. Note that you still cannot read and write from a depth texture simultaneously, so your application will need to make use of two depth textures, one for the scene rendering pass and another for postprocessing.

Putting It All Together

Now that we have an alternative method for obtaining scene depth and blur factor, let us put this into practice by describing a depth-of-field algorithm that incorporates this. We base our algorithm on the one described in [Riguer03], but we modify this algorithm by incorporating our alternative means for obtaining the blur factor. We begin with an overview of the modified algorithm and then go on to describe in detail the stages that differ.

Algorithm Overview

We start by doing a full scene render pass to a full-resolution offscreen render and depth target. The full-resolution render target will then need to be downsampled to a separate render target texture that is one-quarter the size of the original. Next we blur the downsampled render target by a user-specified amount with two passes of a Gaussian filter in the *x* and *y* axes. Before the final render pass, we make available the depth buffer used for the initial scene rendering as a texture that can be sampled. We also need to set back the default render and depth targets as the rendering destinations for the final pass. By now we have all the ingredients to perform the final depth-of-field render pass. During this pass, the depth texture is first sampled to obtain pixel scene depth and blur factor. The blur factor is then used to linearly interpolate between the full-resolution scene render and the quarter-size downsample to obtain the final depth-of-field rendered pixel. Figure 3.1.2 helps illustrate this process.

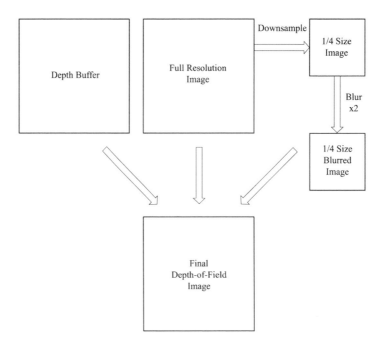

FIGURE 3.1.2   The necessary postprocessing steps involved in producing a
depth-of-field rendered scene.

2x2 Downsampling Pass

Downsampling of the full-resolution scene render is achieved the same way as in the
[Riguer03] technique, where the original full-resolution scene render is sampled and
rendered onto a render target one-quarter its size. Both vertex and pixel shader code
can also be obtained from the same article.

Gaussian Filter Pass

Again, Gaussian blurring of the downsampled render target is achieved as described in
[Riguer03], so refer to that article for the theory behind Gaussian filtering and the
accompanying vertex and pixel shader code.

Depth-of-Field Pass

Once we have made available as a texture the depth buffer that was used to render the
full-resolution scene, we have the necessary ingredients needed to perform the final
depth-of-field render pass. We start by rendering a full-screen quad using the same
vertex shader that is used to perform the downsampling. The pixel shader begins by

calculating the scene depth for the current pixel by back-transforming the value-sampled depth buffer texture. Blur factor is then computed using scene depth. Finally, the blur factor is used to linearly interpolate between the full-resolution scene texture and the blurred downsample to obtain the final pixel value. Again, all texture sampling should be performed using nearest-point filtering.

LISTING 3.1.1   Depth-of-Field Pixel Shader

```
// Depth buffer resolve parameters
// x = focus distance
// y = focus range
// z = near clip
// w = far clip / ( far clip - near clip )
float4 vDoFParams;

// Textures
sampler2D sceneTex;
sampler2D sceneBlurTex;
sampler2D sceneDepthTex;


// —— input structure ——
struct PS_INPUT
{
    float2 vUV : TEXCOORD0;
};


// —— output structure ——
struct PS_OUTPUT
{
    float4 vColor : COLOR0;
};


PS_OUTPUT main( const PS_INPUT input )
{
    PS_OUTPUT output = ( PS_OUTPUT )0;

    float3 vDepthTexel     = tex2D( sceneDepthTex, input.vUV );
    float4 vSceneTexel     = tex2D( sceneTex, input.vUV );
    float4 vSceneBlurTexel = tex2D( sceneBlurTex, input.vUV );

    // Reconstruct depth buffer value from its constituent
    // components
    // This code is assuming 24 bits for depth information
    float fDepth = ( vDepthTexel.x * 255.0 / 256.0 )          +
                   ( vDepthTexel.y * 255.0 / 65536.0 ) +
                   ( vDepthTexel.z * 255.0 / 16777216.0 );
```

```
// This is only required if using a floating-point
// depth buffer format
fDepth = 1.0 - fDepth;

// Back-transform depth into camera space
float fSceneZ = ( -vDoFParams.z * vDoFParams.w ) /
                ( fDepth - vDoFParams.w );

// Compute blur factor
float fBlurFactor = saturate( abs( fSceneZ - vDoFParams.x ) /
                                   vDoFParams.y );

// Compute resultant pixel
output.vColor.rgb = lerp( vSceneTexel.rgb, vSceneBlurTexel.rgb,
                          fBlurFactor );

output.vColor.a = 1.0;

return output;
}
```

In Listing 3.1.1, the global variable vDoFParams is a uniform shader parameter that will require setting from code. The z and w elements store the values used in the equation to back-transform the depth buffer value into camera space. See the comments above its definition on how to set this correctly from client code.

To ensure that the correct depth buffer value is used when calculating pixel scene depth, the depth texture is sampled into a float3 variable. This will force the sampled texel to be split up so that each element of the float3 variable will contain 8 of the 24 depth bits that comprise a depth buffer entry (in a normalized 0–1 range). Using the code in Listing 3.1.2, the value can be consistently reconstructed to be the value that was originally placed into the depth buffer.

LISTING 3.1.2   Code to Reconstruct the Depth Buffer Value from Constituent Components

```
float fDepth = ( vDepthTexel.x * 255.0 / 256.0 ) +
    ( vDepthTexel.y * 255.0 / 65536.0 )  +
      ( vDepthTexel.z * 255.0 / 16777216.0 );
```

This code will obviously change, depending on the format of the depth buffer, but it assumes the most common case of 24-bits of depth. It was found that sampling the depth buffer into a float2 variable to have all depth bits in the x component worked well for HLSL but not for OpenGL/Cg.

If the application is using a floating-point depth buffer, values stored in the depth buffer will probably range from 1 to 0 instead of 0 to 1. Therefore, before calculating camera scene depth, we will need to convert the depth buffer value back into the 0–1 range. See the results in Figure 3.1.3. Please see file DOF_PS.txt on the CD-ROM.

ON THE CD

FIGURE 3.1.3 Screenshot from *MotoGP'06* on the XBox360 using our depth-of-field algorithm to track player vehicle during replays. © 2006 MotoGP'06 for XBox 360, developed by Climax Racing and published by THQ.

Further Improvements

The technique described here provides a convincing effect but is also designed to be quick and minimal. There are several ways in which the algorithm can be improved in terms of both performance and quality:

- Our algorithm uses an approach based on a Gaussian blur filter, but it would also be possible to incorporate our alternative means for obtaining depth and blur factor into an algorithm that uses a circle-of-confusion and Poisson disc filter kernel to achieve blurring [Riguer03] [Scheuermann04]. The added flexibility of this approach would make it possible to eliminate color leaking (when color from in-focus objects leak into background colors). It also allows for more realistic camera lens models, which would give an artist more control over the effect, instead of being limited to focus ranges and amount to blur.
- As the depth of objects in the scene is computed using the depth buffer (or a copy of it), objects that are rendered with *z*-writes turned off will be blurred according to the distance of the last object rendered in their place that had *z*-writes turned on. How much of a problem this is will depend on the application. A possible solution would be to rerender these objects after scene rendering with *z*-writes turned on and color writes turned off.

- The Gaussian filter used in [Riguer03] can be improved upon in several ways, depending on how much blurriness is required. If more and better blur is required, then additional taps and passes can be utilized or one can convert to using a radial blur. However, if only minimal blur is required, a number of optimizations can be performed. One could start by simply reducing the number of taps to 11x11 and so forth, or just do the blur in a single pass by using even fewer taps. An even less expensive approach is to simply sample the downsampled image using a bilinear filter for a subtle blur effect. It all comes down to how much control the application requires over blur.

Conclusion

This article has presented an alternative method to depth-of-field rendering that alleviates some of the constraints of previous techniques by being independent of scene rendering. Exactly how beneficial this approach will be is ultimately dependent on the nature of an application, but the advantages gained should not be underestimated, especially for games. See our results in Figure 3.1.4.

FIGURE 3.1.4   Screenshot from *MotoGP'06* on the XBox360 using our depth-of-field algorithm.
© 2006 MotoGP'06 for XBox 360, developed by Climax Racing and published by THQ.

Acknowledgments

I would like to thank David Jefferies, lead programmer of *MotoGP'06*, for providing me with the original concept that this article is based upon.

References

[Akenine02] Akenine-Möller, T. and E. Haines. *Real-time Rendering,* 2nd ed. A. K. Peters, 2002.

[Baker06] Baker, S. "Learning to Love your Z-buffer." Available online at *http://www. sjbaker.org/steve/omniv/love_your_z_buffer.html,* July 12, 2006.

[Green05] Green, S. "The OpenGL Framebuffer Object Extension." Available online at *http://download.nvidia.com/developer/presentations/2005/GDC/OpenGL_Day/ OpenGL_FrameBuffer_Object.pdf,* 2005.

[Juliano05] Juliano, J., J. Sandmel, et al. "OpenGL EXT_framebuffer_object extension specification." Available online at *http://oss.sgi.com/projects/ogl-sample/registry/ EXT/framebuffer_object.txt,* January 31, 2005.

[Riguer03] Riguer, G., N. Tatarchuk, and J. Isidoro. "Real-time Depth of Field Simulation." *ShaderX²: Shader Programming Tips and Tricks with DirectX 9.* Wordware Publishing, 2003. Available online at *http://www.ati.com/developer/shaderx/ ShaderX²_Real-timeDepthOfFieldSimulation.pdf.*

[Riguer06] Riguer, G. "Depth Textures." *The Radeon X1000 Series Programming Guide.* Available as part of the ATI SDK, *http://www.ati.com/developer/radeonSDK.,* March 2006.

[Scheuermann04] Scheuermann, T. and N. Tatarchuk. "Improved Depth-of-Field Rendering." *ShaderX³: Advanced Rendering with DirectX and OpenGL,* Charles River Media, 2004: pp. 363–377.

3.2

Selective Supersampling

Emil Persson, ATI

Introduction

In the debate between multisampling and supersampling the supporters of supersampling have traditionally argued that supersampling offers better quality. While this is true, it's also the case that supersampling comes with massively worse performance, something supporters of multisampling have been quick to point out. The problem with supersampling is that it runs the pixel shader for every sample location, which means that, for instance, 4x supersampling rendering comes at 4x the pixel shading cost. In many cases this is redundant since the texture filter ensures that texturing aliasing is nearly nonexistent, which makes supersampling much of a brute force approach. Multisampling, on the other hand, only executes the pixel shader once and distributes the result to all covered samples, which ensures that we only anti-alias the polygon edges and not the surface interior, resulting in less performance impact of anti-aliasing. Thus, supersampling has traditionally not been worth the cost since with mostly just texturing in the majority of games there wasn't much internal aliasing to begin with, and the improved texture sharpness could be done better and faster with an anisotropic filter.

However, as shaders get more advanced, there's an increasing risk of running into aliasing problems in the surface interior as well. With shaders supporting fully generic math, there's no guarantee that the given computations won't contain high-frequency components, unlike textures that get sampled at the best possible mipmap level to ensure that under-sampling does not happen. A typical case of this problem is specular highlights on bump-mapped surfaces, where a detailed bump map could cause shimmering in the specular highlights. For this reason many would argue that supersampling should be utilized again, but more advanced shaders also mean higher cost per sample, making traditional driver-side supersampling extremely costly.

To get the best from both worlds, we propose a hybrid solution that uses regular multisampling for edge anti-aliasing and lets the application deal with the internal aliasing in the pixel shader. The application will intelligently apply supersampling only to the materials and shaders that exhibit an aliasing problem, and only to the components of the shaders in question that have a problem, thus reducing the cost of supersampling from being directly proportional to the number of samples to a much more reasonable value. Using dynamic branching can reduce the cost even further by skipping the super-sampling computations where they aren't needed.

Shader-Level Supersampling

First we need to come up with an approach for performing shader-level supersampling. The pixel shader typically gets input in the form of a number of interpolated texture coordinates. If we had the texture coordinates for the subsamples within a pixel, the work would be trivial. We can essentially just put the content of the shader into a function and call that function repeatedly (see Listing 3.2.1 for a pseudo-code example).

LISTING 3.2.1   Example Shader Execution for Supersampling

```
float4 vfSum = 0.0;
for (int i = 0; i < SAMPLE_COUNT; i++)
{
    vfSum += OriginalShader( sampleCoordinate[i] );
}
return vfSum / SAMPLE_COUNT;
```

Unfortunately we don't have access to the sample positions in the pixel shader. We can use the gradients for a given pixel to make a fairly good approximation of the sample positions. This allows us to select the sample positions directly ourselves and gives us control of the amount of samples we may want. This can even be chosen dynamically per pixel using dynamic branching.

Let's talk a bit about the gradients. They are the discrete approximations of the partial derivatives in x and y directions in screen space for a given pixel, computed with the ddx and ddy functions in SM3.0. Typically, this is implemented as follows: pixels go through a programmable pipeline in quads (which means that a given graphics hardware executes pixel shaders for 2×2 pixel regions in parallel). There are several reasons for this, but one of the benefits is that this allows the graphics card to compute the partial derivative cheaply simply by taking the value in any register in the pixel shader in the four pixels in the 2×2 block at any point and computing the difference in x or y between the values. This gives the gradient value. Figure 3.2.1 illustrates this process.

There are many uses of the gradients, including fundamental tasks in 3D graphics such as texture LOD computations, but that's beyond the scope of this article. How do the gradients help us implement supersampling? Let's take a look at Figure 3.2.1 again. The ddx instruction computes the texture coordinate difference to the pixel next to the current pixel. Assume we are shading the upper-left pixel. Computing the texture coordinate of the upper-right pixel would be the regular interpolated texture coordinate plus the result of ddx instruction. Similarly, going to the lower left is the texture coordinate plus the result of ddy. Using this fact, we can estimate that the pixel covers the area of half the gradient in x and y directions around the texture coordinate. Naturally, this math doesn't line up perfectly if we are shading any of the

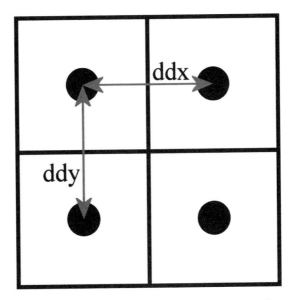

FIGURE 3.2.1 One approach to computing the gradients in a 2 × 2 pixel quad.

other three pixels or even for the upper-left pixel, since we don't take neighbors outside the quad into account, but it will be close enough for our purposes.

Instead of assuming we have a set of sample coordinates (like we did in the previous pseudo-code), we can now supersample in the shader using the available texture coordinate and a set of sample positions of our choice (see Listing 3.2.2).

LISTING 3.2.2 Computing Supersampling Result in the Pixel Shader

```
const float2 fSamples[SAMPLE_COUNT] =
{
    // Sample positions in [-0.5, 0.5] range goes here
    ...
};

// Compute gradients
float2 fDX = ddx( texCoord );
float2 fDY = ddy( texCoord );

float4 vfSum = 0.0;
for ( int i = 0; i < SAMPLE_COUNT; i++ )
{
    // Compute texture coordinates for this sample
    float2 vSampleCoord =
      texCoord + fSamples[i].x * fDX + fSamples[i].y * fDY;
    vfSum += OriginalShader( VfSampleCoord );
}
return vfSum / SAMPLE_COUNT;
```

Notice that although the sample positions are arbitrary, they naturally affect the quality of the resulting rendering. Since we can control the sample positions ourselves, we can select from a number of different choices. For a four-sample pattern, a rotated grid may be a good choice, which could be implemented as shown in Listing 3.2.3.

LISTING 3.2.3   Computing Sample Coordinates Using a Rotated Grid

```
#define SAMPLE_COUNT 4

const float2 fSamples[SAMPLE_COUNT] =
{
    float2( 0.125,  0.375),
    float2( 0.375, -0.125),
    float2(-0.125, -0.375),
    float2(-0.375,  0.125),
};
```

Selective Supersampling

One of the typical cases where you would see internal aliasing is with per-pixel lighting using a normal map. However, all normal maps do not cause aliasing, not every surface on the screen is necessarily normal-mapped, and not all types of lighting computation are prone to aliasing. The diffuse component of lighting typically doesn't exhibit much aliasing, whereas the specular component tends to be more problematic. One of the benefits of implementing the selective supersampling directly in the shader is that we can control where it is applied, rather than blindly applying it to the entire frame. This puts the control over the expensive computations for supersampling into the hands of developers. This means that for the portions of the scene rendering that do not exhibit aliasing artifacts, we can avoid this computation on the GPU and free it up to perform more interesting or complicated shaders or improve existing performance.

One piece of the problem solves itself, namely, the parts of the scene that are totally unaffected by aliasing. We simply don't touch those shaders and render them as usual. For surfaces that require supersampling, the approach is a bit more involved. However, even a naïve implementation that supersamples the entire shader should outperform full-scene supersampling unless most of the screen is covered by surfaces using the supersampling shader.

The most obvious and simplest optimization is to separate the components of shader computations that require supersampling from those that don't. In the per-pixel normal-mapping case, a typical situation is that we only want to compute super-sampling for the specular part. This means we don't supersample diffuse, ambient light-mapping and so on and we don't repeat computation–like normalizing view and light–vectors, unlike in the full-screen supersampling case.

Implementation of this approach is straightforward. Simply put, we convert the portion of the shader computations that we want to compute supersampling for into a function or a macro (for example, as shown in Listing 3.2.4).

LISTING 3.2.4 Creating a Macro for Specular Lighting Computation

```
#define SPECULAR(vNormal)
    pow(saturate(dot(reflect(-vView, vNormal), vLight)), 16.0)
```

Note that the aliasing artifacts appear from the high frequency in the normal sampled from the normal map, so that's what we need to supersample (Listing 3.2.5).

LISTING 3.2.5 Macro for Supersampling the Normal Vector from a Normal Map

```
// Sample the bump-map at given x and y sample positions in
    [-1, 1] range
#define SAMPLENORMAL(x,y) normalize(tex2D(tBump, texCoord +
    (0.5 * x) * fDX + (0.5 * y) * fDY).xyz * 2.0 - 1.0)
```

With these two macros, the final shader with supersampling could look something like Listing 3.2.5.

LISTING 3.2.5 Example of the Shader with Supersampled Specular Component

```
float4 main(float2 texCoord: TEXCOORD0,
            float3 vLight  : TEXCOORD1,
            float3 vView   : TEXCOORD2) : COLOR
{

    // Compute the gradients of the texture coordinates
    float2 fDX = ddx(texCoord);
    float2 fDY = ddy(texCoord);

    // Normalize lighting vectors
    vLight = normalize(vLight);
    vView  = normalize(vView);

    // Compute lighting
    float3 vBase   = tex2D(tBase, texCoord).rgb;
    float3 vBump   = tex2D(tBump, texCoord).xyz;
    float3 vNormal = normalize(vBump * 2.0 - 1.0);

    float3 cAmbient = 0.15 * vBase;
    float  fDiffuse = saturate(dot(vLight, vNormal));

    // Supersample the specular component.
    // Use the center sample and 4 peripheral samples.
    float fSpecular =
        (SPECULAR(vNormal) +
         SPECULAR(SAMPLENORMAL( 0.25,  0.75)) +
         SPECULAR(SAMPLENORMAL(-0.25, -0.75)) +
         SPECULAR(SAMPLENORMAL(-0.75,  0.25)) +
         SPECULAR(SAMPLENORMAL( 0.75, -0.25))) / 5.0;

    return float4(cAmbient + fDiffuse * vBase + fSpecular, 0);
}
```

Note that in Listing 3.2.5 we're only computing the subsample texture coordinates for the normal map. We could use the subsample coordinates to compute the new light vector and view vector for each subsample. In practice, however, the visual difference is minimal. It's not necessary to always compute extra sample values for all inputs. For best performance, this should only be done for the attributes that really need the extra accuracy. In this case only the normal-map coordinates need it.

Dynamic Branching for Selective Supersampling

Being selective about where to apply supersampling doesn't have to be limited to a per-pass decision. It is often possible to use dynamic branching to ensure that we only do this extra work where necessary within a surface. Since we already require SM3.0 for the gradient instructions, we can safely use dynamic branching too without adding to the hardware requirements. There's no generic answer to exactly how a dynamic branching statement should look to do its job and achieve maximum performance. That's something that has to be figured out on a case-to-case basis depending on what is being supersampled. A good tool that can help us out in many cases is yet again the gradients. As discussed, gradients measure at what rate a value is varying between pixels. A sharp variation means a greater chance that we'll have aliasing. We don't have to use it on an interpolator, but we can apply it to any value in our shader, such as, for instance, the specular result. Thus, we can compute the specular lighting for the center sample, and if it varies a lot between the pixels in the quad, we may need to take more samples. In Listing 3.2.5 we can just change the specular part to Listing 3.2.6.

LISTING 3.2.6   An Approach Using Gradients to Figure Out Where to Apply Supersampling

```
// Center sample
float fSpecular = SPECULAR(vNormal);

// Compute specular gradients
float2 ds = float2(ddx(fSpecular), ddy(fSpecular));

// If it's above the threshold, then take the other four samples too
if (dot(ds, ds) > 0.0002){
    fSpecular += SPECULAR(SAMPLENORMAL( 0.25,  0.75));
    fSpecular += SPECULAR(SAMPLENORMAL(-0.25, -0.75));
    fSpecular += SPECULAR(SAMPLENORMAL(-0.75,  0.25));
    fSpecular += SPECULAR(SAMPLENORMAL( 0.75, -0.25));
    fSpecular /= 5.0;
}
```

The value 0.0002 is not based on any exact science but is derived from testing and tweaking. It was chosen because that's about the largest value that could be used without affecting image quality. A larger value results in better performance since then more pixels fall below it and skip the extra samples. To see any performance improvement at all, we need to tweak the SAMPLENORMAL macro:

```
#define SAMPLENORMAL(x,y) normalize(tex2Dgrad(Bump, texCoord +
    (0.5 * x) * fDX + (0.5 * y) * fDY, fDX, fDY).xyz * 2.0 - 1.0)
```

ON THE CD

The only change is that we now use `tex2Dgrad` instead of `tex2D` because the regular `tex2D` function implicitly computes gradients for the LOD computation, and gradients are undefined inside a dynamic branch statement. This is because if pixels within a quad took different paths through the shader, some pixels would not have a useful value to use to compute the difference. The only time this can be done is when the variable in question is an interpolator, in which case it's perfectly legal and well defined to compute the gradients on it inside a dynamic branching statement. In other cases the result would be random. This may not be immediately obvious and could fool even the experienced programmer. Also, we should keep in mind that the HLSL compiler doesn't issue an error or even a warning when we put `tex2D` calls inside a branch. Instead, the compiler will modify the code to a legal result, which often involves moving the `tex2D` call and possibly large chunks of code before it is outside the branch. In some cases the entire branch could get eliminated, and as a result we won't see any performance increase at all, or even a performance decrease. The solution to that problem is to use `tex2Dgrad` instead, which takes explicit gradients, which makes the gradients well defined even inside a branch.

The resulting performance may vary wildly depending on the situation. In various tests for the specular lighting case the costs have generally been fairly moderate. Only multisampling the scene resulted in about 15% performance loss at four samples. Adding selective supersampling with four samples to the mix ended up about 30% slower than no anti-aliasing. This is in contrast to full-scene supersampling that would normally result in about a 75% loss, assuming fragment processing is the bottleneck.

Conclusion

A technique has been presented that can deliver the quality of supersampling without the massive performance loss normally associated with it. By utilizing multisampling for edge anti-aliasing and selective supersampling for various forms of internal aliasing, better performance can be achieved than the traditional supersampling approach.

3.3

Jump Flooding: An Efficient and Effective Communication Pattern for Use on GPUs

Guodong Rong and Tiow-Seng Tan,

School of Computing,

National University of Singapore

Introduction

With the rapid advancement of the computing capability of GPUs, general-purpose computation using GPUs has become a new research focus in recent years. A survey of such research can be found in [Owens05]. Currently, GPUs are used not only to generate rendering results on the screen, but also as single instruction multiple data (SIMD) processors to perform various general-purpose tasks. When using a GPU as an SIMD processor, every pixel can be seen as a processing element (PE). A fragment program is executed on all the pixels simultaneously to process different data stored either in textures or in per-pixel variables such as texture coordinates. The communication between PEs is crucial to such a computation. Different communication patterns can greatly affect the quality and the speed of the computation. In this chapter, we introduce an efficient and effective communication pattern, the jump flooding algorithm (JFA), and demonstrate some of its applications.

The Jump Flooding Algorithm

Suppose we have a seed at the lower-left corner of an $n \times n$ screen and we want to propagate its information (shown as the shaded regions in Figure 3.3.1) to all the other pixels of the screen. In other words, we want to fill the whole screen with the same pattern as the seed. One simple way is to use standard flooding as shown in Figure 3.3.1a. In every pass the information is passed forward by one pixel. After $n-1$ steps, we fill the whole screen. The number of passes required is linear to the resolution of the screen.

When considering the standard flooding process carefully, we find that every pixel is used effectively only once. In every pass only those on the front of the propagation

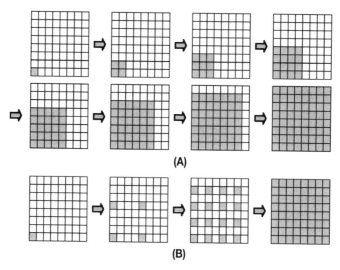

FIGURE 3.3.1   The process of applying **(A)** standard flooding and
(B) jump flooding to a seed at the lower-left corner of an 8×8 screen.

are useful, while the other shaded pixels are not. This is not an effective use of the computational cycles. To remedy the situation, we introduce the JFA.

In the case of standard flooding, a pixel (x, y) passes its information to its (maximum) eight neighbors at $(x + i, y + j)$, where $i, j \in \{-1, 0, 1\}$. We call this a pass with a *step length* of 1. In the JFA we reduce the number of passes and change the step length in every pass. The number of passes is logarithmic to the resolution of the screen, and the step lengths of these passes are $2^{\lceil \lg n \rceil - 1}$, $2^{\lceil \lg n \rceil - 2}$, ..., 1. In a pass with a step length of k, a pixel (x, y) passes its information to the other (maximum) eight pixels at $(x + i, y + j)$, where $i, j \in \{-k, 0, k\}$. Figure 3.3.1b shows the process of the JFA in an 8×8 screen. The step lengths of the passes are 4, 2, and 1 respectively. After only three passes, we complete filling the whole screen.

The above discussion can be generalized to work on more than one seed. In such a case two or more pixels may pass their (possibly different) information to a particular pixel at the same time during the flooding process. This pixel must use a certain criterion to select the information from the "best" seed, and pass on this information in the subsequent passes. The choice of such a criterion depends on the application. We will show two applications of the JFA later.

Implementation of the JFA on GPUs

Owing to the limitations of current GPUs, we need to adapt the JFA to be implemented on GPUs. In particular, current GPUs do not allow *scatter* operations (Figure 3.3.2a), but do allow *gather* operations (Figure 3.3.2b). In other words, a fragment

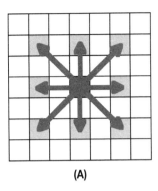 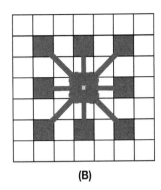

FIGURE 3.3.2   (**A**) The scatter operation and (**B**) the gather operation.

program executing on a certain pixel p can read from many other positions (pixels) but can only write information into the position of p. So when we want to pass the information from one pixel q to eight other pixels around it, we cannot run a fragment program on q to write the information to the eight pixels. Instead, we must reverse the process and run the fragment program on the eight pixels to read the information from q.

With the above understanding, the JFA can be implemented as follows. We use two textures of the same size as the screen. In every pass we read information from one texture (the read texture), perform the computation, and write the results into another texture (the write texture). Then we exchange the roles of these two textures in the next pass. Such a pair of textures is known as a *ping-pong buffer*. In the initialization step, the information from the seeds is written into the read texture for use by the first pass of the JFA.

In every pass of the JFA we draw a quad of the same size as the screen. Thus, we can trigger a fragment program on all the pixels. In the fragment program running on the pixel at (x, y), we read the information from the read texture using texture coordinates of $(x + i, y + j)$, where $i, j \in \{-k, 0, k\}$ and k is the current step length. Using the information, we perform the computation to find the best seed. Then we write the information from this best seed into the write texture.

To avoid calculating the eight texture coordinates on every pixel, we move the calculation into a vertex program. Thus, we do such a calculation only four times (on the four vertices of the quad). The results on these four vertices are correctly rasterized into all the pixels. Figure 3.3.3 shows the vertex program in Cg where we pack the eight texture coordinates into four `float4` variables.

Figure 3.3.4 shows the fragment program. This is a general prototype of the fragment program of the JFA where we include pseudo-codes written in italic. These pseudo-codes are to be replaced by the real codes according to the application, as explained next.

```
void main(float4 position        : POSITION,

          out float4 oPosition : POSITION,
          out float4 oCoord01  : TEXCOORD0,
          out float4 oCoord23  : TEXCOORD1,
          out float4 oCoord56  : TEXCOORD2,
          out float4 oCoord78  : TEXCOORD3,

          uniform float4x4 cameraModelViewProj,
          uniform int2     screenSize,
          uniform int      k)   // k is the current step length
{
    // Transform position from object space to clip space
    oPosition = mul(cameraModelViewProj, position);

    // map the position from [-1, 1]*[-1, 1] to
    // [0, screenWidth]*[0, screenHeight]
    float2 posRECT = (oPosition.xy+1.0)/2.0*screenSize;

    float4 pos4 = float4(posRECT, posRECT);
    oCoord01 = pos4 + float4(-k, -k, 0, -k);
    oCoord23 = pos4 + float4(k, -k, -k, 0);
    oCoord56 = pos4 + float4(k, 0, -k, k);
    oCoord78 = pos4 + float4(0, k, k, k);
}
```

FIGURE 3.3.3　Vertex program of the JFA.

```
void main(float4 position : WPOS,
          float4 Coord01  : TEXCOORD0,
          float4 Coord23  : TEXCOORD1,
          float4 Coord56  : TEXCOORD2,
          float4 Coord78  : TEXCOORD3,

          out float4 oColor : COLOR,

          uniform samplerRECT  readTex)
{
    SomeType Information;

    Information = tex2D(readTex, Coord01.xy);  // neighbor 0
    Compute a criterion value using Information;
    Information = tex2D(readTex, Coord01.zw);  // neighbor 1
    Compute a criterion value using Information;
    Information = tex2D(readTex, Coord23.xy);  // neighbor 2
    Compute a criterion value using Information;
    Information = tex2D(readTex, Coord23.zw);  // neighbor 3
    Compute a criterion value using Information;
    Information = tex2D(readTex, position.xy); // itself
    Compute a criterion value using Information;
    Information = tex2D(readTex, Coord56.xy);  // neighbor 5
    Compute a criterion value using Information;
    Information = tex2D(readTex, Coord56.zw);  // neighbor 6
    Compute a criterion value using Information;
    Information = tex2D(readTex, Coord78.xy);  // neighbor 7
    Compute a criterion value using Information;
    Information = tex2D(readTex, Coord78.zw);  // neighbor 8
    Compute a criterion value using Information;

    float4 bestInfo;
    Using the criterion values to select the "best" seed, and
        store its Information into bestInfo;

    oColor = bestInfo;
}
```

FIGURE 3.3.4　Fragment program of the JFA.

Applications

Voronoi Diagram and Distance Transform

A Voronoi diagram is a partition of a plane into *n* polygons, called *Voronoi cells*, according to *n* sites. The pixels in the *i*th Voronoi cell are not farther away from the *i*th site than from the other sites. The distance transform is an operation that takes the sites as input to compute a grayscale image. The value of every output pixel records the distance from itself to its nearest site. Figure 3.3.5a shows a Voronoi diagram of a set of 10 sites (the white dots), and Figure 3.3.5b shows the distance transform of the same set of 10 sites. The colors in Figure 3.3.5b represent the modulated distances. Brighter colors represent farther distances, and darker colors represent nearer distances. The Voronoi diagram has many applications in various areas (see [Aurenhammer91]). Distance transforms also have many applications in image processing, computer graphics, pattern recognition, and so on. See, for example, [Donnelly05] and [Qin06].

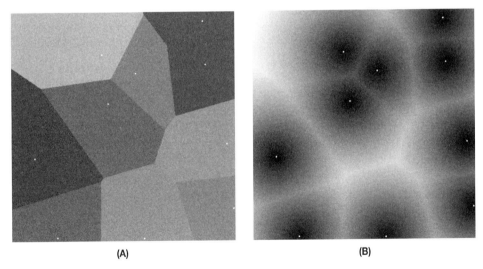

(A)   (B)

FIGURE 3.3.5 (A) Voronoi diagram and (B) distance transform of 10 sites.

Once we have the Voronoi diagram of a set of sites, it is straightforward to compute the corresponding distance transform. We only apply the JFA on the computation of Voronoi diagrams as follows. In the initialization step we write the coordinates of the sites into the read texture at the positions where they are located. In the fragment program of Figure 3.3.4 SomeType can be replaced by float2, and Information is just the coordinate of the site. The criterion value is the distance from the current pixel to the seed, and the seed with the nearest distance known so far is selected as the best seed. With these replacements, the fragment program can be used to compute Voronoi diagrams. The first step length of the JFA is set to half of the resolution of the screen, so that we can guarantee that the whole screen be filled after the last pass with a step length of 1. See Figure 3.3.6 for an example.

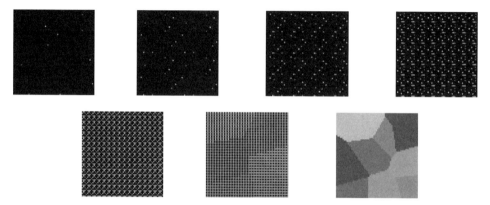

FIGURE 3.3.6   The process of the JFA computing the Voronoi diagram of 10 sites in a 64×64 screen. The leftmost picture shows the 10 sites, and the other six pictures show the results after the passes with step lengths of 32, 16, 8, 4, 2, and 1, respectively.

As shown in [Rong06], the JFA does not generate results identical to those of standard flooding. There may be some errors in the results of the JFA. (It is easy to prove that the results of standard flooding have no errors.) However, the error rate of the JFA is extremely low (see [Rong06]), and the computed Voronoi diagram remains useful for many applications.

Soft Shadows

In Eurographics 2004, Arvo et al. presented an algorithm using standard flooding to compute soft shadows [Arvo04]. The flooding part of their algorithm can be improved with the JFA as discussed in the following.

We first generate the hard shadows using the standard shadow-mapping technique. Then, in the initialization step of the JFA, we write the 3D coordinates of the occluders corresponding to the boundaries of the hard shadows into the read texture. In the fragment program of Figure 3.3.4, SomeType can be replaced by float3, and Information is the 3D coordinate of the occluder. Additionally, the criterion value is the intensity value computed using the occluders' information and the coordinate of the current pixel (see [Arvo04]). Then the seed that generates the maximum (or the minimum) intensity value is selected as the best seed when the current pixel is inside (or outside) a hard shadow. With these replacements, the fragment program can be used to compute soft shadows. Note that we do not need to start the JFA with a large step length here. For example, starting with a step length of 32 can generate penumbra regions with widths as large as 63 pixels, which is good enough for most applications. See Figure 3.3.7 for an example.

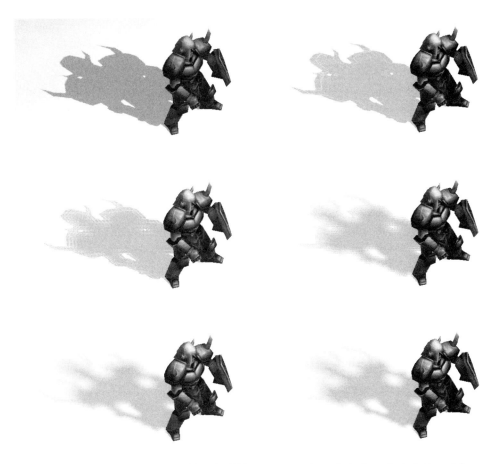

FIGURE 3.3.7   The process of applying the JFA to compute the soft shadow of a knight model (available at *http://www.fileplanet.com/*). The six pictures (left to right, top to bottom) show the results after the passes with step lengths of 32, 16, 8, 4, 2, and 1, respectively.

Conclusion

In this chapter, we introduce the jump flooding algorithm (JFA) as an efficient and effective communication pattern for use on GPUs. The implementation details of the vertex program and the fragment program are provided. We also present two applications of the JFA. The JFA may have other interesting applications. For further updates on the JFA, refer to *http://www.comp.nus.edu.sg/~tants/jfa.html*.

References

[Arvo04] Arvo, J., M. Hirvikorpi, and J. Tyystjärvi. "Approximate Soft Shadows Using Image-Space Flood-Fill Algorithm." *Computer Graphics Forum 23*(3) (2004): pp. 271–280 (Proceedings of Eurographics 2004).

[Aurenhammer91] Aurenhammer, F. "Voronoi Diagrams: A Survey of a Fundamental Geometric Data Structure." *ACM Computing Surveys 23*(3) (1991): pp. 345–405.

[Donnelly05] Donnelly, W. "Per-Pixel Displacement Mapping with Distance Functions." *GPU Gems 2: Programming Techniques for High Performance Graphics and General-Purpose Computation*, edited by M. Pharr and R. Fernando. Addison-Wesley, 2005: pp. 123–136.

[Owens05] Owens, J., D. Luebke, N. Govindaraju, M. Harris, J. Krüger, A. Lefohn, and T. Purcell. "A Survey of General-Purpose Computation on Graphics Hardware." *Eurographics* (2005): pp. 21–51. (State of the Art Reports).

[Qin06] Qin, Z., M. McCool, and C. Kaplan. "Real-time Texture-Mapped Vector Glyphs." *Proceedings of the Symposium on Interactive 3D Graphics and Games*. ACM Press, 2006: pp. 125–132.

[Rong06] Rong, G. and T.-S. Tan. "Jump Flooding in GPU with Applications to Voronoi Diagram and Distance Transform." *Proceedings of the Symposium on Interactive 3D Graphics and Games*, ACM Press, 2006: pp. 109–116.

SHADOWS

Introduction

Tom Forsyth

Creating shadows at interactive rates continues to be an active area of exploration. This section offers a few new tools for improving how shadows are generated and displayed.

The first article, "Cascaded Shadow Maps," by Wolfgang Engel, covers how the resolution of several shadow maps can be distributed along the view frustum by slicing the view frustum parallel to the near and far clipping plane into several pieces and applying a shadow map to each of those pieces. Additionally, it presents how to use those shadow maps in a cache-friendly way.

Christian Schüler presents in his article, "Multisampling Extension for Gradient Shadow Maps," an extension to gradient shadow maps, a technique he already covered in *ShaderX⁴*. Gradient shadow maps are a set of techniques to reduce *surface acne*—false shadowed spots on surfaces, mostly at grazing angles in shadow mapping. This article is dedicated to bringing multisampling to gradient shadow maps.

The article "Alias-Free Hard Shadows with Geometry Maps," by László Szécsi, presents an approach that uses, instead of depth values, a better-sampled representation with the help of geometry maps. This way they achieve a better representation of the geometry intersected by the ray connecting the light source and the center of the lexel. Additionally, they use a better mechanism to query, instead of depth comparisons.

John R. Isidoro explains two methods of edge filtering and propagating the edge and depth information to encompass the boundary region that requires more processing in his article "Edge Masking and Per-Texel Depth Extent Propagation For Computation Culling During Shadow Mapping." The first generates a mipchain for the shadow map edge mask and simply fetches from a lower miplevel to effectively dilate the edge mask. The second propagates the min and max of the depth extent of the shadow map texels to generate subsequent levels of a depth extent mipchain.

The article "Queried Virtual Shadow Maps" by Markus Giegl and Michael Wimmer presents a new real-time shadow mapping algorithm capable of shadowing large scenes by *virtually* increasing the resolution of the shadow map beyond the GPU hardware limit. They achieve this by partitioning the shadow map into tiles.

László Szirmay-Kalos and Barnabás Aszódi present in their article "Real-time Soft Shadows with Shadow Accumulation" a way to store visibility information from the shaded point. By knowing the portion of the light source occluded from the shaded point, they can accumulate shadow data for each lexel.

4.1

Cascaded Shadow Maps

Wolfgang Engel, Rockstar, San Diego

Cascaded shadow maps are useful in a large outdoor environment, where shadows should be visible across huge distances and where changing lighting conditions such as different times of day require dynamic shadows over the whole scene.

Background

Cascaded shadow maps were first mentioned by John Carmack in his QuakeCon 2004 speech. They are utilized in 3DMark06 [3DMark06], and it seems like they are also used in several upcoming games.

The main idea of cascaded shadow maps is to slice the view frustum into multiple slices (usually three to six) and write shadow data for each of these slices into a dedicated shadow map. Figure 4.1.1 shows a view frustum sliced into four pieces.

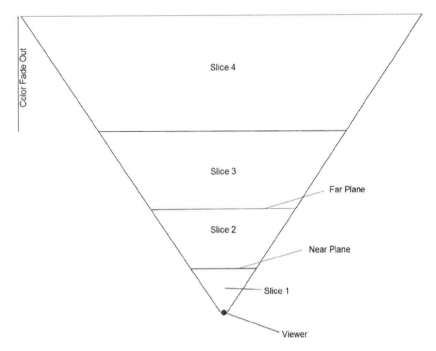

FIGURE 4.1.1 Cascaded shadow maps: sliced view frustum.

The distance between the far plane of each view frustum slice and the far plane of the previous view frustum slice is usually doubled or tripled each time. For example, the first map might go out to 10 meters, the second map up to 30 meters, the third map up to 90 meters, and the fourth map up to 270 meters or more. The exact values depend on the world units, shadow map resolution, and image quality settings. The advantages of using cascaded shadow maps are:

- Large shadow distance
- Scalability
- Reduced dueling frusta problems
- Robustness

Large Shadow Distance

It is possible to cover very large distances with just four or five shadow maps. Because each slice covers a depth range proportional to its distance from the viewer, texels are distributed to give a consistent texel-to-screen pixel ratio. Each additional shadow map triples the distance of the furthest shadows, so relatively few are required to cover a huge view distance.

Scalability

Cascaded shadow maps scale with hardware capabilities very well. Based on the required shadow map distance, the number of view frustum slices/shadow maps can be increased or decreased per level. Additionally, the near and far plane of each slice's frustum, which represents a frustum, can be adjusted during game play. The near and far plane can be moved in for cut scenes or if the viewer approaches a building or an object that is nearer than the first or second shadow map far plane.

The near and far planes can be moved outward if it is not necessary to have sharp shadows close to the viewer. This might be the case in a racing game that uses a tunnel motion blur at speed. Because the tunnel motion blur softens near shadows, shadow map resolution can be dedicated to objects that are farther away than the motion blur effect, and the application can dynamically adjust the shadow resolution along the view frustum or use other algorithms to do so [Zhang].

Dueling Frusta

If the light view frustum is facing the light source, stretched shadow map texels often become visible. This is called *dueling frusta*. Cascaded shadows have numerous texels distributed along the view frustum. In other words the texel-to-pixel ratio decreases more slowly over the view distance, and the cascaded shadows do not suffer as much from this problem as shadow map approaches with a lower number of texels.

Robustness

All the approaches that warp shadows, such as in [Kozlow] and [Wimmer], show huge quality differences between best and worst cases. This quality change can even happen very abruptly. The uniform transformation used for cascaded shadow maps offers a well-balanced quality without noticeable worst-case scenarios.

Implementation

Cascaded shadow maps are mostly like any common shadow map implementation as covered in many introductory texts on shadow maps [Engel]. The major difference is the challenge of dynamically generating efficient light view frusta that capture the view frustum the player sees. Additionally, this chapter will introduce a way to use several large shadow maps in a hardware-cache friendly way and discuss the cascaded-shadow-map-specific challenges for common shadow map problems such as surface acne, soft penumbra, and shadow caster culling.

Constructing a Light View Frustum

Cascaded shadow maps provide a shadow solution for outdoor environments with a visible change in time of day. They partition a scene with several light view frusta and follow the principle of shadow buffer frustum partitioning as described in [Forsyth]. The main improvement is to provide a near-optimal partitioning for large complex scenes and a distant light source with far less computation.

To construct all the light view frusta, the viewer's frustum is first sliced into several pieces. Each of these slices represents a piece of the viewer frustum but at the same time is itself a frustum. To construct such a frustum, the same methods are applicable as for any frustum construction.

Figure 4.1.2 shows a frustum that covers the third slice of the viewer's frustum. It has a near and a far plane that are parallel to the near and far plane of the viewer's frustum and are scaled with a sensitive value to catch shadow casters that are outside of the viewer's frustum on the left and right side of the viewer and a small overlap with the previous slice to simplify the transition phase between the two.

Each of the frusta is then transformed into light space, and the extrema points in light space are used to construct a bounding box. This bounding box represents the orthographic frustum. Figures 4.1.3 and 4.1.4 show how the extrema points of these view frusta are used to create a light view frustum in light space.

The extrema points will be the same from four light directions, because without the y axis, the 2D view should look the same.

Figures 4.1.3 and 4.1.4 also show how using multiple shadow maps focuses on the viewer's frustum more closely than a single one and therefore uses the available texture memory more efficiently. This effect increases with the number of shadow maps used.

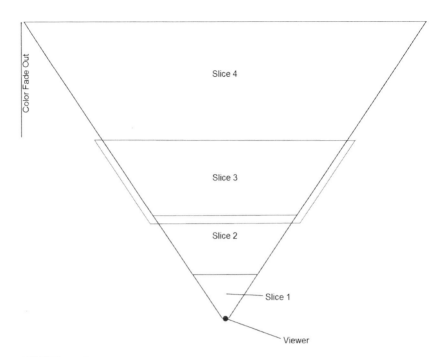

FIGURE 4.1.2   View frustum slice.

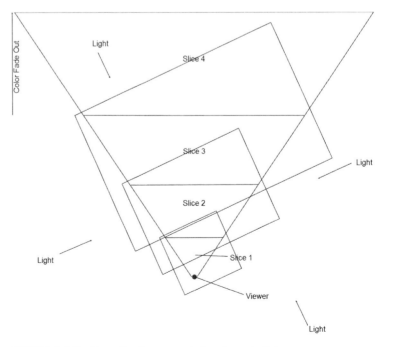

FIGURE 4.1.3   Bounding box around view frusta in light space.

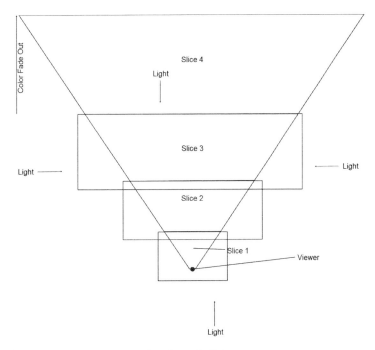

FIGURE 4.1.4 Bounding box around view frusta in light space.

ON THE CD

The code snippet in Listing 1 of the file CascadedShadowMaps.txt on the CD-ROM shows how to construct the frustum for each slice, how it is transformed into light space, and how the view and projection matrices are set up.

Shadow Prepass

Using several large shadow maps can substantially reduce the performance of a game. One reason for this might be that the GPU cannot efficiently cache several large shadow maps being fetched in a random pattern. Shadow map texels are significantly larger than those in most standard texture formats and cannot be compressed well, if at all. If also reading diffuse, normal, and other standard texture maps, the GPU texture cache is often too small to work effectively.

To relieve this problem, the solution proposed here renders all shadow-map-related data in a preprocess (also called deferred shadowing). Like all other shadow map approaches, a light-space pass is done by drawing the depth values from the point of view of the light source into the shadow maps. Depending on the underlying hardware platform, this might be a depth-buffer-only write. The scene is then rendered from the camera's point of view, calculating whether each pixel is in shadow or not, using the shadow maps and writing out the resulting shadow factor into a screen-sized texture. Finally, the scene is rendered again using this texture along with the diffuse, specular, and normal textures performing full lighting.

While the light-space pass renders each of the shadow maps into a simple and fast texture atlas, the subsequent pass sets this atlas once and renders all objects from the viewer's perspective. To pick the right shadow map from the texture atlas, multiple light projection matrices are set, incorporating the correct offsets to address one of the shadows.

 A common trick to make shadow maps more cache friendly is to mipmap them. This might be a good option on certain hardware platforms if there are only a small number of shadow maps. Generating mipmaps for a large number of shadow maps can become expensive.

The shadowing screen-space pass is fast, because it uses small pixel shaders that only do the depth comparison and calculate a shadow fade-out value based on camera distance. Additionally, only one texture is set in these pixel shaders for all objects drawn, allowing the entire GPU texture cache to be used for shadow maps.

With an upper limit of four shadow maps, we can use a conditional instruction in the pixel or vertex shader on a variable that keeps the distance of the four shadow maps in each of its channels to choose between the four light matrices without having to use any branches. The code snippet in Listing 2 of the file CascadedShadowMaps.txt on the CD-ROM shows a pixel shader that can be used with four shadow maps and provides a fade-out for the last map. The source snippet with the conditional that picks the right shadow map looks like this:

```
// start distance of 4 shadow maps
float4  zGreater = (StartShadows < camDistance);
float   mapToUse = dot(zGreater, 1.0f );

// Get pixel depth from the point of view from the light camera
float4 pos = mul(float4(WorldSpace.xyz, 1.0f),
LightMatrixArr[mapToUse - 1]);
```

One disadvantage of a shadow prepass is that tweaking the texture coordinates of shadow map fetches while rendering into the frame buffer is not possible. Thus, shadows that follow a parallax map are not as easily achieved as with the common approach.

Surface Acne

Maybe the biggest challenge with any shadow map approach is *depth aliasing* or *surface acne*. Sampling depth values happens in a stair-stepped manner because of the nature of sampling [Schueler][Schueler2] as shown in Figure 4.1.5.

Because the continuous surface of a polygon is compared to the sampled surfaces, a random point of the polygon might be behind the sample surface, and therefore a false shadow is applied. This effect is emphasized on curved surfaces.

Increasing the shadow resolution along the view frustum makes depth-aliasing artifacts look smaller, owing to the higher sampling density, but it does not remove them.

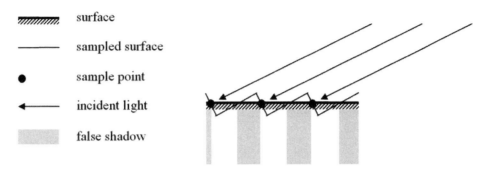

FIGURE 4.1.5 Surface acne. (Courtesy of Christian Schueler.)

 In the case of the popular perspective shadow map approaches, depth-aliasing arti-facts might be emphasized owing to the perspective distortion, because some parts of the scene will receive less shadow resolution than others.

This leaves us with the common ways to fight surface acne. If the shadow data are rendered into depth buffers, all decent hardware offers two render states that are called depth-slope scale bias and depth bias. In Direct3D they are called `D3DRS_DEPTHBIAS` and `D3DRS_SLOPESCALEDEPTHBIAS`, and in OpenGL there is a function called `glPolygon Offset()`. Both approaches use the following formula to decrease depth aliasing.

```
m * D3DRS_SLOPESCALEDEPTHBIAS + D3DRS_DEPTHBIAS
```

where $m = \max(\, | \, \partial z/\partial x \, | \, , \, | \, \partial z/\partial y \, | \,)$.

This offset is added before the depth test and before depth values are written into the depth buffer, so it only works with the depth buffer.

 Kozlow shows how to calculate a depth bias value in world space based on light direction and pixel size [Kozlow].

In case these render states are not available or if the scene still shows too much depth aliasing, an approach called gradient shadow maps can be utilized [Schueler][Schueler2]. Instead of using a constant depth-bias value, Schueler scales the depth-bias value with a gradient value and adds a small constant on top of the gradient scaled bias to account for cases in which the gradient becomes zero and clamps this value at grazing angles. This clamping is chosen similarly to the depth bias value to fit the whole scene.

For a shadow map approach that offers support for shadows at large distances, any form of constant bias value will be valid only for certain distances but not for all. Setting those values separately for each of the cascaded shadow maps offers a better level of control over distance.

Soft Penumbra

The penumbra of a shadow is in real-life quite often softer with increasing distance between the shadow caster and the shadow receiver. This is due to global illumination effects affecting the shadow. In computer games the shadows are commonly softened by using a technique called percentage closer filtering (PCF) [Reeves]. This technique averages the binary result from, for example, a 3×3 block of texels as shown in Figure 4.1.6.

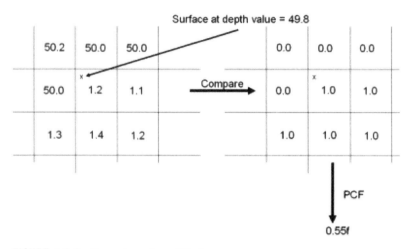

FIGURE 4.1.6   Percentage closer filtering.

Cascaded shadow maps, like any shadow map approach that tries to distribute the shadow map resolution evenly along the view frustum, need at least a visible shadow shape on distant objects that is perceived as a believable shadow. Large filter kernels with a fixed size and based on PCF or even more advanced filters based on a Poisson disk distribution of sampling points [Mitchell] might influence or destroy the shadow shape on distant objects owing to the low density of shadow samples. There are several strategies to cope with this problem. Using just a simple four-tap PCF filter on all shadow maps works very well in practice. Using an adjustable filter kernel over the whole distance should show better results but increase the cost.

Culling Shadow Casters and Other Objects

The number of objects that get rendered into one or more shadow maps is an index of the performance of any shadow map approach. Assuming a shadow map approach with a large shadow distance, the light view frusta for each of the shadow maps may cover many more objects than are visible to the viewer. Additionally, there will be shadow casters that are not visible but cast shadows into the scene and should therefore be considered by the shadow map. Therefore, in most cases more objects will be rendered into the shadow maps than into the frame-buffer. A culling system that culls away objects efficiently for each of the shadow map light frusta is therefore essential (see [Picco] for a good overview of low-level culling mechanisms).

A good approach is to use a dynamic system that is based on an octree as a hierarchy culling method. Breaking down the world into a tree-like structure offers the ability to cull a top level node without culling lower level nodes since they cannot be visible anyway. On a lower level a sphere that surrounds the light frustum can be culled against the bounding sphere of the objects, maybe followed by the cone that surrounds the light frustum culled against the bounding sphere of objects, and then maybe the frustum itself can be culled against the bounding sphere.

An even more efficient approach might use the fact that the position of the sun is known through the time of the day to precalculate visibility. If the viewer always stays on the ground, this would open up even more opportunities to precalculate the visibility of objects.

A good culling system might even determine how many shadow maps need to be used and prevent rendering into shadow maps that would store object shadows that are not visible.

Further Considerations

A shadow prepass can be considered as a Z-prepass or even a first stage of a preprocessing pipeline that is used to achieve different depth buffer effects. Seeing the shadow prepass in the wider perspective of the preprocessing pipeline amortizes some of its cost.

Any perspective [Wimmer] or warped shadow map approach can be cascaded as long as it is stable enough to cover a full time-of-day circle with an acceptable level of depth aliasing. Interesting future approaches that utilize the cascaded shadow map idea are based on a logarithmic distribution of shadow map resolution [Lloyd].

Conclusion

This article covers a proven approach to cascade shadows around the viewer frustum with a simple uniform distribution of shadow map resolution. The main advantage of this approach is that it is very generic compared to other shadow map approaches that offer shadows at large viewing distances. The distribution of quality is quite even, and there are no obvious worst-case scenarios. Additionally, the scalability makes cascaded shadow maps a perfect solution for different scenarios in a game. Adding key-frame support to the parameters that control the view frustum construction allows the game to distribute shadow quality based on the viewer being in a certain area or the existence of occluding objects. Paired with a capable occlusion culling system, the performance will scale well with the view distance and the quality of the shadows.

Acknowledgments

I thank Tom Forsyth and Stefan Krause for reviewing the article and John Carmack for inspiring the technique. I am thankful to Alan Wasserman, Steve Reed, Derek Tarvin, David Etherton, and Eugene Foss for allowing me to write this article. A big thank you goes out to Ron O'Hara for help with the view frustum code. Additionally, I thank Mark Robinson, Raymund Kerr, Ben Padget, Christina Coffin, Alexander Ehrath, and Michael Krehan for discussing with me many aspects of the featured method and widening my view to see the various aspects of the approach.

References

[3DMark06] Futuremark Corporation. "3DMark06 Whitepaper v1.0.2." Available online at *http://www.futuremark.com/companyinfo/pressroom/companypdfs/3DMark06_Whitepaper_v1_0_2.pdf?m=v.*

[Engel] Engel, Wolfgang. *Programming Vertex and Pixel Shaders.* Charles River Media, 2004: pp. 287–301

[Forsyth] Forsyth, Tom. "Shadowbuffer Frustum Partitioning." *ShaderX⁴*, edited by Wolfgang Engel. Charles River Media, 2006: pp. 289–297.

[Kozlow] Kozlow, Simon. "Perspective Shadow Maps: Care and Feeding." *GPU Gems.* Addison-Wesley, 2004: pp. 217–244.

[Lloyd] Lloyd, Brandon, David Tuft, Sung-Eui Yoon, and Dinesh Manocha. "Warping and Partitioning for Low Error Shadow Maps." Available online at *http://gamma.cs.unc.edu/wnp/.*

[Mitchell] Mitchell, Jason. "Poisson Shadow Blur." *Shader X³*, edited by Wolfgang Engel. Charles River Media, 2005: pp. 403–409.

[Picco] Picco, Dion. "Frustum Culling." Available online at *http://www.flipcode.com/articles/article_frustumculling.shtml*

[Schueler] Schueler, Christian. "Eliminating Surface Acne with Gradient Shadow Maps." *ShaderX⁴*, edited by Wolfgang Engel. Charles River Media, 2006: pp. 15–23

[Schueler2] Schueler, Christian. "Multisampling Extension for Gradient Shadow Maps." *ShaderX⁵*, edited by Wolfgang Engel. Charles River Media, 2007: pp. 207–218.

[Reeves] Reeves, William, David Salesin, and Robert Cook. "Rendering Antialiased Shadows with Depth Maps." *SIGGRAPH 1987*, pp. 283–291.

[Williams] Williams, Lance. "Casting Curved Shadows on Curved Surfaces." *Computer Graphics, 23*(3) (1978): pp. 270–274.

[Wimmer] Wimmer, Michael and Daniel Scherzer. "Robust Shadow Mapping with Light-Space Perspective Shadow Maps." *ShaderX⁴*, edited by Wolfgang Engel. Charles River Media, 2006: pp. 313–330.

[Zhang] Zhang, Fan, Hanqiu Sun, Leilei Xu, and Lee Kit Lun. "Parallel-Split Shadow Maps for Large-scale Virtual Environments." Available online at *http://appsrv.cse.cuhk.edu.hk/~fzhang/pssm_vrcia/.*

4.2

Multisampling Extension for Gradient Shadow Maps

Christian Schüler, Phenomic

Introduction

ShaderX⁴ included the article "Gradient Shadow Maps" [Schueler05], describing a set of techniques to reduce *surface acne*—false shadowed spots on surfaces, mostly at grazing angles in shadow mapping and often incorrectly attributed to a precision problem. The scope of the original article didn't include multisampling, which is often used in shadow mapping to approximate *percentage closer filtering* (PCF), which gives a smoother look to shadow edges. In hindsight this was a significant omission, as the integration of the two techniques is sufficiently not obvious. Therefore, this article is dedicated to bringing multisampling to gradient shadow maps.

Overview of Gradient Shadow Maps

We assume the canonical shadow map algorithm, which renders a depth map from the light's perspective in a first pass and does a comparison against this depth map in a second pass to determine whether a fragment is lit or in shadow [Williams78] and recent overviews in [Moeller02] and [McReynolds05]. In this context, we use *depth* as a measure for the distance from the light source. A pixel shader function to compute the light visibility during the second pass could look like this:

```
float lightVisibility( float3 lightCoord )
{
    return lightCoord.z < tex2D( depthMap, lightCoord.xy ).x;
}
```

ON THE CD

Here, `lightCoord` contains the interpolated light space coordinate for the rendered fragment. Without loss of generality, we assume that the light space is affine and omit cluttering up the code with division by *w* (the full shader code on the CD-ROM of course contains this division). The function returns 1 when the fragment is lit and 0 when it is in shadow.

We observe that this naïve implementation casts false shadows onto half of the rendered surface. See Figure 4.2.1 for an illustration and explanation of why this effect is not a resolution or precision problem.

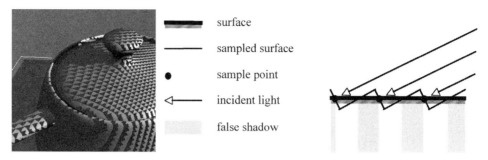

FIGURE 4.2.1   The imperfect reconstruction of the shadow-casting surface gives rise to self-shadowing artifacts.

The well-known remedy for this artifact is to add a small bias value large enough to push the reconstructed surface underneath the reference surface, so we hope no comparisons can fail. However, too much of a bias produces the opposite artifact, called *light bleeding*, at the back face of an occluder. Everyone who has implemented shadow maps will probably remember tweaking the bias value back and forth, alternating between the frying pan and the fire.

Gradient shadow maps address this issue with a combination of three measures that turn out to be mutually beneficial. A central element is the *depth gradient*, which measures the steepness of the surface as seen from the light or mathematically as a vector

$$\nabla z = \left(\frac{\partial z}{\partial x}, \frac{\partial z}{\partial y} \right)$$

with x, y, and z in light view coordinates, z being the depth. This gradient can either be generated from derivative instructions in the first pass and stored with the depth map or estimated from local differences when reading the depth map in the second pass (it may even be calculated from derivative instructions in the second pass if you're willing to solve a set of linear equations). With either method of obtaining a gradient in place, the three improvements are:

Slope-scale depth bias: The bias should be scaled in proportion to the local gradient. This alone can be a potent remedy to some of the nastiest surface acne problems, and it is directly supported for hardware depth maps via the polygon offset feature.

Fuzzy depth comparison: The hard-edged depth comparison (the "less than" operation) should be replaced with a smoother function so that a small numerical error will produce only a small visual error. The range within which the light is attenuated (the fuzzy region) should be proportional to the local gradient.

Linearly filtered depth values: Depth maps are traditionally point sampled. The discontinuous nature of the reconstruction from point sampling is disadvantageous. For instance, if the shadow-casting surface is planar, a bilinear filter over the depth map can reconstruct the original surface perfectly. Further analysis shows that bilinear filtering of the depth map is in no way harmful, even when the underlying surface is not planar. This allows more aggressive reduction of the bias.

The combination of all three measures results in a fuzzy band close underneath the reconstructed surface within which the light visibility gradually falls to zero, allowing for much improved shadow mapping, as shown in Figure 4.2.2. The pseudo code for an improved visibility function might look like this (for the sake of clarity, the code does not consider depth bias):

```
float lightVisibility_GSM( float3 lightCoord )
{
        // get the magnitude of the gradient, by either method
        float gradient = length( getGradientVector( lightCoord ) );
        // get the difference between stored and interpolated depth
        // (depthMap should have LINEAR filtering enabled)
        float diff = tex2D( depthMap, lightCoord.xy ).x -
        lightCoord.z;
        // replace the less-than operator with a smooth function
        // for diff >= 0 the result is 1
        return saturate( diff / gradient + 1 );
}
```

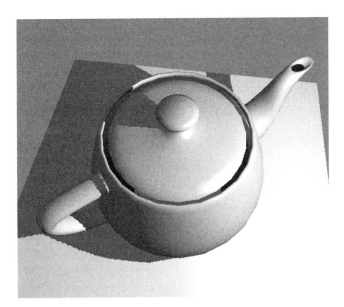

FIGURE 4.2.2   Artifact-free shadow mapping with a just a tiny amount of depth bias needed.

Multisampling and Percentage Closer Filtering

If we consider a given area on the depth map, the term *percentage closer filtering* refers to estimating the fraction of that area that is closer to the light than a given reference depth [Reeves87]. This can be implemented either as an integral over an implied continuous function (which is what bilinear PCF in hardware effectively reduces to) or as a discrete sum over a set of individual samples. In the latter case it is simply the number of depth comparisons that succeed. A visibility function that implements PCF via direct summation may look like this:

```
float lightVisibility_PCF( float3 lightCoord )
{
    float result = 0;
    for( int i = 0; i < n; ++i )
    {
        float3 offCoord = lightCoord + offset[i];
        result += lightCoord.z < tex2D( depthMap, lightCoord.xy ).x;
    }
    return result / n;
}
```

Here, the number of samples taken is n, the light space coordinate is displaced by some offset[] before texture lookup takes place, and the results are averaged. PCF improves shadow mapping by making shadow edges appear less jagged and aliased.

As can be seen from the code above, it would make perfect sense to substitute the less-than operator for any other visibility function, with possible outcomes between 0 and 1. In this case the PCF algorithm is no longer counting a closer-than relation. Instead it accumulates an average visibility, so it really should be called along the lines of *average visibility filtering*. For this article we will stick with the term *PCF*.

Merging the Algorithms

As outlined above, PCF can be seen as an average of light visibility, so it is natural to construct an algorithm that averages the results of our GSM visibility function:

```
float lightVisibility_PCF_with_GSM( float3 lightCoord )
{
    float result = 0;
    for( int i = 0; i < n; ++i )
        result += lightVisibility_GSM( lightCoord + offset[i] );
    return result / n;
}
```

Much to our dismay, the result of a simple code substitution is not what we were expecting. Instead of smoothed shadow edges, it looks like surfaces are now covered with a dark layer that approximately halves the light intensity (see Figure 4.2.3).

FIGURE 4.2.3 Reduced light intensity from PCF disk intersection with the shadow volume.

Further analysis shows what has gone wrong. As in traditional PCF, the offset added to the interpolated light space coordinate only affects texture coordinates x and y, not the depth. In this case a constant depth is tested against samples from different locations. Without a sufficient depth bias, the PCF area will eventually intersect the shadow volume (see Figure 4.2.4a). Since the depth biases used with GSM are very small, the PCF almost always intersects the shadow volume, and the average light intensity is reduced. This is the cause of the visual disruption seen in Figure 4.2.3.

A correction is needed. When offsetting the x and y coordinates, we must also offset the depth coordinate z to follow the local depth gradient and prevent intersection with the shadow boundary, as shown in Figure 4.2.4b. This is effectively following a plane that extends from the local surface. A modified PCF framework therefore needs to make the offset known to the visibility function, so that the visibility function can make the necessary adjustments. The offset will become the second parameter to the visibility function:

```
float lightVisibility_PCF_modified( float3 lightCoord )
{
    float result = 0;
    for( int i = 0; i < n; ++i )
        // forward the offset into the visibility function
        result += lightVisibility_GSM_modified( lightCoord,
        offset[i] );
    return result / n;
}
```

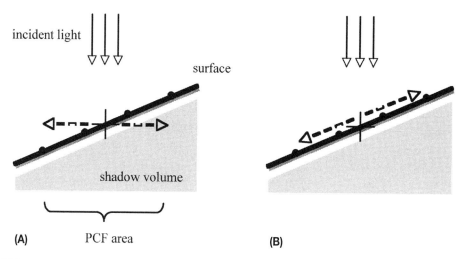

FIGURE 4.2.4   Uncorrected (**A**) and slope-corrected (**B**) offset lookup for PCF. The crosshair indicates the position of the fragment being rendered.

A modified visibility function will use the offset to adjust the depth z. The gradient vector points in the direction of increasing depth, while the magnitude of the gradient vector is the slope. Therefore, a simple dot product between the offset vector and the gradient vector will give the desired z offset:

```
float lightVisibility_GSM_modified( float3 lightCoord, float2
offset )
{
    // get the gradient, by either method
    float2 gradientVector = getGradientVector( lightCoord );
    float gradient = length( gradientVector );

    // calculate an offset coordinate
    // the z coordinate is moved along with the local gradient
    // (this is equivalent to having a local plane equation)
    float3 offCoord = float3(
        lightCoord.xy + offset,
        lightCoord.z + dot( offset, gradientVector ) );

    // the rest is straightforward
    float diff = offCoord.z - tex2D( depthMap, offCoord.xy ).x;
    return saturate( diff / gradient + 1 );
}
```

Finally, we need an analysis of what happens when the modified PCF algorithm encounters a concave surface. As shown in Figure 4.2.5a, the entire PCF area is underneath the concave surface, and the outer regions of the PCF area touch the shadow volume, causing self-shadowing artifacts. Whether the PCF area reaches into the shadow volume or not depends on the curvature of the surface and the bias and range of the shadow boundary, but since the surface is no longer planar, it is clear that a simple linear extension of the PCF area is insufficient. There is no upper limit on the curvature of a concave surface, so any amount of biasing might eventually fail. In practice, this effect results in dark contours at concave polygon intersections, which can be seen as rings around the neck of the knob in Figure 4.2.5b. The obvious improvement is to consider higher-order derivatives to better approximate the local curvature. Another possible improvement is to use the average gradient of the entire PCF area, rather than the gradient at the queried point. As shown in Figure 4.2.5, using the average gradient results in less severe intersections with the shadow volume than if the PCF area followed the gradient of the point where the crosshair is.

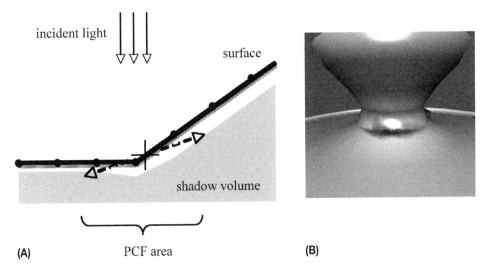

(A) **(B)**

FIGURE 4.2.5 Schematic (**A**) and example (**B**) of PCF look-up at a concave intersection. The crosshair indicates the position of the fragment being rendered.

Optimizing Texture Look-ups

All code samples so far have been presented with clarity in mind, not performance. There is much redundancy and opportunity for optimization. If we do not store the gradient vector with the depth map, but only the scalar depth, then we need to perform at least three texture look-ups to compute the gradient vector. Add one texture look-up for the depth sample itself, and we have four look-ups per PCF iteration. Texture look-ups are an expensive resource and should be used more economically.

Since we would like an average gradient over of the entire PCF area, it is possible to use the depth samples to calculate it. What we're trying to do is to estimate a plane equation from a cloud of point samples. The canonical tool for this task is a *linear regression* to find a least squares approximation. We're not going to do a full regression in our shader code, but the theoretical foundation serves us to understand the shortcuts we're going to take. Consider the following closed-form solution for a two-dimensional regression centered around zero, where Δx_i and Δy_i are components of offset vectors $\Delta \mathbf{p}_i$ while Δz_i is depth differences along corresponding offset vectors:

$$\begin{bmatrix} \partial z/\partial x \\ \partial z/\partial y \end{bmatrix} = \begin{bmatrix} \sum \Delta x_i^2 & \sum \Delta x_i \Delta y_i \\ \sum \Delta x_i \Delta y_i & \sum \Delta y_i^2 \end{bmatrix}^{-1} \begin{bmatrix} \sum \Delta z_i \Delta x_i \\ \sum \Delta z_i \Delta y_i \end{bmatrix}$$

$$\downarrow$$

$$\nabla z = \left(\sum \Delta \mathbf{p}_i \Delta \mathbf{p}_i^T \right)^{-1} \sum \Delta z_i \Delta \mathbf{p}_i.$$

The column vector on the left is the estimate for the gradient vector. The matrix in the middle is the *covariance matrix*. The column vector on the right contains the offset vectors weighted by their corresponding depth difference. Observe that the covariance matrix can be diagonalized if the off-diagonal terms $\sum \Delta x_i \Delta y_i$ vanish. This is the case, for instance, if all offset vectors are either horizontal or vertical or if the point cloud is circular symmetric. The inverse of a diagonal matrix is then a diagonal matrix with inverted elements, and the equation becomes

$$\begin{bmatrix} \partial z/\partial x \\ \partial z/\partial y \end{bmatrix} = \begin{bmatrix} \sum \Delta z_i \Delta x_i / \sum \Delta x_i^2 \\ \sum \Delta z_i \Delta y_i / \sum \Delta y_i^2 \end{bmatrix}.$$

Figure 4.2.6a shows an example of eight PCF samples arranged in a circular pattern where we can use the simplified regression formula. The arrows in the diagram indicate suitable paths for differentiation; these are our Δx_i and Δy_i (they need not be rooted at the center). To efficiently compute an average gradient vector according to this scheme, the loop of the PCF function is unrolled and differences are assigned to components of the gradient vector:

```
float lightVisibility_unrolled_circular8( float3 lightCoord )
{       const float displace = .5 / depthMapResolution;
    const float displaceLong = 1.41421 * displace;
    float depths[8] = {
        tex2D( depthMap, lightCoord.xy + float2( -displaceLong,
        0 ) ).x,
        tex2D( depthMap, lightCoord.xy + float2( displaceLong,
        0 ) ).x,
        tex2D( depthMap, lightCoord.xy + float2( 0,
        -displaceLong ) ).x,
        tex2D( depthMap, lightCoord.xy + float2( 0,
        displaceLong ) ).x,
        tex2D( depthMap, lightCoord.xy + float2( -displace,
        -displace ) ).x,
        tex2D( depthMap, lightCoord.xy + float2( displace,
        -displace ) ).x,
        tex2D( depthMap, lightCoord.xy + float2( -displace,
        displace ) ).x,
```

```
            tex2D( depthMap, lightCoord.xy + float2( displace,
            displace ) ).x
    };
    const float inverseCovariance = 1. / ( 1 + 1 + 2 );
    float2 gradientVector = float2(
            depths[1] * 1.41421 + depths[5] + depths[7]
          - depths[0] * 1.41421 - depths[4] - depths[6],
            depths[3] * 1.41421 + depths[6] + depths[7]
          - depths[2] * 1.41421 - depths[4] - depths[5] ) *
            inverseCovariance;

    // continue with summation over PCF samples using the
    // average gradient
}
```

Basically, each sample contributes to each component of the gradient vector based on the sign of the corresponding component in the offset, while the squares of the path lengths are collated into a single renormalizing factor. Observe that no additional texture lookups are needed besides the ones already used for the PCF samples, unlike the previous case if we had stored the gradients into the depth map.

If the PCF pattern is irregular, for instance, if the sample locations constitute a Poisson disk, it would be possible to precompute the inverse of a covariance matrix. The most straightforward solution to calculate a regression is then to sum the products of all or some of the depths with their corresponding offset vectors and multiply the result with the precomputed covariance matrix. If the PCF pattern is sufficiently circular, the covariance matrix may even turn out to be close to diagonal, reducing it to a scale factor. An alternative method is sort of a hack: to use the simplified regression formula in this case while staying approximately accurate, select some difference paths in the point cloud that already are almost horizontal or vertical and then weight them so that their vector sum becomes aligned. For instance, to compute the x-component gradient vector from a large irregular PCF pattern, select a number of difference paths already approximately horizontal and weight them such that their y-component vanishes, as is illustrated in Figure 4.2.6b.

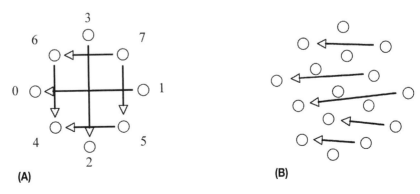

FIGURE 4.2.6 Difference paths in regular (**A**) and irregular (**B**) PCF patterns.

Optimizing with SIMD Vectorization

The shading languages of today's graphics processors are structured around four-way *single instruction multiple data* (SIMD) instructions. With proper SIMD vectorization, batches of similar operations can be calculated in parallel, and summation and averaging can be performed by dot products. We begin by loading the PCF samples into a two-array of four-vectors, which does not look very different from the previous version:

```
float lightVisibility_unrolled_circular8_SIMD( float3 lightCoord )
{
    const float displace = .5 / depthMapResolution;
    const float displaceLong = 1.41421 * displace;
    float4 depths[2] = { float4(
        tex2D( depthMap, lightCoord.xy + float2( -displaceLong,
        0 ) ).x,

        tex2D( depthMap, lightCoord.xy + float2( displaceLong,
        0 ) ).x,
        tex2D( depthMap, lightCoord.xy + float2( 0,
        -displaceLong ) ).x,
        tex2D( depthMap, lightCoord.xy + float2( 0,
        displaceLong ) ).x
    ), float4(
        tex2D( depthMap, lightCoord.xy + float2(
        -displace, -displace ) ).x,
        tex2D( depthMap, lightCoord.xy + float2( displace,
        -displace ) ).x,
        tex2D( depthMap, lightCoord.xy + float2( -displace,
        displace ) ).x,
        tex2D( depthMap, lightCoord.xy + float2( displace,
        displace ) ).x
    ) };
    ...
```

Observe that the sample that used to be depths[0] is now depths[0].x, the sample formerly in depths[1] is now depths[0].y, and so on. The first optimization is to compute both components of the gradient vector in parallel:

```
    const float inverseCovariance = 1. / ( 1 + 1 + 2 );
    float2 gradientVector = float2(
        depths[0].yw * 1.41421 + depths[1].yz + depths[1].ww
      - depths[0].xz * 1.41421 - depths[1].xx - depths[1].zy )
            * inverseCovariance;
    ...
```

The second optimization is to parallelize the computation of the depth differences. Recall that in this step we need to move the light space coordinate along the local gradient to the offset position and then subtract it from the depth found there. The dot products between the offset and gradient vectors can be collated into a series of 2×4 matrix multiplies. This step produces eight depth differences, stored in two four-vectors, `diffs[0]` and `diffs[1]`:

```
// these matrices mirror the offsets in convenient ordering

const float2x4 offsData[2] = {

    float2x4( float4( -1, 1, 0, 0 ), float4( 0, 0, -1, 1 ) )
    * 1.41421,

    float2x4( float4( -1, 1, -1, 1 ), float4( -1, -1, 1, 1 )
    ) };


// aggregate dot( offset, gradientVector ) done by mul(...)
float4 diffs[2] = {
    depths[0] - lightCoord.z - mul( gradientVector,
    offsData[0] ),
    depths[1] - lightCoord.z - mul( gradientVector,
    offsData[1] ) };
...
```

In the last step the calculation of the visibility function is done in parallel for batches of four PCF samples. To accumulate the result and return an average visibility, we can use dot products by observing that a dot product of a four-vector with the vector $(1,1,1,1)$ is in effect the sum of its components, while a dot product with the vector $(0.25,0.25,0.25,0.25)$ is the average of its components. Therefore, we use a series of four-vector and two-vector dot products to compute the average of the eight visibility functions:

```
    return dot( .5, float2(
        dot( .25, saturate( diffs[0] / gradient + 1 ) ),
        dot( .25, saturate( diffs[1] / gradient + 1 ) ) ) );
}
```

ON THE CD The shader code on the CD-ROM contains an implementation of this function augmented with adjustable bias and adjustable radius of the PCF pattern.

Conclusion

This article showed how to add multisampling to gradient shadow maps to achieve a smoother look for shadow edges. We ended up with a substantial reduction in depth aliasing and a good-looking shadow penumbra.

References

[McReynolds05] McReynolds, Tom and Blythe, David. *Advanced Graphics Programming Using OpenGL*. Morgan Kaufmann Publishing, San Francisco, 2005.

[Moeller02] Möller, Tomas and Haines, Eric. *Real-time Rendering*. A K Peters Ltd, Natick, MA, 2002.

[Reeves87] Reeves, W. T., D. H. Saselin, and R. L. Cook. "Rendering Antialiased Shadows with Depth Maps." *ACM SIGGRAPH Computer Graphics, 21,* (1987): pp. 283–291.

[Schueler05] Schüler, Christian. "Eliminating Surface Acne with Gradient Shadow Mapping." *ShaderX⁴*, edited by W. Engel. Charles River Media, Hingham, MA, 2005.

[Williams78] Williams, Lance. "Casting Curved Shadows on Curved Surfaces." *Proceedings of the 5th Annual Conference on Computer Graphics and Interactive Techniques,* 1978: pp. 270–274.

4.3

Alias-Free Hard Shadows with Geometry Maps

László Szécsi, Budapest University of Technology and Economics (szecsi@iit.bme.hu)

Introduction

Rendering shadows is an essential part of generating a properly illuminated, realistic image. In order to shade a surface fragment, we have to check what parts of the light sources are visible. The standard GPU pipeline supports local illumination: if we want to use anything but local surface properties, we have to store them in textures. For point-like light sources, this is a feasible task, with well-known implementations such as shadow maps. In this chapter we investigate the options for storing scene geometry information beyond simple depth maps and present implementations that render superior shadows without a severe impact on performance.

Object Precision and Sampled Geometry Representation

In order to determine whether a light source illuminates a shaded point, we should check if the geometry is intersected by the ray segment between the shaded point and the light source. For this computation, the inputs are the representation of the scene geometry and the definition of the ray segment. The efficiency of the computation is improved if the scene geometry is prepared for this particular computation. The prepared representation may keep object precision or may be a sampled, approximate form. Object precision representations include space-partitioning data structures, such as kd-trees, octrees, regular grids, or shadow volumes storing the extended silhouette edges. Object precision schemes preserve geometric information and thus are able to render geometrically accurate shadow boundaries. However, such schemes require complex algorithms, which are hard to implement on current GPUs, and the performance of the GPU implementation is not necessarily better than the CPU version. Building the data structure on the CPU would make the incorporation of hardware displacement mapping impossible, along with other algorithms that change the geometry on the GPU.

The size and query time of the data structures also grow with the geometric complexity of the scene, making complex scenes problematic.

Shadow volumes using the stencil buffer are the most successful object-precision scheme, used in a multitude of computer games [Crow77]. Shadow volumes are 3D meshes generated by extruding silhouette edges of shadow caster objects along the light vectors. Rendering them through the depth buffer of the scene (without color writes), the stencil buffer is set up to flag shadowed areas. In this case, though indirectly, we manage to render geometry information into the stencil buffer, which is accessible via the stencil test when rendering the scene in subsequent passes. Shadow volumes are effective but have some of the flaws of object precision schemes. The silhouette edges have to be identified, and the volume geometry has to be assembled—usually on the CPU, though modern hardware with shaders alleviates this limitation somewhat. Fill-rate demands are considerable with shadow volumes, and only a single bit of information is available about lighting, making any evolution toward more convoluted shadowing models, such as soft shadow edges or transparency, problematic.

Alternatively, shadow algorithms using a sampled geometric representation are simple and well suited for GPU implementation. These representations can be generated on the GPU in linear time. More important, the query time is constant and independent of the scene geometry. However, sampled representations can never be fully accurate, so we can expect discretization errors in the shadow boundaries. A typical representative of the category of sampled representations is the shadow map algorithm, which rasterizes the scene from the point of view of the light source and stores the distance of the shadow casters in pixels, also called lexels in this case. When the shadow map is queried to find out whether or not a shaded point is in shadow, we have to find the lexel in which this point is seen from the light source. Then we compare the distance of the shaded point to the distance of the point visible from the light source in the center of the lexel. This means that all points visible in this lexel are assumed to be at the same distance. Unfortunately, this assumption is wrong at silhouette edges that are responsible for shadow boundaries.

FIGURE 4.3.1 Depth map shadow with percentage closer filtering (160 fps).

Considering these facts, shadow maps could be much better than object-precision approaches in terms of implementation flexibility, algorithmic complexity, and eventual performance. Their only drawback is shadow aliasing showing up in the form of jagged shadow boundaries. Our goal is to keep all the benefits of shadow mapping but to get rid of these jaggies. The key recognition is that we should not only blame sampling, but we should find a better sampled representation instead of depth values and a better query instead of depth comparisons.

Basic Depth Shadow Implementation

All more advanced algorithms are based on the depth map technique (shown in Figure 4.3.2), and they may also use classic depth maps as a part of their geometry representation. In this section we briefly review the required shader techniques.

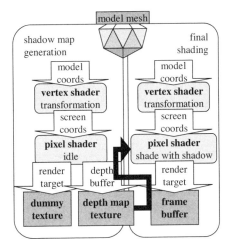

FIGURE 4.3.2 Data flow in depth map generation and shading passes.

There are two passes: the first rendering the depth map and the final shading pass using the depth map. In the first pass the depth map texture is bound to the depth-stencil buffer as we render the scene from the light. Color writes are disabled, the vertex shader performs standard model-view-projection transformation to the light camera's clipping space, and the pixel shader is idle.

In the second pass the depth map texture is assigned to a sampler in the final shading pass. The vertex shader is a generic one, passing position and normal in world coordinates for shading and the position in the depth map's projective space for shadowing. Note that more complex techniques will use the same vertex shader: only the shadow computation in the pixel shader will differ. In the case of simple depth shadows, shadowing is found using a texture lookup, with `depthTexPos` storing the currently shaded point's position in the depth map's texture coordinates:

```
float visibility = tex2Dproj(depthMapSampler, depthTexPos);
```

In DirectX 9 if the texture is a depth texture, the hardware performs a depth comparison instead of a projective texture lookup. It fetches the lexel's depth from the depth map, compares it to `depthTexPos`, and returns a boolean result as a floating point number, which can be used to modulate shading. If we set linear filtering, four depth comparisons will be made and the boolean visibility results interpolated, performing percentage closer filtering.

Geometry Maps

In the classic shadow map algorithm data stored in a lexel are limited representations of the geometry intersected by the ray connecting the light source and the center of the lexel. This information is assumed to be valid for all other points within the lexel's shaft (Figure 4.3.3). The key to improving the method is to store more information about what is happening inside the shaft. In particular, we want to know the exact geometry of visible silhouette edges responsible for shadow boundaries. Storing a complete description of the geometry within the shaft is not feasible with the rasterization hardware of current GPUs, which relies basically on point sampling.

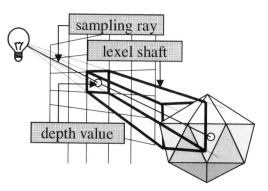

FIGURE 4.3.3   The relation of light shafts and geometry data in classic depth maps.

A better approach still involves sampling the geometry at discrete points, but when the data structure is queried for a point, instead of finding the closest lexel center, multiple enclosing lexels are queried. This means that the information needed for shadowing surfaces in a shaft is stored for its four corners (Figure 4.3.4). Note that accessing neighboring texels in a texture is usually extremely fast because of texture caching. This idea is also exploited in percentage closer filtering. However, percentage closer filtering uses the same geometry representation as the classic shadow map algorithm. It ignores real silhouette edges and bilinearly filters information that is not close to linear at all.

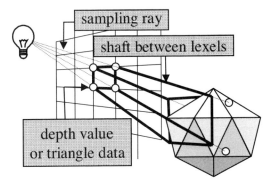

FIGURE 4.3.4 The relation of light shafts and geometry data in filtered depth maps and geometry maps.

Shadow maps that store more than a depth value may be called geometry maps. In the following we describe geometry maps that store sampled representations of triangles, silhouette edges, and silhouette points.

Triangle Map

The most straightforward, but challenging, option is to store the complete geometry visible in a lexel. This idea is called the Haines light buffer [Haines86], and it would require us to store a list of triangles in every geometry map texel. While this is not a possibility on the GPU, a point-sampled version storing one triangle at each shaft corner can be implemented. When a point in a shaft of four sample points is shaded, its shadow ray is tested against the four triangles at the corners.

As with any shadow map algorithm, we need two passes: the triangle map generation and the final shading using the map as shown in Figure 4.3.5. In this second pass, when shading a fragment, we need to access the complete geometry data of possible caster triangles. In every texel of the triangle map texture, we have to store a sufficiently complete representation of a triangle, which is also preprocessed for an effective ray-triangle intersection. A complete description would require nine values: the coordinates of the vertices. However, storing nine values in a single texel would require more than two four-channel textures. We can use multiple render targets to output data into up to four textures, but accessing many textures during rendering would reduce the rendering speed. Thus, we should find a way to encode a triangle with a minimal number of values.

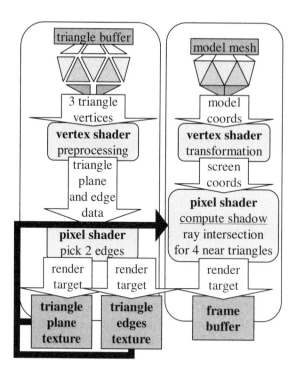

FIGURE 4.3.5 Data flow in triangle map generation and shading passes.

A triangle map contains light-source-dependent data. It is reasonable to store primitives in normalized screen space of the light source camera. This means that light rays are always parallel to the depth axis, and whether a triangle contains an intersection point can be determined in the 2D space of the light source camera screen. In order to render such a map, we render shadow caster meshes, in which each vertex contains all the geometry data associated with its triangle. These meshes are constructed at loading time, in modeling-space coordinates, to be transformed in the shaders. All shared vertices of the original model mesh are split, and each triangle uses three unique vertices, where each vertex contains all three vertex coordinates for the triangle. The vertex shader is responsible for transforming these coordinates to the triangle map's screen space and preprocessing the representation for the pixel shader.

Ray-triangle intersection can be decomposed into two steps: finding the intersection of the ray and the plane of the triangle and checking whether this intersection is within the triangle. This second step usually requires three tests against the three edges of the triangle. We perform these tests on the triangle projected onto the $z = 0$ plane of the light's screen space. Intuitively, this means we check whether the transformed position of the shaded surface point is within the triangle in the triangle map. Our basic assumption with the discretized triangle map is that the sampling density is generally better than the size of the projected triangles; otherwise we could miss some triangles, causing light leaks through surfaces. Additionally, when we check whether a point is within a triangle found in a lexel, it is enough to check it against those edges of the triangle that intersect the lexel. Assuming the triangles are large enough compared to the lexels, it is sufficient to store only two edges out of the three.

Therefore, we need two four-channel textures to store triangle data for the ray-triangle intersection. One texture stores triangle plane data: the plane normal and offset (the distance from the origin). The other one stores two edges projected to $z = 0$, encoded as angle and offset. A direction in 2D can be described by a single angle. In HLSL, a normalized `float2 edgeNormal` can be converted to `float edgeAngle` using

```
edgeAngle = atan2(edgeNormal.y, edgeNormal.x);
```

and converted back with

```
sincos(edgeAngle, edgeNormal.y, edgeNormal.x);
```

The two textures are set as render targets when computing the triangle map and will be assigned to samplers during the final shading. Remember, the light rays are parallel to axis z. With this setup, point clipping tests for the edges in 2D or the plane in 3D consist of comparing the offset to a dot product with the normal. The shadow ray is intersected if the shaded point is behind the triangle plane and within all edges on $z = 0$. If any of these tests fail, the triangle does not shadow the surface element. If none of the four candidate triangles occlude the surface, it is considered lit.

Our assumption that the triangle map resolution is high enough to always contain the actual caster among the four candidates will be violated by thin triangles, or near acute angles, and this will cause light leaking. Therefore, we have to account for the cases where a continuous surface of triangles occludes the shaded fragment but the actual caster triangle is not stored in the triangle map. If the behind-the-triangle-plane test is fulfilled for all four candidates (that is, they are all closer to the light than the shaded fragment), the fragment is considered to be in shadow regardless of the 2D edge tests. This is a safeguard fallback to regular depth testing, but with accurately reconstructed depth values.

Unfortunately, the straightforward triangle map implementation suffers from some persistent artifacts as shown in Figure 4.3.6. Although depth map jaggies are eliminated, sampling of the shadow caster geometry is not guaranteed to be sufficient. Triangles near silhouettes are usually almost perpendicular to the light direction and will be rasterized to a few random pixels. This may be improved by rendering the caster meshes to the triangle map in wireframe mode. Scalene triangles will be rasterized more robustly as line segments. However, multiple overlapping triangle candidates may still occur. This can be improved by storing more triangles in the triangle map, but using high-precision floating point textures costs bandwidth. All of these issues are resolved by rendering the silhouette edges only.

FIGURE 4.3.6   Triangle map shadow with light leaks where sampling of overlapping silhouettes is insufficient (140 fps).

Silhouette Edge Selection on the GPU

Examining the triangle map approach, we may conclude that although we store elaborate geometric information in all four corners of a every shaft, we only really use information about visible silhouette edges. In order to alleviate issues of z-fighting or missing potential shadow casters, we have to make sure that the information near the edges is conservatively rasterized and that no nonsilhouette edges are drawn. In order to achieve this, we will render the edges as line segments instead of triangles. This means we are sampling the one-pixel-wide edge strips at the corners of the lexel grid. If a silhouette edge is visible in the shaft, it will be rasterized into at least one of the four lexels.

In order to render the edges, and the silhouette edges only, we need to create a new representation of the mesh. We have to solve a task that is very similar to constructing shadow volumes. However, we want to avoid processing the mesh geometry on the CPU and assembling a light dependent edge buffer for every frame. We do not need to extrude the edges, as in the shadow volumes algorithm. Therefore, the vertex buffer containing the edges can remain static and be assembled when loading the model mesh.

Rather than storing vertices for triangles, we now store vertices for line list primitives. That is, every vertex specifies a line containing the coordinates of the end points and the coordinates of the third vertex of the triangles on each side. This is a version of a winged-edge mesh format. All vertex data are in modeling space coordinates and transformed to normalized screen coordinates later in the vertex shader. We also need to be able to identify silhouette edges in the vertex shader. Silhouette edges have a front-facing triangle on one side and a back-facing one on the other. That is why the data in the vertex buffer have to contain information about the triangles next to each edge.

Storing the normals of the triangles is not an option, as there is no easy way to transform them into the edge map's screen space, and even if there was, complex animation can deform meshes in nonlinear ways. However, storing the four vertices of the two triangles sharing the edge is sufficient. By transforming all four vertices in the vertex shader, the complete geometry will be known and the silhouette edge can be identified. If the edge is not a silhouette edge, the vertex shader discards the vertex (for example, by setting its position behind the camera) and the edge is not drawn.

We render all the lines by drawing the vertex buffer as line primitives. However, every vertex needs to be considered twice to give every line two end points. For every second vertex in the vertex shader, we exchange the two end points and, similarly, the wing triangle vertices. This can be accomplished without duplicating every vertex in the buffer by using hardware instancing [Gosselin04]. The instanced object will be single line, defined by the two-element index buffer [0,1] and a two-element vertex buffer:

```
[{0.0 : PSIZE}, {1.0 : PSIZE}].
```

The instance data stream will be the edge vertex buffer. For every vertex in the buffer describing a line, two vertices will be rendered, forming the end points of a line primitive, and the vertex shader will receive information about the parity of the vertex in the PSIZE register as shown in Figure 4.3.7.

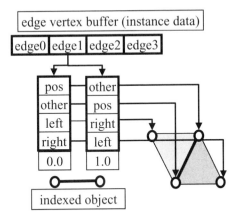

FIGURE 4.3.7   The vertex shader receives the combination of object and instance data. Coordinates are interpreted differently for odd and even vertices.

Edge Map

Unlike the triangle map, we only store the relevant part of the geometry information: the silhouette edges. In every lexel, where a silhouette edge is rasterized, we store information about its geometry. For the inner part of shadows, the classic hardware-supported depth map is sufficient. Where the four depth map comparisons at the corners of the shaft do not agree, the geometry map will be queried for the accurate edges. When the edge map is used in combination with the depth map, it does not need to store 3D information. Only the silhouette edge data in shadow map texture space are necessary as shown in Figure 4.3.8.

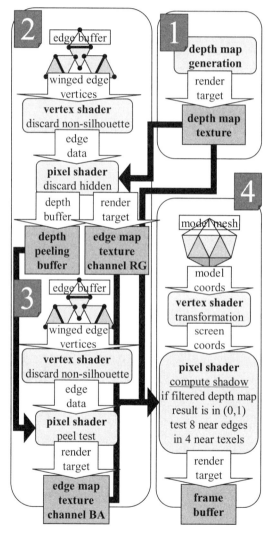

FIGURE 4.3.8   Data flow in edge map generation and shading passes.

As with any shadow map algorithm, we need two stages: the geometry map generation (including the depth map and the edge map) and the final shading using them. In this final pass, when shading a fragment, we need to access the description of possible shadow edges in the shaft the shaded point is in. The rendering only needs to consider the shadow edges that have been rendered to the four nearest texels.

By storing edge map data in texture-relative coordinates, we can use an extremely compact representation: the description of a single edge without depth data, relative to the lexel center, takes only two 8-bit integers. This also makes it easier to handle pixel-level calculations. The light rays are always parallel to the depth axis, and whether the geometry corresponding to a silhouette edge occludes a point can be determined in the 2D texture space. In a four-channel texture we can efficiently store two edges in a single lexel, allowing for more complex geometries where multiple possible silhouette edges cross each other.

As we are able to store two edges in a single lexel, we will render the silhouette edges twice when generating the edge map using a depth-peeling technique [Everitt01]. In the first pass we use conventional Z-buffering, rendering the first peel of visible edges. It is possible that multiple silhouette edges will overlap in some lexels and that some silhouette details will be lost. Therefore, in the second pass those edges hidden behind the previously rendered ones are drawn. The depth peeling works as follows: we store the depth buffer in a texture after rendering the first peel. In the second pass we use a clean depth buffer, but the fragment is discarded in the pixel shader if its depth is not greater than the one stored in the texture. This comparison is identical to the one performed when using a depth map for shading. As a result, the second-closest fragments will be rendered in the second pass. So that we only render to the appropriate channels in each pass, we use the color-write mask-render state. In each pass we render the winged-edge representation of the shadow caster geometry. The vertex shader computes the neighboring triangle plane normals, decides whether the vertex belongs to a silhouette edge, and if so, passes the texture-space edge normal (as an angle) and offset to the pixel shader. We also elongate edges somewhat to ensure a continuous contour.

In the second pass we need to read the depth value for the previous peel. Then we can discard fragments already rendered in the previous pass.

```
void psEdgeMapPeeled( … in float2 screenPos  : VPOS … ) { …
    float2 texPos = mul(float3(screenPos, 1), screenToTexMatrix);
    if( tex2Dlod(peelingDepthMapSampler, texPos) > 0.5 )
      discard;
… }
```

This completes edge map generation. In the final pass, in the pixel shader we evaluate visibility using the depth map first. We use a linearly filtered sampler, providing percentage closer filtering. If the visibility is not 0 or 1, the four samples did not return a unanimous result, and we are on the silhouette. This is the case when we need to carry out the silhouette intersection tests for every edge (Figure 4.3.9). This test will be identical to the point-clipping test we used for triangle edges, and the same angle-and-offset representation is used for the edges, encoded in two channels. If none of the silhouette edges occlude the light, the surface fragment is not in shadow, and we do regular shading. To save precision, we store data not in texture coordinates, but relative to the upper-left corner of the lexel (Figure 4.3.10). The offset and the angle are now in a manageable range and precision and can be stored in 8 bits, which is the minimum channel width for a render target.

FIGURE 4.3.9   The edge map shadow copes well with overlapping silhouettes and self-shadowing (155 fps).

FIGURE 4.3.10   Artifacts appear at shadow corners with a low-resolution edge map.

The edge map is more capable of handling complex silhouette patterns than the triangle map. Owing to the compact representation, its performance is practically identical to that of the depth map. However, the geometry representation is not complete, and it is possible that a surface fragment is behind a silhouette edge but not behind the object itself. This happens if multiple edges appear in the same lexel at very thin model parts or at shadow corners. Depending on geometry and resolution, artifacts may still appear. Although there is no way to reconstruct a shadow with topology finer than the sampling density, correct boundary at shadow corners is possible using the silhouette map and storing points instead of edges.

Silhouette Map

The silhouette map was proposed in 2003 by Sen et al. [Sen03]. Though the basic concept of storing additional information along with the depth map is the same as previously described approaches, the construction is slightly different. One of the ideas is to store sample points along silhouettes. While edges can still be reconstructed from a sufficient number of points, at shadow corners the silhouette point can be placed exactly at the corner. Furthermore, geometry information is not stored along with depth map lexels, at the four corners of a shaft, but on a grid shifted by half a texel. The process can still be seen as reading a number of nearby samples for a depth shaft to determine geometry, but a fundamentally different interpretation is also possible: the depth map grid is distorted so that lexel boundaries (that is, shadow boundaries, too) coincide with the contour samples.

Rendering a silhouette map is a complex task, where contour edges have to be rasterized to create an adequate point sampling for the reconstruction of the geometry. In the original algorithm the silhouette edges were identified on the CPU. Using a modified version of the vertex shader introduced for the edge map, we can port this task to the GPU. The silhouette map is also required to have four-connectivity: edges have to be rasterized so that at least two neighbors also contain silhouette information. Classic hardware-supported edge rasterization does not guarantee this, so in the original algorithm thin quads were rendered instead of line segments. This would require another data structure to be assembled on the CPU. To avoid that, we rasterize double-width lines by drawing two slightly offset ones, with some modification to the vertex shader. With these important implementation improvements, we perform the silhouette map algorithm completely on the GPU as shown in Figure 4.3.11.

The silhouette map can be thought of as a distortion grid for the depth map, where every texel contains the coordinates of a translated grid point. Originally, depth map lexel corners lie on a uniform square grid. If we move these lexel corners to nearby silhouette edges, leaving the topology intact, we get a mesh aligned on scene objects as shown in Figure 4.3.12. Lexel centers not near edges are not affected. It is important that a quadrangular cell still corresponds to a depth sample and that it still includes the original lexel center. First, we discuss how such a distortion map is used for shadowing and then detail the intricacies of generating such a map as shown in Figure 4.3.13.

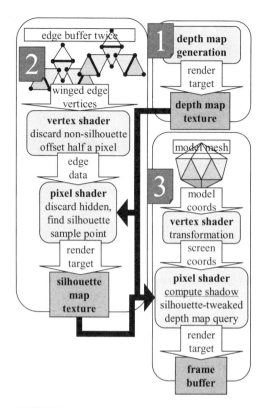

FIGURE 4.3.11   Data flow in silhouette map generation and shading passes.

FIGURE 4.3.12   The distorted grid projected onto a shadow receiver. Edges follow silhouettes.

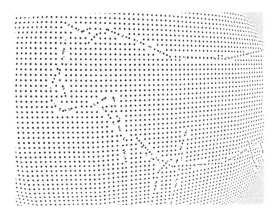

FIGURE 4.3.13 Silhouette map sample points can be interpreted as nodes of a distorted square grid.

When we shade the scene using the silhouette map, we need to find out in which distorted cell the shaded point actually is. A silhouette map texel always overlaps with four cells, the relevant edges of which are defined by the grid points stored in the current and neighboring texels. We divide the texel into eight triangles, pairs corresponding to cells. A point given by its texture coordinates is within such a triangle if

$$\frac{p \cdot c_\perp}{n \cdot c_\perp} > 0 \ \text{ and } \ \frac{p \cdot n_\perp}{c \cdot n_\perp} > 0, \text{ with } \begin{bmatrix} x & y \end{bmatrix}_\perp = \begin{bmatrix} -y & x \end{bmatrix}$$

are true, where p, n, and c are the positions of the shaded point, the neighbor silhouette point, and the corner, respectively, all relative to the central silhouette point (Figure 4.3.14).

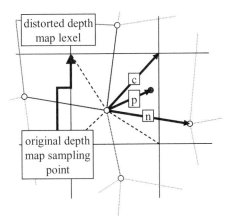

FIGURE 4.3.14 Finding the cell corresponding to a shaded point •, using distorted grid nodes °.

Having found out which cell the shaded point belongs to, we can simply query a nonfiltered depth map at the original cell center (Figure 4.3.15).

FIGURE 4.3.15   Silhouette map shadow (155 fps).

Silhouette Map Generation

To create the distortion grid described above, we need to render silhouette edges, adjusting grid nodes in the pixel shader. Before the pass, the render target is cleared with [0.5, 0.5], specifying the lexel center. In every pixel we have to find a point on the currently rendered silhouette edge. Such a point is found by intersecting the edge with the diagonals of the texel (Figure 4.3.16). However, if one of the edge vertices is within the texel, it is taken as a sample point. Should both diagonals intersect the edge, an average is taken.

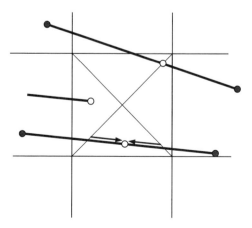

FIGURE 4.3.16   Three cases of finding a point along the edge in the pixel shader.

However, as shown in Figure 4.3.17, the grid will not be properly distorted where a silhouette edge travels between two texels without being rasterized to any of them. We have to ensure four-connected silhouette edges, and we can do it by rendering two edges, half a pixel away from the original one (Figure 4.3.18). The offset must be horizontal or vertical, depending on the slant of the edge, as dictated by line rasterization rules [Bresenham65].

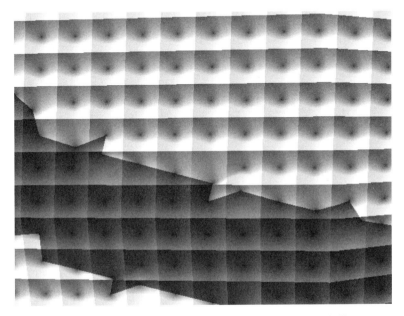

FIGURE 4.3.17   Artifact caused by not rendering four-connected silhouettes.

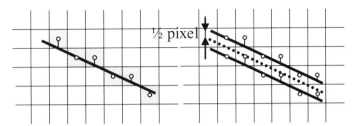

FIGURE 4.3.18   Rendering two line segments ensures four-connectivity.

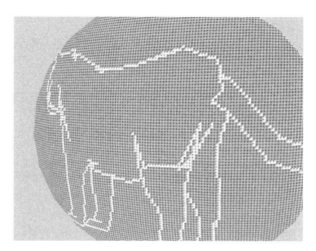

FIGURE 4.3.19   Silhouette texels rendered with conventional rasterization.

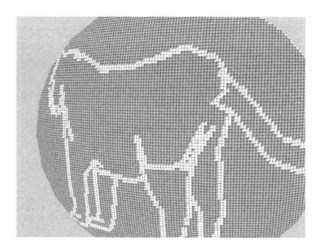

FIGURE 4.3.20   Silhouette texels rendered with double-edge rasterization.

Conclusion

Out of the three extensions of the shadow map algorithm we have presented, the triangle map is of didactic significance, but the edge and silhouette maps have minimal overhead over simple depth maps and provide far superior results. The main advantage of both methods is that low-resolution maps can be used, reducing the cost of texture fetches, practically increasing performance over that of huge depth maps. Any sampled geometry map has a limited accuracy, and artifacts are unavoidable if map resolution becomes comparable in size with object features. Therefore, techniques making better use of map resolution such as light space perspective shadow maps [Wimmer04] should be combined with alias-free shadows.

References

[Bresenham65] Bresenham, J. "Algorithm for Computer Control of a Digital Plotter." *IBM Systems Journal 4*(1) (1965): 25–30.

[Crow77] Crow, F. C. "Shadow Algorithms for Computer Graphics." *Proceedings of the 4th Annual Conference on Computer Graphics and Interactive Techniques* (San Jose, California, July 20–22, 1977). SIGGRAPH '77. ACM Press, New York (1977): 242–248.

[Everitt01] Everitt, Cass. "Interactive Order-Independent Transparency." Technical report, NVIDIA Corporation, May 2001. Available online at *http://www.nvidia. com/. http://citeseer.ist.psu.edu/everitt01interactive.html.*

[Gosselin04] Gosselin, D., P. Sander, and J. Mitchell. "Rendering a Crowd." *ShaderX³: Advanced Rendering with DirectX and OpenGL*, edited by W. Engel. Charles River Media, 2004: pp. 505–517.

[Haines86] Haines, E. and D. Greenberg. "The Light Buffer: A Shadow-Testing Accelerator." *IEEE Computer Graphics and Applications*, September 1986, pp. 6–16.

[Sen03] Sen, P., M. Cammarano, and P. Hanrahan. "Shadow Silhouette Maps." *ACM Trans. Graph. 22*(3) (July 2003): pp. 521–526.

[Wimmer04] Wimmer, M., Scherzer, D., and Purgathofer, W. 2004. "Light Space Perspective Shadow Maps." *Rendering Techniques 2004* (Proceedings of Eurographics Symposium on Rendering), edited by A. Keller and H. W. Jensen. Eurographics Association, June, 2004: pp. 143–152.

4.4

Edge Masking and Per-Texel Depth Extent Propagation For Computation Culling During Shadow Mapping

John R. Isidoro, ATI Research Inc.

An important feature of Shader Model 3.0 is the ability to perform conditional processing within the pixel shader using true flow-control constructs. This type of computation culling can be particularly beneficial for shadow mapping, where anti-aliasing for shadow boundary regions requires significantly more texture fetches and processing than regions completely inside or outside the shadow.

This article explains two methods for edge filtering and propagating the edge and depth information to encompass the boundary region that requires more processing. The first generates a mipchain for the shadow-map edge mask and simply fetches from a lower miplevel to effectively dilate the edge mask. The second propagates the min and max of the depth extent of the shadow map texels to generate subsequent levels of a depth extent mipchain. The second approach is particularly beneficial for complex scenes with high depth complexity, as it only applies the complex processing within a particular depth range per texel, and thus only the shadow map depths where the shadow boundaries appear in the final scene.

These textures are subsequently used in the scene rendering pass of shadow mapping to provide efficient computation culling that allows portions of the scene completely in or out of shadow to be rendered using the simpler single shadow-map sample branch of the conditional shader.

Conditional Processing for Shadow Mapping

A common artifact with shadow mapping is the resulting aliasing artifacts on the shadow map boundaries. The standard solution is percentage closer filtering (PCF), which usually requires taking several (usually 16 or more) samples from the shadow map to completely remove the aliasing artifacts. While using high-quality PCF everywhere in the rendered scene provides correct results, it is not efficient. High-quality filtering is only required for the regions of the scene where the shadow edges are.

One simple and effective method for doing this is to only perform the high-quality filtering in regions front-facing to the light. If a projective spotlight texture or other form of gobo is used to light the scene, the shadow mapping computation should only be performed in the regions onto which the filtered light projects.

Incorporating both of these can really speed things up, especially when the camera is facing the light and most of the visible surfaces in the scene are back-facing with respect to the light.

Computation Masking and Edge Dilation Using Mipchain Generation

Another observation is that high-quality PCF is really only required near shadow boundary regions. In typical implementations of PCF for anti-aliasing, the filtering kernel has a fixed width in shadow map space, so only regions within a certain distance from shadow boundaries in shadow map space need to be processed using the high-quality PCF kernel. Regions completely inside or outside the shadow require only a single fetch from the shadow map to determine whether they are inside or outside the shadow.

To determine the amount of filtering required per pixel, we will build a computation mask in a texture to mask off regions that require higher-quality filtering. We use a couple of approaches to determine these regions.

The first technique involves edge-filtering the shadow map and propagating the filtered regions outward. A standard technique for propagating edge information outward is to perform some form of dilation operator multiple times on the image. Doing this is expensive since the operator would have to process all the texels in the computation-mask texture multiple times. However, since we are using this edge information for computation masking, the dilation operation does not have to be exact. We do not need to know exactly which texels are within N texel lengths from an edge. As long as our computation mask encompasses the regions that require higher-quality filtering, the results will still be correct.

A simpler operation, which is optimized for graphics hardware, is to build a mipchain from the edge mask. By going down levels in the resulting mipchain, we have a lower resolution representation of the edge mask, where each texel occupies four times the area of texels in the previous level.

This effectively approximates the dilation of the shadow mask. Each time the image is filtered to go down a miplevel, the texel is dilated to twice its original size. Thus, a dilation of eight pixels in size can be achieved by going down $\log2(8)$, or three miplevels. However, a few implementation details need to be considered.

The first is that the original edge filter for the highest-resolution miplevel should first be thresholded so that edge pixels have a value of one and nonedge pixels have a value of zero. Then, when generating the subsequent miplevels, the filtering will average edge and nonedge pixels together, which will result in values between zero and one. To account for this, all nonzero pixels in the filtered edge mask should be considered to be in the dilated region.

The second consideration is that with standard fast 2×2 box filtering for mipchain generation, texel values only take into account texels from subsequent levels that project to within its footprint. For example, suppose we have a 16×16 texture that is completely black except for a single bright pixel at location $(7, 7)$ (e.g., as close to the center as possible in the upper-left quadrant). When generating the mipchain, intensity from the single bright texel is not propagated to the texels in the other three quadrants until the 1×1 miplevel as shown in Figure 4.4.1.

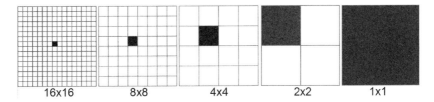

16x16   8x8   4x4   2x2   1x1

FIGURE 4.4.1 Results of standard mipchain generation on an image where only a single texel is non-zero. In order to allow for propagation of non-zero values in all directions for dilation, the lower miplevels should be sampled using bilinear filtering.

To allow for correct propagation of intensity to implement dilation, bilinear filtering should be used when fetching from the edge mask texture. Using bilinear filtering gives an extra texel width of dilation, with the texel width determined by the miplevel. For instance, a single texel from the mipmap three miplevels down is eight texels from the topmost miplevel in width. Since only a subset of the mipchain is used as the computation culling mask, the box filtering used for mipchain generation is only performed up to the required level of the mipchain.

During the scene rendering pass in the pixel shader, the correct level of the mipchain is fetched from the tex2dLOD function. If the result of the fetch is nonzero, more complex PCF is performed; otherwise, standard single-sample shadow mapping is used.

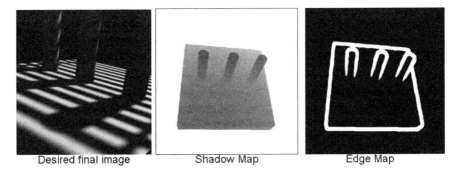

Desired final image   Shadow Map   Edge Map

FIGURE 4.4.2 An image using shadow mapping, the shadow map used to generate that image, and an edge map showing the regions in the shadow map, which may require high quality PCF filtering.

Depth-Extent Propagation for Computation Masking

Although using the dilated shadow map edge mask to limit the number of pixels that use high-quality PCF is effective, there is still room for improvement. One issue is that the computation masking is based on the position of the projection of the current pixel into the computation mask. Any given texel in the computation mask can be thought of as cutting a narrow light frustum through the scene, within which all texels either perform high-quality PCF or basic one-sample shadow mapping. In the case where this texel frustum intersects many objects in the scene, the complex shadow mapping is applied to all pixels rendered within that frustum. Since this frustum emanates from the light source, the shadow boundary should only lie on the first or second object from the light source. To try to limit the high-quality PCF processing to only the layer where it is required, we replace the dilated edge mask with a min and max distance from the light where the shadow can exist. We call this two-channel texture the *depth extent map*.

To generate the depth extent map, the shadow map is edge-filtered. If an edge is detected, the value on the edge that is closest to the light is determined to be the blocker distance. Within the 3×3 neighborhood of the texel, the min and max of any shadow map depth values significantly greater than the blocker value are stored. These can be considered to be the local range of depths for the receiver (the surface the shadow is cast onto), and are written out to the depth extent map. The receiver depths are used, since the shadows lie on the receiving surface rather than the blocking surface. If an edge is not detected in the pixel shader, a degenerate depth range (min = 1.0, max = 0.0) is written into the depth extent map.

To propagate the depth extent outward in texture space to generate the computation mask, we use a similar mipchain technique as before. However, in this case lower miplevels will be used to store the overall depth extent of all the depth extent texels in a small neighborhood. Because of this, we need to compute the mipchain using our own pixel shaders.

Since we are propagating neighborhood min and max values, using bilinear or box filtering will not work correctly. Our solution is to compute the region min and max of the depth extents of a 3×3 neighborhood in the previous miplevel. The 3×3 neighborhood is used rather than a 2×2 neighborhood since bilinear filtering cannot be used when sampling the texture to propagate depth extent information. The 3×3 neighborhood extends one extra pixel to the right and downward to pull depth extent information from other quadrants and subquadrants. Since we use min and max operations over the neighborhood, nonedge pixels (which have degenerate depth extents having a max of 0 and a min of 1) do not affect the depth extent. If all texels in the 3×3 neighborhood are nonedge, it naturally falls out of the math that the resulting texel in the next level is nonedge and has a degenerate depth extent.

Just as in the previous section, the dilation amount should be determined by the width of the PCF kernel in shadow map space. The number of the miplevel chosen in the min-max depth extent mipchain is equal to the log2 of the kernel width. Neighborhood min-max mipchain generation only proceeds until this miplevel.

The depth extent is fetched using the same texture coordinates used to fetch from the shadow map. When rendering the scene pass, the high-quality PCF is only performed if the current depth value is within the depth extent fetched from the depth extent mipchain. If not, basic single-sample shadow mapping is used.

Results

In most cases we have seen an overall performance increase (up to 3× speedup) from using these approaches in our test scenes. Generally, adding conditionally based computation masking to a shader will help the average case but make the worst-case performance worse owing to the additional overhead of the conditional instructions.

Any performance increases are dependent on the scene and viewing angle. A complex scene consisting mostly of shadow edges may require high-quality filtering over nearly the entire image and might not see an overall improvement in performance.

One interesting about these approaches is that they are all image-processing-based operations, and no additional passes using the scene geometry are required over standard shadow mapping approaches. This can be useful when the scene geometry is complex and the cost of rerendering the scene is high.

Shaders

```
//─────────────────────────────────
//Generate edge map from depth map.  The edge map is represented
//in min/max form, where
//  the min and max of the far pixels are stored for edges.
//─────────────────────────────────
float4 ps_EdgeMapRGMinMax(float2 oTex : TEXCOORD0) : COLOR0
{
  float4  neighborOffsets[4] = {
      { 1.0,  0.0, 0, 0},
      {-1.0,  0.0, 0, 0},
      { 0.0,  1.0, 0, 0},
      { 0.0, -1.0, 0, 0}
      };
  float   centerTapDepth;
  float   currTapDepth;
  float   depthDiff = 0;
  float   maxDepthDiff = 0;
  float   furthestTapDepth;
  float   furthestTapDepthMin;
  float   furthestTapDepthMax;

  float4 outColor = {0, 0, 0, 0};

  //Sample depth from shadow map
  centerTapDepth = tex2D(ShadowSampler, oTex).r;
```

```
      furthestTapDepthMin = 1;
      furthestTapDepthMax = 0;

      for(int i=0; i<4; i++)
      {
        currTapDepth=tex2D(ShadowSampler,
        oTex+(g_vFullTexelOffset*neighborOffsets[i] )).r;
        depthDiff = abs(centerTapDepth -  currTapDepth);
        maxDepthDiff = max(depthDiff, maxDepthDiff );

        //If the difference between the current and center tap are
        //significant enough to comprise an edge keep track of min
        //and max tap values that comprise the furthest texels that
        //make up the edge. Only the furthest texels of the edge are
        //stored in the edge map seen as the shadow boundary that
        //requires extra filtering is only projected onto the far
        //depth of the edge.
        if(depthDiff > g_fMinEdgeDelta) //g_fMinEdgeDelta
        {
          furthestTapDepth = max( currTapDepth, centerTapDepth);

          furthestTapDepthMin = min(furthestTapDepthMin,
          furthestTapDepth);
          furthestTapDepthMax = max(furthestTapDepthMax,
          furthestTapDepth);
        }
      }

      outColor.r = furthestTapDepthMin;   // min tap depth
      outColor.g = furthestTapDepthMax;   // max tap depth

      return outColor;
    }


    //----------------------------------------------------
    //ps_MipLevelMinMaxRG
    // generates miplevel from subsequent miplevels by using the
    // min and max of the values in a 3x3 neighborhood
    //----------------------------------------------------
    float4 ps_MipLevel3x3MinMaxRG(
        float4 oTex0 : TEXCOORD0,
        float4 oFullTexelOffset : TEXCOORD1 ) : COLOR0
    {
      float4 outCol = 0;
      float2 tapVals;

      float4 tapOffset = oFullTexelOffset;

      outCol.rg = tex2Dlod(ShadowMipPointSampler, oTex0).rg;

      tapVals = tex2Dlod(ShadowMipPointSampler, oTex0 + (tapOffset *
      float4(1,1,0,0)) ).rg;
      outCol.r = min( outCol.r, tapVals.r );
      outCol.g = max( outCol.g, tapVals.g );
```

```
      tapVals = tex2Dlod(ShadowMipPointSampler, oTex0 + (tapOffset *
      float4(0,1,0,0)) ).rg;
      outCol.r = min( outCol.r, tapVals.r );
      outCol.g = max( outCol.g, tapVals.g );

      tapVals = tex2Dlod(ShadowMipPointSampler, oTex0 + (tapOffset *
      float4(1,0,0,0)) ).rg;
      outCol.r = min( outCol.r, tapVals.r );
      outCol.g = max( outCol.g, tapVals.g );

      tapVals = tex2Dlod(ShadowMipPointSampler, oTex0 + (tapOffset *
      float4(-1,1,0,0)) ).rg;
      outCol.r = min( outCol.r, tapVals.r );
      outCol.g = max( outCol.g, tapVals.g );

      tapVals = tex2Dlod(ShadowMipPointSampler, oTex0 + (tapOffset *
      float4(-1,0,0,0)) ).rg;
      outCol.r = min( outCol.r, tapVals.r );
      outCol.g = max( outCol.g, tapVals.g );

      tapVals = tex2Dlod(ShadowMipPointSampler, oTex0 + (tapOffset *
      float4(1,-1,0,0)) ).rg;
      outCol.r = min( outCol.r, tapVals.r );
      outCol.g = max( outCol.g, tapVals.g );

      tapVals = tex2Dlod(ShadowMipPointSampler, oTex0 + (tapOffset *
      float4(0,-1,0,0)) ).rg;
      outCol.r = min( outCol.r, tapVals.r );
      outCol.g = max( outCol.g, tapVals.g );

      tapVals = tex2Dlod(ShadowMipPointSampler, oTex0 + (tapOffset *
      float4(-1,-1,0,0)) ).rg;
      outCol.r = min( outCol.r, tapVals.r );
      outCol.g = max( outCol.g, tapVals.g );

      return outCol;
   }


   //───────────────────────────────────────//
 ps_LightPassPDisk12RandRotPCFCondEdgeDepthExtent
   //
   // Percentage closer filtering using a poisson disk, with a
   // per-pixel rotation of the sampling disk using a randomized
   // rotation texture.
   //
   // This shader uses dynamic flow control in a similar way to the
   // previous shader (Cond2)
   // but also performs computational culling based on min/max depth
   // ranges of an edge propagated along with the edge information
   // when building the edge mipchain.
   //
   //──────────────────────────────────────--
```

```
float4 ps_LightPassPDisk12RandRotPCFCondEdgeDepthExtent(
      float3 oTex0 : TEXCOORD0, //normal in world space
      float4 oTex1 : TEXCOORD1, //shadow map tex coords
      float3 oTex2 : TEXCOORD2,
      float2 vPos : VPOS)          //world space light vector (not
                                     normalized))
      : COLOR0
{
  float4   shadowMapVal;
  float    dist;
  float3   lightVec;
  float4   inLight;
  float    percentInLight;
  float4   projCoords;
  float4   lightingVal;
  float2   offsetInTexels;

  float2   quadOffsets[12]={
    {-0.326212f, -0.40581f},
    {-0.840144f, -0.07358f},
    {-0.695914f, 0.457137f},
    {-0.203345f, 0.620716f},
    {0.96234f, -0.194983f},
    {0.473434f, -0.480026f},
    {0.519456f, 0.767022f},
    {0.185461f, -0.893124f},
    {0.507431f, 0.064425f},
    {0.89642f, 0.412458f},
    {-0.32194f, -0.932615f},
    {-0.791559f, -0.59771f}
  };

  //variables used for random rotation of pcf kernel
  float2 rotOffset;  //rotated offset
  float4 randRot;     //random rotation matrix sampled from tex-
  ture using screen pos
  float2 edgeValMinMax;
  float4 lightVal;

  //project texture coordinates
  projCoords.xyz = oTex1 / oTex1.w;
  projCoords.w = 0;

  // Return distance from the origin in light's view space
  dist = sqrt( dot(oTex2, oTex2) ) * g_fDistScale;

  //compute lighting val
  lightVal = ComputeLighting(oTex1, dist, oTex2, oTex0 );

  if( dot(lightVal, float3(1, 1, 1)) == 0 )
  {
    return 0;
  }
```

```
       else
{
  //note: have to point sample depth range seen as bilinear
  //filtering with non-edge pixels makes the depth range
  //invalid
  projCoords.w = g_fEdgeMaskMipLevel - 1;   //3x3 propagation
                                               for mipchain
                                               generation
                                            //lets us get away
                                               with going up 1
                                               miplevel
  edgeValMinMax = tex2Dlod(EdgeMipPointSampler, projCoords).rg;

  //extend depth range by 1 grayscale value (8-bit) (this can
  //be done in the edge
  //filtering step instead if desired)
  // 0.005 is one grayscale value for 8-bit depth range map
  edgeValMinMax += float2(-0.005, 0.005);

  //extend depth range upward by depth bias amount (this can be
  //also done in the edge filtering step instead if desired)
  edgeValMinMax -= g_fDistBias;

  projCoords.w = 0;
  percentInLight = 0.0f;

  //If the current pixels distance from the light source is
  //outside the depth range,
  // use a simple shadow map test; otherwise use more complex
  // processing
  if( (edgeValMinMax.r > projCoords.z ) || (edgeValMinMax.g
  < projCoords.z ) )
  {
    shadowMapVal = tex2Dlod(ShadowSampler, projCoords );

    inLight = ( projCoords.z < shadowMapVal );
    percentInLight = dot(inLight, 0.25f );

    return( percentInLight * lightVal );
  }
  else
  {
    randRot = BX2( tex2Dlod(RandRotSampler, float4(vPos *
    g_vFullTexelOffset, 0, 0) ));

    for(int i=0; i<12; i++)
    {
      rotOffset.x = randRot.r * quadOffsets[i].x + randRot.g *
      quadOffsets[i].y;
      rotOffset.y = -randRot.g * quadOffsets[i].x + randRot.r *
      quadOffsets[i].y;

      offsetInTexels = g_fStochSampRadius * rotOffset;
```

```
        shadowMapVal = tex2Dlod(ShadowSampler,
            projCoords + float4(g_vFullTexelOffset * offset-
            InTexels, 0, 0 ) );

        inLight = ( projCoords.z < shadowMapVal );
        percentInLight += dot(inLight, 1.0f/( 12.0f * 4.0f ));
      }

    return( percentInLight * lightVal );
    }
  }
}
```

4.5

Queried Virtual Shadow Maps

Markus Giegl, Michael Wimmer

Vienna University of Technology

Introduction

Shadowing scenes by shadow mapping has long suffered from undersampling artifacts owing to too low shadow map resolution, leading to so-called perspective and projection aliasing.

In this article we present a new real-time shadow mapping algorithm capable of shadowing large scenes by *virtually* increasing the resolution of the shadow map beyond the GPU hardware limit (see Figure 4.5.1(b)). We start with a brute force approach that uniformly increases the resolution of the whole shadow map. We then introduce a smarter version that greatly increases runtime performance while still being GPU-friendly. The algorithm contains an easy to use performance/quality-tradeoff parameter, making it tunable to a wide range of graphics hardware.

Queried virtual shadow maps have the following advantages:

- They can take advantage of characteristics of the scene, such as areas that have no shadow boundaries (i.e., are completely in the shadow or in the light).
- They can remove projection aliasing (as opposed to perspective aliasing only).
- By guaranteeing subpixel shadow map accuracy, they solve the problem of non-static shadows when using the shadow-map-focusing optimization [Brabec02].

They have the following additional advantages over global sample redistribution methods (such as trapezoidal shadow maps [Martin04] or lightspace perspective shadow maps (LiSPSMs) [Wimmer04]) alone:

- They increase the resolution, and therefore quality, of the resulting shadows for any light direction (whereas the effect of global sample redistribution methods diminishes to nil when the light direction approaches the view direction).
- They work for scenes that, even with an optimal global sample redistribution, are too large to give acceptable shadow quality.

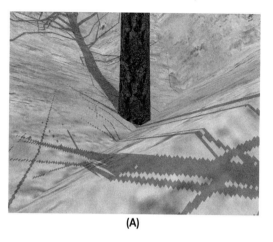 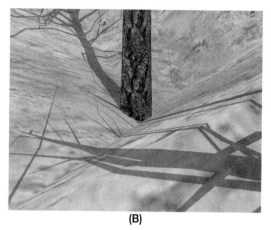

(A)   (B)

FIGURE 4.5.1   **(A)** Undersampling artifacts: perspective aliasing in the lower-right corner and projection aliasing on the slope in the middle of the scene. Projection aliasing occurs when the normal of the shadow receiver surface is nearly perpendicular to the light direction. Shadow map entry rearrangement techniques such as lightspace perspective shadow maps (LiSPSMs) [Wimmer04] cannot help against projection aliasing. Even in this moderately large scene, LiSPSM cannot prevent perspective aliasing artifacts, even though the shadow map resolution used is the maximum supported in hardware. **(B)** Queried virtual shadow maps prevent both types of undersampling artifacts.

Virtual Tiled Shadow Mapping

Virtual tiled shadow mapping is a brute force approach for increasing the resolution of the shadow map beyond the maximum texture size supported by the hardware. The basic algorithm is as follows:

1. Allocate the biggest shadow map texture supported by the GPU, for example, 4096×4096.
2. Partition the shadow map along the shadow map x- and y-axes into $n \times n$ (e.g., 16×16) equally sized tiles (each tile using the full shadow map texture resolution of, for example, 4096×4096 texels; that is, the effective resolution of the full shadow map in this example is $(16*4096) \times (16*4096) = 65536 \times 65536$.
3. For each tile
   a. Render a shadow map into the shadow map texture (overwriting the shadow map for the previous tile).
   b. Use it immediately to shadow (modulate) the part of the scene that is covered by the current shadow map tile.

Virtual shadow map generation can be applied in two ways: shadow map tiling and shadow map slicing. Tiling partitions the shadow map into tiles, whereas slicing partitions the view frustum into several parts. We believe shadow map tiling is the superior approach, so the remainder of this article deals only with virtual tiled shadow mapping.

There are two ways to implement the loop over the tiles: multipass shadowing and virtual deferred shadowing.

Multipass Shadowing

One way to apply successive shadow map tiles to the scene is by multipass rendering. In the first pass the scene is rendered normally (with full shading and depth-writes enabled), with the first shadow map tile applied to it. For each subsequent shadow map tile, the scene is rendered again, but only shadow mapping using the relevant tile is applied to the frame buffer. Pixels falling outside the shadow map tile are suppressed. Depth-writes and shading are disabled, and the depth comparison function is set to EQUAL in those passes (depending on driver support, it can make sense to substitute LESSEQUAL for EQUAL).

Deferred Shadowing

Multipass shadowing, although easy to implement, comes with a significant performance overhead of rendering the whole scene several times. To speed up the application of the shadow map tiles to the scene, we use what we call *deferred shadowing*, where the shadowing is done using a linear depth buffer of the scene instead of rerasterizing the scene geometry and the information needed to do the next shadowing pass; that is, the next shadow map tile is created on the fly between the passes (for shadow map slicing, the slicing can also be deferred, by shadowing only the pixels whose depths lie inside the current view frustum slice).

The scene is first rendered to a texture that stores eye-space depth, called the *eye-space depth buffer*. Each subsequent tiled shadowing pass can then read this texture and calculate the world-space position of the visible surface at each pixel, using the screen coordinates and the depth stored in the eye-space depth buffer. The world-space position is then shadowed using the shadow map tile as before.

Note that storing the unmodified eye-space z-coordinate in the eye-space depth buffer guarantees that the shadow map lookup produces the same results as if the original scene objects were used for shadow mapping. This is important because any other method of obtaining the z-value, for example, using window-space z-coordinates (which is highly nonlinear) or a fixed-precision w-buffer (if it were still supported on current hardware) would inevitably lead to image artifacts.

In detail, this works as follows:

1. In the first pass render the scene as described above, but into a 4-component 32-bit floating point render target. In the pixel shader store the unmodified eye-space z-coordinate into the α-component. This component forms the eye-space depth buffer (for simplicity, we refer to the whole four-component target as the eye-space depth buffer). The color of each pixel in the object when lit by the light (ignoring shadowing) is written to the RGB channels.
2. For each shadow-map tile
   a. Render a shadow map into the shadow map texture as with multipass shadow mapping.
   b. Instead of rendering the geometry for the whole scene again, render a full-screen quad with the eye-space depth buffer bound as a texture.
   c. In the pixel shader for each fragment, look up the eye-space depth of the fragment in the eye-space depth buffer's α-channel and unproject it into world space (see below). Using the unprojected fragment, calculate the shadowing term. Then modulate the already-shaded RGB value from the eye-space depth buffer with the shadowing term.
   d. The resulting shaded and possibly shadowed fragment is then written to the frame buffer.

The pixel shader operations in the individual passes are quite straightforward, with the exception of the unproject operation. Unlike a standard viewport unprojection, which transforms from window (x_w, y_w, z_w)-coordinates to eye space (x_e, y_e, z_e)-coordinates, this operation has to deduce eye space (x_e, y_e, z_e) from (x_w, y_w) (given as texture coordinates, that is, running from 0 to 1) and z_e. This can be done using the following matrix transform:

$$
\begin{pmatrix} x_e \\ y_e \\ z_e \end{pmatrix} = z_e \cdot \begin{pmatrix} \frac{1}{a_x} & 0 & -\frac{b_x}{a_x} \\ 0 & \frac{1}{a_y} & -\frac{b_y}{a_y} \\ 0 & 0 & 1 \end{pmatrix} \cdot \begin{pmatrix} 2 & 0 & 1 \\ 0 & 2 & -1 \\ 0 & 0 & 1 \end{pmatrix} \cdot \begin{pmatrix} x_w \\ y_w \\ 1 \end{pmatrix}
$$

where the parameters a_x, a_y, b_x and b_y in the first matrix should be taken from the projection matrix $\mathbf{P}$ supplied to the graphics API:

$$
P = \begin{pmatrix} a_x & 0 & b_x & 0 \\ 0 & a_y & b_y & 0 \\ 0 & 0 & \dots & \dots \\ 0 & 0 & 1 & 0 \end{pmatrix}
$$

See Figure 4.5.2 for a comparison of multipass and deferred shadowing.

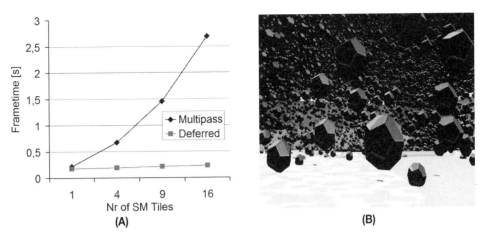

FIGURE 4.5.2   **(A)** Performance comparison of multipass and deferred shadow map tiling. Shadow mapping of scene **(B)** on a GeForce 6600GT with 256MB, Pentium4 2.4GHz (1GB).

Queried Virtual Shadow Mapping

Problems with Brute Force Refinement

One might think that the fill-rate requirements of tiled shadow maps increase with n^2, n being the number of tiles along each shadow map axis. However, to get a noticeable increase in shadowing quality, one has to effectively double the number of tiles along each axis, which leads to a quadrupling in the number of shadow map tiles (i.e., the number of shadow map textures that need to be generated each frame). The refinement level n_r is a much better measure of the shadowing quality than n, and the fill-rate requirements are proportional to 4^{n_r}. This means that even for frame times of about 1 second, the achievable maximum virtual shadow map resolution is limited. In addition, for a typical scene, a lot of unnecessary shadow map tiles are generated, owing to the brute force nature of the approach.

Smart Refinement Preferred

What we would like to do is adaptively refine the shadow map only where necessary: near the eye-point, and in regions with high projection aliasing. We would like to refine to a high level ($n \geq 16$) but do it fast enough so it can be done each frame—and without breaking the GPU friendliness of the algorithm.

One hypothetical way to do this is as follows. Do not shadow the scene directly, but write the results of the shadowing passes into an extra texture the size of the frame buffer (*shadow result texture*). Then refine the shadow map in quad-tree fashion: First, shadow the whole shadow result texture with a single shadow map tile. Then split the tile into 2×2 subtiles and shadow the shadow result texture with each subtile, noting how much the increase of the effective shadow map resolution improves the shadow result texture in each tile. If the improvement achieved by the refinement is small enough, stop processing this tile further. If not, split this tile again into 2×2 subtiles, and so on.

Compared to the brute force approach, this would lead to a greatly reduced number of required shadow map tiles. Unfortunately the GPU is very limited in its ability to execute such "smart" algorithms efficiently, especially those using even moderately complex data structures such as quadtrees.

Therefore, we need to move the decision whether to further refine a shadow map tile to the CPU. The problem is that there is no straightforward way to pass the necessary information to the CPU except by reading back the whole shadow result texture after each refinement step and counting changed pixels, which would be prohibitively expensive.

Queried Refinement: GPU Friendly and Smart

Instead, we have come up with a novel use of the GPU occlusion query mechanism, which counts the number of fragments emitted from the pixel shader. Occlusion queries were introduced to support image-space bounding-volume visibility tests and have seen mainstream support by graphics hardware vendors for some time now. We use the mechanism for another purpose: when applying a shadow map subtile to the shadow result texture, we instruct the pixel shader to produce a fragment only if the resulting shadow value differs from the previous refinement step (this can easily be done by accessing the previous shadow result texture in the shader). The number of produced fragments η, which is identical to the number of changed pixels in the shadow result texture, is found by bracketing the application of each shadow map tile with an occlusion query. The CPU can then decide whether to further refine a tile by comparing the value returned by its corresponding occlusion query with a threshold value η_{min}. If a number of pixels larger than η_{min} have changed, the tile is split into four subtiles; otherwise, the refinement of this tile stops. In addition, we use the maximum number of tiles allowed per shadow map axis, ξ_{max}, as a second refinement termination criterion.

Thus, the decision whether or not to refine a shadow map tile can be made without any frame buffer readback, which allows the whole algorithm to produce larger effective shadow map resolutions in real-time.

In detail, the basic version of queried virtual shadow maps works as follows (the following is schematic C++ code, to facilitate the understanding of the core algorithm, not the actual implementation):

```
const int nr_tile_per_axis_max = 16;
const int nr_pixel_min_changed = 300;

ShadowResultTexture& srt = GetShadowResultTexture();
ShadowResultTexture& srt_old = GetShadowResultTextureOld();

// Set the current shadow result texture to "completely lit"
ClearTexture(srt,1.0);
```

```
// Render Scene, including the linear viewspace depth into
// (r,g,b,a=depth)-float texture with attached
// conventional depth buffer (clear both before rendering)
RenderSceneIntoEyeSpaceDepthBuffer();

// Calculate the light-space matrix
// and focus the whole shadow map
D3DXMATRIX light_space;
CalculateLightSpace(&light_space);

// Queue holding the shadow map tiles to be rendered
SmTileRefinementQueryContainer smtrqc_render;
// Queue holding the shadow map tiles with pending queries
SmTileRefinementQueryContainer smtrqc_pending;

// Prepare the initial SM tile covering the whole
// SM for rendering
smtrqc_render.AddQuery(
  new SmTileRefinementQueryPixelCount(
    new SmTile(0,0,1) // tile at (0,0), nr_tile_per_axis = 1
  )
);

// Refine & Render SM-Tiles

while(!smtrqc_render.empty() || !smtrqc_pending.empty()) {

  // Copy current shadow result texture to
  // old shadow result texture. The "old" is used
  // as an input to the pixel shader to decide
  // whether or not to reject the new fragment.
  // On a NV GF6600 and ATI X1900, it is faster
  // to not copy and use SRT_old = SRT instead.
  CopyTextureFromTo(srt,srt_old);

  // Shadow the current ShadowResultTexture with all
  // pending shadow map tiles
  while(
    SmTileRefinementQuery* p_smtrq_render =
      smtrqc_render.PopNextQuery() )
  {
    // Create the shadow map texture for the current tile
    const SmTile& sm_tile = p_smtrq_render->GetTile();
    const ShadowMapTexture& smt =
    RenderSceneInLightFrustrumIntoShadowMap(sm_tile);
    // Shadow shadow result texture with the just created
    // tile SM, clamped with occlusion queries
    p_smtrq_render->QueryStart();
    ShadowShadowResultTextureWithSmTileShadowMap(
      sm_tile.ProjectionMatrixGet()*light_space, // light
      frustrum
      smt, // do SM lookups here
      srt, srt_old  // write into srt, compare with srt_old
    );
    p_smtrq_render->QueryEnd();
    // Add query to the pending occlusion query queue
    smtrqc_pending->AddQuery(p_smtrq_render);
```

```
            }

            // Wait until the first occlusion query is ready
            while( !smtrqc_pending.FinishedQueryAvailableQ() );

            SmTileRefinementQuery* p_smtrq_ready =
              smtrqc_pending.PopNextFinishedQuery();

            // Decide whether to split the tile int 2x2 subtiles
            if(p_smtrq_ready->NrTilePerAxis() < nr_tile_per_axis_max &&
               p_smtrq_ready->NrPixelChanged() > nr_pixel_min_changed)
            {
              SmTile&  sm_tile = p_smtrq_ready->GetTile();
              // the subtiles live in a virtual space 2x
              // as large in each dimension as the parent
              int ix_sub = 2 * sm_tile.TilePosX();
              int iy_sub = 2 * sm_tile.TilePosY();
              int nr_tile_per_axis_sub = 2 * sm_tile.NrTilePerAxisGet();
              for(int ix_rel=0; ix_rel < 2; ++ix_rel) {
                for(int iy_rel=0; iy_rel < 2; ++iy_rel) {
                  smtrqc_render.AddQuery(
                    new SmTileRefinementQueryPixelCount(
                      new SmTile(
                        ix_sub + ix_rel,
                        iy_sub + iy_rel,
                        nr_tile_per_axis_sub
                      )
                    )
                  );
                }
              }
              DEL(p_smtrq_ready); // this tile query is finished ;-)
            }
          }

          // Shadow the scene by modulating it with the ShadowResultTexture
          // FrameBuffer.RGB = ShadowResultTexture *
        //EyeSpaceDepthBuffer.RGB
          ShadowSceneWithShadowResultTexture();
```

Jump Optimizations

One fact that might not be immediately obvious is that using the maximum shadow map texture size supported in hardware for the virtual shadow map texture is, in general, not the best choice. This is because the minimum number of virtual shadow maps that will be created is $1 + 4 = 5$ (the initial shadow map plus one refinement step). If all of these were maximum size, then the minimum fill-rate requirement of the algorithm would be five times that of conventional shadow mapping. With ever-rising fill-rate capabilities, using the maximum shadow map texture size will become possible, but currently it is better to start the refinement process using a smaller shadow map texture.

At the same time, using four virtual shadow maps of size $n/2$ is more costly than using one shadow map of size n, so we would like to use larger shadow maps whenever possible.

We have come up with two optimizations, both of which exploit the fact that we do not initially use the maximum shadow map texture size the GPU supports. In the following, s denotes the shadow map texture size used for the tiles, and s_{max}, the maximum shadow map texture size that the GPU can still handle well; see the Results section for recommended values.

Maximum Refinement Jump

This optimization makes use of the maximum tile refinement criterion ξ_{max}, the maximum allowed number of tiles per shadow map axis. Before splitting a tile, we first test whether the maximum virtual shadow map resolution $\xi_{max} \cdot s$ could also be reached in one step by switching to a larger shadow map texture (i.e., a higher shadow map resolution) instead of splitting the tile. With ξ as the current tile refinement level, we make the jump if $\xi_{max} \cdot s \leq s_{max} \cdot \xi$. Since we know that we will reach the maximum user-defined virtual shadow map resolution for this tile and therefore will not refine this tile further, we turn off querying for the shadowing step.

Opportunity Jump

The opportunity jump optimization uses a heuristic criterion to predict the future development of η (the number of pixels in the shadow result texture that changed through the last refinement step). If the prediction is that η will become smaller than η_{min} within a *jump distance* (number of refinement steps) $\frac{s_{max}}{s}$, then we again do not refine the tile, but increase the shadow map texture size instead.

Having observed the behavior of η in the vicinity of η_{min}, we currently use the assumption that η decreases at least by a factor of one-half in each refinement step, so we make the jump if $\eta \cdot \left(\frac{1}{2}\right)^{\frac{s_{max}}{s}} \leq \eta_{min}$.

We again turn off querying for the shadowing step and stop any further refinement because in the unlikely case that the tile does not reach the intended resolution, it would be disproportionately expensive to split the tile further, because we would have to use four shadow maps with $s = s_{max}$.

Comparison with Adaptive Shadow Maps

Our algorithm is similar in spirit to "Adaptive Shadow Maps" [Fernando01] and its GPU-based implementation, "Dynamic Adaptive Shadow Maps on Graphics Hardware" [Lefohn05] in that it also uses a quadtree scheme to refine the shadow map (which is a more or less obvious choice). However, instead of trying to predict the required shadow map resolution for each camera pixel, we simply stop the refinement when we discover that the resolution is high enough. The efficiency of this mechanism allows us to perform the complete refinement procedure for each frame. This is in contrast to adaptive shadow maps, which have to cache the recently used shadow tiles for best performance—an approach that is not well suited to dynamic scenes (see the large performance drop for this case in [Lefohn05], even though the test scene consists only of a single tree on a small quad). This also means that we do not need persistent video memory for cached tiles.

Results

Figures 4.5.3 and 4.5.4 show a comparison between different shadow mapping approaches on an ATI Radeon X1900XTX with 512 MB of RAM (Pentium4 3.4 GHz with 2 GB RAM) for different frame buffer resolutions and maximum refine-

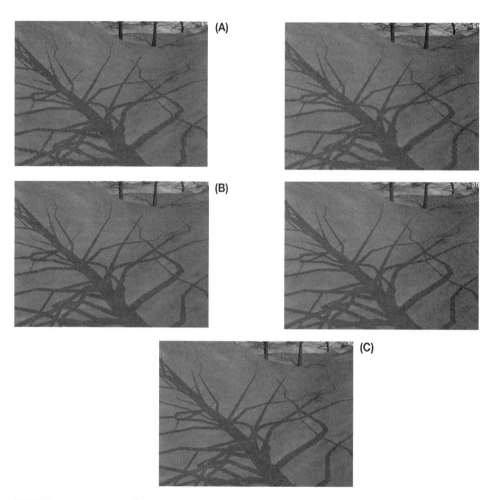

FIGURE 4.5.3 (A) 4096^2 uniform shadow map. (B) 4096^2 LiSPSM shadow map. (C) 4×4 4096^2 virtual tiled shadow map. Quality and performance comparison of shadow mapping techniques at 1024×768 resolution (speed in frames per second [fps] is displayed in the upper right corner). LiSPSM improves the quality, but even at 4096^2 still suffers from strong undersampling; brute force virtual tiling gives greatly improved quality but falls below 10 fps; queried virtual shadow maps give good quality while improving the rendering speed: 27 fps with the basic algorithm, 40 fps with jump optimizations.

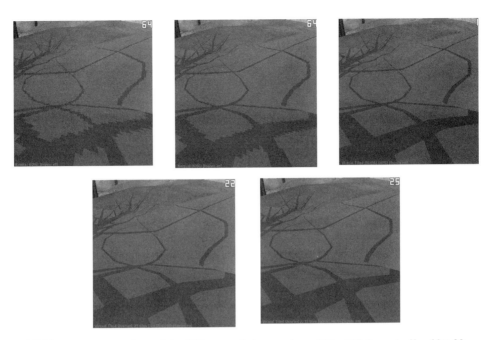

FIGURE 4.5.4 Comparison of the different techniques using a 512×512 frame buffer, 32×32 tiles maximum refinement, and a 2048^2 shadow map texture.

ON THE CD

ment level ξ_{max}. One can see that sample redistribution methods, represented here by LiSPSM [Wimmer04], cannot sufficiently increase the effective shadow map resolution for all view directions.

Shadow mapping and its artifacts (or absence thereof) are best observed in motion. For further results, we therefore refer you to the companion CD-ROM.

For the refinement parameter η_{min}, we found that for an NVidia GeForce 6600GT with 256MB of RAM, 1024×1024 shadow map textures together with $s_{max} = 2048$ proved to be efficient, whereas for an ATI Radeon 1900XTX with 512MB of RAM, using 2048×2048 with $s_{max} = 4096$ proved to be the best choice (both graphics cards support a maximum texture resolution of 4096×4096).

For the threshold parameter η_{min}, we found that a value of 300 works well for a 512×512 frame buffer, whereas $\eta_{min} \approx 1000$ was a good choice for a resolution of 1024×768.

Our tests show that both jump optimizations can be active at the same time, combining their potential to increase the frame rate of the application.

Further Optimizations

The following further optimizations can be applied to the algorithm:

- If there is enough texture memory available, shadow map tile generation can be interleaved with a tile application to the eye-space depth buffer by using two or more shadow maps. Alternatively, in the case of queried shadow maps (for which it is not necessarily the best choice to the use the maximum resolution shadow map texture supported by the GPU; see "Results" above), parts of a larger shadow map texture can be used for virtual shadow map generation.

- If each area in the scene is only influenced by a single light source with a small ambient term (for instance, an outdoor scene lit by the sun) and a diffuse shading model is used, then many problematic polygons with large projection aliasing will be hidden because the dominant $\hat{n}_{polygon} \cdot \hat{d}_{light}$ term in the diffuse shader will cause them to be very dark. In this case one can extend the queried virtual shadow map algorithm. When deciding whether to write a pixel to the shadow result texture, first look up the color of the corresponding pixel in the texture containing the unshadowed scene (created in the first pass). If the largest of the color components is below a certain threshold, skip the shadow map lookup for this pixel and do not write it to the shadow result texture. To make the state switch less abrupt, one could fade out the influence of the shadow map shadow term across a certain region around the threshold.

- Using the relative metric $\eta_{rel} < \frac{n_{pixels\_changed\_in\_tile}}{n_{pixels\_in\_tile}}$ instead of the absolute $\eta_{abs} < n_{pixels\_changed\_in\_tile}$ could be a better choice for deciding whether to further refine a shadow map tile. The problem is to get $n_{pixels\_in\_tile}$:

  1. One possible way would be to reapply the shadow map tile to the eye-space depth buffer (without shadow map lookups, of course), again bracketed with an occlusion query, but always emitting a fragment in the pixel shader if it lies within the current tile. The result of the occlusion query would then be $n_{pixels\_in\_tile}$. We have tried this, and unfortunately it seemed that the practical cost of this operation is too high. See "Hardware Extensions" for a potentially better way to achieve this.

  2. A less accurate but faster method would be to calculate the number of screen-space pixels in the projection of the shadow map tile onto the ground plane of the scene (trapezoid clipped to screen-space coordinates) and use this as an approximation for $n_{pixels\_in\_tile}$. Whether this approximation works well or not would, of course, depend on the characteristics of the scene.

Hardware Extensions

We use the hardware occlusion query mechanism as a counter to efficiently pass back information from the GPU to the CPU. This mechanism is like a tiny loophole, since only one value can be passed back per rendering pass, and increasing the counter is linked to emitting a color value from the pixel shader (which, fortunately, in our case is what we want to do anyway).

We are sure that many more smart, adaptive algorithms could be combined with fast GPU rendering if this GPU functionality would be extended to include several registers like the occlusion query fragment counter, which could, for example, be incremented/decremented (possibly by an arbitrary amount) and which would support atomic min/max operations. Since these operations are independent of the order of execution (with the exception of overflows in the case of decrement/subtraction), they would be compatible with the highly parallel vector processor design of modern GPUs.

With just one additional counter register, one could, for instance, count the total number of pixels corresponding to the current shadow map tile in addition to the number of pixels that have changed in the last refinement step, allowing us to employ different refinement metrics. With four additional registers with min/max support, one could find the screen-space bounding box around the area influenced by a shadow map tile, reducing the number of pixels that need to be touched when applying a shadow map tile to the scene.

Acknowledgments

We thank Albrecht Kadlec for insightful discussions about vector processor design with regards to the "Hardware Extensions" section.

This work was supported by the European Union in the scope of the GameTools project (*www.gametools.org*) (IST-2-004363).

Further Material

ON THE CD

You can find additional material on the companion CD-ROM and at *http://www.cg.tuwien.ac.at/research/vr/vsm/*.

References

[Brabec02] Brabec, S., T. Annen, and H.-P. Seidel. "Practical Shadow Mapping." *Journal of Graphics Tools* 7(4) (2002): pp. 9–18.

[Fernando01] Fernando, Randima, Sebastian Fernandez, Kavita Bala, and Donald P. Greenberg. "Adaptive Shadow Maps." *Proc. ACM SIGGRAPH*, 2001, pp. 387–390.

[Lefohn05] Lefohn, Aaron, Shubhabrata Sengupta, Joe M. Kniss, Robert Strzodka, and John D. Owens. "Dynamic Adaptive Shadow Maps on Graphics Hardware." *ACM SIGGRAPH 2005 Conference Abstracts and Applications.*

[Martin04] Martin, T. and T.-S. Tan. "Anti-aliasing and Continuity with Trapezoidal Shadow Maps." *Eurographics Symposium on Rendering*, 2004, pp. 153–160.

[Stamminger02] Stamminger, M. and G. Drettakis. "Perspective Shadow Maps." *ACM Transactions on Graphics* (Proceedings of SIGGRAPH 2002), *21*(3), (2002): 557–562.

[Wimmer04] Wimmer, Michael, Daniel Scherzer, and Werner Purgathofer. "Light Space Perspective Shadow Maps." *Eurographics Symposium on Rendering*, 2004: pp. 143–151.

[Wimmer05] Wimmer, Michael and Jiri Bittner. "Hardware Occlusion Queries Made Useful." *GPU Gems 2*, Addison-Wesley, 2005: pp. 91–108.

4.6

Real-Time Soft Shadows with Shadow Accumulation

László Szirmay-Kalos and Barnabás Aszódi,

Budapest University of Technology and Economics, Hungary

Introduction

Realistic light sources have nonzero area, resulting in *soft shadows* having continuous transitions, called *penumbra*, between the fully illuminated region and the occluded, *umbra* region. Soft shadow algorithms should handle the visibility between shadow receiver points and all points of area light sources. *Multisample approaches* [Hasen03] [Zhengming02] [Ass03] compute hard shadows from different light source samples and average the partial results. *Single-sample approaches* [Brabec02] [Kirsch03] [Fernando05], on the other hand, process the scene from only one light source sample and apply this information for all light source points. Single-sample algorithms often ignore an important fact. A shadow map describes the visibility *from the light source*. However, in soft-shadow generation we need to know the portion of the light source occluded from the shaded point; that is, we need visibility information *from the shaded point*. While point-to-point visibility is mutual and symmetric, point-to-region visibility is not (Figure 4.6.1).

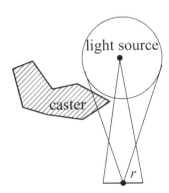

FIGURE 4.6.1 Point-to-region visibility is not symmetric. The center of the light source is visible from all points of a surface element, but not all points of the light source are visible from the center of this surface element.

The algorithm in this article is also a single sample approach that morphs the shadow map to obtain visibility information from the shaded points. The algorithm estimates the solid angles in which the total light source and its occluded part are visible.

The New Algorithm

Consider a homogeneous area light source illuminating receiver point $\vec{r}$ (Figure 4.6.2). If the light source is partially or fully occluded from point $\vec{r}$ by shadow caster c, then the reflected radiance decreases. We will assume that the light source emission is approximately uniform, the surface is diffuse or only moderately glossy, and the light source is not too close to the illuminated surface. Given this, the ratio of the radiances in the occluded and nonoccluded cases is equal to the ratio of the solid angles in which the nonoccluded and the total light sources are visible from point $\vec{r}$. The difference between 1 (a fully-lit surface) and this ratio is the *shadowing factor*, and is denoted by $s(c,\vec{r})$.

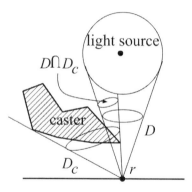

FIGURE 4.6.2 Computation of shadowing factors as the ratio of solid angles of the occluded $\left| D_C \cap D \right|$ and the total $\left| D \right|$ light source part.

Let D be the set of directions from which the light source may illuminate shaded point $\vec{r}$ if no occlusion occurs. This set can also be imagined as the set of those rays that originate at $\vec{r}$ and intersect the light source. Similarly D_C is the set of directions from which caster c is visible or the set of rays that originate at $\vec{r}$ and intersect caster c. A natural measure $|.|$ of these sets is the solid angle. According to its definition, the shadowing factor can also be expressed as:

$$s(c,\vec{r}) = \frac{\left| D_C \cap D \right|}{\left| D \right|}$$

Lighting is an additive phenomenon. Shadows are caused by "missing lighting," so they are also additive if their casters do not occlude each other. Let us consider two shadow casters c_1 and c_2 and express their joint shadowing factor:

$$s(c_1 \cup c_2, \vec{r}) = \frac{\left| \left(D_{C1} \cup D_{C2} \right) \cap D \right|}{|D|} \qquad (4.6.1)$$

If casters do not occlude the light source from each other, then

$$s(c_1 \cup c_2, \vec{r}) = \frac{\left| \left(D_{C1} \cap D \right) + \left(D_{C2} \cap D \right) \right|}{|D|} = s(c_1, \vec{r}) + s(c_2, \vec{r}) \qquad (4.6.2)$$

On the other hand, when caster c_1 occludes all points of c_2, then

$$s(c_1 \cup c_2, \vec{r}) = \frac{\left| \left(D_{C1} \cap D \right) \right|}{|D|} = s(c_1, \vec{r}) \qquad (4.6.3)$$

To compute the shadow factors, we need the visibility information from each shaded point $\vec{r}$, but the shadow map provides visibility information obtained from the light source. However, distances stored in lexels (in the shadow map) together with the positions of the lexels and the center of the light source can also be interpreted as a discretized version of the shadow caster geometry. The main idea here is to take a single shadow map as the geometric description of the scene, assume that each lexel represents a small surface area, compute shadowing factors of these elementary surfaces, and add up their shadowing factors using Equation 4.6.1 or preferably Equations 4.6.2 and 4.6.3 if their requirements are met. From another point of view, this means that when a point is shaded, all lexels that possibly contain geometric information relevant to the shadowing of the given point are read. Note that conventional shadow mapping would read only a single lexel per shaded point.

The evaluation of the shadowing factor requires the identification of the direction sets and the execution of set operations. If the ray origin of a direction set is fixed, then the ray direction can be defined by a point on a plane not containing the ray origin. To discretize this set, a raster grid is imposed on this plane, so each pixel corresponds to a small directional set. Note that a shadow map also uses this representation.

To represent the visibility information from shaded point $\vec{r}$, we need a plane with a raster grid. A straightforward solution is to use the same plane and raster grid for this purpose as was used to identify the points visible from the light source, that is, the same one used by the shadow map. This means that a single point on a shadow caster may correspond to two points of the projection plane, depending on whether the projection is performed from the light source center or the shaded point. The information stored in the lexels of the plane must be transformed to reflect the differences of the two tasks.

Let us examine point $\vec{c}$ on the shadow caster surface, which is projected onto $\vec{l}$ of the shadow map plane with the light source as the center of projection and onto $\vec{l}_{\vec{r}}$ if shaded point $\vec{r}$ is the center of projection. Suppose that these points are given by Cartesian coordinates in the light's camera space. In this coordinate system the origin is the center of the light source, and axis z is perpendicular to the plane of the shadow map (Figure 4.6.3). Denoting the distance of the projection plane from the light source center by n, the projection of caster point $\vec{c}$ from the light source center onto the shadow map plane is

$$\vec{l} = \vec{c} \cdot \frac{n}{c_z} \tag{4.6.4}$$

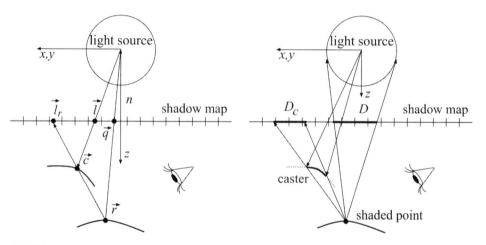

FIGURE 4.6.3   Notations used in the discussion of the shadow accumulation algorithm. An elementary caster is a surface area visible from the light source center in a single lexel. This caster is seen from the shaded point in solid angle D_C defined by other lexels on the shadow map plane.

When the same point is projected from shaded point $\vec{r}$, we compute the intersection between the line through both $\vec{c}$ and $\vec{r}$ and the shadow map plane. The line can be given in parametric form, $\vec{c} \cdot t + \vec{r} \cdot (1-t)$, where t is a scalar parameter. The equation of the shadow map plane is $z = n$, resulting in the following intersection point:

$$\vec{l}_{\vec{r}} = \frac{n - c_z}{r_z - c_z} \cdot \vec{r} + \frac{r_z - n}{r_z - c_z} \cdot \vec{c}$$

Using Equation 4.6.4, we obtain

$$\vec{l}_{\vec{r}} = \frac{n - c_z}{r_z - c_z} \cdot \vec{r} + \frac{r_z - n}{r_z - c_z} \cdot \frac{c_z}{n} \cdot \vec{l}$$

Note that this equation defines a scaling and a translation between $\vec{l}$ and $\vec{l}_{\vec{r}}$. A lexel is a rectangular area whose points correspond to an elementary shadow caster surface, which is projected back to the shadow map from the shaded point. Thus, the mapping of the points corresponding to a lexel results in another, roughly rectangular, area representing those directions from which this caster may occlude shaded point $\vec{r}$. The approximate center of this area is obtained by transforming the center of lexel $\vec{l}$. By definition, the elementary caster covers a single lexel from the point of view of the light source. Consequently, it covers roughly $\left(\frac{r_z - n}{r_z - c_z} \cdot \frac{c_z}{n} \right)^2$ number of lexels when it is seen from shaded point $\vec{r}$.

The shadowing factor caused by this caster is the ratio of the number of lexels in which both the caster and the light source are seen (the light is occluded) to the number of lexels where only the light source is seen (the light is not occluded). In order to process all potential casters, a neighborhood is searched on the shadow plane around $\vec{q}$, which is the projection of shaded point $\vec{r}$. This neighborhood should be large enough to include all casters that can possibly occlude the light. When processing a lexel of the neighborhood, its elementary caster is examined and we check whether it can occlude any part of the light source from the shaded point. The caster is also represented by lexel's on the shadow plane, whose occlusion bits are then set (obit). Note that a lexel's occlusion bit might be set several times, since a light source point might be occluded by several casters from the shaded point, which corresponds to the intersection set operation $D_C \cap D$.

The following algorithm finds the solid angles of the light source (D) and its occluded part (DcD). The solid angles are represented by the lexels, and set operations are executed on the plane of the shadow map.

```
Set obits to zero in D
for each lexel l in D
    for each caster c of lexel l
        size = (r.z-n)/(r.z-c.z) * c.z/n;
        lr = (n-c.z)/(r.z-c.z) * r + size * l;
        for each lexel l' closer to lr than size
            if (l' is in D) obit[l'] = 1;
DcD = 0;
for each lexel l' in D if (obit[l']) DcD++;
s = DcD / number of lexels in D;
```

This algorithm evaluates Equation 4.6.1 and is quite difficult to implement on the GPU because of the complicated conditions. Another problem is that several casters may correspond to a single lexel, so classic shadow maps storing only the closest caster cannot be used. Instead, we should store all casters in a kind of layered depth image.

In order to make the algorithm faster and the implementation easier, we make several simplifying assumptions. These assumptions will replace Equation 4.6.1 with Equations 4.6.2 and 4.6.3, and allow us to get rid of the complicated conditions:

- The light source is assumed to be a sphere of radius R. Setting the shadow map plane distance n proportional to R, the neighborhood in which the light source is visible from $\vec{r}$ can be covered by the same number of lexels, $K \times K$, where K is called *kernel size*.
- We keep only the closest caster in each lexel and assume that they do not occlude each other. Note that if the light source is reasonably sized, then most of the shadow casters belonging to the second and further layers are occluded from all points of the light source, so their contribution to the shadowing factors is already zero (Equation 4.6.3).
- The casters in the first layer are assumed not to occlude each other from the point of view of the shaded point. This allows the application of Equation 4.6.2. Note that by definition, these casters do not occlude each other from the point of view of the light source.

Taking advantage of the simplifying assumptions, the pseudo-code of the computation of the shadowing factor is:

```
R'= R * (r.z-n)/r.z;
s = 0;
for each lexel l of square KxK
    size = (r.z-n)/(r.z-c.z) * c.z/n;
    lr = (n-c.z)/(r.z-c.z) * r + size * l;
    if (|lr - q| < R') s += size * size;
endfor
s /= R' * R' * PI / K / K;
```

Conclusion

The proposed method has been implemented on an NV7800GT graphics card and compared to percentage closer soft shadows (PCSS) [Fernando05] and to a multisample reference solution obtained with 64 light source samples. The images generated with different kernel sizes are shown in Figure 4.6.4. Note that our results are closer to the reference solution and faster than percentage closer soft shadows. Please refer to this article's folder on the CD-ROM.

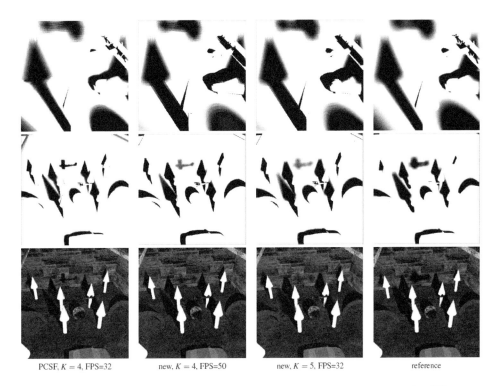

PCSF, $K = 4$, FPS=32   new, $K = 4$, FPS=50   new, $K = 5$, FPS=32   reference

FIGURE 4.6.4   Soft shadows generated with a 512×512 resolution shadow map with different kernel sizes (K), as compared with percentage closer soft shadows and with a reference solution.

References

[Ass03] Assarsson, Ulf and Tomas Akenine-Möller. "A Geometry-Based Soft Shadow Volume Algorithm using Graphics Hardware." *ACM Transactions on Graphics,* *22*(3) (2003): pp 511–520.

[Brabec02] Brabec, Stefan and Hans-Peter Seidel. "Single Sample Soft Shadows Using Depth Maps." *Graphics Interface* (GI 2002 Proceedings), (2002)" pp. 219–228.

[Fernando05] Randima Fernando. "Percentage-Closer Soft Shadows." *SIGGRAPH* *'2005 Sketches*, 2005.

[Hasen03] Hasenfratz, Jean-Marc, Marc Lapierre, Nicolas Holzschuch, and François X. Sillion. "A Survey of Real-time Soft Shadow Algorithms." Eurographics 2003 Conference. State of the Art Reports. 2003.

[Kirsch03] Kirsch, Florian and Juergen Doellner. "Real-time Soft Shadows Using a Single Light Sample." *Journal of WSCG, 11*(2), (2003): pp 255–262.

[Zhengming02] Ying, Zhengming, Min Tang, and Jinxiang Dong. "Soft Shadow Maps for Area Light by Area Approximation." *Proceedings of the 10th Pacific Conference on Computer Graphics and Applications*, 2002, pp. 442–443.

ENVIRONMENTAL EFFECTS

Introduction

Matthias Wloka

Welcome to a fantastic collection of environmental effects. This section of the *ShaderX* series of books explains how to render the showcase effects in games—the things that draw you into a game, the things that make you say: "Wow." *ShaderX⁵* is no exception.

Tamás Umenhoffer, László Szirmay-Kalos, and Gábor Szíjártó start us off: their article "Spherical Billboards for Rendering Volumetric Data" shows how to banish traditional billboard clipping and popping artifacts when rendering particle systems. Their solution still renders billboarded quads, but each quad represents a spherical volume that is approximated using a pixel shader. While the technique requires a distance map of the scene, this distance map can be generated on the fly, or one can reuse the depth buffer when working on a gaming console. The authors demonstrate the practicality of their technique as they apply it to rendering explosions.

In the following article, "Per-Pixel Lit, Light Scattering Smoke," Aurelio Reis focuses on the lighting of particle systems to achieve realistic-looking smoke. He simulates light scattering per pixel and combines the result with a per-pixel direct illumination term. His results speak for themselves.

"Volumetric Clouds and Mega-Particles" by Homam Bahnassi and Wessam Bahnassi, investigates how to use fewer but larger mega-particles to render volumetric effects. This novel approach has plenty of benefits including improved rendering performance and more manageable animation controls for artists. The technique renders the mega-particles into a separate render target, blurs the result, and applies a noise texture before compositing the resulting render target texture with the frame buffer. Ideally only objects behind the volumetric effect are rendered before this process to avoid depth-ordering artifacts near the edges of the particles. The authors describe the details of how the technique works, using clouds as the specific volumetric effect to render.

Natalya Tatarchuk abandons particle systems altogether for her implementation of rain in "Rendering Multiple Layers of Rain with a Postprocessing Composite Effect." She instead generates rain in a postprocess. Her article shows how to simulate multiple layers of falling rain in a pixel shader and how to shade rain drops to create a high-fidelity rain effect. The effect runs in real-time.

Stefano Lanza describes a simple, yet highly effective, technique to animate and render god rays in "Animation and Rendering of Underwater God Rays." He models these light shafts as a collection of parallelepipeds that a vertex shader positions, extrudes, and animates. These parallelepipeds then render into a reduced-resolution render target to accumulate information about their location in screen space. A second rendering pass then computes lighting information for the god rays as it composites the generated render target with the frame buffer. This two-pass approach thus limits the cost of overdraw generated by overlapping light shafts to the first pass, which only uses an inexpensive pixel shader and operates at reduced resolution. Only the second pass makes expensive lighting calculations. The resulting god rays are beautiful and inexpensive enough to be a must for any underwater game.

ON THE CD

To see these effects in motion, please refer to the book's CD-ROM. All articles in this section provide an associated sample application. Enjoy!

5.1

Spherical Billboards for Rendering Volumetric Data

Tamás Umenhoffer, László Szirmay-Kalos, and Gábor Szíjártó

Budapest University of Technology and Economics

Introduction

Many types of natural phenomena are participating media [Blinn82]; examples include fire, smoke, explosions, fog, and clouds. Participating media can be simulated by animating and rendering a particle system [Reeves83]. A particle is an animation and rendering primitive whose geometric extent is small, but that possesses certain properties such as position, speed, color, and opacity.

Formally, a particle system is a discretization of a continuous medium, where each particle represents a spherical neighborhood in which the volume is locally homogeneous. This formulation allows us to replace differentials of the equations governing the motion and light scattering with finite differences during simulation and rendering.

In this article we focus on rendering such systems in real-time; that is, we solve the volumetric rendering equation. The discretization of the volumetric rendering equation thus leads to the following equation expressing *outgoing radiance* $L(j,\vec{\omega})$ of particle j at direction $\vec{\omega}$ (with the *density, albedo,* and *phase function* of this particle given by $\tau_j, a_j,$ and P_j, respectively, and the length of a ray segment intersecting the sphere of particle j given by Δs_j):

$$L(j,\vec{\omega})=I(j,\vec{\omega})\cdot(1-\alpha_j)+\alpha_j\cdot a_j\cdot C_j+\alpha_j\cdot(1-a_j)\cdot L^e_j(\vec{\omega}), \qquad (5.1.1)$$

where $I(j,\vec{\omega})$ is the *incoming radiance* from direction $\vec{\omega}$,

$$\alpha_j=1-e^{-\int_{\Delta s_j}\tau(s)ds}=1-e^{-\tau_j\Delta s_j} \qquad (5.1.2)$$

is the *opacity* that expresses the decrease of radiance caused by this particle due to *extinction*, L^e_j is the emission radiance, and

$$C_j = \int_{\Omega'} I(j,\vec{\omega}') \cdot P_j(\vec{\omega}',\vec{\omega}) \, d\vec{\omega}' \qquad (5.1.3)$$

is the total contribution from *in-scattering*.

Splatting [Schaufler95] [Reeves83] [Wei02] is one solution to this problem. It renders particles as semi-transparent, camera-aligned rectangles, also called billboards. When such a billboard is rasterized, the in-scattering term attenuates according to the total opacity of the particles that are between the camera and the current billboard. To obtain a reasonable approximation to the in-scattering term thus requires billboards to be sorted and rendered in back to front order. Rendering a billboard adds its in-scattering and emission terms (Equation 5.1.1) to the frame buffer.

Billboard Clipping Artifact

Billboards are planar rectangles with no extension along one dimension. This two-dimensional representation causes artifacts when billboards intersect opaque objects (see Figure 5.1.1). The root cause of this clipping artifact is that billboards assume that all objects are fully behind the sphere of the particle. Objects in front of the billboard plane are not affected at all, and thus transparency changes abruptly at all object–billboard intersections.

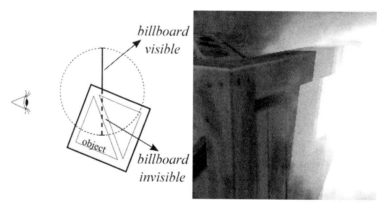

FIGURE 5.1.1   A billboard clipping artifact. When the billboard rectangle intersects an opaque object, transparency becomes spatially discontinuous.

Billboard Popping Artifact

When the camera moves into the simulated medium, billboards also cause popping arti-facts. In this case, the billboard is either behind or in front of the front clipping plane; transitioning between these two states is instantaneous. The particle thus switches from fully visible to fully invisible, resulting in an abrupt change (see Figure 5.1.2).

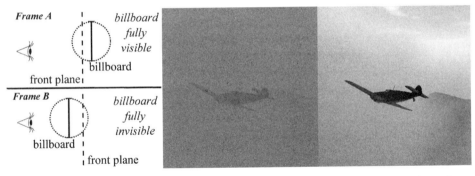

FIGURE 5.1.2 A billboard-popping artifact. When the billboard switches sides of the front clipping plane, the transparency is discontinuous in time (the figure shows two adjacent frames in an animation).

To solve these problems of clipping and popping, we introduce spherical billboards in the section "Spherical Billboards." We apply the proposed idea to render realistic explosions in the section "Rendering Explosions." Figure 5.1.3 shows a few frames of an animation that uses this technique to render explosions.

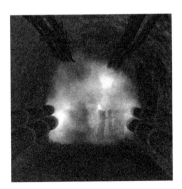

FIGURE 5.1.3 Rendered frames from an animation sequence showing an explosion.

Spherical Billboards

To solve the billboard-clipping artifact we calculate the path length a light ray travels inside a given particle. This length determines the correct opacity value during rendering. Instead of representing particles as planar rectangles, we assume particles to be spherical. To keep an implementation simple and fast, however, we still render particles as quadrilateral primitives and only take their spherical shape into account during fragment processing.

Opacity Calculation

To find out where opaque objects are during particle rendering, the algorithm first renders all objects of the scene and saves the camera-space distance to the origin of the visible points. These saved values are real Euclidean distances $\sqrt{x^2 + y^2 + z^2}$ for a point having (x, y, z) coordinates in camera space. We call the texture storing these distance values a distance map. Then we render the particles as quads placed at the farthest point from the camera of the particle sphere (to avoid unwanted front plane clipping) and rotated toward the camera via the vertex shader. To eliminate incorrect object–billboard clipping, we also disable the depth test.

When rendering a fragment of the particle, we compute the interval the ray travels inside the particle sphere in camera space. This interval is obtained by considering the saved distance values of opaque objects and the camera's front clipping plane distance (see also Equation 5.1.4 below). From the resulting interval, we compute the opacity for each fragment in such a way that both fully and partially visible particles display correctly, resulting in the illusion of a volumetric medium. During opacity computations we assume that the density inside a particle sphere is uniform.

We use the notations of Figure 5.1.4: a particle of center $\vec{P} = (x_p, y_p, z_p)$ renders as a quad perpendicular to the view ray, and a ray intersects a point $\vec{Q} = (x_q, y_q, z_q)$ of the quadrilateral. All coordinates are in camera space where the eye is at origin $\vec{O}$. The radius of the particle sphere is r. The closest point on the ray from the particle center is $\vec{C}$, which $\vec{Q}$ closely approximates as long as the particle's distance to the camera is large compared to the particle's size. Another way to formulate this approximation is to say that we assume that the angle $(\vec{O}, \vec{Q}, \vec{P})$ is close to 90 degrees.

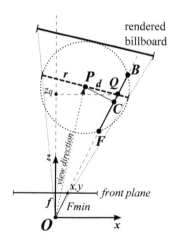

FIGURE 5.1.4   Computation of the length of the ray segment traveling inside a particle sphere in camera space.

The distance d between the ray and the particle center is

$$d \approx |\vec{P} - \vec{Q}|.$$

The ray thus travels inside the particle in the interval $\left[|\vec{F}|, |\vec{B}| \right]$, where $|\vec{F}| \approx |\vec{Q}| - \omega$, $|\vec{B}| \approx |\vec{Q}| + \omega$, and $\omega = \sqrt{r^2 - d^2}$ as long as neither the front clipping plane nor the scene objects intersect the particle sphere.

To take the front clipping distance f into account, we ensure that $|\vec{F}|$ is no smaller than $F_{\min} = \frac{f}{z_q} |\vec{Q}|$.

For the ray passing through point $\vec{Q}$, the distance D_s of the visible surface is stored in the distance map. To take scene objects into account, we thus ensure that $|\vec{B}|$ is no greater than D_s. These distances allow us to compute a very good approximation of the distance a ray travels inside a particle sphere:

$$\Delta s = \min(Z_{s_i}, |\vec{B}|) - \max(F_{\min}, |\vec{F}|). \tag{5.1.4}$$

If we assume that the density inside a particle is homogeneous, although the accumulated opacity at the contour of a particle sphere does become zero, it does not diminish smoothly, making the contour of a particle sphere clearly visible for a human observer. We can eliminate this artifact if the density decreases linearly with distance from the particle center. Instead of Equation 5.1.2, we modulate the accumulated density by a linear function and use the following formula to obtain the opacity of particle j:

$$\alpha_j \approx 1 - e^{-\tau_j (1 - d/r_j) \Delta s_j}, \tag{5.1.5}$$

where d is the distance between the ray and the particle center, and r_j is the radius of this particle.

GPU Implementation of Spherical Billboards

A custom fragment shader program executes an appropriate function that efficiently evaluates the length a ray travels in a particle sphere and the corresponding opacity. This function needs the following inputs, which are calculated in a corresponding vertex shader: the particle position in camera space (P), the shaded billboard point in camera space (Q), the particle radius (r), and the screen coordinates of the shaded point (screenCoord). The function uses uniform parameters, such as the texture of the distance values of opaque objects (Dist), the density (tau), and the camera's front clipping-plane distance (f). The Cg function to determine the opacity is the following:

```
float Opacity(float3 P, float3 Q, float r, float2 screenCoord)
{
    float alpha = 0;
    float d = length(P.xy - Q.xy);
    if(d < r)
```

```
{
  float Ql = length(Q);
  float fMin = f * Ql / Q.z;
  float w = sqrt(r * r - d * d);
  float F = Ql - w;
  float B = Ql + w;
  float Ds = tex2D(Dist, screenCoord).r;
  float ds = min(Ds, B) - max(fMin, F);
  alpha = 1 - exp(-tau * (1 - d / r) * ds);
  }
}
```

The shader program thus obtains the real ray segment length (ds) and computes the opacity alpha of a given particle that controls blending of the particle into the frame buffer. The consideration of the spherical geometry during fragment processing eliminates clipping and popping artifacts (see Figure 5.1.5).

FIGURE 5.1.5   Particle system rendered with planar (left) and spherical (right) billboards.

Rendering Explosions

We now apply spherical billboards to rendering realistic explosions. An explosion consists of dust, smoke, and fire. All these effects are modeled with specific particle systems. Dust and smoke absorb light; fire emits light. We render these particle systems separately and then composite their rendered images to obtain the final result.

Dust and Smoke

Smoke particles absorb light in a fire. These particles typically have low albedo and high density values $(a = 0.2, \tau = 0.25)$. On the other hand, high-albedo and low-density $(a = 0.95, \tau = 0.03)$ dust further improves the realism of explosions (see Figure 5.1.6 for examples).

FIGURE 5.1.6 Low-albedo smoke (left) and high-albedo dust.

When rendering dust and smoke, we assume that these particles do not emit radiance; that is, their emission term is zero. To calculate their in-scattering term, the length that light travels inside a particle sphere, the albedo, the density, and the phase function (see Equation 5.1.1) are needed. We use the Henyey-Greenstein phase function [Henyey40] [Cornette92]:

$$P(\vec{\omega}', \vec{\omega}) = \frac{1}{4\pi} \cdot \frac{3(1-g^2) \cdot (1 + (\vec{\omega}' \cdot \vec{\omega})^2)}{2(2+g^2) \cdot (1 + g^2 + 2g(\vec{\omega}' \cdot \vec{\omega}))^{3/2}} \tag{5.1.6}$$

where $g \in (-1, 1)$ is a material property describing how strongly a material scatters forward or backward. To speed up rendering, these function values are fetched from a 2D texture addressed by $\cos\theta = \vec{\omega}' \cdot \vec{\omega}$ and g, respectively. We find that setting g to constant zero gives satisfactory results for both smoke and dust.

The length that light travels inside a smoke or dust particle is computed by the proposed spherical billboard method.

In order to maintain high frame rates, the number of particles must be limited, which compromises high-detail features. To address this problem, we increase the particles' radii as we decrease their number. To increase variety, we perturb the opacity values computed by the spherical billboards. Each particle has a unique, time-dependent perturbation pattern. This perturbation derives from a greyscale texture called a *detail image*, which depicts real smoke or dust (see Figure 5.1.7). The perturbation pattern of a particle is taken from a randomly placed, small quad-shaped part of this texture. (Off-line renderers use a similar technique for the same purpose [Apodaca00].) To provide variety in the time domain, this texture is updated as time advances. These animated 2D textures are obtained from real-world videos and are best stored as a volume texture: a GPU's texture sampling unit can then provide interframe interpolation and looping.

 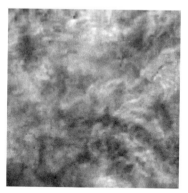

FIGURE 5.1.7   Images from real smoke and fire video clips, which are used to perturb the billboard fragment opacities and temperatures.

Fire

We model fire as a black body radiator rather than a participating medium; that is, we set the albedo in Equation 5.1.1 to zero, so that only the emission term is required. The color characteristics of fire particles are thus determined by the physics theory of black body radiation. Planck's formula computes the emitted radiance of a black body for wavelength λ:

$$L_{e,\lambda}(x) = \frac{2C_1}{\lambda^5 (e^{C_2/(\lambda T)} - 1)} \tag{5.1.7}$$

where $C_1 = 3.7418 \cdot 10^{-16} Wm^2$, $C_2 = 1.4388 \cdot 10^{-2} m^\circ K$, and T is the absolute temperature of the radiator [Siegel81]. The RGB components for different temperature values are obtained by integrating the spectrum multiplied by the color-matching functions. These integrals are precomputed and stored in a texture.

Similar to smoke and dust particles, we add detail to fire particles by perturbing their opacity, as well as their emission radiance. Sampling color directly from a video does not allow us to control the temperature range or color for different explosions. We instead store temperature variations in a detail texture (see Figure 5.1.7); the stored temperature values are scaled and used for color computation on the fly. A randomly selected, small quadrilateral part of the detail video is assigned to each fire particle to control the temperature perturbation of the fragments of a particle billboard. The resulting temperature thus determines the color of a fragment according to the above black body radiation function.

A fragment program to compute fire particles receives as input a fire particle position in camera space (P), a shaded billboard point in camera space (Q), a particle radius (r), screen coordinates of the shaded point (screen), a position of the detail image in the texture (detail) (with starting time in its z coordinate), and the current time of the animation (time). This fragment program also reads uniform parameters, including the texture of the fire video (FireVideo), the black body radiation (BBRad) map, and the temperature scale (T1) and bias (T0). The fragment program calls the Opacity() function, which computes the opacity using the spherical billboard method described above and then calculates the color of a fire particle using the following shader program:

```
float alpha = Opacity(P, Q, r, screen);   // opacity of particle
float3 detuvw = detail + float3(0,0,time);// texcoords of the
                                                detail
float fireVideoSample = tex3D(FireVideo, detuvw).r; //video sample
float T = T0 + T1 * fireVideoSample;       // perturbed temperature
alpha *= fireVideoSample;                   // perturbed opacity
return float4(tex1D(BBRad, T).rgb, 1) * alpha; // emitted color
```

Layer Composition

To combine the above smoke, dust, and fire particle systems with the image of opaque objects, we use a layer composition method. We render the opaque objects and the particle systems into separate textures and then blend the particle texture on top of the opaque objects. This approach thus consists of three rendering passes: one pass to render the opaque objects; one pass to render the dust, smoke, and fire; and one final pass for composition. The first pass computes both the color and the depth of the opaque objects.

One advantage of rendering a participating medium into a texture is that this render pass may use a lower-resolution rendering target than the final display resolution, which speeds up rendering since rendering billboard particles typically overdraws a single pixel multiple times and uses blending (see Figure 5.1.8).

FIGURE 5.1.8 Effect of render-target resolution on rendering throughput. As render-target resolution decreases from full-screen resolution (left) to one-eighth the screen resolution (right), rendering performance increases. On each picture the frame buffer has resolution 512×512. The render-target resolution and fps changes are (from left to right): 512×512, 30 FPS; 256×256, 40 FPS; 128×128, 50 FPS; 64×64, 60 FPS.

The complete rendering process is shown in Figure 5.1.9.

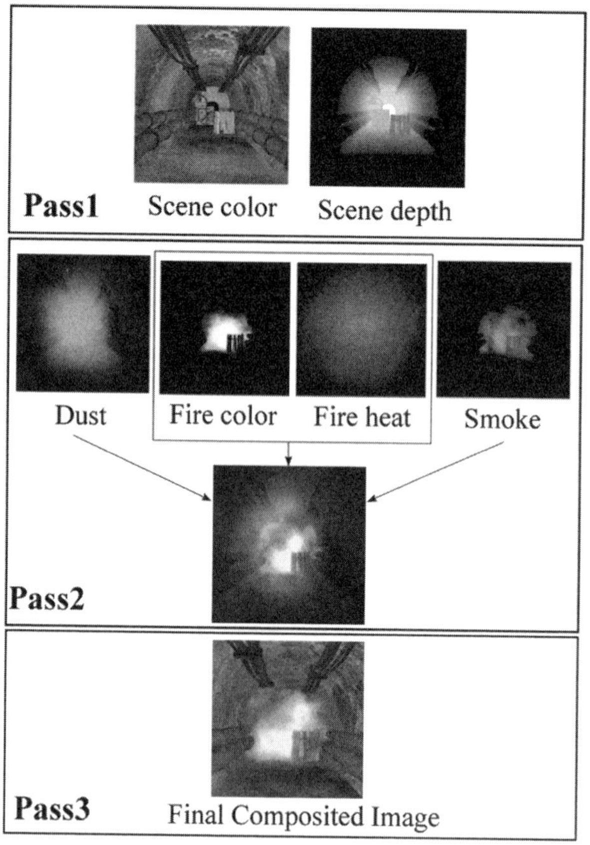

FIGURE 5.1.9 The rendering algorithm.

Conclusion

We introduce an improved billboard rendering method that splats particles as camera-aligned quadrilaterals but takes into account the spherical geometry of the particles during fragment processing. This new method eliminates the billboard clipping and popping artifacts of previous techniques. We show how to apply this new technique to render high-detail explosions consisting of fire, dust, and smoke at high frame rates. Please refer to this article's folder on the CD-ROM for tutorial files.

ON THE CD

References

[Apodaca00] Apodaca, A. A. and L. Gritz. *Advanced RenderMan: Creating CGI for Motion Picture*. Academic Press, 2000.

[Blinn82] Blinn, J. F. "Light Reflection Functions for Simulation of Clouds and Dusty Surfaces." *SIGGRAPH '82 Proceedings*, 1982: pp. 21–29.

[Cornette92] Cornette, W. and J. Shanks. "Physical Reasonable Analytic Expression for Single-Scattering Phase Function." *Applied Optics*, *31*(16), (1992): pp. 31–52.

[Henyey40] Henyey, G. and J. Greenstein. "Diffuse Radiation in the Galaxy." *Astrophysical Journal*, 88, (1940): pp. 70–73.

[Reeves83] Reeves, W. T. "Particle Systems: Techniques for Modelling a Class of Fuzzy Objects." *SIGGRAPH '83 Proceedings*, (1983): pp. 359–376.

[Schaufler95] Schaufler, G. "Dynamically Generated Impostors." *I Workshop: Virtual Worlds*. Distributed Graphics, 1995: pp. 129–136.

[Siegel81] Siegel, R. and J. R. Howell. *Thermal Radiation Heat Transfer*. Hemisphere Publishing Corp., Washington, D.C., 1981.

[Wei02] Wei, X., W. Li, K. Mueller, and A. Kaufman. "Simulating Fire with Texture Splats." *IEEE Visualization '02*, 2002.

5.2

Per-Pixel Lit, Light Scattering Smoke

Aurelio Reis, Firaxis Games

Introduction

We define smoke as a dense collection of particulate matter suspended in air. Steam or even clouds are similar, and we include them in our definition of smoke. Smoke particles are small yet large enough to be influenced by Mie scattering [Nave05]. Accordingly, they exhibit strong forward scattering; that is, all light frequencies scatter roughly in the same direction. Light entering a cloud of smoke reflects, refracts, and is absorbed.

Reeves [Reeves83] was the first to introduce pixel-sized particles to computer graphics; however, they prove too expensive for real-time use. Most past and current games thus model smoke as a few modestly sized, screen-aligned billboards [Moller02]. Although modern processors are ever more powerful, allowing for many more on-screen billboards [Latta04], pixel-sized particles continue to be impractical for today's real-time games. The emphasis is thus on making these multipixel-sized billboards look as much like smoke as possible. For example, using texture maps and texture animations on these billboards is standard practice. We continue this emphasis and introduce per-pixel lighting and light-scattering for smoke particles.

Lighting a screen-aligned particle per pixel requires per-pixel normals. How should one orient the normals of a screen-aligned particle? Erez [Erez05] suggests a number of possible solutions, for example, copying a particle's normals from the surface that emits it or using a particle's velocity vector as a normal. While this solution works modestly well, it leads to artifacts: particles using their velocity vectors as a normal and moving away from a light source remain dark, although intuitively the particle's back should be brightly illuminated.

To allow for normal-mapped lighting, we also require a tangent-basis matrix that transforms a light vector into texture space. ATI's *ToyShop* demo [Tatarchuk06a] includes a particle simulation for running water and raindrops. Since the raindrop particles are screen-aligned, Tatarchuk uses the view matrix as the tangent basis. Because the normal is now screen oriented, the particle always appears to be facing the user. Since smoke billboards simulate a voluminous spherical mass receiving light from every direction, we employ the same trick.

Another aspect of smoke is its light-scattering property. A standard diffuse illumination model covers light reflection, but in- and out-scattering, as well as absorption, are equally important for smoke. Harris [Harris03] describes a technique in which imposters are used to render complex cloud groups: each cloud particle within a group subdivides the scattering equations. This technique allows for an efficient real-time algorithm for single and multiple scattering but relies upon intermittent update rates to minimize the performance burden. This solution offers impressively accurate results yet is only feasible for slowly evolving environments, such as clouds. It also assumes that sunlight is the major light influencing the particles. Harris's method thus does not easily generalize for simulating smoke.

Although per-pixel lighting has become something of a standard rendering technique, lit smoke still remains outside the realm of most rendering engines. Using graphics hardware that supports Shader Model 3, we show how to light particle systems in a single pass, thus allowing for any blend mode to composite these particles into a scene. We examine how to calculate single scattering for a smoke particle, that is, as if it was a volumetric medium. We then offer a fast, yet faithful, approximation of this calculation. In the appendix, we also mention a technique to procedurally generate smoke textures to help alleviate the next-generation art bottleneck.

This article only examines the lighting of smoke. For guidance on how to avoid clipping and popping artifacts when using billboarded particles, see "Spherical Billboards for Rendering Volumetric Data" [Umenhoffer06] in this book.

Making Better Smoke

Equation 5.2.1 describes subsurface scattering of skin [Struck04] but works equally well to approximate light-scattering of smoke. The light vector **L**, the view vector **E**, and a translucency map determine how much light is scattered through and around a smoke particle.

$$\text{translucency} = \min(0, E \cdot L) * \text{translucencyMap} \qquad (5.2.1)$$

Standard per-pixel lighting then adds the influence of direct light reflection. The result of this simple technique is shown in Figure 5.2.1.

Our technique treats each puff as a cloud mass; large masses of smoke particles thus do not influence their neighbors' brightness. A solution to that problem is outside the scope of this article.

Direct Illumination of Smoke

We calculate all of our lighting contributions in a single rendering pass. Multiple light attributes are set as shader parameters (i.e., uniform constants), and the pixel shader iterates over all lights to calculate the lighting function for each. We find that four lights

FIGURE 5.2.1   Applying standard diffuse and wrap-
around lighting to smoke particles lit from below.

suffice to provide realistic illumination. The remainder of this article thus assumes four
light sources. Per-pixel normals are specified through use of a 2D normal map encoded
in the DXT-NM format for highest visual quality at the smallest texture size.

The pixel shader evaluates Lambert's diffuse lighting model for each of the four
active lights in the scene:

$$\text{diffuse} = N \cdot L \tag{5.2.2}$$

Light attributes (e.g., light direction or position) are passed in as world-space coordinates. Per-pixel normals, however, use tangent space, so we transform these to world
space using the inverse-transpose of the tangent matrix. The vertex shader calculates
this matrix and then passes it to the pixel shader using texture coordinate interpolators.
The vertex shader simply uses the view matrix as the tangent matrix since smoke billboards are always screen-aligned [Tatarchuk06a].

Light Scattering of Smoke

We evaluate Equation 5.2.1 for each light source in the pixel shader. If a light is in front
of a smoke particle, then it does not add a scattering contribution. To test for this case
we evaluate the dot product of the view vector and the light vector (Figures 5.2.2 and
5.2.3).

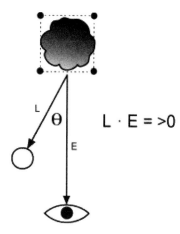

FIGURE 5.2.2   If the cosine of the angle between the light vector
and the eye vector is negative, the light is behind the particle.

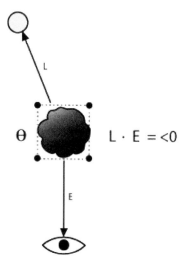

FIGURE 5.2.3   Otherwise the light is in front of the smoke particle.

Then we determine the contribution of the subsurface scattering. For the backlit
term we take the dot product between the surface normal (which we sample per pixel
in tangent space) and the eye vector. Using an exponential function or remapping the
results to a color ramp allows for special effects such as bright light halos around
smoke particles.

To hint at the smoke makeup and overall darkness we use a standard diffuse map
where the color channels store smoke brightness and the alpha channel stores translucency. To simulate thickness within the smoke volume we sample our translucency
map and modulate it by the previous results.

We compute a wrap-around contribution to represent light diffusing through smoke. Equation 5.2.3 generates a light term scale and bias.

$$scale = 1.0 / (1.0 + w)$$

$$bias = w / (1.0 + w) \tag{5.2.3}$$

where w represents the wrap-around coefficient, which can range from 0.0 to 1.0 (a constant value of 0.6 is used in the demo program). The scale and bias is then applied to the lighting term given in Equation 5.2.2, which results in Equation 5.2.4.

$$diffuse = (N \cdot L) * scale + bias. \tag{5.2.4}$$

Even though the wrap-around term works best with the diffuse lighting term, it can also be used with the backlighting term given in Equation 5.2.1 (although subjectively the results aren't as effective).

More Realistic Scattering

To improve the light-scattering component of our lighting equation, we project a ray from the light source and trace it per pixel through a height field using a pixel shader. As the ray intersects with the voxels of the height field, a light absorption factor accumulates (Figure 5.2.4). We use this absorption factor to determine how dark a pixel should be owing to smoke thickness as represented by the height field. The main problem with this ray-casting approach is the large number of steps required to integrate along the height field to avoid stepping artifacts. The high number of texture samples required incurs high rendering overhead.

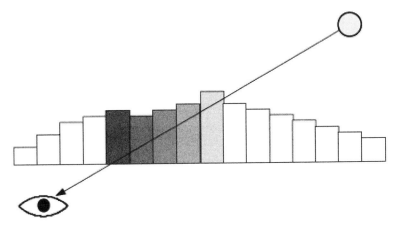

FIGURE 5.2.4 As the eye ray marches through the pseudo-volume it collects the light absorption factor when it intersects with any voxel.

McGuire [McGuire05] employs a similar per-pixel ray-tracing technique to solve parallax bump mapping. Tatarchuk [Tatarchuk06b] improves upon per-pixel ray marching by removing the need for a high and fixed number of ray steps. Using a dynamic sampling rate, it is possible to determine the minimum number of steps for any camera perspective based on the angle between the normal and the view direction:

$$n = \text{nMin} + N \cdot \mathbf{V}(\text{nMax} - \text{nMin}), \tag{5.2.5}$$

where n is the number of steps to use, nMin is the minimum number possible, nMax is the maximum allowed, N is the normal, and $\mathbf{V}$ is the normalized view vector. It is also possible to adjust the sampling rate based on the current mip-level. This feature is only present on Shader Model 3 hardware, however, since it requires dynamic looping. Tatarchuk [Tatarchuk06b] presents a comparison of three possible hardware implementations of such a technique and describes the tradeoffs and advantages.

This technique generates excellent results and more accurately represents the amount of light potentially scattered through a smoke medium. Despite its high cost, it performs reasonably well on modern graphics hardware and scales gracefully with the number of samples used, using either Shader Model 2 or 3. A major drawback of this algorithm is that it represents only the scattering for an individual particle and not a group of particles. Spawning a large number of particles thus does not occlude adjacent particles' lighting contributions. We are, however, able to dampen the lighting based on the number of particles generated via a dampening parameter passed to the light scattering pixel shader.

Conclusion

In this article we show how to implement realistic-looking smoke. Taking advantage of the relationship between a light, the viewer, and the smoke particle, we create an illusion of light scattering. Adding per-pixel lighting to smoke particles via pixel shaders and using tricks to simulate subsurface scattering, we are able to increase the realism of smoke particles. For a sample implementation of the above technique, examine the accompanying source code and demo application in the article folder on the CD-ROM. We hope you find this technique useful in your own smoke implementations.

ON THE CD

References

[Ebert94] Ebert, David, Kent Musgrave, Darwyn Peachey, Ken Perlin, and Steven Worley. *Texturing and Modeling: A Procedural Approach.* Academic Press, 1994.

[Erez05] Erez, Eyal. "Interactive 3D Lighting in Sprites Rendering." GDC, 2005. Available online at *http://www.gamasutra.com-gdc2005/features/20050308/erez_01. shtml.*

[Harris03] Harris, Mark J. "Real-time Cloud Simulation and Rendering." Ph.D. dissertation, University of North Carolina, Technical Report #TR03-040, 2003.

[Hicks03] Hicks, O'dell. "Screen-Aligned Particles with Minimal VertexBuffer Locking." *ShaderX²*, edited by Wolfgang Engel. Wordware Publishing, 2003: pp. 107–112.

[Latta04] Latta, Lutz. "Building a Million Particle System." GDC, 2004. Available online at *http://www.2ld.de/gdc2004.*

[McGuire05] McGuire, Morgan and Max McGuire. "Steep Parallax Mapping." I3D 2005 Poster, 2005. Available at *http://www.cs.brown.edu/research/graphics/games/SteepParallax/index.html.*

[McGuire06] McGuire, Morgan and Andi Fein. "Real-time Rendering of Cartoon Smoke and Clouds." NPAR, 2006. Available at *http://cs.brown.edu/research/graphics/games/CartoonSmoke.*

[Moller02] Akenine-Moller, Tomas. *Real-time Rendering*, 2nd ed. AK Peters, Ltd, 2002: Section 8.3 "Billboarding," pp. 318.

[Nave05] Nave, C. R. "Mie Scattering." Georgia State University, 2005. Available at *http://hyperphysics.phy-astr.gsu.edu/hbase/atmos/blusky.html.*

[Reeves83] Reeves, William T. "Particle Systems: A Technique for Modeling a Class of Fuzzy Objects." *Computer Graphics, 17*(3), (1983): pp. 359–376, 1983.

[Reichert] Texture Maker, Reichert Software Engineering. Available at *http://www.texturemaker.com.*

[Struck04] Struck, Florian, Christian-A. Bohn, Sebastian Schmidt, and Volker Helzle, "Realistic Shading of Human Skin in Real-time." *Proceedings of the 3rd International Conference on Computer Graphics, Virtual Reality, Visualisation and Interaction in Africa*, 2004: pp. 93–97.

[Tatarchuk06a] Tatarchuk, Natalya. "Artist-Directable Real-time Rain Rendering in City Environments." GDC, ATI Research, Inc., 2006.

[Tatarchuk06b] Tatarchuk, Natalya. "Practical Parallax Occlusion Mapping for Highly Detailed Surface Rendering." GDC, ATI Research, Inc., 2006.

[Umenhoffer06] Umenhoffer, Tamás, László Szirmay-Kalos, and Gábor Szijártó. "Spherical Billboards for Rendering Volumetric Data." *ShaderX⁵*, edited by Wolfgang Engel. Charles River Media, 2006.

Appendix

Generating Smoke Textures

There are a variety of ways to generate good-looking smoke textures. The main rule is to reduce prelighting of a texture while still providing interesting detail. The easiest technique is to start with a photograph of smoke and create an alpha mask to delineate the smoke area. This approach yields good results as long as contrast and brightness of the photograph are adjusted so that any built-in prelighting does not dominate the computed lighting. A high-contrast, monochrome version of the same image is useful as a rough approximation of a normal map.

Another solution is to use procedural texturing techniques. [Ebert94] is an excellent reference for procedural techniques including cellular texturing and multifractal noise. Fractal Brownian motion and turbulence functions (with results weighted by the distance to the center of the image) can be used to great effect. Traditional art packages such as Photoshop and their plug-ins, such as, for example, Photoshop's built-in Clouds or Difference Clouds, are also useful. New procedural art packages (e.g., Texture Maker [Reichert]) generate procedural textures in a WYSIWYG environment using premade noise functions.

Finally, McGuire [McGuire06] employs an interesting technique for his smoke texture generation. He utilizes an artist-specified base 3D shape that is cloned and randomly dispersed throughout a volume. Separate textures then capture the color, normal, and depth information. This technique produces excellent results, although care must be taken if the base model is overly complex. We believe this technique is the most versatile and yields the best results, as it offers artistic freedom and quick turnaround.

Special Effects

In our implementation, particle systems are represented through *special effects*. A special effect is a dedicated system that plays back any number of special effect steps, which may include particle emitters, sounds, lights, screen space effects such as flashes, or even geometric debris. For the purpose of this article we only focus on emitters. Our special effects are exposed through a special effect file format (spfx) that uses XML as a base structure. Examples can be found in the "media/spfx" directory of the accompanying demo program.

The ParticleEmitter step type is a straightforward, yet general particle system implementation. In practical use, however, we urge tailoring a general system to your specific needs. For example, if the particles in your system do not need collision detection, then the existing implementation should be improved to work exclusively on the graphics card, thus reducing the number of vertex/index buffer locks, which are expensive since they consume bandwidth. Hicks [Hicks03] describes how to implement just such a system. Our implementation instead maintains general flexibility. Extending it to support full collision detection is a minor task.

5.3

Volumetric Clouds and Mega-Particles

Homam Bahnassi, InlFramez
Wessam Bahnassi, Electronic Arts

Introduction

Volumetric effects are an important part of 3D game scenes. The two most common approaches for implementing these effects are screen-aligned particles and sliced volumetric rendering. Other approaches exist but are mostly variants of these two.

This article lists drawbacks of existing techniques and then introduces a novel, yet simple, technique that overcomes many of these drawbacks (see Figure 5.3.1). This novel technique targets volumetric effects and phenomena that range from clouds to thick smoke, dust, fog, and even space nebulae.

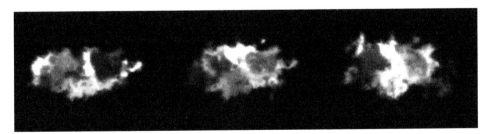

FIGURE 5.3.1   A volumetric cloud rendered using the described technique, featuring correct lighting and depth interaction.

The Problems

Many attempts have been made to make volumetric effects real-time in computer graphics. There always is, however, a catch. Either the output is a crude approximation or it lacks flexibility or other important features. The following categorization summarizes common drawbacks of existing implementations.

Rendering Artifacts

Missing lighting: Most particle sprite approaches are unlit. This lack of lighting is usually due to missing information (e.g., no normals) or due to calculations being too expensive for real-time execution [Laeuchli05].

No proper depth interaction: The implementation is 2D in nature. Existing objects in the scene are not taken into account. Techniques based on fractal generation [Pallister01] typically suffer from this limitation.

Sharp cutouts: Cutouts are common with most sprite-based techniques. The problem is obvious whenever particle sprites intersect the ground or other objects.

User Inconvenience

Camera placement limitations: Several slice-based approaches require that the camera never enters the volume of a cloud. Alternatively, these approaches increase rendering complexity to handle this case [Baker01].

Unintuitive controls and inflexibility: Fractal-based approaches typically suffer from this problem.

Performance

High fill-rate requirements: Particle-based approaches typically consume large amounts of fill rate. High overdraw and the cost of alpha-blending combine to cripple frame rate.

Expensive dynamics calculations: This drawback is specific to particle-based approaches. Simulating a large number of particles consumes a lot of CPU processing power.

Unfriendly to GPU optimizations: Some volumetric techniques alter pixel depth in the pixel shader, which forces graphics hardware to abandon early-z optimizations, resulting in suboptimal rendering speed.

Hardware Requirements

Requirement of advanced GPU capabilities: Navier-Stokes fluid simulations [Stam00] and GPU-generated fractals [Tarantilis04] fall into this category because they require high GPU programmability to execute their algorithms.

High demand of hardware resources: Techniques incorporating volumetric textures typically suffer from this drawback. For example, ray-tracing into volume textures [Gottlieb04] requires large texture dimensions to render a cloud with enough detail. Large volumetric textures tend to suffer from cache misses, thus reducing performance.

The Approach

Most existing particle-based techniques build on the concept of "more is better" to produce good results. The approach presented here is also particle based, yet it depends on rendering a small number of large particles instead. These so-called mega-particles are not 2D billboards, but rather 3D spheres. The spheres render close to each other in different sizes and layouts to give a cloud a basic structure. Later, these grouped spheres turn into a puffy, realistic-looking cloud through a series of operations, outlined below and shown in Figure 5.3.2.

Generating cloud color and depth information: Mega-particles render to a
    separate render-target texture, while using the scene's depth buffer. The particles
    render as lit 3D spheres, just like any other object in the scene. Z-test and
    z-write are enabled for proper interaction with the scene's depth buffer.

Blurring and fractal distortion: Next, the render-target texture is blurred using
    your favorite blurring method (e.g., separable Gaussian and down-sampling
    [Mitchell04]), followed by rendering a 3D box covering all the mega-particles.
    A fractal texture textures this 3D box to add detail to the result.

Final blending: Finally, the blurred texture is blended with the original back buffer.
    The blending is done by rendering a single, full-screen quad over the existing
    color information of the back buffer.

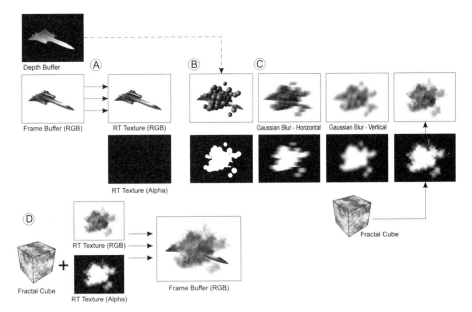

FIGURE 5.3.2   The pipeline for rendering volumetric clouds using mega-particles.

Ingredients and Workflow

This technique requires a render-target texture that is of the same dimensions as the back buffer. The format of this texture depends on the planned effect usage: colored clouds require three channels of color information, while grayscale clouds only need a single channel. Coloring here means variance of chromacity (e.g., differently colored lights or mega-particles). Simple color tinting, however, is still achievable with a single color channel for intensity. The format must also contain an additional alpha channel.

Another requirement is the mega-particles' geometry. These 3D spheres shape the cloud and therefore should be created and sized under artistic control. Animation may be procedural or under artists' control, and may cover all aspects of rendering of these spheres (e.g., position, size, and color).

The final requirement is a 3D box that encloses all mega-particles of a single cloud. This box is textured with a fractal map that covers all faces seamlessly. This texture may be a pregenerated fractal of moderate size (e.g., 256×256 texels for each face). A single-channel alpha format, such as A8, suffices for this texture.

The time for cloud rendering should be chosen carefully. The ideal rendering order is to first render all objects that are behind the cloud (from the camera's viewpoint) or that could potentially penetrate it. Next, the cloud's rendering process is carried out. Finally, the remaining objects in front of the cloud are rendered.

The following sections provide a detailed description of the technique's rendering steps.

Generation of Cloud Color and Depth Information

The operation starts by filling the render-target texture with the current color contents of the back buffer and an alpha value of 0. Next, this texture is set as the current render target, while ensuring that the existing depth buffer is still intact and active.

Now the cloud renders all of its mega-particle spheres with full lighting just like any other scene object. The cloud spheres thus test against existing depth values and write to the depth buffer. During rendering, sphere pixels that pass the depth test also write the value 1.0 into the alpha channel of the render-target texture (i.e., alpha-blending and testing is disabled).

Blurring and Fractal Distortion

At this point, the render-target texture contains the existing scene and the newly rendered mega-particles. The next step is to blur this texture, that is, not only the color channels, but the alpha channel as well. While any blurring technique works, a separable Gaussian blur with down-sampling [Mitchell04] is used in the sample application, which quickly produces a good amount of blurring. Note that the sampling kernel should be big enough to remove any sharp edges that interpenetrating mega-particles might create, yet not so big as to smudge lighting details. The sample application on the companion CD-ROM exposes the parameter `g_BlurAmount` to control this kernel size per cloud.

Color Plate 1 This screenshot shows how a local deformation of an animated mesh can be employed to create believable fold. This technique is described in the article "Dynamic Wrinkle Patterns and Hatching on Animated Meshes."

Parallax occlusion mapping used to render woodcut raised text for a sign

Color Plate 2 Parallax occlusion mapping used to render woodcut rased text for a sign. This technique is described in the article "Practical Parallax Occlusion Mapping." © ATI Research Inc. Reprinted with permission.

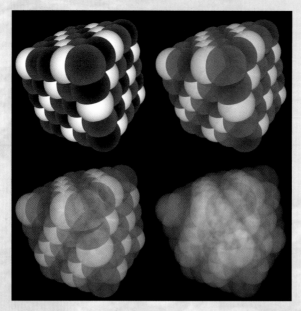

Color Plate 3 General transparency algorithm described in the article "ZT-Buffer Algorithm."

Color Plate 4 *MotoGP'06* for XBox360, developed by Climax Racing and published by THQ using the depth-of-field algorithm described in the article "Real-time Depth-of-Field Implemented with a Post-Processing-Only Technique." © 2006 *MotoGP'06* for XBox360, developed by Climax Racing and published by THQ.

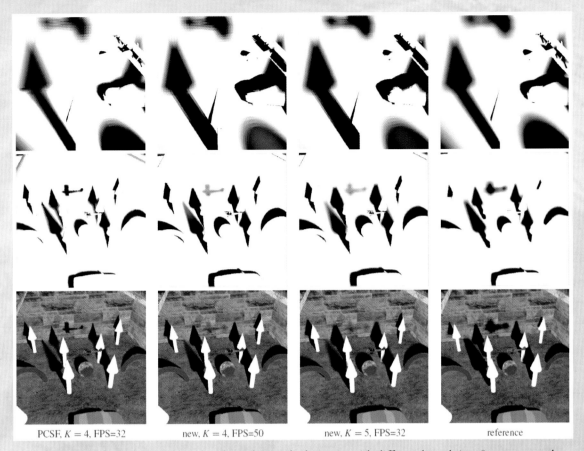

| PCSF, $K = 4$, FPS=32 | new, $K = 4$, FPS=50 | new, $K = 5$, FPS=32 | reference |

Color Plate 5   Soft shadows generated with resolution shadow map with different kernel sizes (), as compared with Percentage Closer Soft Shadows (PCSS) and with a reference solution. Described in "Real-time Soft Shadows with Shadow Accumulation."

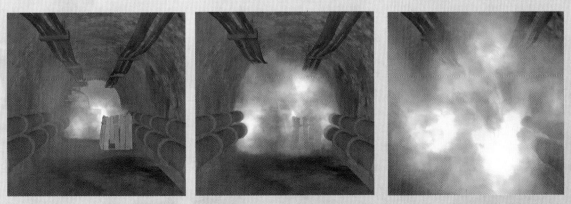

Color Plate 6   Rendered frames from an animation sequence showing an explosion. The underlying technique is described in "Spherical Billboards."

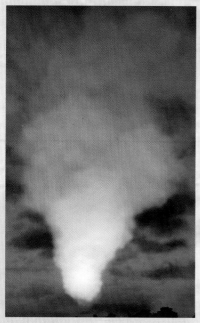

Color Plate 9 God rays are a truly beautiful phenomenon underwater. They are beams of sunlight that filter through water and then dance underwater in many directions. You can admire them in many underwater documentaries and movies, or better, by diving in deep water and then looking up towards the sun. The article "Animation and Rendering of Underwater God Rays" describes the technique that was used to render the screenshot.

Color Plate 7 Applying standard diffuse and wrap-around lighting to smoke particles lit from underneath. Described in "Per-Pixel Lit, Light Scattering Smoke."

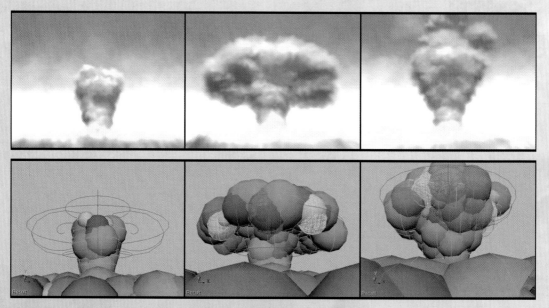

Color Plate 8 This explosion has been rendered with the technique described in the article "Volumetric Clouds and Mega Particles." The scene started from simple shaded spheres, and was post-processed to obtain the final look using the following chain: Gaussian Blur -> Turbulent Distortion -> Radial Blur -> HDR Tone Mapping.

The next step renders the fractal-textured 3D box so that it bounds all cloud spheres (i.e., by applying the required transformations). The purpose of rendering this box is to add detail to the render-target texture's alpha channel. Two techniques achieve this goal: using alpha-modulation or using displacement.

With alpha-modulation, the box is rendered using the scene's camera with z-test and z-writing disabled. Alpha blending is set to a multiplicative blending mode (e.g., ColorOut = ColorSrc × ColorDest + ColorDest × 0), and the color-write mask is set to only write the alpha channel. Backface culling is enabled if the camera is outside of this box or disabled if the camera is within the box.

When using displacement, the fractal box is used as a source to displace pixels in the alpha channel, which gives better results if tuned correctly. [Hargreaves04] describes a similar technique in its "Displacement Effects" section. This technique requires a two-channel format for the fractal texture.

The fractal-box rendering operation guarantees that as the camera orbits around a cloud, it sees true 3D details that identify each part of the cloud.

Final Blending

At this point we have a texture containing blurred and fractal distorted spheres. The final step is to combine this texture and the back buffer. Rendering a full-screen quad to the back buffer that samples the texture at a 1-to-1 texel-to-pixel ratio achieves this combination. During this blit, alpha blending is on, and the blending mode is:

$$Color_{Out} = Color_{Src} \times Alpha_{Src} + Color_{Dest} \times (1\text{-}Alpha_{Src})$$

Z-test and z-write are disabled (see Figure 5.3.3).

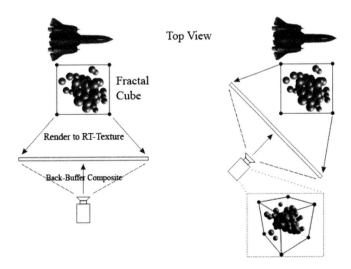

FIGURE 5.3.3 Data setup for the final blit.

Discussion of Results

The described technique has many advantages over existing approaches. The following list shows the differences using the categories mentioned in the preceding section "The Problems."

Rendering

Depth interaction: Rendering clouds using this technique interacts correctly and accurately with depth values of existing objects in the scene.

Colored clouds: Each sphere can be colored independently to give variation over the whole cloud (e.g., dark and bright areas or lightning, causing flashing areas).

Fully lit: The 3D spheres are lit using your favorite lighting calculations; these lighting calculations directly influence the cloud's final coloring. For more complex lighting effects, shadowing and ambient occlusion can be included.

3D and volumetric: The cloud is viewable from any camera angle. Cameras are free to move inside a cloud as long as the fractal texture-mapped box correctly overlays the blurred render-target texture.

User Convenience:

Flexibility and control over shape and animation: The generic layout of the spheres shapes a cloud. Because the number of spheres is small, shaping a cloud is manageable. Spheres can gradually spread and scale over time to fade out a cloud. Moreover, animating the fractal details gives an additional sense of motion (e.g., rotating the fractal box).

Does not require a specific scene setup: The technique fits into existing rendering mechanisms.

Performance:

Low fill-rate consumption: The amount of alpha-blended overdraw is limited to at most two full-screen blits even when clouds fill the whole screen.

High potential for optimization: Sorting the spheres in front-to-back order saves overdraw. Blurring can be limited to the cloud-covered portion instead of the whole screen.

GPU friendly: The technique takes advantage of optimizations offered by today's graphics cards, for example, early z-rejection.

GPU Requirements:

Does not require advanced shader models: The technique is achievable on DirectX 7 hardware or GameCube, Playstation 2, or XBox consoles as long as a simpler blurring method is used.

A side-effect of blurring and fractal distortion is that clouds fuzzily interact with objects interpenetrating them. Instead of a sharp cutout, a cloud smoothly climbs an object's edges, resulting in a realistic look (see Figure 5.3.4).

FIGURE 5.3.4   Clouds climb an interpenetrating object's edges in a fuzzy way.

For more interesting results, a second fractal box can be added. The purpose of this second box is to rotate slowly over time and blend with the first box's values, resulting in apparent internal structure changes of the cloud.

For this technique to work, clouds must render in a certain order within the scene. This order is necessary because the fuzzy-edge-climbing effect should not happen to objects totally in front of a cloud. Since these fuzzy edges are generated by the blur spreading color values outside of the mega-particles, they are not backed up by z-values. Thus, they always blend with what is underneath them, even if it is closer to the viewer. Failure to render in the appropriate order eliminates the fuzzy edges feature, which may still be acceptable if changing the rendering order is not an option.

Clouds rendered with this implementation are fully opaque except at the edges. Constant translucency is achievable during the final back buffer blend, but varying translucency should be handled by changing translucency of each mega-particle.

Conclusion

This article presents a simple technique to render volumetric clouds cheaply. The core concept is to render fully lit mega-particles that are blurred, fractal-distorted, and then alpha-blended with the frame buffer. The technique eliminates many drawbacks of previous volumetric rendering approaches and offers artistic control and flexibility. Finally, performance overhead of this technique is low; in particular, its fill-rate consumption is small and almost constant.

Acknowledgments

Special thanks to Sergei Savchenko of Electronic Arts and Abdo Haji-Ali of In|Framez for their guidance and their reviews of this article.

References

[Baker01] Baker, Dan and Charles Boyd. "Volumetric Rendering in Real-time." Available online at *http://www.gamasutra.com/features/20011003/boyd_01.htm*, 2001.

[Gottlieb04] Gottlieb, Eli Z. "Rendering Volumes in a Vertex & Pixel Program by Ray Tracing." *ShaderX²: Shader Programming Tips & Tricks with DirectX 9*, edited by Wolfgang Engel. Wordware Publishing, 2004: pp. 177–184.

[Hargreaves04] Hargreaves, Shawn. "Non-Photorealistic Post-processing Filters in MotoGP 2." *ShaderX²: Shader Programming Tips & Tricks with DirectX 9*, edited by Wolfgang Engel. Wordware Publishing, 2004: pp. 469–480.

[Laeuchli05] Laeuchli, Jesse. "Volumetric Clouds." *ShaderX³: Advanced Rendering with DirectX and OpenGL*, edited by Wolfgang Engel. Charles River Media, 2005: pp. 611–616.

[Mitchell04] Mitchell, Jason L., Marwan Y. Ansari, and Evan Hart. "Advanced Image Processing with DirectX9 Pixel Shaders." *ShaderX²: Shader Programming Tips & Tricks with DirectX9*, edited by Wolfgang Engel. Wordware Publishing, 2004: pp. 450–452.

[Pallister01] Pallister, Kim. "Generating Procedural Clouds Using 3D Hardware." *Game Programming Gems 2*, edited by Mark A. DeLoura. Charles River Media, 2001: pp. 463–473.

[Stam00] Stam, Jos. "Interacting with Smoke and Fire in Real-time." *Communications of the ACM, 43*(7), (2000): pp. 76–83.

[Tarantilis04] Tarantalis, Georgios E. "Simulating Clouds with Procedural Texturing Techniques Using the GPU." Naval Postgraduate School Master Thesis, September 2004.

5.4

Rendering Multiple Layers of Rain with a Postprocessing Composite Effect

Natalya Tatarchuk, ATI Research

Introduction

Our goal is to create a moment in a dark downtown during a rainy night (see Figure 5.4.1 for an example). Investigating the concept for this demo in the middle of October in Boston fortunately provided many opportunities for research. Figure 5.4.2 shows a comparison between a photograph of the theater district of downtown Boston and the final rendering of the *ToyShop* demo [ToyShop05].

FIGURE 5.4.1   Example of rendering rain in a city scene in real time. (© ATI Research Inc. Reprinted with permission.)

(A)   (B)

FIGURE 5.4.2   Comparison of (**A**) a photograph of a real city during a rainy night versus (**B**) a synthetic rendering of the interactive environment of *ToyShop*. ([a] © Natalya Tatarchuk, 2005. [b] © ATI Research Inc. Reprinted with permission.)

Some games incorporating rain in their worlds use a straightforward approach: rendering stretched, alpha-blended particles to simulate falling raindrops. This approach fails to create a convincing or interesting rain impression. Frequently, these stretched alpha-blended particles and perhaps a simple CPU-based water puddle animation are the only attempt at simulating a rainy environment. These limited attempts result in an unrealistic rendering, with rain not reacting accurately to scene illumination (such as lightning or spotlights). Notable exceptions are the recently released *Splinter Cell* [SplinterCell03] and *Need for Speed: Most Wanted* [NeedForSpeed05] that showcase much improved rain rendering.

Rain is a complex visual phenomenon composed of multiple components. Rainfall consists of specially distributed water drops falling at high velocity. Each drop refracts and reflects the environment. As raindrops fall, they create the perception of motion blur and generate ripples and splashes in puddles on the ground. Rain effects are extensively studied in the context of atmospheric sciences [Wang75] [Mason75], as well as in the field of computer vision [Garg04]. We develop a number of effects for rendering rain in our interactive environment in real-time, consisting of a compositing effect to add rainfall to the final rendering, a number of particle-based effects, and dynamic water effects that are simulated on the GPU.

In this chapter we focus on adding rain to a scene via a compositing postprocess. Our technique provides artist-directable controls and respects the rules of physics for simulating rainfall. It utilizes light reflection models to allow rain to respond dynamically and correctly to lighting changes in the complex environment of the ATI *ToyShop* demo [ToyShop05], for example, owing to illumination from atmospheric effects such as lightning. For more details about the other approaches used to create the rainy environment of *ToyShop*, see [Tatarchuk06] and [Tatarchuk06a].

Rendering Multiple Layers of Rain with a Postprocessing Composite Effect

We develop a novel postprocessing rain effect that simulates multiple layers of falling raindrops in a single compositing pass over the rendered scene (see Figure 5.4.3). We create motion parallax for raindrops utilizing projective texture reads. The illumination for rain is computed using water-air refraction for individual raindrops as well as reflection caused by surrounding light sources and the Fresnel effect. We provide a set of artist knobs for controlling rain direction and velocity, as well as rainfall strength. The raindrop rendering receives dynamically updated parameters such as lightning brightness and direction from the lightning system to allow correct illumination resulting from lightning strikes.

FIGURE 5.4.3   Example of creating an illusion of rain with a postprocessing based effect. (© ATI Research Inc. Reprinted with permission.)

Creating Rainfall

We render a composite layer of falling rain as a full-screen pass before the final postprocessing of the scene. Rainfall is simulated with an 8-bit texture (see Figure 5.4.4 for an example texture and the resulting rain scene). To simulate the mistiness of the raindrops, we blur the rain by using a postprocessing system such as that in [Kawase03]. The artists specify rain direction and speed in world space to simulate varied rainfall strength.

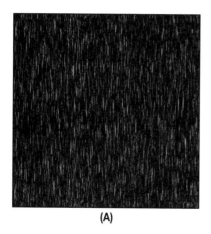
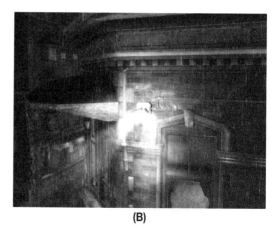

(A)   (B)

FIGURE 5.4.4   Rainfall texture applied for a composite rain effect in the interactive scene.
(A) Rainfall texture. **(B)** Rendered scene using this rainfall texture. Note that the image intensities
have been brightened for better contrast since this is a static capture of rain. (© ATI Research Inc.
Reprinted with permission.)

Although so far this approach sounds rather straightforward, several challenges are
associated with rendering rain via a composite layer. The first difficulty lies in minimizing repeating patterns that are inevitable when using a single static texture to model
dynamic textured patterns. The second concern is that the rain pass is a full-screen
pass, that is, this rain shader processes every pixel on screen. This shader therefore has a
direct effect on performance, and we must design the composite rain rendering so that
it gives pleasing visual results without being expensive.

Computer vision analysis of rain models [Garg04] and video rain synthesis
[Starik03] help us observe that one cannot easily recognize rainfall from a single static
frame; rather, rain is easily noticeable in a dynamic simulation or a video. Perceptual
analysis of rain videos shows that individual raindrop motion cannot be tracked by
human perception owing to the swift movement and density of raindrops. This result
allows us to assume temporal independence of rain frames. Our empiric experiments,
however, show that purely random movement of raindrops yields unsatisfactory
results (generating excessive visual noise). Therefore, to simulate strong rainfall we
simultaneously use the concepts of individual rain drop rendering and of stochastic
distribution for simulation of dynamic textures [Bar-Joseph01] [Doretto03].

The first part of our algorithm simulates individual rainfall movement. We use
the artist-specified rain direction (after transforming it from world- to clip-space) to
determine a raindrop position in screen space by using the current position in clip
space, the specified rainfall velocity, and the current time. Given these parameters and
computation of the raindrop position, we can scroll the rainfall texture using the specified velocity vector. Although texture scrolling is straightforward, even with several
texture fetches in varied directions with slight randomization, repeating rain patterns
become rather obvious in a full-screen pass.

Multiple Layers of Rain

Our goal is to simulate several layers of raindrops moving with different speeds at varied depths in a single rendering layer. This approach better approximates real-life rain movement and allows us to create a feeling of raindrop motion parallax (a strong visual cue in any dynamic environment). The artists can specify a rain parallax parameter that provides control for specifying the depth range for the rain layers in our scene. Using the concepts of stochastic distribution for simulation of dynamic textures, we compute a randomized value for an individual raindrop representation to use in the rain shader. Using the rain parallax value, the screen-space individual raindrop parameter, and the distribution parameter, we can model multiple layers of rain in a single pass with a single texture fetch. This allows us to simulate raindrops falling with different speeds at different layers. The rain parallax value for the raindrop, multiplied by a distribution value, is used as the w parameter for a projective texture fetch to sample from the rainfall texture. Note that we use the same directional vector for all of our raindrops, which is crucial for creating a consistent rainfall effect. This approach creates excellent visual effects of random streaking for the raindrops. Refer to Appendix A for implementation details.

Raindrop Shading

Raindrops behave like lenses, refracting and reflecting scene radiances toward the camera. They refract light from a large solid angle of the environment (including the sky) toward the camera. Specular and internal reflections further add to the brightness of a drop. Thus, a drop tends to be much brighter than its background (the portion of the scene it occludes). The solid angle of the background occluded by a drop is far less than the total field of view of the drop itself. Thus, despite the raindrop being transparent, the average brightness within a stationary drop (without motion-blur) does not strongly depend on its background.

Falling raindrops produce motion-blurred intensities owing to the finite integration time of a camera. Unlike a stationary drop, the intensities of a rain streak depend on the brightness of the (stationary) drop and the background scene radiances, as well as the integration time of a camera. We simulate the motion blur for the raindrops by applying blurring via postprocessing after the rain pass has been blended onto the scene rendering. This simulates both raindrop motion-blur and multiple-scattering glow for individual raindrops.

To shade an individual raindrop, we use a tangent-space normal map corresponding to the rainfall texture. Note that since this is a full-screen pass, the tangent space is simply specified by the view matrix. For each pixel in the rain pass, we compute a reflection based on the individual raindrop normal and air-to-water refraction. Both are attenuated toward the edges of the raindrop by using the Fresnel effect [Akenine-Möller02].

Raindrop Transparency

An interesting observation is that as lightning strikes, raindrops should appear more transparent. In other words, the opacity of each raindrop is a function of lightning brightness; otherwise, water surfaces appear too solid. Our rendering script propagates the lightning system parameters to all of our rain shaders, as well as the material shaders. For the raindrop rendering, we use a combined lightning brightness parameter (mixing all lightning light sources as they flash in the environment) to compute the bias value to adjust the amount of reflection and refraction.

Realistic rain is very faint in bright regions but tends to appear stronger in dark areas. If modeled exactly, however, rain appears too dim and unnoticeable in many regions of a scene. Instead of rendering a precise representation, we simulate a Hollywood film trick for cinematic rain sequences: film crews add milk to water to make the rain appear stronger and brighter on film. We similarly bias the computed rain drop color and opacity toward white. Although this may seem exaggerated, it creates a perception of stronger rainfall.

Compositing Rain via Blending

We would like to make a few notes on how to blend the rain pass with the rest of the scene. The rain layer is rendered as an object that is transparent as well as glowing (for further postprocessing). However, since we want to render the rain layer in a single pass, we are constrained to using a single alpha value. Controlling both opacity and glow with a single alpha blend setting is rather difficult. We would like to blend it using one setting for the amount of glow/blurring via the postprocessing and use a separate blending function to blend the rain into the environment. Despite that, we want to render transparent objects that glow, controlling each state separately for better visual results. We use two sets of blending parameters to control blending for glow and for transparency for all rain effects (i.e., composite rain, raindrops, splashes). DirectX 9.0c supports a rendering state for separate alpha blending (D3DRS_SEPARATEALPHABLENDENABLE). Using this state along with the regular alpha-blending function (via D3DRS_ALPHABLENDENABLE) allows us to specify two separate blending functions for the regular opacity blending and for the alpha used for glow for the postprocessing blurring pass.

Conclusions

Rain is a complex phenomenon, and this chapter presents an effect that creates an illusion of strong rainfall for computer-generated scenes. We successfully used this effect to create an extensive, detail-rich urban environment in stormy weather in the ATI *ToyShop* demo [ToyShop05]. Rich, complex environments demand convincing details. We hope the technology presented here is successfully used in the next generation of games and real-time rendering.

Acknowledgments

We thank the ATI *ToyShop* team, whose hard work and dedication resulted in the striking images of this interactive environment. The artists: Dan Roeger, Daniel Szecket, Abe Wiley, and Eli Turner; the programmers: John Isidoro, Daniel Ginsburg, Thorsten Scheuermann, Chris Oat (who have developed some mathematical helper functions used by the shaders in Appendix A), and David Gosselin (currently at MadDoc Software); and the producers: Lisa Close and Callan McInally.

References

[Akenine-Möller02] Akenine-Möller, T. and E. Haines, E. *Real-time Rendering*, 2nd ed. AK Peters, Ltd., 2002: pp. 194–201.

[Bar-Joseph01] Bar-Joseph, Z., R. El-Yaniv, D. Lischinski, and M. Werman. "Texture Mixing and Texture Movie Synthesis Using Statistical Learning." *IEEE Transactions on Visualization and Computer Graphics*, 7(2), (2001): pp. 120–135.

[Doretto03] Doretto, G., A. Chiuso, Y. N. Wu, S. Soatto. "Dynamic Textures." *International Journal of Computer Vision*, 51(2), (2003): pp. 91–109.

[Garg04] Garg, K., S. K. Nayar. "Detection and Removal of Rain from Videos." *IEEE Conference on Computer Vision and Pattern Recognition*, 2004: pp. 528–535.

[Kawase03] Kawase, M. "Frame Buffer Postprocessing Effects in DOUBLE-S.T.E.A.L (Wreckless)." GDC 2003 lecture, San Jose, CA, 2003.

[Mason75] Mason, B. J. *Clouds, Rain and Rainmaking*. Cambridge Press, 1975.

[NeedForSpeed05] *Need for Speed: Most Wanted*. EA, 2005. Available online at *http://www.ea.com/official/nfs/mostwanted/us/home.jsp*.

[Starik03] Starik, S., and M. Werman. "Simulation of Rain in Videos." Texture 2003. (The 3rd International Workshop on Texture Analysis and Synthesis), 2003.

[SplinterCell03] *Tom Clancy's Splinter Cell*. Ubisoft. 2003. Available online at *http://splintercell.us.ubi.com/splintercell.php*.

[Tatarchuk06] Tatarchuk, N. "Artist-Directable Real-time Rain Rendering in City Environments." *ACM SIGGRAPH 2006: Proceedings of the Conference on SIGGRAPH 2006 Course Notes, Course 26, Advanced Real-time Rendering in 3D Graphics and Games*. 2006: Chapter 3, pp. 29–70.

[Tatarchuk06a] Tatarchuk, N. and J. Isidoro. "Artist-Directable Real-time Rain Rendering in City Environments." *Proceedings of Eurographics Workshop on Natural Phenomena*, Vienna, Austria, 2006.

[ToyShop05] Toyshop Demo. ATI Research, Inc., 2005. Available online at *http://www.ati.com/developer/demos/rx1800.html*.

[Wang75] Wang, T. and R. S. Clifford. "Use of Rainfall-Induced Optical Scintillations to Measure Path-Averaged Rain Parameters." *JOSA*, (1975): pp. 927.

Appendix A

Here are the example shaders used to render this rain effect in our demo:

LISTING 5.4.1   Composite Rain Pass Vertex Shader

```
float4x4 mViewProjection;
float4x4 mView;
float4   vRainDirection;
float3   vWorldCamPos;
float3   vViewCameraPos;
float4   vLightPos0;

struct VsInput
{
  float4 pos      : POSITION0;
  float2 texCoord : TEXCOORD0;
};

struct VsOutput
{
    float4 pos            : POSITION0;
    float4 vRainDirection : TEXCOORD0;
    float2 vRainPosition  : TEXCOORD1;
    float3 vTangent       : TEXCOORD2;
    float3 vBinormal      : TEXCOORD3;
    float3 vNormal        : TEXCOORD4;
    float3 vLightPos      : TEXCOORD5;
    float4 vPosition      : TEXCOORD6;
};

VsOutput main (VsInput i)
{
    // Define output structure
    VsOutput o;

    o.pos       = float4( sign( i.pos.xy  ), 0.0f, 1.0f );
    o.vPosition = i.pos;

    float4 vRainDirectionW = vRainDirection;

    // Rain direction in clip space:
    o.vRainDirection  = mul( vRainDirectionW, mViewProjection );

    // Get into range [0,1]
    o.vRainPosition = ( float2( o.pos.x, -o.pos.y ) + 1.0f ) / 2.0f;

    // In the case of screen aligned quad the tangent space basis is
    // the same as the view basis vectors. Since we are actually
    // going to use this as a transformation matrix to world,
    // it's transposed in the vertex shader:
    o.vTangent  = mView._11_12_13;
    o.vBinormal = mView._21_22_23;
    o.vNormal   = mView._31_32_33;
```

```
        // The object ambient light vector for rain
        o.vLightPos = (float3) mul( vLightPos0, mViewProjection );

        return o;
    }
```

LISTING 5.4.2   Composite Rain Pass Pixel Shader (note that tone mapping is application specific)

```
// Computes an approximated fresnel term ==
// [((1.0f - N.V)^5) * 0.95f] + 0.05f
float SiComputeFresnelApprox (float3 normalVec, float3 viewVec)
{
    // (1-N.V)^4
    float NdotV5 = pow (1.0f - SiDot3Clamp (normalVec, viewVec),
    4.0f);

    // scale and bias to fit to real fresnel curve
    return (NdotV5 * 0.95f) + 0.05f;
}

float3 SiTransmissionDirection (float fromIR, float toIR,
                                float3 incoming, float3 normal)
{
    float eta = fromIR/toIR; // relative index of refraction
    float c1 = -dot (incoming, normal); // cos(theta1)
    float cs2 = 1.-eta*eta*(1.-c1*c1); // cos^2(theta2)
    float3 v = (eta*incoming + (eta*c1-sqrt(cs2))*normal);
    if (cs2 < 0.) v = 0; // total internal reflection
    return v;
}

sampler tBase;
sampler tEnvironment;
sampler tBump;

float    fSpecExp;

float2   vRainSpeed;           // Rain speed in X and Y. We used
                               // .x = 2.41 and .y = 158.1
float4   vTime;                // Current time counter defined as
                               // follows:
                               // vTime.x = object time [0;1]
                               // vTime.y = object time [0;120]
                               // vTime.z = sin(time) [0; 60]
                               // vTime.w = object time
float4   vRandom;              // Random value from a normal
                               // Gaussian distribution
float4   vLightColor0;         // Light color
float4   vRainDirection;       // World-space rain direction
                               // Example: (1, -100, 0, 0 )
float4   vWorldTime;
float    fRainParallax;        // A heuristic value for setting
                                  rain
```

```
                                    // drop stretchiness (ex: 3.5)
    float4x4 mViewProjClipSpace;    // Transformation matrix
    float4x4 mView;                 // Transformation matrix
    float4x4 mViewProjection;       // Transformation matrix

    float2   vLightningBrightness;  // Lightning brightness parameter
                                    // Driven from the rendering engine,
                                    // can be 1.0 for fully bright or
                                       0 for no lightning
    float    fRainContrast;         // Controls contrast for brigher
                                    // rain during lightning (ex: 3.0 )
    float    fRainBias;             // Rain brightness bias (ex: 0.7)

    struct PsInput
    {
       float4 vRainDirection  : TEXCOORD0_centroid;
       float2 vRainPosition   : TEXCOORD1;
       float3 vTangent        : TEXCOORD2_centroid;
       float3 vBinormal       : TEXCOORD3_centroid;
       float3 vNormal         : TEXCOORD4_centroid;
       float3 vLightPos       : TEXCOORD5_centroid;
       float4 vPosition       : TEXCOORD6_centroid;
    };

    float4 main( PsInput i ): COLOR
    {
       // View vector in world space:
       float3 vViewWS = normalize( -mView[2] );

       float4 cBase = float4( 0, 0, 0, 1 );
       float3 cResult;

       // The rain position rotated in the direction of rain fall in
       // screen space is this:
       float2 vRaindropPosition = i.vRainPosition;

       // Move rain direction vector into clip space:
       float2 vRainDirectionCP = normalize( i.vRainDirection.xy );

       // Move the position using rain direction and speed:
       vRaindropPosition += vRainDirectionCP * vRainSpeed * vTime.x;

       float4 texCoord = float4( vRaindropPosition, 0,
                                 fRainParallax * frac( vRandom.x ) );

       cBase   = tex2Dproj( tBase, texCoord ).rrrr;
       cResult = fRainBias * cBase.rgb;

       // Light vector in clip space is:
       float3 vLightCS = ( float3 ) (i.vLightPos -
                                  float3( vRaindropPosition, 0 ) );

       // Light vector in world space:
       float3 vLightWS = normalize( mul( vLightCS,
                                    mViewProjClipSpace ) );
```

```
// Retrieve the normal map normal for rain drops:
float3 vNormalTS = tex2Dproj( tBump, texCoord ).xyz;
vNormalTS = SiComputeNormalATI2N( vNormalTS );

// Compute normal in world space:
float3x3 mTangentToWorld = float3x3( normalize( i.vTangent ),
                                     normalize( i.vBinormal ),
                                     normalize( i.vNormal ));
float3   vNormalWS = normalize( mul( mTangentToWorld,
                                     vNormalTS ));

// Compute the reflection vector:
float3 vReflectionWS = SiReflect( vViewWS, vNormalWS );

// Compute the specular contribution:
float  fRdotL    = SiDot3Clamp( vReflectionWS, vLightWS );
float3 cSpecular = saturate( pow( fRdotL, fSpecExp ) );

// Environment contribution:
float3 cReflection = texCUBE( tEnvironment, vReflectionWS );

// Determine the brightness of lightning
float fLightningBrightness = ( vLightningBrightness.x +
                                 vLightningBrightness.y );
float fLightningBias       = 1.0 + fRainContrast *
                                 fLightningBrightness;

// The lightning brightness affects the strength of reflections.
// Note that for rain the general effect is to flip the
// reflections in the vertical directions
cReflection *= fLightningBias;

// Approximate fresnel term
float fFresnel = SiComputeFresnelApprox( vNormalWS, vViewWS );

// Compute refraction vector: 0.754 = 1.003 (air) / 1.33 (water)
float3 vRefractWS = SiTransmissionDirection( 1.003, 1.33,
                           vViewWS, vNormalWS );

// Refraction contribution:
float3 cRefraction = texCUBE( tEnvironment, vRefractWS );
cRefraction *= fLightningBias;

cResult *= cSpecular + saturate(
(cReflection * fFresnel * 0.25f) +
        cRefraction * (1.0f - (fFresnel * 0.75 )));

// Final color composite:
float4 o = 0;
o.rgb = ToneMapHDRColor( cResult.rgb );
o.a = cBase.r;

return o;

}
```

5.5

Animation and Rendering of Underwater God Rays

Stefano Lanza

God rays are a truly beautiful phenomenon in underwater scenes (see Figure 5.5.1 for an example). They are beams of sunlight that filter through water and then dance underwater in many directions. You can admire them in many underwater documentaries and movies, or better, by diving in deep water and then looking up toward the sun.

FIGURE 5.5.1   A sample screenshot of our god ray–rendering technique.

This article describes an inexpensive yet visually convincing technique to animate and render underwater god rays in real-time. It requires a graphics card supporting DirectX 9 Shader Model 2. This article also provides HLSL shaders to allow games or simulators to easily adopt this technique.

The Physics of Underwater God Rays

The physical explanation of god rays is clear: beams of sunlight initially refract at the air-water interface and then travel underwater in different directions. Light underwater is partly attenuated and partly scattered by particles or other suspended substances before it eventually reaches an observer. The amount of light reaching an observer depends mainly on the water characteristics and the viewing direction. We ignore second-order physical effects such as multiple scattering and the contribution of skylight. We also ignore the conservation of energy when light shafts diverge or converge, which maintains a constant intensity area over cross sections of a light beam.

Mathematical models accurately describe each of these physical phenomena [Deepocean] [Premoze00]. For refractions, the following formula returns the refracted vector $\mathbf{T}$ given the incident vector $\mathbf{I}$, surface normal $\mathbf{N}$, and the refraction index η_1 for the first medium (1.05 for air) and η_2 for the second medium (1.3333 for water).

$$\mathbf{T} = \eta\mathbf{I} + \left(-\eta\mathbf{I}\cdot\mathbf{N} - \sqrt{1 - \eta^2\left(1 - \left(\mathbf{I}\cdot\mathbf{N}\right)^2\right)} \right)\mathbf{N}, \qquad (5.5.1)$$

where $\eta = \eta_1/\eta_2$.

The amount of light $T(\theta)$ transmitted from air to water depends on the angle between the incident direction and the water normal; we use Schlick's approximation [Schlick94] to calculate this term (called the Fresnel term):

$$R(\theta) = R_0 + (1 - R_0)(1 - \cos(\theta))^5, \qquad (5.5.2a)$$

$$T(\theta) = 1 - R(\theta) \qquad (5.5.2b)$$

where R_0 is 0.0204 for water and $\cos(\Omega)$ is the dot product between the water normal and the incident vector.

We model light extinction, which includes losses owing to absorption and scattering, with an exponential attenuation:

$$I_L(\lambda) = I_0(\lambda)\exp(-c(\lambda)L). \qquad (5.5.3)$$

Here λ is the light wavelength (red, green, or blue), $c(\lambda)$ is a wavelength-dependent extinction coefficient, and L is the total distance traveled by light in the attenuating medium. We can use hard-coded or artist-defined coefficients (less for blue, more for red and green) or derive them from the water characteristics, for example, using the physical model described in [Premoze00].

Light scattering is mathematically described by an isotropic phase function $F(\theta)$ that returns the amount of light that scatters toward the viewer, given the angle θ between the light direction and the viewing direction. Among the several functions proposed in the literature, we adopt the Henyey-Greenstein phase function [Henyey41] for our technique; this function is roughly wavelength independent and provides strong forward scattering, which is consistent with god rays being brighter when one is looking towards the sun. This function is:

$$\text{F}(\theta) = \beta_M \frac{1 - g^2}{(1 + g^2 - 2g\cos(\theta))^{3/2}} \qquad (5.5.4)$$

where β_M is the Mie coefficient and g is the eccentricity, which controls the power of forward scattering. For our purposes we can ignore β_M and use g equal to 0.5.

DirectX's HLSL includes all intrinsic functions necessary to reproduce these formulas in a shader. In particular, the refract instruction is an exact implementation of Equation 5.5.1.

Previous Work

Other work in computer graphics already addresses the problem of rendering god rays. Iwasaki [Iwasaki02] describes a physically based model for rendering underwater light shafts, making use of graphics hardware to accelerate the computation. The technique models each god ray as a parallelepiped that is subdivided into subvolumes. It accurately calculates the light intensity for each subvolume and accumulates the results in the frame buffer by using hardware color blending. It also simulates shadows via shadow mapping. The accuracy of this technique comes at the cost of prohibitively high rendering times.

NVIDIA simulates god rays with an image filter in the demo *Nalu* [NVIDIA04]. The *Nalu* demo first renders the bright region corresponding to the refracted sun to a render target, then renders shadow casters and subtracts them from the bright pixels. Finally, it radially blurs the image, creating an illusion of god rays. This technique is quite simple but only works when the sun is visible. It is also impossible to control the animation of god rays, as it indirectly depends on the rendering of the refracted sun disk.

Mitchell [Mitchell04] and Dobashi [Dobashi02] render light shafts by slicing the view frustum into a set of parallel planes. For each plane, they discretize the integrals of the mathematical simulation of god rays and accumulate the resulting intensity into the frame buffer. Shadows are simulated with shadow mapping. This technique is rather expensive, as many planes are necessary to obtain high-quality visual results that are free from severe aliasing. Apart from performance issues, this technique also cannot directly control the animation of light shafts.

Jensen [Jensen01] simulates underwater god rays by slicing the view volume into many (e.g., 32 in the paper) planes and projecting an animated caustics texture onto each plane, assuming that this texture represents the intensity of god rays for each plane.

Our Technique

Our technique is loosely inspired by [Iwasaki02] and works as follows: some light shafts, geometrically modeled as parallelepipeds, are animated in a vertex shader by refracting their supporting vectors against a procedurally animated water surface. They then render to a texture with additive alpha-blending that takes their depth attenuation and other physical phenomena into account. We simulate shadows via standard shadow mapping [Everitt00]. The resulting texture accumulates the approximate intensity of god rays in the scene. In a second pass we additively blend a full-screen quad to the frame buffer; for each pixel we calculate the amount of light scattered toward the viewer and multiply this result with the light intensity fetched from the first texture, obtaining an approximation of the god rays' intensity at that pixel. The following paragraphs describe each step in detail.

Geometrical Model

Each light shaft is modeled as a parallelepiped, as shown in Figure 5.5.2. The top face lies on the water surface, and the lateral edges correspond to refracted sun rays extending underwater to a certain depth.

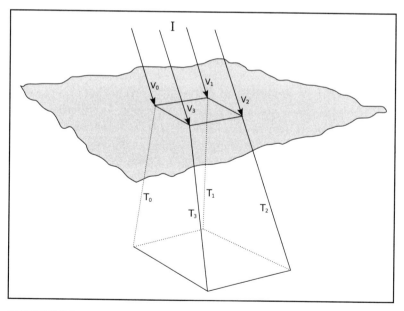

FIGURE 5.5.2   Geometrical model of a god ray. $\mathbf{V}_i$ stand for vertices, $\mathbf{T}_i$ for the corresponding refracted vectors, and $\mathbf{I}$ is the incoming sunlight, assumed constant for all god rays.

We render many god rays with a single indexed primitive. Two sets of vertices represent the god rays' geometry, one set for the top faces and one for the bottom faces. These vertices are arranged on a regular square grid located on the water surface; the top vertices are assigned a depth of 0, while the bottom vertices are assigned a maximum depth (e.g., 30 m). This depth value is used in the vertex shader to move the bottom vertices down along the direction of the refracted sunlight, creating an extruded parallelepiped for each god ray.

A static vertex buffer stores all vertices centered around the point $(0, 0, 0)$ with a spacing of 1. A vertex shader translates and scales these vertices according to the current viewer's position and depth to optimize the distribution of light beams over the visible water surface. The vertices are first recentered around the image of the sun on the water surface, which corresponds to the point $\hat{\mathbf{P}}$ given as the intersection between the water plane and a ray traveling from the viewer in the direction of the refracted sunlight, assuming flat water (see Figure 5.5.3). It equals

$$\hat{\mathbf{P}} = \mathbf{E} + \mathbf{T}\left(h_0 - \mathbf{E}_y\right)\big/\mathbf{T}_y, \tag{5.5.5a}$$

$$\mathbf{T} = \text{refract}(\mathbf{I}, \mathbf{N}, 1/1.333), \tag{5.5.5b}$$

where $\mathbf{I}$ is the incident sunlight, $\mathbf{N} = (0,1,0)$ is the normal for flat water, $\mathbf{E}$ is the viewer position, and h_0 is the water altitude.

God rays are arranged optimally when they completely cover the visible water surface. Assuming that the viewer looks upward, the spacing between god rays should thus be linearly proportional to the viewer's depth, because the area of the visible water surface over which the god rays are arranged increases as the viewer moves deeper. The following formula computes the optimal spacing:

$$S = K \frac{2d \tan\left(fov/2\right)}{N} \tag{5.5.6}$$

where d is the viewer's depth, fov is the field of view, N is the number of god ray vertices along the grid and K is an adjustment factor (around 0.8).

Animation

We mentioned in the previous section that the parallelepipeds representing god rays extrude in the direction of sunlight refracted by an animating water surface.

How to animate water is outside the scope of this article. For example, many recent games use a statistical model evaluated with an FFT [Jensen01]. This method generates heights and normals for a realistic simulation of water but comes at a high cost for our simple needs and does not work well on Shader Model 2 GPUs, where vertex shaders cannot access textures.

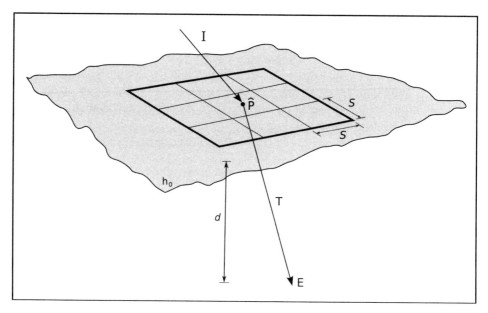

FIGURE 5.5.3   Central position and spacing of vertices on the water's surface.

We propose a procedural way to animate water entirely on the GPU. We model water as a sum of Gerstner waves [Hinsinger02]. Given a point $\mathbf{P} = (x_0, y_0, z_0)$ on the water surface, this point displaces as follows:

$$
\begin{cases}
\varphi_i = \mathbf{K}_i \cdot \mathbf{X}_0 - w_i t + \varphi_i^0 \\
\mathbf{X} = \mathbf{X}_0 - \displaystyle\sum_{i=1}^{N} a_i \frac{\mathbf{K}_i}{\|\mathbf{K}_i\|} \sin\left(\varphi^i\right) \\
y = y_0 + \displaystyle\sum_{i=1}^{N} a_i \cos\left(\varphi^i\right)
\end{cases}
\tag{5.5.7}
$$

where $\mathbf{X}_0 = (x_0, z_0)$ is the location of the point at rest, y_0 is its altitude at rest and a_i, w_i, $\mathbf{K}_i$, and φ_i^0 are the amplitude, frequency, wave number, and initial phase of the ith wave, respectively. The resulting shape is similar to a sinusoid for very small amplitudes, but is sharper otherwise.

From Equation 5.5.7, we obtain an analytical expression for the gradients $\mathbf{T}$ and $\mathbf{B}$ through differentiation:

$$
\begin{cases}
\mathbf{T}_x = -\sum_{i=1}^{N} \dfrac{a_i (\mathbf{K}_{ix})^2}{\|\mathbf{K}_i\|} \cos(\varphi^i) \\[2mm]
\mathbf{T}_z = -\sum_{i=1}^{N} \dfrac{a_i \mathbf{K}_{ix} \mathbf{K}_{iy}}{\|\mathbf{K}_i\|} \cos(\varphi^i) \\[2mm]
\mathbf{T}_y = -\sum_{i=1}^{N} a_i \mathbf{K}_{ix} \sin(\varphi^i) \\[2mm]
\mathbf{B}_x = -\sum_{i=1}^{N} \dfrac{a_i \mathbf{K}_{ix} \mathbf{K}_{iy}}{\|\mathbf{K}_i\|} \cos(\varphi^i) \\[2mm]
\mathbf{B}_z = -\sum_{i=1}^{N} \dfrac{a_i (\mathbf{K}_{iy})^2}{\|\mathbf{K}_i\|} \cos(\varphi^i) \\[2mm]
\mathbf{B}_y = -\sum_{i=1}^{N} a_i \mathbf{K}_{iy} \sin(\varphi^i)
\end{cases}
\qquad (5.5.8)
$$

The water normal is the normalized cross product of the two gradients. The following HLSL function optimally computes the water normal by considering four waves at a time.

```
// Waves constants
// kx, ky, A/sqr(kx*kx + ky*ky), A, wt+phi0
float4   waves[NUM_WAVES/4 * 5];

float3 CalculateWaterNormal(float x0, float y0) {
  float3 t1 = float3(1,0,0);
  float3 t2 = float3(0,0,1);

  for (int i = 0, j = 0; i < NUM_WAVES/4; i++, j += 5) {
    float4 kx    = waves[j];
    float4 ky    = waves[j+1];
    float4 Ainvk = waves[j+2];
    float4 A     = waves[j+3];
    float4 wt    = waves[j+4];
    float4 phase = (kx*x0 + ky*y0 - wt);
    float4 sinp, cosp;
    sincos(phase, sinp, cosp);

    // Update tangent vector along x0
    t1.x -= dot(Ainvk, kx*cosp*kx);
    t1.z -= dot(Ainvk, ky*cosp*kx);
    t1.y += dot(A, (-sinp)*(kx));

    // Update tangent vector along y0
    t2.x -= dot(Ainvk, kx*cosp*ky);
    t2.z -= dot(Ainvk, ky*cosp*ky);
    t2.y += dot(A, (-sinp)*(ky));
  }
```

```
// Calculate and return normal
return normalize( cross(t2, t1) );
}
```

The CPU has to generate the parameters a_i, $w_i t + \varphi_i^0$, and $\mathbf{K}_i$ for some number of waves (eight typically suffices) and pass them to vertex shader constants in the appropriate format. The code on the accompanying CD-ROM provides the data structures and utility functions.

ON THE CD

The vertex shader processing the god rays' vertices calculates a new position in world space for each vertex. First, the spacing and position of vertices on the water surface is adjusted. Next, for the bottom vertices, we refract the incoming sunlight direction against the water normal using the HLSL instruction refract. We then obtain the final vertex position in world space by multiplying the refracted vector by the extrusion length stored in the vertex structure passed to the shader. This position is finally transformed to clip space and passed as output. The shader also calculates the total light attenuation from the water surface to the vertex position and from the vertex to the viewer, as well as the Fresnel term for the amount of light transmitted from air to water. The rasterizer then linearly interpolates the resulting light intensity over the polygon and passes it to the pixel shader. Using vertex computations and subsequent interpolation is cheaper than calculating the intensity in the pixel shader, although that would be more correct. The final HLSL vertex shader is:

```
// Constants
float3   origin;          // central position of vertices
float    spacing;         // new spacing between vertices
float3   extinction_c;    // extinction coefficient
float3   viewer;          // viewer in world space
float3   sunDir;          // sunlight direction
float4x4 shadowmapMatrix; // projective shadowmap matrix


// Input and output vertex structure
struct VS_INPUT {
  float4 pos      : POSITION;
  float  length   : TEXCOORD0;
};

struct VS_OUTPUT {
  float4 pos           : POSITION;
  float3 intensity     : TEXCOORD0;
  float4 shadowmapPos  : TEXCOORD1;
};


// Fresnel approximation, formula 2
float FastFresnel(float3 I, float3 N, float R0) {
  return R0 + (1-R0)*pow(1-dot(I, N), 5);
}
```

```
VS_OUTPUT VS(const VS_INPUT input) {
  VS_OUTPUT output = (VS_OUTPUT)0;

  // Scale and translate the vertex on the water surface
  float3 worldPos = input.pos.xyz*float3(spacing,1,spacing);
  worldPos += origin;

  // Calculate the water normal at this point
  float3 normal = CalculateWaterNormal(worldPos.x, worldPos.z);

  // Extrude bottom vertices along the direction of the refracted
  // sunlight
  if (input.length > 0) {
    // Calculate refraction vector and extrude polygon
    float3 refr = refract(sunDir, normal, 1./1.333);
    worldPos += refr*input.length;
  }

  // Calculate transmittance
  float tr = 1-FastFresnel(-sunDir, normal);

  // Calculate god ray intensity
  float totalDist = input.length + length(worldPos-viewer);
  output.intensity = exp(-totalDist*extinction_c)*tr;

  // Calculate position in light space for shadowmapping
  output.shadowmapPos = mul(shadowmapMatrix,
  float4(worldPos,1) );

  // Transform position from world to clip space
  output.pos = mul(viewProjMatrix, float4(worldPos, 1) );
  // Tweak z position not to clip shafts very close to the viewer
  output.pos.z = 0.01;

  return output;
}
```

With reference to the above code, `extinction_c` is the attenuation coefficient from Equation 5.5.3, while `shadowmapMatrix` is a matrix that transforms the vertices to light space as part of shadow mapping (see the following "Rendering" section).

Rendering

Underwater god rays extend in many directions and usually cover the entire view volume. As a result, their rendering involves processing every screen pixel. When light shafts overlap, screen pixels are processed multiple times. To achieve high frame rates, it is thus imperative to adopt approximations that reduce the cost of rendering god rays. For this purpose, we break their rendering into two steps. The first step blends shadowed light shafts into a temporary render target using a relatively inexpensive pixel shader. The second step operates in image space; it reads the previous step's render target for each screen pixel and modulates the result with a phase function that improves the realism of the rendered scene. The resulting color is blended into the frame buffer, adding the light shafts on top of a previously rendered scene.

Overall, this approach greatly reduces fill rate, which tends to be the bottleneck when rendering god rays. By moving most of the calculations from the pixel to the vertex shader, we sacrifice physical accuracy in favor of rendering performance. We now discuss this approach in more detail.

Since we adopt shadow mapping to simulate shadows, the first step implies rendering the shadow casters to a texture from the point of view of the light source $\hat{P}$ (Equation 5.5.5a), storing the distance to the nearest caster for each pixel.

Next, a number of underwater light beams (e.g., 100) are rendered to a temporary render target with additive blending and z-buffering disabled, using the vertex shader described in the previous section. This step accumulates an approximate light intensity in the render target without relying on complex physical models. Because we use additive blending, the render target contains high values where many light beams overlap, and low values where few or no beams exist.

For performance reasons, it is convenient to use a render target smaller than the current frame buffer, because rendering many alpha-blended polygons stresses the fill rate and bandwidth of graphics cards, especially older ones. We find a quarter of the frame buffer to be a good compromise between rendering performance and quality. The format of this texture (D3DFMT_A8R8G8B8 in DirectX) has 8-bit precision per channel, resulting in a range of 0 to 255 for each color, providing enough precision to represent the average number of god rays overlapping at each pixel. Furthermore, all graphics cards support alpha blending on render targets of this format.

The pixel shader that renders the light shafts is simple and efficient. It first determines whether the pixel is in shadow or not (by comparing its distance from the light source to the corresponding distance stored in the shadow map). We do not filter the shadow map, as that degrades performance without noticeable quality improvements. The pixel shader then multiplies the result of the shadow comparison with the interpolated per-vertex color. The pixel shader is

```
texture shadowmap;

sampler2D shadowmapSam = sampler_state {
  Texture = <shadowmap>;
  MinFilter = Point;
  MagFilter = Point;
  MipFilter = Point;
  AddressU  = Clamp;
  AddressV  = Clamp;
};


float4 PS(VS_OUTPUT input) : COLOR {

  // Calculate distance to light source
  float z = input.shadowmapPos.z/input.shadowmapPos.w;
```

```
         // Fetch shadowmap
         float sz = tex2Dproj(shadowmapSam, input.shadowmapPos).x;

         float lit = (z < sz)? 1 : 0;
         return float4(input.outScattering*lit, 1);
     }
```

A second rendering pass then completes the rendering of god rays. We render a quad covering the entire screen with additive alpha-blending turned on. For each pixel, we read four bilinear samples from the previously rendered texture and average them. This averaging blurs the god rays' intensities. This averaged intensity is then modulated with the percentage of light scattered toward the viewer. The phase function takes as input two arguments: the view direction and the light direction. We calculate the former for each pixel by performing an inverse projection from screen to view space. The light direction theoretically differs from shaft to shaft, but this information is unavailable. We therefore use a constant light direction calculated according to Equation 5.5.5b. As a final touch, we add a small bias to the god rays' intensities that greatly minimizes their aliasing where scattering is strong (see the pixel shader below). The complete vertex and pixel shaders for the second pass follow.

```
     // Constants
     float4x4 invViewProjMatrix; // matrix from clip to world space
     float3   HGg;               // packed Mie parameters
     float3   refrSunDir;        // refracted sun direction
     float3   intensity;         // god rays intensity
     float2   invTexWidth;       // inverse of texture width, height
     float3   viewer;            // viewer in world space

     // Input and output vertex structure
     struct VS_INPUT {
       float4 pos         : POSITION;
       float2 uv          : TEXCOORD0;
     };

     struct VS_OUTPUT {
       float4 pos         : POSITION;
       float4 uv[2]       : TEXCOORD0;
       float3 viewVector  : TEXCOORD2;
     };


     // Mie phase function
     float ComputeMie(float3 viewDir, float3 sunDir) {
       float den = (HGg.y - HGg.z*dot(sunDir, viewDir));
       den = rsqrt(den);
       float phase = HGg.x * (den*den*den);
       return phase;
     }
```

```
VS_OUTPUT VS(const VS_INPUT input) {
  VS_OUTPUT output = (VS_OUTPUT)0;

  output.pos = input.pos;

  // Calculate texture coordinates for four samples
  output.uv[0].xy = input.uv;
  output.uv[0].zw = input.uv + float2(invTexWidth.x, 0);
  output.uv[1].xy = input.uv + invTexWidth;
  output.uv[1].zw = input.uv + float2(0, invTexWidth.y);

  // Transform input position from clip to world space
  output.viewVector = mul(invViewProjMatrix, input.pos)-viewer;

  return output;
}

float4 PS(VS_OUTPUT input) : COLOR {
  // Read godrays intensity, averaging four samples to
  // reduce aliasing
  float4 shafts = 0;
  for (int i = 0; i < 2; i++) {
    shafts += tex2D(godraysSam, input.uv[i].xy);
    shafts += tex2D(godraysSam, input.uv[i].zw);
  }
  shafts /= 4;

  float3 viewVector = normalize(input.viewVector);
  float phase = ComputeMie(-viewVector, refrSunDir);

  // Calculate final color, adding a little bias (0.15 here)
  // to hide aliasing
  float3 color = (0.15 + intensity*shafts.xyz)*phase;
  return float4(color, 1);
}
```

In the code above `invViewProjMatrix` is the inverse of the transformation matrix from world to clip space, `HGg` is the vector $(1-g^2, 1+g^2, 2g)$, where g is the constant from Equation 5.5.4, intensity is a user-defined multiplication factor, and `invTexWidth` is the inverse of the width and height of the render target storing the shafts' intensities.

Conclusion

This article describes an inexpensive way of simulating underwater god rays on common graphics hardware. The proposed technique takes advantage of reasonable approximations to greatly accelerate the rendering of god rays and makes it feasible for interactive applications such as games or simulators. Our technique works entirely on the GPU by exploiting programmable vertex and pixel shaders and render-to-texture capabilities. Although our implementation works with DirectX and HLSL, the described algorithms and shaders easily port to other rendering APIs, for example, OpenGL. The demo on the companion CD-ROM features an underwater scene powered by the

ON THE CD

Typhoon engine developed by the author, with caustics, underwater scattering, and god rays simulated using the described technique.

References

[Deepocean] Available online at *http://www.deepocean.net*.

[Dobashi02] Dobashi, Y., T. Yamamoto, and T. Nishita. "Interactive Rendering of Atmospheric Scattering Effects using Graphics Hardware." *Proc. Graphics Hardware* (2002): pp. 99–108.

[Everitt00] Everitt, C., A. Rege, and C. Cebenoyan. "Hardware Shadow Mapping." Tech. rep., NVIDIA Corp., 2000. Available online at *http://www.nvidia.com*.

[Henyey41] Henyey, L. G. and J. L. Greenstein. "Diffuse Radiation in the Galaxy." *Astrophysics Journal 93* (1941): pp. 70–83.

[Hinsinger02] Hinsinger, D., F. Neyret, and M. P. Cani. "Interactive Animation of Ocean Waves." *Proceedings of the ACM SIGGRAPH Symposium on Computer Animation*. 2002: pp. 161–166.

[Iwasaki02] Iwasaki, K., Y. Dobashi, and T. Nishita. "An Efficient Method for Rendering Underwater Optical Effects Using Graphics Hardware." *Computer Graphics Forum*, Volume *21*(4) (November 2002).

[Jensen01] Jensen, L.S. and R. Golias. "Deep Water Animation and Rendering." Available online at *http://www.gamasutra.com/gdce/2001/jensen/jensen_01.htm*.

[Mitchell04] Mitchell, J. "Light Shafts Rendering Shadows in Participating Media." Available online at *http://www.ati.com/developer/gdc/Mitchell_LightShafts.pdf*.

[NVIDIA04] NVIDIA's *Nalu* Demo. Available online at *http://www.nzone.com/object/nzone_nalu_home.html*.

[Premoze00] Premoze, S. and M. Ashikhmin. "Rendering Natural Waters." *Proceedings of Pacific Graphics*. 2000, pp. 23–30.

[Schlick94] Schlick, C. "An Inexpensive BDRF Model for Physically-Based Models." *Computer Graphics Forum*, 1994.

GLOBAL ILLUMINATION EFFECTS

Introduction

Carsten Dachsbacher

Each new generation of GPUs provides programmable flexibility and computational power exceeding previous generations. Hence, graphics hardware is capable of executing increasingly costly and complex algorithms. Rendering and lighting techniques that are traditionally offline processes migrate into real-time applications. Nevertheless, full global illumination is still not affordable; radiosity and ray tracing usually do not fit into the traditional rendering pipeline. As a result, most interactive applications tend to render plausible realism using clever ideas to map subproblems of global illumination to graphics hardware or storing precomputed solutions in an appropriate manner.

Chris Oat, in his article "Irradiance Volumes for Real-time Rendering," covers how to use adaptively subdivided octrees as spatial partitioning structures to store and approximate the irradiance distribution function. Irradiance volumes are used to illuminate dynamic objects moving through a static scene with precomputed global illumination.

The article "Indirect Diffuse and Glossy Illumination on the GPU," by István Lazányi and László Szirmay-Kalos, shows how to obtain fast approximations of indirect diffuse and glossy reflections on dynamic objects. For this, they use localized lookups in a single, down-sampled cube environment map per object storing irradiance and depth.

In his article "Interactive Refractions and Caustics Using Image-Space Techniques," Chris Wyman presents a clever idea to approximate image-space refractions using standard rasterization and shaders. Once refractions are computed, he shows how to go one step further and render caustics in real-time based on the first technique.

Our article, "Splatting of Diffuse and Glossy Indirect Illumination," presents a technique for rendering one-bounce indirect lighting from diffuse and glossy objects in real-time. Surfaces are sampled using an extended shadow map and replaced by adaptively placed point light sources. Their contribution is accumulated with deferred shading techniques using optimized per-light bounding volumes.

ON THE CD

Source code for all of these articles is provided, and you are invited to run the demo programs to fully appreciate the authors' work and to see what we hope next-generation games will look like.

6.1

Irradiance Volumes for Real-time Rendering

Chris Oat, ATI Research, Inc.

FIGURE 6.1.1   (Left) An adaptively subdivided octree is used to place irradiance sample points in the environment. The octree is finely subdivided in areas where irradiance changes quickly and is coarsely subdivided in areas where fewer samples are necessary because irradiance changes more slowly. (Center and Right) An irradiance volume is used to render a dynamic object (teapot) in a static scene. As the teapot moves through the scene, irradiance samples are chosen from the pre-computed volume and used to compute illumination.

Introduction

Real-time rendering relies on a host of tricks, optimizations and approximations to bring interactive graphics to consumer PCs. As each new generation of consumer graphics hardware exceeds the previous generation in terms of programmable flexibility and computational power, many traditionally offline rendering algorithms migrate out of backroom render farms and into the world of real-time. One of the many remaining discontinuities between real-time and non-real-time rendering is the use of global illumination for physically based, realistic lighting. While techniques such as light mapping can faithfully store global illumination on the surface of static scene geometry, light maps do not address the problem of lighting dynamic objects that move through the scene, and thus we are left with beautifully rendered, globally illuminated scenes that contain unrealistic, locally lit dynamic objects. This problem is addressed by the irradiance volume [Greger98], which captures the effects of global illumination within a bounded 3D space by storing captured lighting samples for discrete locations within its bounds.

Irradiance Volumes

Irradiance volumes have been used by the film industry as an acceleration technique for high-quality, photo-realistic offline rendering. These volumes store irradiance distribution functions for points in space by utilizing some spatial partitioning structure that serves as a cache. Sampling the volume allows the global illumination at a point to be quickly calculated. Until recently, irradiance volumes were impractical for interactive rendering because of their high storage and bandwidth requirements, but it has been shown that spherical harmonics may be used for efficiently storing and evaluating irradiance samples, thus making precomputed irradiance volumes practical for real-time rendering. The remainder of this article deals with generating and using irradiance volumes for a static scene for which it is assumed that light maps have already been generated. An adaptive spatial subdivision scheme is presented, along with several subdivision heuristics, as a way of efficiently sampling an environment that contains varying degrees of geometric density. This subdivision scheme creates more sample points in areas where irradiance changes quickly in the spatial domain and creates fewer sample points in areas of slowly changing irradiance. Techniques for higher-ordered interpolation of irradiance samples within the volume using spherical harmonic irradiance gradients will also be discussed.

Before diving into the details of irradiance-volume generation, compression, and sampling, it is necessary to have a basic familiarity with the physical quantities we seek to represent: *radiance* and *irradiance*.

Radiance and Irradiance

Radiance is the emitted energy per unit time in a given direction from a unit area of an emitting surface [Cohen93]. Don't be confused by the term *emitting surface*. This doesn't mean that the energy originates at the surface in question; it could have arrived there as the result of multiple bounces. The important thing to understand is that there's some light energy coming from some surface in some direction. We could capture radiance at a point for *all* directions by placing a camera at the point and rendering the surrounding scene into a cube map. We would then scale every texel in that cube map by its projected solid angle (i.e., the projected solid angle of the rectangular texel onto a unit sphere located at the center of the cube map). This cube map would represent the radiance for all directions for the point at which it was captured. This is known as the radiance distribution function [Greger98] [Arvo95].

Once the radiance distribution function (L) is known, it may be used to compute irradiance. For a point p on a diffuse surface where the surface normal is N, irradiance is defined as the integral over a hemisphere of incident directions, centered at p and oriented around N, of the radiance distribution function multiplied by the cosine of the angle of incidence (Lambertian term).

$$I(p,N_p) = \int\limits_{\Omega^+} L(p,\vec{\omega}_i)(N_p \cdot \vec{\omega}_i)d\omega_i$$

We could compute irradiance at a point for *all* normal directions by performing a convolution of the radiance distribution function with a cosine kernel. The result of this convolution (see Figure 6.1.2) would be an irradiance distribution function that would look sort of like a radiance distribution function, except much blurrier.

FIGURE 6.1.2 The Eucalyptus Grove Light Probe. (Top left) Captured radiance. (Bottom left) Irradiance map generated from captured radiance data. (Right) A sphere rendered using the resulting irradiance map. (Courtesy of Paul Debevec; *www.debevec.org/Probes/*.)

Just as the radiance distribution function can be stored in a cube map, so can the irradiance distribution function. A cube map could be generated at an object's centroid and reused for all points on the surface of that object. This cube map could be used for real-time rendering. It would be indexed by the surface normal of the point you're rendering, and it would return the sum of all diffuse illumination at that point [Brennan02] [Debevec98].

We could take this idea one step further and store irradiance cube maps for many points in a static scene and we will have created an irradiance volume. There are only two small problems. First, storing many cube maps for an entire scene would quickly fill up the video memory of your graphics card, and rendering would slow to a halt. The second problem is that we've made the assumption that irradiance changes slowly with respect to p's position in space. This allows us to generate a single cube map at our object's centroid but use this same cubemap for all points on the surface of the object. In general this is not a bad assumption to make since in many cases irradiance really does change very slowly with respect to position, but it certainly is not true in *every* case.

Consider a spotlight that's aimed at an actor on a stage. The actor's "centroid" is fully contained by the spotlight's cone, but if the actor reaches out his or her hand, the actor's fingertips might end up outside of the spotlight's cone. In this case the irradiance distribution function sampled at the actor's centroid (inside the light cone) won't work well for computing irradiance at the tip of the actor's outstretched hand (outside the light cone). In this case irradiance changes quickly over a short distance, and a single sample taken at the actor's centroid is insufficient for computing lighting at the actor's fingertip. Both of these issues are addressed in the next section; spherical harmonics are used for compressing irradiance maps so that we can precompute and store many of them for use at render time, and spherical harmonic gradients are used to encode the rate at which irradiance changes around a given point.

Spherical Harmonics

Precomputation works well for eliminating the cost of dynamically generating diffuse environment maps, but we're still left with the cost of storing maps for many different points in our scene as well as the bandwidth overhead of indexing these maps at render time. Compressing irradiance maps by representing them as a vector of spherical harmonic coefficients allows us to reduce both the storage and bandwidth costs. Spherical harmonics are an infinite series of spherical functions that may be used as basis functions to store a frequency space approximation of an environment map [Ramamoorthi01]. Microsoft's DirectX 9.0 SDK includes functions for projecting a cube map into a representative set of spherical harmonic coefficients as well as functions for scaling and rotating spherical harmonics. For a more in-depth look at the theory, as well as code snippets for writing your own spherical harmonic helper functions, see Robin Green's *Spherical Harmonic Lighting: The Gritty Details* [Green03].

Using Microsoft's DirectX 9.0 SDK, a cube map may be projected into spherical harmonics using the D3DXSHProjectCubeMap() function. Once the captured cube map (representing incident radiance) is projected into spherical harmonics, the methods described in [Ramamoorthi01] may be used to approximate an irradiance distribution function.

Reconstructing from Spherical Harmonics

Once the irradiance distribution function has been found, it can be efficiently evaluated in a pixel or vertex shader, in the direction of the surface normal, for all surface locations on our model [Sloan04]. It's no longer necessary to store and sample irradiance from a cube map. We can instead store just nine spherical harmonic coefficients for each color channel of our irradiance distribution function. In fact, because spherical harmonic evaluation doesn't require texture lookups, we can now compute irradiance per-vertex if we want and avoid per-pixel irradiance computation all together. Shader code for evaluating irradiance samples stored as spherical harmonic coefficients is provided in [Sloan04] and is also included in the sample on the companion CD-ROM.

Irradiance Gradients

Irradiance samples only store irradiance for a single point in space. If an irradiance sample is used to shade the surface of an entire object, the potential error increases as we move farther away from the original sample point. Irradiance gradients allow us to store the rate at which irradiance changes with respect to translation about the irradiance sample (Figure 6.1.3) [Ward92].

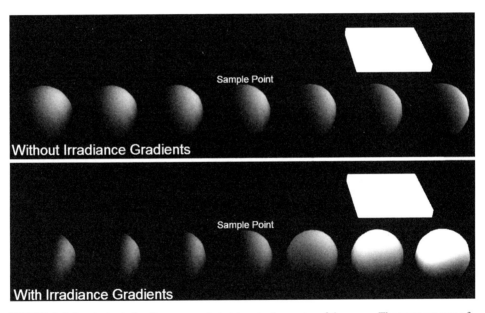

FIGURE 6.1.3 A single irradiance sample is taken in the center of the scene. The topmost row of spheres demonstrates how the irradiance error increases as the single irradiance sample is used to render a sphere that moves to either side of the sample location. The bottommost row of spheres uses the same irradiance sample as the top row but also stores a translational irradiance gradient and more accurately reflects the changes to irradiance as it moves to either side of the original sampling location.

Translational gradients for spherical harmonic irradiance samples may be computed in a number of ways [Annen04]. One simple way to find the gradient is to use central differencing to estimate the partial derivatives of the irradiance function as shown in Figure 6.1.4.

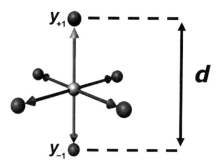

FIGURE 6.1.4   Central differencing may be
used to compute a 3D gradient vector for each
spherical harmonic coefficient.

Because our irradiance functions are stored as spherical harmonic coefficients, we
need to project six additional irradiance functions into spherical harmonic coefficients (an additional sample for each of the $\pm x$, $\pm y$, and $\pm z$ world-space axes) and perform central differencing on each of the coefficients.

$$\nabla_y = \frac{y_{+1} - y_{-1}}{d}.$$

Once the gradient has been found, the six extra samples may be discarded. At render time, a new irradiance function may be extrapolated by computing a world-space
vector from the location at which the sample was generated to the point being rendered. The dot product of this vector and the gradient vector is used to extrapolate a
new irradiance function.

$$I_i' = I_i + (\nabla I_i \cdot d),$$

where I_i' is the ith spherical harmonic coefficient of the extrapolated irradiance function, I_i is the ith spherical harmonic coefficient of the stored irradiance sample, ∇I_i is
the irradiance gradient for the ith irradiance coefficient, and d is a nonunit vector
from the original sample location to the point being rendered.

Irradiance Volumes

By compressing our irradiance functions using spherical harmonics, it is possible to
precompute and store an entire volume of samples for many points throughout a
static scene. This precomputation step is key to real-time applications of irradiance
volumes since, at run time, there may not be sufficient time to compute new irradiance values. An efficient data structure for storing the irradiance volume is needed so
that samples in the volume may be quickly indexed using their world-space positions.

Uniform Subdivision

Subdividing a scene into evenly spaced cells is one way to generate and store irradiance samples. At preprocess time, the scene's bounding box is uniformly subdivided into a grid of cells. Irradiance samples should be computed for each of the eight corners of all the cells. At run time an object's world-space centroid may be used to traverse the grid's hierarchy to determine which cell contains the centroid. Now the eight samples at the cell's corners are used to perform trilinear interpolation (or higher-ordered interpolation if you've also stored irradiance gradients), and the approximate irradiance at the object's centroid is found.

The degree to which you should subdivide a given volume is dependent on the complexity of the scene you are sampling. Simple scenes may only need a few levels of subdivision, while large, complex scenes will require higher levels of subdivision to reduce lighting error. A uniform grid is easy to implement but quickly becomes unwieldy for large, complex scenes that require many levels of subdivision (see Figure 6.1.5). Choosing an adaptive subdivision scheme such as an octree will allow you to only subdivide the volume where subdivision is beneficial.

FIGURE 6.1.5   A uniform subdivision of this scene would be inefficient. Ideally, more irradiance samples would be stored in and around the central building structure, where lighting changes more rapidly than in areas such as the sky or outlying areas of the scene.

Adaptive Subdivision

Knowing which areas of your scene need further subdivision is a challenge. For example, a character standing just inside a house will appear shadowed on a sunny day, but if the character moves over the threshold of the door and into the sunlight, he should appear much brighter; irradiance can change very quickly. We need a way to find areas of rapidly changing irradiance so that these areas can be more finely subdivided.

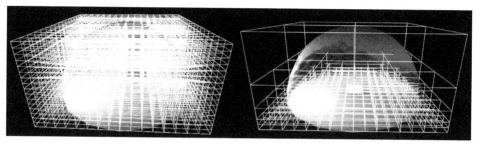

FIGURE 6.1.6   The scene on the left uses a uniformly subdivided irradiance volume. The scene on the right uses an adaptively subdivided irradiance volume.

Since irradiance sampling is done as a preprocess, one option is to use a brute force method that starts by super-sampling irradiance using a highly subdivided uniform grid. After this super-sampled volume is found, redundant cells may be discarded by comparing irradiance samples at child nodes using some error tolerance to determine if a cell was unnecessarily subdivided. This brute force method isn't perfect, though, because it assumes you know the maximum level of subdivision or super-sampling that is needed for a given scene. Instead, certain heuristics may be used to detect cells that might benefit from further subdivision.

Adaptive Subdivision Heuristics

Measuring irradiance gradients and flagging cells where the irradiance is known to change quickly with respect to translation (large gradient) is one way to test if further subdivision is necessary [Pharr04]. Testing gradients isn't perfect, though, because this will only subdivide areas where you know that irradiance changes rapidly. There may still be areas that have small gradients but contain subregions with quickly changing irradiance.

Greger [Greger98] suggests subdividing any cells that contain scene geometry, while Pharr and Humphreys suggest in [Pharr04] that it's better use the sample's distance from nearby geometry to determine when subdivision is needed. They use the harmonic mean of the depth values as their heuristic (explained below). The idea is that areas that contain a lot of geometry will have more rapidly changing irradiance. This assumption is based on the observation that the more geometry there is surrounding a sample point, then the more opportunities there are for shadows and bounced lighting to occur. We can test for this by rendering the scene's depth into a cube map at each irradiance sample point. This depth cube map is then read back into system memory, and the harmonic mean of the depth values is found:

$$HM = N \bigg/ \sum_i^N 1\big/ d_i \, ,$$

where N is the total number of texels in the cube map and d_i is the depth value of the ith texel. The harmonic mean gives us a maximum distance for the sample's usefulness. If the neighboring irradiance samples are further away than this maximum distance, their associated cells should be subdivided. Subdivision may also be desirable if the harmonic mean changes dramatically between neighboring samples. The harmonic mean is chosen over the arithmetic mean (or linear average) because large depth values—owing to infinite depth if no geometry exists in a given direction—would quickly bias the arithmetic mean to a large value. For our purposes, samples with small harmonic means are very important because they indicate potential changes in irradiance that need to be accounted for.

We can further subdivide by testing for cells that contain scene geometry. This test can be performed by examining the depth cube map that we read back. Care must be taken here since the depth cube maps are sampled at each corner of the cell, so some of the texels in the cube map don't correspond to areas within the cell. Alternatively, occlusion queries (which are supported by many consumer-level GPUs these days) can be used to detect scene-cell intersections. We perform occlusion queries by placing a camera at the center of the cell we want to test, and for each face of the cell we render a quad that covers the cell's face and then render the scene. If any of the scene's draw calls pass the occlusion query, we know that a part of the scene must penetrate the cell and thus the cell should be subdivided.

When writing a preprocessing tool for automatically subdividing and sampling a scene, it is important to provide your artists with controls for specifying a minimum and maximum level of subdivision. A minimum subdivision control is extremely useful since frequently the subdivision heuristics will fail to detect that the coarsest cell (i.e., the scene's bounding box) needs further subdivision since the cell corners are typically very far from the majority of the scene's geometry. You will also want to provide thresholds for each of your subdivision heuristics so an artist can control how strongly a particular heuristic can influence whether subdivision should occur. Finally, after you've fully subdivided and sampled the volume, it's useful to go back through the octree and reject any redundant samples; if a cell has been subdivided and its children do not differ significantly from the parent, these child samples may be culled.

Render Time

Now that we have a volume of irradiance samples, we'll want to use this volume for lighting the dynamic objects in our scene. Because we've used an octree to store the irradiance samples, searching the tree for the cell that contains an object's centroid is straightforward. We start at the root of the tree and determine which one of the root's eight children contains our object's centroid. If this child node is subdivided, we then perform the same test on each of its eight children. This traversal continues down the octree's hierarchy until we reach a node that hasn't been subdivided. This will be the smallest cell in the octree that contains our object's centroid, and we can use this cell's eight irradiance samples (one at each corner) to interpolate an irradiance distribution function at our object's centroid. Some care must be taken when interpolating the irradiance samples for a particular cell. It's important to realize that simple trilinear interpolation may only be used with a uniformly subdivided octree, or popping will occur in our lighting results as an object passes between cells that have different levels of subdivision, as shown in Figure 6.1.7.

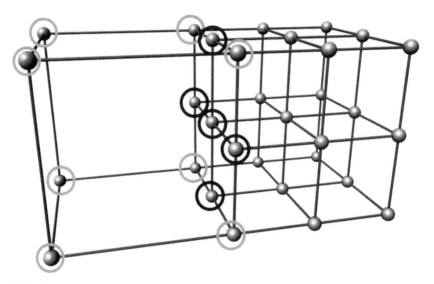

FIGURE 6.1.7   When transitioning between cells that have been adaptively subdivided, trilinear interpolation can produce popping artifacts. The large cell on the left uses the samples marked with gray circles, while the smaller cells use additional samples that have been marked with black circles. When moving from a small cell to the large cell, the additional samples will suddenly be ignored. Popping may be reduced by using a distance-weighted average of all nearby samples. To eliminate popping entirely, methods for scattered data interpolation may be used (a full survey and description of which is beyond the scope of this article).

Instead of using trilinear interpolation, a distance-weighted average of all nearby samples (including samples from neighboring cells) may be employed. Annen et al. [Annen04] describe a method that may be used in a vertex shader for computing an interpolated irradiance sample at each vertex. This scheme requires that a set of nearby irradiance samples, along with their gradients, is sent to the GPU. A vertex shader then uses a distance weighting scheme to perform per-vertex interpolation of the spherical harmonic coefficients.

$$I_i' = \sum_j w_j \left(I_i^j + (\nabla I_i^j \cdot d_j) \right).$$

At each vertex we find the weighted sum of each extrapolated irradiance sample. I_i' is the ith spherical harmonic coefficient of the extrapolated irradiance function, I_i^j is the ith spherical harmonic coefficient of the jth nearby irradiance sample, ∇I_i^j is the irradiance gradient for the ith irradiance coefficient of the jth sample, and d_j is a nonunit vector from the original sample location to the point being rendered. Each sample's weight w_j is computed based on its distance from the sample point s_j to the point p being rendered. Annen et al. [Annen04] use the following weighting:

$$w_j = \frac{(1 / \| p - s_j \|)^b}{\sum_j \left(1 / \| p - s_j \| \right)^b}.$$

The exponent b controls the distance falloff of the weighting function. Larger values of b will decrease the importance of samples as they increase in distance from p and will increase the importance of samples that are closer to p.

Conclusion

A realistic lighting technique using irradiance volumes for rendering dynamic characters in static scenes has been presented. This irradiance volume uses spherical harmonics to compactly store and efficiently evaluate irradiance samples for many points in a scene. Along with irradiance samples, irradiance gradients may also be stored to increase the usefulness of each irradiance sample by allowing for new irradiance samples to be extrapolated from stored irradiance samples. Gradients also allow for more accurate interpolation of irradiance samples, which will help reduce popping when interpolating samples stored in an adaptively subdivided octree. A sample application, with source code, is provided (on the CD-ROM that accompanies this book) that implements many of the techniques described in this article.

ON THE CD

References

[Annen04] Annen, Tomas, Jan Kautz, Fredo Durand, and Hans-Peter Seidel. "Spherical Harmonic Gradients for Mid-Range Illumination" *Proceedings of Eurographics Symposium on Rendering*, June 2004.

[Arvo95] Arvo, J. "Analytic Methods for Simulated Light Transport" PhD thesis, Yale University, December 1995.

[Brennan02] Brennan, C. "Diffuse Cube Mapping." *Direct3D ShaderX: Vertex and Pixel Shader Tips and Tricks*, edited by Wolfgang Engel. Wordware Publishing, 2002: pp. 287–289.

[Cohen93] Cohen, Wallace. "Radiosity and Realistic Image Synthesis" Academic Press Professional, Cambridge, 1993.

[Debevec98] Debevec, Paul E. "Rendering Synthetic Objects into Real Scenes: Bridging Traditional and Image-Based Graphics with Global Illumination and High Dynamic Range Photography." *SIGGRAPH* 1998.

[Green03] Green, R. "Spherical Harmonic Lighting: The Gritty Details." 2003. Available online at *http://www.research.scea.com/gdc2003/spherical-harmonic-lighting.html*

[Greger98] Greger, G., P. Shirley, P. Hubbard, and D. Greenberg. "The Irradiance Volume." *IEEE Computer Graphics & Applications, 18*(2), (1998): pp. 32-43.

[Pharr04] Pharr, M. and G. Humphreys. "Physically Based Rendering" Morgan Kaufmann, San Francisco, 2004.

[Ramamoorthi01] Ramamoorthi, R., and P. Hanrahan. "An Efficient Representation for Irradiance Environment Maps." *SIGGRAPH*, 2001: pp. 497–500.

[Sloan04] Sloan, P.-P. "Efficient Evaluation of Irradiance Environment Maps." *ShaderX²: Shader Programming Tips and Tricks with DirectX 9*, edited by Wolfgang Engel. Wordware Publishing, 2004: pp. 226–231.

[Ward92] Ward, G. and P. Heckbert. "Irradiance Gradients." *Third Eurographics Workshop on Rendering* (1992): pp. 85–98.

Indirect Diffuse and Glossy Illumination on the GPU

István Lazányi and László Szirmay-Kalos

Budapest University of Technology, Hungary

Introduction

This article presents a fast approximation method to obtain the indirect diffuse or glossy reflection on a dynamic object that is caused by a diffuse or a moderately glossy environment. Instead of tracing rays to find the incoming illumination, we look up the indirect illumination from a cube map rendered from the reference point that is in the vicinity of the object.

To cope with the difference between the incoming illumination of the reference point and that of the shaded points, we apply a correction that uses geometric information also stored in cube map texels. This geometric information is the distance between the reference point and the surface visible from a cube map texel. The method computes indirect illumination, although approximately, providing a very pleasing visual quality. The method is well suited to the GPU architecture and can render these effects interactively. The primary application area of the proposed method is the introduction of diffuse and specular interreflections for games.

Indirect Diffuse and Glossy Illumination

To start, let us consider an ideally reflective, mirror-like object. To calculate the illumination of a surface point of this object, we just have to take the viewing direction at that point, mirror it to the surface normal to get the ideal reflection direction, and trace a ray toward that direction to determine the illumination coming from the environment (Figure 6.2.1, left side).

In the case of diffuse and glossy objects, life gets a bit more complicated since there are many incoming directions that contribute to the illumination of a single surface point. Namely, all indirect light sources that are visible inside the hemisphere drawn above the surface point (i.e., $\mathbf{N} \cdot \mathbf{L} > 0$, where $\mathbf{N}$ is the surface normal at that point and $\mathbf{L}$ points toward the indirect light source) must be taken into account (Figure 6.2.1, right side). We have to identify these directions, calculate their contributions by tracing

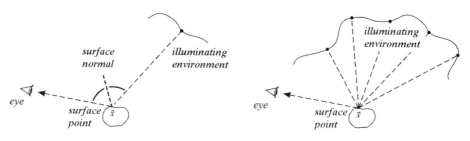

FIGURE 6.2.1   Indirect illumination with sampling rays.

rays toward the illuminating environment, and sum these contributions. Furthermore, all contributions are BRDF- and cosine-weighted before the summation, making the whole process similar to a convolution operation.

This process, also called final gathering, is one of the most time-consuming steps of realistic rendering, since the number of sample directions is about a hundred or a thousand for each surface point and the number of surface points visible from the camera can be over hundreds of thousands or millions. However, in games and in real-time systems, rendering cannot take more than a few tens of milliseconds, which does not allow us to trace all sampling directions for all surface points.

To speed up the computation, the dynamic objects of the scene are usually separated and assumed to be significantly smaller than their static illuminating environment (this is a valid assumption for most computer games). Thus, not being affected by the smaller dynamic objects, the global indirect illumination of the static environment can be precalculated independently, using a radiosity solution, for example. Furthermore, owing to the small sizes of the dynamic objects, illumination information obtained for a single point of a dynamic object can possibly be reused to shade other points of the same object as well.

Diffuse and Specular Environment Maps

Environment mapping is a hardware-accelerated technique to approximate general secondary rays without expensive ray tracing. Images from the environment are taken from the center of the object (also called the reference point), and the environment of the object is replaced by a cube (or a sphere) textured by these images. As long as the environment is very far from the object, this approximation is acceptable.

Diffuse or specular environment maps are derived from the original environment map by calculating the convolution (BRDF- and cosine-weighted sum) for many directions. These convolution results are stored in the texels of the resulting map. In the diffuse case, the surface normal is used as a query direction to read one of these precalculated values, while in the specular case, assuming the Phong BRDF model, the ideal reflection direction can be used for the same purpose.

As an illustration, Figure 6.2.2 shows a simple scene and the corresponding diffuse and specular environment maps, generated from the middle of the room. The tiny ball at the middle of the room is rendered using the environment map.

FIGURE 6.2.2   The original scene (left) and the generated diffuse (middle) and specular (right) environment maps. The lamp in the corner is included only for easier interpretation.

A fundamental problem of environment mapping is that the generated environment map correctly represents the direction-dependent illumination only at a single point: the reference point of the object. For other points, the environment map is only an approximation, where the error depends on the ratio of the distances between the point of interest and the reference point and between the point of interest and the surfaces composing the environment. Thus, if the object size or the scale of its movements are comparable with the distance from the surrounding environment, errors occur, which creates the impression that the object is independent of its illuminating environment.

Thus, when the object is moving, the diffuse (or specular) environment maps have to be frequently regenerated. This may cause a performance bottleneck unless the resolution of the environment map is kept low and fast algorithms are applied (e.g., spherical harmonics [Ramamoorthi01]).

However, if the object is large compared to the distance from the environment (Figure 6.2.3), a single environment map—even if frequently updated—will not provide sufficient information to shade the entire object properly.

Using Multiple Environment Maps

For dynamic scenes, a possible alternative is to use multiple environment maps. In this case the scene is subdivided into a grid, and a separate environment map is generated for each grid vertex [Greger98, Mantiuk02]. Then, during run time the illumi-

FIGURE 6.2.3 A diffuse knot displayed with the classic environment mapping method (left) and with our localized method (right).

nation of a point is determined by linearly interpolating the values obtained from the neighboring environment maps.

Using Environment Maps with Depth Information

Another approach is to use a single environment map "smartly" so that it provides different illumination information for different points [Szirmay05]. To achieve this, the environment map is extended to store depth information about the environment. These extended environment maps will provide precise illumination results not only in the reference point, but for other, slightly different points as well. That is, the environment map can "tolerate" small-scale object movements, so it has to be regenerated less frequently. Details of these extended environment maps are discussed in the next section.

If only one-bounce indirect illumination is considered, we can use a shadow map instead of an environment map. As pointed out in [Dachsbacher05], points where the light is bounced for the first time are stored by default in the shadow map. By adding illumination information to the depth values, the indirect illumination, that is, the secondary light transport, can be computed as the reflection of the shadow map.

The New Algorithm

Let us assume that we use a single environment map to perform illumination calculations. This map records illumination (and depth) information for reference point $\vec{o}$ of the dynamic object. Our goal is to reuse this environment map to shade other nearby points of the object as well. To do so, we apply the following approximations.

First, the environment is decomposed into smaller directional domains where each domain corresponds to a texel in the environment map. Thus, the contribution of the environment will be expressed as the sum of the contributions of the directional domains, where the contribution of a domain (supposing diffuse reflection) is as follows:

$$\int_{\Delta\omega_i} L^{in}(\omega) \cdot k_d \cdot \max(\mathbf{N} \cdot \mathbf{L}, 0) \, d\omega$$

where

- $\Delta\omega_i$ is the solid angle occupied by the domain (i.e., the area belonging to the domain on the surface of a fictitious unit-sized sphere).
- $L^{in}(\omega)$ is the incoming illumination from a specific direction.
- k_d is the diffuse reflection coefficient.
- $\mathbf{N}$ is the unit surface normal at the shaded point.
- $\mathbf{L}$ is the unit illumination direction starting from the shaded point.

Let us examine these factors. Supposing that the domain is small, the incoming radiance $L^{in}(\omega)$ is roughly uniform inside a domain. Thus, as an approximation, the incoming radiance can be assumed constant and factored out.

$$\int_{\Delta\omega_i} L^{in}(\omega) \cdot k_d \cdot \max(\mathbf{N} \cdot \mathbf{L}, 0) \, d\omega \approx \overline{L}^{in} \cdot \int_{\Delta\omega_i} k_d \cdot \max(\mathbf{N} \cdot \mathbf{L}, 0) \, d\omega$$

where $\overline{L}^{in}$ is the average incoming radiance that can be calculated as follows (ΔA_i is the area of the indirect light source, i.e., the surface visible in solid angle Δw_i):

$$\overline{L}^{in} = \frac{1}{\Delta A_i} \cdot \int_{\Delta A_i} L^{in}(\omega) \, dA$$

Calculating Average Incoming Illumination

Owing to the factorization discussed above, average incoming radiance values $\overline{L}^{in}$ can potentially be reused for all shaded points. To identify these values, first we choose a reference point $\mathbf{o}$ in the vicinity of the shaded object and render the scene from this point onto the six sides of a cubic environment map (cube map). In each pixel of these images we store the radiance of the visible point (in the RGB channels of the map) and the distance from the reference point (in the alpha channel). The pixels of the cube map thus store the radiance and encode the position of small indirect light sources.

Then, these small indirect light sources are clustered into larger area light sources while their radiances are averaged. This step corresponds to down-sampling the cube map; that is, a pixel of the lower resolution cube map is computed as the average of the higher-resolution pixels. Since both radiance and distance values are averaged, we obtain large area lights with the average radiance of the small lights and placed at their average position.

Calculating Solid Angles

To perform illumination calculations, solid angles subtended by the area light sources must be determined. Unfortunately, the geometry of the cube map only determines the solid angles when the shaded point is the center of the cube map. For other shaded points, special considerations based on the distance values stored with the cube map are required.

From the reference point $\mathbf{o}$, the solid angle subtended by an area light source can be easily determined by considering the solid angle of the corresponding texel in the cube map:

$$\Delta\omega_i \approx \frac{\Delta A_i^{texel} \cdot \cos\vartheta_i^{texel}}{\left(r_i^{texel}\right)^2}$$

where

- $\Delta A_i^{texel} \cdot \cos\vartheta_i^{texel}$ is the projected size of the texel as seen from the reference point.
- r_i^{texel} is the distance between the reference point and the texel center.

Assuming the cube map coordinates to be in range of -1 to 1, the formula simply becomes $\Delta\omega_i \approx 4/M^2/|\mathbf{L}^{texel}|^3$, where M is the resolution of a single cube map face and $\mathbf{L}^{texel}$ is a nonnormalized vector pointing from the middle of the cube map to the texel center. (We assume that the largest component of $\mathbf{L}^{texel}$ is equal to ± 1.)

Instead of working with texels in a unit-sized cube map, the same solid angle $\Delta\omega_i$ can be expressed with the properties of the area light source. Supposing that the area of the light source is small compared to its distance from the reference point (this assumption will be discussed later), the solid angle approximately equals

$$\Delta\omega_i \approx \frac{\Delta A_i \cdot \cos\vartheta_i}{r_i^2}$$

where $\Delta A_i \cdot \cos\vartheta_i$ is the projected size of the area light source as seen from the reference point and r_i is the distance between the reference point and the center of the light source. What we are interested in is a similar solid angle but measured from surface point $\mathbf{x}$, expressed as

$$\Delta\omega_i^* \approx \frac{\Delta A_i \cdot \cos\vartheta_i^*}{r_i^{*2}}$$

where $\Delta A_i \cdot \cos\vartheta_i^*$ is the projected size of the same area light source as seen from surface point $\mathbf{x}$, and r_i^* is the distance between the center of the light source and surface point $\mathbf{x}$. Supposing that the environment surface is not very close compared to the distances of the reference point $\mathbf{o}$ and shaded point $\mathbf{x}$, cosine values $\cos\vartheta_i$ and can be assumed to be approximately equal [Szirmay06]. Thus, the solid angle can be expressed from $\Delta\omega_i$ as

$$\Delta\omega_i^* \approx \Delta\omega_i \cdot \frac{r_i^2}{r_i^{*2}}$$

Calculating Solid Angles with Disc-to-Point Approximations

If the distance between the shaded point and the area light source is small ($r_i^* \approx 0$), the previous formula cannot be used, since the resulting solid angle will approach infinity. Instead, a disc-to-point approximation is applied. That is, assuming the area light source to be circular in shape, the subtended solid angle can be analytically calculated (the interested reader is encouraged to derive it in Maple or Mathematica, for example). The result is exact if $\cos\vartheta_i$ (the orientation angle measured at the center of the area light source) equals 1 and is a good approximation in other cases:

$$\Delta\omega_i \approx 2\pi \cdot \left(1 - \frac{1}{\sqrt{1 + \Delta A_i \cos\vartheta_i \big/ r_i^2 \pi}} \right)$$

Note that if distance r_i tends to zero, the resulting solid angle $\Delta\omega_i$ remains bounded and tends to 2π instead of infinity. An analogous equation can be derived for $\Delta\omega_i^*$:

$$\Delta\omega_i^* \approx 2\pi \cdot \left(1 - \frac{1}{\sqrt{1 + \Delta A_i \cos\vartheta_i^* \big/ r_i^{*2} \pi}} \right)$$

Using the same assumptions as above, that is, $\cos\vartheta_i$ and $\cos\vartheta_i^*$ are similar, we can derive the solid angle $\Delta\omega_i^*$ from $\Delta\omega_i$ without knowing the area and orientation of the area light source:

$$\Delta\omega_i^* \approx 2\pi \cdot \left(1 - \frac{1}{\sqrt{1 + \left(4\pi^2 \big/ \left(2\pi - \Delta\omega_i \right)^2 - 1 \right) \cdot r_i^2 \big/ r_i^{*2}}} \right)$$

Calculating Reflectivity

Since the incoming radiance is assumed to be constant inside a directional domain, the reflectivity term can be separated, resulting in the following reflectivity integral in the diffuse case for solid angle $\Delta\omega_i$:

$$k_d \cdot \int_{\Delta\omega_i} \max(\mathbf{N} \cdot \mathbf{L}, 0) d\omega$$

Supposing that the object does not approach the environment excessively, the reflectivity can be assumed to be constant in a domain and can be approximately calculated using only one directional sample (e.g., considering the center of the domain) and multiplying it with the size of the integration domain ($\Delta\omega_i$).

However, if the object may approach the illuminating environment, using only one sample causes the centers of the area light sources to become visible (Figure 6.2.4, middle). To avoid this, the reflectivity integral can be precisely precalculated for all possible values and stored in a 2D texture, where one of the texture coordinates corresponds to the size of the integration domain while the other corresponds to the cosine of the angle between the surface normal $\mathbf{N}$ and the illumination direction $\mathbf{L}$ pointing to the center of the area light source. Using this texture makes it possible to greatly reduce artifacts (Figure 6.2.4, right).

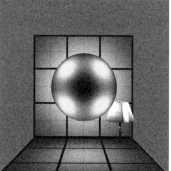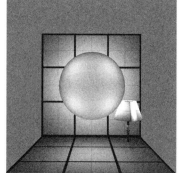

FIGURE 6.2.4   The diffuse ball at the wall (left image) demonstrates the importance of an accurate reflectivity calculation. Compare the side view of the same scene with simplified (middle) and texture-based (right) reflectivity calculations.

Speeding it Up

Since the incoming illumination values get weighted with the reflectivity, the number of area light sources (i.e., texels) that may have a significant contribution depends on how quickly the average reflectivity changes. For diffuse materials, the reflectivity is a simple cosine term that changes slowly, so we can obtain good results using a low-resolution map (4×4 or even 2×2 texels per cube map face).

For specular materials, the reflectivity changes quickly and is nonzero only for a few texels. Therefore, a high-resolution environment map is needed to provide these quickly changing regions with detailed illumination information. However, since the reflectivity is mostly zero, there is no need to visit all texels. We set the resolution of the map according to the specularity of the material and evaluate just a few (for example, five) terms.

Implementation

In our implementation first we render a cube map from the reference point of the object. It stores radiance and distance values and has 256×256 pixels per face. Then it is down-sampled to $M \times M$ pixels per face (e.g., 4×4), and the resulting low-resolution cube map is called LRCubeMap.

To calculate the illumination of a surface point, all texels are visited using two nested for loops in the diffuse case. In the specular case only the most important five texels are taken into account. The contribution of a single texel is calculated using the HLSL function shown below with the following arguments:

- x is the position of the shaded point (relative to the reference point).
- L is the nonlocalized illumination direction pointing from the reference point to the texel center (this vector is strictly nonnormalized, and its largest component equals ± 1).
- N is the unit surface normal at the shaded point.
- V is the unit view direction at the shaded point.

This implementation obtains the average reflectivity on the fly by taking one sample.

```
half3 GetContribution(half3 x, half3 L, half3 N, half3 V)
{
    half l = length(L);
    L /= l;
    half dw = 4 / (M*M*l*l*l);                  // solid angle from o

    half doy = texCUBE(LRCubeMap, L).a;    // r
    half dxy = length(x - L * doy);        // r*
    half den = 1 + doy * doy / (dxy * dxy) *
               ((2*PI)*(2*PI) / ((2*PI-dw)*(2*PI-dw)) - 1);
    half dws = 2*PI * (1 - 1/sqrt(den));        // solid angle from x

    half3 I = L * doy - x;                      // x -> texel center
    half3 R = reflect(-V, N);                   // reflection direc-
                                                //  tion
    half3 a = kd * max(dot(N,I),0) +            // diffuse
              ks * pow(max(dot(R,I),0), s);     // specular
    half3 Lin = texCUBE(LRCubeMap, L).rgb;      // incoming
                                                //  illumination
    return Lin * a * dws;
}
```

First, the solid angle subtended by the texel from the reference point is computed (dw), and then the position of the area light source is determined by looking up the distance value of the cube map. The distances between the reference point and the indirect light source and between the shaded point and the indirect light source are put into doy and dxy, respectively. These distances are used to calculate solid angle dws subtended by the illuminating surface as seen from the shaded point. The Phong BRDF model is used with diffuse coefficient kd and specular coefficient ks, and shininess s.

Results

To demonstrate the results, we took a simple environment consisting of a colorful cubic room with fireballs. Each of the dynamic objects consists of approximately 50–60 thousand triangles. Frame rates were measured in 800×800 windowed mode on an NV6800GT graphics card and P4/3GHz CPU.

The first set of pictures (Figure 6.2.5) shows three diffuse dwarves (borrowed from the DirectX Samples) next to a fireball. In the case of classic environment mapping (Figure 6.2.5a), since the incident illumination is independent of the dwarves' location, all dwarves look identical. Using our method, however, nice localization effects occur even with an extremely low resolution (2×2). Increasing the resolution to 4×4 and 8×8, the results get more realistic at the cost of a reduced frame rate. (Frame rates apply to the rendering of a single dwarf in the room.)

The second set of pictures (Figure 6.2.6) shows glossy skulls (borrowed from the DirectX Samples) between fireballs. Again, the first image presents the classic environment mapping technique (340 fps for a single skull). The second image shows our method optimized for glossy materials, that is, considering only the five "most impor-

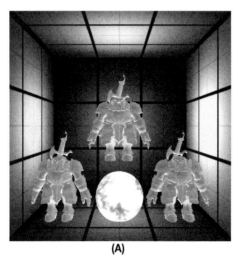 

| (A) | (B) |

FIGURE 6.2.5 Diffuse dwarf at different positions in the scene. Comparing classical environment mapping and our method at different resolutions. (**A**) Classical environment mapping; (**B**) our method (2×2 at 90 fps).

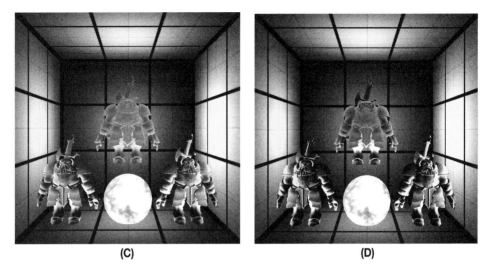

FIGURE 6.2.5 (cont.)   Diffuse dwarf at different positions in the scene. Comparing classical environment mapping and our method at different resolutions. **(C)** our method (4×4 at 26 fps); **(D)** our method (8×8 at 7 fps).

tant" directional domains during the calculation and producing approximate localization effects at a reasonable speed (264 fps for a single skull). The other two images perform a full convolution on the fly, resulting in a better approximation at the cost of reduced frame rates.

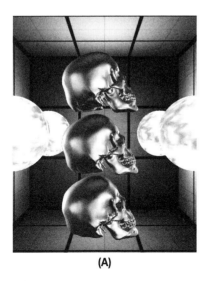 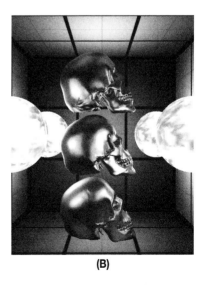

FIGURE 6.2.6   Glossy skull at different positions in the scene. Comparing classical environment mapping and our method at different resolutions. **(A)** Classical environment mapping (340 fps); **(B)** our method (most important contributions only) (4×4 at 264 fps).

(C)

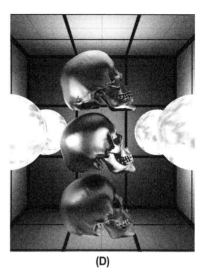
(D)

FIGURE 6.2.6 (cont.)   Glossy skull at different positions in the scene. Comparing classical environment mapping and our method at different resolutions. **(C)** our method (all contributions) (4×4 at 22 fps); **(D)** our method (all contributions) (8×8 at 6 fps).

On the CD-ROM

ON THE CD

On the companion CD-ROM you will find the demo program that was used to generate the color plates. DirectX 9 and Shader Model 3.0 are required to run the demo. Feel free to experiment with the adjustable parameters of the application and then press S to save a screenshot onto the disk. All parameters including camera position are also saved so that the screenshot can be reproduced any time.

Conclusion

In this article we presented a localization method for computing diffuse and glossy reflections of the incoming radiance stored in environment maps. Instead of using multiple environment maps, the presented method proposes the application of a "smart" environment map that provides localized illumination information based on the distance values also stored in the environment map texels. The method runs in real-time and provides visually pleasing results.

Acknowledgments

This work has been supported by OTKA (T042735) and GameTools FP6 (IST-2-004363) project.

References

[Dachsbacher05] Dachsbacher, Carsten and Marc Stamminger. "Reflective Shadow Maps." *Proceedings of the 2005 Symposium on Interactive 3D Graphics and Games*, 2005: pp. 203–231.

[Greger98] Greger, G., P. Shirley, P. Hubbard, and D. Greenberg. "The Irradiance Volume." *IEEE Computer Graphics and Applications*, *18*(2) (1998): pp. 32–43.

[Mantiuk02] Mantiuk, R., S. Pattanaik, and K. Myszkowski. "Cube-Map Data Structure for Interactive Global Illumination Computation in Dynamic Diffuse Environments." *International Conference on Computer Vision and Graphics*, (2002): pp. 530–538.

[Ramamoorthi01] Ramamoorthi, R. and P. Hanrahan. "An Efficient Representation for Irradiance Environment Maps." *SIGGRAPH 2001* (2001): pp. 497–500.

[Szirmay05] Szirmay-Kalos, L., B. Aszódi, I. Lazányi, and M. Premecz. "Approximate Ray-Tracing on the GPU with Distance Impostors." *Computer Graphics Forum*, *24*(3) (2005): pp. 695–704.

[Szirmay06] Szirmay-Kalos, L. and I. Lazányi. "Indirect Diffuse and Glossy Illumination on the GPU." *Spring Conference on Computer Graphics* (2006): pp. 29–35.

Interactive Refractions and Caustics Using Image-Space Techniques

Chris Wyman, University of Iowa

Introduction

Realism plays an important role in virtually all computer graphics applications, but owing to computation constraints, most applications limit realism to that achievable with only a few milliseconds of computing time. Commonly, applications limit material properties and complex illumination, often allowing only diffuse or Phong surfaces under rather simplistic local lighting models, sometimes augmented by simple mirrors. Yet other specular effects such as refraction and caustics play important roles in many real scenes that one may want to simulate.

One of the major problems with such complex effects is their global nature. In the case of caustics, the reflective or refractive focusing of light, specular surfaces virtually anywhere in the environment potentially play an important role. Absent this complex focusing of light, even the simpler problem of rendering the distortion caused by refraction involves recursive ray-object intersection queries that are difficult to evaluate efficiently using GPUs.

Fortunately, most interactive applications aim to achieve only plausible realism instead of photo-realism. This allows the use of approximate techniques for effects such as soft shadows [Hasenfratz03], ambient occlusion [Bunnell05], indirect illumination [Dachsbacher05], et cetera. This article describes an approximate technique for rendering plausible refractions at interactive rates, using an image-space technique. After introducing this approach, we show how this method may be applied to render caustics at interactive rates. Figure 6.3.1 shows examples combining these methods.

FIGURE 6.3.1   Interactive renderings achievable using image-space refraction and caustics.

Approximate, Image-Space Refraction

Approximate image-space refraction [Wyman05] aims to solve one of the major problems of previous GPU-based refraction techniques (e.g., [Lindhom01] [Oliveira00] [Schmidt03] [Sousa05]), namely the limitation to refract through only a single interface. While these existing approaches work well when rendering pools of water, most other refractive geometry involves light that passes through at least two interfaces. The primary difficulty for rendering, of course, is determining the location of additional refractions; Snell's law can easily be applied repeatedly inside a pixel shader. Ray tracing allows arbitrarily complex refractions, but most applications cannot afford GPU-based ray tracing.

The observation underlying our approach is quite simple. Standard rasterization finds the location of the initial intersection with scene geometry, and shaders can compute a refraction direction. Once the refracted direction is known, the problem of finding the second refraction reduces to a question of distance: how far along the refracted ray the second surface is located.

Unfortunately, without knowing the refractor geometry inside the pixel shader, we cannot determine this distance exactly. Only very simple refractors can currently be stored explicitly for efficient traversal inside shaders. When explicit representation proves infeasible, rasterization techniques often fall back on image-space approximations. Our approach represents the refractor geometry using an image and approximates the location of the second refraction using distances easily computed on the GPU. Snell's law can be applied a second time, and the twice-refracted ray can be intersected with the background, using a variety of techniques. While it may be possible to extend this work to more than two refractive interfaces, we assume only two refractions occur along any given ray. Despite this limitation, our approach produces plausible results that compare well with ray-traced images.

Refraction Algorithm

Given our assumption that two refractions occur along the path of the ray, the basic steps in computing a pixel's color are as follows:

1. Find the initial intersection point $\mathbf{p}_1$ with the geometry.
2. Find the surface normal $\mathbf{N}_1$ at point $\mathbf{p}_1$.
3. Refract according to Snell's law to compute the transmitted vector $\mathbf{T}_1$.
4. Intersect the ray $\mathbf{p}_1 + d_1\mathbf{T}_1$ with the refractor to find the second intersection $\mathbf{p}_2$.
5. Find the surface normal $\mathbf{N}_2$ at point $\mathbf{p}_2$.
6. Refract according to Snell's law to compute the transmitted vector $\mathbf{T}_2$.
7. Intersect the ray $\mathbf{p}_2 + d_2\mathbf{T}_2$ with the background geometry at $\mathbf{p}_3$.
8. Compute shading at point $\mathbf{p}_3$.

Steps 1 and 2 are performed by the rasterizer, assuming normal information is passed into OpenGL or DirectX, and step 3 is straightforward to implement using pixel shaders [Oliveira00]. Steps 4 and 5 are discussed in the following sections, after which the application of Snell's law in step 6 can again be performed in a pixel shader. Step 7 is a difficult problem currently under active research, but a number of existing techniques give good results in certain circumstances. Depending on the complexity, the shading at the final point $\mathbf{p}_3$ can be computed in advance and stored in a texture, determined in the refraction shader, or performed in a deferred shading pass. The first six steps are depicted graphically in Figure 6.3.2.

Approximating Distance d_1

Given that both $\mathbf{p}_1$ and $\mathbf{T}_1$ are straightforward to compute, the difficulty in allowing rays to refract twice is identifying the value of d_1 when the transmitted ray again intersects the refractor. As ray tracing currently lacks sufficient speed, we propose approximating this distance with values easily computed or identified with a GPU.

One easily computed value is d_v, the distance between front and back surfaces of the refractor along the viewing direction (see Figure 6.3.3). Depth-peeling techniques can easily determine this value. Clearly, this approximation of d_1 is exact when the incident and transmitted indices of refraction (n_i and n_t) are equal. However, as n_i and n_t diverge, this approximation becomes more inaccurate.

Assuming that the refractor is more dense than its environment (i.e., $n_t > n_i$), the refracted ray $\mathbf{T}_1$ bends towards the negative normal $-\mathbf{N}_1$. In other words, as n_t increases toward infinity, $\mathbf{T}_1$ approaches $-\mathbf{N}_1$. Thus, for very large indices of refraction, the distance d_N shown in Figure 6.3.3 approximates the distance d_1 reasonably

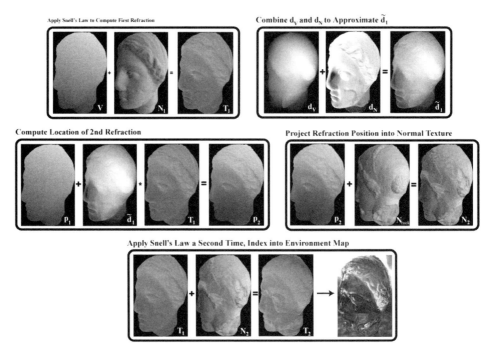

FIGURE 6.3.2   A graphical overview of rendering image-space refraction.

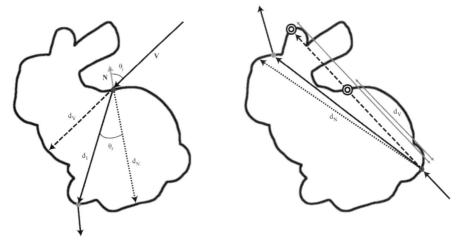

FIGURE 6.3.3   The two distance approximations d_v and d_N and interpolating between them based on θ_i and θ_t. In the case of concave refractors, we set d_v to either the distance to the furthest surface or the distance to the second surface.

well. Again, the approximation d_N is only accurate in those circumstances and loses validity as n_t decreases.

Because these two values give good approximations in the extreme cases, we propose interpolating between them based on the angles between the vectors $\mathbf{V}$, $\mathbf{N}_1$, and $\mathbf{T}_1$. Given the angles shown in Figure 6.3.3, a straightforward linear interpolation gives the approximate distance, $\tilde{d}_1$:

$$\tilde{d}_1 = \frac{\theta_t}{\theta_i} d_V + \left(1 - \frac{\theta_t}{\theta_i}\right) d_N. \tag{6.3.1}$$

When combined with the scheme for identifying the surface normal $\mathbf{N}_2$ discussed below, the approximation $\tilde{d}_1$ gives quite plausible results. Note, however, that this distance is not a physically based approximation, as the structure of the secondary refracting surface is not considered.

Approximating Surface Normal N$_2$

Given the distance approximation $\tilde{d}_1$, point $\mathbf{p}_2$ can be trivially computed as $\mathbf{p}_1$ + $\tilde{d}_1 \mathbf{T}_1$. Without knowing the triangle containing $\mathbf{p}_2$, however, exactly determining $\mathbf{N}_2$ proves difficult since normals are associated with vertices in OpenGL and DirectX. Furthermore, owing to inaccuracies in the computation of $\tilde{d}_1$, $\mathbf{p}_2$ is unlikely to lie exactly on the refractor's surface.

Fortunately, a cheap multipass approach neatly sidesteps the issue. By first rendering a buffer storing surface normals at potential back-facing refractions, a simple texture lookup allows determination of $\mathbf{N}_2$. This can be implemented (typically concurrently with the depth peeling required for computing d_v) as follows:

1. As a first pass, render back-facing surface normals to texture map (see Figure 6.3.2).
2. After computing $\tilde{d}_1$, apply the projection matrix to $\mathbf{p}_2$ to determine texture coordinates.
3. Index into the texture map to find the normal $\mathbf{N}_2$.

Note that computing $\mathbf{N}_2$ this way masks some of the physical inaccuracies of the distance approximation. Slight deviations in $\tilde{d}_1$ still project to the same texel. Furthermore, the texture map captures some of the discontinuities not captured by the $\tilde{d}_1$ approximation.

Fixing Problem Cases

As with all image-space approximations, the algorithm has a few problems and limitations. The first two are straightforward. We have not addressed how to deal with total internal reflection or with nonconvex refractors. The third problem is a bit trickier: what happens if, owing to an inaccurate $\tilde{d}_1$, the texel we index into for $\mathbf{N}_2$ contains no valid normal. Intuitively, this happens when $\tilde{d}_1$ is too large and we index into a black texel in Figure 6.3.2.

Because graphics applications have survived for years using only a single refraction, simply ignoring total internal reflection seems viable. Unfortunately, ignoring the issue leads to the image in Figure 6.3.4, where regions of total internal reflection have been rendered in black. Until someone develops extensions that handle recursive reflections and refractions, we suggest using one of three ad hoc methods to fill these regions with plausible colors:

- Degenerate to previous methods and use only a single refraction. This is equivalent to defining $\mathbf{T}_2 = \mathbf{T}_1$.
- "Refract" so that $\mathbf{T}_2$ leaves the surface perpendicular to the surface normal. Effectively, this clamps the incident angle at $\mathbf{p}_2$ to the critical angle.
- Compute a reflection vector (instead of a refraction vector) at $\mathbf{p}_2$ and ignore any additional interactions with the refractor.

Figure 6.3.4 compares these approaches. We recommend using the second or third approach, depending on application requirements, as the first behaves poorly in dynamic scenes.

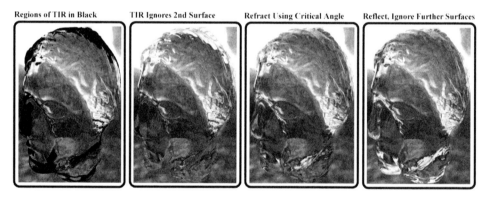

Regions of TIR in Black   TIR Ignores 2nd Surface   Refract Using Critical Angle   Reflect, Ignore Further Surfaces

FIGURE 6.3.4 Regions of total internal reflection (TIR) can be handled in three ways: ignoring the second surface and continuing in direction $\mathbf{T}_1$, clamping to the critical angle and refracting, or reflecting and ignoring further ray-surface interactions.

The second problem occurs with nonconvex refractors. For these objects, the depth complexity is sometimes greater than 2, and it is unclear which surface to use as the second refractive interface (see Figure 6.3.3). In our experiments we used either the surface farthest from the eye or the surface closest to the front interface. Both approaches give plausible results but can lead to objectionable artifacts for refractors with long, narrow protrusions. Subjectively, we prefer using the surface farthest from the eye as the second refractive interface.

Finally, when the approximation $\tilde{d}_1$ overestimates the true distance, $\mathbf{p}_1$ may not project onto a texel containing a valid surface normal. Without using a better approximation or an iterative process to correct the overestimation, little information is available to fix the problem. Fortunately, this situation occurs relatively rarely for most objects, and many occurrences fall in regions of total internal reflection, where refractions naturally appear chaotic. Intuitively, these rays have exited the side of the refractor, where the surface normal is perpendicular to the viewing direction. Thus, instead of using a normal from the texture map, we construct a surface normal $\mathbf{N}_1$ perpendicular to $\mathbf{V}$ and refract as usual. We define $\mathbf{N}_2$ as follows:

$$\mathbf{N}_2 \equiv \mathbf{T}_1 - \left(\mathbf{V} \cdot \mathbf{T}_1\right)\mathbf{V}. \tag{6.3.2}$$

Putting it Together

Given the previous discussion, implementing approximate two-sided refraction is straightforward. The method requires two passes. The first pass renders the back refractor surface, with surface normals stored in the color channel. Both the color buffer and the depth buffer are stored in textures for use as input to the second pass.

The second pass renders the refractor using a fragment shader similar to the following snippet of Cg code. Note that Fresnel reflection and solutions to the three problems discussed above can easily be added, though we have removed them for brevity.

```
// Inputs:
//   Matrix: projectionMatrix
//   Texture: backfaceDistTex, backfaceNormalTex, environmentMapTex
//   Computed in rasterization: P_1, N_1, V, d_N, screenSpaceCoord
void main( ... )
{
  // Find the refraction direction T_1
  T_1 = refraction( V, N_1, index_i, index_t );

  // Compute d_V, the weights for d_V and d_N, and d_tilde, and P_2
  distToBackFace = tex2D( backfaceDistTex, screenSpaceCoord.xy );
  distToFrontFace = screenSpaceCoord.z;
  d_V = unproject( distToBackFace ) - unproject( distToFrontFace );
  weight_dV = Compute θ_t Over θ_i ( );
  d_tilde = weight_dV * d_V + (1 - weight_dV) * d_N;

// Compute our approximate location for the 2nd reflection
  P_2 = T_1 * d_tilde + P_1;

  // Project P_2, scale and bias to get a valid texture coord
  normalTexCoords = ScaleBias( mul( projectionMatrix, P_2 ) );
  N_2 = tex2D( backfaceNormalTex, normalTexCoords.xy );

  // Refract at the second surface, index into environment map
  T_2 = refraction( T_1, -N_2, index_t, index_i );
  outputColor = texCUBE( environmentMapTex, T_2 );
}
```

Examples and Discussion

Our images for this chapter were all captured during interactive sessions of our demo application, either running at a 512^2 or 1024^2 image resolution. Timings even for high polygon count models (like the 100,000 triangle Venus head) remain above 50 frames per second on a GeForce 6800 when the geometry covers the entire screen. Please refer to the folder for this article on the CD-ROM. Simpler models, like those shown in Figure 6.3.5, currently render at speeds of up to 300 frames per second.

FIGURE 6.3.5   Further examples of interactive image-space refraction.

While allowing refractive objects to be suspected inside an infinite environment map is academically interesting, it isn't particularly useful. However, there are a number of existing techniques for intersecting $\mathbf{T}_2$ with other scene geometry, allowing for much more complex refractions, as shown in Figure 6.3.1. Intersections with a small number of planar surfaces can be done explicitly with ray-plane intersections in the fragment shader. Alternatively, a number of image-space search techniques for intersecting more complex geometry have been proposed, including techniques based on linear search [Wyman05b], binary search [Policarpo05], or secant root finding [Szirmay-Kalos05].

A couple of additional implementation notes:

- Refraction with high indices of refraction (>1.2) will require supersampling to improve temporal coherence in regions of total internal reflection.
- We precomputed d_N via ray tracing and stored it in the surface normal's w-component. Depending on model complexity, we found that using $\tilde{d}_1 = d_V$ or $d_N = 0$ often gives acceptable results when precomputation is impossible.

Approximate, Image-Space Caustics

Dynamic global illumination has long remained the realm of offline renderers that can afford to spend minutes or hours per frame. A variety of recent techniques have suggested that caustics, the focusing of light from a specular object, can be interactively rendered. However, these techniques limit light to a single bounce, just as in traditional interactive reflection and refraction schemes.

The key idea motivating this section is that interactive reflection and refraction techniques are vital to quickly rendering high-fidelity caustics. The rest of this chapter investigates an image-space approach for rendering caustics [Wyman06], similar to [Szirmay-Kalos05], that can easily be applied with any interactive reflection or refraction scheme, though we show results using the refraction method presented above (as in Figure 6.3.1).

Again, the observation underlying our approach is quite simple. Caustics are the focusing of light off a specular surface. This means light travels multiple paths in space to reach a focal region. Note that this is a visibility problem—we want to determine how many times a point is visible from the light. A common technique that determines visibility from the light is shadow mapping, but it only determines a binary visibility value. If we could augment shadow mapping to instead count the light rays reaching a given point, we could render both shadows and caustics.

Caustics Algorithm

Fortunately, render-to-texture and render-to-vertex-array allow a relatively straightforward implementation of such an algorithm, which borrows from the two-pass approach of photon mapping [Jensen01]. The idea is to render the scene once from the light, storing where photons land, then render a second time gathering nearby photons to determine a final color.

Given an interactive technique for rendering reflections or refractions, the difficult part is efficiently storing and gathering the photons. Photon map implementations typically use balanced kd-trees to hold photons, but building such trees is slow ($O[N \log N]$ at best). Instead, we propose adding a third render pass, which renders photons into a *caustic map* that counts photons reaching each point visible in the corresponding shadow map. The basic algorithm follows and is depicted graphically in Figure 6.3.6:

1. Render scene from the light, storing locations of photon hits (instead of pixel colors) in a vertex array. We call this the *photon buffer*.
2. Render the photons (as points or splats) into a light-space caustic map, using alpha-blending to count the number of photons affecting each texel.
3. Render the scene from the eye, applying shadowing and adding in the contribution from caustic photons. The caustic map is projected onto the scene using projective texturing.

Rendering From the Light

The goal of the first pass is to determine the photons' final locations. The leftmost bubble in Figure 6.3.6 shows a glass gargoyle rendered from the light's point-of-view using the refractive technique described above, as well as two buffers used in the second and third steps: a depth map and the photon buffer.

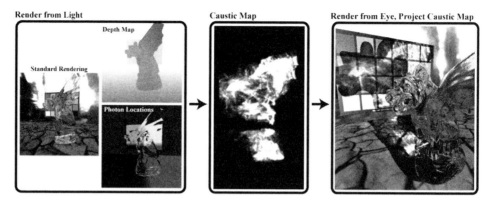

FIGURE 6.3.6   A graphical overview of rendering image-space caustics.

The depth map is a standard z-buffer, used for shadow mapping. The photon buffer stores the per-pixel positions, p_3, computed during refraction. In Figure 6.3.6, (x, y, z) values are mapped to (r,g,b). So, to render from the light:

1. From the light's position, render the scene using reflection and/or refraction.
2. Instead of storing a final color in each pixel, output the location, p_3, where the photon hits the opaque background geometry.

For scenes with pixels that both reflect and refract (i.e., have a Fresnel effect), two photon buffers are necessary (one for the reflected photons and one for the refracted photons).

To achieve more complex effects, additional data may be required. For example, another buffer might store photon attenuation (to simulate colored glass) or each photon's incident direction at the hit point (to simulate caustics on nondiffuse surfaces). These buffers can be generated in a single render pass using multiple render targets.

Rendering the Caustic Map

Using the photon buffer as input, the second pass gathers individual photons into the caustic map. Ideally, the caustic map augments the light's depth map; the depth map determines if photons *directly* hit a surface, and the caustic map determines if photons *indirectly* hit the surface. The idea is to count how many photons indirectly hit each point.

Given a buffer storing photon locations (as shown in Figure 6.3.6),

1. Treat each photon as a point primitive.
2. Ignore photons that are not reflected or refracted (i.e., that directly hit a surface).
3. Render the remaining points into the caustic map, with additive alpha-blending enabled to determine a total per-pixel count.

To reduce noise in the caustic map, each photon should be treated as a splat, with energy distributed over multiple texels. We used a splat with Gaussian weights. Note that there is a tradeoff between noise and caustic crispness. If very sharp caustics are desired, a large number of relatively small splats must be used to create a high-resolution caustic map. For very blurry caustics, a small number of splats in a coarse caustic map are sufficient. Most of our examples use 512^2 photons with 7^2 Gaussian splats.

To preserve energy, the weights of the Gaussians must sum to 1 when the resolutions of the photon buffer and caustic map are the same. Otherwise, the weights should sum to $R = pixelsInCausticMap/totalPhotons$. Technically, each photon subtends a different solid angle from the light and should thus be individually weighted, but we found that this effect can be ignored in practice.

Applying the Caustic Map

Once the caustic map has been computed, rendering the scene is straightforward:

1. Render the scene normally, using your favorite technique for shadows, reflections, and refractions.
2. When rendering diffuse surfaces, add the caustic contribution (modulated by the material properties) to the result of each pixel.

Putting it Together

In our implementation, we only update the caustic map after changes to the light or scene geometry. This allows rendering caustics at about the cost of an additional texture lookup in scenes where geometry moves infrequently. Ultimately, rendering caustics relies on an interactive reflection or refraction. Obviously, both the first and last passes use this reflection or refraction routine, so the approach must be quick enough to run twice per frame while maintaining interactivity.

Examples and Discussion

ON THE CD

We typically use 512^2 or 1024^2 resolution for the photon buffer, the caustic map, and the final screen resolution. In fully dynamic scenes like those shown in Figure 6.3.1, we get speeds of around 40 frames per second (on a GeForce 6800) at 512^2, using refractors of roughly 50,000 polygons. At that resolution, the bottleneck in our approach is the vertex processor, as each pixel in the photon map is treated as a point primitive. By reducing the photon buffer resolution, this bottleneck can be moved to the pixel processor, as using fewer points requires larger splats to reduce noise. Figures 6.3.7 and 6.3.8 show the quality difference when using different resolution photon buffers and caustic maps. Note that our implementation couples the photon buffer and shadow map sizes.

FIGURE 6.3.7 A glass F-16 rendered using 64^2, 256^2, and 1024^2 photons in a 512^2 caustic map. Speeds were 80, 50, and 8 frames per second, respectively, on a GeForce 6800.

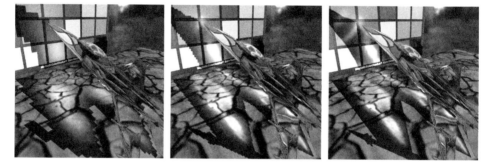

FIGURE 6.3.8 The F-16 with 64^2, 256^2, and 1024^2 photons in a 128^2 caustic map. Speeds are the same as in Figure 6.3.7.

We found that using a photon buffer with twice the resolution of the caustic map generally gives good-quality results, even during animation. Adding more photons does not help, as shown in Figure 6.3.8. Using fewer photons leads to noise and issues with frame-to-frame photon coherence.

Using 128^2 photons for computing a 64^2 caustic map gives good, but very blurry, results. As shown in Figure 6.3.7, using 1024^2 photons for a 512^2 caustic map gives very precise and sharp caustics, at the cost of a significantly lowered frame rate. Varying these values allows each application to find a unique cost-quality compromise. Note that our accompanying demo allows you to vary these parameters interactively to quickly compare settings.

Conclusion

This chapter has presented two image-space techniques, one for interactive refraction through complex objects and one for interactive caustics rendering. These are both multipass techniques that rely on the use of images to store intermediate values. While both approaches exhibit typical image-space aliasing problems, they do not rely on expensive ray casting to determine intersections and therefore provide a viable middle ground in the quality-performance spectrum.

References

[Bunnell05] Bunnell, M. "Dynamic Ambient Occlusion and Indirect Lighting," *GPU Gems 2*, edited by Matt Pharr. Addison-Wesley, 2005: 223–233.

[Dachsbacher05] Dachsbacher, C. and M. Stamminger. "Reflective Shadow Maps." *Proceedings of the 2005 Symposium on Interactive 3D Graphics and Games.* 2005: pp. 203–208.

[Hasenfratz03] Hasenfratz, J.-M., M. Lapierre, N. Holzschuch, and F. X. Sillion. "A Survey of Real-time Soft Shadows Algorithms." *Computer Graphics Forum,* 22(4), (2003): pp. 753–774.

[Jensen01] Jensen, H. *Realistic Image Synthesis Using Photon Mapping.* AK Peters, 2001.

[Lindhom01] Lindholm, E., M. J. Kilgard, and H. Moreton. "A User-Programmable Vertex Engine." *Proceedings of SIGGRAPH 2001.* 2001: pp. 149–158.

[Oliveira00] Oliveira, G. "Refractive texture mapping, part two." Available online at *http://www.gamasutra.com/features/20001117/oliveira_01.htm*, Nov. 17, 2000.

[Policarpo05] Policarpo, F., M. Oliveira, and J. Comba. "Real-time Relief Mapping on Arbitrary Polygonal Surfaces." *Proceedings of the 2005 Symposium on Interactive 3D Graphics and Games*, pp. 155–162.

[Schmidt03] Schmidt, C. M. "Simulating Refraction Using Geometric Transforms." Master's thesis, Computer Science Department, University of Utah, 2003.

[Sousa05] Sousa, T. "Generic Refraction Simulation." *GPU Gems 2*, edited by Matt Pharr. Addison Wesley, 2005: pp. 295–305.

[Szirmay-Kalos05] Szirmay-Kalos, L., A. Aszodi, I. Lazanyi, and M. Premecz. "Approximate Ray-Tracing on the GPU with Distance Impostors." *Computer Graphics Forum, 24*(3), (2005): pp. 695–704.

[Wyman05] Wyman, C. "An Approximate Image-Space Approach for Interactive Refraction." *ACM Transactions on Graphics 24*(3), (2005): pp. 1050–1053.

[Wyman05b] Wyman, C. "Interactive Image-Space Refraction of Nearby Geometry." *Proceedings of GRAPHITE 2005*, pp. 205–211.

[Wyman06] Wyman, C. and S. Davis. "Interactive Image-Space Techniques for Approximating Caustics." *Proceedings of the 2006 Symposium on Interactive 3D Graphics and Games*, pp. 153–160.

6.4

Splatting of Diffuse and Glossy Indirect Illumination

Carsten Dachsbacher

INRIA Sophia-Antipolis

Marc Stamminger

University of Erlangen-Nuremberg

Introduction

Striving for photo-realism in interactive computer graphics and games usually competes against constraints on processing time and hardware capabilities. The major problem with complex lighting and rendering scenarios is the global nature of effects such as indirect illumination, refractions, and caustics. Consequently, compromises have to be found, and usually material properties are simplified and local illumination models are used.

Although photo-realism is a desirable goal, most interactive applications tend to render plausible realism only. To this end, various algorithms exist to approximate global illumination effects. In this article we present a method to render indirect illumination of diffuse and glossy surfaces, that is, caustics, using a GPU-friendly deferred shading method. We describe different ways to obtain secondary light sources, responsible for the indirect lighting, and how their contribution can be rendered efficiently.

Our method is a further development of the idea of *reflective shadow maps* (RSMs), which we recapitulate in the next section.

Reflective Shadow Maps

The RSM approach [Dachsbacher2005] renders one-bounce diffuse indirect illumination without occlusion for indirect lighting. To identify the surfaces where the light bounces, it uses an extended shadow map, which stores not only the depth values, but also the world-space position, the surface normal, and the reflected radiant flux for each visible fragment. Each pixel of an RSM can be considered as a secondary light source (*pixel light*).

In theory, indirect lighting is computed or approximated by considering all secondary lights as local point lights. These point lights represent small surface lights, so they have a hemispherical emission, with the surface normal as main direction. For a diffuse pixel light p with world-space location x_p, direction n_p, and flux F_p, the radiant intensity emitted into direction ω is

$$I_p(\omega) = \Phi_p \max\left(0, n_p \cdot \omega\right) \tag{6.4.1}$$

The irradiance due to p at a surface point x with normal n is then:

$$E_p(x,n) = I_p\left(\frac{x - x_p}{\|x - x_p\|}\right) \frac{\max\left(0, n \cdot \left(x_p - x\right)\right)}{\|x - x_p\|^3} \tag{6.4.2}$$

Since gathering from all pixels is far too expensive, only a subset (typically several hundred pixel lights) is used, which depends on the point to be illuminated. The subset is focused to pixels close to p by sampling the shadow map neighborhood of p. Since the sampling pattern varies across the image, noise and striping artifacts become apparent if the number of samples is too low. This gathering operation is costly in terms of shader instructions and memory bandwidth, and to this end a screen-space subsampling, followed by an adaptive refinement step, is used for speed-up.

Overview

Our new method is similar to the RMSs, in that it uses basically the same extended shadow map to sample the directly lit surfaces of a scene.

The main difference is that we use a shooting approach: we select a subset of the pixel lights, representing the unoccluded indirect illumination of the scene. We can either use a regular distribution of the pixel light samples in the RSM or perform an importance sampling to adapt to surface glossiness and potential proximity of indirectly lit surfaces. The indirect lighting computation is performed using deferred shading techniques, and to maintain high performance, we restrict the lighting computation to the area where a pixel light provides a significant contribution to the final image.

We are not restricted in terms of surface characteristics, and we also render indirect illumination effects from nondiffuse surfaces. For this, we additionally store a glossiness term, similar to the Phong exponent, in the RSM.

Further optimizations and adaptations for static geometry and/or lighting are discussed at the end of this chapter.

Splatting Indirect Illumination

The approach presented in this article reverses the RSM evaluation process: instead of iterating over all image pixels and gathering the indirect light from the RSM, we select a subset of the pixel lights for each rendered frame (not for each shaded pixel) and distribute their light to the image. Basically, this corresponds to a rendering of the scene with a large number of point light sources. This can be done efficiently by using deferred shading techniques. A big advantage of deferred shading is that lighting computations can be restricted to a certain area of the screen if bounding boxes or volumes for the light sources can be determined. The costs for the lighting computations depend on the number of pixels to be shaded, not on the complexity of the scene's geometry.

Deferred shading buffers typically contain the world-space position, surface normals, and the material parameters for each screen pixel as seen from the viewer's camera. They can be created using multiple render targets and are stored as textures. An update is required whenever the camera moves. When rendering the final image, we also use the deferred shading buffers to compute the local illumination with shadowing (of direct illumination) from the light source, before the indirect illumination is computed and blended additively.

The Simple Approach

An important observation is that, in general, a pixel light source only generates a significant indirect illumination in its direct neighborhood or proximity owing to distance attenuation. The easiest way of restricting the number of processed fragments is to render a quadrilateral—the 2D axis-aligned bounding box enclosing the projection of the significant region—in screen space at the position of the point light. It must be big enough to cover all fragments that can receive significant light. This size can be easily computed from the intensity of the pixel light and its distance to the camera. Details on this computation and tighter bounds are described below.

For each covered fragment we retrieve the information of the visible geometry from the deferred shading buffers as shown in Figure 6.4.1. Together with the light source parameters (associated with the quadrilateral), we compute the pixel light contribution

local illumination with shadows   samples placed in light view   created pixel lights in camera view   causing indirect lighting   together with local illumination

FIGURE 6.4.1   The splatting of indirect illumination. Pixel lights are distributed on surfaces captured by the RSM. The region of significant contribution is computed, and the indirect light is computed using deferred shading.

to the underlying fragment according to Equation 6.4.2 and accumulate it in the frame buffer or off-screen render target. This is why we call this process the *splatting* of indirect light, that is, adding the contribution of each secondary light source onto the final image.

The computation of the quadrilateral can be efficiently implemented in a vertex shader. The RSM, storing the information about surfaces causing the indirect illumination, is sampled (using a Vertex Shader 3.0 profile shader) and the quadrilateral positioned. As a vertex shader only processes geometry and does not create geometry, the vertex data for the quadrilaterals is sent through the pipeline and modified accordingly. The sampling pattern for the RSM is provided as a texture, and each quadrilateral has a texture coordinate to select a sampling position from this texture. Using a render-to-vertex-array pass, no texture fetches during vertex processing are required. Geometry instancing, on the other hand, allows specifying the quadrilateral geometry once, and the texture coordinates for the RSM sampling pattern are then provided in another data stream.

Nondiffuse Surfaces

Adapting this approach to indirect illumination effects from glossy or refractive surfaces is easy. To this end, we model such glossy emission characteristics for pixel lights with a Phong-like model (see Figure 6.4.2).

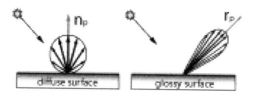

FIGURE 6.4.2   The emission of pixel lights on diffuse and specular surfaces.

The emission of a glossy pixel light p with a Phong exponent P is

$$I_p(\omega) = \Phi_p \max\left(0, r_p \cdot \omega\right)^P,\qquad(6.4.3)$$

where r_p is main light direction of p, which is the reflection direction of light incident at p for reflective surfaces, or the refraction direction for translucent materials. The direction r_p can be computed during the RSM generation per glossy pixel light and is then a parameter of the light source such as P. Note that the emission should also be clamped at the surface of p (this is necessary, e.g., if r_p is close to perpendicular to n_p) so that no light is emitted backwards.

Rendering with such glossy light sources causes, as seen often in global illumination algorithms, problems along common boundaries of walls. This is because the illumination integral has a singularity there, which is difficult to integrate numerically. For RSMs these problems are largely reduced by moving the pixel lights slightly in negative normal direction. This is a possible work-around for diffuse illumination, but with glossy reflection, the problem becomes more apparent. A simple solution to this problem is to reduce these artifacts by widening the narrow high-intensity regions near the glossy pixel light source. This can be easily achieved by replacing the constant Phong exponent P by

$$P_p{}'(x) = \min\left(P, P\|x - x_p\|a\right) \qquad (6.4.4)$$

where $a > 0$ is a user-defined parameter.

Owing to their narrow shape (see Figure 6.4.3), screen space quads very wasteful approximations—especially for glossy pixel lights. A tighter bounding geometry, covering and processing fewer fragments, is mandatory for fast rendering. The computation of tighter bounds is described in the next section.

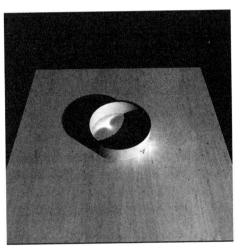 

FIGURE 6.4.3   Axis-aligned bounding quadrilaterals are wasteful approximations, especially for specular pixel lights. The tight bounding volumes are shown as wireframes.

Usually, a higher number of glossy pixel lights is necessary to reproduce the high-frequency caustics, but on the other hand, the region of influence of such a pixel light is smaller and covers fewer fragments. As a consequence, it is possible to render indirect glossy illumination at a similar speed as for the diffuse case when computing tight bounds. Figures 6.4.3 and 6.4.10, below, show examples for caustics generated with our approach.

Tighter Bounding Geometry

With the simple approach, the performance bottlenecks are the fragment shader execution and, especially, the associated memory bandwidth. This is because several hundred to thousands of pixel lights are required for a compelling rendering of indirect illumination. It is obvious that an axis-aligned box in screen space is a wasteful representation, and thus, as long as vertex processing (or generation) does not become a critical factor, we can afford to spend more work on creating tighter bounding volumes. Ideally, these bounds are computed and rendered in world space, which is not only simpler than considering the 2D projection, but also allows us to make use of early-z tests during deferred shading to reduce fragment shader executions.

The goal is to compute a simple bounded region in space, outside of which the illumination drops below a user-defined threshold or cut-off value. As one can see in Figure 6.4.4 this region is egg-shaped for a diffuse pixel light and is similar to a Phong lobe for glossy surfaces. Note that these surfaces are the iso-surfaces of illumination that include spatial attenuation and are not polar plots of exitant radiance. For practical reasons, we use ellipsoids as bounds in both cases. For each pixel light, we have to compute the ellipsoid parameters, and we transform a spherical triangle mesh (with low triangle count) accordingly.

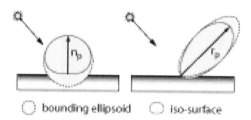

FIGURE 6.4.4   The bounding geometry for the pixel lights adapts to surface characteristics.

In the appendix we describe how the significant regions and parameters of the ellipsoids can be computed quickly for diffuse and glossy pixel lights.

The Extended RSM

In order to splat indirect illumination for diffuse and specular surfaces and with tight bounding volumes, we store more information than for the original RSM approach. For diffuse surfaces, it was sufficient to render RSMs with world-space position (or depth in respect to the primary light source), the surface normal, and the reflected radiant flux. With the new approach, we replace the surface normal by the primary direction of light emission and the Phong-like exponent for the glossy reflections and refractions.

Importance Sampling

To adapt the sampling pattern for the RSM to its actual flux distribution, we perform an importance sampling by hierarchical warping as proposed by Clarberg [Clarberg2005]. Importance sampling is used to obtain a selection of pixel lights that adapts to the scene. It can account for the brightness of surfaces, but also for their glossiness and the likelihood of nearby (and thus likely receiving indirect light) surfaces.

Hierarchical Warping

As a start, we assume that the scene consists solely of diffuse surfaces, and more samples are to be placed at parts of the scene with higher flux; that is, as probability distribution (telling us where to put more pixel lights), we just use the flux taken from the RSM. The resulting set of pixel lights then exhibits a more balanced intensity distribution among the indirect light sources.

Each level of the hierarchical warping consists of a vertical and horizontal warping step according to the flux distribution. We begin with a set of uniformly distributed sample points $s_i = (x_i, y_i)^T$, $x_i, y_i \in [0;1)$ with sample weight $w_i = 1$. Figure 6.4.5 depicts the warping according to the coarsest level; the initial sample set (Figure 6.4.5b) is partitioned into two rows according to the upper and lower average flux (F_{top} and F_{bottom}, Figure 6.4.5a). The sample points are scaled such that the separation border halves the sample area $[0;1)^2$ (Figure 6.4.5c). A new sample point's y_i' is obtained with

$$\Phi_r = \frac{\Phi_{top}}{\Phi_{top} + \Phi_{bottom}} \tag{6.4.5}$$

$$y_i' = \begin{cases} y_i / (2\Phi_r) & \text{if } y_i < \Phi_r \\ (1 + y_i - 2\Phi_r) / (2(1 - \Phi_r)) & \text{otherwise} \end{cases} \tag{6.4.6}$$

To compensate for the varying sampling densities, the sample weights are computed such that the total weight of all samples remains equal:

$$w_i' = \begin{cases} w_i / (2\Phi_r) & \text{if } y_i < \Phi_r \\ w_i / (2(1 - \Phi_r)) & \text{otherwise} \end{cases} \tag{6.4.7}$$

After the vertical warping, the upper and lower halves are warped analogously to obtain x_i' for each sample (Figure 6.4.5d). The warped sampling pattern (Figure 6.4.5e) is then used to obtain the pixel lights from the RSM. The flux taken from the RSM is multiplied with a sample's weight before its contribution to the scene is computed. We refer to this warping strategy as method A. We also experimented with a simpler and thus faster variant (method B) that performs the horizontal warping for all samples, not independently for the upper and lower half. The results are less optimal, yet still useful, and the computation requires fewer instructions.

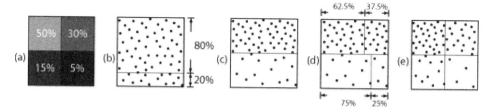

FIGURE 6.4.5   Importance warping for a single level of the hierarchical importance-warping procedure.

In both cases the sample warping is done hierarchically, and after a vertical and horizontal step, we proceed on the four quadrants recursively. The importance sampling is particularly important for scenes with nondiffuse surfaces, as these require more samples to approximate their global illumination effects more accurately. We propose performing the importance sampling according not just to the flux, but to a probability distribution obtained from the product of the flux and the maximum value of the BRDF as shown in Figure 6.4.6, when, for example, using an energy-preserving Phong illumination model, the maximum value of its normalized BRDF is the Phong exponent P.

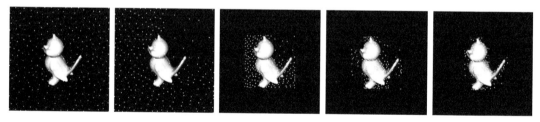

FIGURE 6.4.6   An importance-warped sampling pattern (0, 1, 2, 3, and 4 steps) for a simple example.

Another observation leads to a further criterion for importance sampling: the ambient occlusion term O, used in many computer games and film productions, is the ratio of environment light that a surface point would be likely to receive. This is done by shooting rays into the hemisphere above a surface point and computing the ratio between rays not intersecting other surfaces and the total number of rays. Usually only occluders in near proximity are considered for computing this term. In other words, the ambient occlusion term provides information about whether other surfaces are close to a certain surface point. If no other surfaces are close, secondary light sources positioned there have very little or no contribution to the scene. To account for the aforementioned heuristic during importance warping, we replace the flux for importance sampling by the probability $p_\Phi = \Phi \cdot (1 - O) \cdot P$. The corresponding texture storing this term for the light view is called the importance sampling buffer and replaces the RSM flux for importance sampling.

Warping on the GPU

The warping procedure described above can be easily implemented in a pixel shader, as each sample point can be treated independently. For this, we store the initial list of sampling points, whose locations are precomputed, as a texture. The x- and y-coordinates store the 2D position of the sample, and the z-coordinate stores its weight.

The warping shader is applied by rendering a single quadrilateral to a render target of the same resolution as the initial sample point texture. For each pixel, we retrieve the sample point's data, modify it according to Equations 6.4.5 through 6.4.7, and output the new position and weight. If more recursions are necessary, we can either perform these in separate render passes or within a single, yet longer, shader. As the number of samples in our examples does not exceed 4096, a complex shader has no great impact on performance.

Exploiting Ambient Occlusion

The importance-warping method described above works perfectly well for types of light sources with planar shadow maps; for example, spotlights. For omni-directional light sources, most often, cube shadow maps or dual-paraboloid parameterizations are chosen. Although an importance sampling for each individual quadratic subtexture could be computed or an initial prewarping step could be performed to distribute samples across subtextures, this may reduce performance. Keeping in mind that it is not the geometry processing, that is the number of light sources, but the fragment processing that is usually the bottleneck, there is another way of balancing quality and speed for rendering, although restricted to diffuse surfaces. We use a uniform distribution of light sources in the shadow map and scale the flux by the ambient occlusion term. Secondary light sources that are likely negligible become smaller and thus do not consume valuable rendering time and memory bandwidth. This procedure can be thought of as a replacement for importance sampling, but with results of slightly lower quality.

Indirect Illumination Without RSMs

The rendering part of our method does not necessarily rely on RSMs, and other methods can be applied to determine secondary light sources.

One possibility is to adapt the instant radiosity method [Keller1997] to obtain a light source distribution: a relatively small number of photons are traced stochastically, that is, they are reflected with a probability depending on material properties, from the light source through the scene. Pixel lights are created where photons bounce off or hit surfaces. In most game-typical situations, the best examples are probably indoor games, in which a space-partitioning tree is stored along with the geometry. These data structures may be used for collision detection, but they can also be used to accelerate intersection tests when shooting the photons. Figure 6.4.7 shows a rendering of the famous Cornell box with instant radiosity and the splatting method.

FIGURE 6.4.7   The famous Cornell box rendered with our splatting method and a point light source (left) and with ray-tracing and an area light source (right). Indirect lighting is generated from light sources obtained by instant radiosity.

It is also possible to consider indirect illumination splatting for diffuse parts of a scene on a triangle or patch basis instead of using a point sampling scheme. As a pre-processing step, surfaces that contribute to the indirect illumination of the scene are identified and treated as area light sources. Similar to point light sources, we can determine the significant region and compute a coarse polygonal approximation thereof. The per-pixel computations for area-lights are, of course, more complex (e.g., using area-to-differential-area form factors), but when using the RSM point-light approach, the surface is approximated by several point light sources, causing overdraw and eating up bandwidth.

Results

The rendering speed of our method directly depends on the overdraw caused by the splatting. The number of processed fragments, in turn, depends on the amount of indirect light, that is, its brightness and the cut-off value for bounding the ellipsoids. Figure 6.4.8 shows two renderings with exaggerated indirect illumination and the overdraw caused by 4096 light sources. Figure 6.4.9 shows the impact of choosing different lower thresholds for the indirect light. Supplemental files for this article can be found on the CD-ROM.

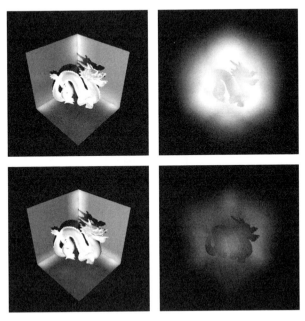

FIGURE 6.4.8 Exaggerated indirect illumination (left) and the resulting overdraw (right). Pure white means 400 times overdraw. In the top row the cut-off value is 0.01, and in the bottom row it is 0.03.

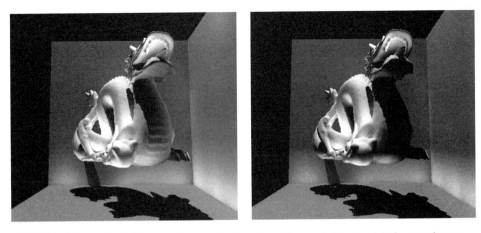

FIGURE 6.4.9 In the left image, the cut-off value is small enough. For the right image a larger cut-off value was used, and as a consequence, light transport over greater distances is lost. A clear boundary of indirect bluish light is visible.

For glossy pixel lights, the bounding volumes are usually very tight and cover only a few fragments on the screen. This allows the rendering of caustics from reflections (see Figure 6.4.3) and refractions (Figure 6.4.10) at high frame rates.

FIGURE 6.4.10   Caustics, obtained from single-sided refraction, can be rendered at real-time frame rates.

Conclusions

In this chapter we presented a GPU-friendly method for rendering approximate indirect illumination from diffuse surfaces and caustics from glossy and refractive objects. All computations can be performed without using the CPU, and an intuitive way of trading speed against correctness or quality of the approximation is inherent.

As in previous methods, we cannot account for self-shadowing for indirect lighting and thus propose to use ambient occlusion methods or combinations with normal shadow mapping techniques; this is the price to pay when approximating global illumination effects in real-time with rasterizing hardware.

Appendix: Bounds on Indirect Light Sources

To derive an easy formula for the significant region for a pixel light p, we use spherical coordinates centered at p; that is, each world-space point is described by a direction ω and a distance r. The exitant light of p depends on ω, as given in Equations 6.4.1 and 6.4.3 and as shown in Figure 6.4.11. The irradiance E at a point with polar coordinates (ω, r) thus depends on ω, but also on the distance to the light source r:

$$E(\omega,r) \propto \frac{I_p(\omega)}{r^2} \qquad (6.4.8)$$

E also depends on the cosine of the incident angle, but we cannot know this in advance when computing the bounding region, and thus we have to use the upper bound of 1 for this cosine term. As a consequence, we can bound the irradiance at (ω, r) by $I_p(\omega)r^{-2}$.

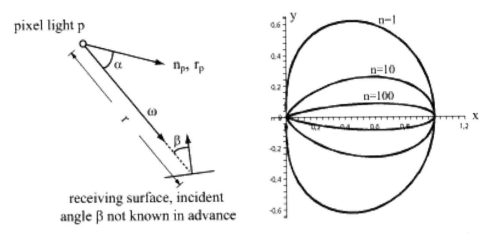

FIGURE 6.4.11   (Left) Quantities required for computing the illumination caused by a pixel light. (Right) Significant regions plotted for pixel lights with different exponents.

In order to obtain a single solution for diffuse and glossy lights, we denote as α the angle to the main light direction; that is, $\alpha = (n_p, \omega)$ for diffuse lights (Equation 6.4.1) and $\alpha = <(r_p, \omega)$ for glossy lights (Equation 6.4.3). If we use an exponent $n = 1$ for diffuse lights, the irradiance can be bounded by the 2D polar function:

$$B(\alpha, r) = \frac{I_0 \cos^n(\alpha)}{r^2} \tag{6.4.9}$$

In the following we restrict our analysis to the 2D case, as the 3D shape is rotationally symmetric. The region of influence of p is then bound by the iso-surface $B(\alpha, r) = I_{low}$. Because B is continuously decreasing with r, we obtain the iso-surface as a polar function:

$$r(\omega) = \sqrt{\frac{I_0 \cos^n(\alpha)}{I_{low}}} \tag{6.4.10}$$

Figure 6.4.11 shows the iso-surfaces for $I_0 = 1$, $I_{low} = 1$ and Phong exponents 1, 10, and 100. The upper half of $r(\omega)$ can be described using the explicit function:

$$F(x) = x^{\frac{n}{n+2}} \sqrt{1 - x^{\frac{4}{n+2}}}$$

(6.4.11)

Now we can fit an ellipse around these shapes with the following heuristic. First, we compute the maximum of F. If the maximum is at x_{max}, we put the center of our ellipse at $(x_{max}, 0)^T$. We use the x- and y-axes as the main axes of the ellipse and select $F(x_{max})$ as the ellipse height. Finally, we select the width, such that the ellipse covers the x-interval [0, 1]. Figure 6.4.12 shows the iso-surfaces in black and the bounding ellipses in gray for $n = 1$ and $n = 10$.

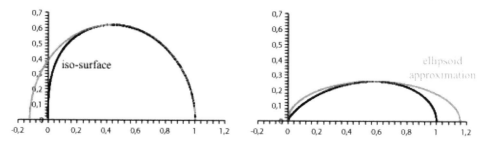

FIGURE 6.4.12   Iso-surfaces and ellipsoid approximations for exponents $n = 1$ and $n = 10$.

The maximum can be found by finding the root of F's derivative. Its x-position is at

$$c(n) = \frac{n}{n+2}^{\frac{n+2}{4}}$$

(6.4.12)

Thus, the center of the ellipsoid is at $[c(n), 0]^T$, its height is $h(n) = F[c(n)]$, and for the width we get $w(n) = \max[c(n), 1-c(n)]$.

References

[Clarberg2005], Clarberg, P. et al, "Wavelet Importance Sampling: Efficiently evaluating products of complex functions," ACM transactions on Graphics, pp. 1166–1175. Available online at *http://portal.acm.org/citation.cfm?id=1073328&dl=ACM&coll=&CFID=15151515&CFTOKEN=6184618.*

[Dachsbacher2005] Dachsbacher, C. et al. "Reflective Shadow Maps." *Proceedings of the 2005 Symposium on Interactive 3D Graphics and Games.* 2005: pp. 203–231.

[Dachsbacher2006] Dachsbacher, C. et al. "Splatting Indirect Illumination." *Proceedings of the 2006 Symposium on Interactive 3D Graphics and Games.* 2006: pp. 93–100.

[Keller1997], Keller, A. "Instant Radiosity." *Proceedings of SIGGRAPH 97, Computer Graphics Proceedings*, Annual Conference Series. 1997: pp. 49–56.

[SHAH2005], Shah, M. et al. "Caustics Mapping: An Image-Space Technique for Real-time Caustics." Technical Report, School of Engineering and Computer Science, University of Central Florida, 2005.

[WYMAN2005], Wyman, C. "An Approximate Image-Space Approach for Interactive Refraction." *ACM Transactions on Graphics*, *24*(3), (2005): pp. 1050–1053.

MOBILE DEVICES SECTION

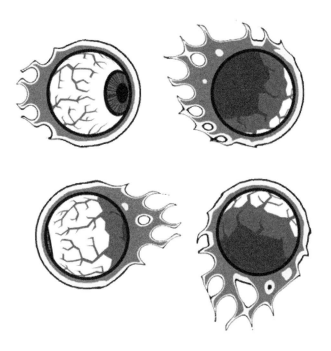

Introduction

Kristof Beets

Welcome to the Mobile Devices section of *ShaderX5*. This section may contain surprises for some readers, covering as it does an area of development in which many coders would not expect to find vertex and pixel shading technologies already in use. You might be very familiar with development for consoles and PCs using shaders. Essentially, developing for mobile is very similar, but because of mobile device constraints you'll have to start to think a little differently.

Why bother? Well, mobile gaming as a whole is a rapidly developing market with many opportunities. According to the research company Informa, mobile gaming sales will generate $7.2 billion a year worldwide by 2011, growing from the $2.4 billion sold in 2006—and that's based on a rather small number of phone users actually playing games. As 3D functionality gets into more handsets, and users realize that they can play the same kind of content in their mobile life that they enjoy at home, the market is likely to boom.

There's real potential for content developers to exploit this market while it's young. Projects started now could ship into an 80–150 million unit OpenGL® ES 1.x market (2007 projections), based on devices from major handset players such as Sony Ericsson and Nokia, or they could ship into the first OpenGL ES 2.0–based shading devices based on silicon from major semiconductor players such as Intel, TI, NEC, or Renesas. The first generation of hardware-accelerated mobiles offers programmable vertex shaders and fixed function multitexturing, while the second generation functionality will exceed Shader Model 3 requirements. Open-standard APIs including OpenVG (vector graphics), OpenMAX (Media Processing) and OpenKODE (media application portability) are all making significant progress, allowing phone multimedia to become ever more advanced and accessible to developers.

Market feedback predicts that 50% of handsets shipped in 2010 will have hardware-accelerated graphics. At Imagination Technologies we've already seen over 20 million phones ship using our 3D acceleration technology, PowerVR. I predict that around 80% of handsets in 2012 will be 3D enabled, and a significant portion of those will be full "shader phones." Most importantly, those shader phones will be sought out by committed gamers—the very people who buy the most high-value content. As well as games, the advent of 3D hardware means that phones will benefit from advanced UI and convergence applications such as navigation, media players, and avatar-based communications.

Ahead of you is a rich feast of articles to help you on your way.

The first article, "OpenGL ES 2.0: Shaders for Mobile Devices," introduces the leading open-standard API, which will enable shader-based graphics on mobile devices: OpenGL ES 2.0.

In "Developing a 3D Engine for OpenGL ES 2.0 and OpenGL v2.0," Daniel Ginsburg builds on the information from the first article to explain the process of creating a game engine that supports both desktop OpenGL 2.0 and mobile OpenGL ES 2.0. He also provides some valuable insights into the process of porting applications between the desktop and mobile market segments.

The next article, "OpenGL ES 2.0 Performance Recommendations for Mobile Devices," dives into the details of getting the best possible performance and visual quality despite the limitations of mobile devices.

Georg Kolling introduces a new image-based texture synthesis method in "Real-time Tile-Based Texture Synthesis Using Nonregular Grids," allowing for substantial savings in the texture memory usage essential in a mobile environment.

To conclude, "Cartoon Fire Effects Using OpenGL ES 2.0," presents a technique to create one of the most enduring graphic clichés of our time: "hotrod flames."

Welcome to the world of mobile shaders!

7.1

OpenGL ES 2.0: Shaders for Mobile Devices

Kristof Beets, Imagination Technologies

Introduction

OpenGL ES (OpenGL for Embedded Systems) defines a streamlined subset of the desktop OpenGL 3D graphics API for embedded devices such as mobile phones, PDAs, and video game consoles. This open standard is defined and promoted by the Khronos Group, a member-funded industry consortium focused on enabling the authoring and acceleration of dynamic media on a wide variety of platforms and devices.

The introduction of OpenGL ES 2.0 in August 2005, based on the desktop OpenGL 2.0 API, replaces the fixed-function pipeline of OpenGL ES 1.x with an entirely programmable model and brings the capabilities of handheld devices in line with the desktop market.

This article will introduce the OpenGL ES 2.0 design philosophy, architecture, and API level differences relative to desktop OpenGL 2.0, in addition to pointing out various online resources for software developers. The content of this article is based on the latest available edition of the OpenGL ES Common Profile Specification 2.0 [Munshi06] and the OpenGL® ES Shading Language Specification [Simpson06].

OpenGL ES 2.0 Design Philosophy

The OpenGL ES 2.0 API aims to bring high-end shader capabilities to the embedded market and achieves this by starting from the desktop market–proven OpenGL 2.0 API specification.

Mobile devices such as smart phones, PDAs, and so on, are increasing their capabilities at an impressive rate, but they remain limited in terms of processing power, system memory, and storage space. The OpenGL ES 1.x specification track defined a streamlined version of the fixed function OpenGL rendering pipeline by removing deprecated, little-used functionality and redundancy from the OpenGL 1.x base specifications [Kari05]. The OpenGL ES 2.0 specification is based on a similar approach applied to the pure programmable model defined by the OpenGL 2.0 base specification. Specifically, all traditional fixed-function capabilities have been removed, thus

creating a parallel API track that no longer aims for backward compatibility with the
OpenGL ES 1.x standard.

OpenGL ES 2.0 Architecture

OpenGL ES 2.0 Pipeline

An overview of the OpenGL ES 1.x fixed-function pipeline can be seen in Figure 7.1.1
versus the OpenGL ES 2.0 programmable pipeline, which can be seen in Figure 7.1.2.
This architecture is almost identical to the OpenGL 2.0 pipeline, with fixed-function
transform and lighting functionality being replaced by the vertex shader. The fragment
shader replaces texture environment, color sum, fog, and alpha-test fixed functionality.

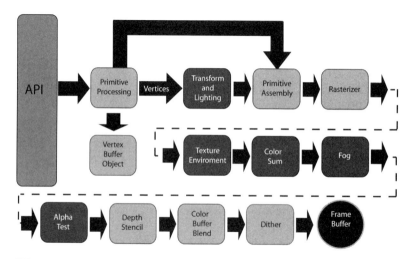

FIGURE 7.1.1   OpenGL ES 1.x fixed function pipeline.

OpenGL ES 2.0 Vertex Shader

The vertex shader takes up to eight user-defined attributes per vertex as inputs. To unify
and simplify the input model for the vertex shader, there are no longer specific attributes
for color, position, normals, and so on. Other inputs to the vertex shader include a minimum of 512 uniform components (float constants) and—optionally—sampled texture
data. To store intermediate results, a number of temporary variables are supported. The
output of the vertex shader is a set of up to eight varyings (four-element vectors). The
minimum required output from the vertex shader is a position. An overview of the vertex shader is shown in Figure 7.1.3.

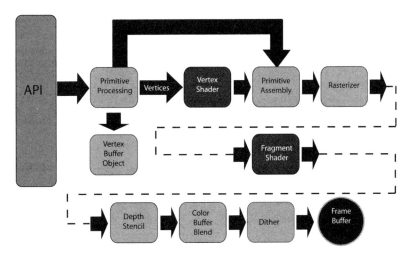

FIGURE 7.1.2   OpenGL ES 2.0 programmable pipeline.

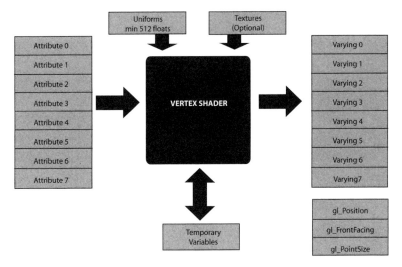

FIGURE 7.1.3   Vertex shader overview.

OpenGL ES 2.0 Fragment Shader

The fragment shader uses per-pixel interpolated varyings as input, and the interpolated position is used to determine the on-screen position of the current fragment. Other inputs to the fragment shader include a minimum of 64 uniform components (float constants) and sampled texture data (minimum of eight texture image units). To store intermediate results, a number of temporary variables are supported. Vertex shader output is a single fragment color that is written to the frame buffer. An overview of the fragment shader is shown in Figure 7.1.4.

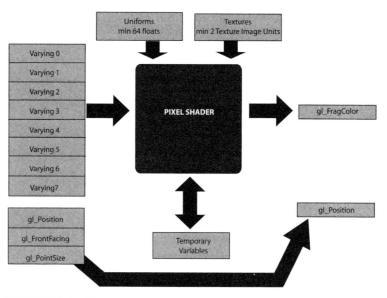

FIGURE 7.1.4   Fragment shader overview.

OpenGL ES 2.0 API and Shading Language

Fixed-Point Support

Historically, mobile applications processors have had limited hardware support for floating-point operations, and system-provided software emulation paths have offered only poor performance. To reduce this performance impact, OpenGL ES 1.1 introduced native support within the API for a fixed-point (signed 16.16) data format that allows mathematical operations to be performed more efficiently on mobile processors.

OpenGL ES 2.0 supports the fixed-point data type for vertex attribute arrays, but not for shader uniforms and command parameters. This simplifies the API and reduces driver complexity. Given the inherent flexibility and programmability of shaders, there is much less need to process data on the CPU, and hence potential performance gains offered by this data type have also been significantly reduced. Additionally, newer generations of mobile applications processors often include full support for floating-point operations, further reducing the need for a fixed-point data type.

Texture Compression

Within the desktop market, texture compression is largely standardized through the Microsoft DirectX API, which mandates hardware support for DXTC (S3TC). Texture compression is also exposed and supported under OpenGL, through ARB and vendor-specific extensions.

The embedded market currently has no comparable dominant texture-compression standard, although the Khronos Group has developed a royalty-free texture compression extension called OES_compressed_ETC1_RGB8_texture. In addition, OpenGL ES, in common with desktop OpenGL, supports a general compressed-texture loading mechanism. Offline precompressed-texture binary data, which can include full mipmap data, can be loaded using the glCompressedTexImage2D and glCompressedTexSubImage2D functions. The formats supported through these APIs are vendor specific, and extensions for them are found in the vendors software development kit (SDK) documentation. Vendors exposing their own formats for current embedded products include NVIDIA (DXT1), ATI (ATITC), Falanx (FLXTC), and Imagination Technologies (PVRTC). In general, the vendor extensions only support precompressed data created using an offline tool, as on-the-fly compression of texture data could exceed the performance levels and memory footprint available on mobile devices.

Shader Compilation and Usage

Desktop OpenGL 2.0 implementations load string-based shader code using the glShaderSource function, requiring a driver-level compiler capable of translating GLSL shaders into assembler-style instructions understood by the graphics hardware. The embedded platforms, targeted by OpenGL ES 2.0, have a limited amount of system memory and limited computational power, which can make on-device compilation difficult, resulting either in long compilation times or less than fully optimized code. For this reason OpenGL ES 2.0 contains two mechanisms to load shaders: the traditional string-based method—which requires an on-device compiler—and a new mechanism that allows precompiled binary shaders to be loaded using the new glShaderBinary function. The OpenGL ES 2.0 specification requires that an implementation must provide at least one or both of these shader loading mechanisms. An overview of each method of shader usage is illustrated in Figure 7.1.5 and Figure 7.1.6.

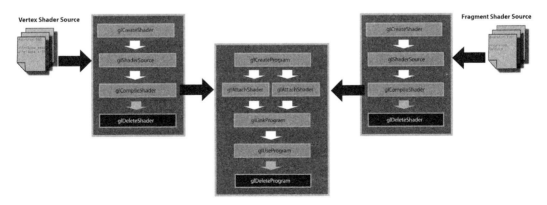

FIGURE 7.1.5 On-line shader compilation overview.

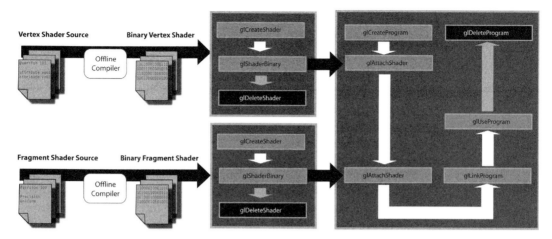

FIGURE 7.1.6   Offline shader compilation.

Precompiled binary shaders can be generated using an off-line optimizing compiler tool provided by the graphics hardware provider. Owing to the platform-specific optimization of the off-line compilation tool, the binary shaders generated for one OpenGL ES 2.0 product are not likely to work on another. Even across OpenGL ES 2.0 products from the same hardware vendor, the binary shaders may not be compatible.

Precision Qualifiers

One of the new features added to the OpenGL ES 2.0 Shading Language is the ability to specify precision qualifiers on variables. Three levels of precision are specified, lowp, mediump, and highp, and they control the range and precision used to store and represent values in both the vertex and fragment shaders. The precision of operations must preserve the storage precision of the variables involved:

```
uniform highp float h1;
highp float h2 = 2.3 * 4.7; // operation and result are highp
mediump float m;
m = 3.7 * h1 * h2; // all operations are highp precision
h2 = m * h1; // operation is highp precision
m = h2 - h1; // operation is highp precision
h2 = m + m; // addition and result at mediump precision

void f(highp p);
f(3.3); // 3.3 will be passed in at highp precision
```

The only exceptions allowed are for a small number of computationally intensive built-in functions, for example, atan(), which may return results at less than the declared precisions.

The introduction of precision qualifiers allows for more efficient hardware implementations for the embedded market, since the qualifiers can influence the storage requirements for constants and temporary variables within the shader in addition to influencing the accuracy and thus potentially the throughput of operations.

The vertex shader must support all three precision levels, and the default precision qualifier is highp for both floating-point and integer values. The minimum precision requirement for highp floating-point variables is a range of at least $(-2^{62}-2^{62})$ and a precision of at least one part in 65,536. Integer highp variables require an integer precision of at least 16 bits, plus a sign bit.

For the fragment shader, highp support is optional and is exposed through the GL_FRAGMENT_PRECISION_HIGH macro, which is defined only on systems that support high precision in the fragment shader. The minimum floating-point precision and range for the fragment shader is represented by mediump and requires a range of at least $(-16,384-16,384)$ and a precision of at least one part in 1024. The minimum integer precision for the fragment language requires a precision of at least 10 bits, plus a sign bit, and is identified by lowp.

Implementations may use greater range and precision than requested, but not less. The actual range and precision provided by a hardware implementation can be queried through the API.

To avoid having to indicate a precision level for each declaration the precision statement can be used to determine the default precision qualifier for both integer and floating-point types:

```
precision precision-qualifier type;
```

The vertex shader has a default precision of highp for both integers and floats, while the fragment shader has a default precision of mediump for integers but has no default precision qualifier for floating-point types.

Invariant Qualifier

Owing to compiler optimizations, it is possible that a set of shaders that contain the same expression do not resolve this expression to the exact same machine language code. This difference is known as *variance* and can cause problems in multipass algorithms that depend on the same results being obtained from a single expression used within multiple shaders. To prevent variance, OpenGL ES 2.0 allows variables to be declared *invariant* either individually,

```
invariant gl_Position;
```

or using a global setting,

```
#pragma STDGL invariant(all)
```

Only variables that are output from a shader can be declared invariant.

To guarantee the invariance of a particular output variable in two shaders, the following requirement must be met:

- The output variable is declared invariant in both shaders.
- The same values must be input to all shader input variables consumed by expressions and flow control contributing to the value assigned to the output variable.
- The texture formats, texel values, and texture filtering are set the same way for any texture function calls contributing to the value of the output variable.

Summary of Changes Relative to OpenGL 2.0

This section gives a brief overview of the differences between OpenGL ES 2.0 and OpenGL 2.0. These differences are summarized in a table format indicating which functionality is included, excluded, or made optional (e.g., through a proposed extension). Where required, a short statement is included to clarify the decision by the Khronos Group to remove certain functionality.

Note that this overview is based on the latest draft specification of OpenGL ES 2.0 available at the time of writing. While no major changes to this specification are expected, minor syntax and functionality changes cannot be ruled out.

Vertex Specification

In	Out	Optional
glVertexAttrib{1234}f[v]	**Immediate mode:** glBegin/glEnd, glVertex	
	All other glVertexAttrib* variants	
	All other fixed function per-primitive attributes: glMultiTexCoord, glNormal, glColor, glFogCoord, glSecondaryColor, etc.	
	Color index mode	

In line with the OpenGL ES 2.0 design philosophy, redundancy has been removed and the only mechanism supported to specify vertex data is through vertex arrays. Because only one type of array is available, the concept of a *provoking vertex* has been removed as well, which means that the array with index 0 no longer receives any special treatment. Immediate mode and fixed-function mechanisms have been removed.

Vertex Arrays and Primitive Types

In	Out	Optional
glVertexAttribPointer glEnableVertexAttribArray glDrawArrays glDrawElements	glVertexPointer glTexCoordPointer glColorPointer glNormalPointer glSecondaryColorPointer	OES_element_index_uint extension: Index Support: uint
Primitive types: Triangles, tri strips, tri fans, line, line strips, line loop, point sprites	glFogCoordPointer glEdgeFlagPointer glEnableClientState, glDisableClientState glArrayElement,	OES_vertex_half_float extension: Data type support: 16 Bit float
Index support: ubyte and ushort	glMultiDrawArrays, glDrawRangeElements	
Data types: byte, ubyte, short, ushort, float, fixed	Primitive types: Quads, quad strips, polygons and points	
	Rectangle support	
	Data types: int, uint	

The OpenGL ES 2.0 specification only supports user-defined vertex attributes. Fixed function support for vertex position, normals, colors, and texture coordinates has been removed since they can be defined using vertex attribute arrays.

Complex primitive types such as quads and polygons and direct rectangle draw commands have been removed since they can easily be emulated using triangles; point support has been replaced by the more advanced point sprite primitive type.

There is optional support for the unsigned int data type for indices, and for a 16-bit float data type that sees widespread use at the vertex attribute level.

Buffer Objects

In	Out	Optional
glBindBuffer glDeleteBuffers glGenBuffers glBufferData glBufferSubData		OES_mapbuffer extension: glMapBuffer glUnmapBuffer

To allow improved performance on systems with a nonunified memory architecture, BufferObject functionality allows vertex and index data to be stored in high-performance server-side memory. MapBuffer and UnmapBuffer support is optional because of possible performance issues relating to reading back from server memory.

Transformation and Clipping

In	Out	Optional
`glViewport`	All other fixed function matrix ops: `glMatrixMode`,	
	`glLoadMatrix`, `glPush/PopMatrix`, `glTranslate/glRotate/glScale`, `glTexGen`, `glFrustum/glOrtho`	
	User-defined clip planes	

Within OpenGL ES2.0 the complete fixed-function transformation pipeline has been replaced by the programmable vertex shader pipeline. Matrices can be uploaded as uniforms to the vertex shader, where specific code is executed to handle vertex transformations.

Viewport transformation happens after the programmable vertex transformation operations, and this fixed-function capability and related command remains.

User-defined clipping planes are used predominantly in engineering and scientific applications, which are not supported on embedded systems. If required, this functionality can be emulated using vertex and fragment shader programs.

Colors and Coloring

In	Out	Optional
`glFrontFace`	All fixed function materials and lights: `glMaterial`, `glLight`, `glLightModel`, `glColorMaterial`, `glShadeModel`	

The fixed-function lighting model is no longer supported in OpenGL ES 2.0; through appropriate vertex and/or pixel shaders, any desirable lighting model can be implemented.

Anti-Aliasing, Points, Lines, and Polygons

In	Out	Optional
Multisampling through EGL	Enable/Disable MULTSAMPLE	
`glLineWidth` `glPointSize`	Point and line smooth	
	`glPointParameters` (now done in the vertex shader)	
Culling `glPolygonOffset`		
	Line and polygon stippling	
	`GL_POLYGON_SMOOTH` `glPolygonMode` (no point or line mode)	

Multisampling is automatically enabled based on the properties of the target render surface, which can be defined through the `Attribute List` submitted to `eglChooseConfig`. Anti-aliased polygons are not supported, because of implementation complexity.

OpenGL ES 2.0 supports aliased point sprites only; traditional points are no longer supported.

Advanced line and polygon stippling can be implemented using pixel shader functionality and has thus been removed.

Culling support remains unchanged and is essential to eliminate unnecessary rasterization. Polygon offset functionality is critical to ensure that coplanar polygons are rendered correctly without the need for application side tricks.

Pixels and Bitmaps

In	Out	Optional
`glPixelStorei` For loading textures and reading from the screen Only supports `GL_PACK_ALIGNMENT` and `GL_UNPACK_ALIGNMENT`	Imaging subset (filters, histograms, minmax)	
	`glDrawPixels` `glCopyPixels` `glPixelZoom` `glBitmap` `glRasterPos`	
`glReadPixels` Color buffer only with a limited number of formats		

OpenGL ES 2.0 offers no support for directly drawing pixel rectangles, given that this functionality can easily be implemented through textured triangles.

`PixelStore` support is retained, but only to allow different pack alignments for `ReadPixels` and unpack alignments for `TexImage2D` to be selected.

`glReadPixels` only supports reading pixels from the color buffer. There is no support for accessing stencil or depth information, owing to implementation complexity and performance considerations. If access to scene depth information is required, this can be handled by writing the depth value to the color buffer from the pixel shader.

Textures

In	Out	Optional
Texture types: 2D, CubeMaps	Texture Types:	OES_texture_3D extension:
	1D, Depth textures, palettized textures	Volume textures
Most common formats: GL_RGB, GL_RGBA, GL_LUMINANCE, GL_ALPHA, GL_LUMINANCE_ALPHA	Texture parameters	glTexImage3D/ glTexSubImage3D glCopyTexSubImage3D
	No LOD control	
Platform-specific compressed texture entry points	No texture border: no clamp-to-border or clamp wrap modes	OES_texture_npot extension: Non–power-of-2 texture
glTexImage/glTexSubImage glCopyTexImage2D/ glCopyTexSubImage2D	Texture priorities: glPrioritizeTextures glAreTexturesResident	OES_texture_half_float, OES_texture_float extensions:
Texture parameters		FP16, FP32 texture formats with point sampling and nearest mipmapping only
All filtering modes	Dynamic texture state queries: glGetTexImage, glGetTexParameter	
Addressing modes: Clamp-to-edge, repeat, and mirror-repeat wrap modes		OES_texture_half_float_ linear, OES_texture_ float_linear extensions:
Non-powerof-2 limitations: No mipmapping support, only clamp to edge		FP16, FP32 texture formats with full texture filtering support

Texturing and high-quality texture filtering are critical features and are fully supported in OpenGL ES 2.0. Limitations are introduced for non–power-of-2 textures because of implementation complexity, but these limitations can be removed through an optional extension. 1D textures have been removed and can easily be emulated through

2D texture functionality. 3D textures, floating point textures, and other complex texture types have been made optional because of memory usage concerns for embedded platforms and implementation complexity.

Per-Fragment Operations

In	Out	Optional
Stencil test	Fixed-function alpha test	Occlusion queries
Scissor test	Texture environment:	
Depth test	No fixed-function texture blending	
Sample coverage		
Alpha-blending through	Color sum	
	Fog	
glBlendFuncSeparate and glBlendEquationSeparate, which only support:	Some alpha blend modes (MIN, MAX, LOGIC_OP)	
Add, Subtract, ReverseSubtract	glDrawBuffer and glDrawBuffers	
Dithering	Multiple render targets	
	Accumulation buffer	

OpenGL ES 2.0 implementations must support a depth buffer (at least 16 bits) and a stencil buffer (at least 8 bits) in addition to scissor support. Fixed-function alpha-test and texture-environment functionality has been removed since these operations are now executed in the fragment shader. Blending is supported through glBlendFuncSeparate and glBlendEquationSeparate with the limitation that min and max modes are not supported; support for logical ops has also been removed. Owing to implementation complexity and memory footprint, support for multiple render targets and an accumulation buffer has been removed.

Frame Buffer Objects

In line with the OpenGL ES 2.0 design philosophy, the Khronos Group is looking for the most efficient way to implement texture renders with minimal overhead and redundancy. The currently proposed mechanism is a simplified version of the Desktop OpenGL EXT_framebuffer_object extension, which is part of the core OpenGL ES 2.0 functionality. Frame buffer objects (FBOs) introduce a mechanism that removes the need for multiple render contexts and expensive memory copy operations that plague other existing render-to-texture methods.

The table below provides an overview of included, excluded, and option functionality relative to the OpenGL 2.0 EXT extension:

In	Out	Optional
IsRenderbuffer, BindRenderBuffer, DeleteRenderbuffers, GenRenderbuffers, RenderbufferStorage, GetRenderbufferParameteriv,	DrawBuffer, ReadBuffer	OES_texture_3D extension: FramebufferTexture3D
IsFramebuffer, BindFramebuffer DeleteFramebuffers,		OES_FBO_render_mipmap extension:
GenFramebuffers,		Allows rendering to any mip-level of a texture.
CheckFramebufferStatus,		OES_rgb8_rgba8, OES_depth24, OES_depth32, OES_stencil1, OES_stencil4, OES_stencil8 extensions:
FramebufferTexture2D,		
FramebufferRenderBuffer, GetFramebufferAttachementParameteriv, GenerateMipmap		Optional internal formats: RGBA8, RGB8, DEPTH_ COMPONENT_{24/32}, STENCIL_INDEX{1/4/8}
Only allows rendering to the base level of a texture		
Supported internal formats: RGB565, RGBA4, RGB5_A1, DEPTH_COMPONENT_16		

Special Operations

In	Out	Optional
glFlush glFinish	Evaluators Selection Feedback Display lists	

Evaluators are rarely used and because of their fixed-function nature do not fit with the programmable model used in OpenGL ES 2.0. Future versions of this API will likely introduce geometry shader functionality to give mobile devices access to the memory footprint and bandwidth advantages offered by procedural geometry. Display lists offer additional performance but have been removed because they are so complex to implement. Selection and feedback mechanisms are rarely used.

OpenGL ES 2.0 Development

Software Development Resources

Khronos Web Site and Developer Events

As the driving force behind the OpenGL ES 2.0 API, the Khronos Group maintains a Web site with the latest OpenGL ES 2.0 specification documents and header files. The Khronos Group also promotes their open standards directly to software developers across the world through their Khronos Developer University—an annual series of educational events often organized at major developer events. More details can be found online at *www.khronos.org*.

PowerVR PC Emulation SDK

The Imagination Technologies PowerVR MBX and SGX families of IP graphics cores have seen widespread acceptance within the market and are supported through an extensive set of SDKs and tools.

Imagination Technologies has already ramped-up developer support for OpenGL ES 2.0 by making a PC-emulation SDK available, which allows developers to create compelling content on any PC with an OpenGL 2.0-compliant graphics card. Through this PC emulation and a shell abstraction framework, it is possible to develop content today and port it quickly to final consumer products when they become available in the market within the next 6 to 12 months.

The OpenGL ES 1.x PC emulation and platform SDKs, in addition to the OpenGL ES 2.0 PC emulation SDK, can be downloaded free at *www.powervrinsider.com*.

Vincent3D Rendering Library

The Vincent project has been working on open source implementations of the OpenGL ES API specifications since 2003. Development of an implementation of the OpenGL ES 2.0 API specification is currently underway, and precompiled versions of the library will be available for download from the project Web site starting September 2006. This distribution will contain a portable and compact runtime implementation written using the C programming language, alongside an offline shader compiler that uses a C-language backend for the generation of optimized shader binaries.

The Vincent project is hosted on Sourceforge.net, and the project home page is located at *http://ogles2.sf.net*.

Hardware

Since the introduction of the OpenGL ES 2.0 standard in August 2005, various companies have announced their support for this new standard that will enable programmable shader graphics on handheld devices.

ATI

ATI's G40 is a fully programmable 2D, 3D, and vector graphics processor with the OpenGL ES 2.0 feature set packed into a small design size with efficient memory bandwidth usage. Programmable vertex and pixel shaders provide for advanced photo-realistic rendering effects and unprecedented visual clarity. The G40 enables a fully visual mobile phone platform. The programmable pixel processor supports pixel shaders, per-pixel executed programs that allow content developers to generate realistic-looking metals, woods, water, lighting effects, and reflections.

For more information or to get ATI's handheld SDK, contact *devrel@ati.com*.

Imagination Technologies

PowerVR SGX, the new generation PowerVR GPU IP core family, is part of the Imagination's PowerVR Series5 scalable and fully programmable shader graphics/video architecture. With state-of-the-art support for 2D and 3D graphics, PowerVR SGX has an industry-leading feature set that exceeds OpenGL 2.0 Shader and Microsoft Vertex and Pixel Shader Model 3 requirements, while maintaining backward compatibility with PowerVR MBX content. The PowerVR SGX family also accelerates vector graphics content processing, including providing class-leading OpenVG performance. The PowerVR SGX family of video/image decode- and encode-processing support covers a broad range of standards such as H.264, MPEG-4/2, VC-1 (WMV9), JPEG, and others. PowerVR SGX family members target mobile, automotive, consumer, and PC markets. PowerVR SGX is based on Imagination's patented tile-based rendering and multithreading technologies.

More information can be found on the Imagination Technologies Web site at *www.imgtec.com*.

Evolution of the Standard and Extensions

The Khronos Group is eager to improve and extend their open standards and welcome developer feedback. This section introduces some extensions that are currently being discussed for OpenGL ES 2.0 and are candidates for inclusion as core functionality in the future.

The Khronos OpenGL ES Working Group welcomes contributions and participation from interested parties. Joining details are available online at *www.khronos.org*.

Occlusion Queries

Owing to the limited available bandwidth and processing power on mobile devices, it is essential to minimize the costly processing of invisible geometry and pixels. Occlusion queries are one of the key mechanisms that allow the reduction of this type of needless processing.

The Khronos group is currently considering an occlusion query extension with three modes of operation. All three modes determine if an object, for example, a bounding box, is visible, and based on this visibility test there are three possible mechanisms to optionally draw further geometry:

Mode 1: Query visibility results are returned to the application for the current frame to allow the application to determine what draw calls to make. This method is highly versatile but is also very sensitive to the latency of the graphics pipeline. This mode should only be used if neither of the other modes can be used.

Mode 2: Query visibility results are returned to the application for use in subsequent frames. This allows the application to determine what draw calls to make in future frames, based on the visibility in the current frame. This mode hides the latency of the graphics pipeline and is thus much more hardware friendly.

Mode 3: The visibility query results are internally used to conditionally draw submitted geometry. This mechanism allows the graphics hardware itself to determine what geometry to process. This mechanism can be implemented to maximize hardware performance with little impact by any pipeline stalls, while minimizing the impact on the CPU at the same time.

The proposed mechanisms are in line with the latest functionality offered in Microsoft DirectX 10.

Uniform Shaders

OpenGL ES 2.0 has removed all legacy fixed-function capabilities including matrix processing, meaning that the complexity of calculating uniform values has been completely moved into the application. Creating an efficient implementation of mathematically complex operations can be difficult on platforms with limited CPU performance (e.g., ~200 MHz) and capabilities (e.g., no floating point). One proposed solution for this problem is the introduction of a new type of shader that would allow the shader hardware to be used as a sort of mathematical coprocessor. These *uniform shaders* would allow specific code to calculate uniforms to be uploaded and executed on the graphics core and the results returned to the application.

Object Shaders

Interest in higher-order surfaces, programmable tessellation, and procedural geometry is high in the mobile market because of the bandwidth and storage reduction introduced by these mechanisms. The Khronos Group is looking into mechanisms to allow this functionality, which is a continuation of the full-programmability philosophy of OpenGL ES 2.0, to be exposed by the API.

Conclusion

This article provided an overview of the OpenGL ES 2.0 API, offering insight into the API design philosophy, an overview of the pipeline architecture, and discussions of topics including texture compression, shader compilation, and qualifiers. A table-based overview of the differences in the desktop OpenGL 2.0 API was provided to allow for a rapid transition from a desktop to a mobile target platform. The article wrapped up with an overview of software development resources, announced hardware support, and future evolution of the standard.

Acknowledgments

The author thanks his colleagues at Imagination Technologies and the members of the Khronos OpenGL ES Group who took the time to provide valuable input for this article, in particular, Daniel Ginsburg and Robert Simpson from ATI, Kari Pulli from Nokia, Tom Olson from Texas Instruments, and Hans-Martin Will from the Vincent Project.

References

[Kari05] Pulli, Kari, Tomi Aarnio, Kimmo Roimela, and Jani Vaarala. "Designing Graphics Programming Interfaces for Mobile Devices." *IEEE Computer Graphics and Applications*, 8(25), (Nov.-Dec. 2005).

[Munshi06] Munshi, Aaftab, Editor. "OpenGL® ES Common Profile Specification 2.0." Available online from the Khronos Group at *www.khronos.org*.

[Simpson06] Simpson, Robert, Editor. "The OpenGL® ES Shading Language." Specification available online from the Khronos Group at *www.khronos.org*.

7.2

Developing a 3D Engine for OpenGL ES v2.0 and OpenGL v2.0

Dan Ginsburg, Imagination Technologies

Introduction

The OpenGL ES v2.0 specification has significantly streamlined the graphics API relative to desktop OpenGL v2.0. Despite the many differences between the APIs, it is still possible to write a 3D engine with largely shared rendering code between OpenGL v2.0 and OpenGL ES v2.0. In the 3D Application Research Group at ATI, we developed a demo engine called Sushi v3.0, which targets OpenGL, OpenGL ES, D3D9, and D3D10. The OpenGL and OpenGL ES rendering layers were written such that the majority of code could be shared between both APIs on multiple platforms. The key to allowing this code sharing was developing a purely shader-based engine.

The purpose of this article is to detail the use of generic vertex attribute arrays, user attributes/varyings, vertex buffer objects, and GLSL shaders to maximize the shared code between the two APIs. The article can also serve as a guide to how to port an existing OpenGL v2.0 engine to OpenGL ES v2.0. By designing an engine without the use of fixed-function and using the highest-performance API paths, much of the code can be shared between both APIs without sacrificing performance on either. This article also deals with the parts of the API that need to be handled differently on OpenGL ES v2.0 such as binary shader compilation, ES GLSL language constructs, and half-float vertex data.

Vertex Attributes and Varyings

To support both OpenGL and OpenGL ES, geometry must be specified using _generic vertex attribute arrays_. In OpenGL ES there is no notion of the semantic binding of vertex attribute data to normal, color, or texture coordinates in the API. Rather, the application is responsible for creating its own per-vertex attributes that can be named arbitrarily and that have no semantic binding. The GLSL shaders should therefore contain only generic vertex attribute names in order to work in both APIs.

For example, below is a simple vertex shader that passes through the position and a texture coordinate that might have been written in desktop OpenGL using built-in vertex attributes.

```
void main()
{
  gl_Position = gl_Vertex;
  gl_TexCoord[0].xy = gl_MultiTexCoord0.xy;
}
```

For this shader to work, the application would have to send vertex data using one of the fixed-function vertex attribute functions. For example, it could use `glVertexPointer` and `glTexCoordPointer` to specify the incoming vertex position and texture coordinate.

To make this shader function on both APIs, it would have to be changed to use generic vertex attributes and user varyings. The GLSL code would change to:

```
// User-defined attribute: vertex position
attribute vec4 vVertex;

// User-defined attribute: texture coordinate
attribute vec2 vInTexCoord0;

// User-defined varying to pass texture coordinate to fragment
    shader
varying vec2 vOutTexCoord0;

void main()
{
  gl_Position = vVertex;
  vOutTexCoord0.xy = vInTexCoord0.xy;
}
```

Several steps need to happen to make this shader work in both APIs. First, the application can bind each of the attributes to a location using

```
void glBindAttribLocation (GLuint program, GLuint index,
const char *name)
```

This function allows the application to specify which generic attribute location to use for each of the attributes. For example, in the case of this vertex shader, the application could call

```
glBindAttribLocation ( progId, 0, "vVertex" )
glBindAttribLocation ( progId, 1, "vInTexCoord0" )
```

Both OpenGL and OpenGL ES will choose default attribute locations for each of the attributes if none is explicitly bound prior to link. The attribute locations chosen by the GL can be queried after linking the program object by using the `glGetAttribLocation` query. Neither API requires calls to `glBindAttribLocation`, except for one special rule in desktop OpenGL. That is, in desktop OpenGL, there is a special meaning to the vertex attribute bound to 0. The attribute bound to location 0 is known as the *provoking vertex,* which is necessary for supporting immediate mode rendering with generic vertex attributes. In some implementations the GL will not automatically choose to assign any of the generic vertex attributes to 0. If this happens, drawing may be undefined. To make an engine work safely between desktop OpenGL and OpenGL ES, it is important to have at least one of the attributes bound explicitly to location 0.

Once the attributes are bound to locations, the vertex data can be specified using the generic vertex attribute array functions `glEnableVertexAttribArray` and `glVertexAttribPointer`.

User-Defined Uniforms

One of the largest tasks for an ES-based 3D engine is the management of global uniform data. In OpenGL the GLSL allows binding to any of the fixed-function states such as the matrix and lighting states. As OpenGL ES removed fixed-function processing, this is no longer possible.

As an example, consider a simple desktop GLSL shader that transforms a position by the model-view projection (MVP) matrix and a texture coordinate by the texture matrix:

```
void main()
{
  gl_Position = gl_ModelViewProjectionMatrix * gl_Vertex;
  gl_TexCoord[0].xy = vec2 (gl_TextureMatrix[0] *
  gl_MultiTexCoord0);
}
```

In order to make this shader work in OpenGL ES, the application needs to manage the equivalent of the MVP matrix and texture matrix and place it in the uniform store. In addition, the shader needs to use a user-named varying for the texture coordinate because the built-in varyings such as `gl_TexCoord` no longer exist.

```
// User-defined uniform: model-view projection matrix
uniform mat4 mMVP;

// User-defined uniform: texture matrix
uniform mat4 mTexMatrix;

// User-defined attribute: vertex position
attribute vec3 vVertex;

// User-defined attribute: texture coordinate
attribute vec4 vInTexCoord0;

// User-defined varying to pass texture coordinate to fragment
  shader
varying vec2 vOutTexCoord0;
```

```
void main()
{
  gl_Position = mMVP * vVertex;
  vOutTexCoord0.xy = vec2 (mTexMatrix * vInTexCoord0);
}
```

This example demonstrates one of the primary aspects of change for a 3D engine using OpenGL ES. The shaders must be written to use no fixed-function state, which means the 3D engine must manage the binding of uniform data. In ATI's Sushi v3.0 demo engine, all shaders are contained inside an effect file that has the ability to bind arbitrarily named uniforms to engine data. The engine then manages all of the necessary matrices, light state, and parameters so that the shader can have access to the uniform data.

As an example, consider a GLSL vertex shader that needs the MVP matrix and a camera position. In the header of the Sushi effect file, there would be variable declarations that have annotations that bind the variables to the necessary engine state:

```
// Declarations for binding uniform variables to engine state
Matrix mMVP <AppUpdate = ViewProjMatrix>
Vector vCamPos <AppUpdate = CameraPosition>
```

The engine has a variety of predefined "AppUpdate" variables that bind to the engine-managed state. The engine replaces the role of fixed-function GL, where it stores all transform matrices, light information, and other data needed by the shaders. In addition, the system is designed to be flexible in that updated uniform variables can also be driven by a Lua script. The idea behind the design is to give the demo creator the ability to easily pass data into uniform store either from the main engine code or a script.

Precision Qualifiers

One of the new features added to OpenGL ES v2.0 is the ability to specify precision qualifiers on variables. As precision qualifiers do not currently exist in desktop OpenGL, this could pose some problems in using the same shaders between both APIs. The fragment shader must have a default float precision declared in OpenGL ES. The vertex shader has a default float precision of highp if none is specified, but in the fragment shader the user must explicitly specify it. To use the same shaders on OpenGL ES and OpenGL, some creative use of the preprocessor can take care of the problem.

In the fragment shader begin with the following block of code:

```
#ifdef GL_ES
  precision highp float;
#else
  #define highp
  #define mediump
  #define lowp
#endif
```

The default precision statement will only be compiled by OpenGL ES because it is enclosed in the `#ifdef GL_ES`. Any GLSL code that is specific to ES should be enclosed inside of a `GL_ES` define, as this is guaranteed to be defined by the preprocessor in the ES GLSL specification. With the precision qualifiers defined away in the desktop GLSL version, any precision qualifiers specified in the shader will be removed. This will allow the shader to successfully compile on both APIs without having to maintain two copies.

In general, unless you need to use precision qualifiers in your shaders, simply having the default precision specified in the fragment shader inside a `GL_ES` define will be sufficient to allow the shaders to compile on both APIs. Precision qualifiers are really not required in OpenGL ES shaders; they are only useful on hardware platforms that support reduced precision of calculations in the shader.

Discard

In desktop OpenGL it was possible to reject a fragment, either by using `alpha test` or by using the `discard` keyword in GLSL. This feature is typically used for rendering surfaces that have transparency. In OpenGL ES, `alpha test` has been removed from the render state, and `discard` is the only method that can be used to perform the equivalent functionality. The easiest way to make the code shared between OpenGL and OpenGL ES is simply to use `discard` where the `alpha test` render state was used.

User Clip Planes

Another fixed-function feature that is not present in OpenGL ES is user clip planes. This functionality was useful in OpenGL for clipping primitives against arbitrary planes. Fortunately, this feature can still be emulated in OpenGL ES. One way to do this is to store the plane equation (Nx, Ny, Nz, D) in a uniform and compute a distance to the plane in the vertex shader, as below:

```
attribute vec4 vVertex;

// Stores the (x, y, z, D) equation for the plane
uniform vec4 vClipPlane;
uniform mat4 mMVP;

// Distance from vertex to plane
varying float fPlaneDist;

void main(void)
{

  // Compute the distance to the clip plane
  fPlaneDist = dot ( gl_Vertex.xyz, vClipPlane.xyz ) +
  vClipPlane.w;
  gl_Position = mMVP * vVertex;
}
```

The `fPlaneDist` varying will hold the distance to the clip plane specified in `vClipPlane`. The fragment shader can then simply evaluate the value of the `fPlaneDist` and discard the fragment if it is behind the plane:

```
// Distance from vertex to plane
varying float fPlaneDist;

void main(void)
{
  // Discard the fragment if it is behind the clip plane
  if ( fPlaneDist < 0.0 )
    discard;

  gl_FragColor = vec4( 1.0, 1.0, 1.0, 1.0 )
}
```

Binary Shader Compilation

In desktop OpenGL shaders are specified to the API via a string using the `glShader-Source` function. This method of loading shaders means that the driver must contain a compiler capable of translating a GLSL shader into machine instructions. Because of the limited memory footprint and performance constraints of embedded platforms, the Khronos Group decided to make online compilation optional. As a result, OpenGL ES v2.0 introduced the notion of loading binary shaders using the `glShaderBinary` function. The OpenGL ES v2.0 specification mandates that an implementation must provide *either* string or binary shader loading (or both).

Each OpenGL ES v2.0 implementer that supports binary shader compilation will provide an offline tool to generate shader binaries. It is important to note that the binary shaders generated for one OpenGL ES v2.0 product are not guaranteed to work on another. The binary shaders are an opaque binary format, and OpenGL ES v2.0 vendors are likely to store hardware-specific shaders in the binary data. Even across OpenGL ES v2.0 products from the same hardware vendor, the binary shaders may not be compatible.

From an engine design point of view, this poses two challenges. First, the engine will need a preprocessing phase that compiles text shaders into binary shaders offline. The other issue is that because the binary shader formats will differ between vendors, the engine will need a way to store hardware-specific binary shader variants. At the time of this writing, the vendor-specific offline compile tools are not yet available. However, ATI plans to release its tools both in the form of a command-line compiler and DLL that should be easy to integrate into a tool chain. Because of the generally limited storage of handheld devices, it is advisable to package hardware-specific binary shaders with each product. If it is not feasible to create device-specific packaging, then providing a package of all shader binaries for all supported devices is another possibility. The engine could choose which to load at runtime by device identification.

The approach that Sushi v3.0 takes to this problem is to allow the loading of shaders either via string or shader binary, depending on what the OpenGL ES implementation supports. In the OpenGL version, shaders are always loaded directly in their text form. Special code for the OpenGL ES variant is capable of loading a shader binary. The offline preprocessing tool selects a binary shader compiler and uses it to generate a binary that can then be loaded at runtime. Sushi uses different packages of binary shaders for the different devices it needs to support.

Compressed Texture Formats

To minimize memory usage and maximize performance on handheld platforms it is important to use compressed texture formats. The OpenGL ES v2.0 specification introduces a new optional extension, OES_compressed_ ETC1_RGB8_texture, for supporting Ericsson texture compression (ETC). Additionally, several OpenGL ES vendors support their own proprietary texture compression formats. For example, some of ATI's products support the ATITC RGB and RGBA color compression formats as well as the 3DC normal compression format.

An engine must be designed in a flexible enough manner to support multiple texture compression formats for different hardware platforms. In ATI's Sushi v3.0 demo engine, the texture formats are chosen inside the effect file. The preprocessor reads this effect file header and compresses images using the chosen texture compression format. To support a variety of platforms, the preprocessor uses a configuration file that can map generic compressed formats to vendor-specific formats. This allows the same effect file to be used on multiple platforms and APIs, although it does require different preprocessed data for each device. An example declaration for a texture is given below.

```
// Texture declaration in Sushi Effect file
Texture2D tBase < format = DXT5 >
```

This declaration inside a Sushi effect file tells the preprocessor that the image data should be stored in DXT5 compressed format. However, the preprocessor is also invoked with a configuration file that can map DXT5 to another format such as ATITC_RGBA. As such, the preprocessor can automatically generate different compressed texture binaries to work on OpenGL and OpenGL ES. This system is highly flexible and eases the burden of having to maintain several effect files for each platform. Instead, the preprocessor configuration file allows the texture format conversion to happen automatically.

Vertex Buffer Objects

To minimize the amount of bus traffic for static vertex data, it is critical to use vertex buffer objects for vertex data. Vertex buffer objects are supported in OpenGL ES, with some minor differences. The glMapBuffer and glUnmapbuffer functions for getting a system memory pointer back to a vertex buffer object are optional. To find out if an

OpenGL ES implementation supports this feature, query for the extension string OES_map_buffer.

If your engine requires dynamic vertex data, and the underlying OpenGL ES implementation does not support mapping vertex data, then traditional system memory arrays can be used instead. The ability of the ES implementation to map buffers can be hidden from the main engine code by keeping a system memory copy of the vertex data. At map time simply return a pointer to the system memory copy to the engine, and at unmap time reload it using the vertex attribute array calls. This piece of the engine code could require different implementations for OpenGL and OpenGL ES in order to not sacrifice any performance in the OpenGL version.

Vertex Data Types

Because of the bandwidth and memory limitations of many handheld platforms, it is advisable to use small vertex data where possible. In OpenGL ES v2.0 two new optional extensions OES_vertex_half_float and OES_data_type_10_10_10_2 were added that allow for reduced vertex data sizes. OES_vertex_half_float introduces half-float vertex data stored in 16 bits. OES_data_type_10_10_10_2 allows for 3-tuples of vertex data to be specified with 10-bits per component. Both of these types can be accessed directly in the shader as floats. These extensions are not directly supported in core desktop OpenGL v2.0, so your engine will have to convert the data from half-float or 10.10.10.2 to float to run on both platforms. In Sushi v3.0 this step is done during the preprocessing phase so that there are different binary vertex data between the OpenGL and OpenGL ES versions. However, an engine could also easily convert between vertex data formats at startup time. The vertex shaders themselves still refer to the data as float, so no changes are necessary to the shader code.

Frame Buffer Objects

The OES_framebuffer_object extension has been integrated into the core specification in OpenGL ES v2.0 so that all implementations must support it. The specification is largely the same as the EXT_framebuffer_object extension on the desktop. The OES_framebuffer_object extension allows for efficient off-screen render-to-texture. The ES version of the spec does add some limitations such as limiting rendering to the base mipmap level of a 2D texture. However, it is still possible to generate mipmaps by using the glGenerateMipmapOES function. Depending on the needs of your 3D engine, most of the FBO code can still be shared. The OpenGL ES spec adds some new internal formats for render-buffer storage that will need to be in ES-specific code.

EGL

One part of code that will have to be different between OpenGL and OpenGL ES is the creation of rendering surfaces and contexts. This is no different than developing an application for desktop OpenGL on Linux and Windows, where the windowing code needs to use GLX and WGL respectively. An engine should be designed to abstract the windowing interface such that an implementation can be written for EGL, WGL, or another window abstraction layer.

Covering the EGL specification in detail is outside the scope of this article. For full details on EGL consult the EGL 1.2 specification available on *www.khronos.org/egl*.

Conclusions

With careful use of the OpenGL API, it is possible to write a 3D engine with mostly shared code between OpenGL 2.0 and OpenGL ES 2.0. In addition, the techniques presented here represent solutions to a large set of the issues that an OpenGL developer will face in porting an OpenGL 2.0 application to OpenGL ES 2.0. The common set of functionality between the two APIs represents a very powerful feature set that enables most of the important rendering techniques a 3D game will need.

7.3

OpenGL ES 2.0 Performance Recommendations for Mobile Devices

Kristof Beets, Imagination Technologies

Introduction

Performance recommendations for the development of 3D applications offer developers a valuable heads-up from graphics hardware vendors that can save frustrating hours trying to figure out why an application runs at only a single-digit frame rate. This article presents a generic overview of performance recommendations for the OpenGL ES 2.0 API for mobile devices.

Mobile Device Limitations

Compared to current PC and console platforms, the resources and capabilities of mobile devices are quite limited. Mobile processors run at low clock speeds, have small cache sizes, and might even be missing native floating-point support. The amount of memory available is limited, and a large chunk will be reserved for the operating system (OS) and various drivers. The available bandwidth is limited by a narrow bus and low clock speed, and in most cases mobile devices have a unified memory architecture. This means that all devices are sharing the same single memory resource, resulting in a higher number of page breaks and page break costs. Data storage is also limited, and data distribution is often limited by cost and carrier restrictions.

Within all these limitations and restrictions, the OpenGL ES 2.0 API introduces graphics capabilities into the mobile space that, in terms of functionality, are on par with the latest PC and console platforms. Despite the limitations, it is not impossible to create stunning, eye-popping, shader-based high-performance 3D graphics. The limitations just mean that extra care and consideration are required from the application developer to ensure high performance is achieved on the target mobile platform.

Identifying the Bottleneck

A mobile device is a complex platform with many parallel blocks, all of which could be the dominant limiting factor within the system. Key bottlenecks within the system are related to running a 3D application include the CPU, memory bandwidth, and the 3D graphics core. Each of these bottlenecks is complex in itself, and multiple subelements can contribute to their load. The CPU is responsible for the overall system, which means it is responsible not only for executing the 3D application, but also for the overall correct operation of the mobile device, which includes spending cycles on the OS, background tasks, and various driver stacks. Given that mobile devices generally have a unified memory architecture, a bandwidth bottleneck is extremely difficult to analyze, given that all the elements, including applications (CPU) and dedicated hardware blocks (GPU, DSP, video core, etc.), within the mobile device are likely to use some fraction of the available bandwidth at any time. The graphics core in itself is also complex, with many possible bottlenecks within its graphics pipeline including the vertex shader, triangle setup, fragment shader, texture filtering, and back-end.

The only way to identify the bottleneck is to decrease the workload of each element within the mobile device and check the resulting impact on performance. If the performance improves greatly when reducing the workload of a specific element, then this block is the bottleneck. The key complexity within this analysis mechanism is the difficulty in being able to separate out each block, since the analysis result depends on not changing the workload of the other blocks.

Application Level Test

An overview of the process of a 3D pipeline bottleneck identification procedure is shown in Figure 7.3.1.

The functionality to support this procedure can be integrated into a 3D application engine during the design phase through the inclusion of some extra OpenGL commands, debug shaders, and debug textures.

A bottleneck may change when rendering a frame that contains multiple primitives. For example, if an application first renders a group of fixed color lines and then a group of shaded triangles, we expect the bottleneck to change. Therefore, the bottleneck identification process may reveal more than one bottleneck.

Dedicated Tools

With the release of OpenGL ES 2.0–compliant hardware, dedicated performance analysis tools, similar to those currently being offered in the desktop space (NVIDIA NVTune, Microsoft PIX, Graphic Remedy's gDEBugger, etc.), will likely be introduced. These tools make bottleneck identification easier by implementing analysis directly at the graphics driver or API level. Additionally, these tools provide further performance-related information based on dedicated internal hardware and driver performance counters.

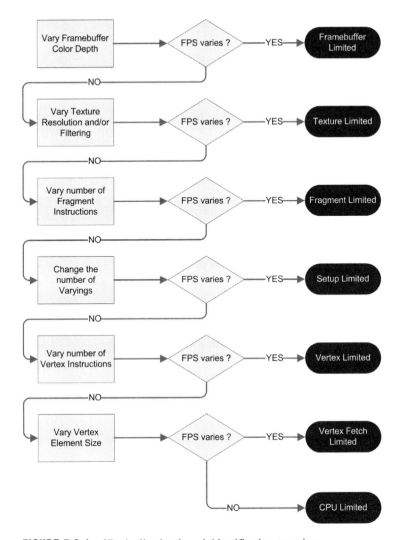

FIGURE 7.3.1 3D pipeline bottleneck identification overview.

Imagination Technologies intends to deliver full performance-analysis tools for their PowerVR SGX family of graphics IP cores, supporting both on-device and remote analysis functionality. NVIDIA has already demonstrated a remote performance analysis tool for OpenGL ES 1.x and is likely to extend the same functionality to future OpenGL ES 2.0–capable products. Other vendors are expected to follow in their footsteps in addition to the support they offer through third-party tools such as gDEBugger from Graphic Remedy.

Performance Recommendations

CPU

Within a mobile device the CPU is responsible for a variety of tasks ranging from running the OS, application, and various device critical threads, in addition to a whole device driver stack. The mobile GPU, on the other hand, is fully dedicated to executing the one task it is designed for: generating graphics. The wide range of tasks running on the CPU makes it the most likely bottleneck when running 3D applications.

Specific performance recommendations for mobile CPUs falls outside the scope of this article, but the CPU is one of the key factors developers should keep in mind when developing their 3D engine architecture. Fully optimized algorithms with minimal bandwidth usage are critical for high performance. Throughout this article further reference will be made to reducing the load of the CPU, specifically from the API side.

Geometry Submissions

Geometry submissions play a critical role in the performance levels that can be achieved on a device. Not only do they involve large amounts of data traffic, but the submission order can also influence the amount of processing required at both the vertex and fragment levels.

Vertex Size and Attribute Compacting

On mobile devices bandwidth is a limited and shared resource, so minimizing the amount of data traffic is essential. This can be achieved in OpenGL ES 2.0 through the use of smaller data types such as *bytes*, *shorts* or the optional *half-float* type rather than the full 32-bit *fixed* and *float* data types.

Vertex attributes can contain between one and four elements. It is important to compact attributes as much as possible and where possible to try to minimize the number of attributes by grouping smaller data elements together into a single attribute. For example, two sets of 2D texture coordinates can be compacted together into a single Vec4 attribute.

Attribute Interleaving

The vertex shader processes vertices one by one and requires all data elements, such as position, normal, texture coordinates, and so on, to be fetched from memory. To maximize preshader cache usage and minimize page breaks, it is important to keep all the attributes of a single vertex together in memory. The OpenGL ES 2.0 `glVertex-AttribPointer` functionality should be used to interleave the attribute data, using a suitable vertex stride rather than spreading the various attribute arrays out in memory.

Optimized Geometry Data Order

Use of a post-vertex shader cache avoids having to recalculate recently processed vertex elements, saving valuable vertex shader clock cycles and vertex fetch bandwidth.

For this caching mechanism to operate effectively, indexed vertex data needs to be used, since the index is used to recognize data already in the cache.

The effectiveness of the postvertex shader cache depends greatly on the vertex ordering and the *optimal* order depends on the actual size and algorithms of the cache implementation itself. For this reason, hardware vendors offer special geometry export tools and/or geometry processing libraries that will optimize generic geometry data into an order optimized for their specific mobile graphics processor. It is important to use these tools within your artwork tool chain to create geometry packages optimized for different devices and to ensure the best possible geometry throughput and performance.

Vertex Buffer Objects

Vertex buffer objects provide a mechanism to store vertex array data in high-performance server memory. This can either be in the form of storage in actual dedicated video memory (rare on a mobile device) or in the form of storage in an optimized ready-for-hardware-usage format in system memory. In either case the use of vertex buffer objects is recommended to reduce driver overhead and thus CPU load.

The creation of vertex buffer objects should always be done up-front and not mid-action to avoid sudden drops in performance caused by the optimization work and/or memory copy operations. Indication of the correct BUFFER_USAGE case (STATIC or DYNAMIC) is also essential. For dynamic vertex array data the optional MapBuffer functionality should be used. If it is not available, regular client memory vertex arrays might be faster for dynamic data.

Submission Order and Batching

All OpenGL ES 2.0 API calls introduce an amount of CPU overhead where standard API calls are translated into registry settings and data formats suitable for use by the graphics hardware. To minimize the CPU load, it is important to minimize the number of API calls, especially the number of draw calls and shader changes. This effect is strengthened by the fact that hardware handles large batches of data much more efficiently than lots of small batches. Hence, similar to the desktop market, it is critical to ensure that the batch size of draw calls is sufficiently large. In overly simplified terms, it is much better to have one draw call that draws 100 triangles than to have 100 draw calls each drawing a single triangle.

A general recommendation for high-level batching is to process all opaque objects first, sorted by shaders, and then process all transparent (alpha-blending and alpha-testing) objects.

Some mobile graphics processors have early-Z functionality that allows them to improve their hidden surface removal (HSR) efficiency. This early-HSR functionality generally depends on the render order (except for tile-based deferred renderers) and gains the most benefit from rendering scene geometry from front-to-back. Front-to-back geometry sorting should be the very last optimization considered as part of batching since it is generally incompatible with other submission-order recommendations and can massively increase the number of draw calls and shader changes. An up-front depth pass to maximize HSR efficiency might be an option in the PC space, but is unlikely to be beneficial in the mobile space because of the duplication of vertex processing and vertex fetch bandwidth.

Important techniques to maximize the batch size and to minimize API overhead include the use of texture pages (Atlas) to minimize the number of texture changes and the usage of über shaders to minimize the number of shader changes.

Culling and Occlusion Queries

Minimizing the data submitted to the graphics hardware for processing is essential, and high-level, intelligent culling algorithms should be used as much as possible. While in the PC space, because of massive CPU and GPU power, it might be possible to submit the whole-world geometry to the GPU. This will likely slow a mobile GPU to a crawl. Hence, potentially visible set and portal techniques should be used where possible.

Occlusion query–based mechanisms, if supported by the mobile GPU, should be considered to further reduce the amount of geometry submitted. When using occlusion queries, it is important to avoid using the result of the query within the same frame, since this can introduce CPU stalls while the GPU flushes its pipeline, thus destroying GPU-CPU parallelism. Where possible, allow the hardware itself to conditionally continue with drawing submitted geometry.

Level of Detail (LOD)

Most mobile devices have a QVGA or VGA LCD display size, and as a result LOD mechanisms are highly recommended because there is no point in investing thousands of triangles into an object that only covers tens of pixels on the screen.

Shaders

Generic shader program recommendations are difficult to give because of the difference in GPU architecture and instruction sets. Refer to the specific recommendations for each platform and use the specific shader compilation and analysis tools provided by the various vendors. A limited number of generic recommendations follow.

Shader Loading

OpenGL ES 2.0 offers two mechanisms to load shader programs: first, on-device compilation from shader source and, second, offline compilation and binary loading on-device. Whenever possible, the binary mechanism should be used since the offline compiler, running on a PC-based platform with considerably more memory and processing power, is likely to offer substantially better-optimized code. Additionally, the binary loading mechanism will also be considerably faster, reducing the loading and waiting times for users.

Über Shaders

Shader changes are complex and can incur a considerable amount of overhead, and this should be taken into account when determining the batching concepts of the 3D engine. One mechanism to deal with implementations suffering from this type of over-head would be to minimize the number of shader changes through the use of über shaders. Über shaders are shaders with multiple paths, each of which can be enabled/ disabled through the use of uniforms (constants). This mechanism allows the same shader to be used for multiple objects, and the shader behavior is influenced by simply uploading a small number of constants to the hardware.

Performance characteristics in this area are likely to be different among hardware implementations, so initial benchmarking is recommended before deploying this mechanism.

Dependent Texture Reads and Lookup Tables

Mobile graphics processors have a limited texture cache size and generally use a unified memory interface (no dedicated video memory), meaning that texture cache misses are more likely to occur and have a higher latency (number of clock cycles to get requested data back from system memory). While mobile graphics processors contain advanced mechanisms to hide this latency, it is important to understand that this latency is likely to limit performance in the case of dependent texture reads, which tend to be unpre-dictable and nonlinear. Dependent texture reads are essential for many of the most visually impressive effects, and as a result, their use is not discouraged, but the devel-oper should be aware of the possible performance implications of excessive use.

The use of texture-based lookup tables to replace complex mathematical opera-tions should be carefully investigated, since simply executing the arithmetic opera-tions is likely to be faster because of the impact of memory latency.

GLSL Discard

Through the use of the GLSL discard command, it is possible to stop the processing of the current fragment. This functionality can be used to implement the equivalent of the fixed-function alpha test and to avoid further processing complex fragment shader instructions. When using GLSL discard, it is important to understand that it seriously reduces the efficiency of the hidden-surface removal capability of the hard-ware since visibility can only be determined after execution of the fragment shader. Use it with moderation.

LOD Shaders

Through the use of GLSL dynamic branching instructions, it is possible to create var-ious paths within a single fragment shader. This can be used to create an LOD imple-mentation and dynamically influence the pixel shader complexity. For example, near the camera an object can use a shader path with full-blown parallax bump mapping and self-shadowing, while further away the shader blends down to simple texture mapping. By using LOD, it is possible to save valuable fragment shader processing cycles and only apply the visually stunning, but costly, effects where they can be seen and appreciated.

Textures

Loading and Usage

Creating a new texture requires a considerable amount of bandwidth traffic and overhead, which should be avoided mid-action. Create and upload all texture data up-front before the actual 3D action starts. Depending on driver implementation, textures might only be fully processed for use by the hardware when they are *used* for the first time, and this can introduce a stuttering effect. To avoid this, touch (use) all textures once before starting the actual 3D application. This is often referred to as a warm-up phase.

OpenGL stores texture filtering and wrapping information on a per-texture basis, not as a "state" (as in Direct3D); hence, it is not necessary to repeat texture filtering and wrapping state when changing texture.

Texture Atlas/Page

To reduce the CPU load, the amount of API overhead associated with changing from one texture to another can be minimized by using a texture atlas (also known as a texture page), which is one large texture containing several subtextures. This mechanism also enables improved batching by allowing multiple objects, with traditionally different textures, to be drawn in a single draw call.

Texture Size

Make sure to use a sensible texture size. There is no need for a 1024×1024 texture for an object that will only ever cover a quarter of a QVGA screen. However, large texture sizes should be used for texture atlases to maximize their benefit.

Texture Compression

Unlike the desktop market, where a dominant texture-compression algorithm has appeared, there are numerous hardware-specific texture-compression algorithms present within the mobile market, allowing textures to be encoded in as few as 2 bits per pixel.

Use of the most optimal texture compression format for each mobile platform is essential to maximize performance and minimize bandwidth, memory footprint, and application distribution size. All vendors provide specific texture compression tools and libraries that can be easily integrated with your artwork tool chain, allowing the creation of specific data packages for each platform.

Mipmapping

Mipmapping not only improves the visual quality of textures by reducing sparkling effects in the distance, but it also plays an important role in texture cache efficiency and, as a result, texture bandwidth. While mipmapping increases storage requirements by 30%, its use is highly recommended to avoid performance drops.

Texture Filtering and Data Formats

Texture formats and filtering modes are likely to have an impact on fill rate because of bandwidth usage and/or filter logic throughput capability. Point sampling and bilinear filtering are likely to be "for free" on all mobile graphics processors. Trilinear filtering, as in the desktop space, will be highly optimized but is likely to introduce some performance reduction. Anisotropic filtering—if supported—is likely to be expensive. Where possible, bilinear filtering with nearest mipmapping should be used:

```
glTexParameterf(GL_TEXTURE_2D, GL_TEXTURE_MAG_FILTER,
                               GL_LINEAR);
glTexParameterf(GL_TEXTURE_2D, GL_TEXTURE_MIN_FILTER,
                               GL_LINEAR_MIPMAP_NEAREST);
```

More advanced filtering modes should only be used after performance analysis.

Texture data formats are also likely to have an impact on performance, again owing to bandwidth usage and/or filter logic throughput capability. The following list orders texture formats from highest throughput to lowest:

1. Hardware-specific compressed texture formats (DTXn, FXTn, PVRTCn, ETCn,...)
2. 8-bit texture formats (I8,...)
3. 16-bit texture formats (RGBA4444, RGB565, RGBA5551, I8A8,...)
4. 24/32-bit texture formats (RGB888, RGBA8888,...)
5. 16-bit floating-point formats (optional)
6. 32-bit floating-point formats (optional)

Non–Power-of-2 Textures

Non–power-of-2 textures can save valuable memory storage space, but their use should be limited to very specific cases since their performance is likely to be lower than power-of-2 textures.

Depth and Stencil Operations

Similar to the desktop, depth-only renders and stencil operations, both with color-write disabled, can, depending on the mobile graphics processor, have a higher fill rate than color operations.

Alpha Blending

Alpha blending potentially increases bandwidth requirements because of the requirement of a read-modify-write operation on the frame buffer in external memory. Because of this increase in bandwidth usage, alpha-blending should only be enabled when required. Leaving the alpha-blend state enabled for opaque objects can have a detrimental impact on the hidden-surface-removal efficiency of the hardware.

Anti-Aliasing

Anti-aliasing considerably increases the memory footprint of color, depth, and stencil buffers on traditional immediate-mode renderers, potentially making this feature impractical because of the reduction in available system memory. Tile-based deferred renderers from Imagination Technologies and hybrid renderers from Falanx avoid this problem.

Additionally, anti-aliasing increases bandwidth and shader processing requirements, and as a result, this highly desirable image-quality feature should be considered on a device-by-device and application-by-application basis.

OpenGL ES API Recommendations

State Thrashing

State thrashing often occurs when render state changes are accidentally included within a loop or through excessive usage of Bind/Enable/Disable functions. For example,

```
glEnableVertexAttribArray( … );
glVertexAttribPointer( … );
glBindTexture(GL_TEXTURE_2D, 1);
glEnable(GL_BLEND );
glDrawElements( … );
glDisable(GL_BLEND);
glDisableVertexAttribArray( … );

// Next Object
glEnableVertexAttribArray( … );
glVertexAttribPointer( … );
glBindTexture(GL_TEXTURE_2D, 1);
glEnable(GL_BLEND);
glDrawElements( … );
glDisable(GL_BLEND);
glDisableVertexAttribArray( … );
```

API calls should be minimized to reduce CPU load introduced by API overhead.

glFinish, glFlush & glReadPixels

The glFinish, glFlush, glCopyTexImage2D, glCopyTexSubImage2D, and glReadPixels API calls force a synchronization between the CPU and GPU, thus destroying the inherent parallelism that should exist between these units. Use of glReadPixels should be limited to screenshot and movie creation code. To maintain maximum performance, glFinish and glFlush should not be used. Use of glCopyTexImage2D and/or glCopyTex-SubImage2D should be limited to up-front creation of textures and should not be used to implement render-to-texture functionality.

glError

During development it is important to check for problems using glError since each error introduces CPU overhead as the driver deals with the issue. Beyond that, in most cases OpenGL ignores API calls that generate errors. When executed correctly, these API calls may have significant impact on application performance. Final applications should, as much as possible, be free of OpenGL error messages.

Extensions

Like the desktop space, OpenGL ES extensions provide extra functionality and performance optimizations for each specific mobile graphics processor. While such extensions potentially fragment the market, their use is highly recommended to get the best out of the hardware both in terms of performance and feature set.

Conclusion

This article provided insight into generic performance recommendations to enable high-performance shader-based 3D graphics on mobile devices, offering recommendations to maximize performance by optimizing CPU load, geometry submission, shaders, textures, back-end frame-buffer operations, and some OpenGL ES 2.0 API-specific recommendations. The recommendations provided allow developers to implement an optimized 3D engine architecture from the start and save valuable time debugging basic performance-related issues.

Acknowledgments

The author thanks his colleagues at Imagination Technologies and the members of the Khronos OpenGL ES Group who took the time to provide valuable input for this article—in particular, Yaki Tebeka from Graphic Remedy.

7.4

Real-time Tile-Based Texture Synthesis Using Nonregular Grids

Georg Kolling, Imagination Technologies

Introduction

The advent of fragment shaders with floating-point precision and generalized dependent texture reads has opened up the possibility of doing image-based texture synthesis on the GPU. Next-generation OpenGL ES 2.0–compliant mobile graphics hardware introduces these capabilities to the mobile space.

Traditional tile-based texture synthesis is similar to the way many 2D games create their game worlds: choosing from a set of small rectangular image blocks, the plane is filled with tiles that form a regular grid. The amount of artwork required to build large worlds this way is small, but care has to be taken to avoid the most obvious repetition artifacts. Using this technique in a fragment shader, generating texels "on demand," can result in substantial savings in texture memory, which is essential in a mobile environment. Additionally, it can help circumvent hardware limitations to texture size.

So far, tile-based texture-synthesis methods have mainly concentrated on laying out rectangular image tiles on a regular grid. This article will show interesting applications for nonregular grids, for example, using tiles that vary in width, including rendering proportional fonts using just a single geometry primitive. A similar method to create a decal layer is presented as well, eliminating the grid entirely.

A Note on Precision Qualifiers and Data-Dependent Branching

The OpenGL ES Shading Language introduces so-called precision qualifiers (`highp`, `mediump`, and `lowp`, with `highp` being optional for the fragment language), each specified with a certain minimum precision and range for integer and floating-point types. It is very likely that many of the first-generation OpenGL ES 2.0–compliant devices will feature multiple precision levels for their shader hardware. However, there is no guarantee that the precision and range will be the same on different devices, so it is possible that shader code tested on one platform will show artifacts on another. For the shader snippets presented in this article, precision qualifiers have been applied very conservatively (and where they are missing, `highp` is assumed to be the default precision). More aggressive use of precision qualifiers may sometimes result in better performance on certain platforms without negatively affecting quality.

ON THE CD

The shaders presented in this article as well as the additional material on the CD-ROM make use of data-dependent branching (if with a non-uniform condition expression) in the fragment part on several occasions. The methods presented here will result in coherent but relatively small blocks of pixels that take the same branch. The thread granularity of the hardware determines whether the presence of data-dependent branching in the shader code will have a positive or negative impact (or none at all if the shader compiler decides to use predicated instructions instead). Not all GPU architectures are well suited for this task, and some testing on the target platform is needed to find the best way to handle it.

Objectives

Many real-world objects are covered with patterns of recurring features. Sometimes these features repeat with precise regularity, but more often they have imperfections, intentional or not. In contrast to these, computer-generated images using simple texture repetition look bland and artificial.

To improve matters without requiring excessive amounts of unique textures, image tiles, carefully crafted to be combined in multiple ways, can be laid out in a random-looking fashion. Methods that place tiles in a regular grid are well researched. This article will thus concentrate on techniques that reduce the limitations of a grid. We target the creation of artist-controlled decal layers where decals can be placed freely. Another main goal is the efficient arrangement of proportional font glyphs to form lines of printed text in a *virtual texture*. Books, signs, newspapers, files, labels, and computer screens all usually feature printed text, and they can certainly help tell a story.

The Basic Idea

Let's begin with the theory. All we have at the start of each invocation of a fragment shader are some constants and linearly interpolated values. If we use these for a texture fetch and don't do any fancy math, we will likely end up with a quite regular distribution of texels over the surface. So how do we get from there to a preferably artist-controlled nonregular arrangement of tiles over that same surface?

Methods of tile-based texture synthesis that use a regular grid, such as [Wei05], usually employ either an index texture where the texels determine which tile from a set of tiles to use at each position in the grid (shown in Figure 7.4.1) or a method to calculate pseudo-random numbers that take the place of the index texels.

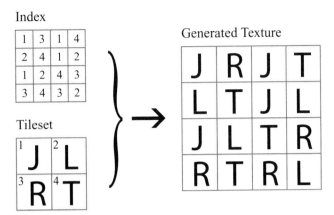

FIGURE 7.4.1   Tile-based texturing with a regular grid. Indices from an index texture determine which tile from a tileset to use at each position of the grid.

Cell Descriptors

The trick now is to consider the texels fetched in a first texture access not just as simple indices, but as complex descriptors of cells that form a regular grid. We remove the fixed relation of one tile per grid cell and replace it with something that is equivalent to a list of tiles per cell, as shown in Figure 7.4.2. In other words, we use a texture of cell descriptors that specify how to place tiles from a tileset freely inside each cell.

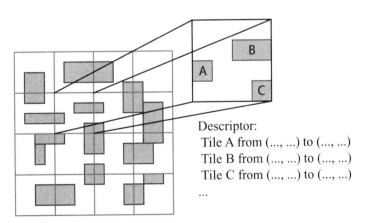

FIGURE 7.4.2   Grid cells can contain several tiles (shown as grey boxes). A descriptor specifies the contents of each tile.

With this approach, regular grid tiling becomes just a special case of using the simplest possible cell descriptor: a single scalar value indexing into the tileset.

Texture bombing [Glanville04] can also be considered a variant of this approach, even though its focus lies more on creating a pseudo-random distribution of features. Nonetheless, the texture used to generate pseudo-random numbers is not much different in principle from a texture of randomly generated cell descriptors.

When trying to find the best cell descriptor layout for a given purpose, we need to keep in mind two main goals:

- Minimize the amount of processing and data required per pixel.
- Minimize the overall amount of data required and optimize for texture cache usage.

While these two goals might appear quite similar at first glance, they can actually be opposing in many cases. They lead to several design decisions to be made to find the optimal cell descriptor for a given purpose. These decisions are outlined below.

Important Design Decisions

Fixed Size versus Variable Size Descriptors

A descriptor of variable size, like a linked list, is more difficult to process in the fragment shader. It may need loops and multiple levels of texture fetch indirection to get all elements of the list but allows great flexibility in choosing the right size for the cells. In contrast, a fixed-size descriptor is easy to process, but it can only have a limited number of "slots" for tiles to be placed in one cell. As a consequence, cell size must be limited so that no cell contains more than this number of tiles. Some of the slots are wasted when cells contain less than the maximum number of tiles. This decision directly influences the choice of texture format(s) to store the cell descriptors. We generally need an accurate representation, so lossy compression is not an option. The commonly supported RGB565 and RGBA8888 formats allow portable implementations, though sometimes it can be preferable to use formats with higher precision.

Tiles that Cross Cell Boundaries

When tiles spread over multiple cells, we can either choose to store their position in each affected cell descriptor, or we could store them in only one cell (e.g., the one that contains the top-left corner of the tile) and let the fragment shader check surrounding cells for tiles that reach into the current cell. In the latter case we avoid storing redundant information, but it comes at the price of adding substantial complexity to the processing required per pixel.

Which Cell Size To Use?

Large cells with potentially many tiles need more complex descriptors and therefore more shader cycles. Additionally, they require more bits to store positional information of tiles than smaller cells. However, large cells also have their advantages. When using fixed-size descriptors, large cells could create a more even distribution of tiles per cell, thus potentially reducing wasted space owing to unused tile slots. Large cells also mean fewer tiles crossing cell boundaries, and if cells are bigger than the largest tile, we never have to look farther than the closest neighboring cells for tiles that may reach into the current cell.

Tiles Overlapping Each Other: Allowed or Not?

Sometimes we need the ability to put one tile on top of another. When the ground is covered with autumn leaves, it is unlikely that none of them will so much as touch each other. To kern a proportional font, it is necessary that the rectangular regions containing the characters sometimes overlap. On the negative side, allowing multiple tiles at any given position adds more instructions and texture fetches to the fragment shader. Especially in a mobile environment, processing resources are in tight supply, so we have to assess carefully what is needed and what is not.

Arrangement of Tiles in the Tileset Texture

When arranging the tiles we want to use in a tileset texture, there are three objectives:

- Wasting as little space as possible
- Making addressing each tile as simple as possible
- Avoiding artifacts from texture-filter kernels extending across tile boundaries, including the filter used to generate mipmaps

When all tiles are of equal size, it is a pretty straightforward decision to arrange them as a grid. However, to avoid artifacts from texture filtering, it is important to place matching tile edges next to each other. For Wang Tiles, Wei [Wei05] presents a comprehensive algorithm for packing the tiles in a tileset texture. "Real" tiles, for example, images of ceramic tiles or bricks that are each surrounded by a natural border, should generally match at every edge and can be arranged in any way. Similarly, if the tiles only contain small features on a transparent background (which font glyphs are a perfect example of), no care needs to be taken to line up matching edges.

Tiles that vary in size could each be given equal space in the tileset texture, or we might try to pack them tightly. By aligning one corner of each tile to n-texel boundaries, we waste some space, but it saves a few bits in the cell descriptor for indexing those tiles. Also, if n is a power of 2, tiles will not bleed into each other when generating mipmaps with a box filter.

Depending on the tile contents, we might still have to treat the tile edges in lower mipmap levels specially, for example, by applying an image filter that reduces the contrast at tile edges at creation time. For tiles like font glyphs, it can help to add a few texels of background color as padding between every tile.

Sometimes the decision can be made whether to arrange the tiles as one long row or in multiple rows and columns. One row makes addressing easy with only one index, but with many large tiles we might exceed the hardware texture size limit. Another possible hardware limitation to have in mind is that of non–power-of-2 textures. Even when they are supported, they might not be as fast as the usual power-of-2 textures.

Furthermore, since batching is very important for good performance, we have to think of putting the tileset and cell descriptor textures into texture atlases. We need to carefully consider how this can affect the interpretation of cell descriptors, and it also means we probably should not rely on texture repeat or clamp in the shader.

Proportional Fonts (Tiles with Varying Width)

Probably one of the most important uses of tiles with varying width is rendering text with a proportional font. This has certain implications. For example, a character set containing all Latin uppercase and lowercase letters, digits, and some punctuation, will easily exceed 64 characters. Therefore, we need at least 7 bits in the cell descriptor to describe which character to use. The characters themselves can usually be stored in a compressed format or as single-channel texture, preferably with some anti-aliasing already applied. Interpreting this as an alpha value, we can smoothly blend between a background color or texture and a font color.

Choosing the Right Cell Descriptor Layout

The easiest decision regarding the cell descriptor layout is that of cell height: one row of cells for each line of text is natural. If we also assume that each character ends where the next one starts, we only need to store one horizontal position for each character (in addition to the character index itself, of course). We will see later that we have to break this assumption if we want to apply kerning, but this only requires a few more bits.

For this example, we decided to favor a simple descriptor that is easy to process over a complex one. This seems reasonable, as the memory space required for storing the cell descriptors is still not excessively large. To keep the processing cost per pixel down, we use a fixed-size descriptor. We also keep the descriptor size at or below 32 bits to minimize texture fetches. If we count at least 7 bits to store which character to use and add some bits for positional information, we're practically limited to two tiles per cell.

How wide can a cell be if we only allow two tiles per cell? The answer is simple: one texel more than the width of the narrowest tile used. That way, if a cell completely contains this narrowest tile, there is a one-texel column left on only one side of it, but not both. Because of this, using fonts with a very slim letter "i," for example, will require more cells and thus more memory space than using fonts with an almost fixed width.

Figure 7.4.3 depicts dividing a line of text in a row of cells, each containing at most two characters. Figure 7.4.4 shows the two positional values we need to store alongside the character indices. The following table outlines how the values are stored in the color channels of a 32-bit RGBA texture.

Red	Character index for the first character in the cell
Green	Distance of the left edge of the first character to the left cell edge (d_1)
Blue	Distance of the left edge of the second character to the left cell edge (d_2)
Alpha	Character index for the second character in the cell

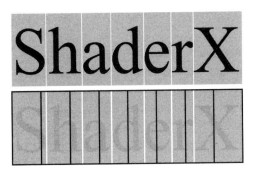

FIGURE 7.4.3 "ShaderX" separated into characters (top) and in cells with each cell containing at most two characters (bottom).

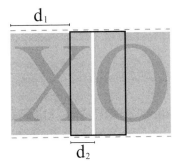

FIGURE 7.4.4 A cell containing two characters needs to store the position of each character. We use the distances from the start of the characters to the left cell edge

By allocating 8 bits for each value, we can access up to 256 different character tiles, and each tile as well as each cell can be up to 256 texels wide. When a cell only contains one character, we simply set d_2 to be larger than the width of the cell and use only the first character.

To keep the indexing of the characters in the tileset texture simple as well, we assume that the characters are arranged as one very long row, even though, given hardware limitations on texture size, this may not always be possible. By horizontally aligning the characters in the tileset texture to n-texel boundaries as shown in Figure 7.4.5, we reduce the number of bits required to store the position of each character in the tileset texture to 8. We then multiply the character index value stored in the cell descriptor by the alignment value to get the horizontal texel offset of the character we want to use. For example, with all characters aligned to 8 texel boundaries and the letter "X" starting horizontally at texel column 80, we store a 10 as the character index in the cell descriptor whenever we want to use the letter "X." The alignment value should be chosen so that we can access all characters required with 8 bits. In the case of 256 characters this means the alignment value has to equal the width of the widest character. That should be avoided whenever possible if we don't want to waste lots of space in the tileset texture.

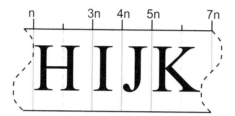

FIGURE 7.4.5   Tile alignment. Each character in the tileset starts at a horizontal position that is a multiple of n.

Storage Cost

With these decisions made, what is the storage cost per character? Let's say we're using a font in which the widest glyph is eight times as wide as the narrowest one. Characters spreading over five cells on average, the first and the last one shared with other characters, might be a reasonable assumption. At 4 bytes per descriptor, this makes about 16 bytes per character—but we have to count all the space at the end of lines or empty lines as well. So depending on the text layout, we could well reach 32 bytes per character of actual text. For rendering a few signs and labels this is surely OK, but if we start with book pages, we might consider trying to store less redundant information. Storing only one tile per cell and relying on information from the left neighbor can be a good idea to reduce storage cost. However, in this case it might be necessary to reduce the cell width by one texel.

Another idea is to add one level of indirection and store each line separately. This way, we can use a *line descriptor* that specifies where each line of text starts and ends, thus eliminating the need to waste cell descriptors on whitespace at the ends of lines. Overall, there are many possible ways of trading storage cost for performance, not all of which can be considered in this article.

Since the placement of character tiles into cells depends on the size of each character, we can't just exchange one font texture for another. Each cell descriptor texture has to be created for use with a certain font, so for each unique string-font combination we want to use, more space is required. Of course, the more text we have, the more substantial are the savings of using each character tile many times compared to using pregenerated textures with text on them.

The Fragment Shader

For the purpose of this article, the vertex shader is hardly worth mentioning. All we need is one set of texture coordinates, and of course the transformed vertex position, so we'll start right with the fragment shader.

To process the cell descriptor outlined above, the following steps are required:

1. Determine which cell the current fragment is in.
2. Get the descriptor for that cell.
3. Find out whether the current fragment lies in the first or the second tile of the cell.
4. Calculate the texture coordinate relative to that tile.
5. Use the right character index value from the cell descriptor to compute the location of the character tile in the tileset.
6. Add the results from steps 4 and 5 and use these coordinates to sample from the tileset texture.
7. Blend the color obtained from step 6 with the background color.

To do this, we need to add some input values to the shader:

```
uniform lowp ivec2 CellSize;
uniform mediump ivec2 NumOfCells;
uniform mediump ivec2 TilesetSize;
uniform lowp int Alignment;

uniform lowp vec4 BackgroundColor;

uniform sampler2D CellDescriptorTex;
uniform sampler2D TilesetTex;

varying vec2 TexCoord;
```

Most of these values are self-explanatory. NumOfCells is the size of the cell descriptor texture. Alignment describes how the tiles in the tileset texture are horizontally aligned to certain texel boundaries; for example, if Alignment is 8, all tiles start at a horizontal position that is a multiple of 8. TexCoord is written by the vertex shader.

It is important that the filter mode for the cell descriptor texture is set to GL_NEAREST, because any kind of filtering would only harm the information in the cell descriptor. For the tileset texture, we should, of course, apply at least bilinear filtering with mipmaps.

Now let's have a look at the main shader.

```
// Get the cell descriptor
// CellDescriptor.x : Index for first character
// CellDescriptor.y : Width of first char inside cell
// CellDescriptor.z : Width of first char outside cell
// CellDescriptor.w : Index for second char
lowp ivec4 CellDescriptor =
    texture2D(CellDescriptorTex, TexCoord) * 255.0;
```

```
// Calculate position inside the cell
vec2 InCellCoord = fract(TexCoord * vec2(NumOfCells));
vec2 TilesetCoord = InCellCoord * vec2(CellSize);

// Are we inside the first or the second tile?
if (TilesetCoord.x > float(CellDescriptor.y))
{
    // Adjustment for second tile
    CellDescriptor.x = CellDescriptor.w;
    CellDescriptor.z = -CellDescriptor.y;
}
// Add position inside tile to position of top-left
// corner of the tile inside the tileset
TilesetCoord.x += float(
    CellDescriptor.x * Alignment + CellDescriptor.z);

// Normalize coordinates: scale to range (0, 1)
TilesetCoord /= vec2(TilesetSize);

// Sample the tileset texture
lowp vec4 TileColor =
    texture2D(TilesetTex, TilesetCoord);
```

The first thing to do is get the cell descriptor and multiply it by 255. That way, we turn the values in the texture that represent a range of 0–1 into integers again. Since the position calculations are based on texels, we later need to divide by `TilesetSize` to get the normalized texture coordinates required for sampling. When it is found that we are inside the second tile of the cell, we simply replace the information describing the first tile with that of the second one. All in all, the process is simple enough to still expect real-time performance on first-generation OpenGL ES 2.0–compliant devices.

Avoiding Artifacts at Tile Edges

Tile-based texture synthesis usually faces the problem of how to select the right mipmap level at tile boundaries. Tiles that are next to each other in the virtual texture might be far apart in the tileset texture, meaning large jumps in the texture coordinates used to access the texture. Since texturing hardware normally uses the differences of texture coordinates between adjacent fragments to derive the level of detail (LOD) value, there can be a huge discrepancy between the LOD you would expect for the virtual texture and the LOD that is computed for fetching from the tileset. As a result, ugly seams might appear around the tiles as shown in Figure 7.4.6.

To work around this problem, the fragment shader can give the texturing hardware the information it needs to select the right mipmap level. With DirectX9 and PS3.0, the most straightforward way would be to calculate derivatives of the virtual texture coordinates and use the `tex1dd` instruction—or the corresponding `tex2Dgrad` HLSL function—to fetch from the tileset texture.

Unfortunately, the OpenGL ES Shading Language in its current incarnation does not provide such a function. Gradient operations are only available as an extension in

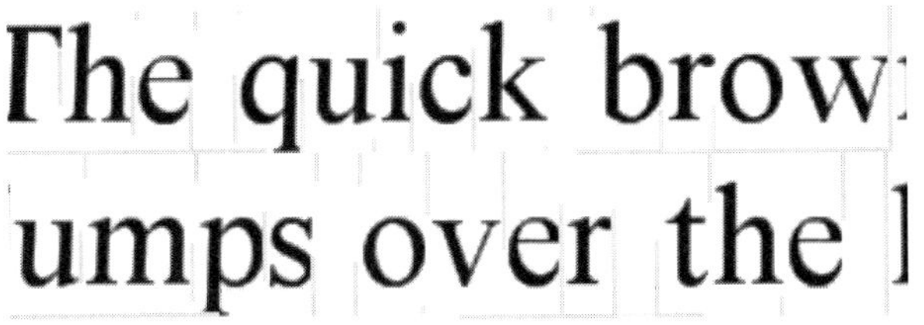

FIGURE 7.4.6   The text shader without LOD correction at the tile edges, showing ugly artefacts.

the desktop space, and most likely there will be a functionally identical extension for the OpenGL ES Shading Language. Until then, though, we want to find a way to avoid artifacts without extensions. For this article, we have explored three approaches to this issue, each being a different trade-off between performance and quality.

Using LOD Bias

The first option, which is the most general-purpose one, is to make use of the optional LOD bias parameter to the sampler functions. The bias value would have to be the difference between the actual LOD and the virtual LOD. How do we get those without gradients? Since the texturing hardware already has the ability to compute the LOD, we use it. All we need is a texture where each mip-level is filled with a constant value representing that level.

The following code snippet shows how to get the right level of detail, given the texture coordinates and the size of the texture to access.

```
uniform sampler2D MipLevelTex;
const mediump float MipLevels = 4.0;
const mediump float MipTexSize = 16.0;

mediump float GetLod(vec2 Coord, mediump vec2 TexSize)
{
    Coord *= TexSize / MipTexSize;
    mediump float Lod = texture2D(MipLevelTex, Coord).x;

    if (Lod > 0.99)
    {
        Coord /= MipTexSize;
        Lod += texture2D(MipLevelTex, Coord).x;
    }
    return Lod * MipLevels;
}
```

The texture used for the sampler `MipLevelTex` should use the highest-compression format available on the target platform. Only a single channel is required, and every mip-level should be filled with a single value, linearly increasing from 0 to 1 from largest to smallest mip-level. This example uses a texture of size 16×16, which has four mip-levels below the base level.

This function can be used to accurately determine the level of detail in a range of 0–1. If we require a larger range, we can either add more sampling steps or use a larger texture with more mip-levels. When trilinear filtering is desired for sampling from the tileset texture, `MipLevelTex` needs to be sampled with a linear mip-filter as well. Otherwise, `GL_NEAREST_MIPMAP_NEAREST` is sufficient as a minification filter mode.

To get the right LOD bias value, we need to call the `GetLod` function twice (once with the interpolated texture coordinates and once with the modified texture coordinates that will be used to access the tileset texture) and subtract one result from the other. This can become quite costly, so usually other methods will be preferable.

With this in place, we get the proper result shown in Figure 7.4.7 and Figure 7.4.8.

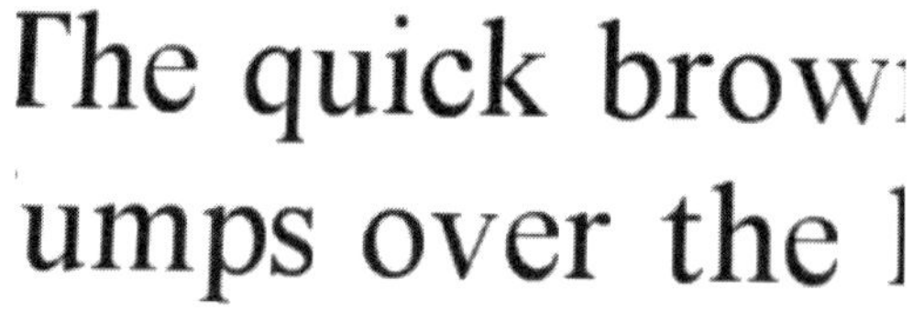

The quick brow

umps over the]

FIGURE 7.4.7   The text shader with LOD correction; the artefacts disappear.

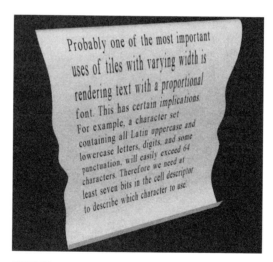

FIGURE 7.4.8   A larger screenshot of the text shader.

Fading Out Tiles

Another option, only suitable for text and other kinds of tiles that are mostly transparent, is to gradually make them completely transparent toward the lower-resolution mip-levels. This way, the text fades out at a distance, and tile edges will appear transparent as well.

ON THE CD

For the sake of not having to edit the tileset mipmap levels, some example shaders on the accompanying CD-ROM map the sampled alpha values so that almost transparent areas will become completely transparent. The effect produced is similar, but it also affects the tiles viewed up close in a way that might sometimes be pleasing to the eye.

Detecting Tile Edges

Similar to the LOD determination method discussed above, we can detect tile edges by first calculating the difference between the texture coordinates and then using this difference to access a special mip-level texture. Inside a tile the difference between virtual and real texture coordinates is a constant, and using constant texture coordinates always results in mip-level zero being used. At tile edges, however, the real texture coordinates take a huge leap, and so does the difference between the two coordinates.

With that in mind, we can use a single-channel 2×2 texture with two mip-levels, the first filled with 0, while the second contains 1. Sampling this texture then returns a truth value indicating whether the current fragment is at a tile edge or not. If it is at an edge, we replace the tile color with a constant edge color, or the background color for tiles with transparent edges.

Unfortunately, this method rapidly breaks down when the tiles become very small on screen. Thus, it is best to combine it with the pregenerated mipmap method presented in the next paragraph.

Fighting Aliasing

Texture aliasing occurs when a texture contains higher frequencies than are displayable using the pixels to which the texture maps. Usually, texture filtering is used to eliminate those high frequencies. However, tile-based texture synthesis exhibits cases of possible texture aliasing that need special attention. When multiple tiles fall into one pixel, for example, at the edge of one tile and another, we would usually need to take texels from each tile into account. Fortunately, if we place font glyphs on a transparent background with some padding around each of them, this will normally not be a problem since it means that all edges are equally showing the background color/texture.

Another issue is tiles becoming smaller than a pixel. It is possible to solve this by pregenerating a small version of the virtual texture. When the tiles become too small, this texture can be used instead of synthesizing the texture on the fly. The decision of when to use this texture as a replacement can be based on special values stored in one channel of the lower mip-levels of the tileset texture. Alternatively, we could use the GetLod function shown above or make the substitution based on the distance of the rendered object from the viewer. Some of the RenderMonkey effect variants provided on the CD-ROM show how to implement this technique.

ON THE CD

Kerning

To make some fonts, especially italics, look better, we might consider kerning. Kerning means that certain character pairs are moved closer together to make them look more

evenly spaced. Figure 7.4.9 shows an example of kerning with the two letters "V" and
"A." As we can see, the rectangular regions containing the characters can overlap with
kerning, so we may need to sample twice from the tileset texture in the shader and
blend the results together. Since kerning will only require a relatively limited span of
overlap, we do not have to spend many bits on storing the width of the overlap region
in the cell descriptor.

FIGURE 7.4.9   The letters "V" and "A" with kerning (right) and without (left).
Kerning avoids excessive spacing between certain character pairs by creating an
area where the bounding boxes of the characters overlap (darker grey).

It can, however, be quite difficult to gather the necessary information for automatic kerning from a font, so we leave this as an exercise for the reader. For small
amounts of text, manual adjustment of the cell descriptors for kerning is an option.

Nontext Uses

Rendering text is not the only use for tiles with varying width. For example, Figure
7.4.10 shows a texture of a brick wall, generated from only 15 different bricks. There are
certainly many more uses to be found for this technique. For tiles without a transparent
background, the methods outlined above to counter aliasing become more important. It
also becomes interesting to try mirroring the tiles for more variation. Beyond that, the
shader itself does not change at all.

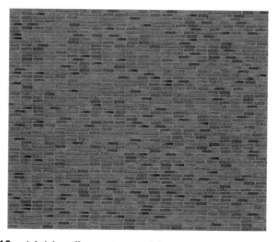

FIGURE 7.4.10   A brick wall texture created from 15 brick tiles with varying width.

A Decal Layer

It is often desirable to be able to add small, not-so-regular features to a surface, such as scratches, holes, dirt marks, bolts, or maybe flowers and leaves. Many games use decal polygons to temporarily add such features to a scene, but these aren't without problems, as they increase the number of draw calls and can suffer from Z-fighting. If we want to add many such features to a surface that is covered with a repeating texture (and thus we don't want to bake these features into the base texture), we may be better off adding them in the fragment shader. We would like to not have to place them on a simple rectangular grid.

Choosing a Cell Descriptor Layout

Again, we can find a good cell descriptor layout for this task, and again we'll try to keep it as simple as possible. This time it means a single tile per cell and only 16 bits per cell descriptor. Using an RGB565 texture gives us enough space to store a tile index value as well as some bits for position. The latter we store as the top-left corner of the tile relative to the top-left corner of the cell. We assume that all tiles have the same size, which is as large as a cell at most. Since we want to be able to place the top-left corner of the tile outside the cell as well, we must store signed position values in an unsigned texture format. That's easily done by adding a fixed bias value and later subtracting it again in the shader. We also consider the position to be in the range of -1 to 1 relative to the cell size.

We have to be careful when interpreting the contents of a RGB565 texture, since the hardware will likely convert it to 8 bits per channel by replicating the most significant bits in the lower ones. This means that, for example, scaling the red channel by 31 will not yield exact integer values. Instead, we will have to multiply by 31.875 (255/8) and round down the results. Alternatively, we can multiply by 255 and then perform an integer division.

The following table summarizes the descriptor layout:

Red	Horizontal position in range of $-16/16$ to $15/16$
Green	Tile index value
Blue	Vertical position in range of $-16/16$ to $15/16$

This approach naturally has some limitations. No tiles can overlap, and when a tile crosses a cell boundary, it needs to be stored in each affected cell, allowing no other tile in those cells. That means there is a kind of border around each tile that must be left blank, which is still good enough for many purposes. Also, positioning is quite coarse with only 5 bits per axis. In comparison, 64 different tile index values might seem like overkill, but we can use these to allow mirrored versions of the tiles quite easily.

We can store an empty cell by using a horizontal or vertical position of –1, which is equivalent to a tile placed entirely outside the cell.

Most decals are similar to font glyphs in that they are arbitrary shapes placed on a transparent background. So again, we don't have to worry about matching tile edges. By storing the decal tiles as a single row in the tileset texture, we avoid having to decompose the tile index value into a 2D position.

Mirroring Tiles

Many decal textures can be mirrored horizontally or vertically to add some diversity. Fortunately, the texturing hardware can do this easily by using the GL_MIRRORED_REPEAT texture wrap mode. Given a tile index value in the range of 0–63 and a tileset texture with 16 tiles of equal size arranged horizontally, we can divide by 16 to get the U coordinate and use either 0 or 1 as the V coordinate, depending on whether the index value is below 32 or not. With a bit of creative placement, this can even work for tileset textures in a texture atlas.

The Fragment Shader

The algorithm doesn't change much from the previous shader, the main difference being that we now have to perform a range check in two dimensions to determine whether we have to sample a tile or not. The steps are:

1. Determine which cell the current fragment is in.
2. Get the descriptor for that cell.
3. Check whether the current fragment lies inside the tile. If not, use background color and go on to next fragment.
4. Calculate the texture coordinate relative to the tile.
5. Use the tile index value from the cell descriptor to compute the location of the decal tile in the tileset.
6. Add the results from step 4 and 5 and use these coordinates to sample from the tileset texture.
7. Blend the color obtained from step 6 with the background color.

This leads us to the following shader snippet:

```
lowp vec3 CellDescriptor =
    texture2D(CellDescriptorTex, TexCoord).xyz;

lowp vec2 InCellCoord = fract(TexCoord * NumOfCells);
// we need floor() because of the way RGB565 is expanded
vec2 TilesetCoord = InCellCoord -
    (floor(CellDescriptor.xz * (255.0 / 8.0)) / 16 - 1);

lowp vec4 Color = BackgroundColor;
// Check if we are inside tile
if (TilesetCoord.x > 0.0 && TilesetCoord.x < 1.0 &&
    TilesetCoord.y > 0.0 && TilesetCoord.y < 1.0)
```

```
{
    // Adjust coordinates to sample from the right tile
    TilesetCoord.x +=
        floor(CellDescriptor.y * (255.0 / 4.0));
    TilesetCoord.x /= NumTilesInTileset;

    Color = texture2D(TilesetTex,TilesetCoord);
    Color = mix(BackgroundColor, Color, Color.w);
}
```

Here we only need two uniforms: NumOfCells, which is again the size of the cell descriptor texture, and the self-explanatory NumTilesInTileset.

Using a 32-bit cell descriptor (or possibly a 16-bit two-channel texture and a single-channel 8-bit texture) can make interpretation of values easier, but it increases bandwidth and storage requirements. Figure 7.4.11 shows a screenshot using this shader, where we used a tileset of 16 flowers and arranged them on a surface.

FIGURE 7.4.11   The decal layer shader using a set of 16 flower decals. The decals were manually placed to create a pattern.

Conclusion

Texture synthesis based on tiles can offer substantial savings in texture memory, not least in the case of textures showing printed text, but it is often important to avoid the regularity of a rectangular grid for an improvement in visual quality. We have presented a very general approach to reducing the grid regularity and accompanied it with two implementation examples. They can be used on mobile platforms that comply with the OpenGL ES 2.0 specification, where texture memory limitations are most pressing.

Material on the CD

ON THE CD

The CD-ROM accompanying this book contains additional material related to this article:

- A RenderMonkey 1.6 workspace containing several variants of the methods presented in this article as GLSL shaders and including some example texture content.
- Two demos with executables based on an OpenGL ES to OpenGL wrapper, along with C++ source code. One demonstrates the use of tiles varying in width to render text, and the other shows the decal layer technique.
- The FontTextureCreator utility with full C# source code and Visual C# 2005 solution. It can be used to generate character tilesets from all installed fonts and matching cell descriptor textures from any string.

Acknowledgments

The author wants to thank his colleagues at Imagination Technologies—the Developer Support team, Ravi Tulsiani for artwork, and Kristof Beets for chocolates and his patience—and Arne Seifert, for their help in the creation of this article.

References

[Glanville04] Glanville, Steven R. "Texture Bombing." *GPU Gems*, edited by Randima Fernando. Addison-Wesley, 2004: , pp. 323–338.

[Wei05] Wei, Li-Yi. "Tile-Based Texture Mapping." In *GPU Gems 2*, edited by Matt Pharr. Addison-Wesley, 2005: pp. 189–199.

7.5

Cartoon Fire Effects Using OpenGL ES 2.0

David Minor, Imagination Technologies

Introduction

Pixel and vertex shaders have given programmers unprecedented control over the visual style of their graphics. No longer restricted by the fixed-function pipeline, we can now control the output down to the last pixel, allowing a range of effects from exquisitely realistic, physically derived lighting at one extreme, to a complete departure from photo-realistic rendering at the other.

Recent 3D technology is allowing developers to create impressive 3D accelerated content on mobile devices such as phones and PDAs, using fixed-function APIs. A new generation of technology currently in development will open up the shader universe to mobile devices, using APIs such as OpenGL ES 2.0—a subset of OpenGL 2.0. This API has no fixed-function pipeline, handling all vertex and fragment processing in shaders, but it is no less powerful than OpenGL 2.0 and can be used to create the same advanced effects as are currently available for desktop PCs.

This article describes how to achieve a non-photo-realistic effect. The example, coded using OpenGL ES 2.0, renders flaming objects in a cartoon style, using a few simple vertex and fragment shaders and the render-to-texture feature.

Visual Style

The ability to create stylized images such as paintings or cartoons on the fly is one of the more impressive things about modern computer graphics. Done well, it can look as if the machine has done hours of work at the touch of a button, and changing the parameters slightly will give you another image, which you've never seen before and will probably never see again.

One of the more enduring graphic clichés of our time has been "hotrod flames"— traditionally used to spice up the décor of everything from motorcycles to underwear. This article describes an algorithm that draws this kind of effect in 3D. An example is shown in Figure 7.5.1.

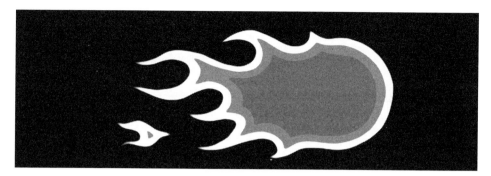

FIGURE 7.5.1   Hotrod flames.

This graphic has two main elements: the smooth, rounded halo on the right and the turbulent flames leaving from the left. The image is made up of successively darker areas of color, one inside another, which are bounded by smooth closed curves, with cusps at the tips of the flames. The flames each have an undulating U shape, and most are joined together in a mass, with some breaking off.

The following pages describe a method of rendering an object enveloped in these flames, which works by first rendering a grayscale image and then passing it through a color lookup table, to create the color banding we see in Figure 7.5.1. The object used in this example is spherical, because of the simplicity of its silhouette, but the technique can also be applied to nonspherical objects.

Principles

Mapping different brightness ranges to different colors in a grayscale image has an effect like a contour plot. For an image with no significant jumps in intensity from one pixel to the next, this will automatically generate sets of curves enclosing each other, separated by colored regions, as seen in the graphic. Discontinuities in the derivatives of the image will lead to kinks and cusps in the curves, which can be put to use drawing the ends of the flames.

We can reproduce some of the character of the flames by applying this method to the pattern in Figure 7.5.2a on the left, which was constructed using 2D Gaussian functions. If you think of it as a height field, it has a series of undulating ridges, where its derivatives are discontinuous, with a few random diagonal connections added between the ridges for some irregularity.

Modulating this pattern with a Gaussian envelope gives us the pattern in Figure 7.5.2b. Figure 7.5.2c shows the result of putting Figure 7.5.2b through a color lookup, mapping all intensity levels below a first threshold to transparent so that the (white) background shows up, mapping the next range to black, for the outline, and the next two ranges to different colors. Note how the "ridges" in the image create undulating features terminated by cusps, like in Figure 7.5.1.

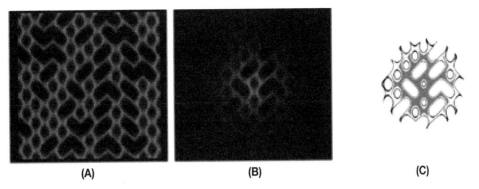

FIGURE 7.5.2 **(A)** 2D Gaussian function. **(B)** Modulated with a Gaussian envelope. **(C)** Applying a color lookup.

To complete the effect, we add a halo on at the bottom by drawing another Gaussian shape over the grayscale image with an additive blend mode, before using the color lookup. If we want to animate the flames, we simply move the ridge pattern while keeping the flame envelope and the halo stationary. This is the basis for the 3D effect.

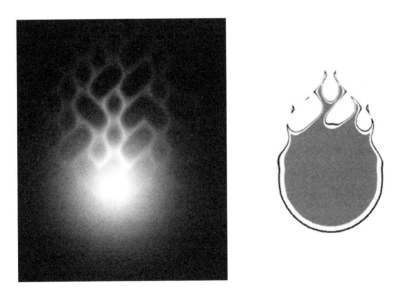

FIGURE 7.5.3 Basis of the 3D effect.

Implementation in 3D

OpenGL ES 2.0, like most current 3D APIs, has a powerful render-to-a-texture feature. This rendered texture can be transferred to the screen via a pixel shader—a quick and easy way to carry out a wide range of image-processing operations. The color lookup is performed in a pixel shader, which acts on a rendered-to-texture grayscale image mapped to a full-screen quad, and indexes a 1D color lookup table with one of the grayscale texture's channels. The GLSLang shader is a one-liner, and is shown below:

```
uniform sampler2D sampler2d;
uniform sampler2D lookupsampler2d;
varying vec2     myTex;

void main (void)
{
gl_FragColor = texture2D
 (
lookupsampler2d,
vec2(texture2D(sampler2d,myTex).r,0)
);
}
```

The problem we are now faced with is rendering the grayscale image while dealing with perspective. The pattern needs to be distorted in an aesthetically pleasing, realistic manner, and it must look sensible from all angles. The desired behavior is shown in Figure 7.5.4:

FIGURE 7.5.4   The view from all angles.

Drawing the Halo and the Flame Envelope

The visual style we are aiming for requires that the halo follow the silhouette of the object to which we are applying the effect. This can be done several ways. The first is to draw the object geometry in place, but with shaders that displace the vertices along their normals, and color the geometry darkly at glancing angles. This rarely looks acceptable, however, as the curvature of the geometry is typically very variable, and if one part of the geometry occludes another, discontinuities in the image will result, creating ugly artifacts. Another method is a 2D process: the object's geometry is rendered to a texture in its on-screen position, using a pixel shader that colors the geometry pure white, for example, and then the texture is convolved with a blurring kernel, creating a grayscale halo. To make this halo appear thicker for objects at close range, as you would expect it to be, the size of the kernel could be varied inversely with the viewing distance. This is a potentially expensive way of doing things, however. A simple and effective alternative is to blend together circular translucent sprites, typically

Gaussian blobs, which tend to blend together well, placed at different points on the object. This is used to create an irregular silhouette in the "Inferno" example demo on the companion CD-ROM. The only requirement for the flame envelope is that it follows the object in the direction the flames are pointing, and it can be rendered in a similar way to the halo.

Drawing the Flame Pattern

To achieve the effect in Figure 7.5.4, the flame pattern itself must be distorted, before being modulated with the flame envelope. A satisfactory distortion can be achieved by rendering a cylinder with the flame pattern mapped to it and flattening or conically distorting the cylinder depending on the viewing angle, as shown from various perspectives in Figure 7.5.5.

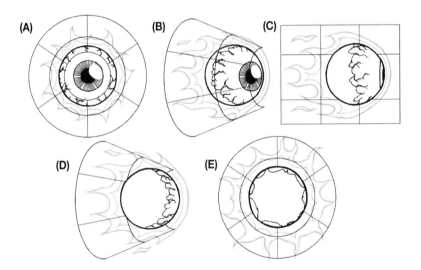

FIGURE 7.5.5   **(A)** Viewed from the front, the cylinder is round and slightly conical. **(B)** Viewed diagonally from the front, only the outer surface of the cylinder is visible, so that its surface curves toward the viewer. **(C)** Viewed from the side, the cylinder is completely 2D and flattened in the plane of the screen. **(D)** Viewed diagonally from the back, the inner surface is visible, curving away from the viewer. **(E)** Viewed from the back, the cylinder is round and slightly conical.

This behavior can be handled by turning on back-face culling, and squashing the cylinder in a direction perpendicular to its axis, lying in the plane defined by the axis and the view vector. This is achieved by modifying the cylinder's world-view matrix. The factor by which it is flattened is dependent on the viewing angle and is allowed to go negative in some cases, turning the cylinder inside out, to achieve the desired effect. The conical transformation can be handled by a vertex shader and is, again, view dependent.

The remaining problem appears when the object is viewed from the front and from the back: the hole at the end of the cylinder comes into view, which leads to discontinuities in the grayscale image and breaks the flame pattern. This can be resolved by capping the cylinder at the visible end, rendering the cap black, and modulating the flame pattern with another texture, such that it fades to black toward the capped end. Screenshots of the final pattern are shown in Figure 7.5.6.

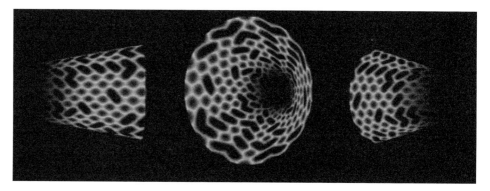

FIGURE 7.5.6   The final flame pattern.

Rendering the Image

We are now ready to render the complete image, as follows:

1. Switch to a texture render target.
2. Clear the render target to black.
3. Draw the flame envelope, without blending.
4. Over the top of this, draw the cylinder with the flame texture mapped to it, in multiplicative blend mode, so it is attenuated by the envelope.
5. Draw the halo on, in additive blend mode.
6. Transfer this image to the screen by mapping it to a full-screen quad and using the color lookup shader.
7. Draw the object to the screen, preferably with some kind of toon shader for visual consistency.

Some screenshots from the "Eyeball" demo, showing a single spherical object, are shown in Figure 7.5.7.

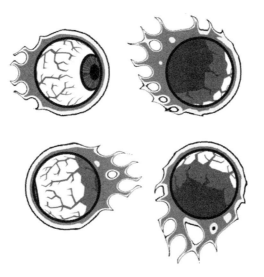

FIGURE 7.5.7 Screenshots from the Eyeball demo.

Rendering Objects in a Scene

The Inferno demo shows an example of an object with an irregular silhouette flying through a scene, emitting cartoon flames. The irregularly shaped halo is drawn by blending together a number of circular sprites, placed at different points on the object, as shown in Figure 7.5.8.

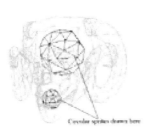

FIGURE 7.5.8 Blending circular sprites.

Currently, in the example code, different flaming objects require separate render-to-texture passes, each of which are transferred to the screen separately. This could be done slightly more efficiently by rendering the flames to different areas of the same render target and then transferring them all to the screen at once.

The transfer of the flames from the texture to the screen must take depth occlusion into account. Because of this, for multiple objects, the flames are depth-sorted and then drawn to the screen, furthest away first, using appropriately mapped screen-aligned quads. Each quad is placed at an appropriate depth, so it is occluded by objects in the scene. A very convenient way of mapping the texture to the screen is by using projective texturing: the x and y positions of the quads in eye space are scaled and shifted, then used as the u and v texture coordinates, and the w texture coordinate is simply set to the w coordinate of the vertex position. This method also has the advantage that the quad does not have to be screen-aligned for the mapping to look correct, which could be advantageous when applying the effect to large objects that wrap themselves around parts of the scenery. Screenshots from the Inferno demo are shown in Figure 7.5.9.

FIGURE 7.5.9   Screenshots from the Inferno demo.

Conclusion

In this article we have demonstrated a shader-friendly way of rendering cartoon fire in 3D, which can be put to use in a game environment. The technique is easily customized by adjusting the lookup colors and the underlying pattern, so a programmer can achieve a wide range of visual styles. This method could also be used to create other effects, such as lightning, force fields, and laser beams.

3D ENGINE DESIGN

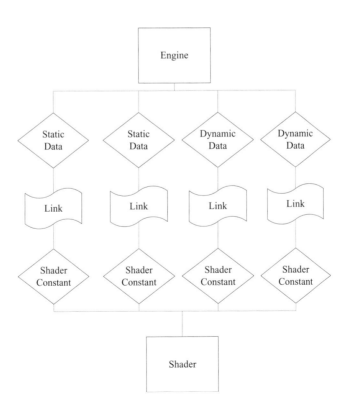

Introduction

Wessam Bahnassi

Among all other subjects in computer graphics (and computer software in general), perhaps the subject of software architecture is the most arguable one. There is no absolute right or absolute wrong, and the validity of the solution changes from one point of view to another.

This situation started a very long time ago with real-world building architecture. A building might be credited by someone to be totally functional from one perspective, but less than perfect from someone else's point of view. This is not a surprise, though, because there is no solid definition of absolute correctness as long as some form of art is involved.

If we look at the heart of architecture, we find the process of design, which exists in both building architecture and software architecture. In *The Ten Books of Architecture (De Architectura),* Vitruvius asserted that under the environment's constraints, a good structure satisfies three principles: firmness, commodity, and delight. This is a good starting point from which to judge the validity of a design. For software architecture, this can translate to stability, functionality, and user convenience. Narrowing it down to our original subject, the design of a 3D engine can be claimed good if, under the constraints of its working environment, it:

- Performs in a stable manner (no crashes or strange skips or pops)
- Properly exposes and performs all of its intended functionality
- Produces the expected results

It is not easy to fully meet all of these goals. Design is a complicated process that involves a lot of forward thinking and deep background knowledge of the environment. Because of its complexity, it is taken with an iterative approach, where each iteration adds finer details and propagates their effect back to the higher levels. This is how the process works, so it really amazes me when I see people trying to come up with a full complete design in only one shot. This is simply not possible with today's requirements and constraints.

That being said, this section is one place where you can increase your design experience by looking at how different people think and what they have achieved with their engine designs.

We begin with Aurelio Reis's article, "Postprocessing Effects in Design." Aurelio proposes a modern design in which postprocessing effects can work effectively. With a clear set of goals, he describes a full XML-based system that has a high degree of extensibility and can include a visual editor for previsualizing and controlling the applied effects.

Next, Dustin Franklin demonstrates a transparent system for binding shader data with hardware constant registers. His article, "Transparent Shader Data Binding" attempts to automate this rather cumbersome task in shader-based 3D engines using a clean and less-intrusive technique, which involves C++ pointer-to-function trickery.

For the third article in this section, Wessam Bahnassi (well, myself) borrows design concepts from well-established offline-renderers to improve real-time shader extensibility with modern high-level shader languages. The article "Designing Plug-in Shaders with HLSL" turns a real-time shader into an expanding function-call tree that can be flexibly grown to express a wide variety of user-defined effects.

As with previous *ShaderX* volumes, we keep the tradition of presenting a case study of an existing 3D engine. This time, Kim Hyoun Woo describes the integration aspect of the Nebula Device engine into 3ds Max™. His article, "Shader System Integration: Nebula2 and 3ds Max" explains an interesting approach that allows exposing shaders to artistic control without being bound to the underlying shader language.

Editing this section has indeed taught me new perspectives in 3D engine design, and I hope you enjoy reading this section and making use of it as much as I did. Remember, you will benefit the most by reading it with an open mentality. Do not reject these techniques just because they do not fit out-of-the-box into your engine. At the very least, they will help increase your confidence over your decisions at the next design iteration for the engine by knowing that you now base these decisions on a broader background of design approaches.

Welcome!

8.1

Postprocessing Effects in Design

Aurelio Reis, Firaxis Games

Introduction

Since the introduction of real-time shaders, postprocessing effects have become a de facto in modern real-time rendering, especially with the arrival of next-generation graphics hardware. Effects such as bloom and depth-of-field can enhance scenes and generally increase visual fidelity in the gaming experience. However, as more and more effects get incorporated into a scene, their management becomes more troublesome, as they can easily get out of control, not to mention the required amount of tweaking to achieve the desired results. Ensuring scalability and peaceful cooperation between the various postprocessing effects also comes with its own set of perils.

In many cases these effects end up being implemented late in the project as a hack to the code or they get implemented so deep in the game that they are hardly reusable in different code bases or projects.

This article demonstrates a system design approach for managing postprocessing effects in modern 3D engines. Extensibility and flexibility are among the primary goals of this system, as well as allowing easy generation of numerous effects under a manageable framework. The design covers all system aspects such as programmatic interfaces and storage, as well as the effects editor itself.

The system is capable of expressing many postprocessing effects such as motion blur, heat haze, night vision, and depth-of-field, as well as HDR tone mapping.

The Goals

A good postprocessing effects system design must fulfill several goals before it proves to be useful. These goals are:

- **Stability:** To perform in a stable manner and offer reliable and consistent results
- **Robustness:** To operate steadily under different usage scenarios and effects
- **Extensibility:** To offer an easy and clear framework for introducing new effects into the system as well as modifying existing ones

- **Performance:** To work as optimally and efficiently as possible
- **Flexibility:** To give enough expressive control for achieving high-quality effects
- **Scalability:** To run gracefully on all supported platforms with regard to underlying limitations. This includes different video card configurations (with each generation being counted as a separate platform).

In practice, some of these goals can occasionally conflict with each other. Thus, balancing is required to achieve the best results based on the specific situation.

Since postprocessing effects by definition operate in screen space, they almost always cause a fill-rate bottleneck as well as consume a large amount of memory. Many approaches can be taken to increase performance (e.g., using down-sampled intermediate buffers); however, most of these optimizations end up as hacks into the original effect's code. For this to be avoided, special consideration to optimizations must be taken into account during the design of the system.

The Design

The design is based on a simple hierarchical system. At the top level, we have an *effect*, which is made of one or more *phases*, where each phase can be made of one or more *steps*. Two or more effects can be chained to each other for cumulative effects. An effect takes a number of inputs and is guaranteed to output results either to a render-target texture or to the frame buffer. A step is the lowest-level element in the system, and it represents a function in the pipeline that needs to be implemented in code and gets exposed for usage by a higher-level interface.

A complex effect can encompass a number of steps. To maintain manageability of such effects, phases are used to assemble the numerous steps into logical groupings. Figure 8.1.1 shows an example of the structure and flow of an HDR effect.

For storage, such a design strongly suggests the use of some kind of a hierarchically templated file format. XML proves to be a suitable fit thanks to its structure and layout [XML01]. Effects, phases, and steps will be expressed with XML elements. However, even with the versatility of XML, we cannot assume that artists will build postprocessing effects by authoring XML files by hand. Thus, this file is considered intermediary and is not intended for direct manipulation by artists. To allow easier authoring, a small user-friendly program can be built to generate these XML effect files.

The design also takes into account one additional element of a special type, which is the RenderTarget element. To declare any required intermediate textures in the effect, the RenderTarget element type must be used. This element generates and tracks a new texture allocated as a render target with the specified format and resolution.

To switch render targets, the special intrinsic *switch render-target* step must be used. Note that there are system-level render-targets that are automatically generated, as in the case of *Framebuffer (the asterisk denotes a render target as being system level to differentiate it from normal user-created render targets).

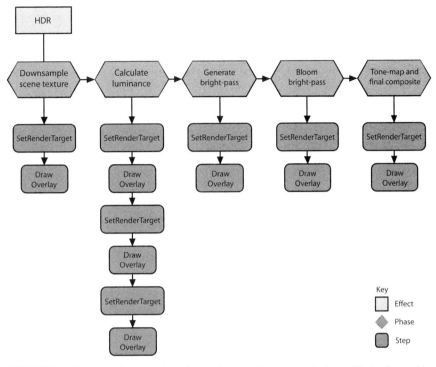

FIGURE 8.1.1 Grouping steps into fewer phases reduces complexity and helps in tracking performance issues.

A Short Test Drive

ON THE CD

To clarify some more design details, it would be best to view the system by example. The "media/PPFX" directory on the accompanying CD-ROM contains a number of different effects that have been created for this purpose. Listing 8.1.1 examines one of the simplest effects in the group, which is the sepia tone effect ("SepiaTone.ppfx").

LISTING 8.1.1 Contents of the SepiaTone.ppfx XML File

```
<Effect Name="SepiaTone" Requirements="DX9" Description="Output a
Sepia-toned image.">
    <Phase Description="">
        <Step Type="SetRenderTarget" Target="*CompositeOut"/>
        <Step Type="Overlay" ShaderTechnique="RenderSepiaTone">
            <Texture Name="*CompositeIn" Alias="g_Texture"/>
            <Texture Name="Media/sepiatone.tga" Alias="g_Depen-
            dantReadTexture" Type="File"/>
            <Param Name="Amount" Alias="g_fBlendAmount"
            Function="FadeIn"/>
```

```
        </Step>
        <Step Type="SetRenderTarget" Target="*Framebuffer"/>
      </Phase>
   </Effect>
```

The general idea is to convert the rendered scene into a grayscale color representation and then use the grayscale values as indices into a color-remap texture [Werle04].

The first element in the file is the Effect element, which contains values from some effect properties such as the name of the effect, the minimum set of requirements for operation, and a description for user convenience.

Inside the effect's declaration, any number of phases can exist. The order of declaring phases is only important when certain phases depend on the output of previous phases (by referencing their output render target for input usage).

A phase can have a description attribute and may contain any number of steps. Each Step must define its Type as a base requirement. Different types of steps can then define additional sets of attributes as needed. In this example, the first step is a SetRenderTarget step, and it takes a mandatory Target as an attribute, which is set to the system level *CompositeOut render target. This tells the system that the output of all following steps (leading up to the next SetRenderTarget step) will directly go to the next effect along the chain.

Some steps require additional information that cannot be expressed conveniently with attributes. Thus, they are represented as child XML elements. In our case, the second step in the phase (the Overlay step) requires two textures to render with the sepia tone shader technique.

A Texture element can express texture data from one of three sources: an existing user-declared render target, an intrinsic render target, or a file loaded from disk (specified by setting the texture's Type attribute to File).

The Alias attribute in the texture element is used to bind the texture to the underlying HLSL texture variable that is declared by the technique used in the parent step.[1]

Back to the Overlay step: two textures are passed to the step's technique. The first is set to use the effect's input image (*CompositeIn) and is aliased to g_Texture within the shader .fx file. The second texture is loaded from a file and contains the color ramp texture that remaps the input image with the sepia tone (aliased as g_DependantReadTexture).

The last element in the Overlay step is the Param element. Similar to the Texture element, a Param can be used to control constants exposed by the underlying HLSL file. For example, a Param named Color can be used to tint an overlay with a color value. The value of the parameter is controlled by a very flexible and extensible system, which allows for the definition of functions to calculate the values of the parameter. The function can

---

[1]It is done this way only for the sake of implementation simplicity. A real-world engine should replace this with its own effect-parameter-binding mechanism.

take a number of arguments, including the parameter's previous value. This means that multiple functions can be used in succession for cumulative calculations or results. For example, the Sin() wave function can take an amplitude, phase, and frequency and then pass the result of the operation to the next function or to the shader.

ON THE CD

One more interesting file to look at is Output.ppfx. This is the simplest effect in the group and is considered the standard output effect, which just writes out the input image without modifications.

Implementation Details

ON THE CD

The companion CD-ROM contains a full code implementation of the described system. The heart of the code begins from the CSceneView class, which represents a specific rendering of the scene and can include things like a standard view, reflections, and shadow map renderings. CSceneManager determines which entities are visible in any given view. These views then render the objects into a texture, which can be accessed by the postprocessing effects system.

The highest level in the postprocessing effects system is the CPostProcessEffects-Manager class (declared as a singleton). This class manages all of the system's functionality such as loading, clean up, tracking, updating, and rendering of all effects. The manager maintains a singly linked list of CPostProcessEffect objects. Each of these objects directly correlates to a postprocessing effects XML file and contains the effect's name, the file it was loaded from, the input and output images, its phases, and the next link along the effects chain (Figure 8.1.2).

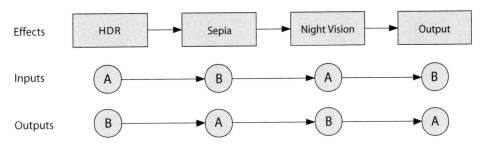

FIGURE 8.1.2 An example effects chain with all effects enabled.

When the CPostProcessEffect object is created, the Parse() function gets called, and it reads all children XML elements from the loaded file. As the elements get parsed, their relevant objects get created. For Step elements, a virtual Parse() method is called to allow parsing of custom data based on the specific requirements of that step's type. The available different step types and their custom parse routines are implemented in PPFXStep_*.cpp files.

A class factory is used to create objects from their relevant elements. Most of the functionality is wrapped up in the REGISTER_PPFX_STEP_ALLOCATOR_CLASS macro, which takes the class type and a proper name to generate a class factory function for it. Factory functions are stored in a global linked list that is iterated by CPostProcessEffectsManager when trying to create step objects (done in the FindStepAllocator() routine).

Finally, after an effect gets loaded, its composite buffer outputs are hooked up with the next effect's inputs in the LinkCompositeBuffers() function. The first effect that links to the composite buffer chain receives the scene image in the frame buffer.

Since the system allows for disabling and enabling effects in a chain at runtime, special care must be taken to maintain valid composite buffer input-output hooks for affected effects (which were determined at load time). Figure 8.1.3 describes the problem.

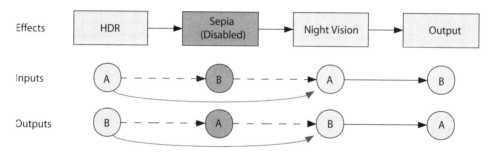

FIGURE 8.1.3   An example effects chain with the sepia-tone effect disabled. Note that the static composite buffer inputs-outputs need to be adjusted for every effect after the sepia-tone effect; otherwise, the first effect on that chain would be pointing to incorrect buffers.

To resolve this issue, it is possible to swap the input and output images for each effect after the disabled (or re-enabled) effect (taking into account the special case of the first effect in the chain). This operation involves correcting pointers to the old input and output images tracked by certain effect steps. The virtual function Fixup-TexturePointers() does this correction and must be implemented for all steps that store any texture pointers. Now effects can be safely enabled and disabled by calling CPostProcessEffect::Enable(bool bEnable) on the relevant effect object.

Performance Considerations

One of the goals of this article is to incorporate an elegant framework for optimization of effects done with this system. In most cases performance can be increased, and memory consumption can be decreased by using down-sampled intermediate buffers.

To be scalable, some method must be established to specify the sizes of these buffers based on the target platform. It is debatable whether it is best to use a constant down-sampling size (e.g., 64 × 64) or, say, a percentage of the current screen resolution.

Although it would be nice to allow scaling the effects quality based on user preferences, it can be difficult to anticipate the difference in memory footprint for such a shift, as well as the additional performance cost or gain associated with it. The preferred method would probably be to use a constant size that is specified for each platform and resolution independently. This can guarantee consistency in appearance, as well as being able to track video memory usage upfront.

For this, the system supports the Screen keyword to fetch the screen's resolution when creating RenderTarget elements. Additionally, it allows the specification of scaling factors to the render target's dimensions.

The Visual Editor

The final piece of the system is the visual editor. Although a discussion of a full implementation of such an editor falls outside the scope of this article, here are a few things that are worth mentioning.

An effective editor interface can provide users with an intuitive nodal system, where nodes express the different parts of the effect hierarchy (the effect, phases, and steps) as shown in Figure 8.1.4. These nodes can be hooked up to each other to build the full effect chain.

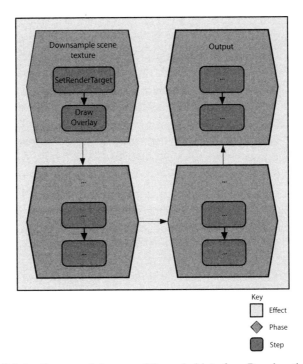

FIGURE 8.1.4   Conceptual diagram of the nodes' interface. Based on their type, nodes can contain children to build the full effect hierarchy. The arrow connections represent the flow in which these grouped steps are executed.

The user should always receive feedback in one form or another. Ideally, the user should be prototyping the effect against an actual in-game scene. If that is not possible, something as simple as captured in-game screenshots from a selection of scenes can be used to maintain appropriate feedback. The screenshots must contain enough information and special rendering inputs in addition to the default color buffer (e.g., the heat scene view for heat vision, or the scene in floating-point format for HDR processing).

The interface must take into account the extensible nature of the system and the fact that new effect steps can be added at any time to the system.

A wide variety of postprocessing effect interfaces can be found in Softimage|XSI's FX Tree, Adobe's AfterEffects, 3ds Max's Video Post, and others.

Also, the recent DirectX 9.0 SDK's sample PostProcess offers a basic user-interface implementation [DXSDK06].

Conclusion

This article demonstrated an extensible postprocessing effects system that allows rapid and easy prototyping and implementation of high-quality postprocessing effects such as HDR bloom, sepia-tone mapping, night vision, and depth-of-field.

The system is based on a composition chain made of one or more effects. The chain is expressed simply in an XML file that contains several types of elements that build the whole chain, starting from the high-level Effect element, to Phases, and down to Steps, which can contain simple inputs such as Textures or Params. Steps are designed to be easily extensible through the use of a class factory system. In particular, Texture inputs can represent intermediate render targets, intrinsic system render targets (such as the frame buffer), or simply textures loaded from file. Params, on the other hand, are values that are calculated from a series of simple functions before being passed to the underlying HLSL shader implementing the relevant effect Step type.

Additionally, the article discussed how the system takes performance optimizations into account by handling special tokens for platform-specific render-target scaling.

Finally, the subject of the visual editor was touched and some references were listed for existing postprocessing effect interfaces in different graphics software.

References

[DXSDK06] "Microsoft DirectX 9 SDK PostProcess Sample." Available online at *http://msdn.microsoft.com/directx/*, 2006.

[Werle04] Werle, Guillaume. "Night Vision: Frame Buffer Post-processing with ps1.1 Hardware." *ShaderX²: Shader Programming Tips & Tricks with DirectX 9*, edited by Wolfgang Engel. Wordware Publishing, 2004: pp. 465–468.

[XML01] "Extensible Markup Language." Available online at *http://en.wikipedia.org/wiki/Extensible_Markup_Language*.

8.2

Transparent Shader Data Binding

Dustin Franklin, Mystic Game Development

Introduction

One of the challenges in operating a fully shader-based material system is to cleanly automate data exchange between the engine and the shaders. Shader data (i.e., constants) can consist of anything from matrices to colors to textures.

To achieve this automation, we need to use an intermediary link system (shown in Figure 8.2.1), which will contain per-data links that retrieve or store the engine-side data and provide it to the shader when queried. This article will describe the linking system and its implementation.

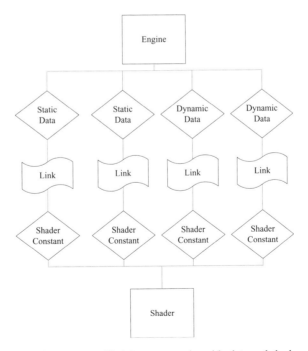

FIGURE 8.2.1   The linking system will sit between engine-side data and shader-side constants.

Overview

The data-linking system must account for the following scenarios:

Static data: Constants that generally do not change. For example, the diffuse color of a material can be static if it remains unchanged after initialization. Textures are static in most cases as well (e.g., diffuse maps, specular maps, normal maps, etc.).

Dynamic data: Constants that are updated from frame-to-frame, for example, transformation matrices, lights, and time variables.

Since we have two different types of data, it is appropriate to have two types of links: *static links* and *dynamic links* as shown in Figure 8.2.2.

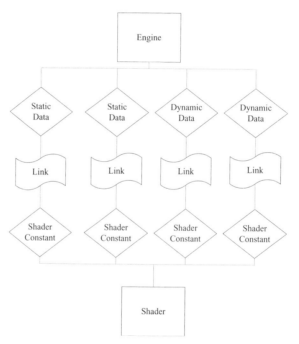

FIGURE 8.2.2   Some shader constants and the path used to retrieve their data.

Details

Following is a description of the two link types in the system:

Static Links

A static link is a simple data container. It stores a pointer to value data, which is initialized at load time. The link also holds a reference to the shader constant to which this data belongs. This is all of the information required to set that particular constant during runtime.

```
class StaticLink
{
    // Simply set the ShaderConstant to our stored data
    void Update()
    {
        mConstant->Update( mData );
    }

    void *mData;
    ShaderConstant *mConstant;
};
```

In practice, this works well because static data (like textures and colors) remains fairly stagnant after initialization; thus, the overhead cost is relatively low.

Dynamic Links

A dynamic link must retrieve its data from the engine each frame, making it more complex than a static link. The problem is that data can come from multiple sources. For example, a `ViewProjection` matrix might exist in a `Camera` object, while a `World` matrix might only be available from the mesh currently being rendered, and a `Directional-Light` might reside inside some lighting system. For future reference, we will refer to a function that returns shader-constant data as a *semantic function* (e.g., `Camera::GetMatViewProjection()`).

To easily retrieve data from an arbitrary data source, we can use function pointers. The dynamic link object will hold a function pointer associated with a specific semantic, so that function pointer can be called at runtime to get the data.

```
// The semantic function-pointer typedef
typedef void* (EngineResource::*DynamicFunctionPtr)();

class DynamicLink
{
    void Update()
    {
        // Get the data from the function pointer
        void* data = (callingObject->*functionPtr)();

        // Set the constant with this data
        // (equivalent of ID3DXEffect::SetValue())
        constant->Update( data );
    }

    DynamicFunctionPtr functionPtr;
    EngineResource *callingObject;
    ShaderConstant *constant;
};
```

Traditionally, C++ function pointers are rigid structures. To enforce type safety, they are essentially uncastable and cannot be manipulated easily. Usually, we would define a generalized function signature and force all semantic functions to be in that form. However, this can pollute the code with redundant functions since it might require an additional data accessor (the first being for normal engine access, and the second for generalized shader access). The code below shows an engine class with non-transparent semantic functions:

```
// Example of semantic functions within a class
class Mesh
{
    Matrix& GetMatWorldViewProjection();
    void* GetMatWorldViewProjectionSF();

    Matrix& GetMatWorldViewInverse();
    void* GetMatWorldViewInverseSF();

    Light* GetSomeLight();
    void* GetSomeLightSF();
};
```

As the engine develops, these function pairs will propagate to the point where it becomes an annoyance to both implement and maintain them. Instead, we will focus on making this dynamic link system transparent to the application. The system should be able to call all of the same existing functions that are normally used.

Unioned Function Pointers

A single function pointer in C++ cannot represent a set of different function signatures. For example, we cannot cast and invoke a void* (BaseClass::*Fnc) signature to accept functions like

```
Matrix& Camera::GetViewInverse();
Matrix** Mesh::GetSkinnedMatrices();
Light* World::GetDirectionalLights();
Vector2& Graphics::GetScreenSize();
float Engine::GetSystemTime();
```

However, if we store all of these different function signatures in a union, then the compiler's type-checking will be subverted, and we can easily cast from more specific signatures into the generalized case (and back again). This union consists of only a small number of members, since shader data types are limited.

```
typedef void* (EngineResource::*DynamicFunctionPtr)();
union DynamicFunctionUnion
{
    DynamicFunctionPtr fp;

    // Our generalized base function
    void* (EngineResource::*DynamicFnc)(void);
```

```
// Now our more specific functions
Matrix& (EngineResource::*DynamicMatrixFnc)(void);
Matrix** (EngineResource::*DynamicMatrixPtrFnc)(void);
Vector2& (EngineResource::*DynamicVector2Fnc)(void);
Vector4& (EngineResource::*DynamicVector4Fnc)(void);
float (EngineResource::*DynamicFloatFnc)(void);
...
};
```

In addition, we compose an enumeration of the different kinds of functions, so that we can maintain the type of a certain semantic function. This type will be needed when the function pointer is to be executed, so that we can select the correct union member to use.

```
enum DynamicFunctionType
{
    FUNCTION_MATRIX,
    FUNCTION_MATRIXPTR,
    FUNCTION_VECTOR2,
    FUNCTION_VECTOR4,
    FUNCTION_FLOAT,
    ...
};
```

Note that MFC uses a similar approach with its message map handlers. Even though its legality can be disputed since type safety is broken, it results in a clean and transparent solution that is easy to use and maintain.

Semantic Function Manager

To automate the process of linking a shader to its engine-side data, we will use a global semantic manager that stores all of the information pertaining to dynamic functions. Then, when a shader is loaded, it will search through this manager to find the appropriate semantic function. The code below shows a basic structure of the semantic function manager:

```
struct DynamicFunction
{
    const char *semantic;
    DynamicFunctionUnion functionPtr;
    DynamicFunctionType functionType;
    EngineResource *callingObject;
};

class SemanticFunctionManager
{
    // Add a function to the manager
    void RegisterFunction(const DynamicFunction& func);

    // Search through the manager for a function
    DynamicFunction* FindFunction(const char* semantic);
```

```
        Array<DynamicFunction> semanticFunctions;
};
```

To set up an object's set of semantic functions, all that is required is to fill the relevant DynamicFunction structures and register them. An example of registering a class follows:

```
class Dummy : public EngineResource
{
    // Some example semantic functions
    Matrix& GetMatrix();
    Vector2& GetVector2();
    Vector4& GetVector4();

    Dummy()
    {
        DynamicFunction func;

        // 'GetMatrix' function
        func.semantic = "MATRIX_SEMANTIC";

        // Cast and assign the particular function. We can cast,
        // because it matches one of the types in the union
        func.functionPtr.fp = reinterpret_cast
                <DynamicFunctionPtr>(&Dummy::GetMatrix);

        // This particular function is the matrix type
        func.functionType = FUNCTION_MATRIX;

        // We want to use this dummy object to call the function
        func.callingObject = this;

        // Register with the semantic manager
        GetEngine()->GetSemanticManager()->
        RegisterFunction(func);

        // 'GetVector2' function
        func.semantic = "VECTOR2_SEMANTIC";
        func.functionPtr.fp = reinterpret_cast
                <DynamicFunctionPtr>(&Dummy::GetVector2);
        func.functionType = FUNCTION_VECTOR2;
        func.callingObject = this;

        GetEngine()->GetSemanticManager()->
        RegisterFunction(func);

        // 'GetVector4' function
        func.semantic = "VECTOR4_SEMANTIC";
        func.functionPtr.fp = reinterpret_cast
                <DynamicFunctionPtr>(&Dummy::GetVector4);
        func.functionType = FUNCTION_VECTOR4;
        func.callingObject = this;
```

```
                        GetEngine()->GetSemanticManager()->
                        RegisterFunction(func);
                }
        };
```

Integrating With Materials

To integrate this system with a material class (or some other object that maintains data pertinent to geometric properties), only a list of static and dynamic links must be added. Generally, all static links are initialized with data loaded from model files or from some other medium. For example, a model might contain its associated textures' file names and their semantics (e.g., diffuse, specular, etc.). When the relevant constant is looked-up in the shader and is found, the texture is loaded and the static link is created, binding both the constant and texture.

Dynamic links can be initialized by searching the semantic function manager for all semantics that are left unbound. The dynamic links are then created from the semantic functions stored by the manager.

When the shader is activated at runtime and the mesh is about to be rendered, the list of links is iterated for update. Static links simply set their constants with the data they already have, while dynamic links retrieve the data from their semantic functions.

Implementation Considerations

This binding mechanism is just a base for what might be used in a real-world engine. Because of the many ways engines handle their shaders, this system should be somewhat customized to fit properly.

One important thing to consider is how the mesh's material properties can change on a per-instance basis. If the same material is applied to all similar mesh instances (i.e., they all use the same shader, textures, and material properties), then it is best to construct one set of links and share it between all instances. Instance-specific data then should be handled by dynamic links. When the engine is rendering these instances, the dynamic links should be called for each instance to set instance-specific data to the shader prior to rendering it (e.g., the transformation matrix).

Hardware instancing usually requires the use of an additional buffer that contains all per-instance data. This system can be tweaked to automatically fill the instancing hardware buffer by flagging the appropriate links as "hardware-instanced." These links in turn will write their data to the buffer instead of sending it to shader registers.

In addition to the traditional geometry material system, a shader-based postprocessing framework might be wanted to integrate into this system as well.

Conclusion

The linking system described in this article helps seamlessly bind shader-side constants to their engine-side data. For data that generally does not change, we use static links.

These links hold references to both the data and their associated shader constants, allowing for a very low runtime cost.

Dynamic links are used to retrieve data that is updated each frame. To support a multitude of data sources, function pointers are stored and later called at runtime. To make this system transparent, all the function pointer types are unioned, allowing us to store many different function signatures in one generalized type.

A global manager is created to register and store semantic functions. When queried, it provides data required to construct dynamic links, including the function pointer and calling object.

This system cleanly allows binding of any type of shader-side constant to custom runtime data and is flexible enough to work with many types of shaders. Overall, it helps reduce the time required to integrate shaders into the engine.

8.3

Designing Plug-in Shaders with HLSL

Wessam Bahnassi, Electronic Arts

Introduction

With the wonderful advances in real-time shader development, engines now compete in the features they offer to game developers, such as advanced lighting calculations, reflections and refractions, postprocessing effects, and so on. Many approaches were developed to expose the high-level of customizability to game developers and shader authors.[1] However, many solutions ended up offering *boxed effects* that can be used just as-they-are without any level of customizability besides the exposed tweakable parameters. Other solutions went totally in the other direction by opening the internal shader code to shader authors. This required additional care and effort to ensure that these shaders are compatible with the engine's requirements. DXSAS [DXSAS01] was an attempt to solve this issue a little bit, but the overall solution was still inconvenient or inefficient for many engines.

So between completely boxed effects and totally open shader code, this article suggests a method that engine developers can adopt to offer convenient customizability for users even without a high level of 3D engineering experience.

Problems at Hand

Perhaps the biggest issue that makes real-world shader authoring so challenging is the issue of possible shader permutations. Throughout the game, a single object using the same material all the time can end up using as many as tens of different variations of the same basic material shader. This is because an object can span different environments. For example, lights have long been a disturbing issue. Add one more light, and you will have to rewrite another shader version that takes this light into account. This can break rendering from single pass to multiple passes. What about skinned characters? That is a whole new headache.

A common way to handle this issue is to use macros inside the shader source code to enable and disable certain calculations or, better yet, static branching (when it is

---

[1]The term *shader author* will be used to reference the person who builds shaders and effects using a 3D engine that was made by an *engine developer*.

available). However, this simply resulted in cluttered shader source code and kept shader authors away from being able to write their own customizations without having good experience on the internals of the rendering engine.

Sneak Peek

It is helpful to look at what our predecessor offline renderers have achieved in their field. Not that real-time shaders are comparable to these juggernauts, but offline renderers have already evolved enough to offer good extensibility experience to shader authors.

Among all of today's offline renderers that offer advanced shader development systems, perhaps the two most popular are RenderMan and mentalRay. Both have a similar design and both expose their customizability in an identical manner.

In short, a mentalRay-RenderMan material can be made of a tree-like hierarchy of connected nodes [Driemeyer05] [Gritz99] (see Figures 8.3.1 and 8.3.2). Each node takes inputs of certain types, does its calculations, and then outputs data through one or more ports, which can be connected to other nodes' input ports and so on.

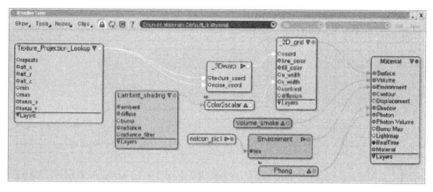

FIGURE 8.3.1   A mentalRay material inside Softimage|XSI's render tree. Note how the nodes are connected together through their ports.

Each node is backed up by a small code snippet, which can be highly specialized (and thus optimized) to do its job. The node does not care (or know) about any other nodes in the hierarchy. Its only purpose is to take the input, perform calculations, and provide output. During these calculations, the node has access to a special state object that aids in making certain decisions or asking certain questions about the object or fragment being rendered.

For example, a bump node can take the object's normal at the current fragment, alter it according to another input value, and then output the result as the new modified object normal prior to including that into the lighting calculations. We can connect the bump source to a texture map (bump mapping) and the bump amount to some other input value such as per-vertex colors.

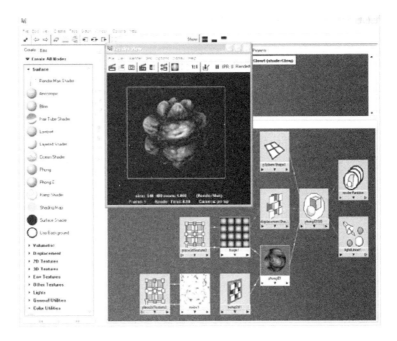

FIGURE 8.3.2   A similar RenderMan material inside Autodesk's Maya.

The code implementing the bump node would be something like Listing 8.3.1.

**LISTING 8.3.1   Sample Code Implementing the Bump mentalRay Node in C
[MentalImages01].**

```
struct mib_bump_map
{
    miVector u;
    miVector v;
    miVector coord;
    miVector step;
    miScalar factor;
    miBoolean torus_u;
    miBoolean torus_v;
    miBoolean alpha;
    miTag tex;
    miBoolean clamp;
};

miBoolean mib_bump_map(miVector *result, misstate *state,
                       struct mib_bump_map *paras)
{
    miTag     tex   = *mi_eval_tag(&paras->tex);
    miBoolean alpha = *mi_eval_boolean(&paras->alpha);
    miVector  coord = *mi_eval_vector(&paras->coord);
    miVector  step  = *mi_eval_vector(&paras->step);
    miVector  u = *mi_eval_vector(&paras->u);
```

```
miVector  v = *mi_eval_vector(&paras->v);
miScalar  factor = *mi_eval_scalar(&paras->factor);
miBoolean clamp  = *mi_eval_boolean(&paras->clamp);
miVector  coord_u, coord_v;
miScalar  val, val_u, val_v;
miColor   color;

coord_u.x = coord.x + (step.x ? step.x : 0.001);
coord_u.y = coord.y;
coord_u.z = coord.z;
coord_v.x = coord.x;
coord_v.y = coord.y + (step.y ? step.y : 0.001);
coord_v.z = coord.z;
if (clamp && (coord.x   < 0 || coord.x   >= 1 ||
    coord.y   < 0 || coord.y   >= 1 ||
    coord.z   < 0 || coord.z   >= 1 ||
    coord_u.x < 0 || coord_u.x >= 1 ||
    coord_v.y < 0 || coord_v.y >= 1))
{
    *result = state->normal;
    return(miTRUE);
}
if (!tex ||
    !mi_lookup_color_texture(&color,state, tex, &coord))
{
    *result = state->normal;
    return(miFALSE);
}
val = alpha ? color.a : (color.r + color.g + color.b) / 3;

if (*mi_eval_boolean(&paras->torus_u))
{
    coord_u.x -= floor(coord_u.x);
    coord_u.y -= floor(coord_u.y);
    coord_u.z -= floor(coord_u.z);
}
mi_flush_cache(state);
val_u = mi_lookup_color_texture(&color, state, tex, &coord_u)
 ? alpha ? color.a : (color.r + color.g + color.b) / 3 : val;

if (*mi_eval_boolean(&paras->torus_v))
{
    coord_v.x -= floor(coord_v.x);
    coord_v.y -= floor(coord_v.y);
    coord_v.z -= floor(coord_v.z);
}
mi_flush_cache(state);
val_v = mi_lookup_color_texture(&color, state, tex, &coord_v)
 ? alpha ? color.a : (color.r + color.g + color.b) / 3 : val;

val_u -= val;
val_v -= val;
state->normal.x += factor * (u.x * val_u + v.x * val_v);
state->normal.y += factor * (u.y * val_u + v.y * val_v);
state->normal.z += factor * (u.z * val_u + v.z * val_v);
mi_vector_normalize(&state->normal);
state->dot_nd = mi_vector_dot(&state->normal, &state->dir);
```

```
        *result = state->normal;
        return(miTRUE);
    }
```

Some attempts have been made to apply this nodal system to real-time shader prototyping [ShaderWorks05], but we are looking for a system that leverages the tedious work of covering every environment possibility from shader authors over to someone else used to this sort of routine work—the computer.

The Goals

The proposed technique will attempt to grant shader authors the ability to build shaders that are:

- Written only once but work in many different environments[2]
- Written with clear, uncluttered, and highly-focused code
- Isolated from 3D engine internals. Authors do not need the experience of the 3D engine developers
- Flexible enough to achieve the widest range of effects
- Fast, with no additional performance cost when compared to a hand-written HLSL variant that is specific to some environment combo

With these goals in mind, it is time to explore the proposed design.

External Shader Functions

This method is our direct reflection of the mentalRay material interface. It operates by having the shader author implement predeclared shader functions that are slipped inside a larger shader block generated by the 3D engine. These functions can be something like "lighting-shader," "displacement-shader," "texturing-shader," "bump-shader," and so on. They only do small specialized calculations that alter the shader's inputs in a way that will effectively change the output.

A call to each of these functions is carefully placed inside a full shader that the engine composes during runtime in accordance to the current environment surrounding the object in question. The calls must be placed at predefined and well-described positions to guarantee consistent operation. Thus, a shader author does not need to care about anything else going on in the full shader except how his own code is modifying the final result.[3]

For example, a displacement shader function could be implemented so that it pushes vertices along the normals by specified amounts based on something else (a texture, per-vertex values, etc). The function can access the input vertex position in model space, do the calculations, and then return the modified value for further processing.

---

[2]Written only, and not compiled. A shader permutation should still somehow be generated and compiled on demand during game play.

[3]Think of the shader as a "base-class" where these functions provide "overrides" to the default implementation.

The exposed set of functions should be carefully defined with vision to avoid putting annoying limits on what the shader author can do inside his implementation. However, exposing too many functions would also clutter the final shader and confuse the shader author, so balance is key to a good implementation of this system.

As is the case with mentalRay, the user always receives the global state structure that contains information about the running context.

On the engine side of the story, it is really simple. The engine receives the definitions for any external shader functions that the author has implemented and puts them into the generated HLSL code prior to sending it for compilation. So, from the engine side, the template shader block would be something like this:

```
struct STATE
{
    float3 vec3Pos;
    float3 vec3Nrm;
    float2 vec2TexUV;
    float4 vec4Color;
    float fTime;
    float3 vec3LightDir[4]; // 4 directional lights
    // ...and the list goes on and on
};

VS_OUTPUT VSMain(VS_INPUT vsInput)
{
    VS_OUTPUT vsOutput;
    float3 vec3Pos = vsInput.vec3Pos;

    // ... some skinning code if necessary

    STATE state;
    state.vec3Pos = vec3Pos; // Model-space position

    // Now call into external displacement shader code
    state.vec3Pos = ExDisplacementShader(vec3Pos, state);

    // Now call into tex-coord generator shader code
    state.vec2UV = ExTexCoordGenShader(vsInput.vec2UV, state);

    // ... rest of shader code

    // Output after all external shader functions are executed
    vsOutput.vec4Pos = mul(state.vec3Pos,g_matWVP);
    vsOutput.vec2UV = state.vec2UV;
}
```

And `ExTexCoordGenShader()` is implemented like:

```
float2 ExTexCoordGenShader(float2 vec2CurUV,inout STATE state)
{
    // Scroll texture based on time...
    return float2(vec2CurUV.x + state.fTime, vec2CurUV.y);
}
```

If the shader author does not provide an implementation for the shader function, the engine just uses a pass-through implementation, like this:

```
float3 ExDisplacementShader(float3 vec3CurPos,inout STATE state)
{
    return vec3CurPos; // Pass through
}
```

It is worth noting that the state parameter has the inout modifier. This is to enable the external shader function to change other pieces of information in the state besides the return value.[4]

As a conclusion, the engine now has the freedom to generate whatever code it needs to get the object render correctly in its environment (e.g., hardware skinning and lights count), while still keeping the essential shader customization intact by correctly placing the relevant calls to the external shader functions defined by the shader author. This whole operation is totally transparent to the shader author and can happen any time the engine makes a decision to transition to a different shader permutation.

Additional Thoughts

Engines utilizing some kind of shader fragment linking make it very straightforward to implement the method presented here. Note that this method does not generate different compiled shader fragments. All the code should be there prior to sending it to the compiler.

To make things more interesting, shader authors can implement the external functions by calling into other external functions that take other parameters and so on. The final result will be a hierarchy of calls that is very similar to the mentalRay nodal hierarchy described before. The method is extensible enough to offer a high amount of customizability and has the potential for various levels of shader authoring,

A careful implementation of this technique can allow the engine to simply move the external shader calls between vertex and pixel shaders. For example, the engine can distribute lighting calculations between being per-vertex and per-pixel in a very dynamic and flexible way, while still maintaining any lighting calculation customizations by simply moving the call to the external lighting shader function between the pixel shader and vertex shader as needed, and all is done transparently.

This method does not incur any performance[5] loss because all the work is done prior to the real shader compilation, which means that the HLSL compiler will receive only one full block of code that can be fully optimized at once. Note that the HLSL compiler is very effective at removing dead code blocks and optimizing and

---

[4]This is totally a personal design decision. This is one place to balance between flexibility and data consistency during shader execution.

[5]In this context, performance refers to how optimized the resulting shader assembly is. The cost of doing real-time compilation for the generated shaders should be handled with the usual hashing and caching and offline compilation methods.

flattening loops and conditions. The end result is high extensibility and flexibility without any performance cost.

Perhaps it is early to introduce this subject today, but such an approach is a first step to maintaining data and code hiding concepts in real-time shader development. The importance of this will keep growing as shaders develop and become more popular to non-engine developers.

On a final note, bringing this method into action inside available real-time shader prototyping tools such as NVIDIA's FXComposer and ATI's RenderMonkey would be an interesting and easy task.

Conclusion

This article has proposed a method to expose real-time shader development in an effective and maintainable way from both sides of the story (the shader author and the engine developers). The method builds upon the concept of generating the final shader code from combined shader functions that are implemented by both parties. From one side, the engine composes a *base shader* that works with the current environment and inserts special calls to externally defined shader functions. The implementation of these functions is provided by shader authors with the purpose of customizing shader calculations in the desirable way.

This technique is executed prior to shader compilation and should produce highly optimized assembly.

Acknowledgments

Thanks to Homam Bahnassi of In|Framez for providing information about mental-Ray shader development, as well as figures and references.

References

[Driemeyer05] Driemeyer, Thomas and Rolf Herken, eds. *Programming Mental Ray*, 3rd ed. (mental ray® Handbooks). Springer, 2005.

[DXSAS01] "DirectX Standard Annotations and Semantics Reference." DirectX 9 SDK Documentation, Microsoft Corp., 2006.

[Gritz99] Apdaca, Anthony A. and Larry Gritz. *Advanced RenderMan: Creating CGI for Motion Pictures*, 1st ed. Morgan Kaufmann, 1999.

[MentalImages01] Available online at *ftp://ftp.mentalimages.com/pub/shaders*.

[ShaderWorks05] Bean, Scott. Available online at *http://www.shaderworks.com*, 2005.

8.4

Shader System Integration: Nebula2 and 3ds Max

Kim Hyoun Woo

Introduction

This article presents ideas for integrating shader systems into DCC tools for artist control. As a case study, we look at the art pipeline workflow established by nmaxtoolbox, the Nebula2 plug-in for 3ds Max. The Nebula Device [Nebula06] is an open source real-time 3D game and visualization engine, written in C++. Version 2 has a modern rendering engine that makes full use of shaders. Because of its shader-centric nature, it is also important to provide a shader-driven system for the 3D art pipeline.

The system described here should be considered by both programmers and artists, as it has the following key features:

- It proposes an easy and flexible way to integrate a shader system into any 3D art package.
- It should take little time to implement and should easily integrate into existing code bases.
- It does not require modifications to existing shader code (e.g., for exposing UI controls in the 3D art package for shader parameters).
- It is independent of the actual shader code. Shaders can be written in any language and still be exposed properly for preview and tweaking.
- It shows how to provide an easy-to-use UI for specifying shader parameters.
- It provides users with instant feedback as they tweak shader parameters from within the 3D art package.
- It does not require the use of DCC tools' SDKs to do the integration.

Art Pipeline Integration

Since artists are the ones responsible for the final quality of art assets, it is important that a 3D art package allows them to tweak shader parameters to obtain the desired look for what they create. For this reason, most DCC tools provide facilities for implementing such systems.

For example, with 3ds Max 6 (or later versions), it is possible to expose HLSL shader parameters from effect files. The effect file is loaded and analyzed with accordance to

DXSAS [DXSAS01] to expose shader parameters for artist control. This is a powerful feature. However, it is limited to DXSAS-compliant shaders only.

In the case of nmaxtoolbox, we use a different workflow, as shown in Figure 8.4.1.

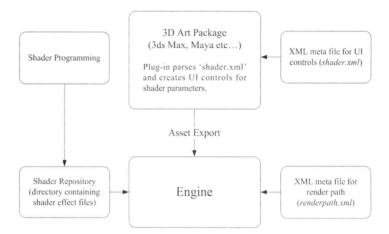

FIGURE 8.4.1   Workflow of the Nebula2 3ds Max toolkit.

The figure shows that effect files (which are written by a shader programmer) are copied to a predetermined location that the game engine knows about. The plug-in inside the 3D art package then dynamically generates UI controls for tweaking shader parameters of a particular shader (in our case this plug-in is nmaxtoolbox). The UI information is extracted by parsing a shaders.xml file (which is created by a programmer). Finally, the game engine depends on the renderpath.xml file to know where it should look for the actual shader code.

To meet artists' needs, the plug-in must support at least two things:

- Easy-to-use user interface for tweaking shader parameters
- Real-time feedback during shader parameter tweaking

In the case of 3ds Max, perhaps one of the easiest ways to provide a decent user interface for editing shader parameters is to use the program's scripting facility.

For nmaxtoolbox, the parameters for each shader are described in an XML metafile (shaders.xml). This metafile contains the name, type, and the default value for each parameter, as well as additional information that is useful for the plug-in.

At load time, the plug-in automatically generates MAXScript code based on the given metafile's contents.

A typical metafile would look like the following:

```
<shader name="Standard" shaderType="default" meshType="default
bsp" file="static">
```

```
...
<param name="MatDiffuse" label="Diffuse Color" type="Color"
gui="1" export="1" def="1.0 1.0 1.0 1.0" />
<param name="MatEmissive" label="Emissive Color" type="Color"
gui="1" export="1" def="0.0 0.0 0.0 0.0" />
<param name="MatEmissiveIntensity" label="Emissive Intensity"
type="Float" gui="1" export="1" min="0.0" max="10.0"
def="1.0" />
<param name="MatSpecular" label="Specular Color" type="Color"
gui="1" export="1" def="0.5 0.5 0.5 1.0" />
...
</shader>
```

For the "Standard" shader, the parameter description for `MatDiffuse` contains the name attribute (which specifies the name of the parameter), the `label` attribute (which specifies the label to use for the corresponding UI control), the `type` attribute (which specifies the data type of the parameter), where `Color` means that a color picker should be used for changing the value of the parameter. Finally, the `def` attribute specifies the initial/default value of the parameter. Figure 8.4.2 shows the user interface that is generated for this shader inside 3ds Max.

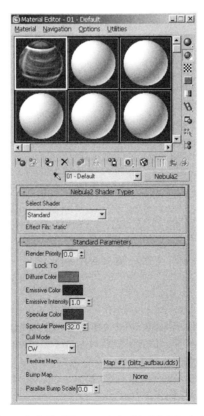

FIGURE 8.4.2 Nebula2's UI controls inside 3ds Max's Material Editor.

The good thing about this design is that it frees the UI from the underlying shader language, so the shader can be freely written in any language (e.g., HLSL or CgFX). Also, the same UI metafiles can be used across different 3D art packages.

ON THE CD

UI controls are added by means of MAXScript. However, it can be tedious to write new MAXScript code every time a new shader is to be exposed. Thus, the plug-in contains logic to automatically generate MAXScript code for UI controls out of metafiles.

The controls created by the plug-in are of different types that suit the underlying data type. These controls include spin buttons, drop-down lists, texture buttons, color pickers, and static labels.

Most 3D art packages have a scripting engine that can be used to dynamically create the UI controls. When scripting is not available, usually plain C++ code generation can compensate for that, but with some added effort.

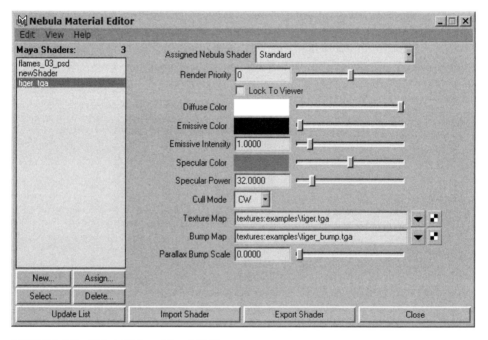

FIGURE 8.4.3 Nebula2 Maya Material Editor.

For Maya, the Nebula2 exporter plug-in uses MEL (Maya's scripting language) to generate UI controls for shader parameters [NebulaMayaTookit06] as shown in Figure 8.4.3. However, the LightWave plug-in uses plain C++ code to achieve the same task as shown in Figure 8.4.4.

In the end, to expose a new shader, we only have to add a new shader entry to the metafile and then specify the shader parameters. The required UI script/code will be automatically generated then. Thus, adding new shaders can be done even by an artist.

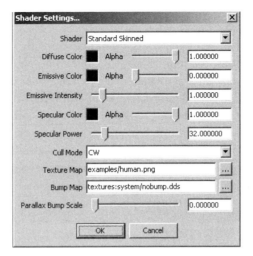

FIGURE 8.4.4 Nebula2 LightWave Material Editor.

As an example, the code snippet below shows the generated MAXScript code for the Standard material:

```
caStandard = attributes "Standard"
(
parameters Standard rollout:rStandard
(
    ...
    MatDiffuse type:#frgba default:[255.000000, 255.000000,
    255.000000, 255.000000] ui:MatDiffuse
    on MatDiffuse set val do
    (
        if loading != true do
        (
            curMaterial = medit.GetCurMtl()
            if classof curMaterial != MultiMaterial do
                if curMaterial.delegate != undefined do
                    curMaterial.delegate.ambient = val
        )
    )
    ...

    rollout rStandard "Standard Parameters"
    (
        ...
        colorpicker MatDiffuse "Diffuse Color" align:#left
        alpha:true color:[255.000000, 255.000000, 255.000000,
        255.000000]
        colorpicker MatEmissive "Emissive Color" align:#left
        alpha:true color:[0.000000, 0.000000, 0.000000, 0.000000]
        ...
    )
)
```

Data Exchange

All exposed shader parameters should be correctly serialized when the 3D model is exported. Thus, the plug-in must be able to access and store shader parameters that are associated with a particular art asset. For 3ds Max, this can be accomplished with *custom attributes*, while Maya uses *extra attributes*. These are additional pieces of information that are saved along with the relevant 3D model in the scene file.

Note that the plug-in exports only the alias of the shader, not the shader code itself. The mapping of shader aliases-to-effect files is specified in the XML metafile (renderpath.xml) that is used by the rendering engine. A typical renderpath.xml meta file might look like this:

```
<RenderPath name="dx9hdr" shaderPath="home:data/shaders/2.0">
    ...
    <!- declare shaders and technique aliases ->
    <Shader name="passes" file="shaders:passes.fx" />
    <Shader name="phases" file="shaders:phases.fx" />
    <Shader name="compose" file="shaders:hdr.fx" />
    <Shader name="static" file="shaders:shaders.fx" />
    <Shader name="static_atest" file="shaders:shaders.fx" />
    <Shader name="environment" file="shaders:shaders.fx" />
    <Shader name="lightmapped" file="shaders:shaders.fx" />
    <Shader name="lightmapped2" file="shaders:shaders.fx" />
    <Shader name="radiosity_normalmapped"
     file="shaders:shaders.fx" />
    <Shader name="skinned" file="shaders:shaders.fx" />
    <Shader name="blended" file="shaders:shaders.fx" />
    <Shader name="alpha" file="shaders:shaders.fx" />
    ...
</RenderPath>
```

Thus, for example, if an exported model specifies `static` as its shader alias, then it will end up using the effect file shaders.fx.

The following Nebula TCL script creates a typical Nebula2 model:

```
new nshapenode model_0
sel model_0
.settexture "DiffMap0" "textures:materials/checker.dds"
.settexture "BumpMap0" "textures:materials/bump.dds"
.setvector "MatDiffuse" 1.000000 1.000000 1.000000 1.000000
.setvector "MatEmissive" 0.000000 0.000000 0.000000 0.000000
.setfloat "MatEmissiveIntensity" 1.000000
.setvector "MatSpecular" 1.000000 1.000000 1.000000 1.000000
.setfloat "MatSpecularPower" 18.160000
.setint "CullMode" 2
.setfloat "BumpScale" 0.000000
.setshader "static"
.setgroupindex 0
sel ..
```

This script shows which texture file to use, as well as the value for diffuse, emissive, specular color, and so on. Most of these settings are passed as parameters to the shader, which is also specified in the script, so model_0 above will be rendered with the `static` shader (found in shaders.fx as specified by renderpath.xml).

Real-time Feedback

Instant feedback for shader parameter tweaks is essential for artists' productivity. The way to achieve this is to use the game engine to display the art asset while the artist is working on it, with shader parameter changes being directly reflected in the view as they occur [Bahnassi05]. However, such an implementation requires the use of the 3D art package's SDK, which can be time-consuming.

In the case of nmaxtoolbox, the asset in question is exported to a predetermined location on disk, from where a preview window picks it up and loads it for rendering using the game engine (Figure 8.4.5).

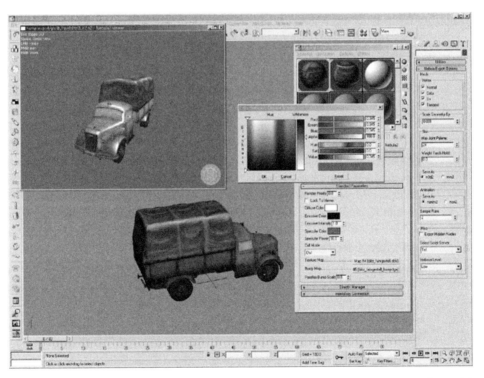

FIGURE 8.4.5   The Nebula2 preview window rendering the exported model. (The opelblitz model is used with permission of RadonLabs.)

In comparison with 3ds Max's hardware plug-in implementation (e.g., the DirectX 9 Material), this method does not provide instant feedback for topology modifications (the model has to be exported again). However, both implementations provide instant feedback for shader parameter value changes that are done inside of 3ds Max's Material Library. Since nmaxtoolbox uses 3ds Max parameter blocks to represent shader parameters, all of these parameters are automatically saved inside the .max file when the scene is saved, which preserves their values across different scene sessions.

As shown in Figure 8.4.5, artists can use 3ds Max's color picker to change the diffuse color of the model. These changes are immediately sent to the preview window for instant feedback on the new model's appearance.

Since the preview window is implemented as an external process, nmaxtoolbox uses interprocess communication (IPC) to communicate shader parameter changes to the preview window. Thus, after an art asset gets exported, the plug-in opens the preview window and connects to it using IPC before it starts to send shader parameter change messages. The underlying mechanism of this feature is based on networking technology (TCP). In 3ds Max, parameter changes trigger a MAXScript that generates a Nebula2 script, which is then sent to the preview window. Below is an example of such MAXScript code:

```
if nIsConnectedIpc() do
(
    nChangeShaderParameter "Standard" "common" "MatDiffuse" "0.5
    1.0 1.0 1.0"
)
```

The script function `nChangeShaderParameter` is a 3ds Max script-callable function. It wraps the Nebula2 API and sends Nebula2 script with the given parameters to the connected preview window. In the code above, the first parameter, `"Standard"`, is the shader type, while the third parameter, `"MatDiffuse"`, specifies which shader parameter to change, and the last parameter is the new value for diffuse.

Implementation Notes

The source code for the Nebula2 engine and the nmaxtoolbox plug-in is available free-of-charge for commercial and noncommercial use at *http://www.nebuladevice.org* [Nebula06].

So far, this article has only described integration with 3ds Max, but the approach here can be easily adopted for other 3D art packages as well (e.g., Maya, Softimage, Lightwave, etc.). nmaxtoolbox uses the same UI metafile that is used by the Nebula2 Toolkit for Maya (a commercial Maya plug-in from RadonLabs) and the Nebula2 Exporter for Lightwave. This method should integrate easily into existing toolchains, including those that use third-party middleware.

One problem with the method described here is that it is hard to have the preview window view and tweak a complex scene containing multiple shaders.

Another potential improvement is to use a third-party script language such as Python or Lua for generating MAXScript out of UI meta files. Currently, whenever the nmaxtoolbox's UI generation code is modified, it needs to be recompiled, and 3ds Max must be restarted. Using a third-party scripting language would allow modifications to the shader UI generation code without recompiling the plug-in or restarting 3ds Max.

Conclusion

This article proposed a system design for integrating game engine visualization services inside DCC tools for artistic shader control and tweaking. The implementation of such a system requires only a small amount of coding. The case of Nebula2 and 3ds Max was taken as an example.

This system is not restricted to a specific shader language. Available shaders are specified in a special file, which is loaded by the nmaxtoolbox plug-in inside 3ds Max. The plug-in then reads meta UI files to render UI controls inside 3ds Max's Material Library by automatic generation of MAXScript instructions.

A preview window is launched after the 3D object gets exported to load and render that object using the game engine. This window is connected to the nmaxtoolbox plug-in to communicate shader parameter changes and give instant feedback as soon as they occur.

Acknowledgments

I thank RadonLabs for their efforts on The Nebula Device open source 3D engine. Also, thanks to Vadim Macagon (author of The Nebula2 LightWave Toolkit for his help with this article.

References

[Bahnassi05] Bahnassi, Homam and Wessam Bahnassi. "Shader Visualization Systems for the Art Pipeline." *ShaderX³: Advanced Rendering with DirectX and OpenGL*, edited by Wolfgang Engel. Charles River Media, 2005: pp. 487–504.

[DXSAS01] "DirectX Standard Annotations and Semantics Reference." *DirectX 9 SDK Documentation*, Microsoft Corp., 2006.

[Nebula06] The Nebula Device. Available online at *http://www.nebuladevice.org*.

[NebulaMayaTookit06] Nebula2 Toolkit 2.0 for Maya®. Available online at *http://www.radonlabs.de/toolkit.html*.

BEYOND PIXELS AND TRIANGLES

Introduction

Sebastien St-Laurent

Graphics processors provide an additional resource that can be harnessed for purposes other than just rendering. This section will cover articles that present techniques that go beyond pixels and triangles.

The section opens with the article "Large Crowds of Autonomous Animated Characters Using Fragment Shaders and Level of Detail," by Erik Millán, Benjamín Hernández, and Isaac Rudomín. The authors implemented agent behavior using finite state machines evaluated by fragment shaders.

Image segmentation consists of grouping pixels into homogeneous regions representing perceptual units using local and/or global cues. Frank Nielsen presents in his article "Interactive Image Segmentation Based on GPU Cellular Automata" a GPU shader implementation for a recent simple yet efficient cellular automata-based foreground/background hard segmentation.

The next article, "Real-time Cellular Texturing," presents two methods for generating 2D Worley-based cellular imagery in real-time using the GPU. The author, Andrew Griffiths, wanted to see what Worley noise would look like animated.

Rahul Sathe's article, "Collision Detection Shader Using Cube-Maps," covers an alternative approach to collision detection that replaces the recursive algorithms with a nonrecursive algorithm that is well suited to run on graphics processors. The algorithm presented here makes use of a hardware-accelerated texturing mode called "cube-map."

The article "A GPU Panorama Viewer for Generic Camera Models," by Frank Nielsen, presents a panorama viewer that allows rendering of several generic camera models in a same view as well converting or remapping on-the-fly complete environment maps on the GPU.

Pedro V. Sander, Natalya Tatarchuk, and Jason L. Mitchell present in their article, "Explicit Early-Z Culling for Efficient Fluid Flow Simulation," an efficient algorithm for simulation and rendering of fluid flow directly on graphics hardware by utilizing early-z culling on current graphics hardware.

The article "Storing and Accessing Topology on the GPU: A Case Study on Mass-Spring Systems," by Carlos A. Dietrich, João L. D. Comba, and Luciana P. Nedel, presents a study case on how to implement mass-spring systems on the GPU, which is a practical technique for implementing deformable systems. They present a critical discussion on the operation that most affects performance in this method: the storage and access of topological information.

Wai-Man Pang, Tien-Tsin Wong, and Pheng-Ann Heng in their article, "Implementing High-Quality PRNG on GPUs," propose using a cellular automata (CA)-based pseudo-random number generator (PRNG) that does not require high-precision integer arithmetic or bitwise operations. It relies only on simple low-precision arithmetic and interconnection of cells (pixels). It generates high-quality random sequences and fits nicely into the architecture of the current GPU.

Finally, the article "Printf Shader for Debugging Pixel Shaders," by Alexander Ehrath, covers a method to visually write numeric shader values directly onto the texture to be debugged while your program runs.

9.1

Large Crowds of Autonomous Animated Characters Using Fragment Shaders and Level of Detail

Erik Millán, Benjamín Hernández, and

Isaac Rudomín, ITESM CEM

Introduction

In motion pictures large crowds of computer-generated characters are often included to produce battle scenes of epic proportions. However, this large number of characters is not yet seen in video games or virtual interactive scenes.

The reason behind this is the resources demanded by crowd simulation. Crowds of hundreds of characters are seen in current video games, but crowds of hundreds of thousands seem prohibitively expensive.

Graphics processors provide an additional resource that can be harnessed for purposes other than just rendering. Shader programs have been, for instance, used to render a variety of characters by modifying colors of clothes, hair, and skin, making it possible to render up to a thousand characters at interactive frame rates [deHeras05]. Geopostors [Dobyn05] also use shader programs to draw a set of impostors, blending normal maps with different-colored regions and detail maps to produce a large variety of virtual characters, and rendering up to 30,000 characters within an urban environment.

However, the power of graphics hardware has not been fully utilized to process the simulation of character behavior. In this chapter we will explain how a large crowd of animated characters can be both simulated and rendered using finite-state machines (FSMs) on the graphics processor.

Simulation of Character Behavior on the GPU

A very common and simple way to define behavior for virtual characters is by using FSMs. In previous work [Rudomin04], we created a system to specify character behavior based on such machines by using a combination of XML scripting and images. From the extensive use of images in this approach, we decided that implementing agent behavior using FSMs evaluated by fragment shaders would be simple and deliver better performance.

Finite State Machines

An FSM can be defined as a set of states and transitions. In the case of animated characters, a state represents a single behavior, such as running or turning left. When certain conditions are met, a transition is triggered. This transition changes the machine to a different state, where a different behavior is performed.

FSMs Using Image Maps

In [Millan05] we implemented an FSM as a fragment shader using three types of image maps: agent-space image maps, world-space image maps, and FSM image maps. The basic idea is to use dependent texture lookups of these maps within a fragment shader.

Agent-space maps contain information about the state of characters. Each pixel from these maps will contain the information for each different character. Initially, they may contain the position (x, y) of the character as well as its current state s within the FSM. This can be extended to include additional information, such as the animation frame or the details of each character.

World-space image maps contain information about the environment. The position (x, y) of a character within a scene will be mapped to a set of texture coordinates (u, v) that will be mapped to each world-space map used. In this way, information about the environment can be obtained and used to influence the behavior of the character.

FSM maps contain information about the behavior for each state and about transitions between states. In our proposed framework rows from the FSM maps will be used to group transitions within the same state, while columns will contain different conditions that will trigger transitions. Then, each pixel in the FSM map will codify, given a state and certain conditions, the behavior and transitions that will occur.

The transition can be stored as the index of the state to which the character will switch, and the behavior can be stored also as an index of a set of behaviors, a displacement for the character, a given animation, or a reference to query a different map to provide the resulting behavior.

The use of these maps to simulate character behavior is illustrated in Figure 9.1.1. For each character in the agent-space map, its state and position are extracted. The position is used to evaluate the environment and query for certain conditions that might trigger a transition. These conditions, together with the character state, will be used to query the FSM map, which will work as a look-up table to obtain the new position and state for the character.

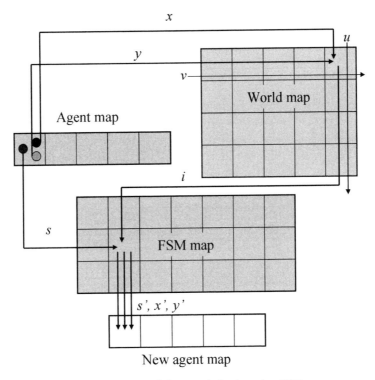

FIGURE 9.1.1   Simulation of character behavior using FSM maps.

The pseudocode for this algorithm is shown in Listing 9.1.1. In this listing, after the state and the position have been calculated, the character should be drawn. This will be addressed in the next section.

LISTING 9.1.1   Simple Pseudocode for FSM on a GPU

```
for_each character in agent_map
  {
    s = character.s;
    x = character.x;
    y = character.y;
    l = world_map[x, y];
    character.sxy = fsm_map[s, l];
    draw character;
  }
```

Level of Detail Techniques

While character behavior can be very efficiently simulated using the proposed algorithm, the geometry for these characters should be animated and rendered efficiently to show a large number of characters at interactive frame rates.

The naïve approach to rendering crowds of characters, consisting of drawing each character with its animated geometry, dramatically increases the number of polygons and, possibly, the amount of data sent from the main memory to the graphics card. In addition, the geometry of animated characters must be modified constantly, which produces constant updates of the geometry for these characters.

Instead, level of detail (LOD) techniques can be used to reduce the number of polygons actually displayed. The objectives of these techniques are to discard objects that are not visible to the camera and to reduce geometric detail in distant objects that are drawn in small areas of the screen.

Object Culling and Detail Selection

A simple approach to determining which characters are visible to a camera, and which uses the machinery already present in the algorithm, is to use a visibility map. To produce this map, the view frustum is intersected with a world-space image map. The polygon where the viewing frustum intersects this plane is then painted in white, with the rest of the map in black. Once this map is generated, a simple query on this map is enough to evaluate whether a character is visible in the current view.

An extension to visibility maps are LOD maps. Instead of drawing a white polygon, each intersection of the viewing frustum will contain a grayscale value w, obtained in this way:

$$w = \frac{z_{far} - z_{int}}{z_{far} - z_{near}}$$

where z_{int} is the distance from the intersection to the camera, and z_{far} and z_{near} are the distances of the corners of the far and near planes to the camera, respectively. The polygon enclosed by these vertices will be drawn on the LOD map, linearly interpolating the colors of the polygon. Darker values on this map denote a lower detail for characters. Characters that are on black areas are culled from the image. An example of an LOD map is shown in Figure 9.1.2.

For renderable characters, a threshold is used to select whether a character is to be rendered at full detail or at a lower detail. In our implementation detailed characters are displayed using a pseudo-instancing technique, while low-detail characters are drawn using impostors.

Impostors

Latest generation hardware supports geometry instancing for static objects under DirectX. In OpenGL pseudo-instancing must be used instead. Any of those techniques

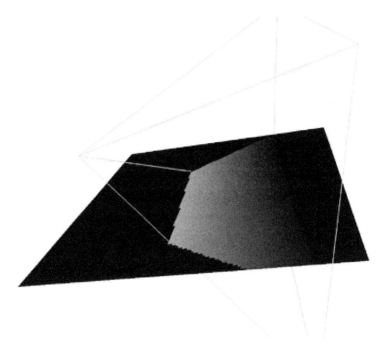

FIGURE 9.1.2 Generation of a LOD map.

can be used to increase the number of full-detail rendered objects. However, graphics hardware still has to deal with a large number of polygons per character. For lower-detail characters, a technique known as impostors is used, reducing the geometry for each character to a single quad.

Impostors for virtual characters were introduced by Aubel et. al. [Aubel98] as an image-based approach to rendering objects. An impostor represents a character as a simple textured plane, which is constantly rotated to face the camera. The texture for this plane is updated with a snapshot obtained according to the relative position of the character to the camera.

Snapshots for impostors are produced in a preprocessing step. This step involves rendering a model using a discrete set of views. For animated characters, models are also rendered in different poses. All these views are stored in a texture and used later in the rendering step. An example of a set of images for an impostor is shown in Figure 9.1.3.

The rendering step involves the display of a textured quad for each character. To generate these quads, the agent-space map is extended so that each character occupies four pixels instead of one. These four pixels are used as the corners of the quad for each impostor.

The extended texture is then used to render all characters. Based on the LOD map, a vertex shader first selects whether the current character will be rendered as an

FIGURE 9.1.3   Images for two animation frames of an impostor.

impostor. If the character will not be rendered as an impostor, the quad vertices are discarded by setting its w component to -1.

For those characters rendered as impostors, a fragment shader uses the camera location and the character direction to select the view that best resembles the appearance of the character. This view, in addition to the current animation frame for the character, will be used to select the texture coordinates within the impostor texture.

Pseudo-Instancing

Object instancing is a technique that can improve the rendering performance of large sets of similar objects [Scott04]. As this example was programmed in OpenGL, a pseudo-instancing approach was used. This approach, similar to the one presented by Zelsnack [Zelsnack04], provides results similar in speed to DirectX instancing.

For nearby characters, a pseudo-instancing technique was used to display the full geometry of the character. The agent map is read into main memory, as well as the details for each character. Details for each character are verified and, for those characters selected for full detail, a display list is rendered, using a shader that will receive the agent displacement for each character.

The display list will be updated at each animation frame. By using a single display list, each character will be shown in the same animation frame. However, better results may be achieved by using a small set of display lists and then selecting the display list of the animation frame closest to the current frame of the character.

Adding Per-Character Attributes

Different attributes for each character may be modified by adding the required agent-space image maps. For instance, color information can be generated randomly for each character. This will produce a different and unique appearance for each character.

This additional information is then used in both the pseudo-instancing fragment shader and in the impostor fragment shader to influence the final color of each pixel. Different parameters can be included in this way to modify different aspects of the final render, such as the animation bias or the size of each character.

Results

ON THE CD

To evaluate this approach, a very simple FSM was implemented. This FSM and the map that represents its behavior are both illustrated in Figure 9.1.4. In this FSM characters simply move from a red area, located on the left side of the screen, toward the green area, on the right side of the screen, and then go back toward the red area.

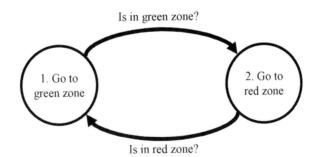

$f(L,S):(S,\Delta x, \Delta y)$	L=Red	L=Yellow	L=Green
S = State 1	**1,1,0** *RGB[0, 255, 0]*	**1,1,0** *RGB[0, 255, 0]*	**2,0,0** *RGB[255, 128, 0]*
S = State 2	**1,0,0** *RGB[0, 128, 0]*	**2,-1,0** *RGB[255, 0, 0]*	**2,-1,0** *RGB[255, 0, 0]*

FIGURE 9.1.4   Example FSM and equivalent FSM map.

The FSM map is composed of two rows, indicating the two different states of the agent: move toward green and move toward red. There are also three different columns, which will be selected according to the information on the world map, seen at the bottom of the simulation in Figure 9.1.5. When characters are found within a red area, a transition in the FSM map is identified by specifying a state different from the current one in the red component of the pixel. According to this map, transitions are triggered in state 1 when the character is walking over a green area and in state 2 when the character is walking over a red area.

In addition, this FSM map includes information on the direction of motion for each character. In the first state, the green component is set to 1, which will move the character right, while on the second state, the green component is set to −1, moving the character to the left.

The system used for the simulation was a Pentium Xeon at 3.2Ghz with a QuadroFX 4400 graphics card, and it was rendered on a 1280×1024 window. Some results of this simulation are shown in Figure 9.1.5, in which a crowd of characters with random colors is displayed. An agent map of 512×512 was used in this simulation. Hence, the behavior of 256K characters was simulated, and characters were ani-

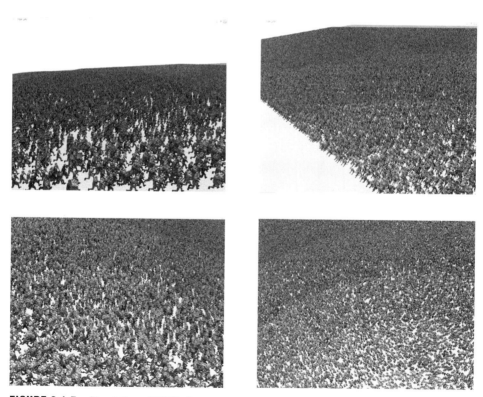

FIGURE 9.1.5   Simulation of 256K characters.

mated and rendered interactively at frame rates between 6 and 15 frames per second within a 1280×1024 window.

Additional frame rates can be seen in Table 9.1.1. Maximum frame rates are obtained when the entire crowd is viewed at a distance, using only impostors in rendering. On the contrary, minimum frame rates combine both impostors and pseudo-instancing for display in a worst-case scenario when most of the characters are seen.

The main drawback of this technique is the additional complexity added by the use of pseudo-instancing. While an impostor requires a single quad to draw a single character, instanced characters have about 300 triangles each. This reduces the frame rate when approaching the crowd.

TABLE 9.1.1 Frame Rates for Different Numbers of Characters (Maximum frame rates use only impostors, while minimum rates use a mix of impostors and pseudo-instancing.)

	Different Colors	Same Colors
256K characters (512^2)	6.5–15.0 fps	8.5–15.1 fps
64K characters (256^2)	19.7–30.0 fps	19.9–30.0 fps
16K characters (128^2)	29.9–60.1 fps	29.9–60.0 fps

Conclusions

We have presented a set of techniques that increase the efficiency of existing methods for simulation and rendering of animated characters by about an order of magnitude compared with existing work. This allows an interactive application to produce large crowds, reducing the resources required for character animation.

The main disadvantage of this approach is that behavior specification is a highly complex process. Every pixel of the FSM should be constructed pixel by pixel within a paint application. A method to automate the creation of this FSM map from a piece of code would highly enhance the usability of this approach.

References

[Aubel98] Aubel, Amaury, Ronan Boulic, and Daniel Thalmann. "Animated Impostors for Real-time Display of Numerous Virtual Humans." *Proceedings of the First International Conference on Virtual Worlds* (VW '98), 1998: pp. 14–28.

[deHeras05] de Heras C., Pablo Sébastien Schertenleib, Jonathan Maïm, Damien Maupu, and Daniel Thalmann. "Real-time Shader Rendering for Crowds in Virtual Heritage." *Proceedings of the 6th International Symposium on Virtual Reality, Archaeology and Intelligent Cultural Heritage* (VAST 2005): pp. 91–98.

[Dobyn05] Dobyn, Simon, John Hamill, Keith O'Conor, and Carol O'Sullivan. "Geopostors: A Real-time Geometry / Impostor Crowd Rendering System." *ACM Transactions on Graphics*, *24*(3) (SIGGRAPH 2005): pp. 933–933.

[Millan05] Millán, Erik, Isaac Rudomín, and Benjamín Hernández. "Fragment Shaders for Agent Animation Using Finite State Machines." *Simulation Modelling Practice and Theory Journal, 13*(8), (November 2005): pp. 741–751.

[Rudomin04] Rudomín, Isaac and Erik Millán. "XML Scripting and Images for Specifying Behavior of Virtual Characters and Crowds." *Proceedings of Computer Animation and Social Agents,* 2004 (CASA 2004): pp. 121–128.

[Scott04] Scott, Phil. "Shader Model 3.0, Best Practices." Technical Report, NVIDIA Corporation, 2004. Available online at *http://developer.nvidia.com/object/SM3_0_best_practices.html,* July 10, 2005.

[Zelsnack04] Zelsnack, Jeremy. "GLSL Pseudo-Instancing." Technical Report, NVIDIA Corporation, 2004. Available online at *http://download.developer.nvidia.com/developer/SDK/Individual_Samples/3dgraphics_samples.html,* July 10, 2005.

9.2

Interactive Image Segmentation Based on GPU Cellular Automata

Frank Nielsen, Sony Computer Science Laboratories, Inc.

Introduction

Image segmentation consists of grouping pixels into homogeneous regions representing perceptual units using local and/or global cues. Although the first segmentation algorithms were introduced in the early 1970s, segmentation is still a hot topic of computer vision. Segmentation can be handled at different image understanding scales [Nielsen05]: (1) *low-level* segmentation uses local pixel neighborhood cues such as color or texture information to infer the global image partition; (2) *middle-level* segmentation considers elements of the Gestalt theory such as symmetry detection and rules thereof to improve the pixel grouping; (3) *high-level* segmentation relies on (re)cognition to improve the overall global segmentation (e.g., recognizing first categories of objects lets us later refine their segmentations). Foreground-background segmentation is a simplified segmentation task that seeks to decompose the image into two planes: the *foreground mask plane* and the *background mask plane*. Finally, we distinguish between *hard* and *soft* segmentation, which depends on whether masks have only 0/1 binary values or potentially float values (by analogy to hard/soft clustering). It is well known that segmentation algorithms are time-consuming and that they may work or simply fail, depending on input images. Thus, it is crucial to allow for a rectification mechanism by letting the user *steer* the segmentation using prior cues [Nock05].

To reduce segmentation computation times, the GPU has already been successfully used in the past for fully automatic segmentation, using for example level sets [Lefohn05]. Here, we present a GPU shader implementation for a recent simple yet efficient cellular automata-based foreground/background hard segmentation: GrowCut [Vezhnevets05]. Figure 9.2.1 displays the compositing result obtained after segmenting of a stuffed furry dog image by a GrowCut shader.

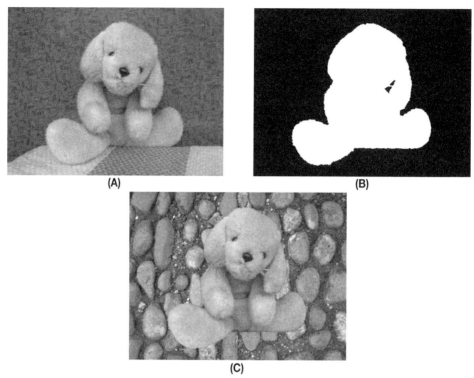

FIGURE 9.2.1   Source image of a **(A)** stuffed furry dog **(B)** with its binary foreground mask obtained from GrowCut. Image **(C)** displays the result of compositing the dog mask with a new background image.

The GrowCut Cellular Automaton Principle

Vezhnevets and Konouchine [Vezhnevets05] recently proposed an elegant and very simple segmentation algorithm, called GrowCut, based on cellular automata. Grow-Cut performs well in practice: A Photoshop® plug-in that can also be used with shareware or freeware software such as Xnview (*xnview.org*), IrfanView (*irfanview.com*), or Paintshop (*jasc.com*) is available [Vezhnevets05]. GrowCut first initializes a cellular automaton (CA) where each cell associated to an image pixel stores its *state* in a three-tuple $(l, s, \mathbf{C})$. Parameter l denotes the label of cell, namely, the foreground ($l = 1$) or background label ($l = 0$) of the underlying cell's pixel. Scalar variable s denotes the strength of the cell, which is related to the stability of the label. Finally, vector $\mathbf{C}$ encodes the color information of the corresponding pixel: A triple of RGB colors. To initialize a GrowCut CA, we set for each pixel p its corresponding CA cell as: $l[p] = 0, s[p] = 0, \mathbf{C}[p] = (R_p, G_p, B_p)$. Then, we require the user to *initially* input foreground and background priors using mouse strokes, as depicted in Figure 9.2.2. We set the corresponding cell states using the stroke label and enforce the initial hard constraints using the maximum strength $s = 1$. Pixel regions not covered by any stroke are labeled unknown ($l = 0.5$) with zero strength. Thus, pixels are initially annotated as being either foreground, background, or unknown (initial trimap). A more flexible initialization will provide a soft background/foreground brush where the strength values may decrease as we near the stroke borders (values within the unit interval).

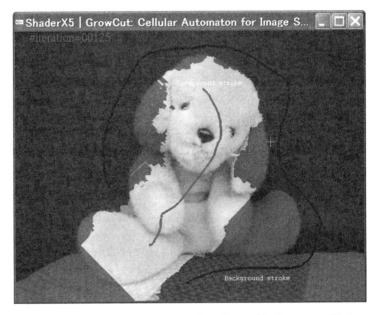

FIGURE 9.2.2   Snapshot of the CPU GrowCut application on a stuffed furry dog image showing the evolution of pixel labels at the 125th iteration.

ON THE CD

Once this initialization step is performed, we let the GrowCut CA evolve on the trimap until it converges into a stable state at which none of the cell states change. Please refer to subfolders, CPU GrowCut UI and CPU Image Composite, in the article's folder on the CD-ROM. The evolution rules are inspired by bacteria behaviors. Bacteria may spread if they can successfully attack some of their neighbors, or conversely, they shrink and potentially vanish if they have been killed by other families of bacteria. Bacteria of a same family are indexed by their common label l. We summarize in pseudo-code the GrowCut CA evolution rule as originally proposed in [Vezhnevets05]:

```
// Pseudo-code for GrowCut CA evolution rules
For all cells
    // Copy the previous state (colors do not change)
```

```
l'[p] = l[p], s'[p] = s[p]
For all C4 or C8 neighbor q of the current cell
if g(Dist(C[p],C[q])s[q]>s[p] then
    // q successfully attacked p
    // update the cell state
    ;'[p] = l[q],s'[q] = g()Dist(C[p],C[q],C[q]s[q]
```

`Dist()` returns the distance between two RGB colors, and function `g()` is a *monotonous decreasing* function bounded to the unit interval $[0,1]$ that guarantees convergence. For example, we can choose $g(x) = 1 - \dfrac{x}{MaxDist} \in [0,1]$.

Choosing the 3D Euclidean distance for comparing (RGB) triples yields $MaxDist = 255\sqrt{3}$ (approximately 441.67). (CIE LAB color space may yield better results, as the Euclidean distance makes sense but would require an extra image conversion step.)

Cellular automata bring to segmentation a *fully dynamic* aspect of region labeling, where pixels' labels may oscillate a few times before reaching their final states. Moreover, at any time, users can further interactively input foreground/background strokes or edit previous strokes to gear the overall segmentation in difficult areas. A naïve CPU implementation (`GrowCutUI`) using a thread for computing the GrowCut cellular automaton yields a low refresh rate. CA, coupled map lattice (CML), or Petri nets are well known to be easily ported to GPU architectures [Harris03] [Lefohn05] (e.g., Conway's game of life). We describe in the next section the GrowCut shader and its performance compared with the nonoptimized CPU version.

A GPU GrowCut Shader

We implemented a simple shader, `growcut.cg`, that examines in a deterministic order the C4 (four-connectivity of pixels) neighbors of a pixel to decide whether to relabel its neighbor. Because computations are carried out in parallel between any two successive iterations, this amounts to deciding for each pixel whether it keeps its label, and updating its strength accordingly. Our shader is a direct translation of the basic C++ loop code. In this implementation we deterministically examine the neighborhood of pixels and store the five parameters (*R*, *G*, *B*, *l*, *s*) into two texture units: the source color image (*R*, *G*, *B*) and the label-strength image (*l*, *s*). Considering a random order of inspection of a pixel's neighborhood will yield a better segmentation but remove privileged-direction-growth artifacts. The shader in the following listing and its accompanying program can further be improved in several ways such as taking into account several objects instead of plain foreground/background segmentation (multi-label), handling 3D volumetric image stacks, and smoothing the object boundaries using a somewhat more complex evolution rule [Vezhnevets05].

```
float Dist(float3 p, float3 q)
{return sqrt((p[0]-q[0])*(p[0]-q[0])+(p[1]-q[1])*
(p[1]-q[1])+(p[2]-q[2])*(p[2]-q[2]));}

sqrt(3) is approximately 1.7321
float g(float x)
{return 1.0-x/(1.7321);}

void GrowCut( float2 texCoord:TEXCOORD0, out float3 color: COLOR,
uniform samplerRECT Image, uniform samplerRECT Label)
{
// Neighborhood in color RGB image
float3 pixel = f3texRECT(Image, texCoord);
float3 neighUp = f3texRECT(Image, texCoord+float2(0,1)) ;
float3 neighDown = f3texRECT(Image, texCoord+float2(0,-1) ) ;
float3 neighLeft = f3texRECT(Image, texCoord+float2(-1,0) ) ;
float3 neighRight = f3texRECT(Image, texCoord+float2(1,0) ) ;

// Neighborhood in (Label,Strength) image
float3 pixell = f3texRECT(Label, texCoord);
float3 neighUpl = f3texRECT(Label, texCoord+float2(0,1)) ;
float3 neighDownl = f3texRECT(Label,  texCoord+float2(0,-1) ) ;
float3 neighLeftl = f3texRECT(Label, texCoord+float2(-1,0) ) ;
float3 neighRightl = f3texRECT(Label, texCoord+float2(1,0) ) ;

// Initialization
float label=pixell[0];
float strength=pixell[1];

float pstrengthUp=neighUpl[1]*g(Dist(neighUp[0],pixel[0]));
float pstrengthDown=neighDownl[1]*g(Dist(neighDown[0],pixel[0]));
float pstrengthLeft=neighLeftl[1]*g(Dist(neighLeft[0],pixel[0]));
float pstrengthRight=neighRightl[1]*g(Dist(neighRight[0],pixel[0]));

float diffUp=pstrengthUp-strength;
float diffDown=pstrengthDown-strength;
float diffLeft=pstrengthLeft-strength;
float diffRight=pstrengthRight-strength;

//
//Neighbor UP tries to attack me
//
    if ((neighUpl[0]!=pixell[0])&&(diffUp>0.0))
        {
        // Neighbor Up succeeded the attack
        label=neighUpl[0];
        strength=pstrengthUp;
        }
        else
        {
```

```
                          // Neighbor DOWN tries to attack me
                          if ((neighDownl[0]!=pixell[0])&&(diffDown>0.0))
                          {
                          label=neighDownl[0];
                          strength=pstrengthDown;
                          }
                          else
                              { // Neighbor LEFT tries to attack me
                                  if ((neighLeftl[0]!=pixell[0])&&(diffLeft>0.0))
                                  {
                                  label=neighLeftl[0];
                                  strength=pstrengthLeft;
                                  }
                                  else
                                  { // Neighbor RIGHT tries to attack me
                                  if ((neighRightl[0]!=pixell[0])&&
                                  (diffRight>0.0))
                                  {
                                  label=neighRightl[0];
                                  strength=pstrengthRight;
                                  }
                              }
                          }
                      }
                  }
              // New LS state for the ImageLS
              color=float3(label,strength,0);
              }
```

For pedagogical reasons, we chose to implement a screen-frame buffer rendering that shows the evolution of the CA state at each iteration. A better-optimized implementation would consider off-screen rendering using common GPGPU techniques: render to pbuffer, render to texture, or use a frame buffer object (OpenGL FBO extension GL_FRAME_BUFFER_EXT [FBO05]).

Finally, we export the foreground mask using the two texture images (ImageRGB, ImageLS) and using another fragment shader, GrowCutExport (see Figure 9.2.3):

```
void  GrowCutExport(float2 texCoord:TEXCOORD0, out float3 color:
COLOR, uniform samplerRECT ImageRGB, uniform samplerRECT ImageLS)
{
float3 pixellabel = f3texRECT(ImageLS, texCoord);

// extract only the foreground object from the image
if (pixellabel[0]==1.0)
        {
        color=f3texRECT(ImageRGB, texCoord);
        }
        else
        {// background color
        color=float3(0.1,0.8,0.1);
        }
}
}
```

(A) (B)

(C)

FIGURE 9.2.3 Snapshot of the GPU GrowCut application (**A**) on a flower image initialized interactively using a foreground/background stroke, (**B**) on a label-strength image after 300 automaton iterations, and (**C**) on an extracted foreground flower.

Conclusion

ON THE CD

We have presented a GPGPU pixel shader for speeding up the simple foreground/background segmentation task using a cellular automaton, which can be found in the article subfolder called GPU GrowCut. The shader implements the simple yet effective GrowCut segmentation method [Vezhnevets05].

References

[FBO05] OpenGL Framebuffer Extension (FBO). Available online at *http://oss.sgi.com/projects/ogl-sample/registry/EXT/framebuffer_object.txt*.

[Lefohn05] Lefohn, Aaron, Ian Buck, Patrick McCormick, John Owens, Timothy Purcell, and Robert Strzodka. "General Purpose Computation on Graphics Hardware." *IEEE Visualization 2005* (VIS'05), 2005.

[Harris03] Harris, Mark J. "Real-time Cloud Simulation and Rendering." University of North Carolina, #TR03-040, 2003. Available online at *http://www.markmark.net/dissertation/*.

[Nielsen05] Nielsen, Frank. *Visual Computing: Geometry, Graphics, and Vision.* Charles River Media, 2005. (*http://www.csl.sony.co.jp/person/nielsen*)

[Nock05] Nock, Richard and Frank Nielsen. "Semi-Supervised Statistical Region Refinement for Color Image Segmentation." *Pattern Recognition,* 38(6), (2005): 835–846.

[Vezhnevets05] Vezhnevets, Vladimir and Vadim Konouchine. "Grow-Cut - Interactive Multi-Label N-D Image Segmentation." Graphicon, 2005. Available online at *http://research.graphicon.ru/growcut/gml-growcut.html.*

9.3

Real-Time Cellular Texturing

Andrew Griffiths, Deep Red Games

Introduction

Cellular texturing describes a type of procedural texture generation based on dividing space up into regions (cells). In 1996 Steve Worley presented a procedural cellular 3D texturing algorithm based on Voronoi cells [Worley96]. His algorithm, often called Worley Noise, is the most well-known implementation of cellular texturing. It has become very popular in the CG industry and is now a cornerstone of procedural basis functions, joining the ranks of Perlin [Perlin02] and Musgrave. One of the main features of the algorithm is its flexibility. It is a basis function with loads of room for experimentation and tweaking, resulting in a huge variety of possible outcomes. This type of texturing is very powerful, but it is also computationally expensive.

This article is the product of wanting to see what Worley noise would look like animated. It turned out that the traditional implementation of Worley noise wasn't suited for animation and was too slow. This article presents two methods for generating 2D Worley-based cellular imagery in real-time using the GPU. The first method is a general solution; the second is more compatible with older hardware and is slightly limited.

Background

Classic Worley noise is a general-purpose texture-basis function. It can be queried for any point in 3D space and will deterministically return a valid texture value. This article will concentrate on generating 2D cellular imagery based on the fundamentals of Worley noise. Luckily, the fundamentals are very simple.

The algorithm works with a set of randomly positioned 2D "feature" points as shown in Figure 9.3.1. For each pixel, the closest of these points is found; the distance to this point is called F_1. Next, the distance to the second closest point is found; this distance is called F_2 as shown in Figure 9.3.2. This can continue on to F_n, the distance to the nth closest point. This is the only data needed to generate cellular textures.

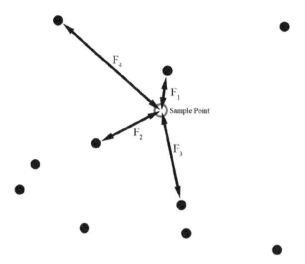

FIGURE 9.3.1   Randomly positioned 2D feature points. The first four feature points closest to the sample point are shown.

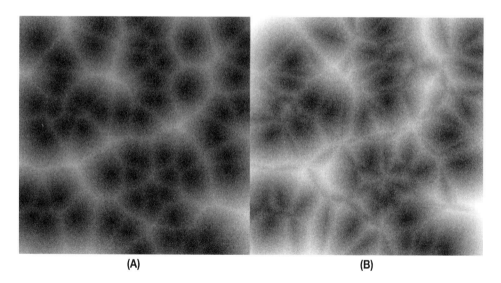

(A)   **(B)**

FIGURE 9.3.2   **(A)** Final F_1 image. **(B)** Final F_2 image.

The final step is completely open. It is up to the individual to decide how to use this distance data to create interesting images. Two of the most commonly used combinations are *flagstone* and *plated*. A flagstone effect (see Figure 9.3.3a) can be achieved by drawing the value of $F_2 - F_1$ per pixel. A plated effect (see Figure 9.3.3b) can be created by using the index of the closest (F_1) feature point to color each pixel. We will only focus on generating grayscale textures, but there is nothing to stop somebody from coming up with colorful variations. The value computed for each pixel can be scaled to bring it between the 0 and 1 range. Scaling and biasing the value is usually needed to bring values into a nice range, and these extra parameters are great for achieving different looks.

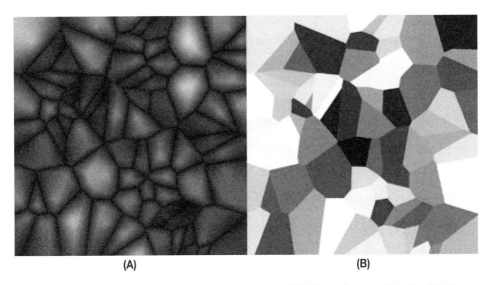

FIGURE 9.3.3 Distance data displayed in various ways. (**A**) Classic flagstone $F_2 - F_1$. (**B**) Classic plated texture.

The great thing is that it's easy to understand and implement this type of cellular imagery. The not-so-great thing is that it's very power hungry.

In a naive implementation each pixel that is sampled would have to do distance calculations to each feature point to find the n-closest point. A 640×480 image with 100 features would need to do 30 million distance calculations. Of course, most implementations use some sort of space segmentation, so the number of distance calculations is much lower than this, but it is still a sizable problem.

GPU Implementation

Our goal is to accelerate the generation of cellular texturing using the GPU. GPUs are massively parallel processors and have huge memory bandwidth compared to CPUs. Let's leverage these features to create some real-time cellular noise.

Generating F_1

For each pixel, F_1 is the distance to its closest feature point. Looking at an example F_1 image (Figure 9.3.4a), we can describe what appears to be happening.

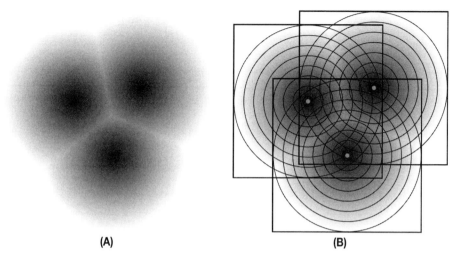

(A)   **(B)**

FIGURE 9.3.4   Three feature points. **(A)** The resulting F_1 image; the pixels are colored by distance to the closest point. **(B)** This can be represented as overlapping circles on each feature point.

Imagine if we render circles centered on each feature point, and if each pixel of a circle is colored based on the distance to its feature point. Each pixel on the resulting image is being assigned a distance to one of the feature points, but we need to make sure that only the distance to the closest (F_1) feature point is left. This can be achieved through a simple comparison before writing the pixel: "Is my value less than the value already at this pixel?"

The GPU's depth buffer is custom built for this type of rejection test and can do it extremely quickly. For each pixel of the circle, write the distance between that pixel and its circle's center pixel position to the depth buffer. With the depth buffer set to the traditional LESSTHAN operation mode, the pixel will only be allowed to pass if the depth value is less than what already exists in the depth buffer for that pixel. This method of using the depth buffer to compute F_1 has been used before [Hoff97] [Warden05].

As shown in Figure 9.3.5, this implementation uses simple rectangles (quads) instead of circles for each feature point, but any 2D shape would do.

The vertex shader outputs the position of the center of the quad and the position of the corner vertex. These values are interpolated across the triangles and are sent to the pixel shader, where they are used to calculate the distance of that pixel from the center of the quad. This process is shown in Figure 9.3.6.

LISTING 9.3.1   HLSL Code for the Vertex and Pixel Shader

```
void
CellularVS_Rect(in float4 center : POSITION,
                in float3 offset : TEXCOORD0,
                out float4 oPos : POSITION,
```

```
                          out float4 oDist : TEXCOORD0)
{
    oPos = center + ( float4(offset.xy,0,0) * rectSize );
    oDist = float4( oPos.xy, center.xy );
}

void
CellularPS_Linear(in float4 dist : TEXCOORD0,
                  out float oDepth : DEPTH,
                  out float4 oColor : COLOR)
{
    float d = distance( dist.xy, dist.zw );
    oDepth=d;
    oColor=d;
}
```

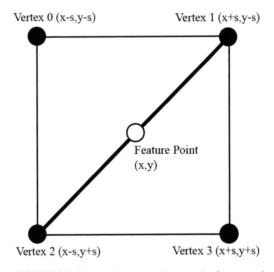

FIGURE 9.3.5   Quad generated around a feature point.

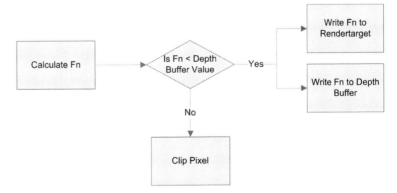

FIGURE 9.3.6   Flow of pixel operations to generate F_1.

If we do this for each feature point, and make sure the quads are large enough to overlap, we end up with an image of the closest feature points (Figure 9.3.2a).

Using Alpha-Blending

As well as using the depth buffer comparison, alpha-blending can also be used to pick the smaller of two values. Setting alpha-blend mode to MIN and source and dest to ONE results in the following pixel blending operation:

```
FinalColor = Min(SourceColor * (1,1,1,1), PixelColor * (1,1,1,1))
```

This post–pixel shader operation is slower than the depth buffer comparison, as the frame buffer has to be read, and the pipeline isn't as highly optimized as depth-buffer reading. We'll come back to this later to show where it can be used in cellular texturing.

F_2 and Beyond

F_n is the distance to the nth closest point and is trickier to calculate than F_1, but luckily not too much. For F_n above F_1, the resulting distances in the image still have to be the smallest distances to a feature point, but they must always be larger than F_{n-1} (since $F_1 < F_2 < F_3 \ldots F_n < F_{n+1}$). If we have already computed F_{n-1}, we can evaluate each pixel with our computed distance values to make sure it is larger than the distance computed for that pixel at F_{n-1}. If it isn't greater than the distance value in the $Fn - 1$ texture, this pixel can be rejected. Otherwise, it is passed down to the depth buffer test as in the previous section.

As shown in Figure 9.3.7, this can be repeated to create images of F_2, F_3, F_4, and so on, but after F_3 the images tend to look very similar and aren't that useful for creating different types of textures.

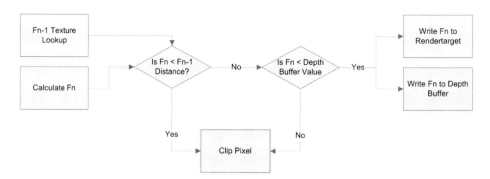

FIGURE 9.3.7   Flow of pixel operations to generate F_n above 1.

Notes

A summary of the algorithm follows:

- Pass for initial F_1:
  1. Set rendertarget to F_1 texture.
  2. Clear depth buffer to 1.0.
  3. Clear rendertarget to 1,1,1,1.
  4. Render rectangles for each feature point.
  5. For each pixel, compute the distance between it and the center of its quad.
  6. Use the depth buffer to test that this distance is less than the depth-buffer value. If it passes, write this distance to the depth buffer and to the render target.

- Passes for F_n where $n > 1$:
  1. Set rendertarget to F_n texture.
  2. Clear depth buffer to 1.0.
  3. Render rectangles for each feature point.
  4. For each pixel, compute the distance between it and the center of its quad.
  5. If this value is less than the corresponding distance value from the F_{n-1} texture, reject this pixel.
  6. Use the depth buffer to test that this distance is less than the depth-buffer value. If it passes, write this distance to the depth buffer and to the render target.

- Combiner pass:
  1. Set rendertarget to frame buffer.
  2. Draw full-screen quad.
  3. For each pixel, blend the previous F_n images in some creative manner.

Because the distance values have a wide range, a lot of precision is needed to avoid artifacts. A 24-bit depth buffer and floating-point textures are ideal.

The size of the quads is also very important; if the quads are not large enough, then discontinuity artifacts will become visible. However, the larger the quads, the more fill rate is used, so it's important to get the balance just right.

A handy note is that for randomly distributed points, the more points you have, the closer they will be, and thus the smaller the rectangles can be. With 10,000 points on screen, the rectangle only needs to be a few pixels wide to find its n closest feature points, so this technique scales well with a large number of points. Also, since $F_n < F_{n+1}$, larger quads are needed for each iteration. Supporting different-sized quads for each iteration can further reduce fill-rate consumption.

Different shapes such as circles could be used instead of quads to cover the surface area more optimally (depending on the distance function used). This technique puts a massive strain on the end of the graphics pipeline and burns a lot of the GPU's fill rate, as it relies on overlapping quads, resulting in massive overdraw. The distance calculation could be moved to the vertex shader, thus alleviating some of the per-pixel burden, but this would impact the quality of the results.

Even more speed can be achieved in some cases by rendering each feature point as a 3D cone [Hoff97]. Creating the cone geometry on the CPU or in the vertex shader tells the GPU that the depth values aren't going to be changing in the pixel shader and can operate much faster. The expensive distance calculations are also not done per-pixel. This can be a massive speed boost; however, it works best for linear or squared distance calculations and makes the technique quite cumbersome for using different distance formulae.

F_1 and F_2 Without Floating Point Buffers

The above method requires high-precision floating-point render targets to produce a useable and artifact-free image. Floating-point surfaces are great, but they do have some limitations. First, they are not as widely supported as integer buffers. Some cards only support lower-precision 16-bit buffers, and the support for different numbers of channels varies too. Second, they tend to be slower than integer buffers and take up much more memory. Taking all this into account, it would be useful to find a way to render cellular textures on the GPU without relying on floating point buffers.

The following techniques achieve the rendering of F_1 and F_2 using 8-bit surfaces, and do not suffer from artifacts, as they use the 24-bit depth buffer to do all of the comparisons. The main limitation is that F_3 can't be generated elegantly after F_2; however there is plenty of room for interesting effect combinations using just these two images.

The F_1 Pass

The F_1 pass is generated the same way as before, but to an integer buffer (e.g., R8G8B8A8). We render the rectangles for each point, calculating the distance from the point per-pixel and writing this distance to the frame and depth buffers if the depth test passes. After this pass our depth buffer is left filled with the F_1 shortest distance values.

1. Set 8-bit rendertarget.
2. Clear rendertarget (clearing to white is good to hide artifacts).
3. Clear depth buffer to 1.0.
4. Render quads for each point, using render states:
5. ZEnable = TRUE
6. ZWriteEnable = TRUE
7. ZFunc = LESS
8. AlphaBlendEnable = FALSE

The F_2 Pass

For F_2 we need to compute the second shortest distance. We need to make sure F_2 is larger than F_1 but also that it's the smallest of all the values tested.

1. Set 8-bit rendertarget.
2. Clear rendertarget.
3. Render quads for each point, using render states:
4. `ZEnable = TRUE`
5. `ZWriteEnable = FALSE`
6. `ZFunc = GREATER`
7. `AlphaBlendEnable = TRUE`
8. `BlendOp = MIN`
9. `SrcBlend=ONE`
10. `DestBlend=ONE`

The depth-buffer test ensures that the pixel that is written has a larger distance value than what is already in the depth buffer (F_1). Values that are higher will pass the depth test and will have their distance value written into the color buffer. This makes sure our distance is greater than F_1, but we will need to make sure it is the smallest remaining distance.

The alpha-blend picks the smallest value of the frame buffer and the pixel that has just passed the depth-buffer test. This leaves us with the second-smallest distance in the color buffer.

Depth writing is turned off on the F_2 pass. If it had been turned on, a depth value greater than F_1 could have been written to the depth buffer, but it wouldn't necessarily be the second-shortest distance (F_2), and this would stop smaller distances from passing.

Increased precision can also be achieved by encoding a float across the 8-bit RGBA channels. This requires some extra computation for packing and unpacking the value on reads and writes [NVFog04] [Baker01].

Tiling

The ability to generate seamless tileable textures is one of the most popular features of procedural texture generation, and cellular texturing is no exception. In the classic algorithms the distance function is modified to wrap around the image area [Scott01]:

LISTING 9.3.2 How the Distance Function Would Usually Be Modified to Generate Wrapped Distance Values

```
float
DistanceWrap(float2 a,float2 b)
{
    float dx = abs(a.x-b.x);
    float dy = abs(a.y-b.y);
    if (dx > width/2)
        dx = width-dx;
    if (dy > height/2)
        dy = height-dy;
    return sqrt( dx*dx + dy*dy );
}
```

Our image-based rendering approach can't use a wrapped distance function.

We create a seamless texture by detecting on the CPU which quads are overlapping the image boundary and render them again at the opposite location. This means we have to do four render calls. It's not very elegant but it works.

If GPUs were able to wrap geometry instead of clipping it, this type of seamless texturing could be achieved very easily and quickly.

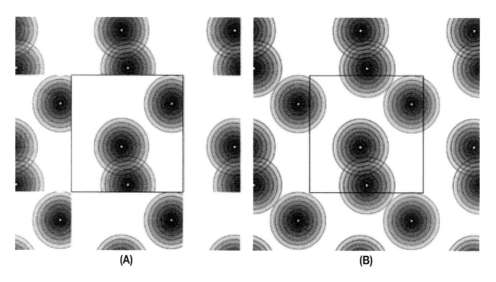

(A)   **(B)**

FIGURE 9.3.8   (**A**) A nontileable texture. (**B**) The same texture, but seamless.

Application

There are countless ways in which cellular texture can be used and combined to form interesting imagery. One of the great things about this type of texture generation is how much scope there is to customize and extend it.

Distance Functions

There is no need to only use the standard Euclidean distance function when plenty of others exist. Simply replacing the distance calculation can completely change the resulting style of texture. Some distance functions to try are:

Distance squared: $F(a,b) = (dx^*dx) + (dy^*dy)$
Manhattan distance: $F(a,b) = abs(dx) + abs(dy)$
Chessboard distance: $F(a,b) = max(dx,dy)$
Minkovsky distance: $F(a,b) = (dx^\wedge e + dy^\wedge e)^\wedge(1/e)$

You can also use a texture as a distance function lookup and create your own bizarre metrics. Usually though, the image won't look good unless the distance value roughly increases, the further you get from the feature point.

Combinations

Figures 9.3.9 through 9.3.12 show some of the many interesting ways to combine the distance images:

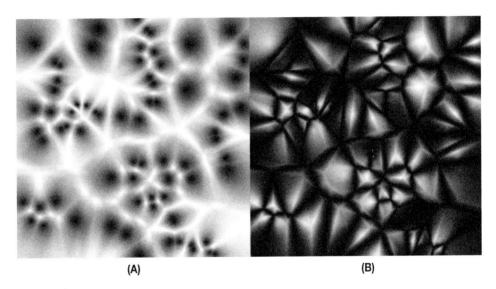

(A)   (B)

FIGURE 9.3.9 **(A)** (f1/f3). **(B)** smoothstep(f1,f3*2,f2).

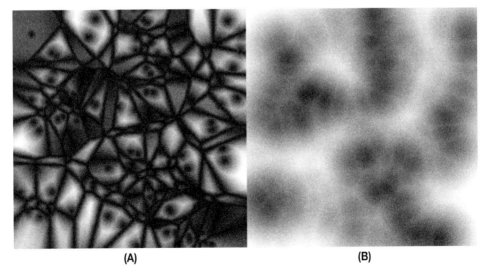

(A)   (B)

FIGURE 9.3.10 **(A)** min(f1,f3-f2). **(B)** length(float3(f1,f2,f3)).

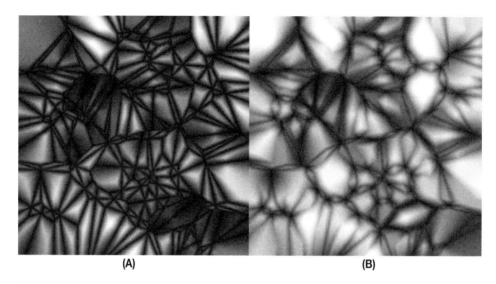

FIGURE 9.3.11   **(A)** min(f2-f1,f3-f2). **(B)** max(f2-f1,f3-f2).

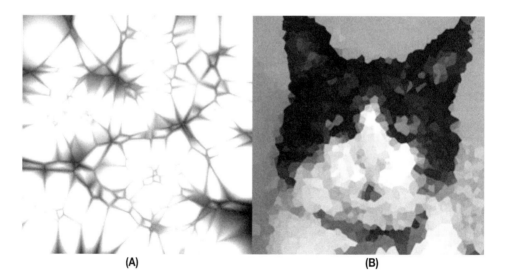

FIGURE 9.3.12   **(A)** abs(f1-f3/f2). **(B)** Mosaic of Pula.

Index and Mosaic

By rendering the index number of the feature point that each pixel is closest to, you can create an interesting indexed image (see Figure 9.3.3b). This looks exactly like a Voronoi diagram and effectively achieves the same effect by segmenting the image into regions (cells), where every pixel in a region is closer to a particular feature point. Extending this to sample a color for each cell from a texture can create a mosaic effect (see Figure 9.3.12b).

Other

There are many other possible applications for this type of pattern generation:

- Repeatedly rendering smaller cells inside larger cells at higher frequencies gives some interesting fractal effects [Shirriff98].
- Cellular textures have been used to synthesize cracks [Mould05].
- Using an animated F_1 fractal image converted into a bump map is a popular way of simulating the surface of the ocean.
- Cellular texture can be used in NPR (non-photorealistic rendering).
- Careful distribution and coloring of the feature points can create interesting patterns [Kaplan00].

Examples

ON THE CD

On the companion CD-ROM you will find several programs (source and binaries) that demonstrate different aspects of this technique. There are also screenshots and a video for those who don't have compatible hardware.

The examples require a Windows PC with DirectX9.0c and a pixel shader 2.0 graphics card. They use the Direct3D sample framework, and the shaders have been written in HLSL.

You can also download the examples from *http://www.rawhed.com/shaderx5/*.

Conclusion

This article has presented a technique to produce images based on classic 2D Worley cellular texturing, using the GPU to accelerate the process to interactive rates. This can allow for rapid experimentation with immediate user feedback when working with this type of procedural texture. The image-based approach and use of a shading language allows for many different derivations from the typical results. A weakness of this technique is that artifacts appear when the rectangles are not large enough, but using large rectangles uses more bandwidth, making it run slower at higher resolutions.

There is still a huge amount of room for investigation and improvement. With the imminent arrival of DirectX 10 Shader Model 4.0 and geometry shaders, it will be interesting to see what can be done with cellular texturing on the GPU in the future.

References and Further Reading

[Baker01] Baker, Dan. "Volumetric Rendering in Real-time." Available online at *http://www.gamasutra.com/features/20011003/boyd_04.htm*.

[Ebert03] Ebert, David et al. "Texturing & Modelling: A Procedural Approach." Morgan Kaufmann Publishers, 2003 (*http://www.texturingandmodeling.com/*).

[Hoff97] Hoff, Kenneth et al. "Fast Computation of Generalized Voronoi Diagrams Using Graphics Hardware." Available online at *http://www.cs.unc.edu/~geom/voronoi/*.

[Kaplan00] Kaplan, Chris. "Voronoi Art." Available online at *http://www.cgl.uwaterloo.ca/~csk/projects/voronoi/*.

[McCombs05] McCombs, Shea. "Introduction to Procedural Textures." Available online at *http://www.newcottage.com/index.php?section=tutorials&subsection=tutorials/3d_procedural4*.

[Mould05] Mould, David. "Image-Guided Fracture." Available online at *http://www.cs.usask.ca/~mould/papers/crack.pdf*.

[NVFog04] NVIDIA. "Fog Polygon Volumes." Available online at *http://download.nvidia.com/developer/SDK/Individual_Samples/DEMOS/Direct3D9/src/FogPolygonVolumes3/docs/FogPolygonVolumes3.pdf*.

[Scott01] Scott, Jim. "Making Cellular Textures." Available online at *http://www.blackpawn.com/texts/cellular/default.html*.

[Perlin02] Perlin, Ken. "Improving Noise." Available online at *http://mrl.nyu.edu/~perlin/noise/*.

[Shirriff98] Shirriff, Ken. "Fractals from Voronoi Diagrams." Available online at *http://www.righto.com/fractals/vor.html*.

[Warden05] Warden, Peter. "Animating Worley Noise." Available online at *http://petewarden.com/notes/archives/2005/05/testing.html*.

[Worley96] Worley, Steven. "A Cellular Texture Basis Function." *Proceedings of SIGGRAPH '96, Computer Graphics Proceedings*, Annual Conference Series, New Orleans, Louisiana, pp. 291–94.

Zaid Mian's and Bryan Chan's implementation of Worley noise using SH. Available online at *http://libsh.org/shaders/*.

Matt Pharr's implementation of Worley noise in C. Available online at *http://pharr.org/matt/code/wnoise.cpp*.

Collision Detection Shader Using Cube-Maps

Rahul Sathe, Intel Corporation

Introduction

With the enormous computing power provided by today's GPUs, virtual worlds are becoming more and more realistic. The two prominent elements in making virtual worlds more realistic are visual appearance of the world at any given instant and the interaction between objects in the world. Advanced rendering techniques help achieve the first element, whereas physics systems take care of the latter. Physics systems simulate object interactions and deal with computationally intensive problems such as collision detection, collision response, and eye candy effects such as fluids, smoke, and so on. Collision detection is very important for the realism of interactive applications, and without collision detection, we would see objects pass through each other.

Why GPU-Based Collision Detection?

Graphics cards, in general, are very good for problems that require floating point operations on large data sets (SIMD), but they do not do as good a job at running general purpose programs that are inherently very "branchy" and often rely on stacks and complicated addressing modes that are supported by CPUs. Conventional collision-detection algorithms (such as OBB, AABB, . . .) are very branchy and recursive in nature, making them difficult for GPUs to handle, but they are also very SIMD in nature because they work on large sets of objects in the virtual world. Because of the recursive and branchy nature of these problems, it makes sense to run them on CPUs. This article proposes a collision detection algorithm that is well suited to exploit the SIMD nature of GPUs.

Problem Statement

Collision detection requires us to determine if two objects are in contact with each other at a given instant in time. In games the virtual world is updated in discrete time steps, so it is more likely that the objects will either intersect each other or be very close to each other and be about to collide. There are two classes of collision-detection algorithms: the ones that determine if objects are intersecting (after the collision) and others that determine if objects are about to collide (before collision). Problems trying to solve collision using the latter approach keep track of some nearest feature such as an edge, a point, or a triangle. They are better for separating vector calculations, but such algorithms (e.g., GJK) are more complex in nature. Another class of algorithms tries to detect if the objects are intersecting. The technique discussed here will discuss a GPU-based algorithm to conduct collision detection by determining if the objects are intersecting.

Background and Definitions

There are two kinds of objects in virtual worlds: rigid bodies and deformable bodies. A rigid body is an object in which the relative position of its vertices do not change with respect to each other over time. The algorithm discussed in this article deals only with rigid bodies, as it relies very heavily on the fact that relative positions of vertices do not change over time. Throughout the discussion, we will be using the terms *objects*, *geometries*, and *polytopes* interchangeably. Geometries can be of two types, namely, convex and concave:

Convex geometry: A geometry (polygon or a polyhedron or anything more general) is convex if with every pair of points that belongs to the geometry, the geometry contains the whole straight line segment connecting the two points. A geometry that is not convex is called concave.

Cube-map: Cube-map texturing is a form of texturing supported by most 3D graphics APIs such as DirectX and Open-GL that uses a 3D direction vector to index into a texture that is six square 2D textures arranged like the faces of a cube. In the simple example that we present, a 3D cube-map is just a set of 2D images of values containing the distance from the centroid.

Conventional collision-detection algorithms eliminate noncolliding objects by bounding sphere tests and use space partitioning structures such as octrees. When simple bounding sphere tests fail to determine collision detection accurately, they invoke more refined algorithms such as oriented bounding boxes (see e.g., [Gottschalk]) or axis-aligned bounding boxes (see e.g., [Bergen]). These algorithms reduce the number of potentially colliding triangles using recursive elimination of noncolliding pieces of the geometry. This article discusses an alternative approach that will replace the recursive algorithms with a nonrecursive algorithm that is well suited to run on GPUs. The algorithm presented here makes use of a hardware-accelerated texturing mode called cube-map.

Actual Algorithm

This technique of collision detection has two steps. The first step is a preprocessing step and can be handled just one time in the game code during initialization or it can be handled by the content creation software. This preprocessing step needs to be done only once per unique object. The second step is the run-time step, which is evaluated for every pair of colliding objects. Thus, the run-time step is run for every instance of a unique object, although it does make use of some common structures for all the instances of unique objects.

Preprocessing

In the preprocessing step we construct a cube-map per unique object. The pixels of the cube-map represent distances. These are the distances from the centroid of an object to its surface in every direction. Let us try to understand what this means and how we go about constructing such a cube-map. Consider a mesh without any transformations applied to it. We calculate the centroid of this mesh by simply adding x, y, and z coordinates of all the vertices and then dividing this sum by the number of vertices. We will do the rest of the preprocessing for this mesh in a reference frame that has its origin situated at the centroid of this mesh. For convex objects, the centroid will always be situated inside of the object.

We then assume a hypothetical cube, such that its centroid is aligned with the centroid of an object and hence is situated at the origin. Sides of the cube are aligned with the axes. Since we are interested in only the directions from origin to some pixel on this cube's faces, the actual size of the cube does not matter. The faces of this cube correspond to the faces of the cube-map that we will be constructing. We then shoot rays from the centroid (which is at the origin), which go through the centers of all the pixels on the faces of this cube. Thus, for a cube-map of size $6 \times 16 \times 16$, we would have 6 times 256 rays. We find the intersection points of these rays with the object's surface using an API such as DirectX's D3DXIntersect() function. We calculate the distance to these intersection points from the centroid and store these distances in the respective pixels of the cube-map. Figure 9.4.1 shows this process of generating a cube-map. Figure 9.4.2 shows a cross section of the cube-map and how these distances are calculated and are stored. DirectX provides a very handy function named D3DXFillCubeTexture() for generating such procedural cube-maps. A couple of important points to note here are that there has to be exactly one intersection point with the mesh for a ray starting at its centroid and going in any direction. This is true only for convex geometries. We can extend our algorithm to concave geometries by using popular computational geometry techniques such as convex decomposition. Alternatively, if approximate collision detection is acceptable, we can store the largest of these distances from centroid to intersection points and thus store a distance map of the convex hull of a concave object.

Creation of this cube-map may sound a little complicated and computationally intensive, but it is done only once and can be completely offloaded to the content-creation software, assuming the APIs are provided to read this information. Figure 9.4.3 explains what this distance cube-map represents in 2D. The process of creating

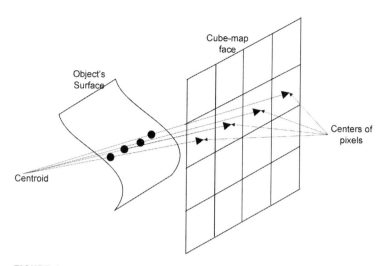

FIGURE 9.4.1   How a cube-map of distances is generated.

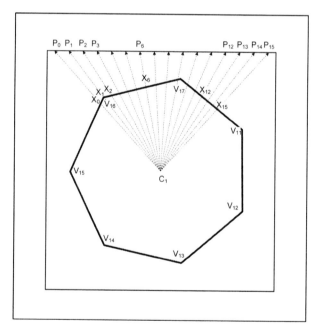

FIGURE 9.4.2 C_1 is the centroid and $P_0, P_1...P_{16}$ are the centers of the pixels. We store distances $C_1X_0, C_1X_1...C_1X_{16}$ at $P_0, P_1...P_{16}$, respectively.

a cube-map of a distance quantizes the continuous "distance from the centroid" function along the cube-map directions. In this example, the distance map is generated using four sample directions along each side of this triangle. As you can see, a triangle is approximated by a figure made of arcs. The arcs have the radii of the distances along the sample directions.

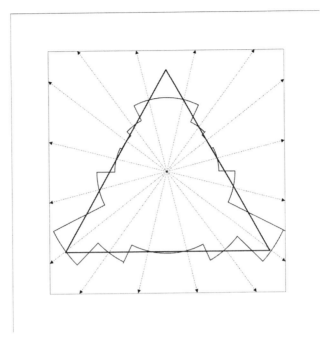

FIGURE 9.4.3   Quantization of the distance function.

Runtime

The runtime step of this algorithm is run once per instance of an object. Bounding sphere tests are done to eliminate objects that are obviously noncolliding. We run our algorithm only for potentially colliding objects. At run time all the calculations are done in the world space. We have access to the world transformation matrices of the objects and their inverses. Figure 9.4.4 explains the algorithm at runtime in 2D. It extends naturally to 3D.

At runtime we shoot a ray from the centroid of object 1, C_1, to all the vertices of object 2 (V_{21}, V_{22}, V_{23}, and V_{24} in this case). We transform these directions back into the original space of object 1, by multiplying by the inverse of object 1's world matrix. Then, using these directions as indices, we look up the cube-map that was constructed in preprocessing step. These are the distances to the object's boundaries in those respective directions. Cube-map looked-up distances are indicated as d_1. We use HLSL intrinsic texCUBE() to do this look-up. We calculate the actual distance in the world space between C_1 and the vertices of the object 2. The actual distances are indicated as d_2. We simply compare these two distances. If the cube-map distance is larger

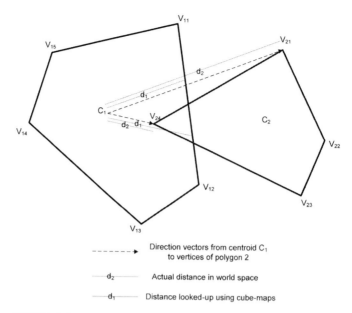

FIGURE 9.4.4   Two intersecting objects and the algorithm in action.

than the actual distance, objects are penetrating each other and there is a collision. We do this for all the vertices of object 2. If there is no collision, then we do the same thing by shooting rays from object 2's centroid C_2 to all the vertices of object 1. A way to further optimize this algorithm for speed and accuracy is included in performance considerations. Pseudo-code for the runtime step is as follows:

```
// Iterate through obj. 2's vertices
for (i=0;i< numVertices2;i++){
    dir = Vertices2[i]-C1;
    dir = Inverse(mWorld2)* dir;
d₂ = distance(C₁,Vertices2[i]);
d₁ = texCUBE(SamplerA, dir);
    if (d₁ >= d₂) {
collision = true
}

// Iterate through obj. 1's vertices
```

The actual pixel shader for collision detection is as shown in code Listing 9.4.1.

LISTING 9.4.1   The Collision-Detection Pixel Shader

```
PS_OUTPUT CollisionDetectionPS( VS_OUTPUT In,
                        uniform bool bTexture )
{
    PS_OUTPUT Output;
    int Index = 0;
```

```
float fActualDist,fCubeMapDist;
float4 temp = (0,0,0,1);
float4 WorldPos,WorldCentroid,dir;
bool collision = false;
float2 tex;

Output.RGBColor.r = Output.RGBColor.g
    = Output.RGBColor.b = Output.RGBColor.a = 0.0;

//Centroid of object 0
WorldCentroid = mul(g_vCentroids[0],g_mWorldMat0);

// This is the displacement to point to the center of the pixel
// for the sampler used for textures containing vertices.

float disp = 0.5/g_iNumVertices[1];

for( Index = 0; Index < g_iNumVertices[1] ; Index++ ) {

    // This is a cheap way to skip the computation,
    // if the collision is already detected.

    if (collision == false) {
        tex.x = Index/(float)g_iNumVertices[1] + disp;
        tex.y = 0.5;
        WorldPos = tex2D(g_samPositions1,tex);

        WorldPos = mul(WorldPos,g_mWorldMat1);
        dir = WorldPos - WorldCentroid;
        fActualDist=
                sqrt(dir.x*dir.x+dir.y*dir.y+dir.z*dir.z);

          // Multiply dir by inverse of world matrix to
          // get the direction in the space that cube-map
          // was created in.

          dir = mul(dir,g_mWorldMat0Inv);
          dir = normalize(dir);

        temp = texCUBE(g_samCubeMapDistance0,dir);
        fCubeMapDist  =  temp.x;
        if (fCubeMapDist > fActualDist) {
            collision = true;
        }
        }
}

// Cycle thru' objects 2's vertices only if Object 1's
// vertex has not penetrated other object's interior.

if (!collision) {
    disp = 0.5/g_iNumVertices[0];
```

```
             WorldCentroid = mul(g_vCentroids[1],g_mWorldMat1);
             for( Index = 0; Index < g_iNumVertices[0]; Index++ ) {

                 if (collision == false) {
                     tex.x = Index/(float)g_iNumVertices[0] + disp;
                     tex.y = 0.5;
                     WorldPos = tex2D(g_samPositions0,tex);

                     WorldPos = mul(WorldPos,g_mWorldMat0);
                         dir = WorldPos - WorldCentroid;
             fActualDist =
                         sqrt(dir.x*dir.x+dir.y*dir.y+dir.z*dir.z);
                     dir = mul(dir,g_mWorldMat1Inv);
                     dir = normalize(dir);

                     temp = texCUBE(g_samCubeMapDistance1,dir);
                     fCubeMapDist  =  temp.x;
                     if (fCubeMapDist > fActualDist) {
                         CollisionDirection = dir;
                         trouble = Index;
                         collision = true;
                     }
                 }
             }
         }

         if (collision == true) {
             Output.RGBColor.r = Output.RGBColor.g =
             Output.RGBColor.b = Output.RGBColor.a = 1.0;
         }
         return Output;
     }
```

In Listing 9.4.1 some things are worth noting. The branch if (collision == true) inside the for loop is executed every time, although the code inside this if will be executed only until collision has not been detected. In normal C style language something like the following would be the right way to stop the loop.

```
for ( Index = 0; Index < g_iNumVertices[1] && !collision; Index++ )
```

This type of loop termination is not allowed by the HLSL compiler, and that's why there is the condition if (collision == true) in the loop body to avoid redundant computation. Also, one may notice that the render target has more space than required for just a boolean value of true or false. This is intentional. Extra space may be used to pass back any additional value such as the direction, separating vector, rebound velocities, and so on.

Since most of today's GPUs provide hardware acceleration for cube-maps, cube-map look-ups are very fast. The result from the collision detection is just one boolean value of true or false. Reading these values back is a little complicated with the algorithms that are run on GPUs. The only way to read the values back is by rendering the outputs to a texture and reading back that texture. Since our result is one Boolean value per pair of colliding objects, one pair of colliding object requires a only one pixel in the render target. Cube-map look-ups (texcube()) are available only in pixel shaders, so our algorithm needs to be written as a pixel shader. To invoke this pixel shader, fake geometry and view frusta must be created, such that the fake geometry always gets rendered into the render target.

This collision detection is run on GPUs and only needs to be evaluated when the scene graph update is done. This technique is an illustration of using GPUs for doing non–graphics-related things. In this case we are doing collision detection.

Performance Considerations

Vertices can be passed as constants to the collision-detection shader, but in doing so, we'll often encounter a constant register number limit. To avoid running into those problems, we can pack the vertex data into textures and access that data using samplers. The number of collisions that a shader can handle in one communication between CPU and GPU depends on number of possibly colliding unique objects, the maximum number of vertices in such objects, and the maximum texture size supported. Since the only thing that is different about multiple instances of unique objects is the world matrices, we only need one distance cube-map per unique object.

This algorithm suffers from minor accuracy problems. When using a sampler for the distance cube-map, we can chose either nearest-point sampling or linear sampling. Both introduce some error. In case of nearest sampling we introduce the obvious error resulting from quantization. In case of linear sampling the distances when linearly interpolated don't generate the original tessellated geometry. We can regenerate fairly accurate tessellated geometry if we store the coordinates of the intersection point relative to centroid in every direction instead of distances. The only exception to the accurate regeneration of the tessellated mesh will be that the vertices that are not sampled get clipped. This will increase the memory requirement, so the vertices that were not along the cube-map–sampled directions will not be regenerated.

This algorithm, in its simplest form, works only on convex polytopes. One key observation about collisions between two convex polytopes is that the points that penetrate into another object are always the farthest points from the respective centroids in the direction of the centroid of the other object. Hence, if we store the indices of the vertices that are farthest in the given direction along with the object surface's distance in that direction, we can quickly know which vertices will be penetrating the other object first when collision occurs. The problem, though, is that depending on the geometry, we can have varying number of vertices that are farthest in any given direction. For example, n-sided prisms will have n vertices farthest in two directions and four vertices that are farthest in n directions. If n is known for a scene and is such that n indices can fit into every entry in a cube-map, we can track the farthest feature (set of points) using another cube-map. This optimization is not implemented in the sample application provided with this article.

Conclusion

This algorithm attempts to solve the collision-detection problem. Once the outcome of collision detection is known, the collision response needs to be evaluated. This collision response requires knowledge of some more parameters such as separating vector, rebound velocities, and so on. One can pass these values along with the collision-detection results by packing some values in render targets. It will be interesting to write a collision response shader.

References

[Bergen] Van den Bergen, G. "Efficient Collision Detection of Complex Deformable Models Using AABB Trees." *Journal of Graphics Tools*, *2*(4), (1997): pp. 1–14.

[Gottschalk] Gottschalk, S., M. C. Lin, and D. Manocha. "OBBTree: A Hierarchical Structure for Rapid Interference Detection." *Proc. SIGGRAPH*, 1996: pp. 171–180.

9.5

A GPU Panorama Viewer for Generic Camera Models

Frank Nielsen, Sony Computer Science
Laboratories, Inc.

Introduction

Digital panoramas are nowadays omnipresent in Internet virtual tours (see *http://www.world-heritage-tour.org/*). A *panorama* basically stores light information arriving at a single position from a wide field of view. Panoramas are particular light fields that conveniently sample the plenoptic function in image-based rendering systems at discrete positions. We distinguish between *spherical panoramas,* which cover the full sphere of directions (4π steradians), from *cylindrical panoramas,* which cover only 360 horizontal degrees over a partial vertical field of view. Panoramas are widely used in computer graphics not only as backdrops (also called skyboxes), but also as *environment maps* for dynamic reflections and more recently as *light probes* for the rendering of convincing lighting. In the old days, environment maps were merely captured using a tele-lens camera (approximating the required orthographic projection), capturing the reflections of a spherical mirror ball [Nielsen05a]. Nowadays, stitching allows us to calibrate and precisely register a sequence of pictures acquired from a same *nodal point*: the *center of projection* (COP) [Nielsen05b]. Thus, an environment map is a *complete panorama ray map* obtained from a single COP, while a pinhole image is interpreted as a *local ray map* partially sampling the environment map from the same COP. The most common environment maps used for simulating real-time reflections in computer graphics are the latitude-longitude map (also called the equirectangular map), the cubic map (six quad faces), and the dual paraboloid map (two images) [Nielsen05a]. Wong et al. further introduced the HEALPix map (12 quads) [Wong05], which improves the spherical ray sampling distribution over the cube map for computing real-time reflections on the GPU.

Figure 9.5.1 depicts a 1024×512 latitude-longitude spherical environment map.

(A)   (B)

FIGURE 9.5.1   Example of **(A)** a latitude-longitude environment map from which **(B)** a virtual pinhole camera image is synthesized. The corresponding border of the virtual pinhole camera is traced in the environment map.

Synthesizing Pinhole Camera Views

To render a view as if obtained by a virtual pinhole camera anchored at the same COP of the environment map, we need to partially remap the ray map using a pinhole camera model. The pinhole camera is defined by a set of *extrinsic parameters* (roll, pitch, and yaw attributes stored in a rotation matrix and defining the aim and orientation of the camera image plane) and *intrinsic parameters* (image dimension, principal point, and focal length). Remapping, a *warping* operation, can either proceed by mapping forward pixels of the environment map to the virtual pinhole camera image (*forward mapping*), or vice-versa (*backward mapping*). This local ray map conversion can be carried out using intensive per-pixel CPU computations, or per-triangle units using the texture primitives of graphics cards (2D or 3D triangles), but this is time consuming. On one hand, per-pixel warping offers the highest picture quality by explicitly controlling the interpolation scheme. On the other hand, texturing triangles allows us to relieve the CPU from excessive computations by leaving the texturing operation of interpolating intermediate values to the graphics engine. The drawback is that texturing uses the standard (trilinear) interpolation scheme. Let us now quickly review the per-pixel backward mapping and the 2D/3D per-triangle forward mapping method before introducing the GPU panorama shader.

A Simple Pinhole Camera Model

The pinhole camera model of image dimension width w and height h and (horizontal) field of view (hfov) maps image pixels to 3D rays anchored at the COP as follows:

$$PinholeXY2TP(x, y) = \left(\arctan\left(\frac{x - c_x}{f}\right), \arctan\left(\frac{y - c_y}{a\sqrt{(x - c_x)^2 + f^2}}\right) \right) = (\theta, \phi),$$

where $(c_x, c_y) = \left(\dfrac{w}{2}, \dfrac{h}{2}\right)$ is the camera principal point, $a = \dfrac{h}{w}$ is the *aspect ratio,* and f is the (horizontal) focal length in pixel units computed from the field of view as:

$$f = hfov2\,fx(w, hfov) = \frac{w}{2\tan\dfrac{hfov}{2}}$$

Conversions between 3D Cartesian and 2D spherical coordinates as shown in Figure 9.5.2 are processed using the conventional formula:

$$Cartesian2Spherical(X, Y, Z) = \left(\arctan\left(\frac{X}{Z}\right), \arctan\left(\frac{Y}{\sqrt{X^2 + Z^2}}\right)\right) = (\theta, \phi)$$

$$Spherical2Cartesian(\theta, \phi) = \left(\sin\theta\cos\phi, \sin\phi, \cos\theta\cos\phi\right) = (X, Y, Z)$$

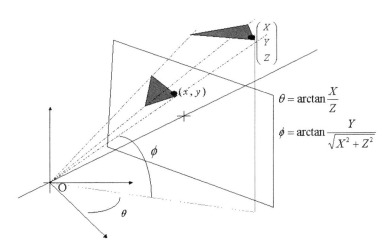

FIGURE 9.5.2 Conversion between spherical and Cartesian coordinates.

Per-Pixel Backward Ray Mapping

We first need to align the principal point of the camera image (image center) with the aim of the camera using a rotation matrix defined as

$$R(r, p, y) = \begin{pmatrix} \cos r\cos y - \sin r\sin p\sin y & -\sin r\cos p & \cos r\sin y + \sin r\sin p\cos y \\ \sin r\cos y + \cos r\sin p\sin y & \cos r\cos p & \sin r\sin y - \cos r\sin p\cos y \\ -\cos p\sin y & \sin p & \cos p\cos y \end{pmatrix},$$

where the roll denotes the angle around the z-axis, the pitch denotes the angular amplitude around the x-axis, and the yaw denotes the inclination around the y-axis. Then we create a *synthetic* pinhole camera view by looking up for each pinhole image pixel xy the corresponding $\theta\phi$ ray, rotating that ray and the original orthonormal frame using the rotation matrix, and finding the corresponding pixel in the environment ray map using the `LatitudeLongitudeTP2XY` function:

$$LatitudeLongitudeTP2XY(\theta,\phi) = \left(w_p\left(\frac{\theta+\pi}{2\pi} \right), h_p\left(\frac{\phi+\pi/2}{\pi} \right) \right),$$

where w_p and h_p denote, respectively, the equirectangular panorama width and height.

Interpolation schemes can be chosen as the nearest neighbor interpolant for speed or bilinear or better interpolation methods (e.g., Lanczos). Listing 9.5.1 shows the source code.

LISTING 9.5.1 Source Code

```
CPUPanoramaViewer.cpp
indexpi=0;
for(y=0;y<hpi;y++)
    for(x=0;x<wpi;x++)
    {
      xy[0]=x;xy[1]=y;

    PinholeXY2TP(xy,tp);
    Spherical2Cartesian(tp,xyz);
    Rotation(xyz,R,xyzrot);
    Cartesian2Spherical(xyzrot,tp);
    LatitudeLongitudeTP2XY(tp,xy);
    // Nearest interpolation scheme for compactness
    xx=(int)xy[0];yy=(int)xy[1];
    indexll=3*(yy*widthpan+xx);

    pinholeimage[indexpi++]=environmentmap[indexll++];// R
    pinholeimage[indexpi++]=environmentmap[indexll++];// G
    pinholeimage[indexpi++]=environmentmap[indexll++];// B
    }
```

ON THE CD Please refer to subfolder CPU Panorama viewer in this article's folder on the CD-ROM.

Per-Triangle 3D Forward Ray Mapping

To speed up the rendering process, we may compute the ray conversion at sparse positions, and let the graphics engine render the textured primitives. A typical example is rendering a 3D unit sphere using texture coordinates of the environment map. We represent the environment map (θ,ϕ) as a grid on a regular mesh and compute the 3D vertex position on the sphere for each 2D grid vertex using the `Spherical2Cartesian` procedure. Deciding whether a triangle is to be rendered or not, and clipping partially visible triangles, is handled by the graphics engine.

Per-Triangle 2D Forward Ray Mapping

Another strategy consists in rendering 2D triangles and determining for ourselves the out-of-view triangles. That is, once we get the 3D triangle vertex positions, we find the angular parameters (θ', ϕ') and project back to the screen space using the `PinholeTP2XY` primitive:

$$PinholeTP2XY(\theta, \phi) = \left(f\tan\theta + c_x, a\sqrt{(x-c_x)^2}\tan\phi + c_y \right) = (x, y)$$

Although the vertex positions are precisely computed, the barycentric 2D triangle interpolation does not produce a perfectly correct result. However, this is quite unnoticeable, and the interpolation approximation error decreases as we refine the triangulation. Note that for textured primitives, backward mapping as shown in Figure 9.5.3 would be challenging, as some 2D *xy* triangles of the pinhole camera image may be cut into several parts in the environment mapping (for example, a triangle containing the latitude-longitude north pole in its interior).

2D Per-pixel backward mapping

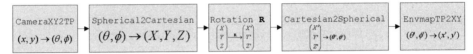

3D Per-triangle vertex forward mapping

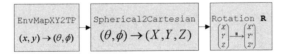

2D Per-triangle vertex forward mapping

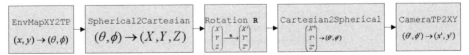

FIGURE 9.5.3   Backward per-pixel and forward per-triangle coordinate pipelines.

A GPU Fragment Shader

In this section, we describe the ray map conversion by a short fragment shader. The parameters of the shader are the rotation matrix and the texture image dimension. Using the shader, we can render at full-screen resolution with maximal frame rate (usually 60 fps, but this may vary according to your monitor's refresh rate).

Zooming in or zooming out is achieved by decreasing or increasing the field of view, which impacts the focal length. This can be implemented using another shader parameter that we omitted here for simplicity. Moreover, rotational motion blur effect can be added purposely using the OpenGL accumulation buffer [Nielsen05b]. Listing 9.5.2 is an excerpt of the file pinhole.cg.

LISTING 9.5.2 Excerpt from pinhole.cg

```
samplerRECT PanoramaImage;
float widthpan,heightpan;
float3x3 R;
float PI=3.14159265;

float2 Cartesian2Spherical(float3 p)
{
float2 tp;

tp[1]=atan(p[1]/sqrt(p[0]*p[0]+p[2]*p[2]));
tp[0]=atan2(p[0],p[2]);

return tp;
}

float3 Spherical2Cartesian(float2 tp)
{
float3 xyz;

xyz[0]=cos(tp[1])*sin(tp[0]);
xyz[1]=sin(tp[1]);
xyz[2]=cos(tp[1])*cos(tp[0]);

return xyz;
}

// Pinhole X-Y -> Theta-Phi -> Panorama X-Y
float2 PinholeXY2TP(float x,float y)
{
// focal length in pixel unit
float f=1000;
// principal point
float cx=widthpan/2.0;
float cy=heightpan/2.0;
// aspect ratio
float aspect=heightpan/widthpan;
float t,p;

t=atan2(x-cx,f);
p=atan2((y-cy)/aspect,sqrt((x-cx)*(x-cx)+f*f));

return float2(t,p);
}
```

```
// Environment map
float2 LatitudeLongitudeTP2XY(float t, float p)
{
float x,y;

x=widthpan*((t+PI)/(2.0*PI));
y=heightpan*((p+PI/2.0)/PI);

return float2(x,y);
}

// Receives RPY in matrix R and warp accordingly
// Backward mapping: Pinhole->Environment mapping
float3  WarpPanorama(float2 texcoord : TEXCOORD0) : COLOR0
{
float3 pp,xyz;
float2 tp,xy;

tp=PinholeXY2TP(texcoord[0],texcoord[1]);
xyz=Spherical2Cartesian(tp);
pp=mul(R,xyz);
tp=Cartesian2Spherical(pp);
xy=LatitudeLongitudeTP2XY(tp[0],tp[1]);

return f3texRECT(PanoramaImage, xy);
}
```

Using the same conversion framework, we can also remove the radial lens distortion effects using the GPU. Let us consider Tsai's radial distortion model [Nielsen05b]. We simply need to define the primitive TsaiXY2TP, which we do by first remapping the (distorted) source image into an undistorted ideal pinhole image and then applying the regular PinholeXY2TP transformation. Please refer to subfolder GPUPanoramaViewer1 on the CD-ROM.

Generic Camera Models

A generic camera model (yielding either a partial or complete environment map) is defined concisely using two change-of-coordinate functions: genericcameraXY2TP and genericcameraTP2XY. These functions are potentially partially defined. For example, the fisheye camera only (re)projects the environment mapping onto an image disk (undefined elsewhere in the rectangular image). Also noteworthy, the origin and axis of the environment map can be readjusted using the GPU by specifying the new origin and frame axes using the rotation matrix. To illustrate the generic camera functions, let us consider the conversion of the latitude-longitude equirectangular map to the front face of the dual paraboloid using the function ParaboloidUpXY2TP. A normalized pixel (x, y) (with $x \in [-1,1]$ and $y \in [-1,1]$) in the front paraboloid maps to a corresponding downward ray direction defined by the following 3D vector:

$$\left(\frac{2x}{x^2 + y^2 + 1}, \frac{2x}{x^2 + y^2 + 1}, \frac{x^2 + y^2 - 1}{x^2 + y^2 + 1} \right)$$

We then need to simply apply the Cartesian2Spherical function to retrieve the corresponding (θ, ϕ) angles. Because we use both back and front paraboloid maps to define a complete environment map, it is enough to consider normalized pixels falling within the unit disk:

```
float3 ParaboloidUpXY2TP(float2 xy)
{
float s,t,X,Y,Z;
float3 tpz;

s=(xy[0]-(widthpan/2.0))/(widthpan/2.0);
t=(xy[1]-(heightpan/2.0))/(heightpan/2.0);

if (s*s+t*t<=1.0)
    {
    X=2.0*s/(s*s+t*t+1.0);
    Y=2.0*t/(s*s+t*t+1.0);
    Z=(-1.0+s*s+t*t)/(s*s+t*t+1.0);
    // Cartesian to spherical conversion
    tpz[0]=atan2(X,Z);
    tpz[1]=atan2(Y,sqrt(X*X+Z*Z));
    tpz[2]=1.0;
    }
    else tpz[2]=0.0;

return tpz;
}

float3  WarpPanorama(float2 texcoord : TEXCOORD0) : COLOR0
{
float3 pp,xyz,tpz;
float2 tp,xy;

xy[0]=texcoord[0];
xy[1]=texcoord[1];

tpz=ParaboloidUpXY2TP(xy);
tp[0]=tpz[0];
tp[1]=tpz[1];

if (tpz[2]==1.0){
xyz=Spherical2Cartesian(tp);
pp=mul(R,xyz);
tp=Cartesian2Spherical(pp);
xy=LatitudeLongitudeTP2XY(tp[0],tp[1]);

return f3texRECT(PanoramaImage, xy);}
else
{
return float3(0,0,1);
}
}
```

The basic difference in the previous `pinhole.cg` shader is that the remapping is only effective inside the image disk. Thus, we need to slightly modify the former `Warp-Panorama` shader to take into account the domain of definition of the mapping functions. The ray remapping shaders can also be combined altogether in a number of scenarios. For example, we can display on each face of a 3D cube a different camera model viewer obtained from a common environment map (see Figure 9.5.4 and shader file `generic-camera.cg`). Please refer to subfolder GPUPanoramaViewer2 on the CD-ROM.

ON THE CD

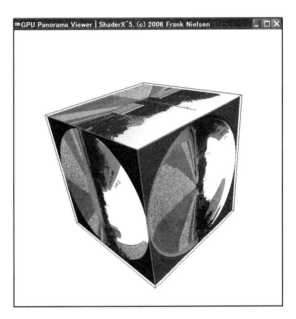

FIGURE 9.5.4   Rendering several generic camera models using the abstract framework.

Conclusion

We have presented an efficient GPU panorama fragment shader for relieving the CPU of the per-pixel and warping procedures. The panorama viewer allows us to render several generic camera models in a same view at maximum frame rate, as well as to convert or remap on-the-fly complete environment maps. The abstraction (θ, ϕ) ray-(x, y) image framework relies on the fact that all rays share a common center of projection. We leave to future work the extension of this abstract camera model and reprojection technique to caustic surfaces particularly observed in catadioptric acquisition systems [Nielsen05b].

References

[Nielsen05a] Nielsen, Frank. "Surround Video: A Multihead Camera Approach." *The Visual Computer, 21*(1-2), (2005): 92–103.

[Nielsen05b] Nielsen, Frank. *Visual Computing: Geometry, Graphics and Vision.* Charles River Media, 2005.

[Wong05] Wong, Tien-Tsin, Liang Wan, Chi-Sing Leung, and Ping-Man Lam. "Real-time Environment Mapping with *equal solid-angle spherical quad-map*." *ShaderX⁴: Advanced Rendering Techniques*, edited by Wolfgang Engel. Charles River Media, 2005: 221–233.

9.6

Explicit Early-Z Culling for Efficient Fluid Flow Simulation

Pedro V. Sander, ATI Research, Inc.,

Natalya Tatarchuk, ATI Research, Inc.

Jason L. Mitchell, Valve

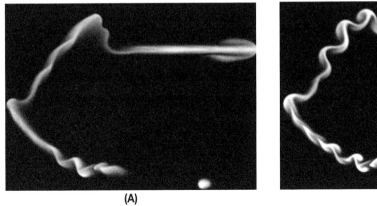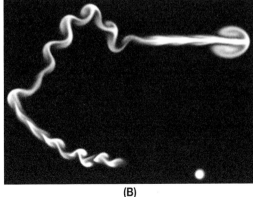

FIGURE 9.6.1 Comparison of fluid flow simulations with and without our early-z acceleration techniques. Both simulations use a 512×512 grid (cropped for the figure) and render at 53fps. **(A)** Brute force. **(B)** Early-z.

Overview

We present an efficient algorithm for simulation and rendering of fluid flow directly on graphics hardware. Our algorithm takes advantage of explicit early-z culling to reduce the amount of computation during the simulation. Our approach is straightforward to implement and speeds up our simulations in some cases by a factor of three. Such an early-z-based technique can be successfully used for general optimization of GPU-based computations.

Introduction

In recent years, graphics processors have been applied to broader areas of computation, such as simulation of natural phenomena. Because of their highly parallel nature and increasingly general computational models, GPUs are well matched with the demands of fluid flow simulation.

In this chapter we present acceleration techniques for simulation of fluid flow. We have implemented a fluid simulation entirely on the GPU based on the solution of Navier-Stokes equations that uses explicit early-z culling as a means of avoiding certain unnecessary computations. More specifically, we present a culling technique for the projection step of the fluid flow simulation.

Fluid flow simulation naturally maps to current graphics hardware by performing the different steps of the simulation using full-screen quadrilaterals and doing all the work in pixel shaders (see [Harris03b] for a thorough description). Prior to execution of a pixel shader, the graphics hardware performs a check of the interpolated z value against the z value in the z-buffer. This occurs for any pixels that are actually going to use the primitive's interpolated z (rather than compute z in the pixel shader itself). This additional check provides not only an added efficiency win when using long, costly pixel shaders, but also provides a form of pixel-level flow control in specific situations. The z-buffer can be thought of as containing condition codes governing the execution of expensive pixel shaders. Inserting inexpensive rendering passes whose only job is to appropriately set the condition codes for subsequent expensive rendering passes can increase performance significantly. This approach is known as *early-z culling* in real-time rendering.

Our technique is based on the observation that fluid flow is often concentrated in subregions of the simulation grid. The early-z optimizations that we employ significantly reduce the amount of computation on regions that have little or no fluid density or pressure, saving computational resources for regions with higher flow concentration or for rendering other objects in the scene.

Previous Work

Simulation of natural phenomena such as water surfaces, smoke, and fire animation have a long history in computer graphics. As early as 1990, Kass and Miller [Kass90] presented a method for animating water by solving a linearized form of a set of partial differential equations approximating the shallow water equations (namely, the Navier-Stokes equations). Furthering their work, Chen et al. [Chen94] solved the Navier-Stokes equations in two dimensions to produce a height field. Foster and Metaxas [Foster96] [Foster97] solved the full three-dimensional Navier-Stokes equations for water and smoke simulation.

These earlier methods of fluid simulation are based on explicit integration schemes. They do not produce a stable simulation unless the simulation time step is very small. Stam [Stam99] introduced an unconditionally stable model for fluid simulation. Stam's approach uses a semi-Lagrangian integration method and a projection step to ensure incompressibility [Chorin67]. This solver allows for much higher time steps, resulting in faster, real-time stable simulations. This seminal work spurred many recent papers on simulation of various natural phenomena with approaches partly based on this solver. As an improvement, Fedkiw et al. [Fedkiw01] suggested using vorticity confinement to preserve the small-scale structure of the flow while simulating fire and smoke phenomena. Enright et al. [Enright02] presented a novel hybridized method for animating and rendering of water surfaces via a combination of marker particles and a level set function representing the surface of the water. Nguyen et al. [Nguyen02] use the incompressible form of the Navier-Stokes equations to model fire (also used by Lamorlette et al. [Lamorlette02]). Many other natural phenomena have been modeled using these techniques, such as clouds [Miyazaki02] [Harris03], particle explosions [Feldman03], and variable viscosity [Carlson02]. We use the solver proposed by Stam [Stam99] as the basis for our acceleration methods for both 2D and 3D simulation. For details on Stam's stable Navier-Stokes solver, we refer the reader to the paper [Stam99]. For a thorough description of fluid simulation on graphics hardware, we recommend [Harris03b].

To address the growing need for heavy use of the computational resources, several approaches were developed using adaptive mesh or level of detail techniques for simulations placing grid cells in regions with visually interesting details for smoke or water simulations. Adaptive mesh approaches for incompressible flow have been described in detail in [Ham02]. As an improvement, Popinet et al. [Popinet03] introduced the first octree implementation of incompressible flow using restricted octrees. Lasasso et al. [Lasasso04] extended Popinet's work by implementing a technique simulating natural phenomena such as water and smoke by using recursive data structures, namely octrees, by extending them to free surface flows to allow modeling of a liquid interface (necessary for modeling accurate simulation of animated water surfaces) and by use of unrestricted octrees. Lasasso et al. [Lasasso04] also address the issue of solving a nonsymmetric system of linear equations while solving for pressure to enforce the divergence-free condition.

Recently presented optimization techniques simulate fluid flow more efficiently by using the graphics hardware. Harris et al. [Harris03] use a red-black Gauss-Seidel relaxation method on their fluid simulation as a vectorized optimization technique. They achieve faster rendering rates by amortizing their simulation over several frames. In their 3D solver they propose using a "flat 3D texture" that stores all slices of a 3D volume to improve the efficiency of their simulation. Rasmussen et al. [Rasmussen03] describe an interpolation method to create high-resolution 3D fields from a small number of 2D fields, significantly reducing computation and memory requirements. Several methods have been proposed to approximate light scattering and other visual phenomena to achieve realistic results in less time (e.g., [Fedkiw001] [Harris03]).

Many techniques have also been developed in recent years to optimize computations by using the GPU for processing. Weiskopf et al. [Weiskopf01] and Jobard et al.

[Jobard00] presented GPU-based approach for accelerating flow visualization using OpenGL 1.2 texture extensions. Bolz et al. [Bolz03] implemented two broadly useful computational kernels on the GPU, a sparse matrix conjugate solver and a regular-grid multigrid solver, by using the fragment shader of a GPU as a stream processor. This design maps the data structures into streams as textures and maps the algorithms (kernels) into fragment shaders operating on the input textures (proposed by Purcell et al. [Purcell02]). These computational kernels are fundamental to many physical modeling applications, and the authors used the common fluid-flow problem from [Stam99] to evaluate the performance of their techniques. Our approach is related to this method in that it also provides an optimization to the pressure computation step.

This chapter presents an acceleration method that takes into account the knowledge of where flow is concentrated to dynamically reduce computation on regions that have little to no fluid density or pressure. Our method is simple to implement and can be used in conjunction with any of the methods outlined above. It also yields good results in little rendering time.

Algorithm Overview

Next, we outline the steps of our algorithm, which simulates incompressible fluid flow. We perform our simulations with no viscosity, so the diffusion step is omitted. All of the steps of our fluid simulation algorithm are implemented on the GPU using HLSL pixel shaders and are executed by rendering full-screen quadrilaterals to renderable textures. For additional details on how such a flow algorithm is implemented on the GPU, please refer to [Harris03b]. First we will describe how the early-z approach optimizes the 2D fluid flow simulation and later briefly show how this approach can be extended to 3D fluid flow.

The first two passes insert flow into the density and velocity buffers based on mouse input:

```
InsertVelocity()
InsertDensity()
```

Next, both the density and velocity buffers are advected based on the content of the velocity buffer:

```
AdvectVelocity()
AdvectDensity()
```

Finally the projection step is computed and the velocity buffer is updated to remain mass conserving. The brute force algorithm for computing pressure is as follows:

```
ComputeDivergence()
for ( i = 0; i < n; i++ )
    UpdatePressure()
SubtractGradient()
```

The UpdatePressure() pass is the bottleneck of the algorithm, as it has to be executed approximately 30 times to yield visually pleasing results. Our algorithm adds a new pass to prime the z-buffer, and employs early-z culling during the pressure computation step:

```
ComputeDivergence()
SetZBufferUsingPressureFromPreviousIteration()
for(int i = 0; i < n; i++)
    UpdatePressureWithEarlyZCulling()
SubtractGradient()
```

After each step of the simulation, we render the density buffer to the screen in a single pass:

```
RenderDensityToScreen()
```

Projection Optimization

In this section we describe an optimization that is performed during the projection step, the most expensive step of the simulation. This step is performed as a series of rendering passes to solve a linear system using a relaxation method. This optimization could also be considered for the diffusion step when simulating highly viscous fluids.

When approximating the solution to this linear system, the higher the number of iterations (rendering passes), the more accurate the result. Instead of performing the same number of passes on all cells, we perform more passes on regions where the pressure is higher and fewer passes on regions with little or no pressure. This is accomplished by performing an additional inexpensive rendering pass that sets the z-value of each cell in the simulation based on the maximum value of that cell and four nearby cells from the pressure buffer of the previous iteration of the simulation. We simply set the z-value for a particular cell x to be

$$depth = \text{saturate}(\alpha P + \beta),$$

where P is the maximum pressure among the neighbors of x, and α and β are constants. We achieved best results with $\alpha = 2.0$ and $\beta = 0.1$. The β value ensures that, even where the pressure is very small, at least some pressure computation passes will be performed.

We take into account the pressure of the neighbors of x, because each relaxation step computes the new pressure for a given cell as a function of their neighbors. Thus, cells with high pressure may significantly increase the pressure of cells around it. In our experiments we looked at neighbors that were two cells away in each of the four directions.

After priming the z-buffer, we perform the pressure computation passes. To reduce this computation, we set the depth compare state to "less than or equal" and linearly increase the z-value on each of the projection passes. On the first pass the z-value is set to $1/N$, where N is the total number of pressure passes. On the second pass it is $2/N$, and so on. Therefore, on the first pass, all cells are processed (because of our β value), and on subsequent passes, the number of cells that are processed gradually decreases. Figure 9.6.2a shows the pressure buffer that is used to set the z-buffer that culls the projection computation. Darker values indicate regions of lower pressure, where fewer iterations need to be performed. Figure 9.6.2b shows that in this scenario pressure is often, but not always, concentrated in regions of high density.

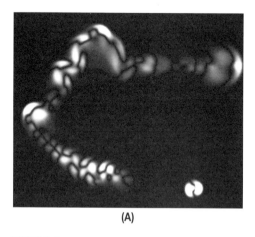

(A)

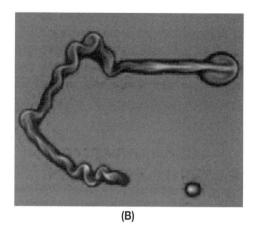

(B)

FIGURE 9.6.2   Visualization of early-z culling. **(A)** Pressure buffer for simulation culling. **(B)** Pixels with very small density shown in red.

The passes that enforce boundary conditions on the pressure computation are not culled. However, since they only affect the pixels on the grid boundaries, it does not hinder the performance of the heavily fill-bound simulation. This optimization provides a win even if the flow spreads across the entire rendered area since in that case the pressure is likely to be located in some regions rather than others, and the computation will be concentrated on the regions with significant pressure.

Note that this optimization is an approximation and does not necessarily yield physically correct results. However, the visual improvement from using this method is evident, and performing 50 pressure computation passes with this culling technique yields more accurate results than performing 10 pressure computation passes with the brute force algorithm in the same amount of time.

Extension to 3D Fluid Flow

We also extended the above optimization to 3D fluid flow simulation. Harris [Harris03] introduces the idea of simulating 3D flow using a tiled 2D texture (Figure 9.6.3a,b). Thus, our optimization naturally extends to 3D flow. As in 2D flow, pressure computation is performed by doing multiple passes to update the pressure buffer (Figure 9.6.3c). Similarly, we perform one pass to prime the z-buffer based on the pressure of the previous simulation iteration, and then, when performing the pressure computation passes, we perform early-z culling the same way we did with 2D flow. More experimentation must be performed to analyze 3D flow results. Currently, we get a significantly higher-quality improvement in our 2D flow experiments, which do not require a "bookkeeping" overhead from the boundaries in the tiled 3D texture and the more expensive 3D rendering.

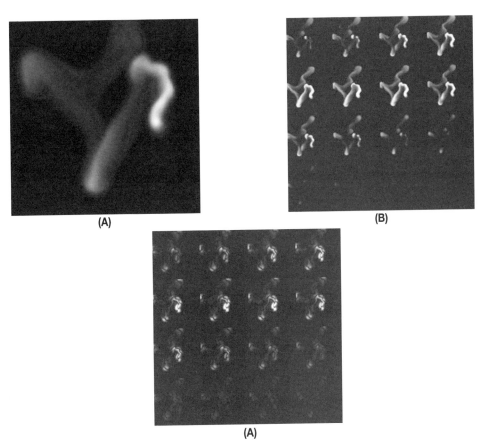

FIGURE 9.6.3 Visualization of 3D flow and the density and pressure buffers. **(A)** 3D view. **(B)** Density buffer. **(C)** Pressure buffer

Results

In this section we present some results of applying the optimizations described in the earlier sections. Figure 6.3.1 compares a brute-force simulation and a simulation with early-z culling. Both examples simulate and render the 512×512 simulation grid at 53 frames per second. Since the brute force approach performs the same number of pressure computation passes on all cells, it only manages 10 pressure computation passes.

Our early-z method performs somewhere between 5 and 50 pressure computation passes, depending on the value in Figure 9.6.2a. Since our optimization allows for a high number of passes on areas of high pressure, it yields a more realistic result. Figure 9.6.4 graphs the performance of our 2D fluid simulation with and without our optimization. The frame rate is on the y-axis, while the resolution is on the x-axis (we have data points for 128×128, 256×256, 512×512, and 1024×1024 simulation grid resolutions). In each case the screen resolution for the rendered output is the same as the simulation grid resolution. Three curves are plotted, one using the brute force method and two using the optimization method. When the optimization method is used, the frame rate is variable, so we use two curves for measuring performance—one without any flow, and one with the entire grid filled with flow. The actual frame rate will be somewhere between these two curves, depending on how much density and pressure is present.

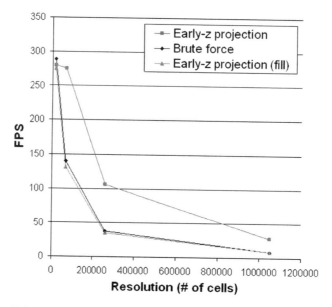

FIGURE 9.6.4   Timings of the different culling methods (screen resolution set to simulation resolution).

As evidenced by the two lowest curves on the graph, the penalty incurred by having the extra pass to set the z-buffer is extremely small. On the other hand, if significant portions of the screen have no flow, the savings can be significant, with no visual loss in quality. At 128×128 the savings from the simulation optimization can be up to a factor of two, with no visual loss in simulation quality. At 1024×1024 the savings can be up to a factor of three.

Figures 9.6.5 and 9.6.6 show different examples in which the pressure buffer is not cleared from one pass to the next (causing extremely swirling-like flow). In Figure 9.6.6 the small number of passes in the pressure buffer coupled with a slow frame rate results in a velocity field that is not mass conserving. In contrast, when using our culling techniques, the result is significantly more stable.

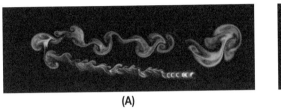
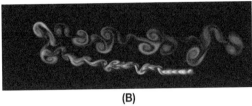

(A)   (B)

FIGURE 9.6.5   Side by side of a 1024×1024 2D simulation. Both simulations render at 25 fps. The small number of passes on the brute force example cause the velocity field not to be mass conserving. **(A)** Brute force (three projection passes). **(B)** Early-z (up to 15 projection passes).

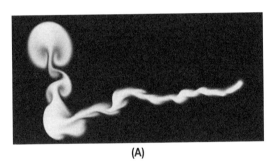
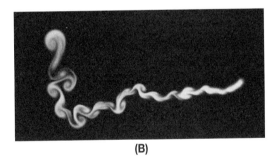

(A)   (B)

FIGURE 9.6.6   Side by side of a 1024×1024 2D simulation. Both simulations have 40 projection passes. The lower frame rate on the brute force example causes artifacts when flow is inserted at a constant, faster rate (e.g., interactive mouse input). **(A)** Brute force (5 fps). **(B)** Early-z (16 fps).

Vorticity Confinement

Figure 9.6.7 shows an example using vorticity confinement on a 512×512 grid. This approach still gives over a factor of two improvement when vorticity confinement is used because the pressure is still more concentrated on regions that have higher density.

Blockers

Our culling technique is also very suitable for fluid flow simulations with blockers. Since no computation needs to be performed on most cells that are blocked (approxi-

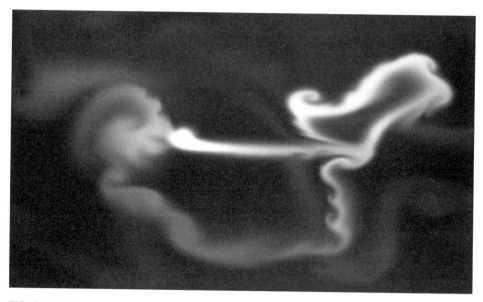

FIGURE 9.6.7   Example with vorticity confinement.

mately half of the cells in Figure 9.6.8), this method can further reduce computational costs. Note that blocked cells that have neighbors that are not blocked cannot be culled and need to be processed to yield the proper effect when fluid collides with the blocker.

FIGURE 9.6.8   Pink flow colliding with blocker in Van Gogh's *Starry Night*.

Conclusion

We have presented a straightforward optimization technique that takes advantage of early-z culling to efficiently simulate and render fluid flow. The method presented in this chapter is easy to implement and yields a significant improvement in rendering speed for the same quality, or conversely, an improvement in quality for a given frame rate. Our results demonstrate that we obtain simulations that look more physically accurate than brute force simulations at a given rendering speed.

Our method excels in scenes where flow is concentrated on specific regions of the grid, such as scenes with blockers. The main limitation of this approach is that it does not yield a significant improvement to simulations that have a large amount of fluid over the entire simulation grid, but even in the worst case our simulations will not significantly impair the quality or rendering speed in such settings, as evidenced by Figure 9.6.4.

For future work, it would be interesting to perform more experimentation on 3D flow acceleration techniques using early-z culling and further investigate other general methods that take advantage of the locality of fluid in the simulation. We are currently investigating a method with adaptive grid sample locations.

The approach presented in this chapter can be adapted to other physically based simulations because of the generalized nature of the main contribution. We hope that we will see more applications of explicit early-z culling in other GPU-based computations.

References

[Bolz03] Bolz, J., I. Farmer, E. Grinspun, and P. Schroder. "Sparse Matrix Solvers on the GPU: Conjugate Gradients and Multigrid." Proceedings of SIGGRAPH 2003, pp. 917–924, 2003.

[Carlson02] Carlson, M., P. Mucha, R. Van Horn III, and G. Turk. "Melting and Flowing." *ACM SIGGRAPH Symposium on Computer Animation 2002*, 2002: pp. 167–174.

[Chen94] Chen, J. and N. Lobo. "Toward Interactive-Rate Simulation of Fluids with Moving Obstacles Using the Navier-Stokes Equations." *Computer Graphics and Image Processing, 57,* (1994): pp. 107–116.

[Chorin67] Chorin, A. "A Numerical Method for Solving Incompressible Viscous Flow Problems." *Journal of Computational Physics*, 2, (1967): pp. 12–26.

[Enright02] Enright, D., S. Marschner, and R. Fedkiw. "Animation and Rendering of Complex Water Surfaces." *Proceedings of SIGGRAPH 2002*, pp. 736–744.

[Fedkiw01] Fedkiw, R., J. Stam, and H. Jensen. "Visual Simulation of Smoke." *Proceedings of SIGGRAPH 2001*, 2001: pp. 15–22.

[Feldman03] Feldman, B. E., J. F. O'Brien, O. and Arikan. "Animating Suspended Particle Explosions." *ACM Transactions on Graphics (SIGGRAPH Proceedings)*, 22(3), (2003): pp. 708–715.

[Foster96] Foster, N. and D. Metaxas. "Realistic Animation of Liquids." *Graphical Models and Image Processing 58,* 1996: pp. 471–483.

[Foster97] Foster, N. and D. Metaxas. "Modeling the Motion of a Hot, Turbulent Gas. *Proceedings of SIGGRAPH 97*, 1997: pp. 181–188.

[Ham02] Ham, F., F. Lien, and A. Strong. "A Fully Conservative Second Order Finite Difference Scheme for Incompressible Flow on Non-Uniform Grids. *Journal of Computational Physics, 117*, (2002): pp. 117–133.

[Harris03] Harris, M. J., W. V. Baxter, T. Scheuermann, and A. Lastra. "Simulation of Cloud Dynamics on Graphics Hardware." *Proceedings of the ACM SIGGRAPH/ EUROGRAPHICS Conference on Graphics Hardware*, 2003: pp. 92–101.

[Harris03b] Harris, M. J. "Real-time Cloud Simulation and Rendering." Ph.D. dissertation. University of North Carolina at Chapel Hill, 2003.

[Jobard00] Jobard, B., G. Erlebacher, G., and M. Y. Hussaini. "Hardware-Accelerated Texture Advection for Unsteady Flow Visualization." *IEEE Visualization,* (October 2000): pp. 155–162.

[Kass90] Kass M. and G. Miller. "Rapid, Stable Fluid Dynamics for Computer Graphics." *Computer Graphics (Proceedings of SIGGRAPH 90), 24*, (1990): pp. 49–57.

[Lamorlette02] Lamorlette, A. and N. Foster. "Structural Modeling of Natural Flames." *ACM Transactions on Graphics (SIGGRAPH Proceedings), 21*(3), (2002): pp. 729–735.

Lasasso, F., and Hoppe, H., 2004: Geometry Clipmap0s: Terrain Rendering Using Nested Regular Grids. In: *ACM Transactions on Graphics, 23(3).*

[Miyazaki02] Miyazaki, R., Y. Dobashi, and T. Nishita. "Simulation of Cumuliform Clouds Based on Computational Fluid Dynamics." *Proceedings of Eurographics 2002 Short Presentation*, 2002: pp. 405–410.

[Nguyen02] Nguyen, D., R. Fedkiw, and H. Jensen. "Physically Based Modeling and Animation of Fire." *Proceedings of SIGGRAPH 2000*, 2002: pp. 736–744.

[Popinet03] Popinet, S. "A Tree-Based Adaptive Solver for the Incompressible Euler Equations in Complex Geometries." *Proceedings of Journal of Computational Physics, 190*, (2003): pp. 572–600.

[Purcell02] Purcell, T. J., I. Buck, W. R. Mark, and P. Hanrahan. "Ray Tracing on Programmable Graphics Hardware." *In Proceedings of SIGGRAPH 2002*, pp. 703–712.

[Rasmussen03] Rasmussen, N., D. Q. Nguyen, W. Geiger, and R. Fedkiw. "Smoke Simulation for Large Scale Phenomena." *Proceedings of SIGGRAPH 2003*, 2003: pp. 703–715.

[Stam99] Stam, J. "Stable Fluids." *Proceedings of SIGGRAPH 1999*, 1999: pp. 121–128.

[Weiskopf01] Weiskopf, D., M. Hopf, and T. Ertl. "Hardware-Accelerated Visualziation of Time-Varying 2D and 3D Vector Fields by Texture Advection via Programmable Per-Pixel Operations." *Workshop on Vision, Modeling, and Visualization VMW,* 2001, pp. 439–446.

Storing and Accessing Topology on the GPU: A Case Study on Mass-Spring Systems

Carlos A. Dietrich, João L. D. Comba, and Luciana P. Nedel, Federal University of Rio Grande do Sul

Introduction

The mapping of a problem into a GPU solution often involves considering several implementation alternatives. In this paper we present a case study on how to implement mass-spring systems on the GPU [Georgii05] [Tejada05], which is a practical technique for implementing deformable systems [Nealen05]. This technique is suitable for GPU implementation since it has an inherent parallelism on its computation. Our goal is to present a critical discussion on the operation that most affects performance in this method: the storage and access of topological information.

A mass-spring system is a simple particle system in which the behavior of a given particle is mainly controlled by the connections it makes using springs with neighbor particles (topological information). In most cases where mass-spring systems are used, the topology information does not change. However, a given particle may have a varying number of neighbors, which needs to be taken into account when storing and recovering topology information on the GPU.

A GPU implementation of a mass-spring system performs all computation inside the pixel shader, where access to all neighbors for a given particle is needed. The way this information is made available at this point of computation has a direct impact on its performance [Calver04]. We discusses several alternatives based on GPU performance results evaluated by measuring GPU performance counters using the gDEBugger® [GraphicRemedy06] interface. Based on these results, we summarize useful guidelines for GPU application development that are valid for a wide variety of applications. In addition, we provide source code for our GPU implementation of mass-spring systems.

Mass-Spring Systems on the GPU

Mass-spring systems are particle systems commonly used to simulate deformable bodies in computer graphics. They are composed of a finite number of particles connected by massless springs (Figure 9.7.1).

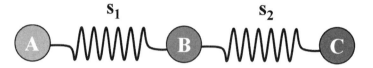

FIGURE 9.7.1   Simple mass-spring system composed of three particles (A, B, and C) and two springs (s_1 and s_2).

The particle motion is affected by both external and neighboring forces. Basically, these forces are (a) the particle inertia, (b) the forces accumulated in springs, (c) the viscous drag (the energy dissipation mechanism), and (d) the external forces that act equally over all particles. Supposing we have a particle p_i with position x_i; we can express the particle energy as

$$m_i \ddot{x}_i - c \dot{x}_i + \sum_{j=0}^{N} F_{spring(p_i, p_j)} - F_{ext(p_i)} = 0 \qquad (9.7.1)$$

where m_i is the p_i mass, c is the damping constant, $F_{spring(p_i, p_j)}$ is the force accumulated in the spring that links the particles p_i and p_j, and $F_{ext(p_i, p_j)}$ is the sum of the external forces that act on p_i. $\sum_{j=0} F_{spring(p_i, p_j)}$ depends on p_i's relationship with all N adjacent particles.

Let's assume that these forces will be integrated in a pixel shader for each particle [Georgii05] [Tejada05]. To accomplish this, all particle data (mass, damping coefficient, external forces, and the incident springs) should be available to the pixel shader. Assuming that each particle can have a different (and unlimited) number of neighbors, how can we represent this information efficiently? This will be discussed in the next section.

Storing and Accessing Topology on the GPU

In this section we present two solutions inspired by the recent work of Georgii et al. [Georgii05] and Tejada et al. [Tejada05] to represent mass-spring models on GPUs:

the vertex representation of individual springs and the texture representation of adjacency lists of springs. In both solutions we represent the geometry (particle positions) using textures but change the way we represent topology information, which plays a major role in the integration efficiency. All results presented in this section were obtained for a model composed of 65K particles and 275K springs (Figure 9.7.2 shows snapshots of this model under deformation).

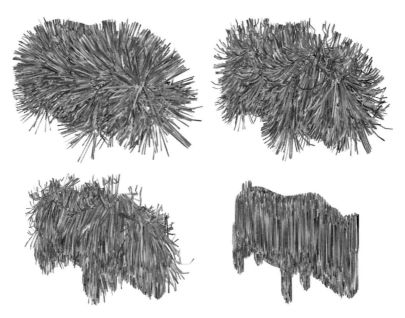

FIGURE 9.7.2   The hairy pig dataset used in performance experiments. Each of its 3,819 hairs is composed of 16 particles and 72 springs, resulting in a structure with 61,104 particles and 274,968 springs.

Using Vertex Attributes

One way to send information to the pixel shader is by sending a vertex primitive through the pipeline with vertex attributes containing the desired information. We can use this approach to send neighbor information encoded at each spring connecting two particles, one at a time. This can be done since spring-force computation can be calculated independently from other springs.

We represent each spring by two vertex primitives, where each vertex accounts for the force exerted by the spring on one particle, containing the particle address, spring stiffness, and rest length. Each vertex is then converted (rasterized) into a pixel associated with the particle on which it acts [Georgii05]. In this solution, the pixel shader integrates the force that one spring exerts over one particle, which is accumulated in the corresponding position in the particle textures (see Figure 9.7.3).

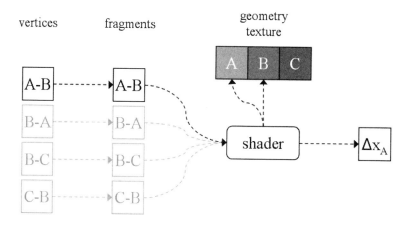

FIGURE 9.7.3   Vertex representation the model springs shown in Figure 9.7.1. The spring forces are represented by vertices, and each vertex stores all the spring data from which it was originated. The pixel shader uses this information to integrate the force at one spring endpoint and accumulates the resultant displacement Δx_A over the corresponding particle position.

Although very intuitive, this approach is not efficient on current GPUs (shader model 3.0 architecture). Mass-spring systems are frequently composed by a huge number of springs; by dividing each spring in two vertices (and thus two pixels), we overload the vertex and pixel shader units. This behavior is illustrated in Figure 9.7.4, where we see that these units are the main bottlenecks.

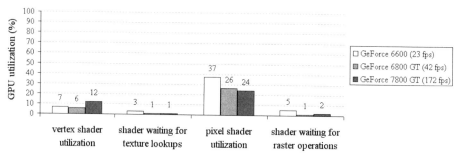

FIGURE 9.7.4   Using vertex primitives. Most of the GPU processing time is concentrated in vertex and pixel shader units, which have greater impact on the integration performance.

Each spring exerts two forces that are equal in magnitude but are in opposite directions. Thus, we can speed up the integration by precalculating the force of each spring instead of calculating it twice in both pixels used to represent each spring. This approach requires an additional rendering step, in which the spring forces are calculated and stored in an additional texture map (Figure 9.7.5).

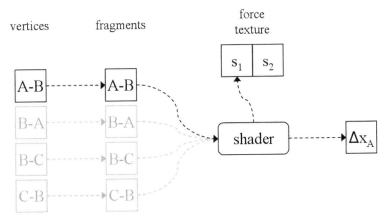

FIGURE 9.7.5   Saving arithmetic effort. Spring forces are precalculated and stored in a new texture map, the force texture, as illustrated to the springs s_1 and s_2. The pixel shader only accumulates the forces of all springs incident to each particle to perform the integration.

Replacing arithmetic effort by texture lookups is a well-known GPU development guideline [Engel04]. However, the performance gain that occurs is due to the reduction of the vertex attribute size. Now, each vertex attribute contains only its corresponding force texture address, which significantly reduces the overload of the vertex processor units (Figure 9.7.6).

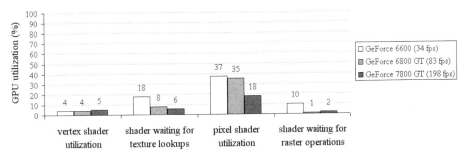

FIGURE 9.7.6   Saving arithmetic effort. Texture lookups allow the reduction of the vertex parameter set and increases the vertex shader unit's performance.

Using Texture Memory

The approaches described in the previous sections, which represent the topological information (springs) with vertex attributes, are based on the assumption that springs are independent. However, one can be interested in using all of the particle neighborhood information to perform the force integration. We can store particle adjacency (list of springs) explicitly in texture memory [Tejada05]. In this approach topology is encoded into two textures, one storing the list of neighbors for all particles (neighbors texture) and a second serving as a neighbors allocation table (neighborhood texture). Each neighborhood texture texel stores a pointer to the neighbors texture texel, where the first of n neighbors of each particle is stored. Each neighbor's texture texel stores a pointer to the adjacent particle and the mechanical parameters of the spring connecting these particles. The number of neighbors is also stored in neighborhood texture, as illustrated in Figure 9.7.7.

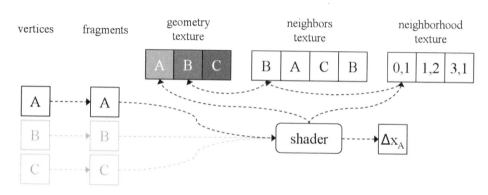

FIGURE 9.7.7   Texture representation of the model springs shown in Figure 9.7.1. Each pixel represents one particle, and the pixel shader is able to recover the information about all incident springs from the neighborhood and neighbors' textures.

If we compare this approach against the ones proposed in the previous sections, we see that we replaced a huge number of vertex primitives and a simple pixel shader with a small number of vertex primitives and a complex pixel shader. This has (at least) one side-effect: the reduced number of vertices and the high number of texture lookups increase significantly the texture unit loading. However, the current GPU pixel shader units are able to deal efficiently with this loading, as can be seen in Figure 9.7.8.

Again, we can save arithmetic effort by precalculating the spring forces. Each spring force is calculated and stored in a texture map, in the same way as before (Figure 9.7.9).

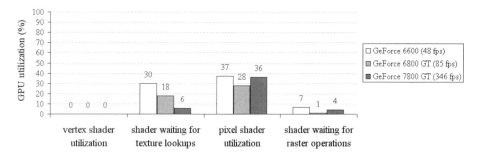

FIGURE 9.7.8 Using texture memory. The reduced number of vertices and the high number of texture lookups increase the texture units loading, although the pixel shader units are able to deal with this added overhead.

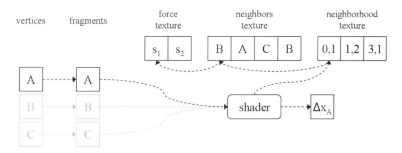

FIGURE 9.7.9 Saving arithmetic effort. The pixel shader loops over all particle neighbors, accumulating the precalculated forces stored in forces texture.

However, this approach does not improve performance, as can be seen in Figure 9.7.10. The texture units' overhead can be attributed to both lack of bandwidth (owing to the new texture lookups) and the high number of texture cache misses (owing to the lookups in different textures).

In the previous approach each pixel represents one particle, and the pixel shader loops over all particle neighbors to integrate the forces acting on each particle. Thus, if we assume that each pixel shader unit (pipe) can be filled with pixels that have a varying number of neighbors, all of them will have to wait for the processing of those with the maximum number of neighbors. We can avoid this by splitting their neighborhood across two pixels, each one representing half of the force that acts on the particle. To accomplish this, both pixels use the same entry in the neighborhood texture (which points to the first particle neighbor in the neighbors texture), and two new parameters—an offset and a new number of neighbors. The first pixel has a null offset and $n/2$ neighbors, which means that it deals with the first $n/2$ neighbors of the particle. Accordingly, the second pixel has a $n/2$ offset and $n/2$ neighbors, corresponding to the remaining neighbors.

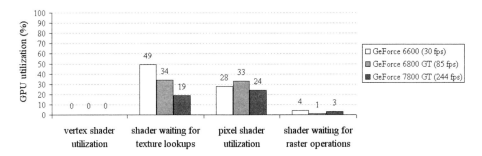

FIGURE 9.7.10   Saving arithmetic effort. In spite of changing the arithmetic efforts with texture lookups, the texture units' overhead stall the integration process.

Thus, the new pixel sets have (nearly) the same numbers of neighbors, which we would assume to be more efficient. However, this does not happen, as can be seen in Figure 9.7.11. One of the reasons for this decrease in performance is a very simple (and also very important) GPU characteristic: texture lookup coherency. The approach proposed here temporally splits the texture lookups to the particle neighbors, causing at least one texture cache miss.

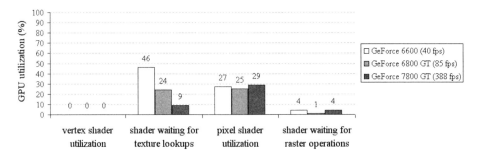

FIGURE 9.7.11   Despite using pixel sets with (nearly) homogeneous numbers of neighbors, the overall performance decreases.

Analysis

The results obtained in the previous sections offer some simple (and useful) conclusions about GPU application development. Some of them are obvious and well-known guidelines, but they deserve to be further discussed in the current scenario (Shader Model 3.0 architecture).

Are Fewer Instructions Always Better?

Engel [Engel04] shows this as a trivial rule, but it should be interpreted carefully. Nowadays, shader assembly instructions are grouped into very large instruction words

(VLIWs). The VLIWs are loaded into the pixel pipes and represent what really happens with each pixel at each GPU cycle. Thus, it is important to *minimize the number of VLIWs of each shader*, although it is hard to say how many VLIWs are necessary to encapsulate an assembly instruction set. Some recent tools such as the NVIDIA NVShaderPerf® [NVIDIA06] can predict the number of cycles for simple shaders and thus are important tools in GPU application development.

It is also important to mention that some optimizations in the assembly instruction set can be very disappointing. The next section discusses the replacement of arithmetic instructions by texture lookups, which effectively reduces the number of assembly instructions but slows down the overall pixel shader performance.

Use (Carefully) Texture Lookups Instead of Arithmetic Instructions

The replacement of arithmetic instructions by texture lookups for precalculated values is a good strategy in many applications [Engel04]. However, in recent GPUs we observe that the processing power has been increasing faster than texture bandwidth [Kilgariff05]. In addition, texture lookups can result in latencies that are very difficult to predict, and they are one of the most common bottlenecks in GPU applications. Thus, this guideline *strongly depends on the available bandwidth of the application*.

This technique was applied in our experiments with very different results. The difference is explained by the *shader waiting for texture lookups* counter. In the first approach, illustrated in Figure 9.7.7, the GPU performance was severely limited by the available bandwidth in the texture units. By including a new texture lookup per pixel (potentially incoherent), we are contributing to the texture units' overhead, and thus the application performance slows down.

Maximize Texture Coherence

This can be the most trivial guideline, but sometimes it can be a very important one. Every time a pixel shader pipe waits for a texture fetch, it becomes idle, and thus we are wasting cycles when doing incoherent texture lookups. Such incoherent lookups usually lead to cache misses because of the small coherence block size implemented in current GPUs.

The approach illustrated in Figure 9.7.7 stores all neighbors in a contiguous array of texels. While splitting this block in half (as discussed in the end of the section "Whether or not to Use Branch Instructions") seems to be a good idea at first, it reduces spatial coherence in the neighbors' texture accesses. This is one of the reasons for the texture misses, as illustrated by the time the shader waits for texture in Figure 9.7.11.

Whether or Not to Use Branch Instructions

The change of flow control introduced by branches reduces parallelism, making it harder to be implemented on GPUs that are essentially parallel stream processors [Harris04]. The branching mechanism as implemented on current GPUs is limited, and its application is only worthwhile in specific situations. Basically, branches should be used when the cost associated with the branch instructions is small compared to the total shader cost. In the approach illustrated in Figure 9.7.7, for example, a branch instruction (break command) allows us to interrupt the access to the particle neighborhood in an efficient way because the number of instructions saved by this command compensates the branch overhead.

Harris [Harris04] says that branches should be used when large blocks of pixels will take the same branch. However, this guideline should also be interpreted carefully. In the approach illustrated in Figure 9.7.7, for example, it is possible to sort the particles according to the number of their neighbors. This leads to large coherent blocks in pixel shader units but breaks the texture coherence in particle texture lookup (particles positions). Again, the texture coherence plays the most important role in the application performance.

Implementation

All the techniques described here are API independent, and we describe our shaders using the Cg language [Mark03]. As discussed before, the pixel shader is responsible for computing the force accumulated in all springs incident to each particle. To achieve this, the shader first recovers the required data (related to the neighboring springs and particles) and then calculates the resultant force over the particle. Since we have assumed that the force computation is the same in all techniques, we choose to outline the particle and spring data lookup from GPU memory. The following sections show how the major techniques perform this task.

Using Vertex Attributes

The storage of topology using vertex attributes has a trivial GPU implementation. Each pixel represents a force exerted by a compressed or stretched spring upon a particle. Thus, the only required parameters are (a) the current particle address, (b) the adjacent particle address, and (c) the spring's mechanical parameters. All of these can be passed as vertex parameters, as illustrated in Listing 9.7.1. Given that, the shader simply recovers the particles' positions and proceeds to the force computation.

LISTING 9.7.1   The Pixel Shader that Integrates the Force that One Spring Exerts over One Particle

```
struct vertexToPixel {
    float2 orgTexCoord;  // address of particle at spring origin
    float2 destTexCoord; // address of particle at spring
                            destination
    float2 param; // spring stiffness and rest length
};

float4 main(vertexToPixel IN,
    uniform samplerRECT geometryTex, // particle geometry texture
```

```
        uniform float timestep)
{
    // particle at spring origin
    float3 org = f3texRECT(geometryTex, IN.orgTexCoord);
    // particle at spring destination
    float3 dest = f3texRECT(geometryTex, IN.destTexCoord);

    // calculate the spring force
    return CalcSpringForce(org, dest, IN.param.x, IN.param.y,
    timestep);
}
```

Using Texture Memory

This implementation requires a more elaborate shader. Each pixel represents one particle, and the shader is responsible for computing the force acting on each particle. To accomplish this, the shader first recovers the location of all neighbors of a given particle in the neighborhood texture and loops over all neighbors to accumulate the force associated with each spring (Listing 9.7.2).

LISTING 9.7.2   Pixel Shader that Accumulates the Force Acting over Each Particle by Recovering the Information about All Incident Springs from Neighborhood and Neighbors' Textures

```
struct vertex2pixel {
    float2 particleTexCoord : TEXCOORD0; // particle address
};

float4 main(vertex2pixel IN,
    uniform samplerRECT geometryTex, // particle geometry texture
    uniform samplerRECT neighborhoodTex, // neighborhood texture
    uniform samplerRECT neighboursTex // neighbors texture
    uniform float timestep)
{
    // address of particle neighborhood and number of neighbors
    float3 index = f3texRECT(neighborhoodTex, IN.
    particleTexCoord.xy);
    // particle at spring origin
    float3 org = f3texRECT(geometryTex, IN. particleTexCoord.xy);

    float4 arrayEnergy = (0.0f).xxxx;
    int i = 0;

    while (i < index.z)
    {
        // particle at spring destination and spring parameters
        float4 destInfo = f4texRECT(neighboursTex,
        float2(index.x + i,
            index.y));

        // particle at spring destination
        float3 dest = f3texRECT(positionTex, destInfo.xy);
```

```
        // calculate the spring force
        arrayEnergy += CalcSpringForce(org, dest, destInfo.z,
        destInfo.w,
            timestep);
    }

    return arrayEnergy;
}
```

Demo

Real-time demos implemented using all approaches described here can be found at *http://www.inf.ufrgs.br/cadietrich/shaderx5*. Images generated with our code is illustrated in Figure 9.7.12.

FIGURE 9.7.12   Grass and cloth scene. This scene illustrates how our mass-spring system models can be used in other modeling scenarios. In this scene the grass and cloths are modeled as mass-spring models, and we use external forces to control their deformation.

Conclusions

In this paper we presented a case study on the implementation of mass-spring systems on the GPU. Implementing deformable models in the GPU can be very useful in several applications, and the source code accompanying this paper can help users integrate mass-spring systems in their applications. Our most important point throughout this paper was that there are several alternatives for implementing such systems in a GPU, and we compared them critically. We expect our discussion to be useful to readers in the development of this and other GPU applications.

References

[Calver04] Calver, D. "Accessing and Modifying Topology on the GPU." *ShaderX³: Advanced Rendering with DirectX and OpenGL*. Charles River Media, 2004: pp. 5–19.

[Engel04] Engel, W. *Programming Vertex And Pixel Shaders*. Charles River Media, 2004.

[Georgii05] Georgii, J. and R. Westermann. "Mass-Spring Systems on the GPU." *Simulation Practice and Theory*, 2005.

[GraphicRemedy06] Graphic Remedy. "gDEBugger." Available online at *http://www. gremedy.com/products.php*, February 20, 2006.

[Harris04] Harris, M. J. "Gpgpu: Beyond Graphics." Available online at *http://www. gpgpu.org*, February 20, 2004.

[Kilgariff05] Kilgariff, E. and R. Fernando. "The GeForce 6 Series GPU Architecture." *GPU Gems 2*. NVIDIA Corporation, 2005: pp. 471–491.

[Mark03] Mark, W., S. Glanville, and K. Akeley. "Cg: A System for Programming Graphics Hardware in a C-like Language." 2003.

[Nealen05] Nealen, A., M. Miller, R. Keiser, E. Boxerman, and M. Carlson. "Deformable Models in Computer Graphics." *Eurographics 2005 State of the Art Report* (STAR), 2005.

[NVIDIA06] NVIDIA. "NVPerfKit 1.1." Available online at *http://developer.nvidia. com/object/nvperfkit_home.html*, February 20, 2006.

[Tejada05] Tejada, E. and T. Ertl. "Large Steps in GPU-Based Deformable Bodies Simulation." *Simulation Practice and Theory*, 2005.

9.8

Implementing High-Quality PRNG on GPUs

Wai-Man Pang, Tien-Tsin Wong, and Pheng-Ann Heng

The Chinese University of Hong Kong

Introduction

A high-quality pseudo-random number generator (PRNG) is essential in many graphics and general purpose applications. It is especially important in rendering algorithms that rely heavily on stochastic sampling, such as distribution ray tracing and photon mapping. However, the lack of high-precision integer arithmetic and native bitwise operations on current GPUs makes it difficult to implement high-quality PRNGs efficiently. For example, the rand() in C is an implementation of linear congruential generator (LCG) that requires high-precision integer arithmetics such as a 32-bit modulo. The build-in Perlin noise [Perlin85] function in shading languages provides a visually smooth noise variation but cannot provide a high-quality random sequence. A high-quality random sequence should have a long repeating cycle and low correlation among subsequences.

In this article we propose to use a cellular automata (CA)-based PRNG that does not require high-precision integer arithmetic or bitwise operations. It relies only on simple low-precision arithmetic and interconnection of cells (pixels). It generates high-quality random sequences and fits nicely with the architecture of current GPUs.

The CA-Based PRNG

The CA-based PRNG was first proposed by Wolfram [Wolfram86]. The basic structure of a CA-based PRNG is illustrated in Figure 9.8.1. It is composed of several interconnected cells, each with the same behavior. Each cell holds a cell state corresponding to a bit of the random number being generated. The number of cells is usually larger than the number of bits of a random number to provide better randomness. The connectivity of cells is defined locally to the cell. Let us consider a simple CA of only four cells, A, B, C, and D (Figure 9.8.1). Each cell connects to its left cell and the second cell on its right. In this case the connectivity is denoted as $(-1,2)$. Notice that the connectivity wraps around when connected to an out-of-boundary cell. For example, the left connection of cell A goes to cell D, and cell D's second right connection should be cell B.

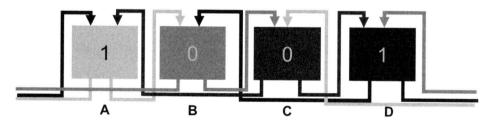

FIGURE 9.8.1   A four-cell CA-based PRNG with input connectivity of $(-1,2)$.

Each cell computes the same cell equation Φ, which is used to update the state of the cell. As illustrated in Figure 9.8.2, the cell equation Φ is a function of cell state values c_i from its connected neighbors. The neighborhood of a cell can include the cell itself. After all cells update their states, a new random number is generated by collecting the bits scattered among the cells.

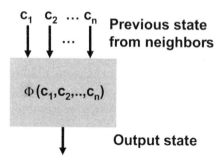

FIGURE 9.8.2   Each cell computes the same cell equation Φ, but with different input c_i from connected neighbors.

Let's demonstrate how the CA-based PRNG works with the four-cell PRNG in Figure 9.8.1. This four-cell PRNG outputs a 3-bit random number by gathering the state values of cells A, C, and D (Figure 9.8.3). The cell's neighbor connectivity is $(-1,2)$, and the cell equation $\Phi = \text{step}(1, 3 - c_{-1} - 2c_2)$. The function $\text{step}(a,x)$ returns 1 if $x \geq a$; otherwise, it returns 0. Like all other PRNGs requiring an initial seed, CA-based PRNG also requires an initialization of cell states. We can simply initialize them with random values as in Figure 9.8.3a. All cell states are updated simultaneously in generating the next random number.

Figure 9.8.3b shows the first computed result and the corresponding new random number. The connected neighbors of cell A are cells C and D, which have the previous state values of 0 and 1, respectively (Figure 9.8.3a). The cell equation updates the state of cell A to 1, as $3-1-2\times0=2\geq1$. Other cells work similarly and simultaneously. Once all cells evaluate the cell equation, a new random number can be obtained by collecting the cell states of A, C, and D, with state of cell A as the MSB and the state of cell D as the LSB. Hence, we get a random number of 111 = 7 (Figure 9.8.3b). To generate the next random number, we simply repeat the process. Figure 9.8.3c shows one more iteration and the corresponding random number 011 = 3.

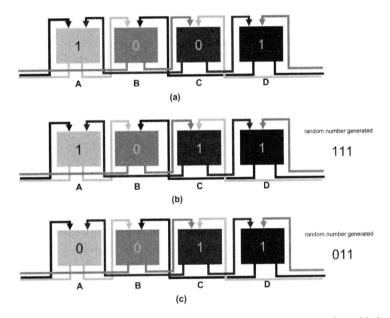

FIGURE 9.8.3 Three iterations of generating a 3-bit random number with the four-cell CA-based PRNG.

The particular connectivity and cell equation in Figure 9.8.3 is only one of the many possible configurations. The configuration of a CA-based PRNG can vary to a large extent and affect the quality of random number generated. It is difficult to find the best configuration analytically. One can find a good configuration by brute force searching or other optimization methods such as genetic algorithms. We introduce here a specific configuration that can generate high-quality 32-bit random numbers. It contains 64 cells, and each cell is connected to 4 neighbors (56,2,21,49). The cell equation is defined below,

```
X          = 8*c[(i+56)%64]+4*c[(i+2)%64]+2*c[(i+21)%64]+
c[(i+49)%64];
newstate = step(0.0,((X/X)/(sin((round((
(cos(X))-X)*(max((ceil(fmod(max(fmod(
```

```
max(cos((sin(X))/(exp(0.71860))),cos(
(-0.99452)/(0.53135/X))),(round(-0.87625))
-(ceil(cos(X))-(sin(X)))),min(-0.33617,
max(min(X+0.84286,X),fmod(X,0.72631)))),
cos(X))))*(0.13350),exp(X+0.84286)))))*
((X+X)*(X-(-0.19354/0.35541)))))));
```

where c[j] is the state value of cell j.

Implementation and Further Speed-Up

The parallelism and homogenous computation of the CA-based PRNG make it fit nicely on the SIMD-based architecture of GPUs. The state of cells can be tightly packed and stored in a texture. Figures 9.8.4a and 9.8.4b show the data organization of the 64 cell states in textures (cells) and the 16-entry lookup table (eqnLUT), respectively. The random number is formed by packing the 32 cell states as in Figure 9.8.4c.

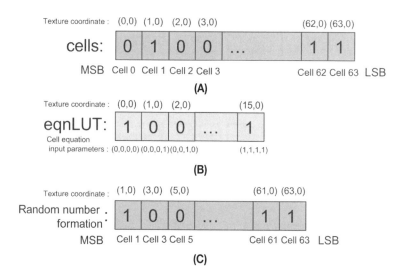

FIGURE 9.8.4   Data organization in the textures. **(A)** Cell organization and **(B)** lookup table for evaluating the cell equation. **(C)** Formation of the random number by 32 cell states.

The computation of the cell equation can be performed in a fragment shader. We speed up the evaluation of the cell equation by replacing the complicated cell equation with a lookup table. Since the cell equation is a mapping of neighbor cell states to an output state that is either 1 or 0, we can precompute the cell equation and store it in a lookup table (texture) to achieve a significant speed-up.

A straightforward implementation is to use an n-dimensional texture if there are n neighbor connections. However, high-dimensional tables are currently not supported on GPUs if the table dimension exceeds 3. Alternatively, we can pack the n bits to form an n-bit index, and the precomputed values are stored in a 1D texture only. In our 4-connected CA-based PRNG, we need only $2^4 = 16$ different output states, so a 16-entry lookup table is sufficient.

As a result, the fragment shader can be as simple as follows

```
float4 caprng( in half2 coords: TEX0,
               in const uniform samplerRECT cells,
               in const uniform samplerRECT eqnLUT) : COLOR0
{
    float2 Connector;
    float4 newState,LUTinput;
    float4 input[4];
    int i;

    // connectivity (56,2,21,49)
    // offset 56
    Connector.x = fmod(coords.x + 56,CA_SIZE);
    Connector.y = coords.y;

    input[0] = round(texRECT(cells,Connector));

    // offset 2
    Connector.x = fmod(coords.x + 2,CA_SIZE);
    input[1] = round(texRECT(cells,Connector));

    // offset 21
    Connector.x = fmod(coords.x + 21,CA_SIZE);
    input[2] = round(texRECT(cells,Connector));

    // offset 49
    Connector.x = fmod(coords.x + 49,CA_SIZE);
    input[3] = round(texRECT(cells,Connector));

    // cell equation evaluation by table lookup
    LUTindex = input[3] + input[2]*2 + input[1]*4 + input[0]*8;
    newState.x = texRECT(eqnLUT, float2(LUTindex.x,0)).x;

    return newState;
}
```

Before executing the above shader, the texture storing the cell states (cells) is initialized with random values, and the lookup table (eqnLUT) is precomputed. The shader first fetches the neighbor cell states by offsetting the current texture coordinate according to the connectivity configuration. Then it packs these neighbor cell states to form the look-up index (LUTindex) for looking up the table (eqnLUT). The output states of the cell equation are stored to the output texture (newState). The roles of newState and cells are then switched.

As the bits of the random number being generated are scattered among different cells (texels), we have to pack them to form the 32-bit integer number. However, the GPU does not support high-precision integer values, so we need to use a floating point to hold the high-precision integer for output. To do so, we pack the generated random number bits, r_i, to a floating point, f, as follows:

$$f = \left(\left(\left(r_0 / 2\right) + r_1\right) / 2 + \ldots\ldots + r_{31}\right) / 2 \qquad (9.8.1)$$

The following simple shader performs the packing.

```
float4 pack(in half2 index : TEXO,
            in const uniform samplerRECT cells): COLORO
{
    int i;
    float4 outbits;
    float4 states;
    float2 texindex;

    outbits = 0;
    // packing all 32 bits
    for (i = 0 ; i < 32 ; i++)
    {
        texindex.x = i*2+1;
        texindex.y = index.y;
        states = texRECT(cells, texindex);
        outbits += states;
        outbits /= 2;
    }
    return outbits;
}
```

Multiple Random-Sequence Generation

Scientific applications usually require a tremendous amount of random numbers. It will be wasteful for the GPU to execute just a single random number generator at a time. We can execute multiple random number generators in parallel. There are two ways to embed more random number generators in a pass.

The first way is to fully utilize the number of texels in a texture allowed by the hardware, which is supposed to be 4096×4096 texels in current GPUs. If we use a 64-cell CA-based PRNG, we can at most store 64×4096 random numbers in a single texture.

The second way is to embed multiple PRNG cell states in a single texel, because a single cell state only occupies a single bit, while a texel consists of at most four floating-point numbers. For simplicity, we demonstrate how to use the mantissa part of a floating point to hold multiple cells; that is we can have 23×4 bits and therefore 92 parallel PRNG cell states in a single texel.

The two approaches can be used simultaneously without conflict, and therefore we can have at most $64 \times 4096 \times 92 \approx 2.4 \times 10^7$ parallel PRNGs. To support this parallelization, we only need to slightly modify the cell equation evaluation part of shader as follows:

```
// cell equation
newState = 0;
for (i = IN_PIXELUNITS-1 ; i >= 0 ; i--)
{
    LUTinput = getBit(input[3],i)   + getBit(input[2],i)*2 +
               getBit(input[1],i)*4 + getBit(input[0],i)*8;

    newState *= 2;
    newState.x += texRECT(eqnLUT,float2(LUTinput.x,0)).x;
    newState.y += texRECT(eqnLUT,float2(LUTinput.y,0)).x;
    newState.z += texRECT(eqnLUT,float2(LUTinput.z,0)).x;
    newState.w += texRECT(eqnLUT,float2(LUTinput.w,0)).x;

}
```

Constant `IN_PIXELUNITS` is defined as the length of the mantissa, that is 23. The code requires a function (`getBit`) to extract a single bit b from the floating-point texel. To do so, we first right-shift the number by b bits. This is equivalent to dividing by 2^b. The last bit of this number is what we wanted. We can perform modulo of 2 to get it. The following code has been tested on different GPUs, and it works properly in all tests.

```
float4 getBit(float4 number, int bit)
{
    float4 div;
    // right shift by "bit" bits
    div = ( number / exp2(float(bit)) ) +0.0000001;
    // get the last bit
    return round(fmod( floor(div), 2.0));
}
```

The purpose of introducing `round`, `floor`, and `+0.0000001` is to make the computation more stable. Similarly, the function `pack` needs a minor change to select the correct bit in each cell state. Only a single line of code,

```
outbits += states;
```

is changed to

```
outbits += getBit(states, fmod(index.x,CA_SIZE));
```

Results

Visual Results

Figures 9.8.5 and 9.8.6 show two photon mapping results, "cross" and "ring," in which photon distributions are generated with the proposed GPU CA-PRNG. In each test scene, we show six snapshots illustrating the convergence.

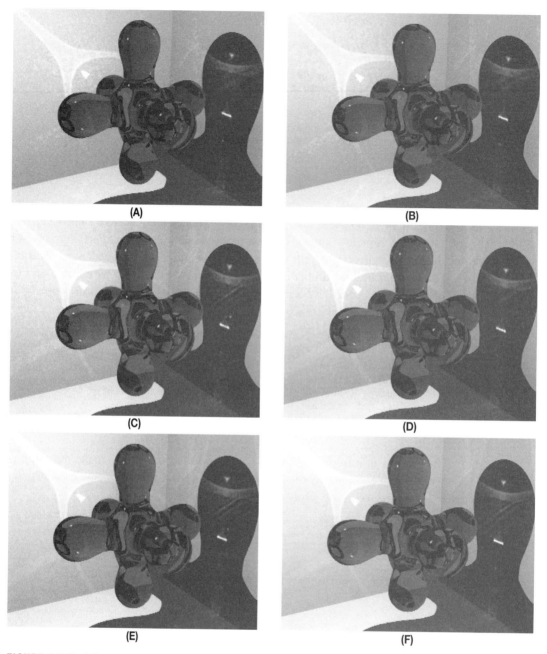

FIGURE 9.8.5　The cross scene. Convergence of photon mapping result with photon distribution generated with the proposed CA-PRNG. (**A**) 100,000 photons. (**B**) 200,000 photons. (**C**) 500,000 photons. (**D**) 1,000,000 photons. (**E**) 1,500,000 photons. (**F**) 2,000,000 photons.

FIGURE 9.8.6 The ring scene. Convergence of the photon mapping result with the photon distribution generated with the proposed CA-PRNG. (**A**) 100,000 photons. (**B**) 200,000 photons. (**C**) 500,000 photons. (**D**) 1,000,000 photons. (**E**) 1,500,000 photons. (**F**) 2,000,000 photons.

Figure 9.8.7 compares the PSNR of images generated with a CA-PRNG and a standard LCG-based PRNG. Different numbers of photons are used to form a curve for each PRNG. The control image is obtained by photon mapping with 10,000,000 photons. In this experiment the ring scene is used. All images are rendered in the resolution of 640 × 480. The statistics show that photon mapping with CA-PRNGs converges faster than photon mapping with LCG-PRNG.

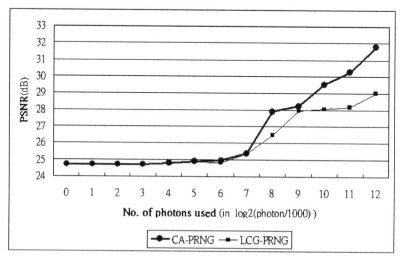

FIGURE 9.8.7   The PSNR of images generated by CA- and LCG-based PRNG.

Quality of Random Numbers

The faster convergence of CA-based PRNG than LCG-based PRNG is mainly due to the higher quality of CA-based random numbers. This quality of random numbers can be measured using empirical tests such as the DIEHARD test suite [DIEHARD]. It is a set of tests tailored for random number sequences. The DIEHARD suite has 14 tests. The basic ideas of these tests are similar, but they have different scenarios and test on different sub-bits in the random sequence. First, they try to extract different subsets of bits in the random sequences. Then, certain transforms are applied to these sub-bit sequences. The *Chi-square* χ^2 test is used to evaluate if the resulting distribution follows the expected one. χ^2 is calculated by finding the square of the difference between observed O_i and expected E_i frequency, divided by expected frequency. Summation of all the results gives χ^2.

$$\chi^2 = \sum_i \frac{(O_i - E_i)^2}{E_i} \qquad (9.8.2)$$

A P-value $\in [0,1]$ can then be computed for each test based on the χ^2 result. The better the expected model matches, the higher the p-value will be. A zero p-value means the sequence is nonuniformly distributed. An overall p-value is computed by performing another χ^2 test over all p-values to see if it matches a Gaussian distribution. The higher the overall p-value, the better the PRNG quality is. The CA-PRNG proposed successfully passes all tests and gets a high overall p-value of 0.962354. In contrast, LCG-PRNG rand() only passes some of the tests, and its overall p-value is zero.

Timing Statistics

For most GPU applications, there is a significant overhead introduced in each pass of the shader. Example overheads include the cost of setup and texture retrieval. Therefore, generating a single random sequence on a GPU is not cost effective compared to a pure software implementation. Table 9.8.1 shows the timing performance for generating a single sequence of random numbers on GPUs and CPUs. The test is performed on a PC with Pentium IV 3.2 GHz CPU and Geforce 7800 GTX GPU.

TABLE 9.8.1 Comparison of Timing Performance

Random Numbers Generated	GPU CA-PRNG	Software CA-PRNG
1,000	0.064s	0.004s
10,000	0.942s	0.042s
100,000	10.081s	0.391s
1,000,000	100.082s	4.163s

Our major performance gain comes from running multiple instances of random number generators in parallel. As shown in Table 9.8.2, we compare the running time for a software multisequence CA-based PRNG and the GPU version. We list their times (in seconds) for generating certain numbers of random numbers. Both PRNGs generate 1000 random sequences simultaneously.

TABLE 9.8.2 Comparison of Running Times

Random Numbers Generated	GPU CA-PRNG	Software CA-PRNG
10,000	0.004s	0.043s
100,000	0.031s	0.425s
1,000,000	0.31s	4.274s
10,000,000	3.098s	43.003s
100,000,000	31.875s	430s

From the statistics, the speed of the GPU version CA-PRNG is roughly 10 times faster than the software version. The difference will be even larger if we generate more random sequences in parallel.

Conclusion

In this article, we demonstrate how to implement a high-quality PRNG shader on GPUs. By exploiting the homogenous cell behavior of CA-based PRNGs, we successfully avoid high-precision integer operations and bitwise operations for generating high-quality random numbers. Speed-up is achieved by replacing the costly evaluation of cell equations with a lookup of precomputed tables. The source code and demonstrative program are available on the companion CD-ROM.

ON THE CD

Acknowledgments

We thank Sebastian Fleissner for sharing part of the code used in this project. This project is supported by the Research Grants Council of the Hong Kong Special Administrative Region, under RGC Earmarked Grants (Project No. CUHK417005) and Direct Allocation (Project No. 2050345). This work is affiliated with the CUHK Virtual Reality, Visualization and Imaging Research Centre as well as the Microsoft-CUHK Joint Laboratory for Human-Centric Computing and Interface Technologies.

References

[DIEHARD] Marsaglia, G. "DIEHARD battery of tests." Available online at *http://stat.fsu.edu/pub/diehard/*.

[Perlin85] Perlin, K. "An Image Synthesizer." *SIGGRAPH '85: Proceedings of the 12th Annual Conference on Computer Graphics and Interactive Techniques.* ACM Press, New York, 1985: pp. 287–296.

[Wolfram86] Wolfram, S. "Random Sequence Generation by Cellular Automata." *Advances in Applied Mathematics, 7* (June 1986): pp. 123–169.

9.9

Print Shader for Debugging Pixel Shaders

Alexander Ehrath, Rockstar, San Diego

Introduction

Often it can be very difficult to debug pixel shaders because of the limited debugging mechanisms currently available on the hardware. This is especially true when you need to look at shader register values in real-time.

Tools such as Microsoft's PIX let you look at some of this data, but you have to stop your application and inspect values after your program runs.

This article presents a method to write numeric shader values visually directly onto the texture to be debugged while your program runs. Because of the complex nature of this shader, a minimum of PS 3.0 hardware is required to run it.

Once integrated into an application, all the Printf shader needs is a font texture from which to fetch the printed characters. After that, it is trivial to change the layout (location and size) of the output and the number of registers to be simultaneously displayed.

Make sure the value you are trying to debug stays constant per frame as the hardware draws the texture. Otherwise, the text will appear garbled, as the font texture will be fetched from different locations. In the example code, the UV coordinate of the pixel of interest is passed in as a shader constant.

Setting Up the Debug Shader

The application using the printf shader needs to supply the appropriate font texture data (one debug font is included on the CD-ROM) and set up a few preprocessor variables used by the printf shader.

ON THE CD

These variables are:

- UV location of the debug text
- Size and scale of the debug text
- Number of lines to be displayed (defines how many different values you can evaluate at once)
- Number of digits per debug value to be printed to the screen (defines the range of possible debug values)
- Position of the decimal point (defines the precision of debug values)

We chose to use preprocessor values to set up these parameters because they usually do not need to change per-shader. If the need arises, these could easily be replaced with variables.

After the setup, you simply need to call the `DebugValues` function after the shader has executed. Simply pass in the current texture coordinate, the current pixel color (as output by the regular shader), and a float array containing the values of interest.

```
//////////////////////////////////////////////////////////////////
//          debugging values (to be set up by programmer)
//

//////////////////////////////////////////////////////////////////

    // Specify the UV coordinates of the location where you want to
    // display the debug text
    #define DebugStartU 0.2
    #define DebugStartV 0.5

    // Total number of digits to be displayed as debug text
    // including decimal point.
    #define NumDigits 9

    // Total number of lines. Basically the number of debug values
    // that are to be displayed.
    #define NumLines 3

    // Opacity of Debug values on top of original texture (0.0-1.0)
    #define DebugAlpha 0.8

    // Font size (1.0 = original size)
    #define FontScale 1.0

    // Position of Decimal Point
    #define DecimalPoint 1
    .

    .
    // original shader code sets the OUT.color value above. Now
    // lets look at some values.
    DebugArray[0] = debugnormal.x;
    DebugArray[1] = debugnormal.y;
    DebugArray[2] = debugnormal.z;

    // DebugValues() either passes OUT.color through, or fetches
       character
    // color from font texture, based on DebugArray inputs.
    OUT.color = DebugValues(IN.texture0, OUT.color, DebugArray);
    .

    .
```

Implementation

The printf shader first evaluates if the current texture coordinate is within the location and size of the debugging area defined within the texture to be debugged. If the current texture coordinate is outside this area, the debug shader simply exits. However, if it does fall within the debugging area, it first evaluates which line (you can print multiple lines of debug values) and which digit this texture coordinate falls into.

Digits to the left of the decimal point need to be treated slightly differently than the ones to the right of the decimal point.

The digit of the value to be displayed is isolated in the shader by multiplying or dividing the value by a power of 10 and then using it to compute an index into the debug font texture. Finally, it subindexes the proper pixel of the character to be printed and uses this as its final color value to be output by the printf shader fragment (see Figure 9.9.1).

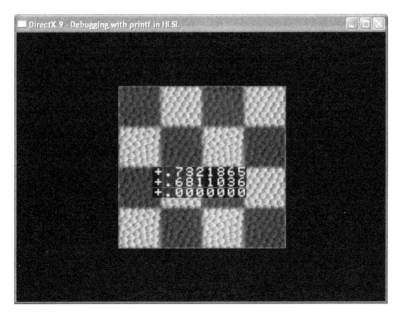

FIGURE 9.9.1 Screenshot of Example Program.

Example Code

The example shader code simply uses a bump map to generate per-pixel normals to implement per-pixel lighting. It first loads the font texture for printf to use, as well as the normal and diffuse textures for the example shader. After loading and setting up the shader, it sends down the UV coordinate of the pixel to be debugged.

Finally, it displays the x-, y-, and z-components of this pixel's normal vector using the DebugValues function as described in the "Setting up the Debug Shader" section.

The location of the debug pixel can be controlled by pressing Q, W, A, and S. The shader shows the location of this pixel in pink.

Use the cursor keys to rotate the object. Notice how the components of the screen space normals change as you rotate the texture and/or change the debug pixel's location.

Conclusion

Until pixel shader debuggers become more advanced, this method provides a solid base to do pixel shader debugging in real-time. The code is meant as a base component for the reader to change and apply. It is fairly small and can easily be extended.

APPENDIX

About the CD-ROM

The CD-ROM contains the example programs with source accompanying the chapters. The directory structure closely follows the book structure by using the chapter number as the name of the subdirectory. You need to download the DirectX 9 June 2006 update SDK.

General System Requirements

To use all of the files on the CD-ROM, you will need:

- The DirectX 9 June 2006 update SDK
- OpenGL 1.5-compatible graphics card
- A DirectX 8, 8.1, or 9.0-compatible graphics card
- Windows XP with the latest service pack
- Visual C++ .NET 2003 or Visual C++ 2005
- 512 MB RAM
- 500 MB of free space on your hard drive
- Pentium IV/ATHLON with more than 1.5 GHz
- The latest graphics card drivers

Updates

Updates of the example programs will be available on *www.shaderx5.com* and on *www.charlesriver.com*.

Comments, Suggestions

Please send any comments or suggestions to *wolf@shaderx.com*.
Have fun!

—Wolfgang Engel

INDEX

3D engine design
    postprocessing effects in, 463–470
    transparent shader data binding,
      471–477
3D engines, developing for OpenGL ES
    2.0, OpenGL 2.0, 411–419
3ds Max v6, 487–495

A

adding
    bump detail to skinned joints,
      49–57
    decal layer to surfaces, 447–450
Adobe Photoshop, 93
agent-space maps, 502
algorithms
    See also specific techniques
    alpha blending, 69
    jump flooding (JFA), 185–192
    per-pixel ray-tracing, 75
    ZT-buffer, for rendering transparent
      objects, 151–157
aliasing
    and anti-aliasing, 113, 128–129,
      403, 430
    depth, 202
    texture, 445
alpha blending, 299, 429, 524
alpha testing, 69, 127
alpha-to-coverage technique, 70–74
ambient occlusion, 381
analytical prefiltering, 46
animation and rendering underwater
    god rays, 315–326
anti-aliasing, 113, 128–129, 403, 430
API, OpenGL ES 2.0, 393–406
approximate image-space refraction,
    caustics, 360–370
area lights, rendering, 63–67
art pipeline integration, 487–491
artifacts at tile edges, 442–443
Aszódi, Barnabás, xv
ATI's handheld SDK, 408

B

Bahnassi, Homam, xv
Bahnassi, Wessam, xiii, xv
barycentric, and Gregory coordinates,
    9–10
batching with OpenGL ES v2.0,
    425–426
Beets, Kristof, xiii, xv
beveling
    described, 23–24
    micro-beveled edges, 24–30
Bezier patches, 9
billboards described, 275
binary shader compilation (OpenGL ES
    2.0), 416–417
blending
    alpha, 299, 429, 524
    alpha-to-coverage technique,
      70–74
Blinn-Phong lighting, 136
blur factor in depth-of-field, 163–164
blurring, Gaussian, 170–173
Botorabi, Ali, xv
branching
    data-dependent, 433–434
    dynamic, 124, 182–183
Brauwers, Maicon, xvi
buffers
    color, normal, depth, and position,
      108–109
    depth, 164–169
    eye-space depth, 251
    geometric (G-buffer), 116–117,
      119–120
    high-precision floating-point,
      526–527
    photon, 367, 370
    ping-pong, 187
    spherical harmonics, 110
    stencil, 220
bump detail, adding to skinned joints,
    49–50, 57
bump mapping, 31, 44–45, 77, 78, 79

C

CA-based PRNG (pseudo-random
    number generator), 579–590
cameras
    GPU panorama viewer for generic
      camera models, 543–551
    rotating, 112
Carmack, John, 197
cartoon fire effects using OpenGL ES
    v2.0, 451–458
cascaded, shadow maps, 197–205
caustics, rendering, 360–370, 384
CD-ROM, about, 595
cells, Voronoi, 189
cellular automata, interactive image
    segmentation based on, 511–517
cellular texturing, real-time, 519–531
characters, large crowds using fragment
    shaders and LOD, 501–509
cloth, rendering techniques, 49–57
clouds
    smoke, 73
    volumetric, and mega-particles,
      295–302
collision detection shader using cube-
    maps, 533–542
color, cloud, 297
color buffer, 108
color channels, alpha testing, 69,
    127
colored lights and SH (spherical
    harmonics), 113
Comba, João Luiz Dihl, xvi
compression, texture, 428
convex geometry, 534
Cornell box, 382
CPU (central processing unit)
    and hardware occlusion query
      mechanism, 260
    mobile device recommendations,
      424
crowds of autonomous characters,
    generating, 501–509